2 MOS

Personnel and Human Resource Management

FOURTH EDIT

Personnel and Human Resource Management

FOURTH EDITION

Randall S. Schuler
New York University

Vandra L. Huber
University of Washington

West Publishing Company
St. Paul ■ New York ■ Los Angeles ■ San Francisco

Copyeditor: Sheralyn Goldbecker
Cover Design: Pete Thiel
Composition: Carlisle Communications, Ltd.

COPYRIGHT ©1981,
1984, 1987   By WEST PUBLISHING COMPANY
COPYRIGHT ©1990   By WEST PUBLISHING COMPANY
                    50 W. Kellogg Boulevard
                    P.O. Box 64526
                    St. Paul, MN 55164–1003

Printed in the United States of America

97 96 95 94 93 92 91 90   8 7 6 5 4 3 2 1 0

Library of Congress Cataloging-in-Publication Data

Schuler, Randall S.
    Personnel and human resource management / Randall S. Schuler,
  Vandra L. Huber.—4th ed.
        p.   cm.
    Includes bibliographical references.
    ISBN 0-314-56277-X
    1. Personnel management.   I. Huber, Vandra L. (Vandra Lee), 1949–
    II. Title.
  HF5549.S249   1990
    658.3—dc20   89-22735
                                                     CIP

Dedicated to:
Susan, John, and Bob for continued support and inspiration—R.S.S. And
to Michael for encouragement, Sandy and Maripi for motivation, and my
parents, Fred and Twila Huber—V.L.H.

Contents

III

IV

Appraising and Compensating 187

V

Improving 361

VI

Establishing and Maintaining Effective Work Relationships   463

Chapter 14: Employee Rights   464

Chapter 15: Unionization and Collective Bargaining   484

Preface

Organizations today are confronted with several major challenges: raising productivity, enhancing innovation, improving production and service quality, and meeting the intense level of international competition never before seen. At the same time, organizations are being asked to provide higher quality of work life for their employees and to comply with laws, guidelines, and court decisions that govern the utilization of human resources. Because people are central to these organizational challenges these issues comprise the heart of personnel and human resource management (PHRM) today. As a result, personnel and human resource management has an opportunity to enable organizations to survive, grow, and be competitive and profitable. PHRM can do this by helping organizations to utilize their human resources productively. However, PHRM practitioners can be effective only if they have the appropriate knowledge related to personnel and human resource management and are able to implement this knowledge in the work place. This fourth edition of *Personnel and Human Resource Management* has been written to provide that knowledge and assist in implementing it as effectively as possible. To further these goals, several features are incorporated into this new edition.

The first is the addition of Vandra Huber as coauthor. She brings a great deal of the academic knowledge and professional work experience that are reflected in this edition. As in the third edition of *Personnel and Human Resource Management*, this edition contains the feature entitled "PHRM in the News." Also in the fourth edition, these glimpses of real-life issues are taken from such sources as *Business Week, The Wall Street Journal, Fair Employment Report,* and *Bulletin to Management.* This feature illustrates the current realities and applications of personnel and human resource management. New to this edition is the feature "International PHRM in the News." The world is becoming the relevant environment for organizations today, and it seems useful to know as much about it as possible. This new feature is incorporated throughout the book to facilitate the acquisition of this knowledge.

Another feature of this edition is the cases that appear at the ends of most chapters. The cases in this edition are like those in the third edition in that they present true-to-life personnel and human resource issues and challenges based on real-life events, although the names and places have been disguised. The majority of the cases in this fourth edition are new.

In addition to these features incorporated to provide knowledge and assistance in implementation, this fourth edition of *Personnel and Human Resource Management* has several other important characteristics. Each chapter contains an extensive list of up-to-date, important references. These are provided in the Notes at the end of each chapter, along with commentary to expand on material in the chapter. Thus, these notes are a valuable source of information in themselves, indicating information that supplements topics presented in the chapter. The references reflect many of the best research and theoretical works, as well as many of the most current articles on personnel and human resource management application.

Each chapter also contains a discussion of the following in relation to the activity being considered: its importance and purpose, its important relationships with other PHRM activities and with the internal and external environments, and the relevant legal considerations. These characteristics are included because they reflect current thinking in personnel and human resource management and the reality of a dynamic, international, and highly competitive environment. Included for the same reason is the section on trends located near the end of each chapter. Within this section are three topics of special importance to the field of PHRM: (1) techniques for assessing the effectiveness of each activity, (2) human resource information system needs and computer technology applications, and (3) how each PHRM activity can be used more strategically in organizations.

The organization of the chapters in this fourth edition is similar to that in the third edition. There are, however, several significant changes. First of all, the international personnel and human resource management material has been woven into the chapters throughout the book, rather than including it all in one chapter at the end of the book. There is also more international material in this edition than there was in previous editions. The separate chapters on unionization and collective bargaining have been combined into a single chapter to improve the flow and presentation of this material. To enhance the flexibility of this edition, the "PC Projects" feature has been removed. However, the importance of PC technology in personnel and human resource management continues to grow, and this is reflected in the revision of *PC Projects for Human Resource Management.* The previous three appendixes have been trimmed back to one; however, this does not mean a loss of information because the deleted material has been included in the chapters where it is discussed. Also trimmed back is some of the material describing the relationships existing among PHRM activities and the environment.

These changes have been made to make it easier for the reader while not resulting in any loss of substance. To the contrary, we really think that there is more substance to each chapter in this fourth edition than there was in previous editions. Nevertheless, we could not include all the personnel and human resource management information in this one textbook. Consequently, we have made available three other books that provide more detail and more PC applications:

- *PC Projects for Human Resource Management,* 2d ed., by Nicholas J. Beutel
- *Readings in Personnel and Human Resource Management,* 3d ed., by Randall S. Schuler, Stuart A. Youngblood, and Vandra L. Huber
- *Case Problems in Personnel and Human Resource Management* by Randall S. Schuler and Stuart A. Youngblood

In summary, this fourth edition of *Personnel and Human Resource Management* represents a substantial change from the third edition. The fourth edition is meant to be more extensive, more current, more challenging and useful, and much more readable. We hope that these goals have been attained.

ACKNOWLEDGMENTS

As with the third edition, many people were of critical importance in the completion of this fourth edition.

Providing important contributions to this third edition were Robert Kerr of the University of Windsor, Mike Burke of New York University, Robert Faley of Kent State University, Peter Dowling of Monash University in Australia, and Robert Davies of New York University. Robert Davies, Peter Dowling, and Robert Kerr contributed some materials on international personnel and human resource management. Robert Faley and Mike Burke provided helpful comments on the content and organization of Chapters 3–5. In addition, Mike prepared the chapter on personnel research. The following individuals contributed the new cases which added greatly to the quality of this edition: Steve Hanks, Gaylen Chandler, Marcia Micelli, Karen Witta, Kay Stratton, Janina Latack, Kyle Steadman, Robyn Sutton, Von Madsen, and Robert McDonough.

Additional thanks should be given to the following former students at the University of Utah and University of Washington from whose class projects, cases, and research projects examples and illustrations were taken: Steve Barfuss, Gregory Love, John Paul, Doyle Riley, Ann Lewis, Gaylen Chandler, and David Officer.

The following individuals also provided many good ideas and suggestions in their roles as reviewers and evaluators of the third edition:

Rick Abderholden, United States Air Force Academy
Steven H. Barr, Oklahoma State University
Debra J. Cohen, George Mason University
Joan G. Dahl, California State University-Northridge
Jeannette A. Davy, Arizona State University
Gregory G. Dell'Omo, Canisius College
Angelo DeNisi, Rutgers University
Diane Franklin, Northeastern University
Rodger W. Griffeth, Louisiana State University
Rudolph L. Kagerer, University of Georgia
Daniel J. Hoys, Marquette University
John Lenti, University of South Carolina
Sharon A. Lobel, University of Michigan
Gene Murkison, Georgia Southern College
Jerry Shuttle, Eastern Montana College

Several personnel and human resource practitioners and practicing managers also provided many good practical examples. These individuals include Jim Walker, The Walker Group; Michael Mitchell and Jerry Goodman, Swiss Bank Corporation; Tessa Jolls, *HR Reporter;* Chuck Ballard and Kay Henry, The Equitable Financial Companies; Frank Berardi and Nancy Berry, Allstate; Bill Reffett, Grand Union; Jim Stahler, J. C. Penney; Chad Frost and Gary Weeda, Frost, Inc.; Steve Rutherford, Federal Express; Tom Moyers, Perdue; Stewart Cole,

American Express; George Ackerman, Westvaco; Dick Parker, Merck; Art Maine, Revco; Joel DeLuca, Sun Company; Jack Berry, Coca Cola; Denny Scott, Goldman, Sachs; Bill Maki, Weyerhaeuser; William Hauser, Pfizer; John Lynch, North American Life Assurance; Hank Goodstein, Third National Bank; Don Laidlaw, IBM; John Bradley, J. P. Morgan; Donald Brush, Barden Corporation; Sharon Ritter, American Red Cross; Robert Harris, Underwriters Laboratories; Michael Robinson, Marriott's Mark Resort; Tom Hoskison, Schnuck Markets; Greg Dawe, Clark Materials Systems Technology; Dave Knibbe, Frito Lay; Lourdes Cooke, KSL Television; Jean Bishop, Bonneville International Broadcast Co.; and Gaylan Moffat, Utah Transit Authority. We would also like to express special thanks to all those who granted us permission to use their materials.

The support and encouragement of John Dutton and Oscar Ornati of the Department of Management at New York University, and Dick West, Dean of the Stern School of Business at New York University, are sincerely appreciated. We are also grateful for the fine secretarial support at New York University, which made the preparation of this manuscript a great deal easier. Those who provided special assistance in preparing the manuscript are Lou DeCaro and Marcia Winward. Special thanks should also be extended to University of Washington graduate research assistant Susan Crandall who painstakingly read some chapters and to Sean Kennedy who prepared reference lists and the integrative case. The support of Gary P. Latham, of the Management and Organizations Department at the University of Washington, and his colleague Tom Lee is appreciated. Manuscript preparation help was also provided by Tovah Gaidos, Darmes Skeeter and Michael Krolewski who worked long hours helping to retype manuscripts and prepare the Instructor's Manual. Also, several people at West Publishing deserve our special thanks for their help and support over many years: Richard T. Fenton, acquisitions editor; Esther W. Craig, developmental editor; Jeff Carpenter, production editor; and Beth A. Kennedy, promotion manager. Without their professional dedication and competence, this book would not have been possible.

Randall S. Schuler
New York City
Vandra L. Huber
Seattle
January 1990

Introduction to Personnel and Human Resource Management

CHAPTER 1
Personnel and Human Resource Management

CHAPTER

1

Personnel and Human Resource Management

PHRM FUNCTIONS AND ACTIVITIES

Planning for Human Resource Needs
Staffing the Organization's Personnel Needs
Appraising and Compensating Employee
 Behavior
Improving Employees and the Work
 Environment
Establishing and Maintaining Effective
 Working Relationships

OBJECTIVES AND PURPOSES OF PHRM
FUNCTIONS AND ACTIVITIES

Objectives of PHRM
Purposes of PHRM

RELATIONSHIPS INFLUENCING PHRM
FUNCTIONS AND ACTIVITIES

Relationships among the Functions and
 Activities
Relationships with the Internal
 Environment
Relationships with the External
 Environment

PHRM's GROWING IMPORTANCE

Events Influencing PHRM's Importance

TRENDS IN PHRM

Assessment of PHRM
Computer Technology and HRIS
Strategic Involvement
Customerization

ORGANIZING THE PHRM DEPARTMENT

Personnel and Human Resource Roles
PHRM in the Organization
Centralization Versus Decentralization
Who Is Responsible for PHRM?
PHRM Budgets

STAFFING THE PHRM DEPARTMENT

Qualities of the PHRM Manager and Staff

PHRM JOBS

How Much Do They Pay?
PHRM Budgets
Professionalism in Personnel
Professional Certification

PLAN OF THIS BOOK

Purposes
Themes
For Whom Is This Book Written?

Managing Human Resources in Flat, Lean and Flexible Organizations: Trends for the 1990s

Companies in every sector of our economy are changing the ways they manage in order to be more competitive. They are striving to manage with fewer employees, fewer management levels, and more flexibility in management practices. What new management practices are applied in these organizations? What role do human resource strategies play when conditions are rapidly changing? What do top executives expect of the human resource function in this new environment? The flat, lean, and flexible organization poses difficult challenges to managers and human resource staff.

Management Expects HR Initiatives

How can companies become more flexible? Because most management effectiveness issues are both general management concerns and human resource issues, a key role of human resource staff is to help managers define "how we want to manage differently" and help achieve desired changes. Senior management expects the human resource function to provide leadership and support in addressing "people-related business issues." The function is being asked to help chart the course for managing human resources as conditions change.

Senior executives expect human resource staff to help management consider key issues and shape strategies for enhancing management effectiveness. "We expect the ideas, leadership, and support we get from our best staff and consultants," one CEO said in describing his view of the human resource function. In the flexible organization, human resource staff are involved in or leading organization planning, productivity, quality, culture, restructuring, downsizing, reskilling, merger or acquisition, and other management initiatives.

Additionally, human resource staff are seeking to keep basic human resource programs current and in tune with changing business needs. They keep executive compensation, salary, incentive, and benefit programs competitively attractive and in legal compliance. New programs are developed to address such concerns as child care, benefits cost containment, union avoidance or decertification, substance abuse, and other needs. In some companies, such as Xerox and Motorola, initiatives result from "competitive bench marking," a process of assessing the best of competitor practices and acting to reduce their competitive advantage while also building on unique company strengths.

Many companies are adopting flexible employment as a human resource strategy. They focus recruitment, retention, and development on a core of talent with critical skills required. They staff variable needs with talent on contingent employment arrangements—fixed term, temporary, part time. Many services that do not require day-to-day management supervision by the company are contracted out. Additionally, many firms permit variable working hours and schedules, work at home or client sites, and diversity in working conditions (e.g., office arrangements).

Companies are minimizing the levels and complexity of the organization structure and encouraging delegation, initiative, and innovation. Jobs, too, are often flexible. Companies change job responsibilities and activities to fit changing business needs and employee capacities and interests. They believe this fosters innovation and flexibility in job performance. Roles of managers are changing under changing conditions (e.g., brokers, negotiators, coaches, consultants, individual contributors).

To be more flexible, many companies are encouraging informal, direct contacts across organizations (multiple, changing matrix of relationships). Communications, too, are more

continued

flexible, providing staff the information they need to do their jobs and to feel they are fully informed. They are providing new processes for employee involvement in communications and decisions.

Flexible compensation is widely used to assure competitiveness of rewards and to contain costs. Multiple compensation programs are widely used, emphasizing incentives, special awards and recognitions, and wide ranges for base pay levels and adjustments. Flexible ben-

efits contain rising costs and respond to employee preferences for different types of benefits. To support compensation actions, companies are using varied formats and approaches in performance appraisal and are obtaining inputs from different sources (managers, peers, customers, etc.).

SOURCE: J. Walker, "Managing Human Resources in Flat, Lean and Flexible Organizations: Trends for the 1990s," *Human Resource Planning* 11, no. 2 (1988): 125–26. Reprinted by permission of *Human Resource Planning*, copyright 1988.

T HE preceding "PHRM in the News" reflects on several significant areas: (1) organizations are more concerned than ever about managing human resources effectively; (2) personnel and human resource management (PHRM) is seen as the department that has the expertise in managing human resources effectively; (3) personnel and human resource management is critical to organizations because of the importance of productivity and the vital link between using human resources effectively—the essence of effective PHRM—and improving productivity; (4) the PHRM profession is growing, and PHRM's importance and contribution to organizations are increasing; and (5) a major trend in PHRM is managing human resources in organizations that are much flatter and more flexible than ever. Together these areas help organizations to be more competitive and profitable as well as to survive and grow. Effective PHRM also enables organizations to enhance the quality of work life for their employees because it is based on respect and concern for individuals' rights and preferences. Although some organizations still use the term *personnel* to refer to the department that deals with such activities as recruitment, selection, compensation, and training, the phrase "personnel and human resource management" is rapidly supplanting it. This change recognizes the vital role that human resources play in an organization, the challenges in *managing* human resources effectively, and the growing body of knowledge and professionalism surrounding PHRM.[1] In return for this recognition, PHRM departments must successfully address the areas listed earlier. Nonetheless, effective PHRM is still implemented through numerous functions and activities.[2]

PHRM FUNCTIONS AND ACTIVITIES

This book describes five functions and activities, which generally include all the functions and activities that personnel and human resource management departments actually perform. (The specific jobs found in these departments and their salaries are described later in this chapter.) These functions are as follows:

- Planning for human resource needs
- Staffing the organization's personnel needs
- Appraising and compensating employee behavior
- Improving employees and the work environment
- Establishing and maintaining effective working relationships

Although the PHRM departments of many organizations may not be currently performing all these functions, the trend is clearly moving in that direction. Consequently, describing them here is useful.

Planning for Human Resource Needs

The function of planning for human resource needs involves two major activities: (1) planning and forecasting the organization's short- and long-term human resource requirements and (2) analyzing the jobs in the organization to determine their duties and purposes and the skills, knowledge, and abilities that are needed. These two activities are essential for effectively performing many other personnel and human resource management activities. For example, they help indicate the organization's present and future needs regarding numbers and types of employees. They also help to determine how the employees will be obtained (e.g., from outside recruiting or by internal transfers and promotions) and what training needs the organization will have. These two activities can be viewed as the major factors influencing the staffing and development functions of the entire organization.

In spite of their importance, most organizations have only recently incorporated these planning activities. Five years ago human resource managers had responsibility for human resource planning in only a handful of companies. Today almost all the nation's five hundred largest industrial companies are relating human resource planning to corporate goals or strategies. They have come to recognize the importance of people to an organization's survival. As Walter Wriston, former Citicorp chief executive officer, commented, "I believe the only game in town is the personnel game. . . . My theory is if you have the right person in the right place, you don't have to do anything else. If you have the wrong person in the job, there's no management system known to man that can save you.[3]

Staffing the Organization's Personnel Needs

Once the organization's human resource needs have been determined, they have to be filled. Thus, staffing activities become necessary. These include (1) recruiting job applicants (candidates) and (2) selecting from among the job applicants those most appropriate for the available jobs.

These staffing activities apply to external candidates (those not currently employed by the organization) as well as to internal candidates (those currently employed by the organization). After the candidates have been identified, they must be selected. Common selection procedures include obtaining completed application forms or resumes; initially interviewing the candidates; checking education, background, experience, and references; conducting various tests; and holding a final interview. These procedures must be related to the job to serve equal employment opportunity (EEO) laws and regulations. In other words, selection procedures must result in a match between a candidate's abilities and the skills that the job requires.

Appraising and Compensating Employee Behavior

After employees are on the job, determining how well they are doing and rewarding them accordingly become necessary. If they are not doing well, the reasons must be determined. This determination may indicate that the reward structure needs to be changed or that employee training is necessary. To these ends, this function incorporates several activities associated with appraising and several associated with compensating. Activities associated with appraising include (1) appraising and evaluating employee behavior and (2) analyzing and motivating employee behavior. Although performance appraisal can be painful for both supervisor and employee, it is a critically important activity, especially because legal compliance dictates that employment decisions be made on the basis of performance. For example, if someone is to be selected for a promotion, the decision should be based on an evaluation of that employee's potential performance in the new job.

Not all employees are good performers. Some may be continually absent or late to work, and some may be chemically dependent. With the rise of employee rights, greater social responsibility, and the cost of replacing employees, however, organizations may prefer to assist employees in correcting their undesired behavior, rather than to terminate them.

Employees are generally rewarded on the basis of their jobs' value as well as on their performance level. Rewards—namely, indirect compensation—provided just for being a member of the organization, however, are rapidly increasing. Which form of compensation is most fair? Which form is most effective for the organization? By what methods can jobs be evaluated fairly to determine their value? These concerns and others are part of the compensating activity, which includes (1) administering direct compensation on the basis of job evaluation, (2) providing performance-based pay, and (3) administering indirect compensation benefits to employees in the organization.

Improving Employees and the Work Environment

In recent years, PHRM interest has grown in these areas: (1) determining, designing, and implementing employee training and development programs to increase employee ability and performance; (2) improving the work environment, especially through quality of work life and productivity improvement programs; and (3) improving the physical work environment to maximize employee safety and health. Training and development activities include training employees, developing management, and helping to develop careers. These activities are designed to increase employees' abilities in order to facilitate employee performance. Concern for employees' careers extends from the organization to the employees themselves.

In addition to providing training and development programs to improve conditions, organizations also provide programs to improve safety and health, productivity, and quality of work life. The federal regulations specified in the Occupational Safety and Health Act of 1970 have special influence in improving employees' work environments. These improvements directly and positively influence employees' physical safety and security as well as their sociopsychological well-being (and thus their productivity and quality of work life).

Establishing and Maintaining Effective Working Relationships

When the organization has obtained the employees it needs, it must take care to bring them into the organization, compensate them, and provide conditions that will make it attractive for them to stay. As a part of this function, organizations must establish and maintain effective working relationships with employees. Although this is formally required for union employees, establishing and maintaining effective working relationships with nonunion employees is also useful. Regarding all employees, this function involves five activities: (1) recognizing and respecting employee rights, (2) understanding the reasons and methods that employees use in organizing, (3) bargaining and settling grievances with employees and the organizations representing them,(4) understanding and learning from PHRM activities in other countries, and (5) conducting research in PHRM activities.

Because employees are increasingly gaining more rights, employment decisions such as discharges, layoffs, and demotions must be made with care and be supported by evidence. The managers of the organization must be aware of their employees' rights. The personnel and human resource manager is in an excellent position to inform line managers of these rights.

A union contract often protects unionized employees' rights. Human resource department staff must become familiar with that contract and the issues related to how employees organize themselves in dealing with the organization and how the organization bargains and negotiates with its organized employees. Familiarity with the formal union-management relationship is necessary because, on the one hand, this relationship can effectively define the extent to which other PHRM functions can be applied to the work force. On the other hand, the union-management relationship can be instrumental in developing new PHRM programs (e.g., programs to improve compensation, productivity, quality of life and employee equity).

OBJECTIVES AND PURPOSES OF PHRM FUNCTIONS AND ACTIVITIES

The five separate PHRM functions and their related activities are important because they fulfill several organizational objectives and purposes. These are shown in Exhibit 1.1.

Objectives of PHRM

The three major objectives are to attract potentially qualified job applicants, retain desirable employees, and motivate employees. PHRM functions and activities are important because they serve to attract, retain, and motivate employees. Their growing importance in organizations is also attributed to the recognition that PHRM can and does have an impact on the bottom line of the organization. The term *bottom line* refers to the organization's survival, growth, profitability, flexibility, and competitiveness. In the case of nonprofit and governmental organizations, the term refers to survival and the ability to do more with the same or fewer resources.[4] Focusing on the bottom line and being results-oriented are key ways in which PHRM can gain recognition and respect in organizations. Generally, the bottom line can be influenced through improved productivity, improved quality of work life, and legal compliance—the purposes of personnel and human resource management.

Purposes of PHRM

The three purposes are to improve productivity, to improve quality of work life, and to ensure legal compliance. Although the several PHRM functions and

---

EXHIBIT
1.1

Objectives, Purposes, and Relationships of
PHRM Functions and Activities

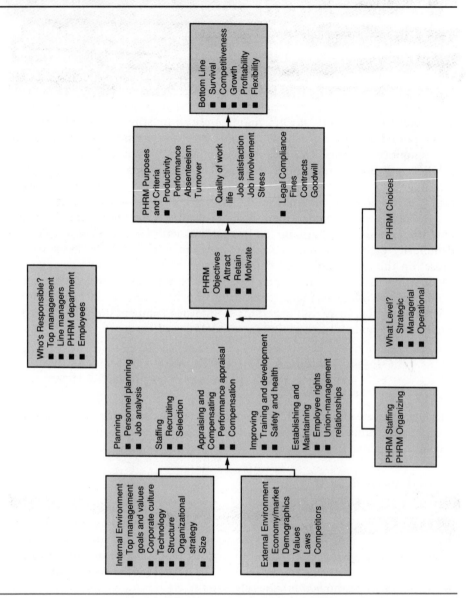

---

activities may serve the three objectives discussed above, each may also serve
these three purposes, and thus the bottom line of the organization.

Productivity.   Without a doubt, productivity is an important goal of organizations. PHRM can do many things to improve productivity. The most productive organizations in America know this and treat their personnel and human resource departments in ways that are different from those of less productive organizations. Recently, A. T. Kearney examined how highly productive American corporations are run. In comparing well-run corporations with those less well run in the same industries, Kearney found that the leaders in productivity have a unique set of personnel and human resource management practices. In particular:

- They define the human resource role according to its level of participation in business decisions that implement business strategies.
- They focus the current resources devoted to the human resource function on important problems before they add new programs or seek additional resources.
- Their human resource staffs initiate programs and communication with line management.
- Line management shares responsibility for human resource programs.
- The corporate staffs share responsibility for human resource policy formation and program administration across organizational levels.[5]

Today, PHRM has a unique and timely opportunity to improve productivity, as described in the "PHRM in the News" feature at the start of this chapter. Increasingly, however, improving productivity does not mean just increasing output. It also means increasing output with higher quality than ever before. This new emphasis on quantity with quality is one of the many forces increasing the need for effective personnel management:

> Nobody is against quality. But to many manufacturers quality has meant something they could do to a badly designed, poorly made product to help hold it together until the buyer got it home. Some companies are now remembering that quality—in appearance, function, and durability—must be built in, not pasted on. Design and manufacturing must be united. Managers and workers at every stage of production must be motivated to contribute to the goal of quality. Above all, top management must be genuinely committed. If executives mouth the right words but signal that they really want products slapped together as fast as possible, everybody gets the message.[6]

But although companies recognize the importance of enhanced quality and quantity, the difficulties and challenges of shifting the way people and the organization are managed are not going unnoticed:

> Sometimes, to their surprise, companies are also discovering that boosting quality saves money. Reducing the cost of fixing mistakes, both before and after a product is sold, can cut production costs as much as 30%. It also increases sales. The rub is that a commitment to improved quality almost always means investing more time and money now for a payoff later. Too many top executives, for a lot of reasons, have chosen not to manage for the long term. Unless it reorients its goals toward building for the future, U.S. industry has little hope of rebuilding product quality, productivity, or its competitive position in world markets.[7]

Part and parcel of many efforts to improve the quality and quantity dimensions of productivity is the improvement of the quality of work life for employees.

Quality of Work Life.   The dissatisfying nature of industrial—or clerical— work is no longer disputed. Many of today's employees prefer a greater level of involvement in their jobs than was previously assumed. Many desire more self-control and a chance to make a greater contribution to the organization. Apparently many employers are equally convinced of the importance of improved quality of work life, and particularly of the importance of greater worker involvement through employee participation in work place decisions. Communicating with employees and encouraging them to communicate their ideas are second only to productivity as a major role that chief executive officers desire to see their personnel and human resource managers play.[8]

Legal Compliance.   In managing their employees, organizations must comply with many laws, executive orders, guidelines, and court decisions. These laws and regulations affect almost all the functions and activities that PHRM uses. Thus, PHRM's constant concern is compliance with current laws, regulations, and court decisions. Additionally, personnel must be familiar with the actions of the Occupational Safety and Health Administration, the Equal Employment Opportunity Commission, the Office of Federal Contract Compliance Programs, the Immigration and Naturalization Service, and the various state and city equal employment commissions and human or civil rights commissions.

RELATIONSHIPS INFLUENCING PHRM FUNCTIONS AND ACTIVITIES

As shown in Exhibit 1.1, PHRM functions and activities do not exist in a vacuum. Indeed, many aspects of the external and internal environment influence the five functions. Presented later in this chapter are discussions of those who are responsible for PHRM and the levels at which it is practiced. Relevant aspects of the internal and external environment are also considered in the remaining chapters. These discussions indicate the multitude of forces and events that help shape an organization's PHRM functions and activities. Although stating precise relationships among aspects of the environment and these activities is impossible, statements of general tendencies can be made. Familiarity with these tendencies is important in understanding how PHRM is practiced in organizations today and how it might be practiced in the future.

Relationships among the Functions and Activities

Although each function and activity is discussed in a separate chapter, each is highly related to the others. That is, the way in which one activity is done often influences the way in which another is done. Because of this interdependence, a section in each chapter describes the most extensive and important relationships of each activity. The chapter sections also describe the critical relationships that each activity has with the internal and external environment. This is done to reflect the complex set of conditions that influence and are influenced by each activity.

Relationships with the Internal Environment

Several features within organizations influence PHRM, including top management, organizational strategy, technology, structure, culture, and size. Although these features are described separately here, they often influence each other. For example, top management's values help shape corporate culture, and strategy helps determine organizational structure.[9] The key focus here, however, is how these features influence the PHRM functions and activities.

Goals and Values.   Top management determines how critical personnel and human resource management will be in an organization. If top management minimizes the importance of people to the organization's overall success, so will the line managers. In turn, those in the personnel and human resource department will perform only the most routine personnel activities. A likely consequence will be minimally effective PHR management.[10]

Strategy. Organizations are increasingly linking PHRM to corporate strategy. Corporate strategy determines which general characteristics organizations need from employees.[11] Exhibit 1.2 lists some of these characteristics. These characteristics contrast with the specific skills, knowledge, and abilities that employees need to perform their jobs—elements that are determined more by technology, organizational structure, and size than by strategy.[12] Because PHRM activities are capable of fostering such employee characteristics, once a strategy is selected, these activities are influenced. The nature of this influence is so important it is described later in this chapter under "Strategic Involvement" and is also described at the end of the remaining chapters.

Culture. Organizational or corporate culture represents the organization's value system.[13] Strongly influenced by top management, corporate culture identifies the value of people to the organization, the assumptions made about people, and the ways in which people are to be treated. Culture often comes to be reflected in the company's personnel practices. For example, companies such as IBM that have a culture of caring for and respecting the individual are likely to offer employment security.

The impact of corporate culture on employees can be significant:

S. C. Allyn, a retired chairman of the board, likes to tell a story about his company—the National Cash Register Corporation. It was August 1945, and Allyn was among the first allied civilians to enter Germany at the end of the war. He had gone to find out what had happened to an NCR factory built just before the war but promptly confiscated by the German military command and put to work on the war effort. He arrived via military plane and traveled through burned-out buildings, rubble, and utter desolation until he reached

---

General Employee Characteristics to Complement an Organization's Strategy		EXHIBIT 1.2

Repetitive, Predictable Behavior	—	Creative, Innovative Behavior
Short-term Focus	—	Long-term Focus
Cooperative, Interdependent Behavior	—	Independent, Autonomous Behavior
Low Concern for High Quantity	—	High Concern for High Quantity
Low Concern for Quality	—	High Concern for Quality
Low Risk Orientation	—	High Risk Orientation
Concern for Process	—	Concern for Results
Preference to Avoid Responsibility	—	Preference to Assume Responsibility
Inflexible to Change	—	Flexible to Change
Low Task Orientation	—	High Task Orientation
Low Organizational Identification	—	High Organizational Identification
Focus on Efficiency	—	Focus on Effectiveness

SOURCE: R. S. Schuler, "Personnel and Human Resource Management Choices and Organizational Strategy," in *Readings in Personnel and Human Resource Management*, 3d ed., ed. R. S. Schuler, S. A. Youngblood, and V. Huber (St. Paul: West, 1988), 27.

what was left of the factory. Picking his way through bricks, cement, and old timbers, Allyn came upon two NCR employees whom he hadn't seen for six years. Their clothes were torn and their faces grimy and blackened by smoke, but they were busy clearing out the rubble. As he came closer, one of the men looked up and said, "We knew you'd come!" Allyn joined them in their work and together the three men began cleaning out the debris and rebuilding the factory from the devastation of war.

A few days later, as the clearing continued, Allyn and his co-workers were startled as an American tank rumbled up to the site. A grinning GI was at its helm. "Hi," he said, "I'm NCR, Omaha. Did you guys make your quota this month?" Allyn and the GI embraced each other. The war may have devastated everything around them, but NCR's hard driving, sales-oriented culture was still intact.[14]

The impact of corporate culture on PHRM functions and activities is similarly significant because these activities articulate corporate culture. The way in which these activities are done is determined by the PHRM practices selected from some of the available choices, described later in this chapter.

Technology and Structure.   Technology generally refers to the equipment and knowledge used to produce goods and services. For example, the technology that has been used to make automobiles is referred to as the assembly line. The use of assembly-line technology has had a distinct impact on the way jobs have been designed and the types of individuals that have been hired. Although it was once believed that the assembly line was the most efficient way to produce automobiles, this belief has been called into question. Times have changed, competition has changed, customers have changed, and employees have changed. Now in the automobile industry, the assembly-line technology is giving way to newer forms of technology, such as craft or batch technology.[15]

Organizational structure describes the number of levels of employees in an organization—both nonmanagement and management levels. The trend has been for companies to restructure themselves to be most effective in terms of quality and cost. They have done this by reducing the number of levels of employees and by decentralizing the decision-making process.

Size.   Organizational size is also an important factor in PHRM activities. Although exceptions exist, generally the larger the organization, the more developed its internal labor market and the lesser reliance on the external labor market. In contrast, the smaller the organization, the less developed its internal labor market and the greater its reliance on the external labor market.

As more reliance is placed on the internal labor market, the organization relies more on itself in determining how to decide issues related to that market. For example, in deciding how much to pay people, job evaluation, job classification, and internal equity would be used. In contrast, as more reliance is placed on external labor market, the rates that other organizations are paying and external equity would be used to decide how much to pay people.[16]

Relationships with the External Environment

Major components of the external environment influencing PHRM functions and activities include the economy, demographics, social values, laws, and national and international competitors. Because the last four components are

major factors contributing to the growing importance of PHRM, they are described in the following section and in Chapter 2.

The national, state, and local economies can have a significant impact. A strong
economy tends to lower the unemployment rate, increase wage rates, make
recruitment more necessary and more difficult, and increase the desirability of
training current employees. By contrast, a weak economy tends to increase the
unemployment rate, diminish wage increase demands and even result in wage
concessions, make recruitment less necessary and easier, and reduce the need
for training and developing current employees.[17] Although a weak economy may
tend to diminish PHRM's importance, other events in the external environment
act to increase its importance. Recently, PHRM has been significantly affected
by the international economy, which has increased the level of competition and
forced U.S. corporations to become more competitive, flexible, and bottom-line
oriented.

PHRM's GROWING IMPORTANCE

Events Influencing PHRM's Importance

Four major events are influential here: (1) increased competition and therefore
the need to be competitive; (2) the costs and benefits associated with human
resource utilization; (3) the increasing pace and complexity of social, cultural,
legal, demographic, and educational changes; and (4) the symptoms of change
in the work place.

Increased Competition.   "The most important characteristic of today's business environment—and therefore the yardstick against which managerial techniques must be measured—is the new competition."[18] The new competition is
from abroad and from within America. Imports of shoes, textiles, and electronics
represent an ever-increasing share of the U.S. market. Less than ten years ago,
American companies dominated the office copier business in the United States.
Today their share is approximately 50 percent. All this is occurring because of
low-priced products or inventive marketing techniques (or both). In China and
India, for example, total compensation per employee is estimated at twenty-five
to thirty cents per hour. The wage disparity between these countries and the
United States is likely to continue, given the fact that between now and the year
2000, 750 million more people will enter the labor force—90 percent of them
outside the industrialized countries. As a consequence:

> The challenge to management in this country has never been greater. Speaking
> about foreign competition in March 1984, John Young, Chairman of Hewlett-
> Packard Company and Chairman of the President's Commission on Industrial
> Competitiveness, commented: "Some competitive disadvantages we'll probably
> have to accept as 'givens.' With our high standard of living, the human resource
> cost is one of those. That means we'll have to find ways to make our labor
> worth what it's paid.[19]

Competition within the United States has increased, in part because of government deregulation in industries such as communications, finance, airlines,
trucking and railroads, bus service, and public construction. In addition, venture
capital has facilitated the rapid growth of new companies and with them, 20

million new jobs since the mid-1970s. New technology and the drive for diversification have also enhanced domestic competition. As a consequence, organizations such as IBM, General Electric, and Hewlett-Packard are using their human resource activities as a weapon in competitive strategy.[20]

Human Resource Costs.   Today, with payroll costs running anywhere between 30 and 80 percent of total expenses, corporations realize that it pays to be concerned with human resources. Two consequences of this are the development of ways to determine the costs of people's behaviors and the development of personnel programs to reduce these costs. Michael Mercer, president of the Mercer Group, a consulting firm near Chicago, describes such programs and their impact:

- For a service company experiencing a 50 percent turnover rate among sales personnel that was costing $250,000 annually. Mercer's firm developed a series of "valid, reliable, and defensible" job selection tests. By using the tests, which cost $15,000 to administer, the company reduced turnover in the sales force to 23 percent a year. The net savings to the company, Mercer says, totaled $105,000.
- To improve white-collar productivity at another organization, Mercer got HR [Human Resources] to implement five quality circles [QCs]. While this step cost the company $47,000 a year, Mercer points out that the productivity gains achieved with the QCs totaled more than $300,000 a year.
- A manufacturer in a slowly growing but highly competitive industry increased its profitability by following up on Mercer's suggestion to conduct intensive one-day team-building sessions with each of the company's 11 department heads. The $4,590 effort improved company sales by $52,000 a week, according to Mercer.[21]

The Pace and Complexity of Change.   Several ongoing changes in the culture, the educational level, and the social order of the United States have contributed to PHRM concerns. For example, because midlife career changes are becoming more common and most occupations require increased knowledge, training and development programs for all employees have developed rapidly. During the 1980's, the number of workers in the eighteen-to-twenty-four age group declined, while the number in the thirty-to-forty-four age group increased. The result has been too few young workers and too many middle-aged workers with potentially frustrated career ambitions.

The current work force is generally becoming more knowledgeable and better informed. Whereas in 1970 only one of every eight workers had a college degree, in 1980 one of every four workers who entered the labor force had one. At the same time, the illiteracy rate and the high school dropout rate are increasing. Skilled laborers, such as auto mechanics and carpenters, are in short supply. Increasingly, it will become more difficult for organizations to count on an already-trained supply of job applicants. Other work force characteristics and their impact on human resource planning are described in Chapter 2.

Symptoms of Change in the Work Place.   Rapid social change has been accompanied by changes in the relationship between workers and their jobs. Some of the changes in the work place involve worker alienation and attitudes toward the organization, which are often associated with decreased motivation, increased counterproductive behavior, and more worker demands. The work ethic remains strong in the United States, with most workers ready to put in long hours to improve their economic positions. But that doesn't mean that wrenching changes in the corporate world over the decade of the 1980's haven't affected employee loyalty.

More than a third of the 1,200 middle managers surveyed by the New York–based National Institute of Business Management, for example, said they would be happier working for other companies. More recent interviews with 1,000 U.S. manufacturing and service employees, conducted by the management consulting arm of Towers, Perrin, Forster & Crosby Inc., turned up similar results. Some 41 percent said they were concerned about job security because of fears of corporate restructuring or foreign competition. More importantly, almost a third said that, given the opportunity, they would "jump ship" and accept a job at the same pay at another company.

Such attitudes hardly enhance worker productivity. Moreover, some of these employees' fears seem all too realistic. In a 1987 survey of top executives at the nation's 500 largest corporations by New York's Penn & Schoen Associates, over half the respondents said more restructuring in their companies is either "certain, likely, or very possible."[22]

Another symptom of change in the work place is the desire for a more explicit statement of employee rights. Among the rights that employees desire are the rights to work, to know what one's job and its requirements are, to participate in decisions, to be appraised fairly and with objective performance criteria, to be accountable, and to be able to take risks and make mistakes.

TRENDS IN PHRM

Several major trends are (1) assessment of PHRM to determine its effectiveness, (2) use of computer technology and creation of human resource information systems, (3) strategic involvement of PHRM in the organization, and (4) customerization.

Assessment of PHRM

PHRM is often considered not vital to organizations because it fails to demonstrate its effectiveness. That is, it sometimes fails to show how it relates to the three objectives and the three purposes shown in Exhibit 1.1. Recognizing this, personnel and human resource managers are starting to demonstrate their effectiveness just as other managers do: by assessing the costs of their activities against the benefits resulting from those activities.[23]

Benefit Criteria.   **Benefit criteria** are those indicators against which comparisons can be made to demonstrate value or benefit to the organization. Three indicators used as benefit criteria are the purposes of PHRM. These indicators and their specific components (and indicated direction for demonstrating effectiveness) are as follows:

Productivity
- Increased performance
- Reduced absenteeism
- Reduced turnover

Quality of Work Life
- Increased job involvement
- Increased satisfaction
- Reduced stress
- Reduced accidents and illnesses
  Legal Compliance
- Reduced or eliminated costs of fines
- Reduced or eliminated costs of lost contracts
- Enhanced community good will and general reputation

In general, productivity represents the efficiency with which an organization uses its work force, capital, material, and energy resources to produce its product. Other things being equal, reducing the work force but getting the same output improves productivity.[24] Similarly, if each employee's performance (quality or quantity) increases, total output increases, and so does productivity. Reducing absenteeism is also a way to increase productivity, as is the reduction in turnover of good employees.[25] Improving the quality of work life may result in increased performance and in reduced absenteeism and turnover, but the results can also be measured in other ways. [26] For example, the more the organization meets individuals' preferences and interests, the more likely the workers will be more involved with their jobs; register higher satisfaction with their jobs, supervisors, and co-workers; suffer less from stress; and have fewer accidents and better health.

Organizations must comply with many laws and regulations. Failure to comply can result in significant settlement costs. Other effects include cancellation of future contracts with federal, state, and local governments. In addition, individual employees can bring suit against the company for violations of some laws and regulations.[27] Finally, good will with potential job applicants and the community can be significantly diminished if a company chooses not to comply with laws and regulations.

Cost Criteria. **Cost criteria** are those indicators against which benefit criteria can be compared to determine **PHRM** effectiveness. Whereas benefit criteria generally apply to all PHRM activities, cost criteria are more specific to each activity. For example, cost criteria appropriate for the safety and health activity may be supervisory training, the addition of newer and safer equipment, the removal of hazards and waste materials, and job redesign. Cost criteria for recruitment may be advertising, training, and recruiters' payroll.

After determining the appropriate cost criteria (based on the specific personnel activity of interest) and the appropriate benefit criteria (not all benefit criteria are equally relevant to each personnel activity), these costs and benefits are compared. This comparison is increasingly being made on the basis of dollars and cents. Thus, the dollars-and-cents values of the cost criteria and benefit criteria must be determined.

Once these values are established, PHRM can demonstrate that the values of the cost criteria are no greater than, or perhaps are even less than, those in other organizations (similar or different). Second, it can enhance the value of those comparisons by including relevant information on benefit criteria.

Although it may be neither feasible to obtain nor valid to use a dollars-and-cents valuation of the turnover of other organizations, it may be useful to compare *rates* of turnover or absenteeism. Thus, the personnel and human resource department could show the organization that the costs for managing its human resources are producing more benefits (using only a comparison of turnover rates) than are those of other organizations.

The department can also demonstrate its effectiveness by comparing changes in benefit criteria levels with specific personnel activities. The valuation of the benefit criteria changes can then be compared with the valuation of the cost criteria associated with the specific personnel activities.

To help prevent erroneous conclusions or false inferences from being drawn, the personnel and human resource manager needs to be aware of varying types of research evaluation designs. These are presented in Chapter 11 on training and development. Other useful research and statistical issues are presented in Chapter 16 on personnel research. Aiding the assessment of PHRM are computer technology and human resource information systems.

Computer Technology and HRIS

PHRM requires a great deal of information. Computer technology enables organizations to combine human resource information into a single data base. A common computer-oriented information system used in the management of human resources is often referred to as a **human resource information system** (HRIS).

> Any human resource information system is logically an inventory of the positions and skills extant in a given organization. However, HRIS is more than a simple aggregation mechanism for inventory control and accounting; it is the foundation for a set of management tools enabling managers to establish objectives for the use of their organization's human resources and to measure the extent to which those objectives have been achieved.[28]

There are four key advantages to HRIS. First, the computer enables the department to take a more active role in organization planning. Forecasting techniques are feasible that would require a significant time investment without the use of computer technology. Second, the computer integrates and stores in a single data base all personnel information previously filed in separate physical locations. Thus, the personnel and human resource department can take a global view of its human resource stock and interpret it in more meaningful ways. For example, data on career interests may be more easily matched with career advancement and training opportunities by creating a simple coding system that automatically identifies candidates. The personnel data that the U.S. State Department gathers include employees' personal preferences, education and training, and experience and skill. The position and personnel data in the HRIS can then be used to make more effective internal selection and placement decisions and career development decisions that are beneficial for both the organization and the individual. Third, the computer speeds the process of comparing costs and benefits in PHRM assessment. Fourth, an HRIS and computer technology facilitate the storage of and access to personnel records that are vital for organizations.[29]

To comply with federal equal employment laws, organizations must follow several personnel record requirements. Title VII of the 1964 Civil Rights Act says that organizations must keep all employment records for at least six months. The Equal Pay Act and the Age Discrimination in Employment Act say that organizations must keep records for three years. Three years, however, isn't always the limit. If an employee or a government agency lodges a charge against a firm, the firm should hold on to all its records until the claim is settled. The organization must keep all records regarding the person making the complaint and records on all other employees in similar positions. The organization must also keep records on seniority, benefit, merit, and incentive plans until at least one year after the plans end.

Besides keeping records, organizations have to fill out reports. Employers of one hundred or more workers must annually file EEO-1 forms. Multiestablishment employers need only file separate EEO-1 forms for each establishment employing fifty or more workers. Organizations with government contracts must fill out affirmative action reports that the Office of Federal Contract Compliance Programs (OFCCP) sends. Government contractors required to fill out Standardized Affirmative Action Formats (SAAFs) for the OFCCP can propose one SAAF to cover all its establishments as long as its personnel practices are homogeneous. Also, employers with $10,000 or more in federal contracts must report annually to the Secretary of Labor the number of Vietnam veterans or special disabled veterans employed, as well as the number hired during the reporting period compared to the total number of new employees.

Among companies using an HRIS and computer technology, relief from "telephone tag" is considered a boon; computer-assisted scheduling of meetings and even computer-based conferences are more advanced advantages. In flexible companies, managers have on-line access to systems for processing pay changes, promotions and transfers, candidate searches, staffing requests, and other transactions that traditionally were paper driven. Some system applications provide direct computer access by employees for flexible benefit enrollments, career planning and self-assessment, job posting, and training.

In addition to internal data management, human resource professionals may benefit from having direct access to external data bases that contain information affecting their work (e.g., literature, demographic data, other company practices, legal requirements), reducing time-consuming steps.[30]

Other potential uses and benefits of the computer in personnel applications are introduced in relation to the central topics in each of the following chapters.

Strategic Involvement

Traditionally, many PHRM departments had a relatively limited involvement in the total organization's affairs and goals. Personnel and human resource managers were often concerned only with making staffing plans, providing specific job training programs, or running annual performance appraisal programs (the results of which were put in personnel files, never to be used). Consequently, these managers were concerned only with the short-term operational and managerial—perhaps day-to-day—human resource needs.

Now, because of the extensive relationships among PHRM activities and the internal and external environment, these managers are becoming more involved in the total organization—where it's going, where it should be going—and are helping it to get there.[31] As a consequence, they and their departments are playing many more roles and utilizing the PHRM functions and activities on a long-term basis as well as the more typical medium- and short-term bases. In utilizing such functions and activities in these three distinct time horizons, personnel and human resource departments are really operating at three organizational levels: strategic, managerial, and operational.

At the operational (short-term) level, these departments make staffing and recruitment plans, set up day-to-day monitoring systems, administer wage and salary programs, administer benefits packages, set up annual or less frequent appraisal systems, set up day-to-day control systems, provide for specific job skill training, provide on-the-job training, fit individuals to specific jobs, and plan career moves.

At the managerial (medium-term) level, these departments do longitudinal validation of selection criteria, develop recruitment marketing plans and new recruiting markets, set up five-year compensation plans for individuals, set up cafeteria benefits packages, set up validated systems that relate current conditions and future potential, set up assessment centers for development, establish general management development programs, provide for organizational development, foster self-development, identify career paths, and provide career development services.

At the strategic (long-term) level, these departments are now just starting to seek ways in which organizations can gain competitive advantage—that is, beat their competitors—and to link their practices (functions and activities) to their organizations' strategies. Because the use of PHRM at the strategic level in organizations is just beginning and is so critical in effectively managing human resources, it is explicitly introduced and described in this chapter and at the end of those to follow. At the operational and managerial levels it is more well established in organizations and is described throughout the remaining chapters.

Gaining Competitive Advantage.   One of the two major ways of using PHRM at the strategic level is to gain competitive advantage.[32] Organizations use one or more PHRM activities to become the lowest-cost producer through increased efficiency or to differentiate their products from those of the competition. For example, Lincoln Electric uses such practices (particularly compensation) to increase production efficiency and thereby lower the cost of its electric motors and arc welders.

Delco-Remy uses its PHRM practices to produce a higher-quality product, thereby differentiating itself from its competitors. When Delco-Remy trained its employees in participative management, it succeeded in differentiating itself from all competitors in the eyes of Honda and others. Delco's Keith W. Wander describes the success of this training and the resultant competitive advantage:

> Honda of America was seeking an American battery manufacturer as a supplier to its auto plant in Maryville, Ohio. Honda wanted a plant which had a participative system of management and a reputation for producing a quality product at a competitive price. After a contact from the Delco-Remy Sales Department, two American representatives from Honda visited the Delco-Remy plant in Fitzgerald, Georgia. This visit was followed by a second one with Mr. Hoshita, President of Honda, in the group.
>
> During the second visit, plant tours were conducted by Operating Team (hourly employees) members. The tours were followed by Operating Team members explaining to Mr. Hoshita how people were involved in the Fitzgerald business, how Fitzgerald and Honda could be mutual resources to each other because of their participative systems, and why a Delco battery was the best-built battery in the world.
>
> Mr. Hoshita returned several months later to ask more questions of the Support team (salaried employees) and Operating Teams. Shortly afterward, Honda of America announced Delco-Remy, Fitzgerald, as its sole supplier of batteries, based upon its (1) culture; (2) quality; and (3) price, in that order.
>
> To date, Honda has had zero returns of batteries and zero complaints on quality or delivery.[33]

Gaining competitive advantage through PHRM activities is extremely advantageous for organizations. A major reason is that a response from competitors is likely to be slow in coming because changing human resource practices consumes vast amounts of time and energy.

Because gaining competitive advantage is so useful for organizations, the following chapters of this book describe how it can be done using specific PHRM practices. The chapters also describe how these practices can be linked with organizational strategy.

Linking with Organizational Strategy. PHRM functions and activities (practices) are increasingly being linked to the organization's strategy. As mentioned under the section entitled "Relationships with the Internal Environment," organizations are recognizing that different employee characteristics are needed with different strategies. As a result, they are using their PHRM practices in different ways, depending on the types of general characteristics (such as those shown in Exhibit 1.2) that they need from employees.[34] This suggests that PHRM activities have major alternatives (choices) and that some may be more appropriate than others for a given strategy. Note that there are many choices in PHRM practices; however, many are not relevant to organizational strategy. Only those few relevant to organizational strategy are discussed here. As a result, they may be referred to as strategic choices in PHRM practices. These are illustrated in Exhibit 1.3, along with five organizational strategies and the needed employee characteristics described earlier.

Exhibit 1.3 suggests that organizational strategy, in part, determines needed employee characteristics, which in turn determine choices in PHRM activities. Because of this, the selection of PHRM practices to match strategy reflects the need for a consistent set of stimuli and reinforcements to be provided or sent to employees. Ideally, then, all such practices are working together to stimulate and reinforce the characteristics that organizations need from their employees to facilitate their strategies.

Customerization

Adding to the personnel and human resource department's ability to gain strategic involvement are its knowledge of the business, its creative insights into how the organization can be more effective, and its familiarity with and acceptance by top management. More and more, these qualities are being found in departments that practice customerization. Customerization means viewing everybody, whether internal or external to the organization, as a customer and then putting that customer first. For personnel and human resource departments, customers are typically other line and staff managers. Increasingly, customers include other organizations and even the nonmanagerial employees. The impact of treating these employees as customers is described in the following "PHRM in the News" feature on Burger King.

An essential underlying ingredient in this philosophy is the recognition and conceptualization of the fact that all personnel and human resource departments produce and deliver products and have customers. Another essential ingredient is the realization that the products they must have to satisfy the customer are determined only by the customer. Giving the customer what is desired results in added value.

PHRM Practice Choices—Organizational Strategy Matches and Needed Employee Characteristics

EXHIBIT
1.3

Organizational Strategy	Needed Employee Characteristics	PHRM Practice Choices
Entrepreneurial Strategy: Projects with high financial risk are undertaken, minimal policies and procedures are in place, resources are insufficient to satisfy all customer demands, and multiple priorities must be satisfied. The focus here is on the short run and getting the operation off the ground.	To varying degrees, employees need to be innovative, cooperative, longer-term oriented, risk taking, and willing to assume responsibility. It is critical that key employees remain.	(1) Planning—formal, tight, implicit, broad, integrative, high participation. (2) Staffing—broad paths, multiple ladders, open, implicit criteria. (3) Appraising—loosely integrated, results criteria; longer term, high participation. (4) Compensation—external equity, flexible, high participation. (5) Training—broad application, informal and high participation.
Dynamic Growth Strategy: Risk taking on projects is more modest. The constant dilemma is between doing current work and building support for the future. Policies and procedures are starting to be written, as the need is for more control and structure for an ever-expanding operation.	Employees need to have high organizational identification, be flexible to change, have a high task orientation, and work in close cooperation with others.	(1) Planning—broad, informal, integrative. (2) Staffing—broad, open, implicit. (3) Appraising—employee participation; combination of individual and group criteria and short- and long-term focus (4) Compensation—employee participation, short- and long-term rewards; internal and external equity. (5) Training—broad application; productivity and quality emphasis, some participation.
Extract Profit/Rationalization Strategy: The focus is on maintaining existing profit levels. Modest cost-cutting efforts and employee terminations may be occurring. Control systems and structure are well developed along with an extensive set of policies and procedures.	The focus is on quantity and efficiency, the short term, and results with a relatively low level of risk and a minimal level of organizational identification.	(1) Planning—formal, narrow, explicit job descriptions, low involvement. (2) Staffing—narrow, closed, explicit criteria, little socialization. (3) Appraising— results criteria, maintenance purposes, individual evaluation. (4) Compensation—short term, internal equity, low participation. (5) Training—narrow application, low participation, productivity focus.

EXHIBIT	PHRM Practice Choices—Organizational Strategy Matches and Needed
1.3	Employee Characteristics (continued)

Organizational Strategy	Needed Employee Characteristics	PHRM Practice Choices
Liquidation/Divestiture Strategy: The focus involves selling off assets, cutting further losses, and reducing the work force as much as possible. Little or no thought is given to trying to save the operation, as declining profits are likely to continue.	Employees need a short-term, narrow orientation, low organizational commitment, a low need to remain, and a limited focus on high quantity.	(1) Planning—formal, segmental, explicit. (2) Staffing—narrow paths, explicit criteria, limited socialization, closed procedures. (3) Appraising—remedial purposes, behavioral criteria, low participation. (4) Compensation—low participation, few perks, fixed package, no incentives. (5) Training—unplanned, narrow application.
Turnaround Strategy: The focus is to save the operation. Although cost-cutting efforts and employee reductions are made, they are short-term programs for long-run survival. Worker morale may be somewhat depressed.	Employees need to be flexible to change, have a high task orientation, have a longer-term focus, and engage in some nonrepetitive behavior.	(1) Planning—informal, loose, high employee involvement. (2) Staffing—extensive socialization, openness, informal, implicit criteria. (3) Appraising—results criteria, group criteria, high participation. (4) Compensation—short- and long-term incentives, high participation. (5) Training—broad focus, high participation, productivity emphasis.

SOURCE: R. S. Schuler,"Personnel and Human Resource Management Choices and Organizational Strategy," in *Readings in Personnel and Human Resource Management,* 3d ed., ed. R. S. Schuler, S. A. Youngblood, and V. Huber (St. Paul: West, 1988), 33–34.

Two ways of adding value are through quality enhancement and innovation. Innovation means creating and doing different things (PHRM practices); quality enhancement means doing things (PHRM practices) better. When a personnel and human resource department adds value, it enables its customers (the rest of the organization) to be more effective and competitive. It enables the rest of the organization to pursue competitive strategies of innovation and/or quality enhancement. This has been happening in such organizations as Ford, Burger King, McDonald's, Carter Hawley Hale, Swiss Bank Corporation, and IBM. And when it does, organizations realize they need different PHRM practices. Consequently, they change their practices and get the employee behaviors they need to implement an innovation or quality enhancement strategy.

In its pursuit of high-quality (dependable) customer service, McDonald's emphasizes training:

Outstanding customer service requires a commitment to ongoing training that stresses workers' job-related skills, positive attitudes toward customers and co-workers, and overall company knowledge, according to Robert L. Desatnick,

Treating Employees as Customers

The fast food and retail industries, faced with a shortage of young people to supply their needs for employees, have developed some creative ways to recruit and retain the ones that are out there. Three years ago, *HR Reporter* reported on Burger King Corporation's challenge to recruit and retain young people.

Still battling a shortage, Burger King is beginning to see a payoff for its efforts in improved retention figures. Since 1985, Burger King has brought its food handler turnover rate down from 300% to 175% annually; and 75% to 40% for managers.

Bob Morrison, director of human resources, focuses entirely on recruitment and retention for the 4,961 restaurants across the country. "At the top of our program is the concept of treating employees as customers," he said. "The way we treat our employees is the way they treat our customers."

Creating a positive work experience begins with orientation training. Burger King is making the training programs more "user friendly"—more fun, interactive and educational, at the same time.

"We have to teach our employees how to flame-broil hamburgers and run the cash register. But, we also want to teach them how to make customers happy," explained Morrison. "Our top management is beginning to understand the importance of treating our human resources as a major asset of the company."

Burger King is promoting three concepts to its work force:

Quality of Work Life (QWL)

The company is developing the environment in the restaurants as a product, just like a new hamburger. The restaurant managers' attitudes and style set that atmosphere. So, Burger King is testing programs in some of the company-owned stores to come up with some measurable programs.

Crew as Family

The crew must feel that they're part of a family—the Burger King family and the individual store family.

Labor Expense as an Investment

"When business is slow on a particular shift," Morrison explained, "we currently send employees home. But, that doesn't help them meet their financial goals. And, they feel that they don't have control of their own time. We're trying to instill in the managers a concept of labor expense as an investment in the future of that employee.

"We feel strongly that we do not have a recruitment problem. We have a retention problem."

A "Senior Management Recruitment and Retention Task Force" has been formed. They have identified three projects that they feel will head Burger King in the right direction:

Blue Ribbon Panel

After assessing all of the 4,961 restaurant managers, the top 20 were selected for an in-depth look at their operation. "We found that

continued

president of Creative Human Resources, and former vice-president of human resources at McDonald's. In his book, *Managing to Keep the Customer,* Desatnick maintains that comprehensive training programs are the key to successful customer service at many leading firms.[35]

There are four major phases in PHRM customerization program: (1) gathering information, (2) developoing action agendas, (3) implementing the action agendas, and (4) evaluating and revising the agendas. To do these successfully, the

the one thing they all do best is the special management of their people," Morrison commented. "We're now in the process of identifying what they're doing that makes it work."

National Orientation Program

The task force has identified the need for a consistent introduction to the Burger King culture.

People Count

This comprehensive package of marketing and training tools is now available to managers. It promotes the philosophy of work as a product, provides self-training programs and contains a summary of every possible recruitment and retention tool available to them.

Source: HR Reporter (June 1988): 1–2. Used by permission of *HR Reporter,* copyright 1988.

personnel and human resource department must learn more about the business, actively seek to develop and deliver new PHRM products (e.g., a new performance appraisal system), and constantly seek feedback from customers. Typically, during customerization the department becomes more effective: it becomes a strategic player, it becomes more responsive, and its staff becomes more committed to the organization.[36]

ORGANIZING THE PHRM DEPARTMENT

Based on our discussion thus far, organizations can apparently benefit the most by allowing their personnel and human resource departments to become proactive and open, to engage in the several functions and activities at each of the three levels (strategic, managerial, and operational), and to demonstrate their effectiveness. Organizations, however, can also benefit by allowing these departments to address several issues associated with organizing the department:

- The number of roles that PHRM plays
- The need for the PHRM staff to be where the action is and to identify with the organization
- The need for a fair and consistent application of personnel policies, regardless of how small or large or diversified the organization
- The need for the department's views to be an integral part of personnel policy
- The need for the department to have sufficient power and authority to help ensure that personnel policies will be implemented legally, affirmatively, and without discrimination
- The need for the department not just to react to personnel crises but also to be active and innovative in dealing with human resource management

These issues, which are the essence of the roles that personnel and human resource departments can play, affect the organization of the department. For example, the department can be organized so that it effectively plays a single role. Or it can be organized so that it plays two or more roles. The number of roles played often depends on the way top management views personnel activities and on what it is willing to let the department do.

Personnel and Human Resource Roles

Personnel can play several roles in an organization.[37] The more roles it plays, the more likely it will be effective in improving the organization's productivity, enhancing the quality of work life in the organization, and complying with all the necessary laws and regulations related to human resource utilization.

The Policy Formulator Role.   One role the department can play is that of providing information for top management's use (at the strategic level). The specific types of information can include employee concerns, the external environment's impact, and how PHRM activities can be used to gain competitive advantage.

The department staff can also advise in the process of policy formulation. The chief executive may still make policy statements, but these could be regarded as drafts of policy. Formal adoption of a final policy can then take place after other executives, such as the personnel manager and line managers, have had a chance to comment. Honeywell has an executive employee relations committee, composed of five operating group vice-presidents and five staff vice-presidents, which is the senior policy board for employee relations issues. This committee not only helps ensure extensive informational input into personnel policies but also increases the input's likelihood of being accepted.

The Provider and Delegator Role.   In reality, PHRM programs succeed because line managers (at managerial and operational levels) make them succeed. The department's bread-and-butter job, therefore, is to enable line managers to make things happen. In the more traditional personnel activities, such as selecting, interviewing, training, evaluating, rewarding, counseling, promoting, and firing, the personnel department is basically providing a service to line managers. In addition, the personnel department administers direct and indirect compensation programs. Because the line managers are ultimately responsible for their employees, many of them see these services as useful. The personnel department can also assist line managers by providing information about, and interpreting, equal employment opportunity legislation and safety and health standards.

The department's responsibilities are to provide the services that the line managers need on a day-to-day basis, to keep them informed of regulations and legislation regarding human resource management, and to provide an adequate supply of job candidates for the line managers to select from. To fulfill these responsibilities, however, the department must be accessible, or the personnel and human resource manager will lose touch with the line manager's needs. The personnel staff should be as close to where the people and the problems are as possible. Because bringing the personnel staff close to the action is important, this is discussed in the section on departmental organizing later in the chapter.

The Auditor Role.   Although personnel may delegate much of the implementation of PHRM activities to line managers, the department is still responsible for seeing that activities are implemented fairly and consistently. This is especially true today because of fair employment legislation. Responses to these regulations can best be made by a central group supplied with accurate information, the needed expertise, and the blessing of top management.

Expertise is also needed for implementing many personnel activities, such as distributing employee benefits. And because having personnel experts is costly, organizations hire as few as possible and centralize them. Their expertise then filters to other areas of the organization.

In organizations that have several locations and several divisions or units, tension often exists between the need for decentralization and the need for having the expertise necessary to comply with complex regulations and advise on the best methods for personnel activities.

The Innovator Role.   An important and ever-expanding role for the personnel and human resource department is that of providing up-to-date application of current techniques and developing and exploring innovative approaches to personnel problems and concerns.

> Naturally, the innovative role must be in tune with the times and the set of issues confronting a particular company. In periods of rising inflation and escalating wage and salary demands, the emphasis may be on compensation issues. In times of retrenchment and falling profits, creative work sharing and lay-off plans may be needed.[38]

Today, the personnel-related issues demanding innovative approaches and solutions center on how to improve productivity and the quality of work life while complying with the law in an environment of high uncertainty, energy conservation, and intense international competition.

The Adapter Role.   It is increasingly necessary that organizations adopt new technologies, structuring processes, cultures, and procedures to meet the demands of enhanced competition. Their personnel and human resource departments are expected to have the skills to facilitate organizational change and to maintain organizational flexibility and adaptability.

Because these departments are facing the same demands as the organizations they work for, they are streamlining and automating their own operations and focusing services on critical tasks. In the flat, lean, and flexible organization, the PHRM function is a small, high-performing, no-hassle staff function. Management wants the staff to dismantle unnecessary institutional trappings—policies, systems, procedures, and the staff finds it essential to reduce the time demands of routine activities in order to find time for initiatives.

The challenge to human resource staff is to perform necessary roles while minimizing the administrative burden on managers and the cost to the organization. Flexible companies seek to streamline, delegate, automate, or eliminate all possible tasks. Thus, the personnel and human resource management staff must review and improve its operations, reduce costs, reduce paperwork, eliminate activities, and contract out services, as appropriate. Not waiting for mandated cutbacks, the department must continually review and evaluate expenses and implement incremental changes to become and stay lean. Through flexible PHRM functions, the department members aggressively seek to be perceived as "bureaucracy busters," setting an example for other staff functions and line organizations.[39] How effective an organization is in addressing these issues depends on how well it organizes and staffs the personnel department.

PHRM in the Organization

The importance that an organization assigns to personnel and human resource management is reflected in the department's status in the hierarchy. To fulfill the five HR roles effectively, the top manager of the department should be at the top of the organizational hierarchy, with line authority to the chief executive officer (CEO).

The top manager and staff of the PHRM department are increasingly expected to be functional experts, capable administrators, business consultants, and problem solvers. In short, management expects human resource staff "to have it all."

As in traditional organizations, administrative skills are essential for efficient human resource management. Specialized human resource expertise is also important, but particularly now in combination with business knowledge and perspective. In flexible organizations, problem-solving and consulting skills are vital in guiding and supporting adoption of new management practices.

Managers would like human resource staff to work closely with them to help solve their people-related problems as efficiently and promptly as possible, allowing them to give more attention to other concerns. Peter Drucker observed that HR staff will "move into line work," making decisions and taking actions, not merely advising. While managers may best understand their own people, they increasingly seek help in handling people problems. As personnel and human resource staff become more capable and effective, managers seek to work with them as partners.[40]

Being at the top and having business skills allows the personnel and human resource manager to play a part in PHRM policy formulation and to have the power necessary to ensure its fair and consistent implementation. When the department has this much importance, it is likely to be performing effectively at the operational, managerial, and strategic levels of personnel activity.

Centralization Versus Decentralization

The organizing concept of centralization versus decentralization relates to the balance between getting personnel to where the action is and applying personnel policies fairly and consistently. It also relates to the balance between the benefits of having personnel generalists and of having personnel specialists. **Centralization** means that essential decision making and policy formulation are done at one location (at headquarters); **decentralization** means that essential decision making and policy formulation are done at several locations (in the divisions or departments of the organization).

With the recent increases in regulatory requirements for use of human resources and the increased expertise necessary to deal with complex personnel functions, organizations are moving away from personnel generalists and toward personnel specialists. And at the same time, organizations—especially larger ones—are moving personnel staff into the organization's divisions. As a result, the trend is to centralize nonroutine aspects of personnel and human resources and to decentralize day-to-day activities.

Thus, in a large, multidivisional organization (which describes most of the largest industrial, retaining, and financial organizations), there is generally a corporate personnel and human resource department staffed largely with specialists and several divisional personnel departments staffed largely with generalists. The headquarters department, then, has two purposes: (1) to develop and coordinate PHRM policy for the personnel staff in all locations, including headquarters, and (2) to execute the PHRM functions and activities for all the employees at headquarters. As the divisions grow, they begin to hire their own specialists and to administer almost all their own personnel functions and activities. The result is several almost complete personnel and human resource departments, similar to what would be found in most organizations without divisions.

Who Is Responsible for PHRM?

Everyone should be responsible, and as organizations demonstrate more openness and mutuality in their human resources policies and practices, everyone is.[41]

The Managers.   Personnel and human resource management is the primary task of individuals who have specialized in and are primarily responsible for this aspect of the organization. But, with the increase in flat, lean organizations, line managers also are becoming more directly involved. As the ratio between personnel and human resource staff and line employees increases, more and more responsibility for human resource administration falls to the line manager. In fact, effective line managers spend at least one-fifth of their time dealing with human resource issues. Routine activities include motivating /reinforcing, disciplining/punishing, managing conflict, staffing and training, and developing staff.[42] This is not meant to imply that the personnel manager never implements personnel functions and activities or that the line manager does not get involved in their development and administration. Indeed, these two managers are interdependent in the effective management of human resources. But the effective management of human resources cannot occur without management's support and direction. Top management influences the number and execution of personnel functions and activities in an organization. This influence is best shown by the roles that top management allows the personnel manager and the line managers to play in the organization.

The Employees.   Employees are increasingly playing a role in personnel and human resource management. For example, employees may be asked to appraise their own performance or that of their colleagues. Employees may also help determine their own performance standards and goals. It is no longer uncommon for employees to write their own job descriptions. Perhaps most significantly, employees are playing a more active role in managing their own careers, assessing their own needs and values, and designing their own jobs. Nonetheless, the personnel and human resource department must help guide this process to ensure that individual plans are congruent with organizational plans.

PHRM Titles.   Several terms are used throughout this text. Note that the terms **personnel manager** (or **executive**), **personnel and human resource manager,** and **HR manager** refer to the person heading the personnel and human resource department. In some organizations, this position may also be called the vice-president of human resources or the vice-president of employee relations.

The term **personnel and human resource department** can be used interchangeably with the term **personnel department** or just **human resources.** Different names are used in different organizations. Nevertheless, all the functions and activities of personnel and human resource management relate to any of these terms. The term **staff** or **personnel staff** refers to the employees in the personnel department (either generalists or specialists).

Line manager (or **supervisor**) refers to the person in charge of the employees who are working directly on the product that the organization produces. The terms **individual, person, worker,** and **work force** refer to anyone in the organization. The term **employee** or **incumbent** generally refers to the person who works for the line manager or the personnel manager; this person may also be called a **nonmanagerial employee.** Use of the term **subordinate** is avoided, except in Chapters 6 and 7, in which the terms **subordinate, incumbent** and **superior** are used.

Perhaps the most effective person to head the personnel and human resource department is an outstanding performer (a superstar) with PHRM expertise who has had line management experience in finance, marketing, and production.

In essence, to be a true professional in many areas of HR management, individuals virtually have to have an advanced degree in the subject and spend full time in that field. Areas like compensation have become incredibly complicated because of their close connection to strategic, legal, financial, and tax matters. [But] with the exception of technical specialists, HR managers need to spend a significant amount of time in line-management positions. It is not enough for senior HR managers to have worked in different areas of the HR function; they must have had some line business experience so that they have a first-hand familiarity with the business operations.[43]

Line experience gives the personnel managers influence over and credibility with other line managers. To understand just how far some companies have gone in this area, consider IBM's policy of assigning line managers to work in the corporate personnel department for two or three years as a part of their career development.

Conversely, the personnel specialist who wants to reach the top may benefit greatly by rotating through a line job in order to increase his or her ability to understand and deal with the entire organization.

STAFFING THE PHRM DEPARTMENT

Qualities of the PHRM Manager and Staff

How effectively an organization's human resources are managed depends in large part upon the quality of the people in the personnel and human resource department.

The PHRM Manager.   These managers need to be effective. They must be able to identify problems, develop alternative solutions, and then select and implement the most effective one. In addition, they must develop and maintain an integrated and effective management information system to help identify prolems and implement policy. They must be innovative, aggressive, and willing to take the risks incurred by serving as the organization's conscience. Furthermore, they must be effective at selecting, building, and developing an entire personnel staff to carry out the five PHRM functions.

PHRM Generalists.   Line positions are one important source for the rest of the personnel staff. A brief tour in a personnel position by a line supervisor, usually as a personnel generalist, can convey to the personnel department the knowledge, language, needs, and requirements of the line. As a result, the department can more effectively fill its service role. Another source of personnel talent is current nonmanagerial employees. In many organizations, PHRM positions are staffed with former hourly employees. Like line managers, these people bring with them information about employee needs and attitudes.

Personnel generalists should possess many of the same qualities as personnel specialists, but the level of expertise in a personnel specialty generally need not be at the same depth. The generalist, however, needs to have a moderate level of expertise in many PHRM activities and must be able to get more specialized knowledge when it is needed.

PHRM Specialists.   Staff specialists should have skills related to their specialty, an awareness of the relationship of that specialty to other PHRM activities, and a knowledge of the organization and where their specialized function fits. Individuals joining an organization for the first time should also have an appreciation for the political realities of organizations. Universities are an important source of personnel specialists. Because specialists may work at almost any personnel activity, qualified applicants can come from specialized programs in law, personnel psychology, industrial and organizational psychology, labor and industrial relations, personnel management, counseling, organizational development, and medical and health science.

PHRM JOBS

As a field of employment, PHRM is becoming very attractive. It offers numerous different types of jobs, many of which are comparable to those associated with other entry-level business career choices such as accounting. Starting salaries for specialists are also competitive—so much so that many master's in business administration (MBA) programs are adding PHRM courses to their curriculum to give students an additional competitive career option.

How Much Do They Pay?

The results of a recent survey, along with the types of jobs in a personnel department, are shown in Exhibit 1.4. In that survey, salaries were generally higher for those individuals in larger organizations, for those with more experience, and for those with more education. In addition, salaries were higher in New York City, Los Angeles, and the states in the South and Southwest.[44]

PHRM Budgets

The amount of money that organizations allocate to their personnel and human resource departments continues to rise yearly. For example, per-employee PHRM costs rose from $582 in 1985 to $601 in 1988. The median department budget went from $575,000 in 1987 to $610,000 in 1988. Median staff size is one personnel staff member for every 100 workers.

Professionalism in Personnel

Like any profession, PHRM follows a code of professional ethics and has an accreditation institute and certification procedures.[45] All professions share the code of ethics that personnel follows:

1. The practitioner must regard the obligation to implement public objectives and protect the public interest as more important than blind loyalty to an employer's preferences.
2. In daily practice, the professional must thoroughly understand the problems assigned and must undertake whatever study and research are required to assure continuing competence and the best of professional attention.
3. The practitioner must maintain a high standard of personal honesty and integrity in every phase of daily practice.
4. The professional must give thoughtful consideration to the personal interest, welfare, and dignity of all employees who are affected by his/her prescriptions, recommendations, and actions.

5. Professionals must make very sure that the organizations that represent them maintain a high regard and respect for the public interest and that they never overlook the importance of the personal interests and dignity of employees.[46]

Professional Certification

The Society for Human Resource Management has established the Personnel Accreditation Institute (PAI) to certify PHRM professionals.[47] The PAI has the following purposes:

1. To recognize individuals who have demonstrated expertise in particular fields
2. To raise and maintain professional standards
3. To identify a body of knowledge as a guide to practitioners, consultants, educators, and researchers
4. To aid employers in identifying qualified applicants
5. To provide an overview of the field as a guide to self-development

The PAI has two levels of accreditation: *basic* and *senior*. The basic accreditation is the Professional in Human Resources (PHR). This designation requires an examination covering the general body of knowledge and four years of professional experience. A bachelor's degree in personnel or social sciences counts for two years of professional experience. The senior level accreditation is the Senior Professional in Human Resources (SPHR). The SPHR requires a minimum of eight years' experience, with the three most recent years including policy-developing responsibility. All professionals receiving accreditation will be listed in the *Register of Accredited Personnel and Human Resource Professionals*.

PLAN OF THIS BOOK

This book is intended to serve readers by fulfilling several specific purposes and by maintaining several themes throughout each of the chapters.

Purposes

The specific purposes are as follows:

- To increase your expertise in the functions and activities of personnel and human resource management
- To assist you in being an effective manager of human resources
- To present the complexities, challenges, and trade-offs involved in being an effective manager of human resources
- To instill a concern for and an excitement over effective personnel and human resource management
- To assist you in being a more effective line manager

Themes

The three major themes in this book are (1) applications and practical realities, (2) international comparisons, and (3) theory and research. Each of these themes is integral in illustrating PHRM's importance and in demonstrating how personnel managers can help organizations effectively use their human resources.

EXHIBIT 1.4   Average Salaries in Human Resource Management

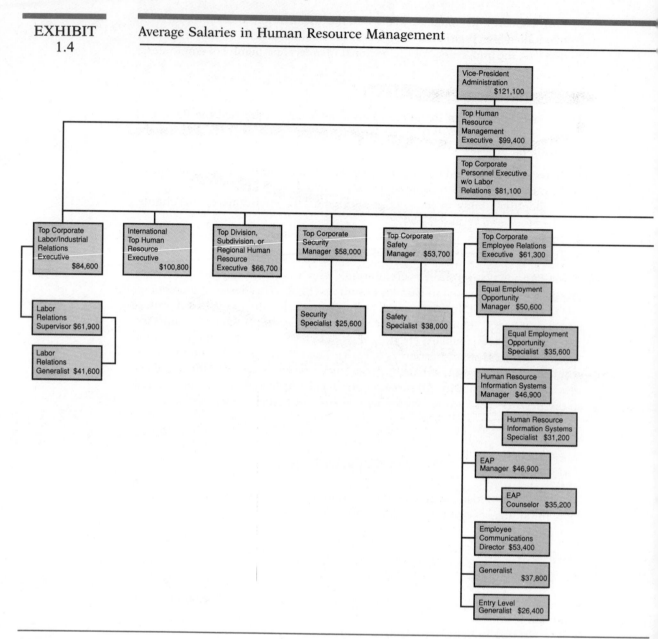

SOURCE: William M. Mercer-Meidinger-Hansen, Inc. Reprinted by permission from the *Bulletin to Management* copyright 1989 by The Bureau of National Affairs, Inc., Washington, DC 20037.

Average Salaries in Human Resource Management (continued)

EXHIBIT
1.4

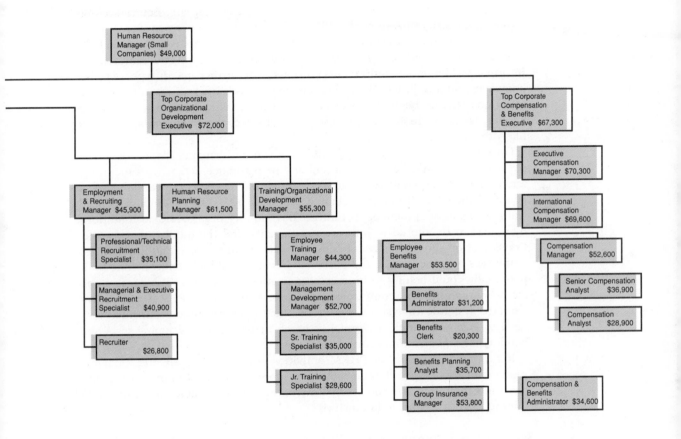

Applications and Practical Realities.   Examples from organizations and human resource managers are used throughout the book to illustrate the practical realities of the personnel activities being examined. Each chapter begins with a real-life scenario or quotation called "PHRM in the News." Additional real-life scenarios and quotations appear throughout each chapter. Cases are included at the end of Chapters 2–16 and at the end of the book to provide you with a firsthand opportunity to deal with the challenges and practical realities of PHRM.

This theme is reflected in the arrangement of the chapters. Before seeking job candidates, organizations should plan for the number and types of employees they need. This includes comparing present and future employee needs in light of information about such concerns as labor market demand and competition. Information about job requirements is necessary to further specify types of skills, knowledge, and abilities. Once this information is gathered, recruitment and selection activities begin. Decisions are made about where and how to seek job applicants. Tests are developed to screen and select those job applicants most likely to succeed.

Once on the job, employees need to be given performance standards. Their performance should be evaluated and any performance deficiencies identified and corrected. A system of direct and indirect pay to the employees also must be established. Conditions may change, requiring new skills, so employees need training and development opportunities. Beyond this, organizational conditions may need to be altered to improve productivity and the quality of work life. Consideration should be given to employee health and safety, and the rights of employees must be known and observed. Because employees may belong to or potentially could belong to unions, organizations may need to engage in collective bargaining and contract negotiations. And because PHRM can benefit from the systemic analysis of conditions, the human resource department may need to engage in such personnel research activities as developing tests and conducting organizational surveys.

Reflecting this model of PHRM activities and functions are the following sections in this book: Planning, Staffing, Appraising and Compensating, Improving Employees and the Work Environment, and Establishing and Maintaining Effective Work Relationships.

International Comparisons.   Because of the increasing level of internationalization of organizations, we should become more aware of how companies in other countries of the world practice personnel management. Consequently, information about how companies in other countries manage their human resources is presented through commentary at the end of sections and through the feature "International PHRM in the News," which appears in many chapters. These comparisons increase our knowledge of the world and offer alternative possibilities for more effective PHR management in the United States.

Theory and Research.   Another major theme of this book is the most current and useful information related to personnel and human resource management. Thus, the book extensively uses current research and theory related to the effective use and management of human resources. You will receive not only an extensive description of all the current PHRM functions and activities but also an understanding of why these functions and activities should work and how they actually do work. With this knowledge, you can decide how to make these functions and activities work better; the section on assessment at the end of each chapter will assist you in this area. This section suggests what data to gather in order to make assessments and, therefore, to improve each activity.

For Whom Is This Book Written?

This book is written for those who are now working or who will one day work in organizations. Knowledge of effective PHRM functions and activities is vital for anyone working in organizations, particularly line managers and especially human resource staff (specialists or generalists) and managers. This is true whether the organization is private or public, large or small, slow-growing or fast-growing.

SUMMARY

This chapter examines the growing importance of the functions and activities of personnel and human resource management, defines what PHRM is, and lists its purposes. Because of the increasing complexity of PHRM, nearly all organizations have established a human resources department. Not all of these departments, however, perform all the personnel functions and activities discussed in this chapter. A department's functions and activities, and the way it performs them, depend greatly on the roles that the department plays in the organization. A human resource department can play five roles, organizations that are most concerned with effective personnel and human resource management allow their departments to play the policy formulator, provider, auditor, innovator role and adapter roles. When this occurs, the departments have most likely demonstrated their value to their organizations by showing how the several PHRM functions and activities influence productivity, quality of work life, and legal compliance—all purposes associated with the organization's bottom-line criteria. In addition, these departments are likely to be operating at all three levels in the organization: operational, managerial, and strategic. Furthermore, they are probably doing this in a proactive manner rather than waiting for the organization to tell them what to do. A human resources department should demonstrate its effectiveness, perform all four roles and operate at all three levels in the organization, and help the organization to attain its goals. In addition, it should customerize its services.

This book is for everyone who is or will be working in an organization, especially those who are responsible for the management and use of human resources: line managers and human resource managers and their staffs. Three major themes are used to make this book as useful and enjoyable as possible: why PHRM functions and activities work, how they work in practice, and how they can be made to work even better.

DISCUSSION QUESTIONS

1. What is the bottom line of an organization, and how can PHRM have a significant impact on the organization's bottom line?
2. What trends and crises are presently influencing PHRM's importance in organizations?

3. How can personnel and human resource managers become proactive in demonstrating their effectiveness?

4. What are some key issues related to the organization of an effective human resources department?

5. What is the difference between personnel generalists and personnel specialists?

6. Why have the top managers of organizations attributed greater importance to the personnel and human resource management function? How will trends in the future influence these perceptions?

7. Briefly summarize the five major functions that PHRM serves.

8. What are some concrete ways in which the human resources department can demonstrate its effectiveness to the organization?

9. What roles does PHRM play in an organization? How are basic functions and activities related to these roles?

10. Why are some PHRM functions centralized while others are decentralized?

NOTES

1. Although the term *personnel* is still used in referring to PHRM or HR departments in organizations, the trend is toward use of the term *PHRM*. See S. J. Carroll and R. S. Schuler, eds., *Human Resource Management in the 1980's* (Washington, D.C.: Bureau of National Affairs, 1983); M. A. Devanna, C. S. Fombrun, and N. Tichy, "Human Resources Management: A Strategic Perspective," *Organizational Dynamics* (Winter 1981): 51–67; and K. M. Rowland and G. R. Ferris, eds., *Personnel Management* (Boston: Allyn & Bacon, 1982). For an excellent description of the evolution of modern PHRM, see J. N. Baron, F. R. Dobbin, and P. D. Jennings, "War and Peace: The Evolution of Modern Personnel Administration in U.S. Industry," *AJI* (Sept. 1986): 350–83; T. A. Kochan and P. Cappelli, "The Transformation of the Industrial Relations and Personnel Function," in *Internal Labor Markets*, ed. Paul Osterman (Cambridge, Mass.: MIT Press, 1984), 133–62; P. R. Lawrence, "The History of Human Resource Management in American Industry," in *HRM: Trends and Challenges*, ed. R. E. Walton and P. R. Lawrence (Boston: Harvard Business School Press, 1985), 15–34; C. Pava, "Managing New Information Technology: Design or Default?" in *HRM: Trends and Challenges*, 69–102; R. E. Thaler, "40 Years of Growth and Service," *Personnel Administrator* (June 1988): 52–158; and S. Zuboff, "Technologies That Informate: Implications for Human Resource Management in the Computerized Industrial Workplace," in *HRM: Trends and Challenges*, 103–40.

2. Effective PHRM implies that whatever PHRM is doing, it is doing it as well as possible (i.e., to attain the maximum benefit possible for the individuals, the organization, and society). Thus, just because a PHRM activity is being done does not mean that the human resources are being used effectively. Only when the activity is done effectively is there effective PHRM.

3. R. S. Schuler and I. C. MacMillan, "Gaining a Competitive Advantage Through Human Resource Management Practices," *Human Resource Management* (Fall 1984): 241–56.

4. K. S. Cameron and D. A. Whetten, *Organization Effectiveness: A Comparison of Multiple Models* (New York: Academic Press, 1983); D. R. Denison, "Bringing Corporate Culture to the Bottom Line," *Organizational Dynamics* (Autumn 1984): 4–22.

5. K. F. Misa and T. Stein, "Strategic HRM and the Bottom Line," *Personnel Administrator* (Oct. 1983): 27–30. See also A. Bernstein, "Can America Compete?" *Business Week*, 20 Apr. 1987, pp. 45–52; T. Peters and N. Austin, *Passion for Excellence* (New York: Warner Books, 1985); T. Peters and B. Waterman, *In Search of Excellence* (New York: Warner Books, 1982); M. J. Piore and C. F. Sabel, *The Second Industrial Divide* (New York: Basic Books,1984); "The Productivity Paradox: Why the Payoff from Automation Is Still So Elusive and What Corporate America Can Do About It," *Business Week*, 6 June 1988, pp. 100–114; "Quality Means a Whole New Approach to Manufacturing," *Business Week*, 8 June 1987, pp. 131–43; and E. Schultz, "America's Most Admired Corporations," *Fortune*, 18 Jan. 1988, pp. 32–53.

6. "Improve Quality," *Business Week*, 8 June 1987, p. 158. See also Bernstein, "Can America Compete?"; and O. Port, "Quality," *Business Week*, 8 June 1987, pp. 131–43.

7. "Improve Quality," *Business Week*, 158.

8. The entire September 1982 issue of *Personnel Administrator* is developed around the roles that PHRM should play in organizations.

9. T. E. Deal and A. A. Kennedy, *Corporate Cultures* (Reading, Mass.: Addison-Wesley, 1982); E. J. Koprowski, "Cultural Myths: Clues to Effective Management," *Organizational Dynamics* (Autumn 1983): 39–51; J. Marin and C. Siehl, "Organizational Cul-

ture and Counterculture: An Uneasy Symbiosis," *Organizational Dynamics* (Autumn 1983): 52–64; R. R. Pascale, "Fitting New Employees into the Company Culture," *Fortune*, 28 May 1984, pp. 28–40.

10. G. R. Ferris, D. S. Cook, and J. Butler, "Strategy and Human Resource Managment," in *Readings in Personnel and Human Resource Management*, 3d ed., ed. R. S. Schuler, S. A. Youngblood, and V. Huber (St. Paul: West, 1988); R. K. Swanson, "Personnel Management: A View from the Top," *Personnel Journal* (Sept. 1984):112.

11. N. Tichy, C. J. Fombrun, and M. Devanna, "Strategic Human Resource Management," in *Readings in Personnel and Human Resource Management*, 2d ed., ed. R. S. Schuler and S. A. Youngblood, (St. Paul: West, 1984).

12. D. C. Funder, "On Assessing Social Psychological Theories Through the Study of Individual Differences: Template Matching and Forced Compliance," *Journal of Personality and Social Psychology* 43 (1982): 100–110; B. Schneider, "Organizational Behavior," *Annual Review of Psychology* 36 (1985): 573–611.

13. Deal and Kennedy, *Corporate Cultures*.

14. Ibid., 3.

15. S. Lohr, "Making Cars the Volvo Way," *New York Times*, 23 June 1987; A. Taylor III, "Back to the Future at Saturn," *Fortune*, 1 Aug. 1988, pp. 63–72.

16. P. Osterman, ed., *Internal Labor Markets* (Cambridge, Mass.: London, 1984).

17. H. R. Northrup, "Labor Market Trends and Policies in the 1980s," in *Readings in Personnel*, 2d ed.

18. D. Q. Mills, *The New Competitors* (New York: Wiley, 1985), 19.

19. Ibid., 23.

20. Schuler and MacMillan, "Gaining a Competitive Advantage"; R. S. Schuler and I. C. MacMillan, "Gaining a Competitive Edge Through Human Resources," *Personnel* (Apr. 1985): 24–29.

21. "Profit Promotion," *Bulletin to Management*, 16 Apr. 1987, p. 11. Reprinted by permission from *Bulletin to Management* copyright 1987 by The Bureau of National Affairs, Inc., Washington, DC 20037.

22. G. Koretz, "The Winter of Workers' Discontent," *Business Week*, 1 Feb. 1988, p. 18.

23. J. Fitz-enz, "Quantifying the Human Resources Function," *Personnel* (March/April 1980): 41–52; J. Fitz-enz, *How to Measure Human Resources Management* (New York: McGraw-Hill, 1984); J. A. Hooper, "A Strategy for Increasing the Human Resource Department's Effectiveness," *Personnel Administrator* (June 1984): 141–48; A. S. Tsui, "Personnel Department Effectiveness: A Tripartite Approach," *Industrial Relations* (Spring 1984): 184–97. For an excellent overview see, A. P. Brief and associates, *Productivity Research in the Behavioral and Social Sciences* (New York: Praeger, 1984); W. F. Cascio, *Costing Human Resources: The Financial Impact of Behavior in Organizations* (Reading, Mass.: Addison-Wesley, 1982); C. R. Day, Jr., "Solving the Mystery of Productivity Measurement," *Industry Week*, 26 Jan. 1981, pp. 61–66; J. E. Hunter and F. L. Schmidt, "Quan-

tifying the Effects of Psychological Interventions on Employee Job Performance and Work-Force Productivity," *American Psychologist* (Apr. 1983): 473–78; R. A. Katzell and R. A. Guzzo, "Psychological Approaches to Productivity Improvement," *American Psychologist* (Apr. 1983): 468–72; F. Krgystofiak and J. Newman, "Evaluating Employment Outcomes: Availability Models and Measures," *Industrial Relations* 21 (1982): 277–92; F. J. Landy, J. L. Farr, and R. R. Jacobs, "Utility Concepts in Performance Measurements," *Organizational Behavior and Human Performance* 30 (1982): 15–40; J. Lapointe and J. A. Verdin, "How to Calculate the Cost of Human Resources," *Personnel Journal* (Jan. 1988): 34–45; J. C. Pingpank, "Preventing and Defending EEO Charges," *Personnel Administrator* (Feb. 1983): 35–40; J. E. Ross, *Productivity, People, and Profits* (Reston, Va.: Reston, 1981); F. L. Schmidt, J. E. Hunter, and K. Pearlman, "Assessing the Economic Impact of Personnel Programs on Workforce Productivity," *Personnel Psychology* (Summer 1982): 333–48; and R. R. West and D. E. Logue, "The False Doctrine of Productivity," *New York Times*, 9 Jan. 1983, p. F3.

24. S. B. Henrici, "How Not to Measure Productivity," *New York Times*, 7 Mar. 1982, p. 2F.

25. D. R. Dalton and W. D. Todor, "Turnover: A Lucrative Hard Dollar Phenomenon," *Academy of Management Review* 7 (1982): 212–18; T. E. Hall, "How to Estimate Employee Turnover Costs," *Personnel* (July/Aug. 1981): 43–52, 212–18; F. E. Kuzmits, "How Much Is Absenteeism Costing Your Organization?" *Personnel Administrator* (June 1979): 29–32; W. Mobley, *Turnover* (Reading, Mass.: Addison-Wesley, 1982).

26. P. H. Mirvis and E. E. Lawler III, "Measuring the Financial Impact of Employee Attitudes," *Journal of Applied Psychology* 62 (1977): 1–8; "The New Industrial Relations," *Business Week*, 11 May 1981, pp. 85–93.

27. B. R. Ellig, "The Impact of Legislation on the Personnel Function," *Personnel* (Sept./Oct. 1980): 49–53; M. D. Levin-Epstein, *Primer on Equal Employment Opportunity*, 3d ed. (Washington, D.C.: Bureau of National Affairs, 1984).

28. E. H. Burack and N. J. Mathys, *Human Resource Planning: A Pragmatic Approach to Manpower Staffing and Development* (Lake Forest, Ill.: Brace-Park, 1979); L. Dyer, "Human Resource Planning," in *Personnel Management*, ed., K. M. Rowland and G. R. Ferris (Boston: Allyn & Bacon, 1982,) 52–77; E. C. Smith, "Strategic Business Planning and Human Resources: Part I," *Personnel Journal* (Aug. 1982): 606–10; E. C. Smith, "Strategic Business Planning and Human Resources: Part II," *Personnel Journal* (Sept. 1982): 680–82; L. J. Stybel, "Linking Strategic Planning and Management Manpower Planning," *California Management Review* (Fall 1982): 48–56.

29. J. Frazee and J. Harrington-Kuller, "Money Matters: Selling HRIS to Management," *Personnel Journal* (Aug. 1987): 98–107; M. MacAdam, "HRIS Training: Keep Documentation on Track," *Personnel Journal* (Oct. 1987): 45–51; J. Pasqualetto, "Computers: No More

Us vs. Them," *Personnel Journal* (Dec. 1987): 61–67.

30. J. Walker, "Managing Human Resources in Flat, Lean and Flexible Organizations," *Human Resource Planning* 11, no. 2 (1988): 125–32.

31. P. F. Drucker, *Innovation and Entrepreneurship* (New York: Harper & Row, 1985); G. R. Ferris, D. A. Schallenberg, and R. F. Zammuto, "Human Resource Management Strategies in Declining Industries," *Human Resource Management* (Winter 1985): 381–94; A. K. Gupta, "Contingency Linkages Between Strategy and General Manager Characteristics: A Conceptual Examination," *Academy of Management Review* 9 (1984): 399–412; J. L. Kerr, "Assigning Managers on the Basis of the Life Cycle," *Journal of Business Strategy* 2, no. 4 (1982): 58–65; J. L. Kerr, "Diversification Strategies and Management Rewards: On Empirical Study," *Academy of Management Journal* 28 (1985): 155–79; J. Lynch and D. Orne, "Managing in the Belly of the Cow," *Management Review* (June 1985): 46–48; M. A. Maidique and R. H. Hayes, "The Art of High Technology Management," *Sloan Management Review* (Winter 1984): 17–31; M. G. Miner, "Legal Concerns Facing Human Resource Managers: An Overview," in *Readings in Personnel*, 3d ed., 40–54.

32. A. K. Gupta and V. Govindarajan, "Build, Hold, Harvest: Converting Strategic Intentions into Reality," *Journal of Business Strategy* 4 (1984): 34–47; A. K. Gupta and V. Govindarajan, "Business Unit Strategy, Managerial Characteristics, and Business Unit Effectiveness at Strategy Implementation," *Academy of Management Journal* 9 (1984): 25–41; T. A. Kochan, R. B. McKersie, and P. Cappelli, "Strategic Choice and Industrial Relations Theory," *Industrial Relations* 23 (1984): 16–39; T. A. Kochan and P. Cappelli, "The Transformation of the Industrial Relations/Human Resource Function," in *Internal Labor Markets*, ed. P. Osterman (Cambridge, Mass.: MIT Press, 1983), 133–62; C. A. Lengnik-Hall and M. L. Lengnik-Hall, "Strategic Human Resource Management: A Review of the Literature," *Academy of Management Review* (July 1988): 454–70; A. R. McGill, "Practical Considerations: A Case Study of General Motors," in *Strategic Human Resource Management*, ed. C. J. Feombrun, N. M. Tichy, and M. A. Devanna (New York: Wiley, 1984,) 149–58; R. E. Miles and C. C. Snow, "Designing Strategic Human Resource Systems," *Organizational Dynamics* (Fall 1984): 36–52; R. E. Miles and C. C. Snow, "Fit, Failure, and the Hall of Fame," *California Management Review* 26 (1984): 10–28; D. Miller, "Configurations of Strategy and Structure: Towards a Synthesis," *Strategic Management Journal* 7 (1986): 233–49.; T. Peters, *Thriving on Chaos* (New York: Alfred A. Knopf, 1987; R. S. Schuler, "Personnel and Human Resource Management Choices and Organizational Strategy," *Human Resource Planning* 10 no. 1 (1987): 1–18; R. S. Schuler, "Personnel and Human Resource Management Choices and Organizational Strategy," in *Readings in Personnel*, 3d ed. 1987; R. S. Schuler and S. E. Jackson, "Linking Competitive Strategies with Human Resource Management Practices," *Academy of Management Executive* 1 (1987): 207–19; R. S. Schuler and S. E. Jackson, "Organizational Strategy and Organizational Level as Determinants of Human Resource Management Practices," *Human Resource Planning* 10, no. 3 (1987): 125–42; J. W. Slocum, W. L. Cron, R. W. Hansen, and S. Rawlings, "Business Strategy and the Management of Plateaued Employees," *Academy of Management Journal* 28 (1985): 133–54. For more discussion of the need for the practice of HR to become more strategic and bottom-line oriented, see M. Beer, B. Spector, P. R. Lawrence, D. Q. Mills, and R. E. Walton, *Managing Human Assets* (New York: Free Press, 1984); F. K. Foulkes, *Strategic Human Resource Management* (Englewood Cliffs, N.J.: Prentice-Hall, 1986); M. Magnus, "Personnel Policies in Partnership with Profit," *Personnel Journal* (Sept. 1987): 102–8; E. H. Schien, *The Art of Managing Human Resources* (New York: Oxford University Press, 1987); and D. A. Stace, "The Value-Added Organization: Trends in Human Resource Management," *Human Resource Management Australia* (Nov. 1987): 52–63.

33. Schuler and MacMillan, "Gaining a Competitive Advantage," 248.

34. L. L. Cummings, "Compensation, Culture, and Motivation: A Systems Perspective," *Organizational Dynamics* (Winter 1984): 33–43; M. Gerstein and H. Reisman, "Strategic Selection: Matching Executives to Business Conditions," *Sloan Management Review* (Winter 1983): 33–49; R. Giles and C. Landauer, "Setting Specific Standards for Appraising Creative Staffs," *Personnel Administrator* 29 (1984): 35–47; E. E. Lawler III, "The Strategic Design of Reward Systems," in *Readings in Personnel*, 2d ed., 253–69; E. E. Lawler III and J. A. Drexler, Jr., "The Corporate Entrepreneur," working paper, Center for Effective Organizations, University of Southern California, 1984; P. Lorange and D. Murphy, "Strategy and Human Resources: Concepts and Practice," *Human Resource Management* 22 (1983): 111–35; J. D. Olian and S. L. Rynes, "Organizational Staffing: Integrating Practice with Strategy," *Industrial Relations* 23 (1984): 170–83; M. E. Porter, *Competitive Strategy* (New York: Free Press, 1980); R. H. Price and T. D'Aunno, "Managing Work Force Reduction," *Human Resource Management* 22 (1984): 413–30; E. B. Roberts and A. R. Fusfeld, "Staffing the Innovative Technology-Based Organization," *Sloan Management Review* (Spring 1981): 19–34; R. S. Schuler, I. C. MacMillan, and J. J. Marocchio, " Strategy Execution and Human Resource Management," in *Handbook of Business Strategy—1985/1986 Yearbook*, ed. W. D. Guth (New York: Warren, Gorham & Lamont, 1985); S. A. Stumpf and N. M. Hanrahan, "Designing Organizational Career Management Practices to Fit Strategic Management Objectives," in *Readings in Personnel*, 2d ed.; A. D. Szilagyi and D. M. Schweiger, "Matching Managers to Strategies: A Review and Suggested Framework," *Academy of Management Review* 9 (1984): 626–37.

35. "Customers for Keeps: Training Strategies," *Bulletin to Management*, 31 Mar. 1988, p. 8. See also R. L. Desatnik, *Managing to Keep the Customers* (San Francisco: Jossey-Bass, 1987).

36. A. Halcrow, "Operation Phoenix: The Business of Human Resources," *Personnel Journal* (Sept. 1987): 92–109; P. Hawken, "The Employee as Customer," *INC.* (Nov. 1987): 21–22; R. S. Schuler and S. E. Jackson, "Customerizing the HR Department," *Personnel* (June 1988): 36–44.

37. M. J. Driver and D. E. Bowen, "Where Is HR Management Going?" *Personnel* (Jan. 1988): 28–31; J. W. English, "The Road Ahead for the Human Resource Function," *Personnel* (Mar./Apr. 1980): 35–39; T. W. Peters and E. A. Mabry, "The Personnel Officer as Internal Consultant," *Personnel Administrator* (Apr. 1981): 29–32; D. Ulrich, "Organizational Capability as a Competitive Advantage: Human Resource Professionals as Strategic Partners," *Human Resource Planning* 10, no. 4 (1987): 169–84; H. C. White, APD, and M. N. Wolfe, "The Role Desired for Personnel Administration," *Personnel Administrator* (June 1980): 87–97.

38. F. K. Foulkes, "The Expanding Role of the Personnel Function," *Harvard Business Review* (Mar./Apr. 1975): 147.

39. J. Walker, "Managing Human Resources in Flat, Lean and Flexible Organizations," 129.

40. Ibid., 131.

41. Beer, Spector, Lawrence, Mills, and Walton, *Managing Human Assets*.

42. F. Luthans, R. M. Hodgetts, and S. A. Rosenkrantz, *Real Managers* (Cambridge, Mass.: Ballinger, 1987).

43. E. C. Lawler III, "Human Resource Management: Meeting the Challenge," *Personnel* (Jan. 1988): 24–27. See also R. E. Walton and P. R. Lawrence, eds., *HRM: Trends and Challenges* (Boston: Harvard Business School Press, 1985).

44. "ASPA–BNA Survey No. 52 Personnel Activities, Budgets and Staffs: 1987–1988," (1 Sept. 1988); S. Langer, "Where the Dollars Are: Annual Salary Survey Results," *Personnel Journal* (Feb. 1986): 92–94; "Personnel and Industrial Relations Survey," *Bulletin to Management*, 5 July 1984, pp. 3–4; "Salary Profile," *Bulletin to Management*, 1 Sept. 1988, p. 273.

45. G. F. Brady, "Assessing the Personnel Manager's Power Base," *Personnel Administrator* (July 1980): 57–61; F. R. Edney, "Human Resources Managers Aren't Corporate Nobodies Anymore," *Business Week*, 2 Dec. 1985, 58–59; L. B. Prewitt, "The Emerging Field of Human Resources Management," *Personnel Administrator* (May 1982): 81–87.

46. D. Yoder and H. Heneman, Jr., *PAIR Jobs: Qualifications, and Careers, ASPA Handbook of Personnel and Industrial Relations*, (Washington, D.C.: Bureau of National Affairs, 1978), 18.

47. C. Haigley, "Professionalism in Personnel," *Personnel Administrator* (June 1984): 103–6; G. B. Hansen, "Professional Education for Careers in Human Resource Administration," *Personnel Administrator* (Jan. 1984): 69–80; J. F. Parry, "Accredited Professionals Are Better Prepared," *Personnel Administrator* (Dec. 1985): 48–52; W. W. Tornow, "The Codification Project and Its Importance to Professionalism," *Personnel Administrator* (June 1984): 84–100.

Planning

Human Resource Planning

Management Practices Are More Flexible

Management is experiencing a radical transformation. The relative stability and predictability of business are being replaced by uncertainty, complexity, and rapid change. Intense global competition, rapidly changing technology, shifting demography, economic fluctuations, and other dynamic conditions require companies to be adaptive and swift. Companies are stripping away long-standing management policies and practices impeding flexibility and are adopting new practices to foster desired initiative, innovation, and change.

In the new environment, strategic business planning has also changed. It is becoming more tentative, short term, and issue focused. Planning is now considered useful more as a tool for provoking thinking and discussion than as a process of determining long-term objectives and courses of action. In this context, strategies are shaped as guides to help organizations recognize and address important changes and opportunities to manage them effectively.

In the flexible organization, the planning horizon is typically no farther than three years, with concentration on the next year. For example, when Hicks Waldron became CEO at Avon, he was asked at an employee meeting what his strategic plan was. He said, "Ask me in five years. I'll tell you what it was." He has since divested Tiffany and other businesses, has acquired new beauty products companies, and has flattened, trimmed, and restructured the company. Human resource management activities have stressed keeping up with the demands of restructuring, staffing changes, and absorption of acquisitions. The experience has been similar in other companies.

Many companies address these issues through human resource planning. Human resource issues and plans are based on analysis of business unit issues, environmental trends suggesting issues of company concern, and forecasts of future staffing and development needs. Typically, human resource plans are developed as functional plans, parallel to strategic plans. In the absence of clear strategic business direction, the human resource function charts its own course, relying on the best available information. The plans provide a basis for discussion and negotiation with unit managers on priorities, activities, and allocation of time and resources. Where business strategic planning is established, human resource strategies are developed as part of this process, with human resource and management effectiveness issues addressed as any other business issues.

In the flat, lean, and flexible organization, the planning process is most valuable as an issue identification and diagnostic process and is necessary to foster management consideration of longer-range vision, strategic direction, and values. In this way, the process helps educate both staff and line on important long-range considerations affecting near term actions. Less time and patience are given formal aspects of planning systems and procedures, detailed data collection and analysis, forecasting, or scanning of external trends and issues. Precision and accuracy are less important than the provocation of considering issues and alternative future projections. Under conditions of rapid change, human resource strategies are long-term views intended to guide today's actions.

J. Walker, "Managing Human Resources in Flat, Lean and Flexible Organizations: Trends for the 1990s," *Human Resource Planning* 11, No. 2 (1988): 125–127. Reprinted by permission of *Human Resource Planning*, copyright 1988.

This "PHRM in the News" highlights several important aspects of human resource planning. One is that this planning is critical to the success of organizational strategy and planning. Second, this planning is tied to the nature of the organization; as the organization changes and becomes more flexible and adaptable, the PHRM planning horizon becomes shorter. Third, line managers and personnel managers share responsibility for effective human resource planning. Fourth, the external environment has to be analyzed and incorporated into an organization's human resource planning.

In general terms, **human resource planning** is the base upon which effective PHRM is contructed. Most specifically, human resource planning involves forecasting human resource needs for the organization and planning the steps necessary to meet these needs. Human resource planning consists of developing and implementing plans and programs to ensure that the right number and type of individuals are available at the right time and place to fulfill organizational needs. As such, human resource planning is directly tied to strategic business planning.[1] Because of the trend toward more strategic involvement by PHRM, discussed in Chapter 1, human resource planning is one of the fastest growing and most important areas in PHRM.

Human resource planning helps ensure that organizations fulfill their business plans—plans that chart the organization's future regarding financial objectives, output goals, product mix, technologies, and resource requirements.[2] Once their business plans are determined, often with the assistance of the personnel and human resource department, "the human resource planner assists in developing workable organizational structures and in determining the numbers and types of employees that will be required to meet financial and output goals.[3] After workable structures and the requirements for needed individuals are identified, the human resource planner develops personnel and human resource programs to implement the structure and to obtain the individuals. Line managers and supervisors, however, are responsible for providing the necessary information for human resource planning, and for working with the human resource manager to ensure that the organization's human resources are used effectively.

PURPOSES AND IMPORTANCE OF HUMAN RESOURCE PLANNING

The general purpose of human resource planning is to identify future organizational demands and supplies of human resources and to develop programs to eliminate any discrepancies, all in the best interests of the individual and the organization. More specifically, the purposes of human resource planning are to

- Reduce personnel costs by helping management to anticipate shortages or surpluses of human resources and to correct these imbalances before they become unmanageable and expensive
- Provide a better basis for planning employee development that makes optimum use of workers' attitudes
- Improve the overall business planning process
- Provide more opportunities for women, minority, and handicapped groups in future growth plans and identify the specific skills available
- Promote greater awareness of the importance of sound human resource management throughout all levels of the organization

■ Provide a tool for evaluating the effect of alternative human resource actions and policies[4]

All these purposes are now more easily attained than ever before, thanks to computer technology. This technology allows vast job-related records to be maintained on each employee, in essence creating a human resource information system. These records, which include information on employee job preferences, work experiences, and performance evaluations, provide a job history of each employee in an organization and a complete set of information on the jobs and positions in the organization. This in turn can be used to facilitate the purposes of human resource planning in the interests of the individual as well as the organization. All these purposes partly explain the recent and growing importance of human resource planning.

A large number of environmental and organizational changes also explain the importance of human resource planning and PHRM. These changes are pushing personnel and human resource management into a future-oriented, comprehensive, and integrative perspective that has a number of fundamental attributes:

1. It considers human resource costs an investment rather than an uncontrollable expense.
2. It is proactive rather than reactive or passive in its approach to developing human resource policies and resolving human resource problems.
3. It is characterized by a change in role perspective from an emphasis on the completion of personnel transactions toward a future-oriented approach in which the personnel department acts as a developer of the organization's human resources.
4. It recognizes that an explicit link must exist between human resource planning and other organizational functions, such as strategic planning, economic and market forecasting, and investment and facilities planning.
5. It recognizes that such PHRM activities as recruitment, selection, labor relations, compensation and benefits, training, organizational planning, and career management must be visualized as dynamic interconnecting activities rather than as a series of separate and nonintegrated functions.
6. It focuses on approaches that further both organizational and individual goals.[5]

One organizational change that is making human resource planning more important is the growing shortage of human resources to fill certain jobs. Currently predicted are shortages in blue-collar occupations and entry-level white-collar occupations, such as tool and die makers, bricklayers, and other skilled crafts workers. In addition, shortages currently exist for shipbuilders, legal secretaries, engineers, robotics engineers, machinists, and mechanics.[6]

Yet while there are shortages of certain types of individuals, there is a growing abundance of another—those in the twenty-five-to-fifty-four-year-old age category. As discussed later in this chapter, the number of people entering this age group is increasing faster than the number of jobs available for them. Consequently, many of these people can probably anticipate relatively static income and rivalry with older workers for some period of time.[7]

The new retirement options available to workers are also causing a shift in concern for staffing positions, but not in the direction once expected. Workers now have options ranging from early retirement in their midfifties to retirement in their seventies. However, more workers are staying on the job longer than anticipated. This fact, coupled with the protection given to employees over the age of forty by the Age Discrimination in Employment Act of 1967 as amended in 1986, has caused organizations to devote more time to managing these senior workers. As a consequence, managers are developing training programs to ensure that senior employees are kept up-to-date and provided with career counseling and pre-retirement planning.[8]

The increasing potential for managerial obsolescence is another critical issue. Rapid changes in knowledge are making it difficult for professionals, engineers, and managers to remain adept at their jobs. It has been speculated that entrants into the labor force in the 1980s will be retrained more than 10 times during their work lives, and half of what today's managers, scientists, and professionals know will be obsolete by the year 2000.[9]

Another change is the growing resistance of employees to change and to relocate. The emphasis on self-evaluation, loyalty, and dedication to the organization also is growing. All these changes are making it more difficult for the organization to assume it can move its employees around anywhere and anytime it wants, thus increasing the importance and necessity of planning ahead.

Because all these changes are increasing PHRM's importance, their implications for planning and program development are described later in the chapter.

THE HUMAN RESOURCE PLANNING PROCESS

As the initial "PHRM in the News" suggests, human resource planning has an extensive set of relationships with aspects of the internal and external environment. These relationships are indicated in Exhibit 2.1.

Relationships with the Internal Environment

Organizational Strategy.   One factor affecting human resource planning more than ever before is the organization's strategy. Four different types of organizational strategy have been identified:

1. Maintaining the status quo by pursuing the same objectives as previously pursued
2. Expanding internally through product diversity or market expansion
3. Growing externally through acquisitions, mergers, and joint ventures
4. Restructuring through cost cutting, downsizing, and diversification[10]

Different types of organizational strategies call for different human resource approaches. However, an organization increases its chances of having the right people at the right place and time to gain a competitive edge if it integrates human resource strategy with organizational strategy. The result is of substantial benefit to the organization:

> Human resources managers who make sure that the "people factor" is integrated into strategic business plans can help the company make more cost-effective and productive decisions, declares John O'Brien, vice-president of human resources planning at Digital Equipment Corp. . . . O'Brien says personnel managers have a responsibility to convince corporate business planners that "human resources represent a major competitive advantage" and are every bit as important as the time, money, and material expended to increase profits.

Aspects and Relationships of Human Resource Planning

EXHIBIT
2.1

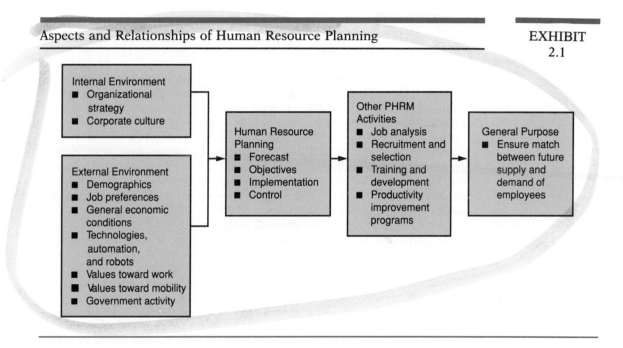

A basic ingredient of an integrated HR-business planning process, O'Brien notes, is personnel managers working side by side with line managers to solve the organization's business and people problems. Jointly, the personnel and line managers strive to:

- Develop business plan strategies for the company's various operating divisions and analyze each unit's strategies to determine what human resources will be needed;
- Collect detailed information on the current workforce and analyze the organization's workforce profile in terms of its future business strategies;
- Identify current and emerging HR issues, and review these with the management committees of units most likely to be affected by changes in the work environment; and
- Develop plans and programs that address the identified issues in support of the business direction.[11]

Corporate Culture.   As Chapter 1 stated, corporate culture reflects the assumptions an organization makes about people and how they are to be treated. Corporate culture provides a vehicle for an organization's continuity, control, integration, and identity. Cultures are expressed in a variety of ways. For example, the rituals associated with organizational entry and promotion signal the values of positions involved. Reward systems based on individual or group performance or seniority act as visible manifestations of what an organization values. Consequently, the nature of an organization's culture influences how PHRM is perceived and functions.[12]

Relationships with the External Environment

As shown in Exhibit 2.1, many aspects of the external environment also affect human resource planning.

Demographics.   American industry is currently faced with a shrinking supply of young workers. After more than two decades of growth, the nation's population between the ages of sixteen and twenty-four has peaked.

Between 1976 and 1980, the labor force grew an average of 2.8 percent, but between 1991 and 1995, the rate of growth will drop to 1.1 percent. Additionally, while over 3 million people joined the labor force in 1978, under 2 million people are projected to enter the labor force each year from 1987 to 1995.

People aged 25 to 54 will constitute a greater percentage of the labor force, increasing from 61 percent in 1975 to 73 percent in 1995. Comparatively, the proportion of younger people (aged 16 to 24) and older people (aged 55 and over) will decline from 24 percent in 1975 to 16 percent in 1995, and from 15 percent to 11 percent, respectively. Between 1984 and 1995, 21.6 million people aged 25 to 54 will enter the labor force, while the number of workers aged 16 to 24, and 55 and over, will decline by 2.7 million and .8 million, respectively.

The combination of an aging baby-boom generation followed by a smaller baby-bust worker group is leading to an increase in the median age of American workers from thirty-five in 1982 to thirty-seven in 1995. Other projections indicate that the first decade of the twenty-first century will mark the graying of the work force, with a 42-percent increase in the fifty-five-to-sixty-five category. The population of persons aged forty-five to sixty-four is expected to increase from 43.6 million in 1980 to 72.9 million in 2010, and the population aged sixty-five and over is expected to increase form 24.5 million in 1980 to 42.8 million in 2020.[13]

The consequence of these population shifts will be a bulge in the twenty-five-to-fifty-four age group, leading to bottlenecks and dissatisfaction among mid-level employees who are fixed in their jobs. Conversely, there will be numerous career opportunities for younger and older people willing to accept entry-level positions as primary or secondary sources of income, respectively. Employers, however, may have to accommodate these employees by making their present jobs more challenging and even by redefining success (in essence, changing the outcomes provided) to remove its association with upward promotions.

A look at the distribution of sex and race in these same age categories shows several other important changes.[14] The total number of white men in the labor force will continue to diminish, while the number of black people and women will continue to increase. As shown in Exhibit 2.2, of the 25 million workers added to the work force between 1985 and 2000, 42 percent are expected to be native white women, and only 15 percent are expected to be native white men.

EXHIBIT 2.2	New Entrants into the Labor Force		
		1985 Labor Force	Net New Workers, 1985–2000
	Total	115,461,000	25,000,000
	Native white men	47%	15%
	Native white women	36%	42%
	Native nonwhite men	5%	7%
	Native nonwhite women	5%	13%
	Immigrant men	4%	13%
	Immigrant women	3%	9%

SOURCE: *Workforce 2000* U.S. Government Printing Office, Department of Labor, Washington, D.C. 1987.

By 1990, families in which only one spouse works will account for only 14 percent of all housholds, compared to 43 percent in 1960. While more than 30 percent of all households are now headed by either a man or a woman without a spouse, this percentage is expected to jump to 45 percent by 1990.

While the education level of the U.S. population has increased over the last seven decades, future generations of employees will be the first with levels of education that are the same as or lower than those of their parents. Current estimates indicate that 26 million adult Americans can't read; another 30 million are functionally illiterate—reading so poorly that they have difficulty coping in everyday life. In fifteen years, functional illiterates are expected to compose more than 70 percent of the population. Thus, the assumption that workers can read, follow instructions, and heed safety warnings is no longer valid. The challenge for management in the 1990's will be to supervise and train the functionally illiterate.[15]

Job Preferences.   Currently, the occupational makeup of the civilian labor force reflects a majority of the female work force in service, clerical (secretarial), nursing, and teaching jobs. The majority of men, on the other hand, are in semiskilled (operative), skilled (crafts), managerial and administrative, and professional and technical jobs. This distribution has, in part, resulted from the notion of **job sex-typing.** That is, a job takes on the image of being appropriate only for the sex that dominates the job. Consequently, once a job becomes sex-typed, it attracts primarily those of that sex. Job sex-typing, combined with **sex-role stereotyping,** has traditionally restricted the perceived job choices and preferences of both men and women. Whereas job sex-typing refers to the labeling of jobs as either "men's jobs" or "women's jobs," sex-role stereotyping refers to labels, characteristics, or attributes that become attached to men and women solely because they are members of their respective sexes.

Evidence now indicates that the range of perceived choices and preferences is expanding for both men and women. This trend has been facilitated in part by the gradual reduction of sex-role stereotyping in our society. In addition, some of the job sex-typing has been reduced through legal mandates that encourage employers to hire females for previously male-dominated jobs, and vice versa.[16]

The amalgamation of more women, single heads of household, older workers, and dual-career families in the work force has also created a demand for alternative work arrangements. The implementation of work alternatives creates added pressure to develop innovative organizational structures that provide for broader sharing of roles. Various alternative work arrangements include **flexible scheduling, the compressed workweek, work-at-home arrangements, job sharing, permanent part-time jobs,** and **self-managed work groups.** These alternatives will be discussed in greater depth in Chapter 12. The challenge of the 1990s will be managing these diverse employment programs to ensure that employees will remain in these nontraditional jobs and perform at high levels.

Job Openings.   According to the Bureau of Labor Statistics, 23.4 to 28.6 million new jobs will be created by 1995. Most of the job growth will be in the service-producing area. Of these, between 1 and 4.6 million will be in high-technology industries. Thus, a substantial number of new jobs will be created in industries other than high technology. Exhibit 2.3 shows the industries that will have the greatest number of new jobs by 2000.[17] Exhibit 2.4 illustrates how this changing job composition is resulting in fewer low-skilled jobs.

EXHIBIT
2.3
Occupations With The Largest Job Growth, 1986–2000
(Numbers In Thousands)

Occupation	Employment		Change in Employment, 1986–2000		Percentage of Total Job Growth 1986–2000
	1986	Projected, 2000	Number	Percent	
Salespersons, retail	3,579	4,780	1,201	33.5	5.6
Waiters and waitresses	1,702	2,454	752	44.2	3.5
Registered nurses	1,406	2,018	612	43.6	2.9
Janitors and cleaners, including maids and housekeeping cleaners	2,676	3,280	604	22.6	2.8
General managers and top executives	2,383	2,965	582	24.4	2.7
Cashiers	2,165	2,740	575	26.5	2.7
Truck drivers, light and heavy	2,211	2,736	525	23.8	2.5
General office clerks	2,361	2,824	462	19.6	2.2
Food counter, fountain, and related workers	1,500	1,949	449	29.9	2.1
Nursing aides, orderlies, and attendants	1,224	1,658	433	35.4	2.0
Secretaries	3,234	3,658	424	13.1	2.0
Guards	794	1,177	383	48.3	1.8
Accountants and auditors	945	1,322	376	39.8	1.8
Computer programmers	479	813	335	69.9	1.6
Food preparation workers	949	1,273	324	34.2	1.5
Teachers, kindergarten and elementary	1,527	1,826	299	19.6	1.4
Receptionists and information clerks ...	682	964	282	41.4	1.3
Computer systems analysts, electronic data processing	331	582	251	75.6	1.2
Cooks, restaurant	520	759	240	46.2	1.1
Licensed practical nurses	631	869	238	37.7	1.1
Gardeners and groundskeepers, except farm	767	1,005	238	31.1	1.1
Maintenance repairers, general utility ..	1,039	1,270	232	22.3	1.1
Store clerks, sales floor	1,087	1,312	225	20.7	1.0
First-line supervisors and managers	956	1,161	205	21.4	1.0
Dining room and cafeteria attendants and barroom helpers	433	631	197	45.6	.9
Electrical and electronics engineers	401	592	192	47.8	.9
Lawyers	527	718	191	36.3	.9

SOURCE: *Bulletin to Management*, 22 Oct. 1987, p. 342. Reprinted by permission from *Bulletin to Management* copyright 1987 by The Bureau of National Affairs, Inc., Washington, DC 20037.

Alternatively, organizational downsizing and flattening have resulted in an estimated drop of one million in the ranks of management since 1979. Thus, while job openings are occurring in many different areas, the need for midlevel managers is expected to shrink further. What will be needed are top-level managers with diversified skills who can handle increasingly complex technology, worker demands, and environments.

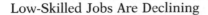

Low-Skilled Jobs Are Declining

EXHIBIT
2.4

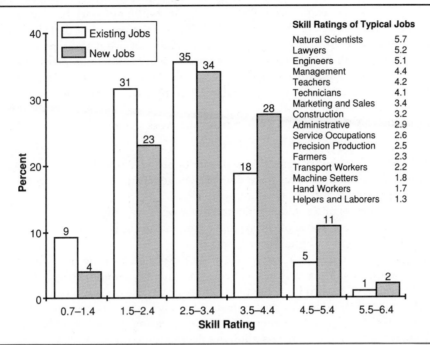

SOURCE: *Workforce 2000* (Indianapolis, Ind.: Hudson Institute, 1987), 100. Used by permission from Hudson Institute, copyright 1987.

General Economic Conditions.   One trend that will affect human resource planning is the relative stagnation in the rate of productivity. Presently, the rate of inflation is at a moderate level and is not a major consideration in human resource planning. Yet if inflation were to increase slightly—say, to 7 percent— the cost of most goods sold would double in about ten years. Similarly, wages and salaries would double to keep up with inflation. High inflation would also influence the cost of employer-paid fringe benefits and would further enhance the need for productivity gains and better work force utilization. Consequently, faced with stagnating productivity rates, the possible renewal of high inflation, and continued intense international competition, organizations are concerned with increasing productivity. This concern has significantly increased the use of automation, robots, and advanced technologies in both white- and blue-collar occupations.

Advanced Technologies, Automation, and Robots.   The U.S. technologies that are advancing most rapidly and that have the most potential for enhancing productivity and work force utilization are microelectronics, artificial intelligence, materials research, material surfaces, biotechnology, and geology.[18] A significant application of microelectronics results in increased use of automation, computerization, and robots. Although using these technologies dramatically increases productivity, it also has a profound effect on the size of the needed work force and on employee pride and self-esteem. When the use of robots is considered, the organization's human resource planning needs must be altered.

Values Toward Work.   Stagnating productivity rates are often related to the decline or disappearance of the work ethic. According to some, however, "The work ethic has not disappeared. People today are willing to work hard at 'good' jobs, providing they have the freedom to influence the nature of their jobs and to pursue their own lifestyles.[19] People still value work, but the type of work that interests them has changed. They want challenging jobs that provide them with freedom to make decisions. Generally, people do not seek or desire rapid promotions, especially when they involve geographic transfers, but they do seek influence and control.[20]

According to a recent study comparing the work values of those over forty years old with those under forty years old

- Members of the older generation, products of the World War II era, accept authority, while employees from the younger generation, who grew up during the Vietnam War, do not trust authority.
- While members of the older generation see work as a duty and a vehicle for financial support, those of the younger generation think work should be fun and a place to meet other young people.
- Employees who are over forty believe that experience is the necessary road to promotion and are willing to spend time in an "apprenticeship," with the expectation of reward for that effort. Younger employees, on the other hand, believe that people should advance just as quickly as their competence permits.
- "Fairness" for the older generation means treating people equally; for the younger generation, it means allowing people to be different.[21]

Government Activity.   The influence of government activity on the human resource function in organizations is greater than ever. In some respects, the requirements of federal and state legislation have shaped the modern corporate personnel department. The remaining chapters will make clear how legislation and regulation (referred to collectively as legal considerations) will continue to influence all PHRM functions and activities.

Changes in these aspects of the external environment are likely to affect human resource management practices significantly. Familiarity with these changes will aid managers to manage their organizations' work force more effectively. Human resource managers must use this knowledge in developing and implementing effective planning programs and related recruitment, selection, compensation, and training programs. Once implemented, these programs need to be evaluated against organizational goals, and then implemented and evaluated again. Only through these continual practices will PHRM be effective in helping organizations gain a competitive edge in today's fast-paced, changing environment.

FOUR PHASES OF HUMAN RESOURCE PLANNING

Determining an organization's human resource needs lies at the base of human resource planning. The two major components of this determination are identifying the human resource supply and identifying the human resource demand—the first phase in human resource planning. Although these determinations are critical, organizations have, until recently, avoided making them.

Indeed, organizations have avoided or at least resisted engaging in any of the four phases of human resource planning.[22] These roadblocks to human resource planning are described later in the chapter.

Human resource planning is generally accomplished in four phases, each of which is discussed below.[23]

Phase 1: Gathering, Analyzing, and Forecasting Supply and Demand Data

The first phase of human resource planning involves developing data that can be used to determine corporate objectives, policies, and plans, as well as human resource objectives and policies. The data developed in Phase 1 represent information retrieved from the past, observed in the present, and forecasted for the future. Obtaining data from the past may be difficult because of inadequate or nonexistent records, and forecasting data with reliability and accuracy may be difficult because of uncertainties. Nevertheless, this data should be provided, however tentatively. The more tentative the data are, the more flexible and subject to revision they should be. Contingencies causing uncertainties in the forecasts should be incorporated, perhaps in the form of estimated ranges. Organizations in unstable, complex environments are faced with many more contingencies than are organizations in stable, simple environments.

Exhibit 2.5 shows the four steps in Phase 1. Each is important for the success of human resource planning and programming. Step 1 consists of analyzing the human resource situation in an organization. As Exhibit 2.5 indicates, this step consists of four aspects.

Analysis. One aspect of a human resource analysis is taking an inventory of the current work force and the current jobs in the organization. Both elements are necessary if the organization is to determine its capability to meet current and future human resource needs.

Use of computers makes compiling inventories much more efficient and allows for a more dynamic, integrative human resource program. Through computers, employees in separate divisions and in different geographic areas find it easier to participate in the organization's network for matching jobs and employees.

A second aspect of human resource analysis is analyzing the probable future composition of society's work force. This analysis is often based on wage, occupational, and industrial groups. Historical data on work force composition, along with current demographic and economic data, are used to make human resource projections. These employment projections are not specific to any single organization, but they can often provide an organization with useful information for its human resource plans, particularly for long-term needs.

Another aspect of human resource analysis is determining labor productivity and probable productivity in the future. Organizations can use their HRISs to measure performance in the process of evaluating the productivity of specific programs, offices, or positions. Related measures are projections of employee turnover and absenteeism. These influence an organization's work force productivity at any one time and, thus, its future human resource needs. These projections might also suggest a need to analyze the reasons for turnover and absenteeism, and then form the basis for strategies to deal with them. Note, however, that at some times and for some employees, increased turnover is

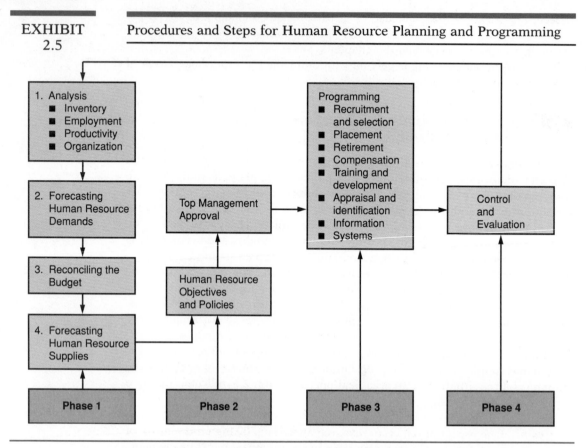

SOURCE: Adapted from E. W. Vetter, *Manpower Planning for High Talent Personnel* (Ann Arbor, Mich.:
Bureau of Industrial Relations, Graduate School of Business, University of Michigan, 1967), 34.

desirable. For example, if an organization suddenly finds itself with too many employees, increased turnover—especially among poor performers—might be welcomed.[24]

Finally, the organizational structure needs to be examined. This helps determine the probable size of the top, middle, and lower levels of the organization, for both managers and nonmanagers. In addition, it provides information about changes in the organization's human resource needs and about specific activities or functional areas that can be expected to experience particularly severe growth or contraction. As organizations become more technologically complex and face more complex and dynamic environments, their structures will become more complex—with more departments and a greater variety of occupations—and they will face more changes in the environment.[25]

Forecasting Human Resource Demands.   A variety of forecasting methods—some simple, some complex—can determine an organization's demand for human resources. The type of forecast used depends on the time frame and the type of organization, its size and dispersion, and the accuracy and certainty of available information. The time frame used in forecasting the organization's demand for human resources frequently parallels that used in forecasting the potential supply of human resources. Comparison of the demand and supply forecasts then determines the organization's short-, intermediate-, and long-term needs. These needs form the basis for human resource programming.

Forecasting results in approximations—not absolutes or certainties. The forecast quality depends on the accuracy of information and the predictability of events. The shorter the time horizon, the more predictable the events and the more accurate the information. For example, organizations are generally able to predict how many MBAs they may need for the coming year, but they are less able to predict their needs for the next five years.

A recent study indicates that 60 percent of major firms conduct some form of human resource forecast. More than half of these firms prepare forecasts for both the short term (one year) and the long term (five years). In conducting forecasts, the emphasis is generally on predicting PHRM demand rather than supply. In fact, more than 50 percent of the firms predicted *only* demand, while only one-third formally forecast supply *and* demand.[26]

Two classes of forecasting techniques are frequently used to determine the organization's projected demand for human resources. These are **judgmental forecasts** and **conventional statistical projections.** Judgmental forecasting employs experts who assist in preparing the forecasts. The most common method of estimating PHRM demand is **managerial estimates.**[27] Estimates can be made by top managers (**top-down**). Alternatively, the review process can begin at lower levels (**bottom-up**) with the results sent to higher levels for refinement. The success of these estimates depends on the quality of the information provided to the judgmental experts. Useful information can include data on current and projected productivity levels, market demand, and sales forecasts, as well as current staffing levels and mobility information.

Experts are also being utilized to make PHRM demand judgments. One way of combining information from experts is called the **Delphi technique.** At a Delphi meeting, experts take turns at presenting their forecasts and assumptions to the others, who then make revisions in their own forecasts. This process continues until a viable composite forecast emerges. The composite may represent specific projections or a range of projections, depending on the experts' positions.

The Delphi technique has been shown to produce better one-year forecasts in comparison with linear regression analysis. But it does have some limitations. Difficulties may arise, for example, in integrating the experts' opinions. This technique, however, appears to be particularly useful in generating insights into highly unstructured or undeveloped subject areas, such as human resource planning.

A related method is the **nominal group technique.** Several people sit at a conference table and independently list their ideas on a sheet of paper.[28] The ideas presented are recorded on larger sheets of paper so that everyone can see all the ideas and refer to them in later parts of the session.

Although the two techniques are similar in process, the Delphi technique is more frequently used to generate predictions, and the nominal group technique is more frequently used to identify current organizational problems and solutions to those problems. Although all these judgmental forecasts are less complex and rely on less data than those based on the statistical methods discussed next, they tend to dominate in practice.[29]

The most common statistical procedures are simple linear regression and multiple linear regression analyses. In **simple linear regression analysis,** a projection of future demand is based on a past relationship between the organization's employment level and a variable related to employment, such as sales. If a relationship can be established between the level of sales and the level of employment, predictions of future sales can be used to make predictions of future employment. Although a relationship may exist between sales and employment, it is often influenced by an organizational learning phenomenon. For example, the level of sales may double, but the level of employment necessary to meet this increase may be less than double. And if sales double again, the amount of employment necessary to meet this new doubling may be even less than that necessary to meet the first doubling of sales. An organizational learning curve can usually be determined by logarithmic calculations. Once the learning curve has been determined, more accurate projections of future employment levels can be established. See Chapter 16 for a more complete description of regression analysis.

Multiple linear regression analysis is an extension of simple linear regression analysis. Instead of relating employment to one variable, several variables are used. For example, instead of using only sales to predict employment demand, productivity data and equipment-use data may also be used. Because it incorporates several variables related to employment, multiple linear regression analysis may produce more accurate demand forecasts than does simple linear regression analysis. Apparently, however, only relatively large organizations use multiple linear regression analysis.[30]

In addition to these two regression techniques, several other statistical techniques are used to forecast staffing needs. Such techniques include productivity ratios, personnel ratios, time series analysis, and stochastic analysis. Currently, little research exists regarding the use of these techniques for human resource planning.[31] These techniques and a brief description of each are presented in Exhibit 2.6. Although most of these techniques are used for forecasting the total organization's human resource demand, parts of the organization use an additional technique. The **unit demand forecasting** technique relies on labor estimates that the unit or functional area managers provide. This technique may produce forecasts of demands that, when added up for all unit managers, are discrepant with the total organization's forecasted demands. However, it encourages unit managers to be more aware of their employees' skills, abilities, and desires. Such an awareness may also produce a higher-quality forecast. Each unit may use the same statistical techniques that are used for the total organization.

Since the use of unit demand forecasting often produces discrepant forecasts, reconciliation of the differences is necessary before planning can be undertaken. The discrepancies, however, can often provide a useful basis for questioning and examining each unit's contributions as compared with its demands.

Reconciling the Budget.   The third aspect in the first phase of human resource planning and programming puts the whole activity into economic perspective. The human resource forecast must be expressed in dollars, and this figure must be compatible with the organization's profit objectives and budget limitations.[32] The budget reconciliation process may point up the importance of adjusting the budget to accommodate the human resource plan. This reconciliation stage also provides an opportunity to align the objectives and policies of the organization with those of the personnel department.

Forecasting Human Resource Supplies.   Although forecasted supply can be derived from both internal and external sources of information, the internal

	EXHIBIT
Statistical Techniques Used to Project Staffing Demand Needs	2.6

Name	Description
Regression analysis	Past levels of various work load indicators, such as sales, production levels, and value added, are examined for statistical relationships with staffing levels. Where sufficiently strong relationships are found, a regression (or multiple regression) model is derived. Forecasted levels of the retained indicator(s) are entered into the resulting model and used to calculate the associated level of human resource requirements.
Productivity ratios	Historical data are used to examine past levels of a productivity index (P): $$P = \frac{\text{Work load}}{\text{Number of people}}$$ Where constant, or systematic, relationships are found, human resource requirements can be computed by dividing predicted work loads by P.
Personnel ratios	Past personnel data are examined to determine historical relationships among the employees in various jobs or job categories. Regression analysis or productivity ratios are then used to project either total or key group human resource requirements, and personnel ratios are used to allocate total requirements to various job categories or to estimate requirements for non-key groups
Time series analysis	Past staffing levels (instead of work load indicators) are used to project future human resource requirements. Past staffing levels are examined to isolate seasonal and cyclical variations, long-term trends, and random movement. Long-term trends are then extrapolated or projected using a moving average, exponential smoothing, or regression technique.
Stochastic analysis	The likelihood of landing a series of contracts is combined with the personnel requirements of each contract to estimate expected staffing requirements. Potential applications in government contractors and construction industries.

SOURCE: Adapted from L. Dyer, "Human Resource Planning," in *Personnel Management*, ed. K. Rowland and G. Ferris (Boston: Allyn & Bacon, 1982). Used with permission.

source is generally the most crucial and most available. As with forecasting demand, two basic techniques help forecast internal labor supply: judgmental and statistical. Once made, the supply forecast can then be compared with the human resource demand forecast to help determine, among other things, action programming for identifying human resource talent and balancing supply and demand forecasts. However, most current forecasting of labor supply and demand is short range and for the purposes of budgeting and controlling costs. Forecasts for periods of five or more years are used in planning corporate strategy, planning facilities, and identifying managerial replacements.[33]

Two judgmental techniques that organizations use to make supply forecasts are replacement planning and succession planning. **Replacement planning** uses replacement charts. These charts are developed to show the names of the current occupants of positions in the organization and the names of likely replacements. Replacement charts make potential vacancies readily apparent and indicate what types of positions most urgently need to be filled. Present performance levels of current employees can be used to estimate potential vacancies. These may occur in those jobs in which the incumbents are not outstanding performers. On the replacement chart the incumbents are listed directly under the job title. Those individuals likely to fill the potential vacancies are listed directly under the incumbents. Such a listing can provide the organization with a good estimate of what jobs are likely to become vacant and indicate if anyone will be ready to fill the vacancy.

Succession planning is similar to replacement planning, except that succession planning tends to be longer term and more developmental and tends to offer greater flexibility.[34] Although succession planning is widely practiced, many employers using it tend to emphasize the characteristics of the managers and downplay the characteristics of the positions to which these managers may eventually be promoted.[35]

Statistical techniques are used less frequently than are judgmental techniques. Still, with the advent of personal computers and the need to gain a competitive edge, organizations are using more sophisticated statistical models to examine the supply of human resources. An important component of these statistical models is a **transition matrix** or **Markov matrix,** which models the flow of human resources. For example, Touche Ross traditionally used a recruitment planning heuristic. However, this method did not account for attrition, expected growth of the firm, or the time needed to reach a specific job level. Now the firm uses a transition matrix similar to the one presented in Exhibit 2.7. The percentages in a transition matrix indicate average rates of historical movement between job categories from one period to the next. The table shows, for example, that a supervisor during year T (the first year) has a 12-percent chance of being promoted to manager, a 60-percent chance of remaining a supervisor, and a 28-percent chance of exiting the firm in the following year.

These data can also be used to estimate future human resource supply and demand (see Part B of Exhibit 2.7). This is done by multiplying the staffing levels at the beginning of the planning period by the probabilities of movement.

| EXHIBIT 2.7 | Transition Matrices for 1985–1989 |

Personnel Classification in Year T		Personnel Classification in Year T + 1					
A:		P	M	S	Sr	A	Exit
Partner		.70					.30
Manager		.10	.80				.10
Supervisor			.12	.60			.28
Senior				.20	.55		.25
Accountant					.15	.65	.20
	Beginning Staffing						
B:	Levels	P	M	S	Sr	A	Exit
Partner	10	7					3
Manager	30	3	24				3
Supervisor	50		6	30			14
Senior	100			20	55		25
Accountant	200				30	130	40
		10	30	50	85	130	—

In this example, the anticipated availabilities are 10, 30, 50, 85, and 130 in the five job categories. To keep staffing levels at the same level as in the initial year, the firm would need to hire 15 senior accountants and 70 accountants. Alternatively, the firm could promote 15 more accountants to senior accountant and recruit 85 accountants. This may be more cost effective. However, if new ideas are needed, the firm may wish to hire at higher levels. The transition matrix also points out rates of turnover. If the firm believes that the 30-percent turnover in partners is too high, it would need to develop strategies to correct the problem.

Markov analysis is also at the heart of **computer simulations** that examine alternative worker flows.[36] Promotion, turnover, and hiring rates can be varied and the effects on the bottom line examined. **Goal programming** is a further extension of Markov analysis.[37] The objective here is to optimize goals—in this case, a desired staffing pattern—given a set of constraints concerning such things as the upper limits on flows, the percentages of new recruits, and the total salary budget. Fortunately, software packages are available to facilitate these processes. IBM has gone so far as to develop personal-computer-based software to be used by managers in all their facilities to simulate HR flows for specific units or facilities.

Phase 2: Establishing Human Resource Objectives and Policies

While Markov-based analysis provides useful information, the actual strategy chosen to fill vacancies or resolve turnover problems depends on corporate goals and their linkage to PHRM goals established in Phase 2 of the planning process (refer to Exhibit 2.5). The importance of an organization's objectives, policies, and plans to human resource planning seems difficult to deny. Yet, only 25 percent of organizations achieve a substantial link between their general institutional planning and their human resource planning.

According to a survey conducted by D. Quinn Mills, a professor at Harvard Business School:

> Of the 291 companies surveyed 40 percent reported that they include a human resources component in their long-term business plans. Just under 50 percent of the respondents draw up a formal management succession plan, and approximately the same percentage prepare training and development plans for managerial employees. Only 15 percent of the surveyed firms do no people planning at all, Mills finds.
>
> Most of the respondents that engage in people planning do so because they believe it "makes their company more flexible and entrepreneurial, not because the environment forces it on them," Mills says. Of the survey respondents that practice people planning, 72 percent emphasized that it improves profitability, and 39 percent insisted that they can "measure the difference on the bottom line."[38]

Phase 3: Human Resource Programming

The third phase in human resource planning, human resource programming, is an extremely important extension. After the assessment of an organization's human resource needs, action programming must be developed to serve those needs. These action programs may be designed to increase the supply of the right employees in the organization (e.g., if the forecasts in Phase 1 showed that demand exceeded supply) or to decrease the number of current employees (e.g., if the forecasts showed that supply exceeded demand). Although many alternative programs could be proposed and evaluated to address these purposes, only two are presented here: to increase the supply of the right employees and to decrease the supply of current employees.

Attraction: Developing Alternative Organizational Structures. As indicated earlier, the human resource planner assists in developing workable organizational structures. Workable structures are those that can serve PHRM's objectives (i.e., to attract, retain, and motivate individuals). Present organizational structures, however, may not be as workable as they once were: "Changes in our society, particularly in the values of the workforce, have seriously undermined the traditional relationship between organizations and their members. This has led to a crisis for organizations that may only be resolved by the evolution of new organizational forms.[39] Some apparent results of this crisis have been the decline in productivity, especially quality of performance, and the increase in absenteeism. Consequently, organizations have been losing their ability to effectively use the human resources available to them.

In general, present organizational structures can be characterized by supervisory control, minimal employee participation in work place decisions, top-down communications, an emphasis on extrinsic rewards to attract, retain, and motivate employees (such as pay, promotion, and status symbols), narrowly designed jobs with narrow job descriptions and a primary concern for productivity and fitting people to jobs. These primary concerns result in selecting and placing people solely on the basis of their knowledge, skills, and abilities to meet the job demands.

Sensing that these organizational structure characteristics are no longer appropriate for attracting, retaining, and motivating individuals, some organizations, such as Honeywell, Control Data, Romac Industries, and Westinghouse, are engaging in alternative structures. These structures can be characterized by greater employee self-control, more employee participation in work place decisions, bottom-up as well as top-down communications, recognition of employee rights, an emphasis on intrinsic rewards (such as responsibility, meaningfullness, and achievement) and extrinsic rewards, more broadly designed jobs allowing for more worker discretion (see Chapter 12), and primary concerns for quality of work life, productivity, and fitting jobs to people. These primary concerns result in selecting and placing people on the basis of their personality, interests, and preferences, as well as their skills, knowledges, and abilities, to meet job and organization characteristics.[40]

Because a growing number of organizations are currently using alternative structures to improve their effectiveness, they apparently offer human resource planners a way of providing workable structures to serve employees. As described more extensively in Chapter 12, alternative structures are proving effective in some organizations.[41] This chapter's second "PHRM in the News" describes how IBM uses alternative structures to retain and motivate its current work force.

Reduction: Dealing with Job Loss. With the need for massive layoffs in the past few years (because of economic or technological conditions), organizations have become increasingly sensitive in dealing with the effects of layoffs on employees and are trying to either minimize these effects or eliminate the

"Alternatives to Hiring" Concept

IBM has developed an "alternatives to hiring" concept—the purpose of which is to motivate management and the support groups involved in hr planning to consider work solutions that maximize the utilization of current employees and minimize the acquisition of new hires.

IBM's basic hiring philosophy includes:

- hire the best
- promote from within
- offer career development within IBM
- make significant investments in training and development

When a position does become vacant, managers consider many options before they hire someone new. Here is an outline of IBM's "alternatives to hiring" concept.

1. Utilize current resources

- *Participative Management:* ask employees how the work can be completed without hiring someone new.
- *Zero Base Planning:* take a fresh look at all department or project activities as if beginning a new operation and justify each on the basis of value, necessity and required resource.
- *Work Elimination:* Can the work be eliminated? Can someone in another department do it?
- *Redefining Priority:* systematically prioritize activities to determine what the exposures are with or without additional resources.
- *Remissioning:* move work from a department/location/division with too much work or excess skills to a department/location/division that needs more work or certain skills.
- *Job Restructuring:* regroup the tasks that make up a given job to match the skill of the resource available.
- *Vendoring:* contracting work to other companies or other IBM locations. Potential work for vendoring is that which is not key to the business, work of a less desirable nature, work requiring skill or equipment that does

not exist internally or work which can be done by a vendor at less cost.
- *Buying:* buying work product to yield productivity gains and avoid needless investment in equipment, space or human resources.
- *Automation:* look for ways to automate a function.
- *Home Terminals:* can have significant potential for increasing productivity and better utilizing critical skills.
- *Overtime:* increases output without adding additional human resources. However, stay within the guidelines—one week in six free from overtime, an average of 10 hours per week in any consecutive three months, fifteen percent on a yearly basis.
- *Reducing Absenteeism:* motivated employees with ownership and pride in their work will avoid excessive time away from the job.
- *Improving Performance of Low Contributors:* produce greater contributions through determining the problem, and assisting and counseling the employee for improvement.
- *Risk Management:* prudent risk-taking by management is a business necessity in today's fast-moving business environment. For example, short-term violations of overtime or supplemental guidelines might be necessary. It could also mean retracting commitments or allowing low priority activities to go undone until a later time.

2. Utilize Non-permanent Resources

- *Supplemental Employees:* non-permanent resources for needs of an indeterminate duration, or special skills needed for a limited period of time, or skills in short supply within the company.
- *Contract Personnel:* people on or off premises for specific projects of a limited duration.
- *Borrowed Resources:* temporary assignment from other departments or locations.

continued

3. Utilize Internal Transfers

The three basic requirements of a good placement and transfer system include:

- a real time requisition system that lists openings;
- a candidate pool by skill, position, level and other identifying characteristics; and
- a real time system/network that matches candidates with requisitions.

SOURCE: "'Alternatives to Hiring' Concept," by IBM *HR Reporter* (Apr. 1988): 3. Used with permission from *HR Reporter*, copyright 1988.

necessity for layoffs. Attempts to minimize these effects are reflected in redundancy planning. **Redundancy planning** is essentially human resource planning associated with the process of laying off employees who are no longer needed (they are redundant). Involved in this planning may be outplacement counseling, buy-outs, job skill retraining opportunities, and job transfer opportunities.[42]

> Handling the wave of layoffs caused by mergers and acquisitions and finding ways to motivate and recruit skilled managers are two of the top human resources problems facing companies today, according to a survey of more than 50 major corporations conducted by Goodrich & Sherwood Co., a New York-based consulting firm.
>
> Layoffs during an employment cutback or downsizing are handled by most of the surveyed firms by eliminating jobs (77 percent) or finding them redundant (71 percent), the study notes. Other factors taken into account include employee performance (25 percent) and length of service (21 percent). The study also finds that 81 percent of the firms provide laid-off workers with outplacement assistance, 56 percent grant regular severance pay, and 48 percent provide special early retirement benefits.[43]

The concern for layoffs and the use of outplacement firms in the United States are reflected in Japan. The "International PHRM in the News" feature describes the unusual layoff situation in Japan.

In addition to using layoffs to reduce the total number of employees, organizations also use early retirement. One approach to early retirement is illustrated by IBM

> Here, nearly 10,000 U.S. employees have entered an early retirement incentive program announced by IBM September 1986. Normally IBM employees may retire after 30 years of service or reaching age 55 with 15 years of service. Under the special program, which nearly doubled the number of employees eligible for retirement, the company added five years to an employee's service and age when calculating eligibility. An employee's benefits under the retirement incentive program also increased, since the credited five years are included in the calculation of benefits.

Similarly, Xerox has offered about 4,000 of its nearly 56,000 U.S. employees an opportunity for early retirement. The Xerox incentive program also adds five years to an employee's length of service and age for retirement-eligibility purposes. Additionally, certain employees will receive a social security supplement from the company until they qualify for benefits under the government program.[44]

Preretirement counseling can help facilitate an employee's transition from work to nonwork and, by so doing, can encourage employee retirement. PHRM

PHRM IN THE NEWS

Saying Sayonara in a Way That Saves Face

Outplacement Firms, Once Shunned, Offer Workers a New Safety Net

Japan has a problem that traditional methods can't solve: excess workers and managers. So during a recent retrenchment, a Japanese truck builder tried something different. It secretly turned over a list of employees it no longer needed to Managemates International, a Tokyo-based version of a U.S. outplacement and executive search firm. Within weeks, thanks to Managemates' efforts, several of the unwanted and unsuspecting employees received and accepted new job offers.

Professional outplacement services, once shunned as alien, are catching on in Japan. The strong yen is forcing many manufacturers to slash thousands of workers from their payrolls to help cut costs. Loath to fire people outright, such companies have been asking employees to retire early or shifting them to subsidiaries, new ventures, or affiliated businesses. But they can no longer afford those security-blanket employment practices. Such companies as Kobe Steel, Mitsui Engineering & Shipbuilding, and Sumitomo Metal Industries are being overwhelmed by excess managers in their 40s and 50s.

"The system isn't working any longer," says Atsuhiko Tateuchi, president of the Tokyo branch of Drake Beam Morin Inc., the sole U.S.-based outplacement firm in Japan. So far, there are only a handful of Japanese firms offering outplacement counseling to employees who are laid off or retire early. But the demand for such services is increasing. Tokyo-based Bright Career's client list has grown from 30 companies in 1985 to 50 now. Since opening its Tokyo office in late 1982, Drake Beam Morin has helped 500 employees from 150 companies polish their resumes and interview skills.

Some overstaffed trading houses have even launched counseling services to help their older employees—and those of other companies—to find new jobs, although usually at lower salaries. C. Itoh, Marubeni, and Mitsubishi all now have majority interests in outplacement businesses. Forced by company rules to retire at age 60, C. Itoh textile executive Tanji Matsumoto found work as an administrator of an educational institute through Career Planning Center Co., which is 90% owned by C. Itoh. "I was lucky because I had general management skills," says Matsumoto.

Hush-Hush

Few Japanese companies will admit publicly that they are using outplacement firms. Most are embarrassed about being unable to honor the promise of lifetime employment. More important, "once they open up about this, their employees' loyalty will disappear," says an outplacement executive.

The growth in outplacement services is also generating more business for headhunters, who have had a difficult time operating in Japan. "We're getting very good candidates now who maybe wouldn't have talked to our counselors four or five years ago," says Paul Penrose, managing partner of KPMG Peat Marwick, which operates an executive search business in Tokyo. As a result, small and medium-size domestic and foreign companies, which rarely get graduates from top Japanese universities, are now snapping up former employees of major Japanese manufacturers. With lifetime employment apparently on the way out, that's good news for at least part of Japan's growing surplus of middle managers.

SOURCE: By Amy Borrus in Tokyo. Reprinted from the Arpil 6, 1987, issue of *Business Week* by special permission, copyright © 1987 by McGraw-Hill, Inc.

may help an organization reduce employee bottlenecks, as well as avoid or reduce the number of redundant workers, by making sure that counseling programs are provided and that potentially redundant employees are identified and made aware of the counseling.

Regardless of the human resource program implemented, it must be monitored and evaluated. This allows for controlling how well the program is being implemented and revising it as appropriate. Thus, the necessary fourth phase in human resource planning is comprised of control and evaluation.

Phase 4: Human Resource Planning—Control and Evaluation

Control and evaluation of human resource plans and programs are essential to effectively manage human resources. Efforts in this area are clearly aimed at quantifying the value of human resources. These efforts recognize human resources as an asset to the organization. An HRIS facilitates program control and evaluation by allowing for more rapid and frequent collection of data to back up the forecast. This data collection is important not only as a means of control but also as a method for evaluating plans and programs and making adjustments.

Evaluation of human resource plans and programs is an important process not only for determining the effectiveness of human resource planning but also for demonstrating the significance of both human resource planning and the personnel and human resource department in the organization as a whole.

Possible criteria for evaluating human resource planning include the following:

- Actual staffing levels against established staffing requirements
- Productivity levels against established goals
- Actual personnel flow rates against desired rates
- Programs implemented against action plans
- Program results against expected outcomes (e.g., improved applicant flows, reduced quit rates, improved replacement ratios)
- Labor and program costs against budgets
- Ratios of program results (benefits) to program costs[45]

An important aspect related to evaluation, revision, and adjustment is the issue of cause and effect. The PHRM model presented in Chapter 1 is based on the notion of integrated, related activities. For example, if the recruiting program is not working well, the conclusion that the program needs revision is invalid. Perhaps the salaries offered to recruits were too low and not competitive with other organizations. Also possible is that despite the best recruiting efforts, few acceptable applicants applied. The integrated approach makes the evaluation of any single program not only complex but also necessary on the basis of the total program. Indeed, evaluation of planning and programming activities may need to consider only the bottom line—the composite results of a set of activities rather than separate results for each activity.

Regardless of whether PHRM *should* establish preretirement counseling programs, alternative organizational structures, or redundancy planning programs, little doubt exists that PHRM will need to consider these and other human resource programs. The many significant changes occurring in society will continue to severely impact human resource needs and supplies, as well as the entire organization's operation.

Roadblocks to Human Resource Planning

A key roadblock to initiating human resource planning is the lack of *top-management support*. PHRM can help remove this roadblock with data and bottom-line facts that demonstrate the effectiveness of human resource planning and PHRM.

Another roadblock is the difficulty in obtaining *integration* with other personnel activites—a necessary step if human resource planning is to work. A challenge for personnel and human resource managers is to create a personnel system in which all the functions and activities discussed in Chapter 1 are integrated and coordinated in conjunction with the organization's business plan.

A third roadblock is line managers' *lack of involvement*. Failure to involve line management in the design, development, and implementation of a human resource planning system is a common oversight for first-time planners. Personnel and human resource managers are often tempted to develop or adopt highly quantitative approaches to planning, which often have little pragmatic value in solving line managers' problems. To be effective, personnel planning must be useful. An integral part of being useful is serving line managers' needs. With this important point in mind, personnel can begin developing human resource plans and programs.

TRENDS IN HUMAN RESOURCE PLANNING

Because of their relevance for the entire area of PHRM, major trends introduced in Chapter 1 are also relevant to human resource planning.

Assessing Human Resource Planning

Human resource planning can make or break an organization, especially over the long term. Without effective human resource planning, an organization may find itself with a plant or an office without the people to run it. On a broad level, then, human resource planning can be assessed on the basis of whether the organization has the people it needs (i.e., the right people at the right place, at the right time, and at the right salary).

At more specific levels, human resource planning activities can be assessed by how effectively they, along with recruitment, attract new employees, deal with job loss, and adapt to the changing characteristics of the environment. Because an important part of human resource planning is forecasting, human resource planning can be assessed by how well its forecasts (whether of specific personnel needs or of specific environmental trends) compare with reality. Several other criteria against which human resource planning can be assessed are presented earlier in the section on human resource planning control and evaluation.

Artificial Intelligence and Planning

Currently, high-level computer languages have been developed that vastly increase the ease with which complex human knowledge can be represented in computer-usable form. This is making it possible to capture and make available expert knowledge about how things work and get done through **artificial in-**

telligence. Artificial intelligence (AI) has gained enough momentum to be considered the second computer revolution. Advances are making possible computer programs that have reliable knowledge about important topics. The field of PHRM is no exception. Interactions with these new AI programs can closely simulate interaction with experts. This is making possible, at least in principle, the attainment of the highly desirable goal of providing "real-time" on-the-job access to people who need PHRM support. The advantage from a PHRM planning perspective is that managers in the field will have optimal planning expertise available at a moment's notice.[46]

Strategic Involvement of Human Resource Planning

Competitive Advantage.   Increasingly, companies are being forced to think about using human resource planning to gain a competitive advantage. Companies are taking note of census data that indicate a decline in the number of young workers and a bulge in the number of middle-aged workers, as well as increases in the ranks of the functionally illiterate. Add to these changes an environment that is becoming more turbulent and more demanding of change. The interaction of these events is producing a need for flexibility and current skills. Such companies as AT&T, Bank of America Corporation, Sun Company, and Eastman Kodak Company are trying to gain this flexibility and skill currency by offering attractive early retirement packages to carefully selected groups of employees. Texas Instruments and New York Telephone are getting into secondary and primary education to help increase the literacy rate of the reduced supply of labor force entrants. McDonald's, confronted with the shortage of young workers, has begun a national advertising campaign designed to lure older workers into part-time employment with the fast-food chain.[47]

Linking with Organizational Strategy.   As introduced in Chapter 1, there are several strategic planning choices. The first choice in the planning menu relates to the extent or **degree of formalization**—ranging from informal to formal. The more formal the planning activity becomes, the more attention and concern that must be given to explicit planning procedures and activities for human resource management. One example of the result of more formal planning is Hewlett-Packard (HP)'s willingness and ability to state and support its human resource policy of not being a "hire and fire company." An advantage of this type of formalized planning is that it enables a company to provide employees with job security—a facet of human resource management critical to the success of such companies as IBM, Dana, and Delta, in addition to HP.

A second choice in the planning menu involves the **degree of tightness.** Establishing a tight rather than a loose link between human resource planning and corporate planning is necessary to the implementation and success of a more formal planning policy.

A third choice is the **time horizon** of the planning. As such, organizations can choose to plan only for short-term human resource needs or to extend themselves much further into the future. However, organizations apparently need to have a longer-term time horizon because their human resource characteristics change so slowly.[48] Nevertheless, because their environment may be volatile, organizations may benefit from some long-range planning considerations with shorter-range flexibility.

A final choice, and one common to all PHRM activities, concerns the **degree of employee involvement** in the planning activity. Organizations can choose to allow employees involvement ranging from extensive to relatively limited.

These four practices in human resource planning offer organizations variety in how they do their planning. The choices they make are likely to depend on several aspects of the environment, such as top management, corporate culture, and organizational strategy.

SUMMARY

Human resource planning is needed because of societal changes: (1) changes in population and labor force characteristics, such as age, sex, and race composition, job preferences, and job openings; (2) changes in general economic conditions and the increased use of automation and robots; (3) changes in social values, especially those regarding work, mobility, and retirement; and (4) changes in legislation and the level of government activity.

These changes mean that personnel and human resource departments must develop strategic and operational plans for all phases associated with using human resources. By moving it into a more vital position in total organization management, PHRM can begin to play the several roles described in Chapter 1, one of which is policy formulation to ensure that the organization's human resources are used as effectively as possible. A major roadblock to PHRM planning is lack of top-management support. Support, however, can be gained by showing top management the potential gains of planning.

The department must pay careful attention to accomplishing each of the four phases of human resource planning. The first phase determines present and future resources in order to develop a forecast of human resource needs. The second phase ensures that PHRM objectives and policies are compatible with the organization's overall objectives. Action programs must be developed and implemented in the third phase. The fourth phase controls and evaluates each program in order to help ensure its effectiveness. Based on the results of the evaluation, the program can then be modified as necessary.

DISCUSSION QUESTIONS

1. If human resource planning is so difficult, why do companies still engage in it?
2. What are the major changes in the demographic, occupational, industrial, and geographic mix of the U.S. labor force? What impact could these changes have on specific human resource functions?
3. What is the difference between judgmental and statistical forecasting? Give examples of how both techniques could be used to forecast human resource demand and supply for an organization.
4. Choose an organization where you work or have previously worked. Assume that you have been given a personal computer and told to create an HRIS. What information would you put into your system? How would you use this information? How could you keep this information current? Would your HRIS make you a better planner? How?

5. Aside from identifying future organizational personnel and human resource needs and establishing programs for eliminating discrepancies while balancing individual and organizational interests, what other specific purposes does human resource planning have?
6. Discuss the roadblocks to human resource planning and how each might be removed.
7. Provide a step-by-step overview of the four phases of human resource planning.

CASE STUDY

What PHRM Strategy Should Techtronics Pursue?

You are the CEO of Techtronics, a ten-year-old mature firm which manufactures computer chips. Because of foreign competition and cheap labor overseas, the business is very competitive. Approximately 75 percent of your firm's costs are salary related. In order to gain a competitive edge, it is critical that you manage your human resources carefully.

To assist you in analyzing your human resource flow, the director of administrative services, Christine Stephens, has prepared a matrix of Techtronics' employee flows for the past year. Listed on the left are the five levels in the organization and the number of employees at each level at the beginning of 1989. The remainder of the table lists employee flows across the different levels for the year. At the administration level, 150 administrators worked for the company at the beginning of 1989. At the end of the year, 120 of the original 150 remained. Thirty employees quit. Ten employees were promoted from midlevel management positions and one from engineering. Consequently, at the end of

1989, there were 131 persons at the administrative level. Your task is to analyze the remaining flows and develop a strategy to meet Techtronics' staffing needs for 1990.

Case Questions

1. How many employees are needed at each level to maintain current staffing levels?
2. What strategies can you pursue at Techtronics to fill all the available positions?
3. Which is preferred? Why?
4. Is turnover a problem at Techtronics? Why or why not?
5. Assume that Techtronics is forced to cut back its work force by 15 percent at all levels except management. At the management level, a 10 percent cutback is anticipated. In light of this, are there surpluses or shortages at other levels? What strategies are available to Techtronics to deal with this impending crisis?

	Number at Start of 1989	Movement of Employees Through the Year					
		Adm.	Mid.	Eng.	Tech.	Prod.	Exit
Administration	150	120	0	0	0	0	30
Midlevel Managers	300	10	225	5	0	0	60
Engineers	500	1	34	350	5	0	110
Technicians	700	0	20	10	500	100	70
Production Workers	1200	0	0	20	30	800	350

NOTES

1. N. L. Bloom, "HRM'S Planning Pays Off: Down-to-Earth Strategies for Your System's Success," *Personnel Journal* (Apr. 1988): 66–70; E. H. Burack, "A Strategic Planning and Operational Agenda for Human Resources," Human Resource Planning 11, No. 2 (1982): 63–69; L. Dyer, "Strategic Human Resources Management and Planning," in *Research in Personnel and Human Resources Management 3*, (Greenwich, Conn.: JAI Press, 1985), 1–30; G. L. Manis and M. S. Leibman, "Integrating Human Resource and Business Planning," *Personnel Administrator* (Mar. 1988): 32–38; G. Milkovich, L. Dyer, and T. Mahoney, "The State of Practice and Research in Human Resource Planning," in *Human Resource Management in the 1980s*, ed. S. J. Carroll and R. S. Schuler (Washington, D.C.: Bureau of National Affairs, 1983).

2. E. H. Burack, "Linking Corporate Business and Human Resource Planning: Strategic Issues and Concerns," *Human Resource Planning* 8 (1985): 133–46; D. Ulrich, "Strategic Human Resource Planning: Why and How?" *Human Resource Planning* 10, No. 1 (1987): 37–56; D. Ulrich, "Strategic Human Resource Planning," in *Readings in Personnel and Human Resource Management*, 3d ed. R. S. Schuler, S. A. Youngblood, and V. Huber (St. Paul: West, 1988): 57–71.

3. L. Dyer, "Human Resource Planning," 57–58.

4. D. B. Gehrman, "Objective-Based Human Resource Planning, "*Personnel Administrator* (Dec. 1982): 71–75; J. W. Walker, "Managing Human Resources in Flat, Lean and Flexible Organizations: Trends for the 1990s," *Human Resource Planning* 11, No. 2 (1988): 125–32.

5. J. Laurie, "Gaining Acceptance for Your HRD Plan," *Personnel* (Dec. 1982): 896–97; J. P. Muczyk, "Comprehensive Manpower Planning," *Managerial Planning* (Nov./Dec. 1981): 36–41; C. F. Russ, Jr., "Manpower Planning Systems: Part I," *Personnel Journal* (Jan. 1982): 40–45; C. F. Russ, Jr., "Manpower Planning Systems: Part II," *Personnel Journal* (Feb. 1982): 119–123.

6. A. Etzioni and P. Jargonwsky, "High Tech, Basic Industry, and the Future of the American Economy, "*Human Resource Management* (Fall 1984): 229–40; L. Greenhalgh, R. B. McKersie, and R. W. Gilkey, "Rebalancing the Workforce at IBM: A Case Study of Redeployment and Revitalization," *Organizational Dynamics* (Spring 1986): 30–47; P. H. Mirvis, "Formulating and Implementing Human Resource Strategy: A Model of How to Do It, Two Examples of How It's Done," *Human Resource Management* (Winter 1985): 385–412.

7. J. F. Coates, "An Environmental Scan: Projecting Future Human Resource Trends," *Human Resource Planning* 10, No. 4 (1987): 209–19; G. F. Gallup, *Forecast 2000: George Gallup, Jr. Predicts the Future of America* (New York: William Morrow, 1984).

8. R. W. Goddard, "How to Harness America's Gray Power," *Personnel Journal* (May 1987): 33–40; J. A. Kingson, "Golden Years Spent Under Golden Arches," *New York Times*, 6 March 1988, p. 26; "Older Minorities in Work and Retirement," *Working Age* (May/June 1988): 1. For information on senior workers, write to the American Association of Retired Persons, 1909 K Street, N.W., Washington, DC 20049.

9. D. W. Allen, "We Don't Know What 50% of the Jobs Will Be in the Year 2000," in *The Changing Composition of the Workforce: Implications for Future Research and Its Applications*, ed. A. S. Glickman (New York: Plenum Press, 1982); S. B. Wehrenberg, "Training Megatrends," *Personnel Journal* 62, No. 4 (1981): 279–80.

10. M. Frohman and A. I. Frohman, "Organizational Adaptation: A Personnel Responsibility," *Personnel Administrator* (Jan. 1984): 45–47, 88; M. Leshner, "The Case of the Missing HRP," *Personnel Journal* (Apr. 1985): 57–64; D. Q. Mills, "Planning with People in Mind," *Harvard Business Review* (July/Aug. 1985): 97–105; R. O'Connor, *Facing Strategic Issues: New Planning Guides and Practices* (New York: Conference Board, 1985); J. W. Peters, "Strategic Staffing: A Key Link in Business and Human Resource Planning," *Human Resource Planning 11*, No. 2 (1988): 151–58.

11. "Planning with People," *Bulletin to Management*, 3 May 1984, pp. 2, 7.

12. M. R. Louis, "A Cultural Perspective on Organizations: The Need for Consequences of Viewing Organizations as Culture Bearing Milieux," paper presented at the National Academy of Management; V. Sathe, "Some Acion Implications of Corporate Culture: A Manager's Guide to Action," *Organizational Dynamics* 12 (Autumn 1983): 7.

13. *American Demographics* (Ithaca, N.Y.: American Demographics, 1982; P.O. Box 68, Ithaca, NY 14850); J. F. Coates, "An Environmental Scan: Projecting Future Human Resource Trends," *Human Resource Planning* 10, No. 4 (1987): 209–19; S. M. Davis, *Future Perfect* (Reading, Mass.: Addison-Wesley, 1987); E. G. Flamholtz, Y. Randle, and S. Sackman, "Future Directions of Human Resource Management from 1985 to the Year 2000: An Environmental Scan Overview," in *Future Directions of Human Resource Management*, ed. E. G. Flamholtz, Y. Randle, and S. Sackman (Los Angeles: University of California Press, 1986); "Labor Force Demographics," *Bulletin to Management*, 23 July 1987, pp. 236–37; "Managing Now for the 1990s," *Fortune*, 26 Sept. 1988, pp. 44–96; "Needed: Human," *Business Week*, 19 Sept. 1988, pp. 100–141; S. Nelton, "Meet Your New Work Force," *Nation's Business* (July 1988): 14–21; "Women in the Labor Market: The Influx Continues," *Fair Employment Practices*, 28 Apr. 1988, pp. 51–52.

14. J. F. Coates, "An Environmental Scan: Projecting Future Human Resource Trends," *Human Resource Planning* 10, No. 4 (1987): 209–19; M. Doering, S. R. Rhodes, and M. Schuster, *The Aging Worker: A Compilation and Analysis of the Literature* (New York: Sage,

1983); J. Lindroth, "How to Beat the Coming Labor Shortage," *Personnel Journal* (Apr. 1982): 268–72; B. Rosen and T. H. Jerdee, "Management of Older Employees," unpublished manuscript, University of North Carolina, 1982; "When Retirees Go Back on the Payroll," *Business Week*, 22 Nov. 1982, pp. 112, 116.

15. E. Flamholtz, Y. Randle, and S. Sackman, eds., *Future Directions of Human Resource Management* (Los Angeles: University of California Press, 1986); D. R. Torrence and J. A. Torrence, "Training in the Face of Illiteracy," *Training and Development Journal* (Aug. 1987): 44–48.

16. For a discussion of these data and issues, see J. Bales, "Sex Stereotyping Data Valid, Brief Says," *Monitor* (Aug. 1988): 23; P. F. Drucker, "Working Women: Unmaking the Nineteenth Century," *Wall Street Journal*, 6 July 1981, p. 12; C. Hymowitz, "More Men Infiltrating Professions Historically Dominated by Women," *Wall Street Journal*, 25 Feb. 1981, p. 23; P. Somers, C. Poulton-Callahan, and R. Bartlett, "Women in the Workforce: A Structural Approach to Equality," *Personnel Administrator* (Oct. 1981): 61–64.

17. A. Feingold, "The Future in Employment and Jobs," *Personnel Administrator* (Dec. 1983): 80; "The 1990 Worker: A Profile of the Future," *Trends* (Theodore Barry & Associates, 1981); "Where the Jobs Are," *Newsweek*, 2 Feb. 1987, pp. 42–48.

18. "Technologies for the '80s," *Business Week*, 6 July 1981, p. 48. See also "Artificial Intelligence: The Second Computer Age Begins," *Business Week*, 8 Mar. 1982, pp. 66–75; "Employment Outlook in High Technology," *New York Times*, 28 Mar. 1982, sec. 12; "Robots Create Changes in Work Force," *Ann Arbor Business-to-Business* (Oct. 1985): 9.

19. "Expectations That Can No Longer Be Met," *Business Week*, 30 June 1980, p. 84. See also J. Andrew, "In High School Today, Youths Are Absorbed with Material Goals," *Wall Street Journal*, 3 June 1981, pp. 1, 22; A. Cherns, "Work Values: Shifting Patterns in Industrial Society," *International Social Science Journal* 32 (1980): 427–41; K. E. Debats, "The Continuing Personnel Challenge," *Personnel Journal* (May 1982): 332–44; R. Dubin, "Industrial Workers," *Social Problems* 3 (1956): 131–42; P. C. Grant, "Why Employee Motivation Has Declined in America," *Personnel Journal* (Dec. 1982): 905–9; R. H. Hannah, "The Work Ethics of Coal Miners," *Personnel Journal* (Oct. 1982): 746–51; J. Holt, "Growing Up Engaged," *Psychology Today* (July 1980): 14–16, 23–24; G. S. Odiorne, "HRM Policy and Program Management—A New Look in the Eighties," in *Human Resource Management in the 1980s*; P. Parrish, "PAIR Potpourri," *Personnel Administrator* (July 1981): 15–16; W. H. Schmidt and B. Z. Posner, *Managerial Values and Expectations* (New York: AMACOM, 1982); M. Sinetar, "Management in the New Age: An Exploration of Changing Work Value," *Personnel Journal* (Sept. 1980): 749–55; J. W. Walker, "Training and Development," in *Human Resource Management in the 1980s*; D. Yankelovich, "New Rules in American Life: Searching for Self-Fulfillment in a World Turned Upside Down," *Psychology Today* (Apr. 1981): 35–91.

20. J. Case, "Why Work?" *INC.* (June 1988): 25–28; C. Hartman and S. Pearlstein, "The Joy of Working," *INC.* (Nov. 1987): 61–71; R. Levering, *A Great Place to Work* (New York: Random House, 1988); M. Maccoby, *Why Work: Leading the New Generation* (New York: Simon & Schuster, 1988); D. Q. Mills, *Not Like Our Parents* (New York: William Morrow, 1987).

21. "Work Attitudes: Study Reveals Generation Gap," *Bulletin to Management*, 2 Oct. 1986, p. 326.

22. C. Mackey, "Human Resource Planning: A Four-Phased Approach," *Management Review* (May 1981): 17–22.

23. For an extensive description of each of these phases, see E. H. Burack, "A Strategic Planning Operational Agenda for Human Resources," *Human Resource Planning* 11, No. 2 (1988): 63–68; L. Dyer, "Studying Human Resource Strategy: An Approach and an Agenda," *Industrial and Labor Relations Review* 23 (1984): 156–69; L. Dyer and N. D. Heyer, "Human Resource Planning at IBM," *Human Resource Planning* 7, No. 3 (1984): 111–26; "Manpower Planning and Corporate Objectives: Two Points of View," *Management Review* (Aug. 1981): 55–61; A. O. Manzini, "Integrating Human Resource Planning and Development: The Unification of Strategic, Operational and Human Resource Planning Systems," *Human Resource Planning* 11, No. 2 (1988): 79–94; G. S. Odiorne, "Developing a Human Resource Strategy," *Personnel Journal* (July 1981): 534–36; J. A. Sheridan, "The Relatedness of Change: A Comprehensive Approach to Human Resource Planning for the Eighties," *Human Resource Planning* (1979) 123–33; N. M. Tichy and C. K. Barnett, "Profiles in Change: Revitalizing the Automotive Industry," *Human Resource Management* (Winter 1985): 467–502.

24. For a discussion, see D. R. Dalton, "Absenteeism and Turnover in Organizations," in *Applied Readings in Personnel and Human Resource Management*, ed. R. S. Schuler, J. M. McFillen, and D. R. Dalton (St. Paul: West, 1980).

25. M. D. Hawkins, "Micros and Mainframes: Emerging Systems to Support HRP's Newer Roles," *Human Resource Planning* 11, No. 2 (1988): 125–32.

26. M. J. Feuer, R. J. Niehaus, and J. A. Sheridan, "Human Resource Forecasting: A Survey of Practice and Potential," *Human Resource Planning* 7, No. 2 (1988): 85–97.

27. For a description of managerial estimates, see J. W. Walker, *Human Resource Planning* (New York: McGraw-Hill, 1980).

28. For a more extensive discussion of group techniques, including the nominal group technique, see A. C. Delbecq, A. H. Van deVen, and D. H. Gustafson, *Group Technique for Program Planning* (Glenview, Ill.: Scott, Foresman, 1977); D. H. Gustafson, R. K. Shukla, A. Delbecq, and G. W. Walster, "A Comparative Study of Differences in Subjective Likelihood Estimates Made by Individuals, Interacting Groups, Delphi Groups,

and Nominal Groups," *Organizational Behavior and Human Performance* 9 (1973): 280–91; J. K. Murnigham, "Group Decision Making: What Strategy Should You Use?" *Management Review* (Feb. 1981): 56–60.

29. H. Kahalas, H. L. Pazer, J. S. Hoagland, and A. Leavitt, "Human Resource Planning Activities in U.S. Firms," *Human Resource Planning* 3 (1980): 53–66.

30. D. M. Atwater, E. S. Bress, R. J. Neihaus, and J. A. Sheridan, "An Application of Integrated Human Resource Planning Supply-Demand Model," *Human Resource Planning* 5 (1982): 1–15; E. P. Bloom, "Creating an Employee Information System," *Personnel Administrator* (Nov. 1982): 67–75; Milkovich, Dyer, and Mahoney, "The State of Practice," in *Human Resource Management in the 1980s*; G. Milkovich and T. Mahoney, "Human Resources Planning and PAIR Policy," in *PAIR Handbook*, vol. 4, ed. D. Yoder and H. Heneman (Berea, Ohio: American Society of Personnel Administration, 1976).

31. J. R. Hinrichs and R. F. Morrison, "Human Resource Planning in Support of Research and Development," *Human Resource Planning* 3 (1980): 201–10; Milkovich, Dyer, and Mahoney, "The State of Practice," in *Human Resource Management in the 1980s*.

32. P. S. Bender, W. D. Northup, and J. F. Shapiro, "Practical Modeling for Resource Management," *Harvard Business Review* (Mar./Apr. 1981): 163–75.

33. "Resource Planning: Forecasting Manpower Needs," *Personnel Journal* (Nov. 1981): 850–57; N. Scarborough and T. W. Zimmerer, "Human Resources Forecasting: Why and Where to Begin," *Personnel Administrator* (May 1982): 55–61.

34. J. Fraze, "Succession Planning Should Be a Priority for HR Professionals," *American Society for Personnel Administration/Resource* (June 1988): 4; G. L. McManis and M. S. Leibman, "Sucession Planners," *Personnel Administrator* (Aug. 1988): 24–30.

35. T. P. Bechet and W. R. Maki, "Modeling and Forecasting: Focusing on People as a Strategic Resource," *Human Resource Planning* 10, No. 4 (1987): 209–19; J. Carnazza, *Succession Replacement Planning: Programs and Practices* (New York: Center for Research in Career Development, Columbia Business School, 1982); Dyer, "Strategic Human Resources"; S. H. Zanski and M. W. Maret, "A Markov Application to Manpower Supply Planning," *Journal of the Operational Research Society* 31 (1980): 1095–1102.

36. G. T. Milkovich and F. Krzystofiak, "Simulation and Affirmative Action Planning," *Human Resource Planning* 2 (1979): 71–80.

37. E. S. Bress, D. Burns, A. Chernes, and W. W. Cooper, "A Goal Programming Model for Planning Officer Accessions," *Management Science* 26 (1980): 773–82.

38. D. Q. Mills, "Planning Policies," *Bulletin to Management*, Aug. 8, 1985; p. 48.

39. E. W. Vetter, *Manpower Planning for High Talent Personnel* (Ann Arbor: Bureau of Industrial Relations, Graduate School of Business, University of Michigan, 1967), 67. See also L. E. Davis, "Individuals and the Organization," *California Management Review* (Spring 1980): 5.

40. Note that although the terms *knowledge, skills,* and *abilities* are used, these can include other characteristics as well. For example, aptitudes can be included because organizations do select on the basis of aptitudes and because some aptitudes may be job related, as discussed in Chapter 5.

41. Organizations are becoming aware of the importance of matching job rewards with individuals' personalities, interests, and preferences, particularly the latter two. This is because of the growing recognition that an individual behaves in an organization on the basis of ability and motivation. Essentially, people do what is rewarded, assuming they believe that they can do what is required to get the reward. See J. R. Gordon, "Using the People/Problem Management Dichotomy," *Personnel Administrator* (Mar. 1983): 51–57.

42. J. P. Bucalo, Jr., "Administering a Salaried Reduction-in-Force . . . Effectively," *Personnel Administrator* (Apr. 1982): 79–89; "Casting Executives as Consultants," *Business Week*, 30 Aug. 1982, pp. 46, 51; G. H. Cauble, "Alternatives to a Reduction in Force," *Personnel Journal* (June 1982): 424–25; D. Henriksen, "Outplacement: Program Guidelines That Ensure Success," *Personnel Journal* (Aug. 1982): 583–88; N. R. Kleinfield, "A Human Resource at Allied Corp.," *New York Times*, 6 June 1982, p. 4F; J. T. McCune, R. W. Beatty, and R. V. Montagno, "Downsizing Practices in Manufacturing Firms," *Human Resource Management* (Summer 1988): 145–61; K. B. Noble, "Study Finds 60% of 11 Million Who Lost Jobs Got New Ones," *New York Times*, 7 Feb. 1986, pp. 1, 11; A. L. Otten, "Many Swedes 60 and Older Cut Working Hours Before Retirement Under Government Program," *Wall Street Journal*, 6 July 1982, p. 46; "The Rise in Worker Buy-Outs," *New York Times*, 23 Feb. 1983, pp. D1, D16.

43. "HR Agenda: Today's Paramount Problems," *Bulletin to Management*, 9 July 1987, p. 223; For other information refer to J. M. Ivancevich, D. M. Schweiger, and F. R. Power, "Strategies for Managing Human Resources During Mergers and Acquisitions," *Human Resource Planning* 10, No. 1 (1987): 19–36.

44. "Early Retirement Incentives: Two Approaches," *Bulletin to Management*, 8 Jan. 1987, p. 15.

45. H. L. Dahl and K. S. Morgan, "Return on Investment in Human Resources," unpublished manuscript, Upjohn Company, 1982.

46. A. O. Putman, C. R. Bell, and J. B. Van Zwieten, "Artificial Intelligence and HRD: A Paradigm Shift," *Training and Development Journal* (Aug. 1987): 28–31.

47. F. K. Foulkes and A. Whitman, "Marketing Strategies to Maintain Full Employment," *Harvard Business Review* (July/Aug. 1985): 30–35.

48. Milkovich, Dyer, and Mahney, "The State of Practice" in *Human Resource Management in the 1980s*.

Job Analysis

Building Competency Models

"Our objective in HR is to be able to have more employees who are capable of delivering superior performance on the job," Donatelli (an Aerojet General Corp. official) said. "We have made quite an investment in taking steps to identifying competency models for key jobs in our organization to help us:

- make better candidate selections, based on facts about what characteristics are necessary to be successful in a particular job;
- know whether we have the needed skills inside the organization—or whether we need to recruit outside;
- know our training needs;
- have realistic expectations for performance evaluations;
- make realistic assessments for promotional possibilities; and
- affect our compensation policies and performance incentives.

"Because the research for building a competency model for a specific job takes about six months, we have been careful to target our efforts to focus on key jobs where we can see meaningful results for our investment—what we call "jugular jobs." The more important the job, the more important and sophisticated competencies are to effective business performance. To date, we have identified three jobs which we have built competency models for—models that are all specific to Aerojet.

"Competencies we look at include knowledge, skills, self-concept, character traits and motivation. We take the following steps to define a competency application:

1. We nominate individuals to serve on an expert panel—those who know and can eval-

uate performance of a job.

2. We interview the expert panel to gain nominations and to use a data-based interview with nominated job incumbents. It takes about two hours for each interview.

3. We get transcripts of interviews, and analyze them thematically and for content. The content is analyzed by expert coders.

4. A committee of three expert coders cross-validates patterns, practices and characteristics identified in the transcripts. They must reach consensus on their conclusions.

5. The expert coders then provide a definition of competency indicators.

6. The competency indicators are put into conceptual clusters. For example, our management competency model has four clusters:

- Commitment to Work Achievement
- Diagnostic and Problem-Solving Skills
- Interpersonal Management
- Leadership and Management

"Each cluster has defined practices associated with it, plus examples of the application of these practices on the job. Practices are behaviors associated with successful—or unsuccessful—execution of the job. For example, we identified a total of 26 practices associated with management at Aerojet.

"By the time we have built a competency model, we know what is required for success in a job—through facts, experience of successful incumbents, and examples of behaviors on the job."

SOURCE: *HR Reporter* (August 1987): 5. Reprinted by permission from *HR Reporter,* copyright 1987.

T HE preceding "PHRM in the News" illustrates the importance of knowing what knowledge, skills, and abilities are needed to perform effectively on the job. It also illustrates the job analysis technique used at Aerojet General Corporation. Not all organizations, however, build competency models to obtain this knowledge. Typically, organizations get this knowledge as a part of doing more extensive job analysis.

Job analysis is the process of describing and recording the purpose of a job, its major duties and activities, the conditions under which it is performed, and the necessary knowledge, skills, and abilities (KSAs).[1] As shown in Exhibit 3.1, job analysis collects information that forms the essential parts of a job description. Job descriptions do not typically include information about performance standards or task design as in Exhibit 1.2. However, job descriptions can be used to generate weighted performance standards and to engineer jobs to attain high productivity and high quality of work life, respectively. The other major purpose of PHRM, complying with legal regulations, is served by generating job descriptions that comply with federal guidelines.[2]

PURPOSES AND IMPORTANCE OF JOB ANALYSIS

As shown in Exhibit 3.1, job analysis is the basis of job descriptions. Job analysis is necessary to legally validate the methods used in making employment decisions, such as selection, promotion, and performance appraisal. Job analysis is also important because it serves several other purposes:

■ Aids the supervisor and the employee in defining each employee's duties and related tasks

EXHIBIT 3.1   Relationships and Aspects of Job Analysis

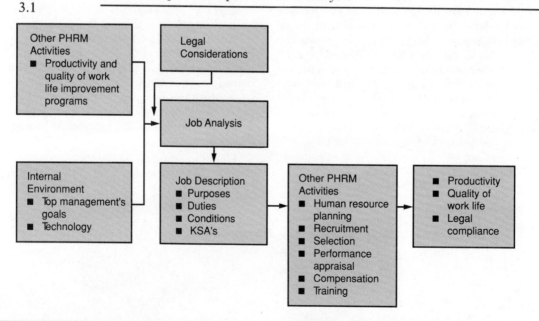

- Serves as a reference guide to move employees in the correct work-related direction
- Prescribes the importance of and time requirements for a worker's effort
- Provides job applicants with realistic job information regarding duties, working conditions, and job requirements
- Provides a justification for the existence of the job and where it fits into the organizational structure
- Identifies reporting relationships for supervisors and subordinates
- Guides change in work design and task management
- Determines the relative worth of jobs to maintain external and internal pay equity
- Ensures that companies do not violate the Equal Pay Act of 1963
- Provides selection information necessary to make employment decisions consistent with the Civil Rights Act of 1964[3]
- Serves as a basis for establishing career development programs and paths for employees
- Identifies worker redundancies during mergers, acquisitions, and downsizing
- Guides supervisors and incumbents in writing references and preparing résumés, respectively, for employees leaving and seeking new employment.[4]

RELATIONSHIPS INFLUENCING JOB ANALYSIS

Job analysis has extensive relationships with other PHRM activities and the internal environment.[5] These relationships are illustrated in Exhibit 3.1.

> The data generated by job analyses have significant use in nearly every phase of human resources administration: designing jobs and reward systems; staffing and training; performance control and more. Few other processes executed by organizations have the *potential* for being such a powerful aid to management decision making.
>
> But the word *potential* must be emphasized. The typical manner in which job analyses are conducted leaves much to be desired because the data tend to be incomplete, inaccurate and inappropriate. Indeed, using job analyses information as it is commonly collected can create as many problems for an organization as it helps resolve.
>
> One reason the analyses data tend to be highly flawed is that the data are often gathered by novices or employees who lack appreciation and understanding of the final use of the facts. Too frequently management delegates the task to a new employee or to someone with little experience, assuming that the procedure is routine and elementary. In reality, data collection for job analyses requires practice and considerable human relations skills.[6]

Relationships with Other PHRM Activites

Job analysis has extensive relationships with PHRM activities as well as with the internal environment (see Exhibit 3.1). The data gathered during job analysis are extremely useful in relation to almost all phases of PHRM: designing jobs, planning to meet staffing needs, setting job requirements, establishing training programs, and instituting performance control systems.

Job analysis is particularly important for establishing compensation. A job's worth is determined on the basis of job analysis. Job analysis also determines whether the pay level is fair in relation to that of other jobs. That is, job analysis ensures that employees in jobs of equal worth receive the same pay, as prescribed by the Equal Pay Act. Job analysis also provides a foundation for human resource planning. Without job analysis and the related planning, an organization would be unable to specify the types of job applicants it needs now and in the future.

Relationships with the Internal Environment

Two aspects of the internal environment that are relevant to job analysis are top management's goals and the technology used to pursue those goals.

Top Management's Goals.   Because they are created by organizations, jobs are top management's explicit statements of what they believe are the most appropriate means for accomplishing their goals. Furthermore, if workers' thoughts and beliefs about their organizations help determine their behavior, then the stated goals and the subsequent standards of excellence that an organization establishes give clear cues to employees about what is important and where their efforts are required. Because goals help determine organizations' products and environments, they also help determine the criteria against which workers will be evaluated—hence, their behaviors. The criteria and goals in turn also determine the kinds of individuals who will be attracted to the organization, evaluated highly, and promoted. Thus, organizational goals can help establish the reasons for jobs, the organization's expectations for workers, and even the legitimacy of the job demands.[7]

Technology.   The type of technology available to and used by an organization is also critical because it determines what types of job designs are possible and what types of jobs are appropriate for various organizational designs. For example, U.S. automobile manufacturers, with huge investments in plants and machinery to make cars on assembly lines, find it almost impossible to convert their car-making technology so that groups of workers make the cars. The result is that most assembly jobs are fairly segmented and repetitive and remain that way. Furthermore, assembly-line technology determines the structure or design of the organization and in turn the most appropriate types of job design. Increasingly, however, technology and the structure of organizations are changing very rapidly. Consequently, the design of jobs is changing rapidly, and with it comes the need to continually analyze jobs.

LEGAL CONSIDERATIONS IN JOB ANALYSIS

In addition to an extensive set of relationships with other PHRM activities and aspects of the organization, job analysis faces several legal considerations and constraints, largely because it serves as the basis for selection decisions, performance appraisals, and training determinations. The *Uniform Guidelines on Employee Selection Procedures* of 1978 and several court decisions have articulated these considerations and constraints. For example, Section 14.C.2 of the *Uniform Guidelines* states:

> "There shall be a job analysis which includes an analysis of the important work behaviors required for successful performance. . . . Any job analysis should focus on work behavior(s) and the tasks associated with them.[8]

Where job analysis has not been performed, the validity of selection instruments has been successfully challenged (*Kirkland v. New York Department of Correctional Services*, 1974; *Albemarle Paper Company v. Moody*, 1975). Numerous court decisions regarding job analysis and promotion and performance appraisal also exist. For example, in *Brito v. Zia Company* (1973), the court stated that the performance appraisal system of an organization is a selection procedure and therefore must be validated—that is, it must be anchored in job analysis. And in *Rowe v. General Motors* (1972), the court ruled that to prevent discriminatory practices in promotion decisions, a company should have written objective standards for promotion. Job analysis can determine these objective standards. In *U.S. v. City of Chicago* (1978), the court stated that in addition to simply having objective standards for promotion, these standards should describe the job to which the person is being considered for promotion. These standards can be determined through job analysis.[9]

ASPECTS OF JOB ANALYSIS

Renewed interest in job analysis has been spurred in part by organizational efforts to become more competitive and profitable and in part by the need to comply with the *Uniform Guidelines*.[10] Interest has also grown because job analysis serves many purposes and has an extensive set of system relationships in organizations. As a consequence, organizations want to know about all aspects fo job analysis, starting with collecting job analysis information.

Collecting Job Analysis Information

As defined earlier, job analysis is the process of describing and recording many aspects of jobs. These aspects vary greatly, often depending on the purposes to be served. Because gathering information on these aspects is necessary to comply with the *Uniform Guidelines*, one must know who collects the information and how it is collected.

Choice of Analyst. Job analysis can be conducted by those in the PHRM department, outside consultants, supervisors, or incumbents or by means of instrumentation—or by combinations of these. Because each person sees the job from a different perspective, job analysis outcomes may differ, depending on the information source. For example, female job analysts may focus on fatigue, visual strain, and interpersonal relations, while male analysts may emphasize working conditions and physical effort. Research also indicates that supervisors and incumbents rate the worth of incumbent jobs more positively than do outside job analysts. And while supervisors and incumbents usually agree about whether an incumbent performs specific tasks and duties, incumbents tend to see their jobs as requiring greater skill and knowledge than supervisors or outside job analysts do.

One reason for these differences is that job specific information is more salient to incumbents who perform the work than to outsiders who observe or interview incumbents. Differences may also be due to a **self-enhancement bias.** Because job analysis is related to many important PHRM outcomes (e.g., performance appraisal, compensation), incumbents and, to a lesser extent, their supervisors may exaggerate job duties in order to maximize organizational rewards and self-esteem.[11]

While incumbent ratings may be slightly enhanced, there are still good reasons to include them in the job analysis process. First, they are the source of the most current and accurate information about the job. Second, by including incumbents in the analysis process, supervisors and incumbents gain a shared perspective of job expectations.

In choosing a job analyst, attention should be paid to the analyst's education and training, degree of job familiarity, and cost of involvement. If incumbents do not have the reading and writing skills necessary to complete task inventories or write job descriptions, it is essential that outside experts intervene. For example, the Position Analysis Questionnaire (PAQ) requires post-college-level reading comprehension and extensive training. To train all employees in PAQ procedures would be inordinately costly.

Communiction about Job Analysis.   The launching of a job analysis program is often unpopular. It is not only time consuming but also potentially threatening to incumbents who perceive that it may lead to changes in job responsibilities, compensation, and training. To defuse resentment and misunderstanding, management should convey to employees the purpose of the job analysis program, who will be involved, and exactly what will happen as a result of the program.[12] Employee involvement also increases perceptions of procedural fairness and reduces resistance to change.

Methods of Gathering Information.   Information is gathered by a number of methods, including (1) interviews with job incumbents, (2) conferences with job analysts/experts, (3) observations by job analysts, (4) diaries kept by job incumbents, (5) structured and unstructured questionnaires filled out by incumbents or by observers, such as supervisors or job analysts, (6) critical incidents written by incumbents or others who know the jobs, and (7) mechanical devices, such as stopwatches, counters, and films. Here again, multiple methods can provide more information that can be used for a variety of purposes. However, the cost is usually high in terms of employees' time spent recording, coordinating, and storing all the information.

Job Descriptions

From the data gathered through job analyses, job descriptions are generated. On the basis of job descriptions, performance appraisal forms can be developed, and job classification systems can be established for job evaluation and compensation purposes. Because job descriptions identify the education and training needed to perform a job, it is also possible to design appropriate recruitment, selection, and training-and-development programs. Typically, a single document describes job duties and underlying tasks. The final job analysis documents should probably include the following:

■ **Job title** refers to a group of positions that are identical with regard to their significant duties. In contrast, a **position description** refers to a collection of duties performed by a single person. A company with fifty accounting assistants has fifty accounting positions but probably fewer than five discernible jobs. Job titles can be deceptive; jobs in different departments or in different organizations may erroneously have the same title but different duties. Thus, in determining whether jobs are similar for purposes of pay or selection procedures, an analyst should focus on the degree of overlap in job duties rather than on the similarity in job titles.[13]

- **Department** or division in which the job is located should be listed.
- **Date** the job was analyzed will cue job analysts as to when the description was and should be updated.
- **DOT code** is a standard job code published in the *Dictionary of Occupational Titles* by the Department of Labor. It provides some desirable but not essential information for validation reports pertaining to the job.
- **EEO-1/AAP categories** are the reporting categories in which the job falls for annual Equal Employment Opportunity (EEO) reporting and Affirmative Action Plans (AAPs).
- **Name of incumbent and name of job analyst** are useful for record-keeping purposes. However, for job evaluation purposes, incumbent names should not be included because they may inappropriately bias evaluators.
- **Job summary** is an abstract of the job; it can be used for job posting, recruitment advertisements, and salary surveys.
- **Supervision received and given** identifies reporting relationships. If supervision is given, the duties associated with that supervision should be detailed under **work performed.**
- **Work performed** identifies the duties and underlying tasks that make up a job. A task is something that workers perform or an action they take to produce a product or service. Duties are a collection of tasks that recur and are not trivial. For maximum informational use, duties should be prioritized in terms of the time spent as well as the importance; a duty may take little time to complete but be critical to job success. Weighted duty statements prioritize work for incumbents, are useful in establishing performance standards, and may be important for determining whether job accommodations for individuals protected under the Rehabilitation Act are reasonable. A concise weighted listing of job duties is also important to determine whether jobs are exempt from overtime provisions of the Fair Labor Standards Act and whether two jobs with different job titles are similar in skill, effort, responsibility, and working conditions, as provided by the Equal Pay Act.[14]
- **Job requirements** delineate the experience, education, training, licensure, and specific knowledge, skills, and abilities needed to perform a job. **Knowledge** relates to a body of information in a particular subject area that, if applied, makes adequate performance of the job possible (e.g., knowledge of Pascal; knowledge of OSHA regulations). The terms **skill** and **ability** are often used interchangeably and relate to observable capabilities to perform a learned behavior (e.g., operating a drill press).

Job requirements should be limited to the *minimum qualifications* a new employee can be expected to bring to the job. Minimum qualifications are likely to be prime focal points for EEO investigations because abuses are common and the potential for adverse impact is great. For example, requiring a high school diploma is unnecessary for the position of janitor. A janitor may, however, need basic reading skills to identify cleaning agents. Thus, an appropriate requirement would be the ability to read labels and instructions, not a high school diploma. Similarly, requiring an M.S. degree in social work may be an inappropriate qualification for the position of child welfare worker if individuals without the degree have been shown to perform the job as well as those with the degree. An M.S. degree *may* be necessary if required by state law. Job requirements are also controversial when employers impose artificially high minimums to reduce the number of applicants to be processed, to justify high salaries, or to enhance the prestige of the job or organization. Acceptable minimum qualifications should also not be incumbent-specific. If an incumbent has a college degree, yet the job requires only a high school diploma, only the high school diploma should be listed as required.

- **Job context** deals with the environment that surrounds the job. For example, work may be conducted outdoors (construction worker), in close quarters (film editor), in romote areas (forest ranger), in high temperatures (chef), or in low temperatures (meat cutter). It may involve extensive standing (sales clerk), sitting (data entry clerk), or exposure to fumes (fiberglass fabricator), noise (drill press operator), electrical shocks (electrician), diseases (laboratory technician), or stress (pension fund manager). Information on these job components provides an understanding of the setting in which work is conducted.[15]

Job descriptions should employ a terse, direct writing style, using present tense and active verbs. Each sentence should reflect an objective, either specifically stated or strongly implied.

Any words that impart unnecessary information should be omitted. Care should be taken to use words that have only one connotation and that specifically describe how the work is accomplished. Task descriptions should reflect the assigned work performed and worker traits ratings.[16] Each task statement should begin with an action verb (e.g., controls, sets up).

Keep in mind that the job should be described in enough detail that the reader can understand (1) what is to be done (the domains, behaviors, results, and duties), (2) what products are to be generated (the job's purposes), (3) what work standards are applied (e.g., quality and quantity), (4) under what conditions the job is performed, and (5) the job's design characteristics. Design characteristics are included so that individuals might select and be placed in jobs that match or suit their personalities, interests, and preferences. Nevertheless, organizations generally do not include job design characteristics in their job descriptions.

Exhibit 3.2 is an example of a typical job analysis document.[17] This job description does not provide information on performance standards, design characteristics, or the job's pruposes. The introductory section, however, implies the job's purposes. Performance standards are typically not specified in job descriptions because organizations prefer to retain flexibility and include standards in the performance appraisal form. Also typically missing from job descriptions is information on employee characteristics, such as degree of risk taking and emphasis on the shorter term or longer term, as presented in Chapter 1.

JOB ANALYSIS METHODS

This section summarizes the most common methods of job analysis. Motion studies focus on job efficiency. Task listings and inventories—the Position Analysis Questionnaire (PAQ), and the Job Element Inventory (JEI)—are structured questionnaires that can be analyzed by computer. Three other methods designed to meet specific PHRM information needs are also described. Finally, three methods that focus specifically on managerial work are examined.

Job Description	EXHIBIT 3.2

1. *Identification*

Job Title: Assistant Vice-President   Code: 186.167-058
Department: Fixed Income   EEO-1/AAP Category 7
Analyst: David Officer   Incumbent: John Smith

2. *Job Summary*

   Under direction of vice-president of fixed income, buys or sells treasury bills/notes in the cash and futures markets. Arbitrages between the cash and futures markets. Researches trading patterns from current publications, charts, and news organizations. Determines daily trends in markets through personal conversations with other traders in the industry. Follows current trading in cash and futures markets to determine arbitrage opportunities on a continuous basis each hour. Monitors other markets, news, and patterns to see how they will impact the future and cash markets on a continuous basis. Should provide a profit from arbitrage activity to the firm. Requires state license, B.S. degree, training. High stress level.

3.   *Supervision*
A.   Supervision Received:

     Immediate supervision _____   General supervision ___x___
     General direction _____   Part-time understudying or
                        assisting supervisor _____

B.   Supervision Given:

     Coordinates operations _____   Supervises assistants _____
     Supervises work group _____   Supervises fellow workers _____
     No. of departments or units supervised _____
     No. supervised: Full-time employees _____
                    Part-time employees _____
     Jobs supervised
   None

4.   *Work Performed*
A.   Coordinates market activity; 60%
     1.   Readies trades (writes up orders to buy and sell securities that were discussed in morning meeting).
     2.   Follows market (i.e, current prices for treasury bills in the cash markets vs. the futures markets).
     3.   Assesses arbitrage opportunities. Buys in the market where the T-bill is lowest and sells in the market where the T-bill is highest.
     4.   Phones other arbitrageurs/traders to make trades (i.e., to buy or sell T-bills in either cash or futures market).
     5.   Writes up transactions for record purposes once trade has gone through.
     6.   Executes orders from other departments regarding T-bills.
     7.   Maintains watch over positions throughout the day. Selling or buying to make a profit.

B.   Converses with other arbitrageurs and traders; 15%
     1.   Talks with traders in the office to see if they have discovered any market patterns.
     2.   Phones other arbitrageurs at other firms to develop contacts and information sources.
     3.   Strives to pick up information before the market reacts through contacts in organization and industry.

**EXHIBIT
3.2**   Job Description (continued)

C.   Stays abreast of current events; 10%
      1.   Reads papers including *Wall Street Journal, Barron's, Investors Daily*.
      2.   Reads financial reports from the firm's analysts.
      3.   Reads and analyzes projected forecasts of economy.
      4.   Follows volume from Japan that occurred during the night.

D.   Closes out daily market activities; 10%
      1.   Determines profits for the day from arbitrage activities.
      2.   Will consult with executive vice-president on day's activities.
      3.   Will research the market for the next day.

E.   Sets stop levels on trading activity; 2%
      1.   From researching the market the arbitrageur will determine price levels at which certain
            securities will be sold or bought if the market hits that level during the day.
      2.   Checks Japan's stops to see if they are consistent.

F.   Meets with department in morning meeting; 3%
      1.   Sets up stragedy for the perceived market trends during the day.
      2.   Receives ideas, news, company information.
      3.   Conveys market information to others.

5.   *Training and Experience*

A.   Previous job experienced desired and/or necessary:
            Two to three years financial trading, specifically with futures, cash markets, primary dealer, or
            some arbitrage background.
B.   Schooling and training:
            B.S. degree in business or finance.
C.   Special training:
            Must have a state of New York security trading license; certification from passing both the
            National Association of Security Dealers and National Futures Associations exams.
D.   On-the-job training:
            Knowledge of securities screens, selling and buying procedures for securities, and other office
            equipment.

6.   *Working Conditions*
      Inside office with noise from phones and loud voices. High degree of stress associated with large
      monetary exchanges, money, and high-risk decisions.

7.   *Physical Demands*
      Requires 90% of time sitting with 10% standing. Telephone use 20% and exposure to CRT 70% of
      the time.

8.   *Relation to Other Jobs*
      The promotion from a fixed income trader to future executive vice-president of fixed income.
      Transfer to other arbitrage activities in other markets is likely.

Methods Analysis   *The need and*

Methods analysis focuses on analyzing **job elements,** the smallest identifiable components of a job. The need for methods analysis often results from (1) changes in tools and equipment, (2) changes in product design, (3) changes in materials, (4) modifications of equipment and procedures to accommodate handicapped workers, and (5) health and safety concerns.

While PHRM managers have downplayed the importance of methods analysis in recent years, it is still widely used in manufacturing settings. In fact, the increased use of new technologies, collectively referred to as **programmable automation,** has increased the need for methods analysis. These new processes include computer-aided design (CAD), computer-aided manufacturing (CAM), computer-aided engineering (CAE), flexible manufacturing systems (FMS), group technology, robotics, and computer-integrated manufacturing (CIM). Unfortunately, manufacturers have acquired new equipment much in the way a family buys a new car. Drive out the old, drive in the new, enjoy the faster, smoother, more economical ride—and go on with life as before. With the new technology, however, "as before" can mean disaster. Executives are discovering that acquiring an FMS or any of the other advanced manufacturing systems is more like replacing that old car with a helicopter. If you fail to understand and prepare for the revolutionary capabilities of these systems, they will become as much an inconvenience as a benefit—and a lot more expensive.

The new manufacturing technologies can shock a business organization because they require a quantum jump in a manufacturing organization's precision and integration. Automated machine tools can produce parts to more exacting specifications than can the most skilled human machinist, but to do so they need explicit, unambiguous instructions in the form of computer programs.

The new hardware provides added freedom, but it also makes possible more ways to succeed or fail. It therefore requires new skills on the part of managers— an integrative imagination, a passion for detail. To prevent process contamination, for example, it is no longer possible to rely on people who have a "feel" for their machines, or just to note on a blueprint that operators should "remove iron filings from the part." When using the new automated machine tools, everything must be stated with mathematical precision: Where is the blower that removes the filings, and what's the orientation of the part during operation of the blower?[18]

Thus, it is increasingly important to study and document work processes. A variety of techniques are available for conducting methods analysis.

Flow Process Charts.   These charts are used to examine the overall sequence of an operation by focusing on either the movement of an operator or the flow of materials. For example, flow process charts have been used in hospitals to track patient movements, in grocery stores to analyze the checkout process, in small-batch manufacturing facilities to track material flows from machine to machine, in banks to examine the sequence associated with document processing, and in general to track supervisor-incumbent interactions during a performance appraisal interview.

Worker-Machine Charts.   Such are useful for envisioning the segments of a work cycle in which the equipment and the operator are busy or idle. The analyst can easily see when the operator and the machine are working jointly or independently. One use of this type of chart is to determine how many machines or how much equipment an operator can manage. A gang process chart is an extension of worker-machine charts. Rather than focusing on the operations of a single operator and a machine, this chart simultaneously plots the man-machine interfaces for a team of workers. Such charts are particularly useful for identifying individuals' utilizations of equipment and pinpointing bottlenecks in interdependent tasks.

Methods Analysis.   Also called **motion study,** this technique has its origins in industrial engineering and the work of Frederick Winslow Taylor and Frank Gailbreth. In essence, work measurement determines standard times for all units of work activity in a given task or job. Combining these times gives a standard time for the entire job. Exhibit 3.3 summarizes the formulas associated with methods analysis. **Observed time** is simply the average of observed times. **Normal time** is the observed time adjusted for worker performance; this is accomplished by determining a **performance rating** (PR) for observed performance. The PR is an estimation of the difference between the normal rate at which a worker could be expected to perform and the observed rate. The adjustment is necessary because workers may deliberately slow down or speed up the processes when observed. For instance, a PR of 1.20 indicates that an observed pace is much faster than normal. By comparison, a PR of .80 assumes that observed performance is slower than normal (a likely occurrence if the job is being studied to set rates of pay).

Standard time is the normal time adjusted for normal work interruptions. These delays may include personal delays (getting a drink of water, going to the washroom) and variable allowances specific to the job (mental or physical effort, lighting, atmospheric conditions, monotony, and detail). Industrial engineers have developed tables listing the allowances for different work delays.

To demonstrate the calculations associated with time study, an example follows:

Observations:

1.	4.50		PR	=	1.10 (Observed performance is faster than normal)
2.	4.32	Allowance	=	15%
3.	4.15	OT	=	T/n	=	21.18/5	=	4.23
4.	4.12	NT	=	OT × PR	=	4.23(1.10)	=	4.65
5.	4.09	ST	=	NT(1 + A)	=	4.65(1.15)	=	5.35
	21.18

In explaining these equations, it should be emphasized that there are several different formulas for determining standard time (see Exhibit 3.3). For example, if the allowance is expressed as a percentage of the normal time, then ST = NT(1 + A). Alternatively, if the allowance is expressed as a percentage of total time, then ST = NT/(1 − A). In both cases, the performance rating and allowance factors are judgment calls made by such experts as trained, licensed industrial engineers or psychologists.

Standard times can be used as a basis for wage incentive plans (incentives are generally given for work performance that takes less than the standard time), cost determination, cost estimates for new products, and balancing production lines and work crews.[19] Establishing standard times is a challenge of some consequence because the time it takes to do a job can be influenced as much by the individual doing the job as by the nature of the job itself. Consequently, determining standard times often requires measurement of the "actual effort"

Summary of Time Computations

EXHIBIT
3.3

Variable	Formula	Note
Observed Time	$OT = t_i/n$	
Normal Time	$NT = OT*PR$	
Standard Time	$ST = NT(1 + A)$	Allowance as a % of NT
	or	
	$ST = NT/(1 - A)$	Allowance as a % total time

Where

A = Allowance percentage
n = Number of observations
NT = Normal time
OT = Observed or average time
PR = Performance Rating
ST = Standard Time
t_i = Time observed for the ith observation

the individual is exerting and the "real effort" required. This process often involves trying to outguess someone else.

Work sampling is not only a technique for determining standard times but also another form of methods analysis. "Work sampling is the process of taking instantaneous samples of the work activities of individuals or groups of individuals."[20] The activities observed are timed and then classified into predetermined categories. The result is a description of the activities by classification of a job and the percentage of time for each activity.

Work sampling can be done in several ways: The job analyst can observe the incumbent at predetermined times; a camera can be set to take photographs at predetermined times; or at a given signal, all incumbents can record their activity at that moment.

Work sampling was utilized in a recent study that examined the differences between successful managers and effective managers. **Successful managers** are those who move up formal hierarchies quickly, while **effective managers** are those who have achieved high levels of quality and quantity of work performance and satisfaction. Managers in general were found to spend their time in the following activities: traditional management (32 percent), routine communication (29 percent), human resource management (20 percent), and networking (19 percent). Successful managers spent more time on networking activities and less on human resource management activities than effective managers did. The latter spent additional time on routine communication and human resource management.[21]

Structured Questionnaires

Task Inventories.   In contrast to the multiple methods that are used in work sampling to gather job data, the task inventories method of job analysis is based solely on a structured questionnaire. As such, task inventories are a listing of tasks for the occupations (jobs) being analyzed, with a provision for some type of response scale for each task listed. Using such a questionnaire, the job incumbent, supervisor, or job analyst performs the job analysis by checking the appropriate scale responses for each task listed. Suppose a specific secretarial job were to be analyzed using a task inventory with only three tasks. A part of the questionnaire might look like that shown in Exhibit 3.4. Because the task inventory method is based on a structured questionnaire, it is easy and quick to score and analyze. The results can be readily processed by computer and used for recruitment, selection, and compensation.

Because the development of task inventories requires large samples of employees and complex statistical analysis, their use is usually limited to organizations that employ many people in the same occupation (police, firefighters, data entry clerks). As a consequence, the use of task inventories is fairly widespread in city and state governments and the military, which typically have many incumbents performing the same job.[22]

Position Analysis Questionnaire (PAQ).   The PAQ is a structured questionnaire containing 187 job elements and 7 additional items relating to amount of pay that are for research purposes only. The PAQ is organized into six divisions, each of which contains some of the 187 job elements. The divisions and a sample of elements include the following:

- **Information input:** Where and how does the worker get the information used in performing the job? Examples are the use of written materials and near-visual differentiation.
- **Mental processes:** What reasoning, decision-making, planning, and information-processing activities are involved in performing the job? Examples are the level of reasoning in problem solving and coding/decoding.
- **Work output:** What physical activities does the worker perform, and what tools or devices are used? Examples are the use of keyboard devices and assembling/disassembling.

**EXHIBIT
3.4**

Sample of a Task Inventory Questionnaire

	Is Task Done?	Importance	Time Spent
			1. Very much below average
		1. Extremely unimportant	2. Below average
		2. Very unimportant	3. Slightly below average
		3. Unimportant	
		4. About medium importance	4. About average
			5. Slightly above average
		5. Important	
		6. Very important	6. Above average
	1. Yes	7. Extremely important	7. Very much above average
	2. No		
Prioritize typing requirements	① ②	① ② ③ ④ ⑤ ⑥ ⑦	① ② ③ ④ ⑤ ⑥ ⑦
Type address labels	① ②	① ② ③ ④ ⑤ ⑥ ⑦	① ② ③ ④ ⑤ ⑥ ⑦
Type business correspondence	① ②	① ② ③ ④ ⑤ ⑥ ⑦	① ② ③ ④ ⑤ ⑥ ⑦

- **Relationships with other people:** What relationships with other people are required in performing the job? Examples are instructing and contacts with the public or customers.
- **Job context:** In what physical or social contexts is the work performed? Examples are high temperature and interpersonal conflict situations.
- **Other job characteristics:** What other activities, conditions, or characteristics are relevant to the job?[23]

Each element is also rated on one of six rating scales: (1) extent of use, (2) importance to the job, (3) amount of time, (4) possibility of occurrence, (5) applicability and (6) other.

Using these six divisions and six rating scales, the nature of jobs is essentially determined in terms of communciation, decision making, and social responsibilities; perfomance of skilled activities; physical activity and related environmental conditions; operation of vehicles and equipment; and processing of information. Using these five dimensions, jobs can be compared and clustered. The job clusters can then be used for staffing decisions and developing job descriptions and specifications.

While task inventories limit comparisons of jobs within occupations, the PAQ is more general and can be applied to a variety of jobs and organizations without modification. Responses to the items are analyzed by computer to produce a job profile that indicates how a particular job compares with other jobs with regard to the six elements detailed above. The PAQ data base also contains information about the relationships among PAQ responses, job aptitudes, and labor market pay rates. These scores can then be used to set qualification or compensation levels for jobs. Thus, the PAQ is a potential selection and job evaluation tool, as well as a job analysis tool.

Using the PAQ to set qualification cutoff levels is less subjective than using a supervisor's opinion. However, there is no direct evidence that obtaining a given test score makes an applicant more likely to perform well. Care is also needed in using the PAQ to set compensation rates because the worth of jobs is not determined independently of the labor market. Thus, jobs highly valued by an organization but less valued in a labor market would be paid the lower market rate. Another concern with the PAQ is that it must be bought from a consulting firm; consequently, direct costs appear high. Finally, a postcollege reading comprehension level is required to respond to the items. Thus, PAQ is not well suited to job analysis situations in which job incumbents or supervisors serve as raters.[24]

Job Element Inventory (JEI).   Closely modeled after the PAQ, the 153-item Job Element Inventory has a readability index estimated to be at the tenth-grade level, and is explicitly designed for completion by incumbents. For example, the PAQ item "Dirty Environment" (situations in which workers and/or their clothing easily becomes dirty, greasy—environments often associated with garages, foundries, coal mines, highway construction, furnace cleaning) is "Work where you easily become dirty" on the JEI. The dimensional structure of the JEI is similar to that of the PAQ. The advantage of this instrument lies in the cost savings associated with having incumbents rather than trained analysts complete the instrument.[25]

Functional Job Analysis (FJA).   The U.S. Training and Employment Service (USTES) developed functional job analysis to describe concerns (people, data, and things) and to develop job summaries, job descriptions, and employee specifications.[26] FJA was designed to improve job placement and counseling for workers registering at local state employment offices. Today, a number of private and public organizations use many aspects of FJA.[27]

FJA is both a conceptual system for defining the worker activity dimensions and method of measuring worker activity levels. Its fundamental premises are as follows:

- A fundamental distinction must be made between what gets done and what workers do to get things done. Bus drivers do not carry passengers; they drive vehicles and collect fares.
- Jobs are concerned with data, people, and things.
- In relation to things, workers draw on physical resources; in relation to data, on mental resources; and in relation to people, on interpersonal resources.
- All jobs require workers to relate to data, people, and things to some degree.
- Although workers' behavior or the tasks they perform can apparently be described in an infinite number of ways, only a few definitive functions are involved. Thus, in interacting with machines, workers feed, tend, operate, and set up; in the case of vehicles or related machines, they drive or control them. Although these functions vary in difficulty and content, each draws on a relatively narrow and specific range of worker characteristics and qualifications for effective performance.
- The functions appropriate to dealing with data, people, or things are hierarchical and ordinal, proceeding from the complex to the simple. Thus, to indicate that a particular function—say, compiling data—reflects the job requirements is to say that it also includes lower-function requirements, such as comparing, and excludes higher-function requirements, such as analyzing.[28]

Exhibit 3.5 lists the worker functions associated with data, people, and things. The USTES has used these worker functions as a basis for describing over thirty thousand job titles in the *Dictionary of Occupational Titles* and for creating job families (groupings of jobs) based on similar data, people, and things. The USTES even provides a simple job description for most job titles.

A PHRM manager who has to prepare job descriptions and specifications might start with the *Dictionary of Occupational Titles* to determine general job

---

EXHIBIT 3.5

Functions Associated with Data, People, and Things

Data	People	Things
0 synthesizing	0 mentoring	0 setting up
1 coordinating	1 negotiating	1 precision working
2 analyzing	2 instructing	2 operating-controlling
3 compliling	3 supervising	3 driving-operating
4 computing	4 diverting	4 manipulating
5 copying	5 persuading	5 tending
6 comparing	6 speaking-signaling	6 feeding-offbearing
	7 serving	7 handling
	8 taking instructions-helping	

Source: Adapted from U.S. Department of Labor, Employment Service, Training and Development Administration, *Handbook for Analyzing Jobs* (Washington, D.C.: Government Printing Office, 1972), 73.

analysis information. The *Handbook for Analyzing Jobs* is used for more specific resource planning, recruitment, selection, placement, performance evaluation, training, and job design.

Critical Incidents Technique (CIT). A job analysis technique frequently used for developing behavioral criteria is the critical incidents technique (CIT). The CIT requires those knowledgeable about a job to describe to a job analyst the critical job incidents (i.e., those incidents observed over the past six to twelve months that represent effective and ineffective performance). Sometimes the job analyst needs to prompt those describing the incidents by asking them to write down five key things an incumbent must be good at in the job to be analyzed or to identify the most effective job incumbent and describe that person's behavior.[29]

Those describing the incidents are also asked to describe what led up to the incidents, what the consequences of the behavior were, and whether the behavior was under the incumbent's control. After the critical incidents (often several hundred for each job) have been gathered and described, they are rated by frequency of occurrence, importance, and the extent of ability required to perform them. Then the critical incidents and their characteristics can be clustered into job dimensions.

These job dimensions, which may often use only a subset of all the critical incidents obtained, can then be used to describe the job.[30] They can also be used to develop performance appraisal forms, particularly behavioral anchored ratings scales and behavioral observation scales (described in Chapter 6). Additionally, critical incidents can be used to develop job-specific situational questions for selection purposes (described in Chapter 5).

With this job analysis method, as with others, the major disadvantages are the time required to gather the incidents and the difficulty of identifying average performance, because these methods often solicit performance extremes (e.g., ineffective or effective, or very bad or very good) and omit examples of average performance. This disadvantage, however, can be overcome by obtaining examples of multiple levels of performance.

Guidelines-Oriented Job Analysis (GOJA). GOJA was developed in response to the *Uniform Guidelines*—hence its name.[30] The several steps in GOJA each involve the job incumbents. Before any of these steps begin, the incumbents indicate their names, their length of time on the job, their experience, and the location of the current job.

In the first step, incumbents list their job domains. Related duties in a job often fall into broad categories. A category with related duties is called a **domain.** For example, a secretary may type letters, contracts, and memos. Since these duties are related, they are put into the same domain—call it typing. Jobs typically have several domains.

After the domains are identified, the incumbents list the critical duties typically performed for successful job performance in each domain. Duties are observable work behaviors that incumbents are expected to perform. Often each domain contains several duties.

Once the critical duties are identified, the incumbents indicate how frequently the duties are performed. Then each duty's degree of importance is determined.

The fourth step is the incumbents' determination of the skills and knowledge required to perform each duty. Only those skills and knowledge that cannot be learned or acquired in eight hours or less are included. This is consistent with the *Uniform Guidelines*. Not selecting an applicant who could have learned the necessary skills in less than eight hours is not a defensible (job-related) practice. This is discussed further in Chapter 5.

The fifth step is determining the physical characteristics that incumbents need to perform their job duties. Here the incumbents respond to five open-ended statements, each related to a physical characteristic.

The sixth and final step is a description of other characteristics necessary to perform the job, such as a listing of any legally required licenses or degrees. It may also inquire about the necessity to work overtime and travel, and if so, when, where, and how frequently.

The result of the six GOJA steps are a job description; a set of individual skills, knowledge, and abilities needed to perform the job; and a basis for developing job-related selection procedures and performance appraisal forms. As with the CIT, GOJA, because it focuses on behaviors, is useful for developing performance appraisal forms and spotting training needs.[31] In addition, because skills (physical and mental) and knowledge are identified, selection procedures can also be developed as described in Chapter 5. As with the CIT, GOJA enhances employee understanding and validity of the job analysis because job incumbents are involved in the process. This involvement, however, takes time.

Managerial Jobs

A number of special concerns arise in analyzing managerial jobs. One is that managers adjust job duties to fit their styles rather than adjusting their styles to fit the job. Also, it is difficult to identify what a manager does over time because activities vary from hour to hour and day to day. As immediate situations or exceptions arise, the content of a manager's job changes. Despite these complications, several methods have been developed to analyze managerial jobs.

Management Position Description Questionnaire (MPDQ). Although the FJA approach is complete, using it well requires considerable training, and its nature is quite narrative. The narrative portions tend to be less reliable than more quantitative techniques, such as the Management Position Description Questionnaire.[32] The MPDQ relies on the checklist method to analyze jobs. It contains 197 items related to managers' concerns, responsibilities, demands, restrictions, and miscellaneous characteristics. These 197 items have been condensed into the following 13 job factors:

- Product, market, and financial planning
- Coordination of other organizational units and personnel
- Internal business control
- Products and services responsibility
- Public and customer relations
- Advanced consulting
- Autonomy of action
- Approval of financial commitments
- Staff service
- Supervision
- Complexity and stress
- Advanced financial responsibility
- Broad personnel responsibility

The MPDQ is designed for managerial positions, but responses to the items vary by managerial level in any organization and also in different organizations. The MPDQ is appropriate for determining the training needs of employees moving into managerial jobs, evaluating managerial jobs, creating job families and placing new managerial jobs into the right job family, compensating managerial jobs, and developing selection procedures and performance appraisal forms.

Supervisor Task Description Questionnaire (STDQ). While MPDQ can be used to describe, compare, classify, and evaluate management jobs at all levels, the STDQ is limited to the work of first-line supervisors. The questionnaire describes one hundred work activities of first-line supervisors in areas such as:

- Working with subordinates
- Planning subordinates' work
- Work planning and scheduling
- Maintaining efficient production and quality
- Maintaining safe and clean work areas
- Maintaining equipment and machinery
- Compiling records and reports

A study of more than 250 first-line supervisors in forty plants showed that these job responsibilities were universal, regardless of technology or product type.[33]

The Hay Plan. Another method of analyzing managerial jobs is the Hay Plan, which a large number of organizations use. Although less structured than the MPDQ and STDQ, it is systematically tied into a job evaluation and compensation system. Thus, use of the Hay Plan allows an organization to maintain consistency not only in how it describes mangerial jobs but also in how it rewards them. The Hay Plan's purposes are management development, placement, and recruitment; job evaluation; measurement of the execution of a job against specific standards of accountability; and organization analysis.

The information gathered relates to four aspects of the incumbent's job: objectives, dimensions, nature and scope of the position, and accountability objectives.

Because the Hay Plan is based on information gathered in an interview (as opposed to the checklist method used by the MPDQ), the plan's success depends on the interviewer's skills. Interviewers can be trained, however, enabling the information to be used for job descriptions, job evaluation, and compensation. The Hay Plan results in one organization can be compared with those in other organizations to ensure external pay comparability. This plan is discussed further in Chapter 8.

INTERNATIONAL COMPARISONS IN HUMAN RESOURCE PLANNING AND JOB ANALYSIS

Not all countries practice job analysis and human resource planning in precisely the way that this chapter has described. In over forty countries, including the USSR, Korea, Japan, Germany, England, and Australia, a type of time-and-motion study called MODAPTS is utilized to assess the elements that make up manufacturing, government, banking, and dental jobs. Little known in the United States, MODAPTS is fundamentally simple. It is based on the assumption that the time taken for any body movement can be expressed in terms of a multiple of the time taken for a simple finger move. The time for a finger move is called a MOD (set at 129 milliseconds). The code of a MODAPTS move consists of a mnemonic character (G = Grasp) and a number, which is the MOD value of that movement. Thus, a hand move becomes M2 (.129 second x 2).

The MODAPTS system answers four questions:

- What is a reasonable time for a "normal" (nondisabled for the task) person to carry out a defined task?
- What is a reasonable output for a "normal" person in a given time period?
- What are the relative efficiencies of two or more ways of performing the task?
- When a particular person takes longer than "normal" to perform a specific task, what is the degree of deficiency?

An advantage of MODAPTS is that a series of twenty-one "workability" tests have been developed to asses the functional capabilities of workers against the performance standard of a "nondisabled" individual. The results of the test can be used to place people on tasks that maximize their strengths, to train workers in areas of identified deficiencies, to redesign jobs to minimize worker deficiencies, and to determine if a performance loss is due to injury or handicap. Testing materials cost less than fifty dollars, and even individuals suffering from cerebral palsy can be tested.[34]

Japanese organizations select individuals on the basis of their fit with the company rather than on the basis of how they can do a particular job. In essence, individuals are organizational applicants rather than job applicants, as in the United States. Consequently, job analysis takes on much less significance. If an individual is unable to perform a job, training is provided.

The Japanese system of lifetime employment also contrasts sharply with human resource management practices in the United States. The commitment to lifetime employment is a distinguishing feature of the Japanese labor market. Described as **Shushin Koyo,** or lifetime employment, the practice comes close to a guarantee that once an employee joins a company, he will stay with it until retirement age. He will not decide halfway through his career to move to another company, nor will the employer decide to dismiss him before retirement, except under extreme circumstances. (In Japan, lifetime employment has not generally applied to women workers, who for the most part have left their jobs once they were married or pregnant.)

With lifetime employment, human resource planning takes on more importance, especially in a dynamic global environment in which products and competitors are constantly changing. Training and development programs must be accurately planned, so that employees will be prepared for new tasks and new environments. Human resource plans thus have to be more closely linked to the plans of the business. Although lifetime employment has been a cornerstone in Japanese employment practices, increasing levels of international competition, shrinking profit margins, and slowing economic growth are making the practice less feasible than before.

Though neither required by law nor formalized by a written contract, lifetime employment is encouraged by and endorsed by the Ministry of Labor and Nikkeiren (the Japan Federation of Employers' Associations) and is practiced by major employers. Lifetime employment does not appear to be practiced within smaller companies, such as vendors and small parts suppliers, although it is not uncommon for a major corporation to provide extra benefits to valued employees within vendor companies as a means of encouraging lasting relationships with important suppliers.[35]

TRENDS IN JOB ANALYSIS

A recent study of exemplary job analysis systems suggests several trends in job analysis. First, the job analysis process is **formal** and **highly centralized** in a specific PHRM unit—usually compensation. The system is formalized to the extent that a structured effort is made to conduct job analysis and update job descriptions for specific purposes. While too strong a linkage between job analysis and a particular application limits the use of job analysis information, locating job analysis functions with the application it must serve ensures that information will be maximally used and that the program will not be eliminated during a period of financial retrenchment.

Second, flagship job analysis programs rely on **highly detailed structured questionnaires**—including task inventories, the PAQ, semistructured position description questionnaires for job evaluation, or some combination of these— to collect job information. **Semistructured interviews** are relied on to construct questionnaires and fill in information gaps. The programs also rely on elaborate **software** to analyze the data collected by the inventories. These PHRM information systems have the capability of creating and accessing large data banks. They can also generate a variety of products, such as job descriptions and job analysis summary sheets.

Third is the **use of consultants** at some point in the development of the job analysis program. This is important because the development of an organization-specific structured questionnaire is extremely time consuming and complicated. Off-the-shelf job evaluation procedures, such as the PAQ or the MPDQ, require extensive training and consequently involve outside experts.[36]

Fourth, a variety of standards have been proposed for analyzing the usefulness of job analysis methods. These include (1) versatility for analyzing a variety of jobs; (2) standardization of procedures for data collection and analysis; (3) user acceptability and involvement; (4) training required by those involved in using the method; (5) readiness for use; (6) time required for completing the method and obtaining results; (7) reliability and validity; and (8) utility or overall benefit of using the method in relation to other methods and the costs incurred in their use.[37] Unfortunately, outstanding organizations did not employ elaborate and formalized evaluation processes. The majority of exceptional organizations relied on job analysis manuals and analyst training to standardize procedures. Regarding outcome standards, statistical analyses were also conducted to assess the reliability of results, and user acceptance was assessed through surveys. Thus, leading organizations still fall short of theoretical recommendations for analyzing job analysis procedures.

Fifth, is the general estimation of costs and benefits of job analysis functions.[38] In the exemplar organizations, precise quantification of benefits was not even attempted. Estimates of costs were made, but only in rudimentary ways. For example, custom-designed qualitative job analysis plans entail direct costs of between $250,000 and $500,000 for development expertise, at least one PHRM professional's time for one year, and about twenty-four months to complete from design through installation. The installation of a computerized job analysis system for one county government required a full-time project director, three to seven job analysts, and a systems analyst.[39] Compared to these costs, the PAQ and the MPDQ are relatively inexpensive; computer processing costs between five dollars and twenty-five dollars. Costs associated with the JEI are even less because incumbents complete the instrument with little or no training.

Assessment of the job analysis methods used by these organizations suggests that, overall, no method is clearly superior to others. Thus, the challenge is finding the best or most appropriate way to analyze jobs. Because jobs can be analyzed in so many ways, first identifying what purposes are to be served becomes important. This knowledge is useful, because the different ways to analyze jobs serve different purposes, such as helping to develop tests for selection, criteria for performance appraisal, and needs for training programs. Once the purposes are decided, the possible ways can be narrowed down. A final selection can then be made with the consideration of several practical concerns.

PHRM IN THE NEWS

Required HR Competencies

Historically, the personnel specialist needed some functional knowledge, people interaction skills and administrative expertise. Today, these competencies are still necessary, but they are not sufficient. Based upon a review of the available literature accompanied by feedback from hr practitioners themselves, the hrm professional of the 1990s will require a broad set of multidisciplinary skills, including:

1. Business Perspective.

The personnel managers of tomorrow must be sensitive to bottom line profit and loss calculations, must understand business terminology and must appreciate what it takes for their employers to succeed in the competitive marketplace.

2. Strategic Orientation.

Every hrm specialist must learn to think strategically, must understand how the organization's people resources interconnect with the firm's strategic plan and must be able to articulate an hr strategy for their particular subfunction.

3. Systems Approach.

Hr practioners must become adept at viewing issues and responses from a broad based, integrated, coordinated whole rather than a narrow, fragmented, parochial direction.

4. Professional Expertise.

Especially as a new employee, the hrm professional will be hired as an individual contributor and valued for functional competencies, e.g., instructor, interviewer, counselor, program designer, etc.

Moreover, this functional knowledge will typically be applied within a specific hr unit such as employment, labor relations or salary administration. Therefore, personnel staff members must be up to date and competent in their professional expertise and be able to relate this expertise to the issues at hand.

5. People Understanding.

Even though the stereotype that the primary requisite for personnel work is liking pople has been refuted, a sensitivity to employee needs and
continued

A final job analysis trend relates to the use of job analysis information to determine competencies. While job descriptions are the most common product and job evaluation the most common use, the "PHRM in the News" presented at the begining of the chapter indicates that organizations are now using job analysis information to identify the competencies necessary for excellent performance. As noted in the section on work sampling, an important determinant of managerial effectiveness is the ability to manage human resources effectively. The final "PHRM in the News" identifies the competencies for successful PHRM professionals of the 1990s. The same competencies can give any manager a competitive edge in the management of human resources.

SUMMARY

The creation and maintenance of organizations today requires that the worker-job interface be understood and managed. The belief that the way jobs are organized and perceived by job incumbents affects job attitudes and behaviors

---

concerns and the ability to effectively match this individual dimension with organizational requirements and demands remains a critical hr skill.

6. Managerial Capabilities.

Today it is recognized that human capital is a resource which can and should be managed like other scarce resources. Thus, the administrative focus of yesterday is gradually being complemented by an emphasis upon such managerial skills as planning, directing organization, coordinating and controlling.

7. Communication Abilities.

Hrm professionals are becoming increasingly skilled at using a variety of verbal and written communication channels to correspond with a diversity of constituencies. Moreover, this need for communication skills encompasses a variety of roles such as trainer, interviewer, negotiator and change agent.

8. Problem Solving and Evaluation Skills.

Increasingly, U.S. business firms expect the personnel function to make a difference and to be able to document the nature and magnitude of that payoff. This requires hr managers with the quantitative skills necessary to measure the costs and benefits of personnel alternatives and the expertise needed to evaluate the efficiency of various hrm programs and practices.

9. Networking Facility.

Human resources management is increasingly viewed as a shared responsibility with senior executives, line managers, hr professionals and even employees themselves having a role in planning the implementing of successful programs for effectively utilizing and developing this key resource.

Therefore, the hr professional must become effective at getting objectives accomplished through others and competent in such interpersonal techniques as networking, influencing, rapport establishing and selling.

10. Consultative Change Agent Focus.

In order to survive and prosper in today's competitive environment, many organizations are undergoing a substantial metamorphosis in terms of their corporate culture, i.e., philosophy, beliefs, values, goals. Moreover, this cultural transition typically means employee value systems must be reoriented to bring them back into harmony with the new culture. The personnel function must serve as an internal consultant and change agent in managing this cultural transformation and in resolving the hr issues which it creates.

SOURCE: *HR Reporter* (August 1987): 3. Reprinted by permission from *HR Reporter,* copyright 1987.

is a compelling reason for understanding job analysis. Job analysis provides information about what jobs are about and what individuals need to perform them. Information can be collected by several individuals using several methods; together, they provide the information for job descriptions and job specifications. These go a long way toward linking the individual to the organization and the job analysis activity to all other PHRM activities.

The choice of a job analysis method should be a product of purpose, as defined by the type of PHRM issue to be served, and practical concerns.

Regardless of the approach, it is important to bear in mind that job analysis serves as the backbone of nearly all the PHRM activities described in the succeeding chapters. The value of job analysis will become even more apparent in the following two chapters on the staffing function.

DISCUSSION QUESTIONS

1. List several purposes of job analysis.
2. How does state and federal legislation affect job analysis?
3. Discuss and review the important considerations in selecting job analysis methods.
4. Briefly, how might job analysis activities be assessed according to their importance to organizations?
5. Are jobs static? That is, will a job change over time? If so, what might cause the job to change? What implications does this have for job analysis?
6. Do you think the existence of job analysis might make a PHRM function (such as recruitment, performance appraisal, or compensation) less legally vulnerable? Explain.
7. Despite the de-emphasis on scientific management in organizations, why is it important that today's organizations have a firm understanding of the elemental motions that comprise many jobs?
8. Why have special job analysis procedures been developed for managerial jobs?
9. Can the reliability of job analysis information be compromised by the individual who provides it? If so, in what way? What can be done to minimize any biasing effects caused by job analysis sources?
10. Why aren't organizations conducting cost-benefit analyses of job analysis when methods exist to evaluate such programs?

CASE STUDY

Job Descriptions at HITEK

Jennifer Hill was excited about joining HITEK Information Services after receiving her MBA. Her job involved examining compensation practice, and her first assignment was to review HITEK's job descriptions. She was to document her work and make recommended changes, which would include reducing more than six hundred job descriptions to a manageable number.

Background

To its stockholders and the rest of the outside world, HITEK is a highly profitable, highly aggressive company in the computer business. In addition to its numerous government contracts, it provides software and hardware to business and individuals. From its inception in the late 1970s, it has maintained its position on the leading edge by remaining flexible and adaptable to the turbulent environment in which it operates. It is a people-intensive organization that relies enormously on its human resources; therefore, it is in HITEK's best interests to establish policies and procedures that nurture productivity and enhance the satisfaction of its employees.

Because the computer industry is growing at an incredible pace, opportunities for placement are abundant, and the competition for high-quality human resources is tremendous. HITEK has grown about 30 percent in the last three years, and its management knows that as easily as it attracts new employees, it can lose them. However, its turnover rate (14 percent) is about average for its industry.

HITEK remains relatively small at one thousand employees, and it prides itself on its "small team company culture." This culture is maintained partly by the use of a computer mail system that can put any employee in touch with anyone at HITEK and by the utilization of open office spaces. The relatively flat lean organizational structure (see Exhibit 1) and the easy accessibility of all corporate levels also promotes an open-door policy. All in all, employees enjoy working for HITEK, and management is in touch with the organization's "pulse."

With the notable exception of the human resource department, there are few rules at HITEK. Work in a department is often shared by all levels of employees, and positions are redefined to match the specific skills, abilities, and interests of the incumbent. "Overqualified" and "overachieving" individuals are often hired but are then promoted rapidly. Nothing is written down, and if newcomers want to know why something is done a certain way, they must ask the person(s) who created the procedure. There is extensive horizontal linkage between departments, perpetuating the blurring of distinctions between departments.

HITEK's Organizational Chart

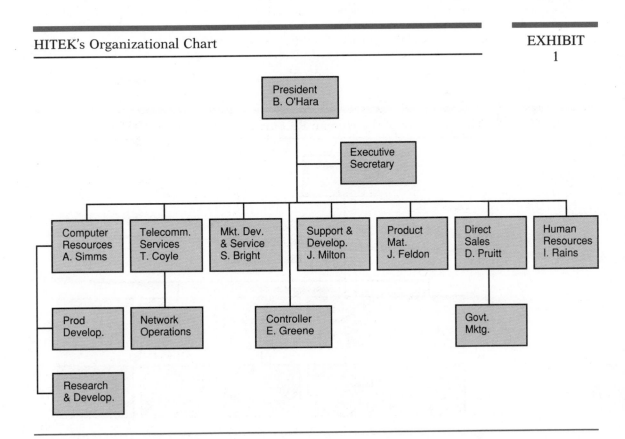

EXHIBIT 1

The Human Resources Department

The human resources department stands in stark contrast to the rest of HITEK. About thirty people are employed in the department, including the support staff members, or about one human resource employee per thirty-three HITEK employees. The vice president for human resources, Isabel Rains, rules the department with an "iron fist." Employees are careful to mold their ideas to match Rains perspective. When newcomers suggest changes, they are told that "this is the way things have always been done" because "it's our culture." Most of the human resources functions are bound by written rules and standard operating procedures, and because department employees know their job descriptions well, there is little overlap in duties.

With the exception of one recruiter, all twelve of the incumbents whose positions are represented in Exhibit 2 are women. Only half of them have degrees in industrial relations or PHRM, and only one-fourth have related experience with another company. Most of them have been promoted from clerical positions. In fact, some employees view the vice-presidency as a "gift" given to Isabel, a former executive secretary, the day after she received her bachelor's degree at a local college. In other departments, it is widely believed that professional degrees and related experience lead to expertise.

One incident that conveyed the department's image to Jennifer Hill occured during her second week on the job. While preparing a job description with Dave Pruitt, Jennifer explained that she would submit the job description to Janet Voris for final approval. Dave became confused and asked, "But Janet is only a clerical person; why would she be involved?"

Jennifer Hill's Duties

At HITEK, the pool of job descriptions had grown almost daily as newcomers were hired, but many of the old job descriptions were not discarded, even when obsolete. Other job descriptions needed updating. Jennifer spent some time thinking about how to proceed. She considered the uses of the job descriptions and what steps she would need to take to accomplish all that was expected of her. Support from within the department was scarce because other employees were busy gathering materials for the annual review of HITEK's hiring, promotion, and development practices conducted by the Equal Employment Opportunity Commission.

After six harried months on the job and much frustration, Jennifer had revised all the descriptions that were still needed (examples of "old" and "new" job descriptions appear in Exhibits 3 and 4. She was also beginning to develop some strong

---

EXHIBIT 2   The Structure of the Human Resources Department at HITEK

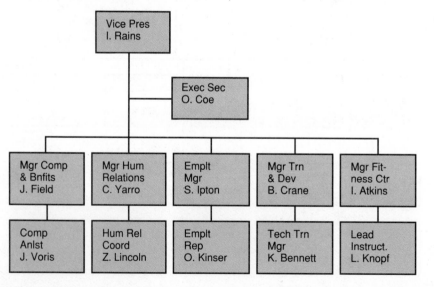

An "Old" Job Description	EXHIBIT 3

ASSOCIATE PROGRAMMER

Basic Objective

Perform coding, testing, and documentation of programs, under the supervision of a project leader.

Specific Tasks

Perform coding, debugging, and testing of a program when given general program specifications.

Develop documentation of the program.

Assist in the implementation and training of the users in the usage of the system.

Report to the manager, management information services as requested.

Job Qualifications

Minimum: (a) BA/BS degree in relevant field or equivalent experience/knowledge; (b) programming knowledge in FORTRAN; (c) good working knowledge of business and financial applications.

Desirable: (a) computer programming experience in a time-sharing environment; (b) some training or education in COBOL, PL1, or assembler languages.

A "New" Job Description	EXHIBIT 4

ASSOCIATE PROGRAMMER

General Statement of Duties

Performs coding, debugging, testing, and documentation of software under the superivsion of a technical superior. Involves some use of independent judgment.

Supervision Received

Works under close supervision of a technical superior or manager.

Supervision Exercised

No supervisory duties required.

Examples of Duties

(Any one position may not include all the duties listed, nor do listed examples include all duties that may be found in positions of this class.)

Confers with analysts, supervisors, and/or representatives of the departments to clarify software intent and programming requirements.

Performs coding, debugging, and testing of software when given program specifications for a particular task or problem.

Writes documentation for the program.

Seeks advice and assistance from supervisor when problems outside of realm of understanding arise. Communicates any program specification deficiencies back to supervisor.

Reports ideas concerning design and development back to supervisor.

EXHIBIT 4	A "New" Job Description (continued)
	Assists in the implementation of the system and training of end users.
	Provides some support and assistance to users.
	Develops product knowledge and personal expertise and proficiency in system usage.
	Assumes progressively complex and independent duties as experience permits.
	Performs all duties in accordance with corporate and departmental standards.
Minimum Qualifications	Education: BA/BS degree in relevant field or equivalent experience/knowledge in computer science, math, or other closely related field.
	Experience: No prior computer programming work experience necessary.
	Knowledge, Skills, and Abilities: Ability to exercise initiative and sound judgement. Knowledge of a structured language. Working knowledge in operating systems. Ability to maintain open working relationship with supervisor. Logic and problem-solving skills. System flowchart development skills.
Desirable Qualifications	Exposure to BASIC, FORTRAN, or PASCAL; some training in general accounting practices and controls; effective written and oral communication skills.

opinions about how the human resources department functioned at HITEK and what needed to be done to improve its effectiveness and its image. She decided to arrange a confidential lunch with Billy O'Hara.

Written By M. P. Miceli, Ohio State University and Karen Wijta, Macy's

Case Questions

1. What are the goals of HITEK? Of the human resources department? Why does the conflict create problems for HITEK?

2. Organization members can draw from several kinds of power, such as referent power and reward power. Is the human resources department powerful? Why is it important for HITEK to maintain a professinal, competent human resources function?

3. Jobs change frequently at HITEK. Shouldn't the human resources department simply discontinue the practice of job analysis and stop writing job descriptions?

4. What steps should Jennifer Hill take in performing the tasks assigned to her? How do your answers to the earlier questions affect your answer?

5. Is the "new" job description (Exhibit 4) better than the "old" one (Exhibit 3)? Why or why not?

6. What should Jennifer suggest to the president concerning the image and operation of the human resources department?

NOTES

1. B. Schnedier and A. M. Konz, "Strategic Job Analysis," unpublished manuscript, University of Maryland, College Park, 1988.

2. More traditional definitions of job analyses are found in S. E. Bemis, A. H. Belenky, and D. A. Soder, *Job Analysis* (Washington, D.C.: BNA Books, 1983); E. J. McCormick, "Job and Task Analysis," in *Handbook of Industrial and Organizational Psychology*, ed. M. D. Dunnette, (Chicago: Rand McNally, 1976), 651–96; E. J. McCormick, *Job Analysis: Methods and Applications* (New York: AMACOM, 1979); C. P. Sparks, "Job Analysis," in *Personnel Management*, ed. K. M. Rowland and G. R. Ferris (Boston: Allyn & Bacon, 1982) 78–100; and C. P. Sparks, "Job Analysis," in *Readings in Personnel and Human Resource Management*, ed. R. S. Schuler, S. A. Youngblood, and V. Huber, 3d ed. (St. Paul: West, 1988). In these sources, job analysis is the process of determining, by either structured or unstructured methods, the characteristics of work, often according to a set of prescribed dimensions, for the purpose of producing job descriptions and job specifications. See J. V. Chorpade, *Job Analysis: A Handbook for the Human Resource Director* (Englewood Cliffs, N.J.: Prentice-Hall, 1988).

3. The essence of the Civil Right Act of 1964, the Equal Opportunity in Employment Act of 1972, and various court decisions is that employment decisions must be made on the basis of whether the individual will be able to perform the job. To determine this, organizations should conduct job analyses to help them determine the skills, knowledge, and abilities needed to perform the jobs. Once this is known, selection procedures can be developed. Chapters 4 and 5 expand on the job relatedness of selection procedures.

4. For more discussion of the purposes of job analysis, see R. A. Ash and E. L. Levine, "A Framework for Evaluating Job Analysis Methods," *Personnel* (Nov./Dec. 1980): 39–53; S. Gael, *Job Analysis: A Guide to Assessing Work Activities* (San Francisco: Jossey-Bass, 1983); P. C. Grant, "What Use Is a Job Description?" *Personnel Journal* (Feb. 1988): 45–53; E. L. Levine, *Everything You Always Wanted to Know About Job Analysis* (Tampa: Mariner Publishing, 1983); E. Prien, "Multi-Domain Job Analysis," paper presented at the National I–O and OB Graduate Student Convention, 23–25 April 1982, University of Maryland; Sparks, "Job Analysis," in *Personnel Management*, 81–88; and Sparks, "Job Analysis," in *Readings in Personnel and Human Resource Management*, 3d ed.

5. L. E. Albright, "Staffing Practices in the 1980s," in *Human Resource Management for the 1980s*," ed., S. J. Carroll and R. S. Schuler (Washington, D.C.: Bureau of National Affairs, 1983); Gael, *Job Analysis*; Sparks, "Job Analysis," in *Readings in Personnel and Human Resource Management*, 3d ed.

6. Grant, "What Use Is a Job Description?" 45–53.

7. S. Lohr, "Making Cars the Volvo Way," *New York Times*, 23 June 1987, p. 1; N. M. Tichy and C. K. Barnett, "Profiles in Change: Revitalizing the Automotive Industry," *Human Resource Management* (Winter 1985): 467–502.

8. Section 14.C.2. of the 1978 *Uniform Guidelines on Employee Selection Procedures*. For more legal review, see D. E. Thompson and T. A. Thompson, "Court Standards for Job Analysis in Test Validation," *Personnel Psychology* 35 (1982): 865–74.

9. W. F. Cascio and H. Bernardin, "Implications of Performance Appraisal Litigation for Personnel Decisions," *Personnel Psychology* 34 (1981): 211–26; D. W. Myers, "The Impact of a Selected Provision in the Federal Guidelines on Job Analysis and Training," *Personnel Administrator* (July 1981): 41–45.

10. See Bemis, Belenky, and Soder, *Job Analysis;* Gael, *Job Analysis;* Sparks, "Job Analysis".

11. R. D. Arvey, "Sex Bias in Job Evaluation Procedures," *Personnel Psychology* 39 (1986): 315–35; A. P. O'Reilly, "Skill Requirements: Supervisor-Subordinate Conflict," *Personnel Psychology* 26 (Spring 1973): 75–80.

12. R. L. Brady, L. N. Persson, and S. E. Thompson, *Comparable Worth Compliance Handbook: A Wage and Salary Handbook* (Stanford, Conn.: Bureau of Law & Business, 1982); V. Huber, "Comparison of Supervisor-Incumbent Job Evaluation Ratings," working paper, University of Washington, 1989.

13. R. D. Arvey, "Sex Bias in Job Evaluation Procedures," 315–35; D. Doverspike, B. Racicot, and C. Albertson, *The Role of Information Processing Variables in the Decision Making Process in Job Evaluation: Results of Empirical Studies on Sex Prototypes, Person Prototypes and the Effects of Training*, First Annual Conference on HRM Decision Making, October 1986, Buffalo, N.Y.; M. K. Mount and R. A. Ellis, "Investigation of Bias in Job Evaulation Rating of Comparable Worth Study Participants," *Personnel Psychology* 40 (1987): 85–96; D. P. Schwab and R. Grams, "Sex-Related Errors in Job Evaluation: A "Real World" Test," *Journal of Applied Pscyhology* 70 (1986): 533–39.

14. Equal Employment Opportunity Commission, "Uniform Guidelines on Employee Selection Procedures," *Federal Register* 43 (1978): 38,290–315; J. Ledvinka, *Federal Regulation of Personnel and Human Resource Management* (Boston: Kent Publishing, 1982).

15. P. C. Grant, "What Use Is a Job Description?" 45–53; *How to Analyze Jobs* (Stamford, Conn.: Bureau of Law & Business, 1982); *How to Write Job Descriptions the Right Way* (Stamford, Conn.: Bureau of Law & Business, 1982); V. L. Huber, "Job Descriptions," in *Cases in Personnel/Human Resources Management;* ed. E. Stevens (Plano, Tex.: BPI, 1986, 278–86; M. A. Jones, "Job Descriptions Made Easy," *Personnel Jour-*

nal (May 1982): 31–34; L. Levine, *Everything You Always Wanted to Know About Job Analysis* (Tampa: Mariner Publishing, 1983); R. J. Plachy, "Writing Job Descriptions That Get Results," *Personnel* (Oct. 1987): 56–63.

16. See note 15.

17. "Job Analysis," *Employee Relations Law Journal* (1981): 586–87.

18. R. H. Hayes and R Jaikumar, "Manufacturing's Crisis: New Technologies, Obsolete Organizations," *Harvard Business Review* (Sept./Oct. 1988): 77–85.

19. E. E. Adam, Jr., and R. J. Ebert, *Production and Operations Management* (Englewood Cliffs, N.J.: Prentice-Hall, 1986); V. L. Huber and N. L. Hyer, "The Human Factor in Cellular Manufacturing," *Journal of Operations Management* 5 (1985): 213–28; V. L. Huber and T. S. Lee, "Job Design: The Airplane Assembly Exercise," *Organizational Behavior Teaching Journal* 7 (1987–1988): 80–91; B. W. Niebel, *Motion and Time Study* (Homewood, Ill.: Richard D. Irwin, 1976); W. J. Stevenson, *Production/Operations Management* (Homewood, Ill.: Richard D. Irwin, 1986).

20. McCormick, *Job Analysis*.

21. F. Luthans, R. M. Hodgetts, and S. A. Rosenkrantz, *Real Managers* (Cambridge, Mass.: Ballinger Publishing, 1988).

22. McCormick, *Job Analysis*, 117–35.

23. E. J. McCormick and J. Tiffin, *Industrial Psychology*, 6th ed. (Englewood Cliffs, N.J.: Prentice-Hall, 1974), 53. Reprinted by permission of Prentice-Hall, Inc. The Position Analysis Questionnaire (PAQ) is copyrighted by the Purdue Research Foundation. The PAQ and related materials are available through the University Book Store, 360 West State Street, West Lafayette, IN 47906. Further information regarding the PAQ is available through PAQ Services, Inc., P.O. Box 3337, the Logan, UT 84321. Computer processing of PAQ data is available through the PAQ Data Processing Division at that address.

   For a description of the validation of a short form of the PAQ, see S. M. Colarelli, S. A. Stumpf, and S. J. Wall, "Cross-Validation of a Short Form of the Position Analysis Questionnaire," *Educational and Psychological Measurement* 42 (1982): 1279–83. The PAQ has been adopted for professional and managerial jobs; for a description, see J. C. Mitchell and E. J. McCormick, "Development of the PMPQ: A Structural Job Analysis Questionnaire for the Study of Professional and Mangerial Positions," Report 1 (West Lafayette, Ind.: Purdue Research Foundation, Purdue University 1979).

24. For discussion of the PAQ, see E. T. Cornelius III, A. S. DeNisi, and A. G. Blencoe, "Expert and Naive Raters Using the PAQ: Does It Matter?" *Personnel Psychology* (Autumn 1984): 453–64; and J. B. Shaw and J. H. Riskind, "Predicting Job Stress Using Data from the Position Analysis Questionnaire," *Journal of Applied Psychology* (May 1983): 253–61.

25. R. J. Harvey, F. Friedman, M. D. Hakel, and E. T. Cornelius, "Dimensionality of the Job Element Inventory, A Simplified Worker-Oriented Job Analysis Questionnaire," *Journal of Applied Pscyhology* 73 (1988): 639–46.

26. McCormick, *Job Analysis*.

27. McCormick, "Job and Task Analysis," in *Handbook of Industrial and Organizational Psychology*, 111.

28. S. A. Fine, "Functional Job Analysis: An Approach to a Technology for Manpower Planning," *Personnel Journal* (Nov. 1974): 813–18. See also Department of Labor, *Dictionary of Occupational Titles*, vol. 2, 3d ed. (Washington, D.C.: U.S. Government Printing Office, 1965); Department of Labor, *Dictionary of Occupational Titles*, vol. 2, 3d ed. (Washington, D.C.: U.S. Government Printing Office, 1965); Department of Labor, Manpower Administration, *Handbook for Analyzing Jobs* (Washington, D.C.: U.S. Government Printing Office, 1972); Department of Labor, *Task Analysis Inventories: A Method of Collecting Job Information* (Washington, D.C.: U.S. Government Printing Office, 1973); and J. Markowitz, "Four Methods of Job Analysis," *Training and Development Journal* (Sept. 1981): 112–21.

29. J. C. Flanagan, "The Critical Incident Technique," *Psychology Bulletin* 51 (1954): 327–58; G. P. Latham and K. N. Wexley, *Increasing Productivity through Performance Appraisal* (Reading, Mass.: Addison-Westley, 1981).

30. GOJA is a specific technique developed by a consulting firm, as is the Hay Plan. GOJA is from Biddle and Associates and is described here with their permission. Although GOJA was developed in response to the *Uniform Guidelines*, this does not mean that it is the only technique that complies with the guidelines. According to the guidelines (Section 14A), "Any method of job analysis may be used if it provides the information required for the specific validation strategy used" (i.e., content, construct, or empirical). See also G. A. Kesselman and F. E. Lopez, "The Impact of Job Analysis on Employment Test Validity for Minority and Non Minority Accounting Personnel," *Personnel Psychology* (Spring 1979): 91–108; and L. S. Kleiman and R. H. Faley, "Assessing Content Validity: Standards Set by the Court," *Personnel Psychology* (Fall 1978): 701–13.

31. When job analysis techniques are used for more than just descriptions and employee specifications, they are often referred to as *integrated techniques*. The Guidelines-Oriented Job Analysis is an example.

32. W. W. Tornow and P. R. Pinto, "The Development of a Managerial Job Taxonomy: A System for Describing, Classifying, and Evaluating Executive Positions," *Journal of Applied Psychology* 61 (1976): 410–18. See also W. F. Cascio, *Applied Psychology in Personnel Management*, 2d ed. (Reston, Va.: Reston, 1982), 61.

33. B. E. Dowell and K. N. Wexley, "Development of a Work Behavior Taxonomy for First Line Supervisors," *Journal of Applied Psychology* 63 (1978): 563–72.

34. J. Shervington, "Return of the Handicapped to Employment," *Australian Occupational Therapy Journal* 30 (1983): 20; M. D. Shinnick and D. L. Gerber, "A Common Language for Analyzing Work," *Journal of Systems Management* (Apr. 1985): 8–13; Y. Yokomizo,

Research Reports (Waseda, Japan: Waseda University Press, 1982).

35. This section on Japan is adapted in a large part from M. S. O'Conner, "Report on Japanese Employee Relations Practices and Their Relation to Worker Productivity," prepared for the study mission to Japan, 8–23 November 1983. M. S. O'Conner's permission to reproduce this material is appreciated. K. J. Duff, "Japanese and American Labor Law: Structural Similarities and Substantive Differences," *Employee Relations Law Journal* (Spring 1984): 629–41; R. Marsland and M. Beer, "The Evolution of Japanese Management: Lessons for U.S. Managers," *Organizatonal Dynamics* (Winter 1983): 49–67; and E. Zussman, "Learning from the Japanese: Management in a Resource-Scarce World," *Organizational Dynamics* (Winter 1983): 68–76.

36. E. L. Levine, F. Sistrunk, K. J. McNutt, and S. Gael, "Exemplary Job Analysis Systems in Selected Organizations: A Description of Process and Outcomes," *Journal of Business and Psychology* 3 (1988): 3–21.

37. R. A. Ash and E. L. Levine, "A Framework for Evaluating Job Analysis Methods,"; E. L. Levine, R. A. Ash, and N. Bennett, "Exploratory Comparative Study of Four Job Analysis Methods," *Journal of Applied Psychology* 65 (1980): 524–35; E. L. Levine, R. A. Ash, and F. Sistrunk, "Evaluation of Job Analysis Methods by Experienced Job Analysts," *Academy of Management Journal* 26 (1983): 339–348.

38. F. Krystofiak, J. M. Newman, and G. Anderson, "A Quantified Approach to Measurement of Job Content: Procedures and Payoffs," *Personnel Psychology* (Summer 1979): 341–57.

39. N. Gambordella and W. G. Alvord, *Ti-CODAP: A Computerized Method of Job Analysis for Personnel Management*, (Prince Georges County, Md.: April 1980); G. Milkovich and J. M. Newman, *Compensation* (Plano, Tex.: BPI, 1987).

CHAPTER

4

Recruitment

Recruitment

In the recruiting area, Burger King managers use many typical tools, such as: high school job seminars, working with local and state agencies to gather referrals, soliciting referrals from politicians who receive work requests from their constituents and job fairs.

In addition, Burger King has some interesting recruiting programs:

- *Handicapped agencies:* The Florida region is experiencing great success with its "Be Capable" program. More than 100 handicapped young people are working in Burger King stores there.

"Early information indicates that we're experiencing much better retention with this group," said Morrison. "They're more loyal and thankful for the company's efforts in hiring and training them."

- *Senior citizens:* This growing population is being reached through senior citizen centers. "We're hoping that they will have a positive influence on the young people," said Morrison. "They are a great opportunity for the fast food industry."
- *Operations recruiters:* Three regions—Boston, Atlanta and Detroit—are experiencing the most severe labor shortage problems. So, Burger King is testing a new position in those areas—operations recruiter. In most regions the store managers do the recruiting as part of their job. This new person is responsible for recruiting in these areas.
- *Theater commercials:* Recruiting commercials are being aired before the main feature in theaters in Detroit and San Francisco.
- *"Ask me . . . ":* Using employees as recruiters is a proven winner. "Ask me about working for Burger King" buttons, t-shirts, posters,

etc., are being successfully used in the Florida region.

- *Crew referral:* Burger King offers cash awards for recruiting. Different regions handle this in different ways. In the areas where young people are exceptionally hard to find, the cash award is simply for bringing in an applicant; in others it's for a new hire.
- *Shift premiums:* Six regions are paying a higher hourly wage for certain less desirable shifts.
- *Providing transportation:* When a store cannot hire from its own community, because it is in an affluent neighborhood where the children don't work, or in an industrial area where there are not many young people, Burger King is providing transportation or bus fare.
- *Applicant sharing:* Restaurants transfer applications to other stores in the area. "Surprisingly, the restaurant industry hasn't done much of this," said Morrison. "Now we're seeing our managers share their applicants."
- *Ex-employee log:* Some stores call back their good ex-employees either to offer them jobs, or ask them to refer their friends.
- *Translites:* Just recently some stores have put recruitment ads in the menu board spot where the pictures of new products usually are.
- *TV Show:* Burger King is working with an advertising agency to develop a 14-minute television program which will promote the idea of learning through work. It will not focus on Burger King, but on the fast food industry and the many advantages for young people found there.

SOURCE: *HR Reporter* (June 1988): 1–2. Reprinted by permission of *HR Reporter*, copyright 1988.

T he preceding "PHRM in the News" illustrates several features about recruiting at Burger King. One is that a wide net is being cast for job applicants of all ages, with and without handicaps. A second is that many methods are being used to identify job applicants. Some methods have never been tried before. Implied in this feature is the fact that it is becoming harder for organizations to identify potentially qualified applicants. This reflects the changing demographics, described in Chapter 2, that are affecting service and manufacturing organizations equally.

Recruitment. is generally defined as the set of activities and processes used legally to obtain a sufficient number of qualified people, so that the organization can select the most appropriate people for its needs. Recruitment should also be concerned with meeting candidates' needs. In this way, recruitment not only attracts individuals to the organization but also increases the chance of retaining individuals once they are hired. Additionally, the recruitment activity must comply with extensive rules and legal regulations.

PURPOSES AND IMPORTANCE
OF RECRUITMENT

The general purpose of recruitment is to provide an organization with a pool of potentially qualified job candidates. The specific purposes of recruitment are as follows:

- To determine the organization's present and future recruitment needs in conjunction with human resource planning and job analysis
- To increase the pool of qualified job applicants at minimum cost to the organization
- To help increase the success rate of the selection process by reducing the number of obviously underqualified or overqualified job applicants
- To help reduce the probability that job applicants, once recruited and selected, will leave the organization after only a short period of time
- To meet the organization's responsibility for affirmative action programs and other legal and social obligations regarding work force composition
- To increase organizational and individual effectiveness in the short and long term
- To evaluate the effectiveness of various techniques and locations of recruiting for all types of job applicants[1]

Effectively meeting all these purposes enables the organization to avoid costly legal battles and settlements and to select only those applicants who are qualified and will thus be productive. Because the recruiting activity is as much concerned with retaining selected individuals as it is with getting an initial pool of potentially qualified job applicants, a higher quality of work life should result. In essence, effective recruiting helps an organization attain the three general purposes of PHRM discussed in Chapter 1: productivity, quality of work life, and legal compliance.

RELATIONSHIPS INFLUENCING
RECRUITMENT

In achieving the purposes listed above, recruitment is influenced by many relationships with other PHRM activities and with the external environment. The most important of these relationships are described next (see Exhibit 4.1).

EXHIBIT
4.1

Relationships and Aspects of the Recruitment Activity

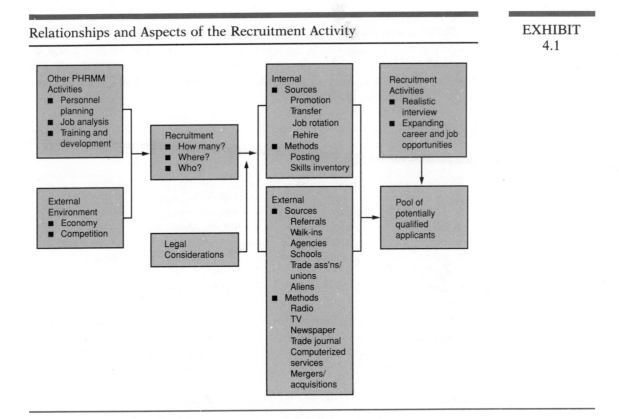

Relationships with the External Environment

The type of employees an organization needs often depends on the external environment. For example, the current shortage of skilled workers has presented organizations such as Burger King with a real challenge as they attempt to recruit skilled workers in sufficient numbers.[2] In times of national economic recession, while most executives are worrying about job security, chief financial officers and others who can cut costs still get calls from recruiters.[3]

Other factors in the external environment also affect recruitment. Consider the results produced by the threatened nationwide boycott of Coca-Cola in July 1981 by the People United to Save Humanity (PUSH). Under the "moral convenant" announced by PUSH founder the Reverend Jesse Jackson and Coca-Cola president Donald R. Keough, Coca-Cola promised to more actively recruit black applicants and promote them into management and to expand the pool of black-owned company distributors.[4]

Relationships with Other PHRM Activities

While recruitment is affected by all aspects of PHRM, three relationships are critical.

Human Resource Planning.   To develop a strategic recruiting program, extensive planning is required. Recruiting programs are developed around three components of organizational planning: (1) strategic business planning, which determines the organization's goals, future products and services, growth rate, structure, and location; (2) job-role planning, which specifies what will be done at different levels; and (3) human resource planning, which determines the types of jobs the organization needs (or will need) to fill, as well as the skills, knowledge, and abilities that job applicants need. All three planning components are interrelated and necessary to determine how many individuals should be recruited to fill specific positions.

Job Analysis.   Job analysis is also important because it identifies the organization's need for jobs and pinpoints the knowledge, skills, and abilities qualified recruits need to possess.

> No internal or external recruiting should begin until there is a clear and concise statement of the education, skills, and experience requirements and the salary range for the job. In larger organizations, this information is readily available in job descriptions and salary structures. Yet numerous hours and dollars are spent in recruiting, particularly recruiting advertising, where the applicant is required to play a "guessing game" about the job qualifications required.[5]

Training and Development.   If recruiting activities produce a large pool of qualified job applicants, the need for employee training may be minimal. But recruiting activities may produce only a large, potentially unqualified pool of job applicants. At this point, the organization may weight the costs of selecting versus those of training. If the costs of selection are deemed greater than those associated with training, the organization may hire all the applicants it needs and train them.

Developing training programs can also be a critical way in which organizations can accommodate handicapped job applicants, thus making it easier to recruit and retain disabled individuals. For example, AT&T has developed a training program for managers who supervise disabled people; Sears, Roebuck & Company has been conducting an affirmative action program for the disabled since 1947; Control Data Corporation provides suddenly disabled employees with computer training to help them get back on the job; and IBM has a program to train and place severely physically disabled people in entry-level computer jobs. The result of all these companies' training efforts is to make employment easier for disabled employees and to encourage those employees to stay on the job. These training efforts help the companies meet equal opportunity employment goals as well.[6]

LEGAL CONSIDERATIONS IN RECRUITMENT

In addition to PHRM activities and the organizational environment, legal considerations must also be considered in developing a recruiting program. Although much of the legal framework facing PHRM is directed at issues involved in hiring, firing, health, and compensation, it essentially begins with the organization's search for job applicants. Fair or equal employment laws affect the selection procedures of all organizations and are described in detail in the next chapter.

Affirmative Action Programs

A subset of these laws, referred to as **affirmative action programs** (AAPs), are directly relevant to recruitment. Affirmative action programs generally arise from the three conditions discussed below.

Federal Contracts.   If a company has a federal contract greater than $50,000 and has fifty or more employees, it is required to file an AAP for each establishment—for example, each plant or field office—with the Office of Federal Contract Compliance Programs (OFCCP). These plans must be filed within 120 days of receiving the contract, and compliance is currently enforced through Executive Order 11246. Those with federal contracts that range from $2,500 to $50,000 are required to include an affirmative action clause in their contracts; they do not have to have a written affirmative action plan. Those who hold contracts or subcontracts of less than $2,500 are not covered by EO 11246. These programs are designed to facilitate an organization's commitment to provide and achieve proportional representation or parity (or to correct underutilization) in its work force for the relevant labor market of protected group members (defined by Title VII to include women, blacks, Hispanics, native Americans, and Asian-Pacific Islanders).

AAPs often contain several important components, including utilization and availability analyses, goals, and timetables. A **utilization analysis** determines the number of minorities and women employed in different jobs within an organization. An **availability analysis** measures how many minorities and women are available to work in the relevant labor market of an organization. If an organization is employing fewer minorities and women than are available, a state of **underutilization** exists.

The **relevant labor market** is generally defined as the geographical area a substantial majority of job applicants and employees come from. To provide initial guidance in determining this area, organizations may look to published population data sources, such as the Standard Metropolitan Statistical Analysis (SMSA). Within a relevant labor market, availability data can be gathered from such sources as the U.S. Census, local and state Chambers of Commerce, and city, county, and state governments. Because organizations may fill some job openings with applicants from the local area and others with applicants from across the nation, organizations may have several relevant labor markets. The relevant labor market is of importance in both developing affirmative action programs and defending cases of prima facie illegal discrimination. This market is discussed further in Chapter 5.

After utilization and availability analyses are completed, **goals** and **timetables** are written to specify how an organization plans to correct any underutilization. Because goals and timetables become the organization's commitment to equal employment, they must be realistic and attainable.[7]

Federal contractors are also required to "take affirmative action to employ and advance in employment qualified disabled individuals at all levels of employment, including jobs at the executive level (Section 503 of the Rehabilitation Act of 1973).

The Rehabilitation Act names three categories of disabled persons protected against employment discrimination:

■ Any individual who has a physical or mental impairment that greatly limits one or more of life's major functions
■ Any individual who has a history of such an impairment
■ Any individual who is perceived as having such an impairment

The impairments in the first category are usually evident conditions such as amputations, Down's syndrome, paralysis, hearing or visual problems, etc. Impairments in the second category can't be readily discerned. Nevertheless, some employers shy away from applicants whose medical histories include cancer, heart disease, diabetes, and similar health problems, perhaps out of fear that a recurrence or other effects of the disease will result in increased insurance costs, a higher rate of absenteeism, and decreased efficiency. In one case, an employer refused to hire a worker who had leukemia because he was prone to infection from even minor injuries. But a Wisconsin circuit court found that because the man was qualified to perform his job, the company could not refuse to hire him (*Chrysler Outboard v. Dept. of Industry,* 1976). An employer's misconceptions can also bring an individual who isn't actually disabled under the coverage of the Rehabilitation Act or a similar state law. That happened when an employee was terminated because his employer thought he had epilepsy. The Washington Court of Appeals awarded the worker two years' back pay and ordered him reinstated[8] (*Barns vs. Washington Natural Gas, 1986*). Also included are individuals who have suffered from alcoholism or drug abuse, and, perhaps eventually, those suffering from acquired immune deficiency syndrome (AIDS) may be covered. While the federal law does not explicitly protect individuals with AIDS, several states have already adopted specific legislation to prohibit discrimination against individuals with AIDS. Individuals who merely test positive for the AIDS virus will likely be covered under the third category of the Rehabilitation Act; this portion of the act protects *any individual who is perceived* as having a disability.

To aid in attaining its specified goals and timetables, it is important for the organization to make sure its employment policies, practices, and procedures are operating to facilitate goal attainment. This generally requires an assessment of current policies, practices, and procedures. This assessment may reveal policies, practices, and procedures that are not operating to facilitate goal attainment if underutilization exists. If so, the policies, practices, and procedures need to be modified.

Consent Decree.   An AAP may also be mandated by a federal court if a discrimination suit against an organization has found evidence of past discrimination. An AAP under these conditions is generally part of a **consent decree,** a statement indicating the specific affirmative action steps an organization will take.

A famous affirmative action program resulting from a consent decree involved AT&T, which the EEOC found to be discriminating against women. Although AT&T neither admitted nor was required to admit any act of discrimination, it entered into a consent decree after the EEOC opposed its application for a rate increase. The cost for the first five years of this settlement (1973–1978) is estimated to have been more than $75 million.[9] State Farm Insurance was involved in a more recent settlement:

> State Farm Insurance Co. agrees to set aside for women half of its new sales agent jobs in California over the next 10 years, and to pay damages and back pay to women who were refused sales jobs during a 13-year period, according to a consent decree settling a long-running sex bias case against the company.
>
> Female employees filed a class action suit in 1979, claiming that State Farm in California had discriminated against women in recruitment, hiring, job assignments, training, and termination decisions. A federal district court found the company had discriminated and was liable for damages to all women who unsuccessfully applied for or were deterred from applying for trainee agent jobs since 1974. The settlement covers 1,113 sales jobs that became vacant and were filled by men between 1974 and 1987, and is expected to result in back pay awards totaling between $100 and $300 million.

The agreement provides that State Farm will use its best efforts to give women 50 percent of the trainee agent appointments each year for the next decade. The company is required to nominate one woman in each of its three California regions to serve as a recruitment administrator to train agency managers to recruit and retain qualified women. In addition, procedures are specified for the company to follow in publicizing openings for sales agent jobs.

Women affected by the decree who wish to make a claim may file for damages during a four-month period beginning May 1. (*Kraszewski v. State Farm . . .* 1988)[10]

Although these goals, as well as those that are a part of the federal contractor's AAP, specify only percentages, in essence they are often seen as establishing **quotas.** That is, the goals establish that no organization must hire a certain number of blacks or minorities to correct underutilization or past discrimination in employment. The courts have generally held in favor of quotas and goals as the only way to reverse previous practices of discrimination (*Detroit Police Officers Association v. Coleman Young,* 1979; *Charles L. Maehren v. City of Seattle,* 1979; and *City of St. Louis v. U.S.,* 1980). Nevertheless, the issue of reverse discrimination is being raised more frequently, as evidenced by a 1985 reverse discrimination case in Washington, D.C.:

Eight white District of Columbia firefighters have won a reverse discrimination suit against the city. U.S. District Court Judge Joyce Green has ruled that the firefighters are eligible for back pay and retroactive pensions estimated to be worth about $160,000 (*Edward Dougherty v. Marion Barry, Jr.,* Civil Action Nos. 82-1687 and 83-0314). The eight are now retired.

Green found that the white firefighters all had more experience and better "objective credentials" than the two blacks who were appointed as deputy fire chiefs in 1980. "Based on the evidence, one conclusion is clear: race was a substantial, significant, determinative factor" in the promotion of the blacks, Green concluded.[11]

In a related case, the U.S. Supreme Court ruled that federal courts could not ignore a seniority-based layoff policy, even though it would mean that blacks hired under an APP would be the first to be laid off (*Firefighters Local Union 1874 v. Stotts,* 1984). The Court reasoned that layoffs impose too severe a burden on the innocent whites who would be retained if it were not for a racial preference policy.

The key considerations in establishing a legal, voluntary AAP are that it be

- Remedial in purpose
- Limited in its duration
- Restricted in its reverse discrimination impact—that is, it should not operate as an absolute ban on nonminorities
- Flexible in implementation

When an organization's voluntary AAP has these characteristics, the risk of losing a reverse discrimination suit may be minimized.

Voluntary AAPs. Organizations may establish their own voluntary affirmative action programs without pressure from the EEOC or OFCCP. In fact, organizations may benefit from using EEOC guidelines that support voluntary AAPs. By doing so, however, they may still run the risk of being charged with reverse discrimination. The key considerations in an organization's establishment of a legal voluntary **AAP** are that it be remedial in purpose, limited in its duration, restricted in its reverse discrimination impact—that is, it does not operate as an absolute ban on nonminorities—and flexible in implementation. When an organization's voluntary AAP has these characteristics, the risk of losing a reverse discrimination suit may be minimized.

Management Commitment. Although equal opportunity employment guidelines, goals, and quotas are usually established for the organization, these efforts are actually implemented by managers. If organizations are really to fulfill the spirit as well as the letter of the law, managers must be committed to implementing these goals. Important characteristics of equal employment efforts that increase managerial commitment include

- Clear goals
- Top-management support for implementing goals
- Managerial accountability for implementing goals
- Managerial participation in setting goals and policies
- Managerial training for implementing goals.

On the basis of several recent court decisions, it appears that AAPs have now become recognized as a critical component of fair employment practices in U.S. companies (*U.S. v. Paradise*, 1987; *Johnson v. Transportation Agency, Santa Clara County*, 1987).[12] Exhibit 4.2 shows the percentages of organizations that had AAPs or statements to this effect in 1988.

EXHIBIT 4.2   Corporate Hiring Practices

The following percentages of surveyed companies have written affirmative-action plans, or goals and timetables for hiring protected groups.

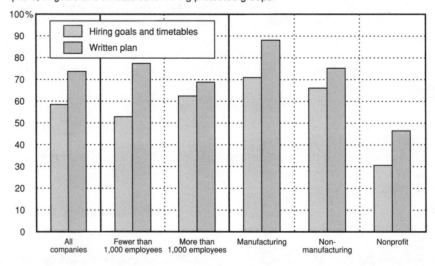

NOTE: Some written affirmative-action plans are merely statements that don't include goals and timetables.

SOURCE: *Bureau of National Affairs*

OBTAINING JOB APPLICANTS:
SOURCES AND METHODS

Internal Sources

Internal sources include present employees, friends of employees, former employees, and former applicants. Promotions, demotions, and transfers can also provide applicants for departments or divisions within the organization.[13] Current employees are a source of job applicants in two respects: they can refer friends to the organization, and they can also become applicants themselves by potential promotion or transfer.

Promotions.   The case for promotion from within rests on several sound arguments. One is that internal employees are better qualified. "Even jobs that do not seem unique require familiarity with the people, procedures, policies, and special characteristics of the organization in which they are performed."[14] Another is that employees are likely to feel more secure and to identify their long-term interests with the organization that provides them the first choice of job opportunities. Availability of promotions within an organization can also motivate employees to perform, and internal promotion can be much less expensive to the organization in both time and money.

By comparison, luring applicants from outside the organization can be an expensive process. Often the new recruit is brought in at a salary higher than that of workers currently in similar positions in the organization, and the costs to the company of relocating the new recruit and his or her family may range from $10,000 to $50,000. Soon other employees learn of this expensive new recruit. The result, especially if the new recruit fails to contribute as expected, is dissatisfaction among the current employees. In addition, the incentive value of promotions diminishes.[15] Disadvantages of a **promotion-from-within** policy may include an inability to find the best-qualified person. Also, infighting, inbreeding, and lack of varied perspectives and interests may result.

Considering these advantages and disadvantages, it is not surprising to find organizations doing some internal promoting while obtaining some applicants from external sources. In addition, organizations tend to obtain particular types of employees from particular sources. For example, many organizations are more likely to hire highly trained professionals and high-level managers from the outside than to promote from within.[16] Further discussion of what sources are used for what applicants is presented later in this chapter. But whether internal or external sources of promotion are used, promotion considerations must incorporate affirmative action and equal employment concerns.

Transfers.   Another critical way to recruit internally is by transferring current employees without promotion. Transfers are often important in providing employees with the more broad-based view of the organization that is necessary for future promotions. A second reason for transferring employees focuses on the changing nature of organizations. Because of the "baby-boom bulge," the trend toward lean, flat organizations, and the increase in professional organizations discussed in Chapter 2, more and more midcareer individuals are expected to be plateaued in positions with little or no advancement opportunity.

With promotional opportunities blocked, a transfer may give these committed employees opportunities for skill diversity and job enrichment.

Job Rotation.   Whereas transfers are usually permanent, job rotations are usually temporary. Job rotation has been used effectively to expose management trainees to various aspects of organization life. Job rotation has also been used to relieve job burnout for employees in high-stress occupations. For example, the Utah Department of Social Services has a job rotation program in which human service workers swap jobs with workers in other divisions or with employees in federal agencies for periods of up to one year. At the end of the contracted year of service, employees have the opportunity to return to their original positions or to remain in the new position. Such programs give employees different perspectives and the opportunity to try our new positions without fear of failure. Management, on the other hand, gets a chance to preview the employee prior to long-term commitment.

Rehires and Recalls.   Each week, thousands of employees are temporarily laid off from work, and others are recalled to former jobs. The rehire of former employees or employees temporarily laid off is a relatively inexpensive and effective method of internal recruiting. The organization already has information about the performance, attendance, and safety records of these employees. Because they are already familiar with job responsibilities, rehires are better performers than recruits from other sources are. They also tend to stay on the job longer and have better attendance records.

In considering rehiring as recruitment strategy, organizations should weigh the costs against the benefits. Rehiring and recalls are particularly beneficial to organizations that have seasonal fluctuations in the demand for workers (e.g., department stores, canneries, construction firms, ski resorts). For example, each summer and fall during the apple harvest, canneries in eastern Washington recall large numbers of employees—some of whom have been employed off and on by the same companies for more than twenty years. This helps reduce labor costs. However, the downside of this recruitment approach is that employee commitment may be low. By the time of the recall, a qualified recruit may have found alternative employment, possibly with a major competitor. Finally, because turnover is occurring, an organization's contribution to unemployment compensation programs is likely to increase.

Internal Methods

Candidates to fill job vacancies can be located by a notice on the bulletin board, word of mouth, company personnel records, promotion lists based on performance, potential ratings obtained from assessment activities, seniority lists, and lists generated by the skills inventory in an organization's HRIS. The most frequently used methods include **job posting** and rehires.

Job Posting.   Job posting, a method of prominently displaying current job openings, extends an open invitation to all employees in an organization. It serves the following purposes:

- Provides opportunities for employee growth and development
- Provides equal opportunity for advancement to all employees

- Creates a greater openness in the organization by making opportunities known to all employees
- Increases staff awareness of salary grades, job descriptions, general promotion and transfer procedures, and what constitutes effective job performance
- Communicates organization goals and objectives and allows each individual the opportunity to find a personal fit in the organization job structure.[17]

Although job postings are usually found on bulletin boards, they also appear in company newsletters and are announced at staff meetings. Sometimes specific salary information is included, but job grade and pay range are more typical. Job posting is beneficial for organizations because it improves morale, provides employees with the opportunity for job variety, facilitates a better matching of employee skills and needs, and fills positions at a low cost.[18]

These benefits are not always realized. Conflicts are sometimes created if an "heir apparent" in the department is passed over in favor of an outside candidates. Conversely, the system may lose credibility if the successful candidate within the department has apparently been identified in advance and the manager is merely going through the motions in considering outsiders. In addition, the morale of the unsuccessful candidates may suffer if feedback is not carefully handled. Finally, choices can be more difficult for the selecting manager if two or three equally qualified candidates are encountered.

Skill Inventories.   Another method of internal recruiting is to use skill-related information buried in personnel files; much time and effort is required to get at it. A formal skills inventory aggregates this information through the use of an HRIS. Any data that can be quantified can be coded and included in a skills inventory.

Common information includes name, employee number, job classification, prior jobs, prior experience, specific skills and knowledge, education, licenses, publications, and salary levels. The results of formal assessments, such as those obtained in assessment centers, during work-sample tests, and with job interest inventories, are usually included. Skill inventories should also include information regarding the employee's job interests, geographical preferences, and career goals. The inclusion of the latter information ensures that potential job assignments meet individual as well as organizational goals.

Skill inventories are only as good as the data they contain. They are also time consuming and somewhat costly to maintain. Still, a skill inventory helps ensure that *any* individual who has the necessary qualifications for a position is considered. IBM's system contains information on more than 100,000 employees, and RCA Service Company relies on its skill inventory to define what businesses it could be in.[19]

External Sources

Recruiting internally does not always produce enough qualified job applicants, especially for organizations that are growing rapidly or that have a large demand for high-talent professional, skilled, and managerial employees. Therefore, organizations need to recruit from external sources. Recruiting from the outside has a number of advantages, including bringing in people with new ideas. Hiring an already trained professional or skilled employee is often cheaper and easier, particularly when the organization has an immediate demand for scarce labor skills and talents. External sources can also supply temporary employees, who provide the organization with much more flexibility than permanent employees.

In general, organizations need to use both internal and external sources of recruitment. A summary of the advantages and disadvantages of each source appears in Exhibit 4.3.

Employee Referral Programs.   Employee referral programs (ERPs) are word-of-mouth advertisements in which current employees refer applicants from outside the organization. Because of the involvement of current employees, this recruiting method blends internal with external recruitment and is a low-cost-per-hire means of recruiting.[20] Informal ERPs inform current employees about job openings and encourage them to have qualified friends and associates apply for positions. Formal ERPs, on the other hand, reward employees for referring skilled applicants. The financial incentive may be as little as fifteen dollars or as much as two thousand dollars for referring someone with a critical skill, such as robotics engineering or specialized nursing care. Financial incentives can be linked to the completion of an application, the acceptance of employment, or the completion of work for a specified period of time.

Compared to other external recruiting methods, employee referrals generally result in the highest one-year survival rates for most occupations. The findings are less clear regarding performance and attendance by source. One explanation for the success of ERPs is that employees provide a balanced view of organizational life. Another explanation is that employees tend to recruit applicants who are similar to themselves in terms of skills, interests, and abilities. Because the employee is already integrated into the organization culture, this matching process increases the likelihood that applicants will also fit into the environment.

EXHIBIT 4.3

Sources of Job Applicants

Internal	
Advantages	Disadvantages
	Inbreeding
Morale of promotee	Possible morale problems of those not
Better assessment of abilities	promoted
Lower cost for some jobs	"Political" infighting for promotions
Motivator for good performance	Need strong management development
Have to hire only at entry level	program

External	
Advantages	Disadvantages
"New blood," new perspectives	May not select someone who will "fit"
Cheaper than training a professional	May cause morale problems for those
No group of political supporters in	internal candidates
organization already	Longer "adjustment" or orientation time
May bring competitors' secrets, new	May bring in an attitude of "This is the
insights	way we used to do it at XYZ
Helps meet equal employment needs	Company."

SOURCE: R. L. Mathis and J. H. Jackson, *Personnel: Contemporary Perspectives and Applications*, 5th ed. (St. Paul, Minn.: West Publishing Co., © 1989). Reproduced by permission. All rights reserved.

On first blush, referring individuals who are similar in type (age, sex, race, and religion) is beneficial. However, such referrals—particularly if they are required for employment—may have effects contrary to AAP and Equal Employment Opportunity (EEO) obligations.[21]

Walk-ins. As illustrated in Exhibit 4.4, the use of walk-ins recruiting is especially prevalent for clerical and production/service job applicants. In the walk-in method, individuals become applicants by walking into an organization's employment office. This method, like employee referrals, is relatively informal and inexpensive and is almost as effective as employee referrals in retaining applicants once hired.[22] Unlike referrals, nonreferred applicants may know less about the specific jobs available and may come without the implicit recommendation of a current employee. This may be a disadvantage in comparison to referrals because current employees may be reluctant to refer or recommend unsatisfactory applicants.

Although walk-ins may be a relatively inexpensive source of applicants, the walk-in method is not used extensively by managerial, professional, and sales applicants. Furthermore, it tends to be a passive source and thus may not provide sufficient numbers of applicants to help fulfill affirmative action and equal employment obligations. These aspects may be reduced by attracting walk-ins through open house events, which can attract all types of applicants from the nearby community.[23] Open houses, however, may not be appropriate for every organization. Even if they are, sufficient numbers of some applicants can be obtained only by using other sources, such as employment agencies.

Employment Agencies. Employment agencies are a good source of temporary employees—and an excellent source of permanent employees. Employment agencies may be public or private. The **public employment agencies** in the United States are under the umbrella of the U.S. Training and Employment Services (USTES). The USTES sets national policies and oversees the operations of state employment services, which have branch offices in many cities. The Social Security Act in general provides that any worker who has been laid off from a job must register with the state employment agency in order to be eligible for unemployment benefits. The agencies then have a roster of potential applicants to assist organizations looking for job applicants.

State employment agencies provide a wide range of services. Most of these services are supported by employer contributions to the state unemployment funds. The agencies offer counseling, testing, and placement services to everyone. They provide special services to individuals, military veterans, minority groups, and college, technical, and professional people. The state agencies also make up a nationwide network of job information and applicant information in the form of job banks. These job banks have one drawback, however: USTES and its state agencies do not actually recruit people but passively assist those who come to them, and often those who do come in may be untrained or only marginally qualified for most jobs.

Private employment agencies tend to serve two groups of job applicants: professional or managerial and unskilled. The agencies dealing with the unskilled group often provide job candidates that employers would otherwise have a difficult time finding. Many of the employers looking for unskilled workers do not have the resources to do their own recruiting or have only temporary or seasonal demands for them.

EXHIBIT
4.4

Organizational Recruiting Sources and Methods by Occupation

	Percent of Companies					
	Any Job Category*	Office/ Clerical	Production/ Service	Professional/ Technical	Commissioned Sales	Managers/ Supervisors
(Number of companies)	(245)	(245)	(221)	(237)	(96)	(243)
Internal Sources						
Promotion from within	99%	94%	86%	89%	75%	95%
Advertising						
Newspapers	97	84	77	94	84	85
Journals/magazines	64	6	7	54	33	50
Direct mail	17	4	3	16	6	8
Radio/television	9	3	6	3	3	2
Outside Referral Sources						
Colleges/universities	86	24	15	81	38	45
Technical/vocational institutes	78	48	51	47	5	8
High schools/trade schools	68	60	54	16	5	2
Professional societies	55	4	1	51	19	37
Community agencies	39	33	32	20	16	9
Unions	10	1	11	1	—	1
Employee referrals	91	87	83	78	76	64
Walk-in applicants	91	86	87	64	52	46
Employment Services						
State employment service	73	66	68	38	30	23
Private employment agencies	72	28	11	58	44	60
Search firms	67	1	**	36	26	63
U.S. Employment Service	22	19	20	11	7	7
Employee leasing firms	20	16	10	6	2	**
Computerized resume service	4	**	—	4	—	2
Video interviewing service	2	**	**	1	—	1
Special Events						
Career conferences/ job fairs	53	20	17	44	19	19
Open house	22	10	8	17	8	7
Other	9	5	5	7	6	7

*Percentages for each job category are based on the number of organizations that provided data for that category, as shown by the number in parentheses.

SOURCE: Reprinted by permission from *Personnel Politics Forum,* Survey No. 146, Recruiting and Selection Procedures, 4–5. Copyright 1988 by The Bureau of National Affairs, Inc., Washington, DC 20037.

Private agencies play a major role in recruiting professional and managerial candidates. These agencies supply services for applicants of all ages; most, however, have had some work experience beyond college. During the past ten years, the executive recruiting industry has grown phenomenally. The fees that these agencies charge range up to one-third of the first year's total salary and bonus package for the job to be filled.[24]

Even if an organization successfully hires an employee, its cost may be much greater than the fees charged. In the prescreening process, for example, the search firm may have erred in rejecting a candidate who would have done well, or by identifying a candidate who will not do well. These errors, discussed in Chapter 5, pose additional costs to the organization.[25] The organization can help minimize these costs, however, by closely monitoring the search firm's activities. Note also that these agencies may prescreen applicants who are already working with other organizations. Consequently, in addition to the expense, this method of dealing with a potential candidate is apt to be secretive and counter to the openness that is desirable in an organization's employment process.

Temporary Help Agencies.   At the same time that private recruiting agencies provide applicants for full-time positions, temporary help agencies provide an ever-increasing number of temporary (temps) or "contingent" workers:

> An increasing number of employers contract out for temporary help, according to a 1988 Administrative Management Society survey of 289 member-companies. Ninety-one percent of the surveyed firms say that they use temps, up from 86 percent in 1987. The survey also finds that 39 percent of the respondents have increased or maintained their use of temporary workers over the 12 months studied.
>
> The principal reason for using temporary workers is to help alleviate work overloads, report 67 percent of the respondents. Employers also hire temps to assist with special projects (61 percent), cover for vacationing employees (43 percent), and fill vacancies left by departing employees (37 percent). Another 36 percent of the surveyed employers indicate that they hire temps to perform duties where permanent positions cannot be justified financially.
>
> The AMS survey also finds that:
>
> - Temps are used every week by 36 percent of the respondents. . . . The usual length of service for a temporary hire is one to four weeks (49 percent).
> - Temps are hired primarily for clerical duties (80 percent) and secretarial help (56 percent). Other functions often performed by temps are word processing (38 percent), accounting (28 percent), and data processing (25 percent).[26]

Temporary help agencies are beneficial because they prescreen candidates, guaranteeing that the temporary workers have the requisite skills. This reduces the search activities of the firm, while retaining flexibility with regard to the size of the work force. These advantages must be weighed against the higher direct compensation rate because both the agency and the temp must be paid. Still, it is unlikely that the total salary plus the agency fee would exceed current outlays for direct and indirect compensation (benefits cost organizations up to 40 percent of direct salary).

Trade Associations and Unions.   Unions for the building trades and maritime workers assume responsibility for supplying employers with skilled labor. This practice takes many labor decisions, such as job assignment, out of company hands. However, the Taft- Hartley Act restricts these "hiring hall" practices to a limited number of industries (see Chapter 15).

Trade and professional associations are also important sources for recruiting. Their newsletters and annual meetings often provide notice of employment opportunities. Annual meetings can also offer employers and potential job applicants an opportunity to meet. Communities and schools have adopted this idea and now bring together large numbers of employers and job seekers at **job fairs.** With only a limited time for interviews, such fairs serve only as an initial step in the recruitment process. Nevertheless they provide an effective means for both employers and individuals.

Schools.   Schools can be categorized into three types: high schools, vocational and technical schools, and colleges and universities. All are important sources of recruits for most organizations, although their importance varies depending on the type of applicant sought.[27] For example, if an organization is recruiting managerial, technical, or professional applicants, then colleges and universities are the most important source.

Unfortunately, the majority of the baby boomers have already passed through the education system. Consequently, each succeeding graduating class through the 1990s is expected to be smaller than its predecessor. The decline in the number of potential college graduates comes during a time of increased demand for white-collar employees.

> The shortage of qualified candidates has resulted in a new level of sophistication in campus recruiting. Companies are reviewing and revising all aspects of the recruiting process from how they identify and screen high potential graduates to how they manage interviews, logistics, recruiting materials and costs. . . .
>
> Most of the changes in the recruiting process are coming at the very beginning and very end of the process: pre-screening and offer-acceptance. By identifying high potential students very early in the year, companies are concentrating their efforts on these students and eliminating the time and money spent on those graduates who would eventually be dropped from the system. The other key factor in improving recruiting effectiveness is increasing the offer-acceptance rate to ensure that once qualified students have been identified and introduced to the company, they are not wooed away by a competitor.[28]

Recruiting at colleges and universities is often an expensive process. The significant figures to review are the costs associated with hires versus the costs associated with nonhires. If an organization is spending more than two-thirds of its recruiting budget on individuals who never join the company, the recruiting program needs serious revamping. Costs reviewed should include the salaries of recruiters and line managers involved in interviewing and selection; mailing, telephone, and recruiting materials; administrative support; and recruiting advertising materials, including receptions, videos, and programs. Companies with successful campus recruiting programs consistently hire 70 to 80 percent of the students they bring to their corporate offices. The cost-per-hire savings of targeted recruiting have been estimated as greater than 90 percent.

Even if the recruiting visit eventually produces job offers and acceptances, approximately 30 percent of the applicants hired from colleges leave the organization within the first five years of their employment. This turnover rate is even higher for graduate management students. Nevertheless, college placement services are helpful to an organization recruiting in particular fields, such as engineering and microelectronics, and to those seeking highly talented and qualified minorities and women.

Aliens.   As indicated in Chapter 2, real shortages of some job applicants exist, including professionals such as chemical engineers, nurses, and geologists. As a result, employers seek to recruit aliens—often overseas or in college placement offices.[29] Organizations use aliens for operations in the United States and abroad. When they work abroad, aliens serve as host-country nationals (person working in their own country, which is not the country of the parent company) or third-country nationals (persons working in a country that is neither their own country nor the country of the parent company). In either capacity, alien employees are critical for any company operating internationally. In the United States, aliens perform many jobs vital to the economy.

Aliens are so critical to U.S. companies that they have made increased efforts to ensure that their alien employees either are or become legal. Under the 1986 Immigration Reform and Control Act, employers are obliged to employ only legal aliens. Fines are levied for violations of the act.[30]

External Methods

Many organizations looking for applicants of all types engage in extensive advertising on radio and television, in the local paper, and in national newspapers such as the *Wall Street Journal*.

Radio and Television.   Of the approximately $2 billion spent annually on recruitment advertising, only a tiny percentage is spent on radio and television.[31] Companies are reluctant to use these media because they fear that the advertising is too expensive, will make the company look desperate, or will damage the firm's conservative image. Yet organizations are desperate to reach certain types of job applicants, such as skilled workers. In reality, using radio or television to advertise is not a desperate measure. Rather, the level of desperation implied depends on what is said and how it is delivered. Recognizing this, organizations are increasing their recruitment expenditures for radio and television advertisements, with favorable results.

Newspapers and Trade Journals.   Newspapers have traditionally been the most common method of external recruiting.[32] They reach a large number of potential applicants at a relatively low cost per hire. Newspaper ads are used to recruit for all types of positions, from the most unskilled to the most highly skilled, including top managerial positions. The ads range from the most matter-of-fact type to the most creative type.[33]

Trade journals enable organizations to aim at a much more specific group of potential applicants. Unfortunately, long lead times are required, and the ads can thus become dated.

Computerized Services.   An external method growing in popularity is the computerized recruiting service. This service provides a place to both list job openings and locate job applicants.

Personnel officers using a Job/Net terminal "can find people in fifteen minutes that it would take eight hours to find going through paper resumes," says Janice Kempf, a vice-president and cofounder. M/A-Com, a microwave and telecommunications company in Burlington, Massachusetts, recently hired a $30,000 quality-control engineer through Job/Net. "If we had paid an agency fee, it would have been $6,500 to $7,000," says Richard L. Bove, the staffing and development manager. He adds that the service lets him see more resumes of qualified people and lets him choose people who don't require expensive relocation.[34]

Acquisitions and Mergers.   A significant result of the merger or acquisition process is a large pool of employees, some of whom may no longer be necessary in the new organization. Consequently, the new organization potentially has a large number of job applicants (although they are current employees) who are already qualified. As a result of the merger or acquisition, however, new jobs may be created in addition to the retention of old jobs. For these new jobs, the pool of employees becomes the pool of potentially qualified applicants. For the old jobs (those unchanged), the pool of employees becomes the pool from which the most qualified people can be identified and selected.

In contrast to the other external methods, acquisitions and mergers may play an immediate role in facilitating an organization's strategic plan by enabling it to quickly obtain a large pool of highly qualified individuals. This pool may enable an organization to pursue a strategic business plan (e.g., entering a new product line that would otherwise be unavailable using other recruiting methods). What these other methods do not present that mergers and acquisitions do, however, is the need to displace excess employees and to quickly integrate a large number of employees into a new organization. Consequently, recruiting via acquisitions and mergers needs to be closely tied in with human resource planning and selection.[35]

JOB SEARCH FROM THE APPLICANT'S PERSPECTIVE

Before considering what the organization can do to attract potentially qualified applicants, looking first at the applicants is useful. That is, if organizations want to attract candidates, they need to know *what* attracts and *how* candidates are attracted. In essence, knowing how candidates are attracted means understanding where they get their information regarding job availability.

Sources Used

As discussed in the previous section, different types of candidates learn about jobs through different sources. Still, informal methods—referrals from friends and relatives, direct applications—top the list of sources used by recruits across all jobs. Additionally, these sources result in the highest one-year job survival rates. However, individuals who get help from friends and relatives in obtaining jobs tends to accept lower wages. It would appear that recruits give into friends and relatives who apply pressure to accept job offers.

More formal sources, such as classified advertisements and private employment agencies, have lower survival rates but are used more often by managerial and clerical employees. Because the recruiter's fee is contingent on the salary level accepted, it can be speculated that salaries secured through private employment agencies may be higher than those obtained through other methods.

This occurs because the recruiter as well as the applicant will be pushing for a higher salary.[36]

Intensity

Individuals also differ in the intensity with which they search for employment opportunities. Several factors are related to job search intensity.

Financial Need.   Intensity is inversely related to financial security. Employed job seekers spend fewer hours on job searches than unemployed workers do. There is also a negative relationship between the weekly hours spent on a job search and the level of unemployment compensation received. And the duration of unemployment compensation benefits is positively related to the duration of employment. One explanation for these results is that as financial stress decreases, job seekers are able to hold out longer for better employment or higher wages. If employed, their job search may even be passive, with no search unless they are contacted by a search firm.[37]

Self-esteem.   Job applicants who have a high need for achievement tend to launch more intensive job searches than applicants who have less drive do. Additionally, high-self-esteem job seekers apply for more jobs than they intended to (prior to the search) and more than low-self-esteem individuals apply or intend to apply for. One reason for this is that job applicants with high self-esteem may have greater feelings of self-efficacy (beliefs about their competency) in terms of job search activities and job competence.[38]

Training.   For individuals low in self-esteem or lacking job search skills, training has been found effective. Interventions that encourage job seekers to locate as many alternatives as possible and provide them with skill building (e.g., grooming tips, résumé preparation, letter writing) lead to more job opportunities and, more importantly, job placements. In one study, the placement rate following two months of search was 90 percent for trained job seekers, compared to 55 percent for untrained job seekers. Thus, for displaced workers, an important organizational strategy will be to provide job search training coupled with skill building. This will increase the likelihood that their job searches will be successful.[39]

Evaluating Job Offers

Just as organizations have ideal requirements for job applicants, recruits have preferences for jobs. Several factors, including occupational choice and organizational choice, influence applicants' evaluations of job options.

Occupational Choice.   Choosing an occupation involves a narrowing process which begins in childhood and continues through adulthood. While almost any occupation a child is exposed to may be a potential choice, people have narrowed their job choices to one or two by young adulthood. These choices are influenced by economic factors, including the realities of the labor market; psychological factors, such as individual needs, interests, and abilities; and sociological factors, including exposure to the occupation. The process draws to a close when an organization offers a position that most clearly meets these needs.[40]

Organizational Choice.   Most individuals make an occupational choice and then choose an organization within that occupation. As noted in Chapter 2, the number of functionally illiterate individuals is on the increase. For these individuals, organizational choice dictates occupational choice. Still, several factors affect organizational choice.

While it has often been assumed that job seekers generate as many options as possible and simultaneously evaluate them, job search activities are usually not this intense. In fact, job seekers typically have only a hazy notion of their options.[41] Thus, the objective of most job seekers is to find a minimally acceptable, rather than optimal job. As a result, job opportunities are usually evaluated *sequentially.* If a job meets minimum qualifications, it is accepted; if it does not, the sequential search process continues.

The exception is job search activities after college. In high-demand fields (e.g., nursing and engineering), new graduates often have more than one offer to consider *simultaneously.* Traditionally, organizations provide these individuals with job information and give them time to consider various job options. Increasingly, however, organizations are adopting strategies that bring high-potential students to the company's attention earlier in the process to ensure acceptance of its job offer.[42]

Organizational choices are also affected by job attributes. An important job attribute is an individual's **noncompensatory reservation wage** (the minimum pay necessary to make a job offer acceptable). Prior compensation levels, the length of unemployment, and the availability of accurate salary information all affect an individual's reservation wage. There is also evidence that males have higher reservation wages than females. One reason is that females have been found to undervalue their work abilities. Reservation wages of males may be higher also because they are exposed to more job opportunities.[43]

Once a reservation wage is met, job seekers adopt a **compensatory approach,** in which trade-offs are made between different job attributes, including higher levels of compensation. In the largest study ever undertaken, more than 50,000 male and female applicants to the Minnesota Gas Company were asked to rank the importance of ten job attributes. For both sexes there was a tendency for individuals to rank the importance of company and co-workers higher for themselves than for others, while benefits, hours, and pay were ranked lower. Job applicants agreed that pay was important to others but were less willing to admit that it was important to them. For females, the type of work was ranked as most important, while job security was ranked higher by males.[44]

INCREASING THE POOL OF POTENTIALLY QUALIFIED APPLICANTS

As the previous sections indicate, recruitment goes beyond choosing between internal and external sources. To gain a competitive edge, organization must also understand and meet the needs of job seekers. To increase the likelihood that high-potential employees will be successfully recruited, hired, and retained, organizations can adopt a variety of strategies.

Conveying Job and Organizational Information

The traditional approach to recruitment involves matching the job applicant's skills, knowledge, and abilities with the demands of the job. The more recent approach to recruitment is also concerned with matching the job applicant's personality, interests, and preferences with the job and with organizational characteristics. For effective PHRM, getting the job applicants to stay is as important as recruiting job applicants who can do the job.

Achieving both is possible by (1) devoting attention to the job interview, (2) having a job matching program, (3) carefully timing recruitment procedures, (4) developing policies regarding job offer acceptances, and (5) expanding career and job options. Other ways are illustrated in the preceding "PHRM in the News" about Burger King.

Job Interview.   A vital aspect of the recruitment process is the interview. A good interview provides the applicant with a realistic preview of what the job will be like. It can definitely be an enticement for an applicant to join an organization, just as a bad interview can turn away many applicants.

The quality of the interview is just one aspect of the recruitment process. Other things being equal, the chances of a person's accepting a job offer increases when interviewers show interest and concern for the applicant. In addition, college students feel most positive toward the recruitment interview when they can take at least half of the interview time to ask the interviewer questions and when the interviewer does not embarrass them or put them on the spot.

The content of the recruitment interview is also important. Organizations often assume that it is in their best interests to tell a job applicant only about the positive aspects of the organization. But studies by the life insurance industry have reported that providing realistic (positive and negative) information actually increases the number of eventual recruits. In addition, those who receive realistic job information may be less likely to quit once they accept the job. The type of interview that conveys positive and negative information is referred to as a **realistic job interview.**

> A realistic preview can be given as part of the recruitment process before an individual has accepted a job, or as part of the orientation or socialization process that takes place after job acceptance. Such previews can take many forms, including written descriptions of the job, film or video tape presentations, and samples of the actual work. Although they may differ in form or mode of presentation, all realistic job previews are alike in presenting all relevant aspects of a job as accurately as possible. Since new or potential employees usually have inflated ideas or expectations about what a job involves, a realistic preview usually *reduces* these overly optimistic expectations. In effect, even though it presents a complete and accurate picture, a realistic preview primarily serves to acquaint new or prospective employees with the previously unknown *negative* aspects of a particular job.[45]

Assuming that job applicants pass on initial screening, they should be given the opportunity to interview with a potential supervisor and even with co-workers. The interview with the potential supervisor is crucial, because this is the person who often makes the final decision.

Job Matching.   Job matching is a systematic effort to identify people's knowledge, skills, and abilities and their personalities, interests, and preferences and to match them to the job openings. Increasing pressure on organizations to effectively recruit, select, and place new and current employees may make an automated job matching system worthwhile. For example, Citibank's job matching system for nonprofessional employees evolved from an automated system designed to monitor requisition and internal placement processes. The system is currently used to identify suitable positions for staff members who wish to transfer or who are seeking another job because of technological displacement or reorganization. The system also ensures that suitable internal candidates won't be overlooked system also ensures that suitable internal candidates won't be overlooked before recruiting begins outside the organization. Thus, the system appears not only to help recruit people and ensure that they stay but also to provide a firm basis for job-related recruitment and selection procedures (job relatedness is an important part of legal compliance and is discussed in Chapter 5).

Timing of Recruitment Procedures.   In markets where recruiting occurs in well-defined cycles (as in college recruiting), organizations have the option of being either early or late entrants into the recruiting process. Assuming that most individuals evaluate job options sequentially, organizations enhance their chances of obtaining high-potential candidates through early entry into the recruitment process. For example, high-technology companies begin the recruitment process by involving high-potential juniors in summer internships or cooperative education programs. Progressive organizations are also bypassing traditional second-semester campus interviews and inviting high-potential candidates directly to corporate headquarters early in the senior year. Most major accounting firms have job offers out and accepted by year-end. Such strategies are designed to induce commitment from top graduates before exposure to competing firms. Organizations that rely on traditional second-semester interviews and long selection processes may find themselves in a less competitive position than that of their more aggressive recruiting rivals.[46]

Policies Regarding Job Offer Acceptance.   Employers can also influence job applicants' selection decisions through the amount of time they allow individuals to ponder their offer (this is referred to as a **recall policy**). Given unlimited time to ponder a job offer, most job seekers will delay decision making until they have heard from all the organizations in the job search net. While potentially advantageous to the job seeker, the lack of a deadline places the organization at a distinct disadvantage. Unless job openings are unlimited, the organization cannot extend an offer to a second-choice candidate until a decision is made by the preferred candidate. Conversely, job applicants may want to delay making a commitment until they have completed all interviews. Thus, most organizations have recall policies, and job seekers find themselves in the dilemma of having to accept or reject a minimally acceptable alternative before receiving an offer from a preferred alternative. The short- and long-term effects of time deadlines need further investigation before definitive conclusions can be drawn about their effectiveness.

Expanding Career and Job Opportunities

By providing career opportunities and child-care assistance, organizations can enhance their attractiveness while increasing their applicant pools.

Career Opportunities.   The decision to provide career opportunities involves several choices for the organization. First, should the organization have an active policy of promotion from within? Second, should the organization be committed to a training and development program to provide sufficient candidates for internal promotion? If the answers to these questions are yes, then the organization must identify career ladders consistent with organizational and job requirements and employees skills and preferences, such as Citibank has done with its job matching program.

An organization may identify several career paths for different groups or types of employees. This concept is based on the premise that an organization cannot afford to recruit applicants for jobs at the lower rungs of the ladder when they already possess those skills necessary for jobs at the higher rungs. This actually occurs, however, with many people recruited from college. Although they are essentially overqualified for their first jobs, the organization hires them for more difficult "future" jobs. This approach is partially to blame for the higher turnover rate of new college graduates and is also a cause for concern regarding legal compliance. Employers may claim that a college degree is necessary for an entry-level managerial job when they may actually consider the degree necessary for the second or third job. Such a policy can lead to discriminatory barriers for recruitment and promotion.

One way to reduce the possibility of discriminatory barriers is for an organization to establish career ladders and paths. When organizations have career ladders and paths with clearly specified requirements anchored in sound job analyses, they can present better legal defenses for their recruitment policies. In essence, organizations establish a case of long-term job relatedness. Organizations with clearly defined career ladders may also have an easier time attracting and recruiting qualified job applicants and a better chance of keeping employees.

Efforts are also being made by many organizations, such as Burger King and McDonald's, to attract and retain older workers. For example, McDonald's now utilizes older workers in its television advertisements. While demonstrating McDonald's attitude to service to the general public, the advertisements also have a secondary focus. The advertisements are designed to encourage older workers to apply for positions at McDonalds. It appears that this will become even more critical than it is today.

Child-Care Assistance.   Along with society and technology, the percentage of wage-earning women in America is rapidly changing. Between 1960 and 1990, for example, the percentage of women working outside the home who are married with children under six years of age who work outside the home jumped from 19 percent to 50 percent. Today more than one child in five lives with a single parent.[47]

More companies than ever before are now providing some kind of child-care service for their employees. Because child-care service is such a critical employee benefit, it is discussed in detail in Chapter 10.

TRENDS IN RECRUITMENT

Key trends in recruitment include assessment of recruiting, contract recruiting, and applicant rejection management. Although some issues of strategic involvement are emerging, they are closely tied to selection and consequently are described in the next chapter.

Assessing Recruitment

The recruitment activity is supposed to attract the right people at the right time within legal limits, so that people and organizations can select each other in their best short- and long-run interests. This is how recruitment should be assessed. More specific criteria for assessing recruitment are shown in Exhibit 4.5, grouped by the stage of the recruitment process to which they are most applicable.

Recruitment is not concerned just with attracting people; it is concerned also with attracting those whose personalities, interests, and preferences will most likely be matched by the organization and who have the skills, knowledge, and abilities to perform adequately. Another criterion by which to assess recruiting is legal compliance. Job applicants must be recruited fairly and without discrimination.

In addition to assessing each benefit criterion of recruitment, each method or source of recruitment can be valued, or "costed out," in terms of its short- and long-term benefit costs. First, the utility of each method is determined by comparing the numbers of potentially qualified applicants hired by each method and by occupational group. These comparisons are referred to as **selection ratios.** The method resulting in the largest number of qualified applicants at the lowest per-hire cost may be deemed the most effective in the short run. The important costs to compare are those associated with hires versus those associated with nonhires. As noted earlier, *if an organization is spending more than two-thirds of its recruiting budget on individuals who never join the company, the recruiting program needs serious revamping.* To reiterate, the items reviewed should include the salaries of recruiters and line managers involved in inter-

EXHIBIT 4.5	Some Criteria for Assessing Recruitment
Stage of Entry	**Type of Criteria**
Pre-entry	Total number of applicants Number of minority and female applicants Cost per applicant Time to locate job applicants Time to process job applicants
Offers and hires	Offers extended by source Total number of qualified applicants Number of qualified female, minority, and handicapped applicants Costs of acceptance versus rejection of applicants
Entry	Initial expectations of newcomers Choice of the organization by qualified applicants Cost and time of training of new employees Salary levels
Postentry	Attitudes toward job, pay, benefits, supervision, co-workers Organizational commitment Job performance Tenure of hires Absenteeism Referrals

viewing and selection; all expenses for mailing, telephone, and recruiting materials; administrative support costs; and all recruiting advertising charges, including receptions, videos, and programs.[48]

Contract Recruiting

In response to employment cycles and the need for cost containment, a trend toward contract recruiting has developed. A contract recruiter is a consultant who accepts temporary assignments with companies (typically three to six months), becomes an integral part of the staff, and addresses problems relating to recruitment.

Although employment activity accounts for a majority of their assignments, contract recruiters are increasingly involved in a variety of PHRM issues, ranging from compensation and benefits to employee relations and EEO/AA programs.

Contractors are available immediately, without the need to hire a full-time employee or the expense of employee benefits. Unlike regular employees, a contractor is easily replaced without the trauma of an employee termination. For example, GTE, in Needham, Massachusetts, won a major contract, assuring the government that 1,200 professionals would be on board within sixteen months. At the peak of recruiting, twelve PHRM contractors worked full time as an instant employment staff, establishing a recruiting and selection system. The number diminished to two at the end of the sixteen months. Before leaving, the consultants recruited, hired, and trained their own replacements.

With the switch to a service economy, financial service, insurance, and health care organizations are also expected to use contract recruiting. Recently, Fidelity Investments opened up a new consumer division in Salt Lake City. Rather than relying on a corporate staff to recruit applicants, the firm trained PHRM graduate students in Fidelity's selection procedures. En masse, these contract recruiters were able to select sufficient job candidates that Fidelity's new office could be operational within two months. Similarly, companies such as Kendall have used contract recruiters to reduce the cost per hire. During downsizing, Kendall has used contractors for outplacement counseling rather than recruiting.[49]

Rejection with Tact   *Job*

When a new Toyota plant opened in Georgetown, Kentucky, the applicant pool reached 40,000 for 2,700 assembly-line openings. Thousands more applied for the 300 office jobs.[50] Similarly, more than 1 million applicants apply annually for between 5,000 and 8,000 positions at International Business Machine (IBM), IBM PHRM officials contend. For these "high-demand," consumer-oriented organizations, there's a new challenge to recruiting—rejection with tact.

Consider a hundred applicants who apply for one position with a bank. Only one applicant out of one hundred will be accepted, leaving ninety-nine potential employees and/or customers. If these rejected candidates feel angry at the rejecting organization, they may never again purchase goods or services from the organization. If procedures are viewed as unfair, too lengthy, or too impersonal, rejected candidates may also share their dissatisfaction with friends and associates.

While research on the rejection process is in its infancy, several characteristics of rejection letters make a difference. Statements that (1) are friendly (e.g., thank you for applying, good luck in the future, (2) include a personalized address and correct salutation (Ms., Mrs., and Miss—versus Mr. to all), and (3) summarize the applicant's job qualifications leave positive impressions. Including statements about the size and excellence of the application pool and the person who was offered the job (e.g., the person had ten years experience and was certified in arbitrage) reduce disappointment and increase perceptions of fairness.

Including a statement that the applicant's résumé will be kept on file increases the likelihood that the applicant will continue to use the organization's services or buy its products. While no court challenges have been launched, promises made in rejection letters (e.g., to keep the résumé on file) can serve as binding contractual obligations. Thus, a promise to keep an application on file should be made only if the organization intends to do just that. The timeliness with which rejection letters are mailed also seems important. Not only should a recruitment and selection timetable be specified to applicants, but also the organization should meet its self-imposed deadlines.[51]

SUMMARY

Recruitment is a major activity in an organization's program to manage its human resources. After human resource needs have been established and job requirements have been identified through job analysis, a recruiting program can be established to produce a pool of job applicants. These applicants can be obtained from internal or external sources.

For recruitment to be effective, it must consider not only the needs of the organization but also those of society and the individual. Society's needs are most explicitly defined by various federal and state regulations in the name of equal employment opportunity. Individuals' needs figure prominently in two aspects of recruiting: attracting candidates and retaining desirable employees. The legal commitments and obligations that influence an organization's recruitment activity most significantly are those associated with affirmative action programs. Such programs result from an organization's being a federal contractor, from entering into a consent decree, or from a voluntary action to provide greater equal employment opportunity. Although not legally imposing on recruitment, they directly influence the establishment and definition of the organization's selection requirements.

Keeping legal considerations firmly in mind, the organization must recruit sufficient numbers of potentially qualified applicants so that the individuals selected are adequately matched to jobs. This matching will help ensure that the individuals will perform effectively and not leave the organization. An organization can attract and retain these job applicants by numerous methods and through various sources. Although some methods and sources are more effective than others, the ones chosen are often necessarily determined by the type of applicant sought.

As with other PHRM activities, recruitment assessment is essential. Recruitment can be assessed by evaluating the associated benefit and cost criteria. For example, the benefits of reduced turnover or enhanced performance can be assessed and compared with the costs of the program to recruit job applicants. Costs of sources and methods can also be assessed and weighed against the benefits, such as the ease of recruiting or the number of qualified applicants obtained. After these assessments are made, recruiting methods and sources can be revised as appropriate. As with the recruitment assessment, however, the revision should be made with consideration for selection, the other half of the staffing function. This is necessary because the two activities are interdependent, as is made more apparent in the next chapter.

DISCUSSION QUESTIONS

1. What are the purposes of recruitment, and how do those purposes affect other organizational activities?
2. Discuss why the cost of employee training and development is so closely tied to recruitment programs.
3. How does human resource planning contribute to effective recruitment? What are the roles of the line and personnel managers in each of these activities?
4. Just-in-time inventory is a concept that enables manufacturers to assemble products from parts that are delivered as needed rather than kept in inventory (which is costly). Could this concept be applied to the recruitment function and human resources? Explain.
5. What is an affirmative action program? Why might a company develop an AAP?
6. Describe and explain the meaning of *utilization and availability analyses goals*, and *timetables* in relation to recruitment.
7. Why do some organizations use an external search, whereas others use an internal search? Can each be best for that particular organization? Explain.
8. The search for job applicants involves finding not only the right number but also the right kind. Are some recruitment sources richer than others—that is, do they yield more information about the kind of applicant needed? Can you give examples?

CASE STUDY

Invisible Ceilings Versus Doors?

Southwestern State University prides itself on its rapid growth and expansion of facilities during the decade of the seventies. Now, in the decade of the eighties, many see Southwestern State poised to become, as college presidents are wont to say, a preeminent university. A traditional land grant university with an emphasis on agriculture, Southwestern State currently boasts one of the largest schools of business and engineering in the country.

John DeNisi, an employee relations specialist in the personnel department at Southwestern, has witnessed firsthand the proud growth and trans-

formation of Southwestern during his eleven-year tenure in university administration at Southwestern. John is less sanguine about the future, though. Growth will continue but at a considerably reduced rate given projected population trends for the region. Moreover, John, like others, is worried about Southwestern's stance toward minority recruitment.

Three years ago, John served on a university-wide committee that examined the status of minorities at Southwestern in staff, faculty, and student areas. The final report his committee delivered to the president was not optimistic, to say the least. Southwestern is predictably underrepresented in all areas with regard to both blacks and Hispanics. Potentially, Southwestern stands to lose federal funds unless the university undertakes significant moves to attract and retain more minorities in the future. Accordingly, the committee's report recommended renewed efforts to recruit aggressively in all areas, to set aside money for minority recruitment, and to set up minority scholarships to attract more students.

Recently, though, John wondered what impact the current administration policy from Washington would have on Southwestern's step toward affirmative action. John had followed closely reports in the *Chronicle of Higher Education* and the College and University Personnel Association newsletter of the battle in Washington over the status of voluntary affirmative action plans. Although professional groups such as the National Association of Manufacturers and the American Society for Personnel Administration support affirmative action as "good business policy," the Department of Justice and the Equal Employment Opportunity Commission (EEOC) seem to have taken a major retreat from earlier administration positions on affirmative action.

The Department of Labor, though, seems to be at odds with the Justice Department and the EEOC by supporting goals and timetables in its enforcement of affirmative action plans for federal contractors. Moreover, the Supreme Court appears to support voluntary affirmative action plans in several recent decisions dealing specifically with such plans. Vocal critics of the new administration stand on affirmative action argue that without affirmative action, minorities will merely bump up against the "invisible ceiling." John wondered what implications these developments could have for Southwestern's stance for the future. If Southwestern initiated such a plan, and then the Department of Justice successfully challenged the constitutionality of affirmative action plans, the university could strap itself with discrimination and reverse discrimination suits well into the twenty-first century.

John's ruminations were abruptly interrupted by a call from the front office informing John that an applicant had requested a meeting. Usually this meant that a disgruntled applicant was unhappy with the impersonal treatment received from the front office. John would then spend a few minutes with the applicant, try to smooth ruffled feathers, and, when necessary, reprimand office staff for rude or discourteous behavior. More often than not, though, John encountered an obnoxious faculty spouse that not only expected immediate employment but also demanded it publicly in a crowded front office.

As John girded himself, he was introduced at the door to Alma Fisher, a well-dressed and attractive black woman. Alma did not beat around the bush. "Mr. DeNisi," Alma blurted out, "this university doesn't want to hire blacks, and I want to know what you're going to do about it!" After a few minutes of discussion, John learned that Alma had previously worked at the university as a secretary and had left two years ago on maternity. Upon reentering the labor force, Alma had visited the university employment office, taken the clerical tests, and qualified, based on her performance, for a senior secretary position, the highest-paid clerical position at the university.

John's office had matched Alma's qualifications to a position request submitted by the Medical College and referred Alma to the dean of the Medical School for an interview. According to Alma, during the interview the dean asked Alma if she had children and how she supported herself. The straw that broke the camel's back, though, came when the dean asked Alma if she was on welfare. At that point, Alma suggested to the dean that his line of questioning was "inappropriate" and asked the dean to stick to job-related questions concerning her qualifications to do the job. "You know, Mr. DeNisi," asserted Alma, "I did not tell the dean that my previous position with the university was as a secretary to the affirmative action officer. I could sue this university based on his behavior!"

John was struck by the irony of this moment. Why worry about invisible ceilings at Southwestern, he thought, when the invisible doors aren't open?

NOTES

1. "Employer Recruitment Practices," *Personnel* (May 1988): 63–65; B. Schneider and N. Schmitt, *Staffing Organizations*, 2d ed. (Glenview, Ill.: Scott, Foresman, 1986).
2. *Basic Skills in the U.S. Work Force* (New York: Center for Public Resources, 1983); L. S. Fink and M. M. Harris, "A Field Study of Applicants' Reactions to Employment Opportunities: Does the Recruiter Make a Difference?" *Personnel Psychology* (Winter 1987): 765–84; G. Gallup, Jr., *Forecast 2000: George Gallup, Jr. Predicts the Future of America* (New York: William Morrow, 1984); R. Stoops, "Are You Ready for the

Coming Recruitment Boom?" *Personnel Journal* (July 1982): 490, 492; R. Stoops, "Recruitment Strategy," *Personnel Journal* (Feb. 1982): 102.

3. H. Klein, "Financial Officers Often in Demand As Companies Seek Cost-Cutters," *Wall Street Journal*, 22 Nov. 1982, p. 33; "When the Slump Helps Service Firms Prosper," *Business Week*, 10 May 1982, p. 42.

4. *Fair Employment Report*, 17 Aug. 1981, p. 3.

5. H. A. Acuff, "Improving the Employment Function," *Personnel Journal* (June 1982): 407. Reprinted with the permission of *Personnel Journal*, Costa Mesa, Calif. All rights reserved. See also M. S. Taylor and T. J. Bergman, "Organizational Recruitment Activities and Applicants' Reactions at Different Stages of the Recruitment Process," *Personnel Psychology* (Summer 1987): 261–86.

6. "Hiring and Disabled: A Firm Commitment," *Fair Employment Practices*, 4 Feb. 1988, p. 16; "Reasonable Job Accommodations for Employers and Employees," *Fair Employment Practices*, 14 Apr. 1988, p. 45; B. Solomon and W. H. Wagel, "Spreading the Word on New Technologies for People with Disabilities," *Personnel* (July 1988): 14–17; W. H. Wagel, "Project Ace: New Opportunities for People with Disabilities," *Personnel* (Jan. 1988): 9–15; J. M. Williams, "Technology and the Disabled," *Personnel Administrator* (July 1988): 81–83.

7. R. H. Faley and L. S. Kleiman, "Misconceptions and Realities in the Implementations of Equal Employment Opportunity," in *Readings in Personnel and Human Resource Management*, 3d ed., ed. R. S. Schuler, S A. Youngblood, and V. L. Huber (St. Paul: West, 1988): 151–61; P. S. Greenlaw, "Labor Relations: Reverse Discrimination: The Supreme Court's Dilemma," *Personnel Journal* (Jan. 1988): 84–89.

8. *FEP Guidelines* (July 1988): 7.

9. AT&T has gone beyond the consent decree and is operating under a new plan that is even more far reaching than the old; see *Personnel Administator* (Oct. 1982): 20, 23.

10. *Fair Employment Practices*, 18 Feb. 1988, p. 23.

11. *Fair Employment Report*, 15 May 1985, p. 76.

12. "Assessing the Progress of Women in America's Corporations," *Fair Employment Practices*, 26 May 1988, p. 63; G. S. Becker, "Productivity Is the Best Affirmation Action Plan," *Business Week*, 27 Apr. 1987, p. 18; "High Court Approves Racial Promotion Quota," *Fair Employment Practices*, 5 Mar. 1987, p. 28; B. Martin, "Personnel Executives Respond to Reaffirmation of Affirmative Action," *Personnel Journal* (May 1987): 9–10, 15. For a discussion of the impact AAP's have had on opportunities for women and blacks in organizations, see "A Nation Divided on Black Progress," *Business Week*, 14 Mar. 1988, p. 65; R. H. Faley and L. S. Kleiman, "Misconceptions and Reality," in *Readings in Personnel and Human Resource Management*, 3d ed., 151–61; L S. Kleiman and R. H. Faley, "Voluntary Affirmative Action and Preferential Treatment: Legal and Research Implications," *Personnel Psychology* (Autumn 1988): 481–97; C. Leinster, "Black Executives: How They're Doing," *Fortune*,

18 Jan. 1988, pp. 109–20; and G. B. Northcraft and B. J. Licata, "Can We Legislate Employment Equity?" in *Readings in Personnel and Human Resource Management*, 3d ed. R. S. Schuler, S. A. Youngblood, and V. L. Huber (St. Paul: West, 1988), 141–50.

13. Only promotions and transfers are considered internal sources for recruitment. Recruiting by demotions is done infrequently. Demotions are discussed in Chapter 7 and in the section on employee rights in Chapter 14.

14. L. R. Sayles and G. Strauss, *Managing Human Resources* (Englewood Cliffs, N.J.: Prentice-Hall, 1977), 147.

15. See A. Patton, "When Executives Bail Out to Move Up," *Business Week*, 13 Sept. 1982, pp. 13, 15, 17, 19. For a review of the costs of relocations, see H. Z. Levine, "Relocation Practices," *Personnel* (Jan./Feb. 1982): 4–10.

16. J. P. Campbell, M. D. Dunnette, E. E. Lawler III, and K. E. Weick, Jr., *Managerial Behavior, Performance, and Effectiveness* (New York: McGraw-Hill, 1970); T. Rendero, "Consensus," *Personnel* (Sept./Oct. 1980): 5.

17. *Recruiting and Selection Procedures: Personnel Policies Forum Survey No. 146* (Washington, D.C.: Bureau of National Affairs, 1988).

18. J. R Garcia, "Job Posting for Professional Staff," *Personnel Journal* (Mar. 1981): 189–92; L. S. Kleiman and K. L. Clark, "An Effective Job Posting System," *Personnel Journal* (Feb. 1984): 20–25; H. Z. Levine, "Job Posting Practices," *Personnel* (Nov./Dec. 1984): 48–52; G. A. Wallropp, "Job Posting for Nonexempt Employes: A Sample Program," *Personnel Journal* (Oct. 1981): 796–98.

19. W. Glueck, *Personnel: A Diagnostic Approach* (Plano, Tex.: BPI, 1982).

20. R. Stoops, "Employees Referral Programs: Part I," *Personnel Journal* (Feb. 1981): 98; B. Stoops, "Employee Referral Programs: Part II," *Personnel Journal* (Mar. 1981): 172–73.

21. R. Stoops, "Employee Referral Programs; Part I."

22. P. J. Decker and E. T. Cornelius, "A Note on Recruiting Sources and Job Survival Rates," *Journal of Applied Psychology* 64 (1974): 463–64; D. P. Schwab, "Recruiting and Organizational Participation," in *Personnel Management*, ed. K. M. Rowland and G. R. Ferris (Boston: Allyn & Bacon, 1982), 103–28.

23. R. Kenney, "Open House Complements Recruitment Strategies," *Personnel Administrator* (Mar. 1982): 27–32.

24. S. Bronstein, "What's New in Executive Recruiting," *New York Times*, 25 Aug. 1985, p. F13; G. P. Craighead, "Are Executive Recruiters Paid Too Much?" *Personnel Journal* (May 1985): 90–94.

25. For a good discussion of the false negatives and positives, see S. Rubenfeld and M. Crino, "Are Employment Agencies Jeopardizing Your Selection Process?" *Personnel* (Sept./Oct. 1981): 70–78. The selection chapter in this text also discusses these decisions. See also W. J. Bjerregaard and M. E. Gold, "Employment Agencies and Executive Recruiters: A Practical Approach," *Personnel Administrator* (May 1981): 127–

31; W. J. Bjerregaard and M. E. Gold, "Executive Utilization of Search Consultants," *Personnel Administrator* (Dec. 1980): 35–39; R. J. Cronin, "Executive Recruiters: Are They Necessary?" *Personnel Administrator* (Feb. 1980): 31–34; and B. Horovitz, "Where Headhunters Hunt," *Industry Week*, 9 Feb. 1981, pp. 43–47.

26. "Temporary Help Becoming Permanent Fixture," *Bulletin to Management*, 9 June 1988, p. 183.

27. L. D. Foxman and W. L. Polsky, "What Are the Best Employment Sources?" *Personnel Journal* (Nov. 1984): 26–27; A. E. Marshall, "Recruiting Alumni on College Campuses," *Personnel Journal* (Apr. 1982): 264–66; T. Rendero, "Consensus," 4–10.

28. M. Hanigan, "Campus Recruiters Upgrade Their Pitch," *Personnel Administrator* (Nov. 1987): 55–58.

29. S. McConnell, "The New Battle over Immigration," *Fortune*, 9 May 1988, pp. 89–102; C. E. Morrissey, "Utilizing U.S. Educated Foreign Nationals," *Personnel Journal* (Nov. 1983): 862–66.

30. "Immigration Reform Compliance: Surprise Visits in Store," *Bulletin to Management*, 1 Oct. 1987, pp. 313–14; F. L. Sullivan, "Immigration Legislation: An Update," *Personnel* (Dec. 1987): 26–32; "Undocumented Workers and the New Immigration Law," *Bulletin to Management*, 6 Aug. 1987, pp. 252–53.

31. R. Stoops, "Radio Advertising as an Effective Recruitment Device," *Personnel Journal* (Jan. 1981): 21; R. Stoops, "Radio Recruitment Advertising: Part II," *Personnel Journal* (July 1981): 532; R. Stoops, "Television Advertising," *Personnel Journal* (Nov. 1981): 838.

32. R. Stoops, "A Marketing Approach to Recruitment," *Personnel Journal* (Aug. 1981): 608. An extension of newspapers and journals is direct mail advertising; for a description, see B. Martin, "Recruitment Ad Ventures," *Personnel Journal* (Aug. 1987): 46–63; and R. Stoops, "More on Direct Mail Advertising," *Personnel Journal* (Mar. 1982): 184.

33. A. Halcrow, "Anatomy of a Recruitment Ad," *Personnel Journal* (Aug. 1985): 64–65; M. Magnus, "Recruitment Ads at Work," *Personnel Journal* (Aug. 1985): 42–63; R. Stoops, "Creative Ad Concepts Are Not Accidents," *Personnel Journal* (Nov. 1984): 86–88.

34. *Wall Street Journal*, 8 Feb. 1983, p. 35. Reprinted by permission of the *Wall Street Journal*. Copyright © Dow Jones & Company, Inc., 1983. All rights reserved.

35. J. M. Ivancevich, D. M. Schweiger, and F. R. Power, "Strategies for Managing Human Resources During Mergers and Acquisitions," *Readings in Personnel and Human Resource Management*, 3d ed., ed. R. S. Schuler, S. A. Youngblood, and V. L. Haber (St. Paul: West, 1988), 92–107; D. M. Schweiger, J. M. Ivancevich, and F. R. Power, "Executive Actions for Managing Human Resources Before and After Acquisitions," *Executive* (May 1987): 127–38.

36. C. Rosenfield, "Job Seeking Methods Used by American Workers," *Monthly Labor Review* (Aug. 1975): 39–42; D. P. Schwab, "Organizational Recruiting and the Decision to Participate," in *Personnel Management*, ed. K. M. Rowland and G. R. Ferris (Boston: Allyn & Bacon, 1982); D. Schwab, S. L. Rynes, and R. J. Aldag, "Theories and Research in Job Search and Choice," in *Research in Personnel and Human Resource Management* (Greenwich, Conn.: JAI Press, 1987), 136–37; M. S. Taylor and D. W. Schmidt, "A Process-Oriented Investigation of Recruitment Source Effectiveness," *Personnel Psychology* 36 (1983): 343–54.

37. P. Burgess and J. Kingston, "UI Benefit Effect on Compensated Unemployment," *Industrial and Labor Relations Review* 20 (1981): 258–70; H. J. Holzer, "Job Search by Employed and Unemployed Youth," *Industrial and Labor Relations Review* 40 (1987): 600–601.

38. R. Kanfer and C. L. Hulin, "Individual Differences in Successful Job Search Following Lay-Off," *Personnel Psychology* 63 (1985): 835–47.

39. N. H. Nazrin, T. Flores, and S. J. Kaplan, "Job-Finding Club: A Group-Assisted Program for Obtaining Employment," *Behavior Research Therapy* 13 (1975): 17–27; J. J. Zandy and L. F. James, "A Review of Research on Job Placement," *Rehabilitation Counseling Bulletin* 30 (1977): 451–61.

40. J. O. Crites, *Vocational Psychology* (New York: McGraw-Hill, 1969); J. P. Wanous, *Organizational Entry: Recruitment, Selection, and Socialization of Newcomers* (Reading, Mass.: Addison-Wesley, 1980); K. G. Wheeler and T. M. Mahoney, "The Expectancy Model in the Analysis of Occupational Preference and Occupation Choice," *Journal of Vocational Behavior* 19 (1981): 113–22.

41. Schwab, Rynes, and Aldag, "Theories and Research," in *Research and Personnel and Human Resource Management*, 129–66.

42. G. T. MIlkovich and J. Newman, *Compensation* (Plano, Tex.: BPI, 1984); Schwab, Rynes, and Aldag, "Theories and Research," in *Research in Personnel and Human Resource Management*, 129–66.

43. C. E. Jurgenson, "Job Preference: What Makes a Job Good or Bad?" *Journal of Applied Psychology* 63 (1978): 267–76; B. Major and E. Konar, "An Investigation of Sex Differences in Pay in Higher Education and Their Possible Cause," *Academy of Management Journal* 4 (1986): 777–92; Schwab, Rynes, and Aldag, "Theories and Research," in *Research in Personnel and Human Resource Management*, 129–66.

44. C. E. Jergenson, "Job Preference,"; Schwab, Rynes, and Aldag, "Theories and Research," in *Research in Personnel and Human Resource Management*; S. L. Rynes, H. Heneman III, and D. P. Schwab, "Individual Reactions to Organizational Recruiting: A Review," *Personnel Psychology* 33 (1980): 529–42.

45. R. D. Arvey and J. G. Campion, "The Employment Interview: A Summary and Review of the Recent Literature," *Personnel Psychology* 35 (1982): 281–322; J. A. Breaugh, "Realistic Job Previews: A Critical Appraisal and Future Research Directions," *Academy of Management Review* (Oct. 1983): 612–23; R. A. Dean and J. P. Wanous, "Effects of Realistic Job Previews on Hiring Bank Tellers," *Journal of Applied Psychology* (Feb. 1984): 61–68; M. D. Hakel, "Employment Interviewing," in *Personnel Management*, ed. K. M. Rowland and G. R. Ferris (Boston: Allyn & Bacon, 1982),

153–54; B. M. Meglino and A. S. DeNisi, "Realistic Job Previews: Some Thoughts on Their More Effective Use in Managing the Flow of Human Resources," *Human Resource Planning* 10, no. 3 (1987) 157–67; B. M. Meglino, A. S. DeNisi, S. A. Youngblood, and K. J. Williams, "Effects of Realistic Job Previews: A Comparison Using an Enhancement and Reduction Preview," *Journal of Applied Psychology* (May 1988): 259–66; G. N. Powell, "Effects of Job Attributes and Recruiting Practices on Applicant Decision: A Comparison," *Personnel Psychology* (Winter 1984): 721–32; S. L. Rynes and H. E. Miller, "Recruiter and Job Influences on Candidates for Employment," *Journal of Applied Psychology* (Feb. 1983): 147–56.

46. Meglino and DeNisi, "Realistic Job Previews." See also S. M. Colarelli, "Methods of Communication and Mediating Processes in Realistic Job Previews," *Journal of Applied Psychology* 69 (1984): 633–42.

47. J. F. Coates, "An Environmental Scan: Projecting Future Human Resource Trends, *Human Resource Planning,* 10, No. 4 (1987): 209–19.

48. J. W. Boudreau and S. L. Rynes, "Role of Recruitment in Staffing Utility Analysis," *Journal of Applied Psychology* (May 1985): 354–66; D. F. Caldwell and W. A. Spivey, "The Relationship Between Recruiting Source and Employee Success: An Analysis by Race," *Personnel Psychology* (Spring 1983): 67–72; D. Dennis, "Are Recruitment Efforts Designed to Fail?" *Personnel Journal* (Sept. 1984): 60–67; P. Farish, "Cost Per Hire," *Personnel Administrator* (Jan. 1985): 16; D. A. Levinson, "Needed: Revamped Recruiting Services," *Personnel* (July 1988): 50–52; M. London and S. A. Stumpf, "Effects of Candidate Characteristics on Management Promotion Decisions: An Experimental Study," *Personnel Psychology* (Summer 1983): 241–60; Taylor and Schmidt, "A Process-Oriented Investigation," 343–54.

49. J. S. Lord, "Contract Recruiting: Coming of Age," *Personnel Administrator* (Nov. 1987): 49–53.

50. R. Koenig, "Toyota Takes Pains and Time Filling Jobs at Its Kentucky Plant," *Wall Street Journal,* 1 Dec. 1987, p. 1.

51. M. J. Aamodt and D. L. Peggans, "Rejecting Applicants with Tact," *Personnel Administrator* (Apr. 1988): 58–60; B. Adair and D. Pollen, "No! No! A Thousand Time No!" *Washington Post,* 25 Sept. 1985, p. 5.

CHAPTER 5

Selection and Placement

Employee Selection Is One Conduit to Tandy's Profitability

The success of the Tandy Corporation is based on the profitability of its retail sales. Retail sales, in turn, are based on the sales ability of individuals backed by a strong corporate commitment to employee selection, training and development.

With more than 80% of Tandy's work force in direct sales, "my job is to work with field sales management to select qualified sales personnel, to train the sales force and develop programs focusing on sales productivity," says George J. Berger, vice president of human resources for the Fort Worth–based company best known by its Radio Shack trademark.

Berger feels a direct responsibility for the profitability of Tandy. More than 75% of the management compensation plans at Tandy, including that of the vice president of human resources, is tied to the company's profit and loss.

Overall Berger works directly with the 167 district managers who manage 25–30 stores each with an average of 75–100 full- and part-time employees. He is responsible for the corporate-wide personnel systems, including the initial selection process to identify qualified salespeople, the development of training programs and the continuing employee skill development.

Berger is concerned with the personnel issues that make salespeople more productive. If they are more successful, their success "makes us all more successful."

For instance, Berger is focusing some of his efforts on the selection process to more closely and clearly identify the sales experience and sales potential of prospective employees. By improving the quality of salespeople and identifying their propensity to succeed in the be-

ginning, he believes he can contribute to overall profitability of the organization.

Berger explains, "I've taken the questions that are asked during the interviewing process and developed a computerized program—which runs on a Tandy computer—to administer as part of the final skill assessment profile" to determine a candidate's aptitude for qualifying customers, making sales presentations, closing sales and after-sales or customer service.

This is not the only selection device used by Tandy, but it is used in making a hiring decision. "There is no flunking or passing. It's just part of the pre-screening process and not the sole criteria for hiring," Berger says.

This skill assessment program is also used "as an after-hire tool to determine where to concentrate the initial training." For instance, if a new hire isn't as strong in closing as in customer service, then the training concentrates on closing sales.

Berger is proud of the company's success and the commitment to its employees. What corporate philosophy lies behind the company's success and how it approaches personnel issues?

"We take a basic approach and try to do things better than they were done before. We try to get more mileage from what works rather than recreate the wheel.

"We take a good, basic standard program and work with that. We don't do traditional things in a traditional way. We try to put a new twist to them."

SOURCE: M. Magnus, "Personnel Policies in Partnership with Profit," *Personnel Journal* (September 1987): 105–6. Reprinted with permission of *Personnel Journal*, Costa Mesa, CA., all rights reserved.

T his "PHRM in the News" feature highlights many aspects of selection that will be discussed in this chapter, including (1) how to collect information on job applicants, (2) how to make selection and placement decisions, (3) how to use selection to improve the profitability of the company, and (4) how to tie selection into the basic philosophy of a company. Other aspects of selection and placement (to be described in Chapter 16) include how to validate tests used in making selection decisions and how to make the entire set of selection and placement procedures more useful. These concerns, along with the extensive legal environment of selection decisions, are the essence of selection and placement and equal employment opportunity.

Selection is the process of gathering legally defensible information about job applicants in order to determine who should be hired for long- or short-term positions. **Placement** is concerned with matching individual skills, knowledge, abilities, preferences, interests, and personality to the job. Effective selection and placement involve finding the match between organizational needs for qualified individuals and individual needs for jobs in which they are interested.[1]

Line managers play an important role in the selection and placement activity. They help identify the need for staffing through the organization's human resource planning activity, assist with job analysis, and evaluate employee performance.

The personnel and human resource department, however, should be responsible for gathering information and should arrange interviews between job applicants and managers for several reasons:

- Applicants have only one place to go to apply for a job and have a better chance of being considered for a greater variety of jobs.
- Outside sources of applicants can clear employment issues through one central location.
- Operating managers can concentrate on their operating responsibilities—especially helpful during peak hiring periods.
- Hiring is done by specialists trained in staffing techniques so selection is often better.
- Costs may be cut because duplication of effort is avoided.
- With increased government regulation of selection, it is important that people who know about these rules handle a major part of the hiring process.

PURPOSES AND IMPORTANCE OF SELECTION AND PLACEMENT

Selection and placement procedures provide the essence of an organization—its human resources. Selecting employees who are likely to perform well may result in substantial productivity improvements and cost savings. For example, in 1978, members of the Edison Electric Institute, a trade association of power companies, began a project to design and validate industrywide assessment tools for positions in several job categories. By analyzing job requirements, developing and administering experimental tests, and correlating the results with performance appraisals by supervisors, the institute created tests measuring decision-making capability and electrical knowledge for systems operators, mechanical comprehension for maintenance workers, and language skills for clerical employees.

By the fall of 1987, many utility companies across the country had adopted all these tests. "If every company in our industry did a separate validity study, it would have cost at least 10 times as much," said David Kleinke, manager of psychological services at Edison. Kleinke estimated that by improving employee selection procedures, the tests should save utility companies at least $20 million in operating costs in 1988.[2]

Effective selection and placement are critical to any organization. Serving the organization's needs and providing effective selection and placement mean attaining several purposes:

- To contribute to the organization's bottom line through efficient and effective production.
- To ensure that an organization's financial investment in employees pays off. For example, hiring an employee with a starting salary of $25,000, annual cost of living adjustments (COLAs) of only 1.5 percent, and no benefits results in an investment of $128,000 in that employee in five years and $578,092 in twenty years.
- To evaluate, hire, and place job applicants in the best interests of both the organization and the individual.
- To minimize multi-million dollar verdicts and settlements in litigation brought by victims of criminal, violent, or negligent acts perpetrated by employees who should not have been hired or kept in their jobs.[3]
- To enable organizations to fulfill their strategies:

  I am the ultimate believer in people first, strategies second. To me, strategy starts with the person you hire. If a business lacks a good strategy, then put in charge of the business someone who will develop one.[4]

- To help fulfill hiring goals and timetables specified in affirmative action programs.

RELATIONSHIPS INFLUENCING SELECTION AND PLACEMENT

To serve these purposes effectively, selection and placement must be congruent with the internal environment and integrated with other PHRM activities (see Exhibit 5.1).

Relationships with the Internal Environment

Organizational Strategy.   Reginald H. Jones, former chairman and CEO of the General Electric Company, has noted that "businesses with different missions require quite different people running them."[5] As a result, particular characteristics, skills, abilities, values, and perspectives of executives need to match particular types of business strategy.[6] For example, a recently released study by the Hay Group reports that when a business is pursuing a growth strategy, it needs top managers who are likely to abandon the status quo and adapt their strategies and goals to the marketplace. Because insiders are slow to recognize the onset of decline and tend to persevere in strategies that are no longer effective, top managers need to be recruited from the outside.

EXHIBIT
5.1

Relationships and Aspects of Selection and Placement

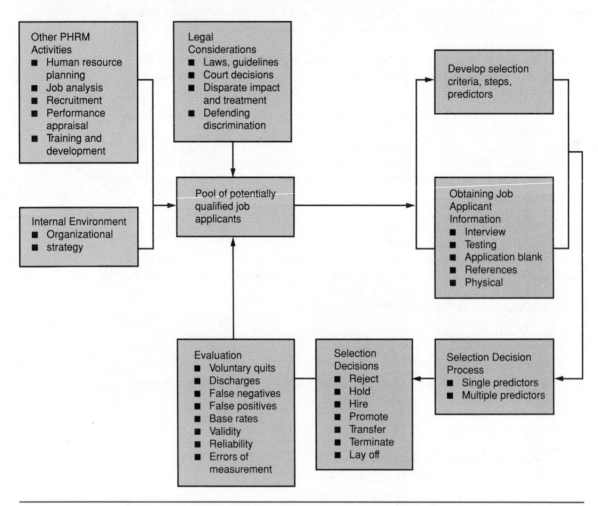

Recruiting outsiders as a part of the strategy has been successful for Stroh Brewing, once a small family-run brewery in Detroit. Some 20 percent of its senior management team of 25 executives, including President Roger T. Fridholm, have been brought into Stroh since 1978. They have been instrumental in transforming it into the third-largest U.S. brewer.[7]

The result of such staffing practices has been rather significant.

Growth companies that staffed 20% of their top three levels with outsiders exceeded their expected return on investment by 10%. Those that relied on inside talent fell short of their goals by 20%. The same holds true for companies within declining businesses. Companies with outsiders in one out of every five top management jobs exceeded expected returns by 20%; those with a low proportion of outsiders fell 5% short.[8]

Outsiders, of course, are not always helpful. When a business is pursuing a mature strategy, what is needed is a stable group of insiders who know the intricacies of the business.

The results of the Hay study suggest that the staffing practices of top management should be tied to the nature of the business; different aspects of business demand different behaviors. The implication of this perspective is to select the right top manager for the nature of the business.

Relationships with Other PHRM Activities

In addition to meshing with an organization's culture, selection and placement procedures need to be integrated with human resource planning, job analysis, recruitment, performance appraisal, and training and development activities.

Human Resource Planning and Job Analysis.   Human resource planning can facilitate the organization's selection decisions by projecting when and how many such decisions will need to be made. When linked with job analysis, planning also helps indicate the worker qualifications necessary for the jobs. With essential worker qualifications known, selection procedures can be developed that are job related and consequently valid.

Recruitment.   As noted in Chapter 4, the success of selection and placement procedures depends on the effectiveness of the recruiting activity. If recruiting does not provide a large pool of potentially qualified job applicants, the organization has difficulty selecting and placing individuals who will perform well and not quit. Even if recruitment does provide some applicants, if the pool is small, the potential effectiveness of the selection and placement procedures is lessened because the selection ratio tends to become large.

Performance Appraisal.   Performance appraisals serve as a source of feedback to show that the selection devices indeed predict performance. If the criteria used in performance appraisal are not job related [e.g., the appraisals are not built on job analysis (see Chapters 3 and 6)] or not communicated, the organization has difficulty developing and using selection devices to predict meaningful employee performance. In other words, performance appraisals serve as criteria for evaluating the predictive and economic utility of selection procedures.

Training and Development.   If recruiting does not provide a large pool of potentially qualified job applicants, an organization may hire underqualified job applicants and then train them. The trade-off between selecting the "right" individual versus training individuals to "perform right" centers around costs and time. For example, Microsoft prefers to hire inexperienced software engineers and train them in the Microsoft tradition. Conversely, a major West Coast bank waits until college graduates have completed a competitor's intensive one-year management training program and then "steals" them at a higher salary. It saves training costs while getting the best and brightest.

LEGAL CONSIDERATIONS IN SELECTION AND PLACEMENT

The legal environment for most organizations is growing so complex that it is a major consideration in making employment decisions. Determining an organization's specific equal employment obligations is made complex by an extensive web of federal acts, federal and state constitutions, state and local legislation, court decisions, executive orders, guidelines, quasi-judicial bodies—such as the Equal Employment Opportunity Commission (EEOC) and the Office of Federal Contract Compliance Programs (OFCCP)—and state equal employment opportunity (EE0) or civil rights agencies.

Congressional Acts

The historical development of equal employment legislation began with the Civil Rights Act of 1866, Section 1981 of which prohibits employee discrimination based on race, color, and national origin. Section 1983 of the Civil Rights Act of 1871 enforces the Fourteenth Amendment to the U.S. Constitution, which has been held to prohibit discrimination based on race, color, national origin, religion, sex, and age. The Equal Pay Act of 1963 prohibits discrimination between employees on the basis of sex by paying a wage rate higher for one sex than another on jobs that are equal in skill, effort, responsibility, and working conditions. The Age Discrimination in Employment Act of 1967, as amended in 1978 and 1986, prohibits discrimination against employees and applicants for employment who are more than forty years old.

The Equal Employment Opportunity Act of 1972 amended the Civil Rights Act of 1964 that had first created the Equal Employment Opportunity Commission. This 1972 amendment expanded the coverage of Title VII to include public and private employers with fifteen or more employees, labor organizations with fifteen or more members, and public and private employment agencies. Elected officials and their appointees are excluded from Title VII coverage but are still covered under the Fourteenth Amendment and the Civil Rights Acts of 1866 and 1871. The 1972 amendment also identified exceptions or exemptions to Title VII, including bona fide occupational qualifications, seniority systems, preemployment inquiries, use of job-related tests for selection, national security interests, and veteran's preference rights.

The Rehabilitation Act of 1973, as amended in 1980, prohibits discrimination against persons with physical or mental handicaps that substantially limit one or more major life activities or are visible to others or against persons who have a history of impairment (see Chapter 4). The Vietnam Era Veterans Readjustment Act of 1974 protects disabled veterans and veterans of the Vietnam era in seeking employment opportunities. In addition, both the Rehabilitation Act and the Vietnam Era Veterans Readjustment Act provide for affirmative action plans. In addition to these major federal acts pertaining to equal employment opportunity, state and local governments also have their own laws that employers must follow.[9]

Executive Orders

The equal employment opportunity acts have been supported by a number of executive orders (EOs). EO 11246 of 1965 prohibits discrimination by federal agencies, contractors, and subcontractors on the basis of race, color, religion, and national origin. In 1966, EO 11375 was signed to prohibit discrimination on the basis of sex in these same organizations. EO 11478 of 1969 prescribes that employment policies of the federal government be based on merit and that the head of each agency establish and maintain a program of EEO.

Guidelines

While acts and executive orders delineate protected classes, guidelines provide the mechanisms by which these acts and orders are implemented. The first set, issued in 1970 by the EEOC, originally intended to provide a workable set of ideal standards for employees, unions, and employment agencies. The guidelines defined a *test* as

> all formal, scored, qualified or standardized techniques of assessing job suitability, including . . . background requirements, educational or work history requirements, interviews, biographical information blanks, interviewer's rating scales and scored application blanks.[10]

Additionally, the guidelines stressed that any test that has an adverse impact on any protected group must be identified.

Following the issuance of the guidelines, the courts began using them as a "checklist" of *minimum* standards for test validation, rather than as a flexible set of ideal standards, as intended. Concern over the court trend prompted the Equal Employment Opportunity Coordinating Council (EEOCC) to develop a set of **uniform guidelines,** to be used by all federal agencies, based on sound psychological principles and technical feasibility. As a result, the *Federal Executive Agency Guidelines* were published in 1976, followed by the *Uniform Guidelines on Employee Selection Procedures* in 1978. The 1978 *Uniform Guidelines* are a fourteen-thousand-word catalog of do's and don't's and questions and answers for hiring and promotion. They contain interpretations and guidance not found in earlier EEOC guidelines.

The EEOC has also published other guidelines. On November 10, 1980, the commission issued *Guidelines on Discrimination Because of Sex* (sexual harassment is discussed further in Chapter 14).[11] These guidelines are premised on the assumption that sexual harassment is a condition of employment if women are exposed to it more frequently than men. Six weeks later, the EEOC issued its *Guidelines on Discrimination Because of National Origin*. The national origin guidelines extended earlier versions of this protection by defining national origin as a *place* rather than a *country* of origin. It also revised the "speak-English-only rules." This meant that employers could require English to be spoken if it was job-related or a bona fide occupational qualification. On September 29, 1981, the EEOC issued guidelines on age discrimination (in essence, identifying what the Age Discrimination in Employment Act meant to do and what it should mean to employers and employees).[12]

Under the *Guidelines on Discrimination Because of Religion,* an employer is obliged to accommodate the religious preferences of current and prospective employees unless the employer demonstrates undue hardship. It appears, however, that if an employer shows "reasonable attempts to accommodate," the courts may be satisfied that no religious discrimination has occurred (*Philbrook v. Ansonia Board of Education,* 1986; *State Division of Human Rights v. Rochester Housing Authority,* 1980).

Professional Standards

Selection processes are also monitored by the American Psychological Association (APA). In 1966 and again in 1974, the APA released its *Standards for Education and Psychological Tests*. These standards were last updated in 1985.

In 1975 and again in 1987, the Society for Industrial-Organizational Psychology (SIOP), a division fo the APA, published its *Principles for the Validation and Use of Personnel Selection Procedures*. Drawing from relevant research, these standards and principles help clarify issues regarding test fairness and discrimination.

Proving Illegal Discrimination

While Title VII prohibits discrimination, nowhere in the law is **discrimination** defined. The guidelines listed above, coupled with a growing body of case law, however, have delineated the intent of the law. Title VII prohibits differences in the treatment of employees based on race, color, religion, sex, or national origin. Discrimination based on age or physical and mental handicaps or against disabled or Vietnam era veterans is prohibited by other acts. Discrimination based on all other criteria is untouched by the law, except when discrimination is based on nonprohibited factors in an attempt to disguise illegal discrimination. For example, using minimum height and weight requirements as surrogate measures of physical strength may adversely affect women and certain groups (Asians, Hispanics). When this occurs, Title VII would be violated.[13]

Prima Facie Case.   A typical discrimination suit involves multiple steps. Initially, a person alleges discrimination due to unlawful employment practices. In the first phase of a discrimination suit, it is the obligation of the plaintiff (the person filing the suit) to establish a *prima facie* case of discrimination. A **prima facie case** of illegal discrimination is established by showing disparate impact or disparate treatment. **Disparate impact** means that discrimination has affected a *group* of employees. **Disparate treatment** means that there is an apparent case of illegal discrimination against an *individual*. The basic criteria were established by the Supreme Court for a *prima facie* case of disparate impact in *Griggs v. Duke Power Co.* (1971) and for a *prima facie* case of disparate treatment in *McDonnell Douglas v. Green* (1973). Because a charge of disparate treatment requires evidence of **intent to discriminate,** it traditionally has been more difficult to establish than a charge of disparate impact. This may not be the situation in the future.[14]

Disparate Impact.   Cases of disparate impact rely on three types of statistical evidence. In *Griggs v. Duke Power,* the focus was the actual impact of employment practices, rather than the intent of these practices. Thus, one approach relies on **comparative statistics** or comparisons of the actual rates or ratios of hiring, firing, promoting, transferring, and demoting for protected and nonprotected groups.

The *Uniform Guidelines* suggest that adverse impact has been demonstrated if the selection rate for any racial, ethnic, or sex subgroup is less than **four-fifths,** or 80 percent, of the highest selection rate for any group. If, for example, a company hires 50 percent of all white male applicants who apply in a particular job category, then it must hire at least 40 percent (80 percent x 50 percent) of all black people who apply and 40 percent of all women and other protected groups. Originally, this bottom-line criterion was aimed at identifying disparate impact only for an entire set of selection procedures rather than for any single part of the procedures. This aim, however, has now been modified to *apply to each part* of the selection procedures, as well as to the entire set (*Connecticut v. Teal*, 1982).[15]

In contrast, the argument using **demographic statistics** centers on the comparison of an organization's work force to the population at large. This argument is rooted in the Civil Rights Act of 1964. For example, an employer's selection procedures could be shown to be discriminatory (*prima facie*) if the employer's work force failed to reflect parity with the race or sex composition of the **general labor market** (*Griggs v. Duke Power Co.*, 1971; *Castaneda v. Partida*, 1977). Historically, then, Title VII reflected an egalitarian presumption (that is, that all individuals are equally qualified for all jobs).[16]

Today, however, the point of comparison for the employer's work force has tended to become the **relevant labor market.** This notion that *prima facie* evidence of discrimination must be based on comparisons with the relevant labor market (that is, the labor market of equally qualified individuals) rather than on those with the general labor market was reflected in *Hazelwood School District v. U.S.* (1977) and *EEOC v. United Virginia Bank* (1980). Thus, an employer's work force should reflect the percentages of groups in the relevant labor market.

> For some, it refers to a given geographic location: i.e., the Richmond, Virginia labor market, the Cleveland, Ohio labor market, etc. In economics, the concept of a labor market is more rigorously defined as the area in which buyers and sellers of labor are in sufficiently close communication that wages tend to be equalized. Equating a labor market with a given geographic area is sometimes a convenient simplification, but it is not accurate. Any given area is composed of a large number of submarkets (partially overlapping but essentially noncompeting) which shade gradually into one another. The more highly trained and paid the workers in a market are, the wider the geographic area of the market will tend to be.[17]

As Exhibit 5.2 shows, the definition of relevant labor market can vary substantially. Consider an organization with 4 percent black managers. According to the **80 percent rule,** black people would be underutilized if U.S. labor force participation rate is used in the comparison (.80 x 10.7% = 8.6%). If the comparison is restricted to the percentage of black managers in the U.S. labor force, adverse impact will *not* be shown (.80 X 5.2% = 4.2%). In fact, parity will be shown. If the relevant labor market is defined as management personnel in a *specific geographical area* (e.g., Utah), a firm with 4 percent black managers substantially exceeds the norm. Determining relevant labor market is often an art rather than a science and is often the source of much debate in Title VII court proceedings.

Example of Availability Statistics Using Different Relevant Labor Markets   **EXHIBIT 5.2**

	% of Labor Force in U.S.	% of Managers in U.S.	% Of Managers in Utah
White	86.4	92.3	96.3
Black	10.7	5.2	.3
Hispanic	6.9	3.7	2.1
Women	44.5	36.8	26.3

SOURCE: Abstracted from 1986 Utah Affirmative Action Information, Utah Department of Employment Security.

Once the relevant labor market has been determined, it is subject to revision because of changing demographic characteristics of the U.S. labor force. Organizations will probably see dramatic demographic changes based on comparisons of the 1980 and 1990 national censuses. As a result of these comparisons, organizations will have to redetermine their relevant labor markets to successfully defend AAPs and refute *prima facie* cases of discrimination.

The third basis for establishing a case of disparate impact uses **concentration statistics.** The argument here is that a *prima facie* case of illegal discrimination exists to the extent that protected group members are all located in one particular area or job category in the organization. For example, equal numbers of male and female employees may be in entry-level jobs in the organization, but the females may be predominantly in secretarial jobs. Such a situation provides a case of disparate impact, but the plaintiff may also need to show that specific policies created the disparities (*Wards Cove Packing v. Atonio,* 1989).

Disparate Treatment.   Illegal discrimination against an individual is referred to as **disparate treatment.** In contrast to cases of disparate impact, a *prima facie* case of disparate treatment exists to the extent that an individual can demonstrate the following:

- The individual belongs to a minority group.
- The individual applied for a job for which the employer was seeking applicants.
- Despite being qualified, the individual was rejected.
- After the individual's rejection, the employer kept looking for people with the applicant's qualifications.

These conditions were set forth in *McDonnell Douglas Corp. v. Green* (1973).

Bases for Defending Illegal Discrimination

Once a *prima facie* case of illegal discrimination is shown, the **burden of proof** (also called the **burden of persuasion**) shifts to the defendant. The defendant must demonstrate that the decision was based on a legitimate nondiscriminatory reason using any of the five defenses summarized below.

Job Relatedness.   Employee qualifications are necessary for many jobs. Thus, employers are interested in measuring them and establishing predictions as to how employees who possess them will "do on the job." To demonstrate **job relatedness,** the company must show that its selection and placement procedures (predictors) are related to an employee's being successful on the job (*Watson v. Fort Worth Bank and Trust,* 1988).

It is important to note, however, that any test used must be related to *important components of the job* as determined through job analysis. For example, a typing test may be an appropriate selection device for a clerk-typist who spends 60 percent of his or her time on data entry. However, it would not be an appropriate selection device for a receptionist who spends less than 5 percent of his or her time on typing.

Business Necessity.   Although showing the job relatedness of a selection procedure is desirable, it may not always be possible. Some courts, recognizing this situation, have allowed companies to defend their selection procedures by showing **business necessity.** Whereas the job-relatedness defense often requires a demonstration of actual predictor-performance relationships, business necessity does not. The decision in *Levin v. Delta Air Lines* (1984) was based on the fact that pregnancy was not shown to affect the essence of the business (safe air travel)—not on the fact that pregnancy failed to affect the ability of a flight attendant to provide service to travelers. In cases in which business necessity clearly is great, demonstrating that a specific selection procedure is job related is not necessary (see *Spurlock v. United Airlines*, 1972, and *Hodgson v. Greyhound Lines* (1974).[18]

Bona Fide Occupational Qualifications.   Another defense against illegal discrimination is **bona fide occupational qualifications (BFOQs).** For example, the EEOC sued the Massachusetts State Registry of Motor Vehicles, charging that denying entry-level jobs to individuals over age 35 violated ADEA. The state argued that the 1986 ADEA amendment exempts all law enforcement officers from the scope of the act for a seven-year period and that, in any event, age is a bona fide occupational qualification for motor vehicle examiners under *Mahoney v. Trabucco* (1987), which upheld a mandatory retirement age of fifty for Massachusetts state troopers. EEOC countered that few motor vehicle examiners perform active law enforcement duties.

Acknowledging that the issue is a close one, the court agreed with the state that motor vehicle examiners, who are authorized to carry weapons, enforce the state's motor vehicle laws and perform many of the same duties that state and local police officers do, are properly classified as law enforcement personnel, and are therefore exempt from ADEA under the 1986 amendment. Even if they were not covered by the amendment, the court said, the evidence suggests the examiners as a unit satisfy the criteria for an age-based BFOQ under *Mahoney* (*EEOC v. Commonwealth of Massachusetts*, 1987).[19]

Bona Fide Seniority Systems.   Closely related to BFOQs are **bona fide seniority systems.** As long as a company has established and maintained a seniority system without the intent to illegally discriminate, it is considered bona fide (*International Brotherhood of Teamsters v. United States*, 1977; *United States v. Trucking Management*, 1981; *American Tobacco v. Patterson*, 1982). Thus, promotion and job assignment decisions can be made on the basis of seniority.[20] Recently, the U.S. Supreme Court ruled in a major decision that seniority can be used in determining which employees to lay off, even if doing so reverses the effects of affirmative action hiring (*Firefighters Local Union 1784 v. Stotts*, 1984).

Voluntary Affirmative Action Programs.   Organizations may establish **affirmative action programs** (AAPs) without pressure from the EEOC or the OFCCP. For these programs to serve as a defense against illegal discrimination, however, they need to be remedial in purpose, limited in duration, restricted in impact, flexible in implementation, and minimal in harm to innocent parties. Although charges of reverse discrimination have resulted from the implementation of voluntary AAPs, the courts appear to be sympathetic to these AAPs, particularly if their impact is on the hiring of new employees, rather than on the laying off of current employees (*Wygant v. Jackson Board of Education*, 1986). The courts are also sympathetic to the defense of AAPs established by consent decrees (*International Association of Firefighters Local 93 v. City of Cleveland* 1986).

Because of a 1989 Supreme Court ruling (*Wards Cove Packing v. Atonio*), the shifting burden of proof model in disparate impact cases may no longer apply. In the *Wards Cove* case, concentration statistics were used to demonstrate disparate impact. Challenging the viability of concentration statistics, the Supreme Court ruled that in this particular instance, the burden of proof should *not* shift to the defendant. Instead, it is up to the plaintiff to show that the practices they were challenging were in fact unnecessary. Thus, the court said that when concentration statistics are used to prove disparate impact, the burden of proof *remains* with the plaintiff and does not shift to the defendant.

What is still undetermined is just how far–reaching this ruling is. Representatives for business groups who filed briefs in this case contend that the decision provides long overdue relief from the threat of costly litigation and defense. They also speculate that the ruling lays the groundwork for business to challenge *all* disparate impact cases—regardless of the method used to show disparate impact.

Civil rights lawyers prefer to interpret the decision in a narrower sense. They stress that the court's ruling only applies to those cases which rely on concentration statistics. Cases showing disparate impact through comparative statistics or relevant labor market comparisons are *not* affected by the decision. Thus, until more legal challenges are presented, it is unclear just how far–reaching the *Wards Cove* ruling really is and what the long term ramifications will be.

Alternative Procedures

In phase III of a discrimination suit the burden of proof is again with the plaintiff. In cases of disparate impact, the plaintiff must identify a less discriminatory alternative that is equally as job related as the challenged practice (*Texas Department of Community Affairs v. Joyce Ann Burdin*, 1981). This is called the **alternative procedures requirement**.

In cases of disparate treatment, the plaintiff must produce evidence that the motive was discrimination. This means that the plaintiff must establish **intent**—not an easy aspect to prove. However, supporting evidence in the form of memorandums and policy statements that disparage protected groups has been accepted as evidence.

CONSIDERATIONS IN CHOOSING SELECTION TECHNIQUES

In choosing the right selection devices to use, several technical factors need to be considered, including the choice of predictors and criterion scores and the relative usefulness of different devices.

Predictors

Selection decisions are generally made on the basis of job applicants' **predictor** scores. These scores predict how well applicants will perform. While a wealth of selection devices (background information, paper-and-pencil tests, work simulations, physical tests, interviews) can be used to predict job performance, the usefulness of these devices depends on their reliablility and validity.

Reliability. The **reliability** of a measurement device is the degree to which it produces dependable or consistent results. Unreliable measurements produce one set of results at one time and a different set of results at another. When a selection device yields equivalent results time after time, it is considered reliable. For example, tests of physical attributions (height, weight, hearing) tend to be more reliable than tests of personality characteristics (neuroticism, flexible thinking, emotional stability).

Two types of reliability are relevant to selection. Consider a cognitive ability test administered to a hundred job applicants. It would be reliable if you retested these job applicants and received similar results the second time. This form of reliability is called **test-retest reliability. Interrater reliability** focuses on the consistency of ratings by different individuals. For example, unstructured interviews tend to be unreliable, with multiple interviewers perceiving the same applicant dissimilarly.[21]

Validity. The term **validity** refers to how well a measure actually assesses an attribute. The validity of a measure is not absolute; rather, it is relative to the situation in which the selection device is being used. For example, a test of aggression may be a valid predictor of police performance, but it may be useless in predicting job success for machinists. Chapter 16 discusses in more depth the different approaches to validating selection devices.

Mathematically, validity refers to the correlation between the predictor score (selection device) and a criterion (job performance, job rating, number of absences, tardiness, or worker compensation claims). Recall from basic statistics that a correlation coefficient can range from -1.00 to 1.00. The closer the correlation coefficient to the absolute value of 1.00, the more valid the selection device. For example, work simulation tests have been shown to have average validity coefficients up to .47. This is substantially higher than the average validity coefficients of .14 for interview. [22]

Criterion Scores

The type of criterion against which a selection device is validated can vary greatly. At one end of the spectrum are direct measures of output (e.g., number of widgets produced, number of trades, number of absences, number of grievances). Unfortunately, for many jobs, direct output measures do not exist. Consequently, performance appraisal ratings become the criterion. As will be discussed in Chapters 6 and 7, performance ratings need to be based on job-related criteria if they are to be useful and valid measures of performance.[23]

SELECTION TECHNIQUES

A variety of selection techniques are available for obtaining applicant information. As Exhibit 5.3 shows each selection technique varies in terms of costs, the number of firms using them, and their usefulness as predictors.[24]

Application Blanks and Background Information

Premised on the assumption that past behavior is a good predictor of future performance, the application blank is a form seeking information about the

EXHIBIT
5.3

Comparison of Costs and Benefits of Various Common Selection Devices

Type of Test	Cost	% of Firms Using Device	Validity
Cognitive ability test	$5.00– $100.00	42	.53
Situational interview	25.00– 50.00	5–20	.54
Work sample test	50.00– 500.00	75	.44
Assessment center	50.00– 2000.00	6	.44
Biodata	5.00– 25.00	11	.37
Background check	100.00– 500.00	8–15	.26
Experience rating	5.00– 50.00	(no data)	.18
Standard interview	25.00– 50.00	70	.07
Interest inventory	25.00– 50.00	5	.10
Education rating	5.00– 50.00	(no data)	.10
Personality test	1.00– 100.00	5	.10–.25
Handwriting analysis	50.00– 250.00	5	.00
Polygraph test	25.00– 50.00	6	.00
Drug screening	35.00– 90.00	25	(varied estimates)
Alcohol screening	10.00– 35.00	13	(varied estimates)
Genetic screening	35.00– 450.00	1	(varied estimates)

SOURCES: Bureau of National Affairs, "Employee Selection Procedures," ASPA–BNA Survey No. 45, 5 May 1983; J. E. Hunter and R. F. Hunter, "Validity and Utility of Alternative Predictors of Job Performance," *Psychological Bulletin* no. 96, 1, (1984): 93; T. Janz, "Initial Comparisons of Patterned Behavior Description Interviews Versus Unstructured Interviews, *Journal of Applied Psychology* 67 (1982): 577–80; J. D. Olian "New Approaches to Employment Screening: Body Over Mind," in *Readings in Personnel and Human Resource Management*, 3d ed., ed. R. S. Schuler, S. A. Youngblood, and V. L. Huber (St. Paul MN: West, 1988); 206–16.

applicant's background and present status. Usually this information is used as an initial or preemployment screen to decide if the candidate meets the minimum job requirements. While not prohibited per se, many traditional questions are now considered "red flags" of discrimination and should be avoided because of their *potential* for producing adverse impacts.[25]

- *Demographic Information.* Questions related to race should be strictly avoided. Because characteristics related to age, sex, religion, and national origin are difficult to prove as BFOQs, questions regarding them should also be avoided. Proof of age and citizenship can be required after hiring.
- *Commitments.* Questions about marital status, dependents, spouse's job, and child-care arrangements need to be asked of *both* men and women and given *equivalent* weight if they are asked at all. It is acceptable to ask if applicants have any social, family, or economic responsibilities that would prevent them from performing job duties.
- *Arrests and Convictions.* Inquiries about arrest records are not permissible under *any* conditions because minorities are often arrested (not necessarily convicted) more frequently than whites. An employer may ask about convictions.
- *Disabilities.* Disabilities may be considered, but general inquiries should be avoided. It is acceptable to ask if there are any disabilities that would interfere with the ability to perform a specific job or if special accommodations are needed.

- *Physical Requirements.* Height and weight measurements are acceptable for a *few* jobs. Care should be taken to ensure that physical requirements (such as height and weight) are valid because they tend to discriminate against Hispanics, Asians, and women.
- *Affiliations.* Catchall questions about organization affiliations (e.g., country clubs, fraternal orders, lodges) should be avoided. However, it is acceptable to ask about *professional* memberships that relate to specific jobs.

The accuracy of applicant-generated information is also a concern. Verified Credentials, Inc., reports that almost 30 percent of the résumés it checks contain false information. Distortions vary from a wrong starting date for a prior job to inflated college grades to actual lies involving degrees, types of jobs, and former employers. The most common distortions relate to length of employment and previous salary.[26]

Biographical Information Blank (BIB) and Other Tests.   In addition to the application blank, or even as a substitute for it, employers may administer a **biographical information blank** (BIB). A BIB generally requests *more* information from the applicant than an application blank does. For example, in addition to requesting information about name, present address, references, skills, and type of education, the BIB may request the applicant to indicate a degree of preference for such things as working split shifts, being transferred, working on weekends, or working alone. Exactly which items are asked should be based on the nature of the job. If the job does require split-shift work, a BIB item that indicates any preference for split shifts may be a good predictor of turnover.[27]

Biodata tests appear to be good predictors of job success (see Exhibit 5.4) and generally have less adverse impact on minorities than many standard tests do. Consider the settlement reached in a recent discrimination suit against the Suffolk County (N.Y.) police department, one of the nation's largest police forces. The police department's unvalidated qualifying examination had an adverse impact on blacks, Hispanics, and females. Under the consent decree that settled the suit, the county agreed to offer the chance to take a biodata test to women and minorities who had taken the earlier test.

This new biodata test calls for applicants to answer autobiographical questions on such subjects as academic achievement, work attitudes, physical orientation, and self-perception. According to Frank Erwin, president of Richardson, Bellows, Henry & Co., which developed the selection device, biodata tests reduce by more than half the scoring differences that routinely result between whites and minorities on traditional general aptitude or intelligence tests (*United States v. Suffolk County,* 1986).

Education and Experience Evaluations.   As part of the initial application process, applicants often complete a form that details their educational achievements and work experience. Validity evidence indicates that education requirements are predictive of job tenure (the average correlation of performance is .10). Like education, experience requirements may be useful in selecting individuals for high-level, complex jobs but not for jobs that require short learning periods (the average correlation is .18).

What is questionable is the *extent* of education and experience required for a specific job. In order to narrow down the application pool, some organizations impose inordinately high experience requirements (e.g., five years or more).

Similarly, higher levels of education than needed are required for many jobs. These requirements serve as artificial barriers to minority, applicants, who generally have less opportunity to acquire education and experience than whites do.[28]

Handwriting Analysis.   In addition to the application blank, an employer may request a special handwriting sample. Handwriting analysis, or graphology, is used by 85 percent of all European companies and is catching on in the United States. An estimated 2,000 to 2,500 U.S. employers use graphology as a selection device.

> The factor most contributing to graphology's growing acceptance is the "chorus of praises by companies that have used the tool and found it works," says Marlais Mayotte, a graphoanalyst certified by the International Graphoanalysis Society in Chicago, Ill. (IGAS is the primary provider of graphology training in the U.S.).
>   Graphology is based on the premise that the strokes of a person's handwriting are subconscious expressions of the individual's personality. In developing their assessments, graphologists examine such items as the slant or angle of letters in a handwriting sample; the spacing between letters and words; the size, shape and length of letters; and the way the writer uses the space on the sheet of paper. While an analysis cannot determine age, sex, or race, it can identify up to 300 different character traits.[29]

Despite the testimonials, there is *no* scientific evidence that graphology can predict job performance. In one controlled study of sales success, applicants provided handwriting samples, and graphologists predicted job success. While there was limited evidence of interrater agreement on observed character traits, there was no relationship between the assessments and three measures of job performances (sales productivity and self- and supervisory performance ratings). Graphology also is costly ($50–$250), considering its poor predictive ability. Therfore, it is *not* recommended as a selection device.

Reference Verification.   Because some job applicants falsify their past and current qualifications, employers are stepping up efforts to check references thoroughly. Instead of relying on unstructured reference letters, which are always positive, some organizations are using outside investigators to verify credentials, others are personally contacting prior employers to get reference information firsthand, and still others have structured the reference process to acquire *only* job-specific information (goals, accomplishments, degree of supervision).

One reason for the increased rigor in reference checking is that reference checks, if done correctly, are quite predictive of performance. Another reason revolves around the recent spate of negligent hiring lawsuits. Consider the following typical case:

> A woman raped by a cable television installer . . . sued the installer's employers—a cable television franchise and its independent contractor. She claimed that they gave the installer a master key to her apartment, which he used to enter her dwelling on the night of the attack. Because his employers gave him a master key to the apartments, the woman argued that they owed their customers a special duty to ensure that he was not a violent criminal. But they had failed to check his criminal record. The employers settled out of court for $250,000.[30]

Samples of Cognitive Ability and Psychomotor Tests

EXHIBIT
5.4

Verbal Comprehension involves understanding the meaning of words and their relationship to one another. It is measured by such test items as

> Which one of the following words means most nearly the same as *dilapidated:*
> (1) new   (2) injured   (3) unresponsive   (4) run-down   (5) lethargic

Word Fluency involves the ability to name or make words, such as making smaller words from the letters in a large one or playing anagrams. For example,

> Using the letters in the word "measurement," write as many four-letter words as you can in the next two minutes.
>
> _____   _____   _____
>
> _____   _____   _____

Number Aptitude involves speed and accuracy in making simple arithmetic calculations. It is measured by such test items as

> Carry out the following calculations:
>
> $\begin{array}{r} 429 \\ +762 \end{array}$ $\begin{array}{r} 7983 \\ -6479 \end{array}$ $721 \times 52 = $ _____ $4920 \div 6 = $ _____

Inductive Reasoning focuses on the ability to discover a rule or principle and apply it to the solution of a problem. The following is an example:

> What number should come next in the sequence of five numbers?
> 1   3   6   10   15
> (1) 22   (2) 21   (3) 25   (4) 18

Memory relates to having the ability to recall pairs of words or lists of numbers. It is measured by such test items as

> You have 30 seconds to memorize the following pairs. When the examiner says stop, turn the page and write the appropriate symbols after each of the letters appearing there.
> A @   C #   E△   G ?
> B >   D *   F +   H $

Perceptual Speed is concerned with the ability to perceive visual details quickly and accurately. Usually these tests are timed and include such items as

> Make a check mark in front of each pair below in which the numbers are identical. Work as fast as you can.
> 1. 755321-------753321
> 2. 966441-------966641
> 3. 334579-------334579

Motor Skill—Aiming involves the ability to respond accurately and rapidly to stimuli. For example,

Place three dots in as many circles as you can in 30 seconds.
O O   O   O   O   OO   O   O

SOURCE: Modified from M. Dunnette, *Personnel Selection and Placement* (Monterey, Calif.: Brooks/Cole Publishing, 1966: 47-49).

Unfortunately, it is getting more difficult to get information because of the potential for defamation of character suits (discussed in Chapter 14). Previous employers are becoming "street-smart" and consequently are limiting the type of information they give out about former employees. However, reference checks of an applicant's prior employment record are not an infringement on privacy if the information provided relates specifically to work behavior and to the reasons for leaving a previous job.

Written Tests

Written testing is another important procedure for gathering, transmitting, and assembling information about applicants. The most common types of written tests measure ability (cognitive, mechanical, and psychomotor), personality, and interests and preferences.

Cognitive Ability Tests.   Ability tests measure the potential of an individual to perform, given the opportunity. Used in the United States and Europe since the turn of the century, these devices are useful and valid (see Exhibit 5.3). Recent studies further suggest that they are equally valid for black and white applicants and that their use can be generalized to different jobs in different situations. Exhibit 5.4 shows sample items for measuring seven types of cognitive abilities.

Tests have also been developed to measure special abilities. For example, sensory tests measure the acuity of a person's senses, such as vision and hearing. These tests may be appropriate for such jobs as wine taster, coffee bean selector, quality control inspector, and piano tuner. Clerical tests focus primarily on perceptual speed. However, specific tests such as the Minnesota Clerical Tests measure these skills in a job-relevant context. Standard Oil has developed a cognitive ability test of management reasoning and judgment, while other firms have developed programmer aptitude tests.[31]

Psychomotor Tests.   Many jobs involve not only a wide range of cognitive abilities but also psychomotor skills. For example, a bank teller needs the motor skills necessary to operate a computer or a ten-key calculator and the finger dexterity to manipulate currency.

There are a variety of psychomotor abilities, each of which is highly specific and shows little relationship to other psychomotor abilities *or* to cognitive abilities. For example, control precision involves finely controlled muscular adjustments (e.g., moving a lever to a precise setting), whereas finger dexterity entails skillful manipulation of small objects (e.g., assembling nuts and bolts).

Ability tests, then, are useful for selecting applicants in many occupations. However, only some categories of ability tests may be predictive of job performance in a specific position.

Personality Tests.   **Personality** refers to the unique blend of characteristics that define an individual and determine his or her pattern of interactions with the environment. While most people believe that personality plays an important role in job success or failure, personality tests have generally not been found viable for employee selection. One reason is that personality variables have not been defined consistently. What we have then is a diverse group of testing devices, each of which was designed to accomplish a different goal, but all of which are called **personality inventories**. The various tests are *not* equivalent, however, in their contruction, their measurement goals, or their underlying theoretical bases.[32] Consequently, inventories often yield different, incompatible, or even conflicting results.

Another problem is that the **wrong types** of personality measurements have generally been used for PHRM selection. The widely used Minnesota Multiphasic Personality Inventory (MMPI) is designed to identify areas of maladjustment. While an appropriate selection device for high-stress jobs (e.g., police, nuclear power plant employees, air traffic controllers), it is not an appropriate selection device for most jobs because the absence of psychopathology does not guarantee the presence of competence. Consequently, an employee can be well adjusted but hopelessly mediocre in performance.

Finally, in highly structured situations controlled by regulations, rules, and guidelines, an individual's personality is unlikely to have an effect. However, in less structured organizations in which individuality and creativity are encouraged, personality attributes are likely to make the difference between job success and job failure.[33]

While less predictive of job success than cognitive ability tests are, carefully developed personality assessments can be inexpensive additions to the selection process for a few jobs. One common multidimensional test of personality that appears useful is the **Ghiselli Self-Description Inventory**. It includes 64 pairs of trait adjectives (equal in social desirability to prevent faking).[34] For each pair, a person is asked to choose the most or least descriptive adjective. Responses are then scored across thirteen personality dimensions (e.g., supervisory ability, decisiveness, achievement motivation) that relate to managerial competence. Ghiselli has shown that successful managers perceive themselves quite differently than unsuccessful managers do on these dimensions. Sample items from the Ghiselli Personality Inventory are as follows

In each of the pairs of words listed below, check the one you think MOST describes you.

| 1 _____ capable | 2 _____ persevering | 3 _____ unaffected |
| _____ discreet | _____ independent | _____ alert |

Interest and Preference Inventories.   While applicants may have the ability to perform in jobs that interest them, interest inventories assess applicants' preferences for different types of work and work situations.[35] Such inventories are useful in matching people to jobs they will enjoy.

Representative items from an interest inventory include the following:

For each set, write an "M" next to the activity you most like and an "L" next to the item you least prefer.

1. _____ go to a concert	2. _____ work in the garden
_____ play tennis	_____ go hiking
_____ read a book	_____ paint a picture

Test Batteries.   It is often beneficial to administer a battery of tests to applicants. The most widely used is the General Aptitude Test Battery (GATB), which measures cognitive abilities—verbal, numerical, spatial, intelligence, form perceptions, clerical perceptions, motor coordination, finger and manual dexterity—and has been found to be useful in matching individuals to a wide array of jobs. Alternatively, an organization can construct its own test battery. For example, Sears has used tests of ability (American Council on Education Psychological Test), values (Allport-Vernon Study of Values), and interest (Kuder Preference Record) since the 1940s to select managers. Similarly, Standard Oil of New Jersey relies on cognitive ability (Miller Analogies, Nonverbal Reasoning, Management Judgment), personality (MMPI), and an individual background survey. Because batteries are difficult to develop, they are usually designed for organizations under the guidance of industrial psychologists.[36]

Work Simulations

Work simulations, often referred to as **work sample tests**, require applicants to complete verbal or physical activities under structured "testing" conditions. Rather than measuring what an individual knows, they assess the individual's ability to do. Still, work sample tests are somewhat artificial because the selection process itself tends to promote anxiety and tension.[37] Exhibit 5.5 shows three sets of work simulation tests.

Because they replicate the actual work, work sample tests are not easy to fake. As a result, they tend to be more valid than almost all other types of selection devices. Additionally, they do not have an adverse impact on minority applicants. Unfortunately, because simulation tests are job specific, they are usually expen-

---

EXHIBIT 5.5   Examples of Physical, Verbal, and Mental Work Sample Tests

Physical

Dental students	Carving Dexterity
Machine operators	Lathe; Drill Press; and Tool Dexterity
Meat scalers	Meat Weighing
Mechanics	Belt and Pulley Installation; Gear Box Repair; Motor Installation and Alignment; Sprocket Reaming
Miners	Two-Hand Coordination
Pilots	Rudder Control; Direction Control; Complex Coordination
Administrative assistants	Word Processing on Specific Equipment; Dictation; Filing

Mental

Magazine editors	Writing Skills; Page Layout; Headline Writing
Administrators	Judgment and Decision Making
Engineers	Processing Mathematical Data
Administrative assistants	Letter Composition; Proofreading

Verbal

Telephone operators	Role Play of Telephone Contacts
Communication specialists	Oral Fact-Finding
Construction supervisors	Construction Error Recognition
Administrative assistants	Telephone Screening

SOURCE: Adapted from J. J. Asher and J. A. Sciarrino, "Realistic Work Sample Tests: A Review," *Personnel Psychology*, 27 (1974): 519–33.

sive to develop unless large numbers of applicants are to be examined. However, by placing work sample tests at the end of a selection process, the number of applicants tested is smaller and the price lower.

Assessment Centers.   This selection device evaluates applicants or current employees with regard to how well they might perform in a managerial or higher-level position. Over twenty thousand companies now utilize this method and its use grows each year because of its validity in predicting which job applicants will be successful and which will be unsuccessful.[38]

An assessment center usually involves six to twelve people who have been chosen or have chosen to attend it. It is most often conducted off the premises by the organization for one to three days. The performance of the attendees is usually rated by managers in the organization who are trained assessors. Typically, the purpose of an assessment center program is to help determine potential promotability of applicants to a first-line supervisor's job.

At a typical assessment center, candidates undergo evaluation using a wide range of techniques. One important activity is the in-basket exercise, which creates a realistic situation designed to elicit typical on-the-job behaviors. Situations and problems encountered on the job are written on individual sheets of paper and set in the in-basket. The applicant is then asked to arrange the papers by priority. Occasionally the applicant may need to write an action response on the piece of paper. The problems or situations described to the applicant involve different groups of people—peers, subordinates, and those outside the organization. The applicant is usually given a set time limit to take the test and is often interrrupted by phone calls meant to create more tension and pressure.

Other tests used in managerial selection are the leaderless group discussion (LGD) and busines games. In the LGD, a group of individuals is asked to discuss a topic for a given period of time. At IBM's assessment center, participants must make a 5-minute oral presentation about the qualifications of a candidate for promotion. During the subsequent group discussion, they must defend their nomination of the candidate with five or more other participants. Participants are rated on their selling ability, oral communication skill, self-confidence, energy level, interpersonal competency, aggressiveness, and tolerance for stress. LGD ratings have been shown to be useful predictors of managerial performance in a wide array of business areas. Additionally, prior experience in LGD does not affect present LGD performance. Business games are living cases. That is, individuals must make decisions and live with them, much as they do in the in-basket exercise.

Because in-baskets, LGDs, and business games tend to be useful in managerial selection, they are often used together in an assessment center.[39] As candidates go through these exercises, their performance is observed by a specifically trained team of observers or assessors drawn from the local management group. After the candidates have finished the program, these assessors meet to discuss the candidates and prepare performance evaluations based on their combined judgments of the candidates in such areas as organizing and planning, analyzing, making decisions, controlling oral communications, conducting interpersonal relations, influencing, and exhibiting flexibility. The composite performance on the exercises and tests is often used to determine an assessment center attendee's future promotability and the organization's human resource planning requirements and training needs, as well as to make current selection and placement decisions. This rating is generally given to the attendee, who in turn can use it for his or her own personal career planning purposes.

Assessment centers have been used effectively in manufacturing companies, government, military services, utility companies, oil companies, the foreign services, and educational institutions. Assessment centers appear to work because they reflect the actual work environment and measure performance on multiple job dimensions. Additionally, more than one *trained* rater with a common frame of reference evaluates each participant's behavior. In terms of cost effectiveness, assessment centers are often criticized as costing too much ($50 to over $2,000 per applicant). However, *annual* productivity gains realized by selecting managers via assessment centers average well above administrative costs.[40]

Interviews

Job offers go to applicants who *appear* most qualified because it is often impossible to determine from available data who really is most qualified. Though appearances can be deceiving, the job interview and the perceptions gained from it still comprise the tool most heavily used to determine who gets the job offer.[41] As shown in Exhibit 5.6, the interview is important at the beginning and the end of the selection procedure.

The reliability and usefulness of the interview really depend on several factors.

Structure.   The unstructured interview involves little preparation. The interviewer merely prepares a list of possible topics to cover and, depending on how the conversation proceeds, asks or does not ask them. While this provides for flexibility, the digressions, discontinuity, and lack of focus may be frustrating to the interviewer and interviewee. More importantly, unstructured interviews result in inconsistencies in the information collected about the candidates.

Alternatively, in a structured interview all applicants are asked the same questions in the same order. While structuring the interview restricts the topics that can be covered, it ensures that the same information is collected on all candidates. As a result, managers are less likely to make snap and possibly erroneous judgments.

A compromise that still minimizes snap judgments is the semistructured interview. Questions are prepared in advance, and the same questions are asked of all candidates; responses are recorded. However, follow-up questions are allowed to probe specific areas in depth. This approach provides enough flexibility to develop insights, along with the structure needed to acquire comparative information.

Job Relevance.   At one extreme, interviewers focus on generalities about qualifications. Such questions help interviewers form an overall impression of the candidate's competence but are not predictive of success in a specific job. A better approach is to use job analysis to generate questions about specific job skills and duties. For example, the critical incident method of job analysis (see Chapter 3) can be used to develop **situational questions** (Exhibit 5.7 illustrates how critical incidents are then transformed into job-specific situational interview questions.)

Systematic Scoring.   Job interviews also vary in the degree to which results are scored. At one extreme, an interviewer merely listens to responses, forms

Possible Steps in the Selection Process

EXHIBIT
5.6

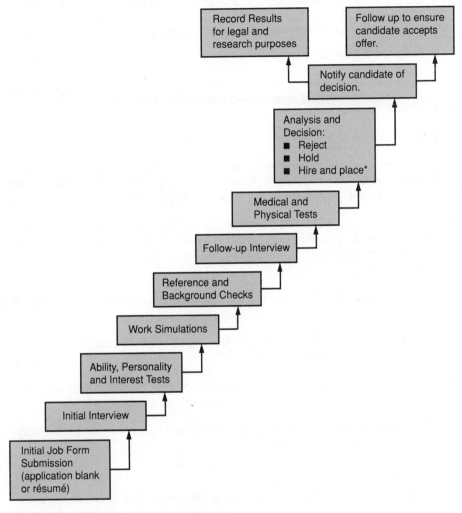

* Note that these decisions could be made in previous steps in the selection
  process; however, they would be based upon less information.

*Note that these decisions could be made in previous steps in the selection process; however, they would be based on less information.

an impression, and makes an accept, reject, or hold decision. Alternatively, raters are given specific criteria and a scoring key to evaluate responses to each question (see Exhibit 5.7). This latter approach is more rational because it helps ensure that applicants are evaluated against the same criteria. Systematic scoring also tends to minimize halo bias, in which an interviewer judges an applicant's entire potential on the basis of a single characteristic, such as how well the applicant dresses or talks.

Number of Interviewers.   Typically, applicants are interviewed by one person at a time. Unfortunately, managers sometimes overlap in their coverage of

Steps in Developing Job-Related Situational Interview Questions

1. Generate the critical incident of good or poor behavior.

"This employee always calls in sick at the last minute for personal reasons."

2. Rewrite the incident as a situational interview question.

"Your husband and children are all sick with the 24-hour flu. Your husband urges you to stay home and take care of them. It's two hours before your shift starts. What do you do?"

3. Develop a weighted scoring key.

Managers and incumbents brainstorm possible answers to the question and then rank them in terms of their appropriateness. Assuming a weight of 5 percent for the situational question above, responses could be scored as follows:

5   "I would call the doctor and see if there is any medication I could get for them before going to work. If it's the flu, there really isn't much I can do by staying home, so I'd go to work as usual. I might call them on break to check on how they are doing."

4   "I'd call the substitution board and see if someone could fill in for me. If not, I'd go to work."

3   "I'd call my supervisor immediately, explain the situation, and stay home and take care of my family. My family comes first."

2   "I'd see if my family got any better in the next two hours. If not, I'd call my supervisor and let him know I won't be coming in due to family sickness."

1   "Because we're allowed so many sick days a year, I'd call my supervisor at the start of my shift and say I was sick."

0   "I'd stay home and take care of my family."

4. *Develop similar questions and scoring keys for all important job duties.*

One of the only three female employees in your group says she is being sexually harassed by some of the male workers. She says the continuous stream of lewd jokes, sexist comments, and pats on the behind are very upsetting. The other two women have not complained. How would you respond?

5. *Total the scores for all questions to arrive at an overall suitability score.*

SOURCE: Adapted from: G. P. Latham, L. M. Saari, E. D. Pursell, and M. A. Campion, "The Situational Interview," *Journal of Applied Psychology* 65 (1980): 422–27.

some job-related questions and miss others entirely. An applicant may have not four interviews, but one interview four times. This is a time-consuming process in which the interviewer's *and* applicant's impressions may vary, depending on what was discussed in the one-on-one interviews. This problem can be overcome by using a **panel interview** in which several individuals simultaneously interview one applicant. Because all decision makers hear the same responses, panel interviews produce more cosistent results. On the other hand, panel interviews are expensive because many people are involved. But, if applicants are to be interviewed by more than one manager anyway, panel interviewing may be more efficient and reliable and as cost effective as individual interviews.

Training.   Left on their own, interviewers tend to form their own impressions based on whatever criteria are most important or salient to them. For example, an applicant might be rejected by one interviewer for being "too aggressive" but accepted by another for being "assertive." Consequently, it is important to train interviewers so that they interpret information consistently.

Frame of reference training, which is also used to reduce inconsistencies in performance ratings, involves teaching interviewers (raters) a common nomenclature for defining the importance of each component of behavior that is to be observed in the interview.[42] This can be accomplished by having potential interviewers develop items and scoring approaches like those in Exhibit 5.7. Alternatively, an interviewer's ratings for "practice" interview questions can be compared to normative ratings given by other interviewers. Such training brings perceptions into closer congruence with those of the rest of the organization.

Medical, Physical, and Polygraph Tests

Although not all organizations require medical exams or physical tests, such tests are being given in increasing numbers. One consequence is a concern about genetic screening as a part of the physical examination process.

Physical Examination.   Because of its high cost, the physical examination is often one of the final steps in the selection process. Many employers give common physical exams to all job applicants, whereas special exams are given to only a subset of all applicants.[43] For example, production job applicants may receive back X-rays, while office job applicants may not. According to the *Uniform Guidelines*, physical examinations should be used to screen out applicants when the results indicate that job performance would be adversely affected.

Guidelines for assessing physical abilities have been developed that detail the sensory, perceptual, cognitive, psychomotor, and physical requirements of most jobs (e.g., police, firefighters, electrical power plant workers, telephone line workers, steel mill laborers, paramedics, maintenance workers, and workers in numerous mechanical jobs). When applied carefully then, these physical requirements (not physical examinations per se) are extremely useful in predicting job performance, worker's compensation claims, and absenteeism. However, arbitrary physical requirements can be a curse, screening out women and minorities who could do a job if given the opportunity. To accommodate handicapped workers, organizations should also explore whether equipment can be "reasonably" adapted to facilitate these workers. Guidelines on inexpensive adaptations for most types of machinery are available from the federal government.[44]

Genetic Screening.   In 1985, there were 390,000 cases of job-related illness and 100,000 deaths. Many of these illnesses and deaths were attributable to chemical hazards. **Genetic screening** identifies individuals who are hypersensitive to harmful pollutants in the work place. Once identified, these individuals can be screened out of chemically dangerous jobs and placed in positions in which environmental toxins do not present specific hazards.[45]

While cost-effective genetic tests have not yet been developed, 1 percent of major firms already use genetic screening, and 15 percent are considering gentic tests in the future. As scientific research on genetic screening continues, the debate over the ethics of basing employment decisions on immutable traits is likely to grow. It also seems probable that pressure will be exerted on organizations to develop engineering controls that minimize or eliminate work place pollutants. These controls would be the preferred alternative to genetic screening, a selection criterion over which which an individual has no control.[46]

Drug and Alcohol Testing.   Alcohol and drug abuse are said to cost American industry more than $100 billion annually. As a result, drug and alcohol testing of job applicants and employees is up, and further increases are likely. According to a survey of 221 organizations conducted by the American Society for Personnel Administrators, more than 25 percent of the 1986 *Fortune* 500 companies required job applicants to submit to urinalysis for drug use and 13 percent for alcohol use. These percentages are expected to increase, the survey says, noting that more than half (53.8) percent) of the companies polled said they are considering adding new tests.[47]

Despite the increase in drug and alcohol testing,

> An employer "is asking for trouble," asserts Robert DuPont, vice-president of Bensigner, DuPont, and Associates, if it follows a policy of "we're just going to test people, period." DuPont notes that there are three levels of drug testing. The first and least controversial level is preemployment testing; the second is testing conducted on a "for cause" basis—e.g., when an accident or serious problem has occurred; and the third is the seldom used policy of random testing of all current employees. There have been a number of problems with the accuracy and credibility of drug testing programs, DuPont adds, stressing that employers must make sure that a "chain of custody" is established with respect to urine test results and that positive test results are rechecked with a confirming test. If a urinalysis testing lab does not provide these two services, DuPont says, "the employer should look elsewhere."[48]

Two newer methods of testing for drug abuse appear promising. Developers of the Veritas 100 scanner have correlated brain-wave patterns with numerous chemicals (e.g., tranquilizers, cocaine, alcohol, marijuana) and claim close to 100-percent validity for the technique. While not generally available yet, this is a promising alternative to traditional urinalysis. Similarly, hair analysis is considered a positive development.

> The test involves radioimmunoassay analysis of drug metabolites permanently embedded in hair. By testing workers' hair, rather than requiring them to provide urine samples, employers can avoid invasion-of-privacy and intentional-infliction-of-emotional-distress claims. Moreover, employees cannot tamper with hair samples in an effort to conceal drug use.[49]

Regardless of what methods are used for drug testing, a key issue in adopting a drug policy is establishing that drug use impairs performance. A description of this issue, along with pointers for adopting a drug policy, is presented in the second "PHRM in the News" feature.

AIDS Testing.   AIDS victims are protected by the Rehabilitation Act of 1973 (*Chalk v. U.S. District Court for Central District of California*, 1987). Because

Drug Policy Pointers

Drug testing policies that hinge on the concept of impairment may be unenforceable, suggests David A. Copus, a Washington, D.C., management attorney with Jones, Day, Reavis & Pogue. Addressing a conference on employment law co-sponsored by BNA and the National Employment Law Institute, Copus asserts that many of the problems employers have with drug testing policies stem from the fact that it's impossible to measure impairment from drugs.

Setting Enforceable Drug Policies

A drug test won't tell you if or when a worker's physical or mental faculties are impaired, only that the employee has tested positive or negative for drug use, Copus explains. Consequently, he adds, if your policy relies on impairment and you can't make the connection between impairment and drug use, the policy may be challenged as unenforceable.

The question for employers, Copus maintains, should not be whether impairment exists, but when disciplinary action can be taken. If a drug policy does not state specifically that disciplinary action will be taken when an employee tests positive for drug use, there's no reason to test. Drug testing doesn't make sense if you're not willing to take disciplinary action based on a confirmed positive test result. Copus tells employers. He adds that a policy calling for discipline in such a circumstance doesn't have to require termination. Rehabilitation can be required as an alternative.

Employer Checklist

Copus offers employers an extensive checklist for determining whether and how to establish an enforceable substance abuse policy. His recommendations include:

■ Decide whether the company's policy will be to discipline or rehabilitate employees who test positive for drug use. In addition, identify which job applicants or employees will be covered, specify the circumstances under which testing will be conducted, and determine appropriate penalties for different kinds of drug-related offenses.

■ Clearly state the policy in writing; then, prior to implementation, inform applicants and employees about the circumstances under which screening will be required, the uses of test results, and the penalties for policy violations. Also, broadly define the substances covered by your policy.

■ Differentiate between employees and job applicants by preparing separate written policies.

■ If you maintain one position on alcohol abuse and a differenct one on drug abuse (e.g., the former leads to rehabilitation, the latter to discharge), provide separate policies and state your rationale for doing so.

■ Specify prohibited conduct. Cover the use, possession, or sale of alcohol or drugs on company premises and during work hours; the unauthorized use, possession, or sale of a controlled substance; being under the influence of either legal or illegal drugs or alcohol; the use, possession, or sale of alcohol or drugs off-premises that adversely affects work performance, safety, or the employer's reputation; switching or adulterating urine samples provided for testing; and refusing mangement's request to provide a urine sample for testing.

■ Make sure that testing is performed by a reputable, independent laboratory, under the direction of a board-certified toxicologist. The laboratory should be accredited and maintain state-of-the-art quality control.

■ Determine, in consultation with the laboratory, what cutoff level will result in a positive test finding; state the standard in writing; and advise employees of the standard.

■ Confirm a positive test with a second test that is at least as sensitive, and preferably more specific than the first, and rely on the results of the second test.

continued

- Reserve the right to conduct drug tests or search company property and personal effects placed in company property, based on a reasonable suspicion of the presence of drugs or alcohol.
- Obtain employees' consent to be tested prior to screening; however, avoid stating that a refusal to give consent or be tested creates a "resumption" of intoxication or drug use.
- Give employees the opportunity to list any drugs they have taken within the last 30 days and to explain why they have used the drugs.

- Inform employees of their test results, and give them a chance to explain or challenge a positive test result.
- Document workers' performance deficiencies.
- Where employees are given a chance at rehabilitation, state in your policy the conditions for receiving rehabilitative treatment, as well as the conditions for post-rehabilitation monitoring and testing.

SOURCE: "Drug Policy Pointers," *Bulletin to Management*, 7 Jan. 1988, p. 8. Used by permission of *Bulletin to Management*, copyright 1988.

AIDS is such a major challenge in today's work place, organizations are establishing guidelines concerning it. Companies such as IBM, AT&T, and Johnson & Johnson have endorsed these guidelines:

- People with AIDs or who are infected with HIV, the AIDS-causing virus, are entitled to the same rights and opportunities as people with other serious illnesses.
- Employment policies should be based on the scientific evidence that people with AIDS or HIV infection do not pose a risk of transmitting the virus through ordinary workplace contact.
- Employers should provide workers with sensitive and up-to-date education about AIDS and risk reduction in their personal lives.
- Employers have the duty to protect the confidentiality of employees' medical information.
- Employers should not require HIV screening as part of general pre-employment or workplace physical examinations.[50]

Lie Detector Tests. With the passage of the Employee Polygraph Protection Act of 1988, employers are restricting their use of **polygraph** or **lie detector tests**. In passing the law, supporters of polygraph restriction claim that the tests are accurate only two-thirds of the time and are far more likely to be inaccurate for honest employees. The new law restricts preemployment screening and random use of the device. Congressional estimates are that the law will reduce polygraph testing by 85 percent. Other provisions of the law are as follows:

- Permits private security firms and drug companies to continue to administer polygraph tests to job applicants and employees
- Exempts federal, state, and local government employers from the ban on polygraph testing
- Prohibits employers from disciplining, discharging, discriminating against, or denying employment or promotions to prospective or current workers solely on the basis of polygraph test results
- Provides that employers that violate any *provision* of the law may be assessed a civil penalty of up to $10,000[51]

Honesty Tests.   Partly as a response to regulatory prohibitions on employers' use of polygraphs, the use of **paper-and-pencil honesty tests** has increased.

> A record 2.3 million employment applicants were given "honesty" tests last year, up from one million in 1981, estimates James Walls, a marketing vice president at Stanton Corp., a psychological testing concern.
>
> Stanton's own evaluations underscore why employers are using the tests more frequently. Thirty-two percent of the employment applicants the company screened last year admitted on signed statements that they had stolen from a previous employer, up from 12% two decades ago. Similarly, a recent survey of 9,000 employees by the Justice Department found that one-third admitted stealing from their current or previous employers.
>
> "More and more employees today have a negative attitude toward their employers," says E. John Keller, a security consultant at Arthur Andersen & Co., the accounting firm. "There's a direct correlation between low morale and high theft." . . .
>
> Sometimes simply giving a test can help solve a company's problems. A convenience food-store chain recently gave an honesty test to a few hundred employees, who were given instructions on how to correct the test themselves. Their exposure to the test and the process of self-correction, according to Mr. Keller, prompted an immediate two-thirds reduction in inventory theft.[52]

Despite endorsements from industry, honesty tests have not been subject to careful validation and are therefore not recommended as a selection device. Depending on the cutoff score an organization chooses to use, anywhere from 25 to 75 percent of job applicants will fail an honesty test. Thus, many people will suffer negative employment repercussions as a result of these tests.[53]

METHODS OF USING INFORMATION FOR SELECTION AND PLACEMENT DECISIONS

As shown above, a variety of devices are available to make selection decisions. The choice of devices depends on job relatedness, related costs, and time constraints. If more than one predictor is used, a decision must be made regarding the order in which selection devices will be administered and how information from the various sources should be combined. Additional considerations center on controlling bias associated with making selection decisions.

The Single Predictor Approach

When only one piece of information is used to make selection decisions, personnel and human resource managers are using the **single predictor approach**. Single predictors are useful for unskilled, simple, or repetitive jobs in which one duty is most important or time consuming.

> A few hiring tests are easy enough to validate, especially those in which the candidate actually performs a task he/she will have to perform on the job. It makes obvious good sense, for example, to require a candidate for a secretarial job to pass a typing test, and generally the equal-opportunity establishment accepts such tests.

The Multiple Predictor Approach

When there is more than one selection device, information can be combined in three ways.

Multiple Hurdles Approach.   In a **multiple hurdles** approach an applicant must exceed fixed levels of proficiency on all the predictors in order to be accepted. A score lower than the cutoff score on one predictor (test) cannot be compensated for by a higher-than-necessary score on another predictor. Underlying this approach is the assumption that a specific skill or competency is so critical that inadequacy guarantees the person will be unsuccessful on the job. This assumption legitimately applies for some physical ability requirements (visual acuity for pilots) and for state-mandated licensing requirements (state licensure for nurses).

Previously, organizations believed that they could construct a multiple hurdles system and escape liability by applying what is called the **bottom line rule**. The rule presumes that an adverse impact found in one component of a selection process (written examination) can be neutralized by favorable treatment overall. Unfortunately, the Supreme Court has ruled that the bottom line rule is no defense when adverse impact is shown for *any* component in a selection process *Connecticut v. Teal*, 1982). Thus it is important to assure that *each* component of selection process does not produce adverse impact.[54]

Compensatory Approach.   Because most jobs do not have truly absolute requirements, a **compensatory approach** is more realistic. This approach assumes that good performance on one predictor *can* compensate for poor performance on another (e.g., a low score on a written examination can be compensated for by a high score on an interview). With a compensatory approach, no selection decisions are made until the completion of the entire process. Then a composite index is developed that takes into consideration performance on all predictors.

The advantage of this approach is that *every* applicant, regardless of race, gets to participate in the *entire* selection process. While more time consuming and costly than a multiple hurdles approach, a compensatory approach is less likely to cause legal problems—provided, that overall hiring rates are equivalent for blacks and whites.

Combined Approach.   Many organizations also use a **combined approach** in which one or more specific requirements (e.g., passing the state bar or CPA examination) must be met. Once these hurdles are jumped, performances on the job remaining predictors are combined into an overall measure of job suitability. Consider college recruiting. Many organizations interview only college students with GPAs that exceed a specific level (first hurdle). To be offered a plant visit, the candidate must then pass a campus interview (second hurdle). At corporate headquarters, the applicant may take aptitude tests, participate in an assessment center, and be interviewed. A composite index that considers performance in all three areas is used to make the final selection (compensatory).

Biases in PHRM Decision Making

In addition to deciding on the order in which selection devices will be administered, managers should make a conscious effort to minimize biases associated with selection. Because of information processing limitations, managers tend to overutilize inferential strategies. As a result, their selection decisions may be biased in a number of different ways. Exhibit 5.8 lists some of the biases that affect selection decisions.

Training.   Despite the susceptibility of PHRM decision makers to these biases, distortions can be minimized in several ways. First, selection biases can be prevented or reduced by direct frontal assault—training decision makers to be aware of and to compensate for their susceptibility to judgmental influences. At a minimum, such training programs need to alert decision makers to the possibility of bias, offer alternative approaches, and give feedback regarding the frequency of bias in their judgments. Unfortunately, because of the range of decision biases, such training may be lengthy and costly.

Decision Aids.   Alternatively, selection biases can be reduced with decision aids. The advantage of decision aids is that they provide an "organizational memory." Because the procedures insulate the decision from the biases of the decision makers, decision aids reduce inappropriate cognitive influences for *any* decision maker who uses them. Decision aids may be as simple as a scoring key for interview questions or as complex as mathematically derived regression equations that indicate how the results from multiple selection devices should optimally be combined.

Unfortunately, few organizations rely exclusively on decision aids. This is because managers do not easily accept the fact that mathematical models provide better predictions than humans do. They contend that the fine nuances of good decision making simply cannot be captured adequately by decision models. This argument is personified in discussions about the viability of the interview as a selection device. Even though the interview is less reliable than cognitive ability tests are, managers persist in using the interview as a primary selection device.

> The argument usually forwarded is that tests really can't assess interpersonal skills (e.g., communication, likeability). Nor can they assess whether the applicant will fit within the organization's culture.
>
> Thus, it appears that removing the possibility of human bias by removing humans from the process may be too large a step at this time.[55]

In sum, when developing a selection process, several questions need to be answered:

- Which predictors are most valid?
- Are predictors correlated with one another? (If so, only one should be used.)
- In what order will predictors be administered?
- How will predictors be scored (multiple hurdles, compensatory, or combined)?
- What strategies will be used to minimize bias in selection decisions?
- Were the desired results attained?

TRENDS IN SELECTION AND PLACEMENT

The trends in selection and placement include assessment of decisions, computer technology, strategic involvement, and expatriate selection.

EXHIBIT
5.8
Description of Cognitive Biases Affecting Selection Decisions

Bias	Definition
1. Illusion of completeness	Decision makers perceive an information set as complete, even in the absence of important information or considerations. Consequently, decisions will be made with incomplete information. For example, a secretary will be selected on the basis of a typing test, even though typing accounts for only 15 percent of work duties.
2. Overconfidence	Decision makers tend to be overconfident in their fallible judgments when answering moderately to extremely hard questions. Personnel and human resource managers have greater confidence in their selection decisions than objectively they should. Recall that the best selection devices (e.g., cognitive ability tests) have a validity coefficient of only .53, which means they account for only 25 percent of the reason someone performs well or poorly on a job.
3. Confirmatory bias	Information that confirms one's hypothesis is taken at face value, while potentially unconfirmatory evidence is subjected to highly critical and skeptical scrutiny. For example, during the initial phase of an interview, a manager makes a judgment about the suitability of an applicant. Information that confirms this judgment is retained, while unconfirming information is more likely to be ignored.
4. Base rate fallacy	Decision makers tend to ignore prior probabilities (base rates) when any—even worthless—situational information is available. For example, in determining whether to use a specific test, managers may fail to consider how many applicants could perform adequately if no test were used. As a result, they may view a test as more useful than it actually is.
5. Law of small numbers	In estimating probabilities, people tend to ignore the importance of sample size and attribute greater stability to results attained from small samples than is warranted. For example, personnel and human resource managers have inappropriately believed that small samples were sufficient to validate a test. Similarly, they have assumed that a 30-minute interview is a representative sample of an applicant's overall job behavior.
6. Framing	Decision makers are likely to treat risks concerning perceived gains differently from risks associated with perceived losses. In the face of losses, they are risk seeking; in the face of gains, risk averse. For example, managers may not narrow down applicant pools sufficiently if they adopt a reject versus an accept selection strategy.
7. Illusion of validity	A good fit between the predicted outcome and input information produces unwarranted confidence. Information that appears consistent (redundant) is weighted more heavily than it should be. For example, managers may erroneously believe that two tests that are highly correlated (e.g., perceptual speed and error detection) predict better than a single predictor or uncorrelated predictors.
8. Anchoring and adjustment	The number of openings to be filled may inappropriately anchor selection decisions. That is, when there is more than one opening to be filled, marginal candidates may be viewed as qualified; if there is only one opening, managers adjust their evaluations upward so that fewer candidates are considered qualified. Consequently, evaluations of candidates are based on the number of openings rather than on the qualifications of the candidates.
9. Career fixation	Following an initial judgment about an applicant's qualifications, an employee is later perceived as incapable of possessing or developing expertise in other areas. As a result, the employee may be pigeon-holed in a particular career track, even when qualified for other positions.

SOURCE: Adapted from: V. L. Huber, G. B. Northcraft, and M. Neale, "Foibles and Fallacies in Organizational Staffing Decisions," in *Readings in Personnel and Human Resource Management,* 3d ed., Ed. R. S. Schuler, S. A. Youngblood, and V. L. Huber (St. Paul: West, 1988); 193–205.

Assessing Selection and Placement Decisions

The quality and effectiveness of selection and placement decisions depend on whether the organization hires applicants who turn out to be good performers. If the organization can select and place applicants who turn out to perform well, organizational productivity will benefit. In addition, if the organization does not select and place applicants who would have performed poorly, organizational productivity will also benefit. The critical point is that when an organization makes selection and placement decisions based on activities that benefit organizational productivity, it is making decisions using predictors that are valid and serve its legal considerations. Using predictors that do not result in selection and placement decisions that benefit productivity is counterproductive and generally is not consistent with legal considerations. Consequently, organizations must use valid predictors. They must also be concerned with the overall costs of the selection devices and weigh these against the benefits.

Because developing valid predictors is a critical activity in personnel research, strategies to validate single and multiple predictors are described in Chapter 16. But obtaining and using valid predictors comprise only part of making effective selection and placement decisions. The other parts include the base rate, the selection rate, the selection ratio, and the overall dollar costs and benefits of the decisions. These are also described in Chapter 16.

Computer Technology

On any given day, a personnel and human resource department will probably evaluate a number of candidates for a variety of positions. Deciding which predictors are relevant (valid) for a particular case and administering a multitude of predictors (tests) make personnel's work challenging. Effective management of predictors is critical in the face of extensive laws and regulations. Doing all of these tasks effectively requires a great deal of information. Computer technology can enhance personnel's ability to coordinate the scheduling, administration, and evaluation of predictors by processing this information in a variety of ways.

For example, personnel could quickly do a validation study by correlating the current job performance data with any of several predictors, if these data were stored in a human resource information system and analyzed by computer. With an HRIS and computers, the utilization rates for affirmative action programs, as discussed in Chapter 4, can also be determined quickly and easily. Results of tests to measure job applicants' skills, knowledge, and abilities, as well as personality, interests, and preferences, can be stored in an HRIS and used together with job analysis data (also in the HRIS) to make better selection and placement decisions. This same information can then be used to help plot career paths for employees when they are hired.

Computers are also being used to reduce **first impression biases** inherent in the interview. Computer-aided interviewing uses a computer to present a structured interview directly to an applicant, without an interviewer present. Although it does not replace the face-to-face interview, it complements it by providing a base of information about each applicant before the interviewer meets the applicant. This provides a first impression based on information that is job relevant rather than anecdotal.

Computer interviewing is also faster. An applicant can complete a one-hundred question computer-aided interview in about twenty minutes. The same information would require a face-to-face interview of more than two hours. In addition to time savings, computer-aided interviewing provides an automatic record of answers, so that they can be compared across applicants. More important, computer-aided interviews have been validated in a number of settings, including manufacturing and service industries.[56]

Strategic Involvement of Selection and Placement

Organizations are increasingly realizing that people make a difference and that different types of people are required to run different types of organizations. They are also learning that the type of culture the organization has influences the type of people it needs. To get the right type of people, organizations can change the criteria that define "successful" and "unsuccessful" to meet their needs. The "International PHRM in the News" feature describes this impact on Pepsi-Cola International.

Gaining Competitive Advantage.   Also growing is the awareness of how staffing can be used for competitive advantage. For example, the American Productivity and Quality Center in Houston utilizes its staffing practices to gain a competitive advantage. Furthermore, it supports its staffing practices with consistent training practices. According to Stu Winby formerly at the Center:

> In hiring consultants we specifically look for the generalist; an individual who has high propensity to learn other areas in the productivity domain; an individual whose appreciation system and skills span both the qualitative and quantitative aspects of productivity and organizational effectiveness. A value of the organization is placed on organizational integration. We promote cross-training and a multi-disciplinary approach to consulting engagements. The competitive advantage is that most members of the consulting staff can "sell" any of the other speciality areas but can also be reasonably effective in the delivery of those specific services.
>
> Against consulting firms that are more specialized and do not seem to have this broad perspective emphasis on hiring generalists and promoting internal integration among consultants has provided competitive advantage.[57]

Expatriate Selection

Although the number of American **expatriate employees** (Americans who work in other countries for U.S. companies) is relatively small, their importance to companies operating in the international markets is relatively great. Without effective expatriate employees—managers and nonmanagers—U.S. companies are essentially unable to operate abroad successfully. Nevertheless, the ineffectiveness of expatriate employees is alarmingly commonplace. Consequently, American-based multinational companies not only need to obtain candidates for expatriate positions but also to ensure they are effective on the job.

A key in selecting any employee is knowing what the job entails. In general, expatriate managers are involved in six major categories of relations: (1) internal relations with their co-workers; (2) relations with their families; (3) relations with the host government; (4) relations with their home government; (5) external

INTERNATIONAL

PHRM IN THE NEWS

Pepsi's Expectations

Pepsi-Cola International always knew it needed a certian kind of savvy, intelligent manager to succeed in the complex world of international production and marketing. But, just to be sure, the international division quantified its values and expectations, says John Fulkerson, hr director for Pepsi-Cola International (Somers, NY).

"We recently studied 100 successful managers and 100 unsuccessful managers, with the help of the Center for Creative Leadership, and came up with 11 qualities that seem to make a differnce in success at Pepsi-Cola International. We looked at very junior to very senior managers over a three year period.

"We were not surprised by any of the qualities - especially the top three:

- The ability to handle business complexities
- The ability to lead and manage people
- Drive and a results orientation. . . .

"All these qualities support our company's success and results orientation, which lies at the heart of our corporate culture. "It sounds hard to maintain a workable corporate culture when doing business across cultures. However, Pepsi International has built a set of values that transcend petty differences and apply to everyone, everywhere. . . .

"What's important is how you treat people. We operate on the principles of telling people what we expect, showing them how to develop and helping them reach the goals. Those ideas work in any of the 150 countries we do business in.

"People are more similar than we think; they want the same things. They want to be successful. That even applies in the Communist bloc countries. After all, they invited us in. They just want to be successful, too.

"Our 1200 international employees help us sell 40 billion 8-ounce servings of Pepsi annually in 145 countries through 16 regional offices. Our people need to be mature and savvy. They must be able to handle complex business issues and understand global issues.

"We need these kinds of people to do business in the complex international arena, and Pepsi-Cola needs people like this to operate in the result-oriented culture that (former Pepsi chairman) Don Kendall pioneered here. We key on results because, especially in international, you quickly learn there are 100 ways to do anything.

"Our culture centers around clear communication of the expected results, and risk taking with no punishment for making mistakes. Along with this expectation that our mature, savvy people will know what to do is another expectation that they'll know when it's time it ask for help. We emphasize the criticality of communication. We make it known that we expect, for example, a manager in Spain to know when its appropriate to check with New York to see what Australia is doing in a certain circumstance. If you talk to others, you lessen the chance of making a mistake.

"Our culture also tells managers that being defensive will get you nowhere and that you are not viewed as being mature if you just complain. Things are very open and above board here, and that is even reflected in a formalized personnel program we call "Instant Feedback." It's a system for reinforcing our desire to have constant, quick communication. If there's a problem, we want to be as quickly responsive as we can.

"Some cultures don't like this, and we are flexible. For example, in the Far East, you can't give feedback in front of peers, you wait until you're alone. In Latin American, on the other hand, people are much more vocal in discussing performance issues. They throw it out on the table and it's a jump ball.

"Though we try to emphasize similarities in our culture, and hope that most of our values cut across cultures, we are not unmindful of varying customs in different cultures and religions. We're willing to modify our practices to get results, because wanting results is at the heart of our culture."

SOURCE: *HR Reporter* (July 1987): 4–5. Used by permission of *HR Reporter*, copyright 1987.

relations with the local culture; and (6) relations with the company's head-quarters. Expatriate managers perform their daily activities in the context of the parent company's headquarters, the host country's government, the parent company's government, and a local culture that is often quite different from their home culture. In addition, expatriate managers typically operate in a culture with a different language—a major obstacle for many of them. Thus, for expatriate managers to be successful, they need the skills not only to perform the specific type of job but also to perform the general duties required by these six categories.[58]

Related to the selection of expatriate employees is the more general issue of staffing operations abroad. Typically, expatriate employees fill only a few positions. A majority of the employees are host-country nationals (HCNs) who are usually selected using host-country practices. A growing but still relatively small number of positions are filled by third-country nationals (TCNs), individuals from neither the host country nor the country of the parent firm. They are often selected by the parent firm, using practices similar to those used in selecting expatriates.[59]

INTERNATIONAL COMPARISONS IN STAFFING

Staffing activities in Japan and Germany present alternatives that could be used in the United States. Canada and Australia provide a useful comparison with this country with regard to equal employment and human rights legislation.

Japan

Because of the lifetime employment policy common in Japan, recruitment there is different from recruitment in the United States, where hiring emphasis is on skill or job qualifications. In Japan, emphasis is placed on the general attributes of the person being hired. All regular employees of the corporation are recruited from either the high school graduate or the college and university graduate level and are hired at one time of the year only (in April, immediately after the end of each academic year). Employees not hired at this time are considered "non-regular" employees (that is, they may have been employed by other companies earlier in their careers or self-employed; in short, they are hired at times other than the beginning of their occupational careers). In addition to "regular" and "nonregular" employees, there are temporary employees and part-time workers.

For the most part, company employment policies are directed toward regular employees, and a great competition takes place at the time of the April hiring, both among the companies, which seek to attract the best candidates (tests are given on academic and basic aptitudes), and among the graduates, who wish to align themselves with growth companies.

This division between "regular" employees (estimated to be between 30 and 50 percent of the total national work force) and the nonregular, part-time, and temporary employees makes the lifetime commitment possible despite economic fluctuations. In times of temporary growth or decline, additional temporary workers may be hired or laid off. Alternative solutions for dealing with down cycles that affect the retention of regular workers include shifting employees to new areas of operation or contracting employees out to other companies in more prosperous industries. The transferred employee continues to remain formally affiliated with the original employer in such cases.

In more serious circumstances, temporary layoffs may be required, though according to Japan's labor standards law, workers receive 60 percent of normal salary during this "vacation," or **kyugyo**. However, because Japanese companies pay close attention to the development of long-term trends, they are generally able to predict a leveling off or decline within an industry and adjust their springtime recruitment efforts accordingly.

In their attention to the long term, many Japanese companies are seeing two major trends. One is the need to redeploy and retrain their employees for different industries. For example, Nippon Steel has been shifting employees out of basic steel production and into electronics. The other major trend is adjusting the management of employees under general economic conditions of relatively slow growth in comparison with the past twenty years.[60]

Increasingly, Japanese companies are locating plants and offices in the United States. Selection is viewed by these companies as one of the most critical factors for the success of their operations here. Consequently, they tend to invest a great deal of time and effort in selection.

Germany

An alternative work arrangement that is being used in Germany is the experimental **flexiyear schedule**. Under flexiyear, employees base their work schedule thinking on a year rather than on a day or a week, as is generally the case in flextime or compressed workweek arrangements. Actual implementation of such schedules may vary across organizations, but typically, employees indicate how many hours they want to work each month. Then the employer and the employees together agree on the exact days and hours of the day to be worked. As with many alternative work plans in the United States, a critical advantage of flexiyear schedules is the choice it provides employees. The results thus far are extremely favorable: reduced absenteeism, reduced conflict between work and family for many employees, and increased accommodation of employees' desires for more leisure time.[61]

Canada

In Canada, most companies use techniques of recruiting and selection similar to those in the United States. At the same time, they face significantly different equal employment legislation or, more broadly, human rights legislation. Relatively comprehensive human rights legislation now exists at the federal level and in each of Canada's ten provinces. This legislation follows a common pattern but has specific deviations in each jurisdiction.

The typical Canadian human rights statute prohibits discrimination based on race, color, religion, ancestry, place of origin, marital status, sex, age, or physical handicap, when such discrimination involves employment or trade union membership, services or accommodations that are available to the public, residential or commercial rentals, or public notices.[62] The statute is enforced by a human rights commission, whose staff investigates and conciliates complaints of statute violations. If the commission staff is unable to conciliate a complaint successfully, an ad hoc tribunal or board of inquiry of one or more members may be appointed to hold a public hearing. The commission normally takes the lead in supporting the complaint at this hearing. If the tribunal finds that discrimination has occurred, it can formulate a remedial order. The legislation varies as to whether the tribunal issues the order of recommends the order to either the human rights commission or a designated cabinet minister, who in turn has the authority to issue it. Normally, the order can be enforced by court proceedings and is appealable to a court. Violations of the statutes are also subject to the ordinary penal process, although consent of either the human rights commission or a designated cabinet minister is usually necessary to begin prosecution.

Some uncertainty exists as to what operations are subject to the federal statute and what operations are subject to the appropriate provincial statute. Federally regulated industries, such as banks and interprovincial transportation and communications, are clearly subject to the federal statute. Unlike most comparable federal legislation, however, nothing in the federal statute expressly limits it to such industries, although tribunals under the statute have held that it is implicitly so limited. All other operations are clearly subject to the provincial statutes. The federally regulated industries have sometimes assumed that they are not subject to the provincial statutes, but some case law indicates that the provincial statutes also apply to federally regulated industries.

In addition to protecting basic human rights, the federal statute prohibits discrimination on the basis of criminal conviction where the person has been pardoned.[63] In the case of the physically handicapped, employment discrimination is prohibited, but not other forms of discrimination, and employers are not compelled to renovate their premises to accommodate the handicapped. A unique feature of the federal statute in the area of sex discrimination is that employers are required to provide equal pay for work of equal value. This contrasts with the provincial legislation, which does not affect pay differentials between different jobs as long as there is no ongoing practice of denying access to these jobs because of sex. Penal proceedings for discrimination under the federal statute are possible only where a person violates the terms of an agreed settlement of a complaint. Otherwise, enforcement must proceed through the hearing procedure and, if necessary, court enforcement of the resulting decision.

Australia

The development of equal opportunity (EO) in Australia has been a rather slow process, with community support and awareness gradually increasing. It was not until the South Australian government passed the Sex Discrimination Act in 1975 that formal sex discrimination machinery appeared in Australia. The impetus for this first act was the personal interest of the state premier and the development of a women's lobby group within the Australian Labor Party (ALP). Two other states enacted EO legislation shortly after the act: the New South Wales government passed the Anti-Discrimination Act in 1977, and the Victoria government passed the Equal Opportunity Act in 1977. All three state acts are "complaint-based" legislation that enables individuals to place grievances before a special board or tribunal. The remaining Australian states have considered the implementation of EO legislation in more recent years.

Within the labor union movement, various women's groups developed a Working Women's Charter to guide policy development in the area of equal opportunity. This charter was adopted by congress of the Australian Council of Trade Unions (ACTU) in 1977. The aims and objectives of the charter include the following:

- Equal access to education, training, and vocational guidance
- Quality child-care controlled by parents and employees
- Elimination of discrimination in conditions of employment
- Flexible working hours
- Adequate paid maternity and paternity leave
- Regular on-the-job medical services for workers
- Increased recruitment, training, and participation of female members in trade unions

As these broad aims and objectives show, the main objective of the charter was to serve as a basis for union activity in the EO area. A somewhat similar task was undertaken by the tripartite National Labour Consultative Council (NLCC), which was established as a consultative forum for EO issues. (The NLCC is comprised of representatives of the Commonwealth government, the ACTU, and the Confederation of Australian Industry.) In 1978, the NLCC issued a booklet entitled "Guidelines for Employers—Equal Employment Opportunities for Women," which encouraged employers to adopt EO practices in their organizations.

Thus, by 1980, EO had emerged as an issue which was "on the agenda" in a number of ways. There was EO legislation in three states and federally established national and state committees on discrimination in employment. On the policy level, the ACTU had endorsed the Working Women's Charter, and the NLCC had endorsed the concept of voluntary acceptance by employers of EO practices. EO was not, however, a high-profile issue. By and large, the state EO legislation emphasized conciliation rather than compulsion, and many private sector employers simply ignored this legislation. The effectiveness of the legislation was further reduced because individuals who lodged complaints felt that they might later be victimized in their employment. Feminist groups within the ALP argued that stronger EO legislation was required if significant EO progress was to be made. These views were reflected in the Sex Discrimination Bill, which was introduced in the Commonwealth Parliament in 1983.

The Sex Discrimination Bill of 1983, introduced by the Federal Labor government, had three main objectives:

- To implement provisions of the United Nations Convention on the elimination of all forms of discrimination against women.
- To eliminate discrimination on the grounds of sex, marital status, or pregnancy in the areas of employment; education; accommodation; the provision of goods, facilities and services; the disposal of land; the activities of clubs; the administration of Commonwealth laws and programs; and discrimination involving sexual harassment in the work place and in educational institutions.
- To promote recognition and acceptance within the community of the principle of the equality of women.

This bill contained no proposals for affirmative action because the government felt it more appropriate that the concept of, and proposals for, affirmative action be the subject of public discussion. A discussion paper on affirmative action for women was issued in mid-1984.[64] Considerable opposition arose to the 1983 bill, taking two forms:

- Particular objections to wording, the procedure specified for dealing with complaints, the inclusion of certain types of discrimination, and the use of the external affairs power of the Australian Constitution as the legal basis of the bill

■ General objections to the whole concept of equal opportunity legislation

Despite such opposition, an amended form of the bill was passed as the Sex Discrimination Act of 1984—the first comprehensive federal equal opportunity legislation to cover the Australian work force.[65]

Affirmative action (AA) has remained a politically controversial issue in Australia.[66] In 1984, the federal government released a discussion paper that announced the introduction of a voluntary pilot program whereby a number of organizations, both private and public, would establish AA programs with assistance from a special affirmative action resource unit. In 1986, the program was followed by the Affirmative Action (Equal Opportunity for Women) Act. This legislation requires all private sector companies with more than one hundred employees and all higher education institutions to implement AA programs. Annual reports on the progress of the programs must be submitted to the Office of the Director of Affirmative Action, and a summary report must be made available to the public. It is important to note that the legislation does *not* set any quotas or targets that must be complied with. The only sanction available to the federal government in dealing with uncooperative companies is to name these companies in the federal Parliament and expose them to pressure groups and the influence of public opinion.

SUMMARY

This chapter examines what selection and placement procedures are and how they relate to other personnel activities. It also examines in detail the legal considerations in making selection and placement decisions, such as BFOQs, business necessity, job relatedness, and bases for illegal discrimination. Organizations want to ensure that they hire job applicants with the abilities to meet job demands. Increasingly, they also want to ensure that job applicants will not only perform well but will also stay with the organization. Thus, organizations may want to attain a match between the job applicant's needs and the rewards that the job qualities and organizational context offer.

To match individual knowledge, skills, and abilities to job demands and individual personalities, interests, and preferences to job and organizational characteristcs, organizations need to gather information about job applicants. The three most common methods—interviewing, testing, and application blanks—must operate within legal regulations. These legal regulations are not intended to discourage the use of these methods but rather to ensure that information is collected, retained, and used in recognition of an individual's rights to privacy and an organization's right to select individuals on the basis of legal considerations. Consequently, the types of information and the methods used to obtain information for selection vary according to the type of job for which the applicants are being selected. For example, assessment centers are apt to be used for managerial jobs, and physical ability tests are apt to be used for manufacturing and public health and safety jobs. Exactly how many predictors are used may depend in part on the type of job, but this is also likely to depend on the selection ratio, the costs associated with the selection tests in comparison to their benefits, and the degree of validity and reliability of the predictors being used. Because these are important concerns in personnel research, they are described in more detail in Chapter 16.

Increasingly, U.S. organizations are operating in other countries. For example, over 40 percent of the five hundred restaurants that McDonald's opens each year are overseas. Because the globalization of many U.S. companies is just beginning, gaining information about managing expatriates and learning how other countries manage their employees are likely to be of interest for some time.

DISCUSSION QUESTIONS

1. Once an organization has had a *prima facie* case of discrimination or adverse impact brought against it, what course does the organization have to defent itself?
2. Where does selection and placement information come from, and what is it used for?
3. Although the interview is still the primary method used in selection and placement, what problems arise from its use?
4. Under what conditions is a multiple hurdles selection procedure more viable than a compensatory selection procedure?
5. What is the relationship between validation and reliability?
6. Why are more and more organizations resorting to drug and alcohol testing? How can such tests best be included in the selection process?
7. What is the bottom-line defense to employee selection processes? Is it still a viable alternative? Why or why not?
8. Compare and contrast unstructured, patterned, and situational interviews.
9. What is genetic screening? How might the employer's rights conflict with the individual's rights?
10. Successful selection and placement decisions are dependent on other personnel functions. Identify these functions and their relationships to selection and placement.

CASE STUDY

Metro Transit Company

Metro Transit is located in a metropolitan area of approximately 250,000 persons with bedroom communities bringing the population up to more than a million. Serving more square miles than any other transit company, Metro provides bus service along an eighty-mile corridor covering three counties. As a recipient of several million dollars from the U.S. Department of Transportation, Metro is required to have an affirmative action plan that includes a set of specific and result-oriented procedures, including a utilization analysis of minorities and women.

In order to comply with federal regulations, Metro's general manager, Gaynord Moppitt, hired Heather Miranda eighteen months ago as Metro's first affirmative action officer. Immediately on accepting the position, Heather put in place a written affirmative action policy. Consistent with the guidelines of the Office of Federal Contract Compliance Programs (OFCCP), she also developed a complete internal and external AA policy dissemination program.

In prior years, Metro relied on advertisements placed in the *Daily Planet* and on employee referrals to fill all openings. One of Heather's first goals was to step up the recruitment of women and minorities for positions as bus operators. During the past year, she gave talks about Metro to more than twenty minority and women-oriented organizations and prepared a new recruitment brochure, printed in Spanish and English. Additionally, written notifications of all openings were mailed routinely to more than thirty minority and women-oriented organizations. Advertisements were also included in the *Minority Voice* and in *Network*, a female-oriented newspaper. Her efforts seem to be paying off. The number of minority applicants is up 22 percent over the previous year. Female applications have increased but not nearly as much (5 percent over the previous year).

Now it was time to see if her hard work had paid off. Before her were the results of the utilization analysis that her assistant Raphael Smith had prepared. The report (Exhibit 1) shows the number of

EXHIBIT 1	Adverse Impact Report for Bus Operators at Each Stage of the Selection Process and Cost of Each Selection Device				

Applicant Group	Applied	Passed Test	Passed Interview	Passed Physical	Passed Training
Cost per Applicant	$25	$54	$60	$175	$2,550
Total	676	481 (68%)	350 (73%)	270 (77%)	100 (37%)
Male	591	421 (88%)	310 (74%)	245 (79%)	85 (35%)
Female	85	60 (71%)	37 (62%)	25 (68%)	15 (60%)
Caucasian	569	410 (72%)	313 (76%)	248 (79%)	85 (34%)
Black	10	6 (60%)	5 (83%)	3 (60%)	2 (66%)
Asian	25	18 (72%)	10 (55%)	8 (80%)	7 (88%)
Indian	8	4 (50%)	2 (50%)	0 (0%)	0 (0%)
Hispanic	53	40 (76%)	20 (50%)	11 (55%)	5 (45%)
Withdrawal	4	3	3	25	105

SOURCE: Metro Personnel Information System.

EXHIBIT 2	Population and Employment by Ethnic Group and Sex— 1990 Annual Average for Metro Area		

Ethnic Group or Sex	Total Population	Civilian Labor Force	Employed as Operatives
Both sexes	698,000	349,190	44,917
Female	353,188 (50.6%)	140,520 (42.8%)	11,062 (24.6%)
Caucasian	636,551 (91.2%)	320,202 (91.6%)	38,450 (85.6%)
Black	4,418 (.6%)	1,960 (.6%)	449 (1.0%)
Asian	17,348 (2.5%)	8,708 (2.5%)	1,707 (3.8%)
Indian	4,880 (.7%)	2,064 (.6%)	494 (1.1%)
Hispanic	34,803 (5.0%)	16,256 (4.7%)	3,817 (8.5%)
Total minority	61,449 (8.8%)	28,388 (8.4%)	6,467 (14.4%)

SOURCE: 1990 Census Equal Employment Opportunity File; prepared by State Department of Employment Security.

protected group members who applied to Metro for bus operator positions. Additionally, the report indicates the number of applicants who passed each stage of the selection process (written test, interview, physical, and training). Exhibit 2 provides relevant information on the metropolitan area's labor market. Exhibit 3 and 4 show samples of the items from the written test and questions from the structured interview, respectively. The physical included a drug screening test. The training program lasts four weeks and includes driving on a practice course, role-plays of customer interactions, and route driving under the direction of an operator/coach.

In presenting the data, Raphael exclaimed, "For the two minority groups which account for more than 2 percent of the labor force (Hispanic and Asian), the percentage of applicants who eventually were employed was 9.4 percent and 28 percent. In both cases, the hiring percentage exceeds the representation of these minority groups in the relevant labor market. We're obviously doing better than

---

Sample Items from Written Bus Operator Test

EXHIBIT
3

Customer Relations Sample Question

Please Pick One Answer.

1. As you are driving the bus, you notice in the rear-view mirror that boys in the back of the bus are cutting the seats with a knife. You should:
   a. Ask a passenger near you to tell the boys to stop cutting up the seats. You have to keep driving the bus.
   b. Quickly stop the bus and tell the boys to get off the bus.
   c. Ignore them.
   d. Call dispatch on your radio for police assistance.

Math Skills Sample Question

2. The fare for one adult is 60 cents. The fare for a child is 40 cents. If two adults and three children board the bus, what will the *total* of the five fares be?

   $ _____

Reading Comprehension Sample Questions

Please Read.

Policy and Procedure Manual for Bus Operators
Section 2B Reporting for Duty

A. Operators will be marked "absent" if:
   1. They are more than one (1) minute late for their report time.
   2. They fail to relieve at the proper place and time.
B. Operators will be charged with an "AWOL" if they fail to report for work within four (4) hours of their reporting time without notifying their on-duty dispatcher.
C. Operators will be charged with an unauthorized absence if:
   1. They leave without being excused from their assignment by their supervisor.
   2. They are on report and absent themselves from the Wait Room without the permission of the shift coordinator.

Based on the Policy and Procedures Manual for Bus Operators, answer the following questions:

1. What will an operator be charged with, given the following situation:
   a. The operator's reporting time is 10:15 A.M.
   b. The operator does not report for work until 1:22 P.M.
   The operator will be charged with _____
2. An operator is on report but wishes to run an errand that will take about 10 minutes. The operator needs to leave Metro and drive just a few blocks. What is the operator's responsibility prior to running the errand?

| EXHIBIT 4 | Sample Structured Interview Questions for Bus Operator |

1. Why do you want to be a bus operator for Metro?
2. What qualifications do you believe qualify you to be professional bus operator?
3. Give us four different words to describe yourself.
4. What did you like most (least) about your last job?
5. Metro requires that operators wear a uniform. Would you have a problem with such a restriction? Would you be able to maintain a uniform once it was assigned to you?
6. There is a five-week training program for bus operator positions. Training is held five days a week including every other Saturday and Sunday and begins each day at 6 A.M. During the training period you will be paid minimum wage. Would you have any problem with these restrictions?
7. Part of that training is in class and requires you to read written material and take a written test. Do you believe you would have any problem with the reading, writing, or tests in the training program?
8. This position will initially affect your life outside work in several ways.
   a. It is a six-day work week.
   b. Work assignments are made the day before each workday, making it difficult to plan ahead.
   c. Much of your work is done in split shifts with an early reporting time (5–7:30 A.M.), several hours of free time, and a return to work to do another shift.
   d. There will be no benefits until you move from the reserve board to the B-Board. This could occur within six months or be delayed as long as two years.
   Is this a job you could live with?
9. Metro requires a physical prior to employment. It includes a drug/alcohol screen. Metro takes a strong position against drug use. If you have smoked marijuana in the last four weeks, it will show up on your drug screen. Do not embarrass yourself or make Metro go to the time and expense of a physical if you use any illegal drugs. Do you have any questions about the physical?

most other companies." Eyeballing the utilization report, Heather was not so sure she agreed with Raphael. She needed to spend more time looking at the numbers.

Case Questions

1. How should Heather determine whether her AAP and selection procedures are working?
2. Metro's selection procedure involves multiple hurdles, each of which must be passed for an applicant to be employed. What are the advantages and disadvantages of this approach? Would a compensatory approach be better? Why or why not?
3. Do you agree with Raphael's assessment that Metro is in good shape regarding the representation of protected groups in its work force? Why or why not?
4. Twenty-five applicants dropped out the selection process when they found out they would have to pass a drug test. Do you agree or disagree that Metro should require a drug test as part of its physical screening program for bus operators? Why or why not?
5. Of 270 applicants eligible for Metro's training, 105 (39 percent) dropped out. Is this a problem? Why or why not? What, if anything, could Metro do about the dropout rate?
6. Should any changes be made in Metro's selection process? If so. what do you recommend?

NOTES

1. L. E. Albright, "Staffing Issues," in *Human Resource Management in the 1980s*, ed. S. J. Carroll and R. S. Schuler (Washington, D.C.: Bureau of National Affairs, 1983); R. D. Arvey and R. H. Faley, *Fairness in Selecting Employees* (Reading, Mass.: Addison-Wesley, 1988); H. S. Field and R. D. Gatewood, "Matching Talent with the Task," in *Human Resource Management: Perspectives and Issues*, ed., G. O. Ferris and K. M. Rowland (Boston: Allyn & Bacon, 1988); M. D. Hakel, "Personnel Selection and Placement," *Annual Review of Psychology* 37 (1986): 351–80; N. Schmitt and B. Schneider, "Current Issues in Personnel Selection," in *Research in Personnel and Human Resource Management*, ed. K. M. Rowland and G. D. Ferris (Greenwich, Conn.: JAI Press, 1983); B. Schneider, "The People Make the Place," *Personnel Psychology* (Autumn 1987): 437–54.

2. *Bulletin to Management*, 12 Feb. 1988, p. 15.

3. M. Miner, "Legal Concerns Facing Human Resource Managers: An Overview," in *Readings in Personnel and Human Resource Management*, 3d ed., ed., R. S. Schuler, S. A. Youngblood, and V. L. Huber (St. Paul: West, 1988), 40–56.

4. J. Welch, quoted in J. W. Peters, "Strategic Staffing: A Key Link in Business and Human Resource Planning," *Human Resource Planning* 11, no. 2 (1988): 155.

5. C. Fombrun, "An Interview with Reginald Jones," *Organizational Dynamics* (Winter 1982): 46.

6. A. K. Gupta, "Contingency Linkages Between Strategy and General Manager Characteristics: A Conceptual Examination," *Academy of Management Review* 9 (1984): 339–412; A. K. Gupta and V. Govindarajan, "Build, Hold, Harvest: Converting Strategic Intentions into Reality," *Journal of Business Strategy* 4 (1984): 34–37; D. C. Hambrick and P. A. Mason, "Upper Echelons: The Organization as a Reflection of Its Top Management," *Academy of Management Review* 9 (1984): 193–206; J. D. Olian and S. L. Rynes, "Organizational Staffing: Integrating Practice with Strategy," *Industrial Relations* 23 (1984): 170–83; A. D. Szilagyi and D. M. Schweiger, "Matching Managers to Strategies: A Review and Suggested Framework," *Academy of Management Review* 9 (1984): 626–37.

7. J. A. Bryne and A. L. Cowan, "Should Companies Groom New Leaders or Buy Them? *Business Week*, 22 Sept. 1986, pp. 94–95.

8. Ibid.

9. Although the Civil Rights Acts of 1866 and 1871 are less frequently discussed, they are important because they permit individuals to win substantial monetary remedies above and beyond back pay awards granted under Title VII. Consequently, they are discussed again in Chapter 14. See also J. Ledvinka, *Federal Regulation of Personnel and Human Resource Management* (Boston: Kent, 1982); M. D. Levin-Epstein, *Primer of Equal Employment Opportunity*, 3d ed. (Washington, D.C.: Bureau of National Affairs, 1984); H. McCarthy, ed., *Complete Guide to Employing Persons with Disabilities* (Albertson, N.Y.: National Center on Employment of the Handicapped, 1985); B. L. Schlei and P. Grossman, *Employment Discrimination Law* (Washington, D.C.: Bureau of National Affairs, 1983); and K. L. Sovereign, *Personnel Law* (Reston, Va.: Reston, 1983).

10. *Uniform Guidelines on Employee Selection Procedures*, 29 Code of Federal Regulations, Part 1607.

11. For an excellent overview of the *Guidelines*, see J. A. Belohlav and E. Ayton, "Equal Opportunity Laws: Some Common Problems," *Personnel Journal* (Apr. 1982): 282–85. See also T. H. Curry II, "A Common-Sense Management Approach to Employee Selection and EEO Compliance for the Smaller Employer," *Personnel Administrator* (Apr. 1981): 35–38. R. H. Faley and L. S. Kleiman, "Misconceptions and Realities in the Implementation of Equal Employment Opportunity," in *Readings in Personnel and Human Resource Management*, 3d ed., ed. R. S. Schuler, S. A. Youngblood, and V. L. Huber (St. Paul: West, 1988) and G. B. Northcraft and B. J. Licata, "Can We Legislate Employment Equity? in *Readings in Personnel and Human Resource Management*, 3d ed., ed. R. S. Schuler, S. A. Youngblood, and V. L. Huber (St. Paul: West, 1988)

12. For more on national origin discrimination, see P. S. Greenlaw and J. P. Kohl, "National Origin Discrimination and the New EEOC Guidelines," *Personnel Journal* (Aug. 1981): 634–36; and O. A. Ornati and M. J. Eisner, "Are You Complying with EEOC's New Rules on National Origin Discrimination?" *Personnel* (Mar./Apr. 1981): 12–20. For more on age discrimination, see P. S. Greenlaw and J. P. Kohl, "Age Discrimination in Employment Guidelines," *Personnel Journal* (Mar. 1982): 224–28. Currently, there is no federal law that prevents employers from discriminating against overweight individuals; see E. Matusewitch, "Employment Discrimination Against the Overweight," *Personnel Journal* (June 1983): 446–50.

13. Arvey and Faley, *Fairness in Selecting Employees*.

14. R. A. Baysinger, "Disparate Treatment and Disparate Impact Theories of Discrimination," in *Readings in Personnel and Human Resource Management*, 3d ed., ed. R. S. Schuler, S. A. Youngblood, and V. L. Huber (St. Paul: West, 1988), 162–77; P. M. Podsakoff, M. L. Williams, and W. E. Scott, Jr., "Myths of Employee Selection Systems," in *Readings in Personnel and Human Resource Management*, 3d ed., ed. R. S. Schuler, S. A. Youngblood, and V. L. Huber (St. Paul: West, 1988), 178–92.

15. "Go Ahead for AA Data Disclosure," *Fair Employment Practices*, 29 Oct. 1987, p. 129.

16. J. C. Sharf, "Personnel Testing and the Law," in *Personnel Management*, ed., K. M. Rowland and G. Ferris (Boston: Allyn & Bacon, 1982), 156–83.

17. H. R. Bloch and R. L. Pennington, "Labor Market Analysis as a Test of Discrimination," *Personnel Journal* (Aug. 1980): 650. Reprinted with permission of *Personnel Journal*, Costa Mesa, Calif. All rights reserved.

18. For an excellent discussion of the impact and interpretation of the *Uniform Guidelines* and many other issues related to selection and testing, see the special October 1981 issue of *American Psychologist*. See also D. D. Baker and D. E. Terpstra, "Employee Selection: Must Every Job Test Be Validated?" *Personnel Journal* (Aug. 1982): 602–4; Baysinger, "Disparate Treatment and Disparate Impact Theories of Discrimination," in *Readings in Personnel and Human Resource Management*, 3d ed.; and Huber, Northcraft, and Neale," Foibles and Fallacies in Organizational Staffing Decisions," in *Readings in Personnel and Human Resource Management*, 3d ed.

19. "Age-35 Job Restriction Upheld," *Fair Employment Practices*, 7 Jan. 1988, p. 2.

20. T. C. McKinney, "The Management of Seniority: The Supreme Court and the California Brewers Case," *Personnel Administrator* (Feb. 1984): 8–14.

21. F. N. Kerlinger, *Foundations of Behavioral Research* (New York: Holt, Rinehart & Winston, 1986).

22. "Uniform Guidelines on Employee Selection Procedures," *Federal Register* 43 (1978): 290–315.

23. For an excellent discussion about criteria for selection and placement decisions, see Schmitt and Schneider, "Current Issues." Important concepts about criteria are contamination, deficiency, sensitivity, discriminability, relevance, and practicality.

24. Arvey and Faley, *Fairness in Selecting Employees*.

25. R. S. Lowell and J. A. DeLoach, "Equal Employment Opportunity: Are You Overlooking the Application Form?" *Personnel* 59 (1982): 49–55; E. C. Miller, "An EEO Examination of Employment Applications," *Personnel Administrator* 25 (1980): 63–69; J. Olian, "New Approaches to Employment Screening," in *Readings in Personnel and Human Resource Management*, 3d ed., ed. R. S. Schuler, S. A. Youngblood, and V. L. Huber (St. Paul: West, 1988), 206–16.

26. D. G. Lawrence, B. L. Salsburg, J. G. Dawson, and Z. D. Fasmen, "Design and Use of Weighted Application Blanks," *Personnel Administrator* (Mar. 1982): 47–53, 101.

27. A. Childs and R. J. Klimoski, "Successfully Predicting Career Success: An Application of the Biographical Inventory," *Journal of Applied Psychology* (Feb. 1988): 3–8.

28. Arvey and Faley, *Fairness in Selecting Employees*.

29. "Handwriting Analysis," *Bulletin to Management*, 8 May 1986, p. 152. Reprinted by permission from *Bulletin to Management* copyright 1986 by The Bureau of National Affairs, Inc., Washington, D.C. See also G. Ben-Shakar et al., "Can Graphology Predict Occupational Success? Two Empirical Studies and Some Methodological Ruminations," *Journal of Applied Pscyhology* (Nov. 1986): 645–53.

30. "Background Checks," *FEP Guidelines* no. 266 (3), 1987, p. 1.

31. C. Sparks, "Paper and Pencil Measures of Potential," in *Perspectives on Employee Staffing and Selection*, ed. G. Dreher and P. Sackett (Homewood Ill.: Richard D. Irwin, 1983), 349–67.

32. R. Hogan, B. N. Carpenter, S. R. Briggs, and R. O. Hansen, "Personality Assessment and Personnel Selection," in *Perspectives on Employee Staffing and Selection*, ed. G. Drebes and P. Sackett (Homewood, Ill.: Richard D. Irwin, 1983), 21–51.

33. H. M. Weiss and S. Adler, "Personality and Organizational Behavior," in *Research in Organizational Behavior*, ed., B. Staw and L. L. Cummings (Greenwich, Conn.: JAI Press, 1984), 1–50.

34. E. E. Ghiselli, *Explorations in Managerial Talent* (Pacific Palisades, Calif.: Goodyear Publishing, 1971); G. S. Taylor and T. W. Zimmer, "Viewpoint: Personality Tests for Potential Employees: More Harm Than Good," *Personnel Journal* (Jan. 1988): 60.

35. J. Hogan, "Interests and Competencies: A Strategy for Personnel Selection," in *Readings in Personnel and Human Resource Management*, 3d ed., ed. R. S. Schuler, S. A. Youngblood, and V. L. Huber (St. Paul: West, 1988): 484–95.

36. J. P. Guilford and W. S. Zimmerman, *Guilford Zimmerman Temperament Survey* (Orange, Calif.: Sheridan Psychological Services, 1976); F. L. Schmidt, J. E. Hunt, R. McKenzie, and T. Muldrow, "The Impact of Valid Selection Procedures on Workforce Productivity," *Journal of Applied Psychology* 64 (1979): 609–26; Sparks, "Paper and Pencil Measures," in *Perspectives on Employee Staffing and Selection*, 349–67; A. K. Wigdor and W. R. Garner, eds., *Ability Testing: Uses, Consequences, and Controversies, Parts I and II* (Washington, D.C.: National Academy Press, 1982).

37. For an extensive review of and guide to these tests, see L. P. Plumke, "A Short Guide to the Development of Work Sample and Performance Tests," 2d ed., pamphlet from the U.S. Office of Personnel Management, Washington, D.C., Feb. 1980. Note the interchangeability of the terms *work sample* and *performance tests*.

38. S. L. Cohen, "Pre-Packaged vs. Tailor-Made: The Assessment Center Debate," *Personnel Journal* (Dec. 1980): 989–95; L. C. Nichols and J. Hudson, "Dual-Role Assessment Center: Selection and Development," *Personnel Journal* (May 1981): 350–86; J. C. Quick, W. A. Fisher, L. L. Schkade, and G. W. Ayers, "Developing Administrative Personnel Through the Assessment Center Technique," *Personnel Administrator* (Feb. 1980): 44–46, 62; J. S. Shippman, G. L. Hughes, and E. P. Prien, "Raise Assessment Center Standards," *Personnel Journal* (July 1988): 69–79.

39. For the LGD, see M. M. Petty, "A Multivariate Analysis of the Effects of Experience and Training upon Performance in a Leaderless Group Discussion," *Personnel Psychology* 27 (1974): 271–82. For business games, see B. M. Bass and G. V. Barnett, *People, Work, and Organizations*, 2d ed. (Boston: Allyn & Bacon, 1981).

40. B. B. Gaugler, D. B. Rosenthal, G. C. Thorton, and C. Bentson, "Metanalysis of Assessment Center Validity," *Journal of Applied Psychology* 72 (1987): 493–511; R. Klimoski and M. Brickner, "Why Do Assess-

ment Centers Work? The Puzzle of Assessment Center Validity," *Personnel Psychology* 40 (1987): 243–60; A. Tziner and S. Dolan, "Validity of an Assessment Center for Identifying Female Officers in the Military," *Journal of Applied Psychology* 67 (1982): 728–36.

41. R. D. Arvey, H. E. Miller, R. Gould, and P. Burch, "Interview Validity for Selecting Sales Clerks," *Personnel Psychology* (Spring 1987): 1–12; M. A. Campion, E. D. Pursell, and B. K. Brown, "Structured Interviewing: Raising the Psychometric Properties of the Employment Interview," *Personnel Psychology* (Spring 1988): 25–42; T. W. Dougherty, R. J. Ebert, and J. C. Callendar, "Policy Capturing in the Employment Interview," *Journal of Applied Psychology* (Feb. 1986): 9-15; R. A. Fear, *The Evaluation Interview*, 3d ed. (New York: McGraw-Hill, 1984); M. D. Hakel, "Employment Interviewing," in *Personnel Management*, ed. K. M. Rowland and G. Ferris (Boston: Allyn & Bacon, 1982), 129–55; S. P. James, I. M. Campbell, and S. A. Lovegrove, "Personality Differentiation in a Police-Selection Interview," *Journal of Applied Psychology* (Feb. 1984): 129–34; G. P. Latham and L. M. Saari, "Do People Do What They Say? Further Studies on the Situational Interview," *Journal of Applied Psychology* (Nov. 1984): 569–73; S. D. Maurer and C. Fay, "Effect of Situational Interviews and Training on Interview Rating Agreement: An Experimental Analysis," *Personnel Psychology* (Summer 1988): 329–44; S. M. Raza and B. N. Carpenter, "A Model of Hiring Decisions in Real Employment Interviews," *Journal of Applied Psychology* (Nov. 1987): 596–603; D. D. Rodgers, "Personnel Computing: Computer-Aided Interviewing Overcomes First Impressions," *Personnel Journal* (Apr. 1987): 148–52; J. A. Weekley and J. A. Gier, "Reliability and Validity of the Situational Interview for a Sales Position," *Journal of Applied Psychology* (Aug. 1987): 484–87.

42. H. J. Bernardin and R. W. Beatty, *Performance Appraisal: Assessing Human Behavior at Work* (Boston: Kent, 1984), 258–60; W. C. Borman, "Format and Training Effects on Rating Accuracy Using Behavior Scales," *Journal of Applied Psychology* 3 (1979): 103–15.

43. The role of the medical doctor in providing the physical exam is an important one. With it, however, is attached responsibility to the employer rather than the employee. See M. S. Novit, "Physical Examinations and Company Liability: A Legal Update," *Personnel Journal* (Jan. 1981): 47–52.

44. E. A. Fleishman, "Some New Frontiers in Personnel Selection Research," *Personnel Psychology* 41, no. 4 (1988): 679–702; E. A. Fleishman, *The Structure and Management of Physical Abilities* (Englewood Cliffs, N.J.: Prentice-Hall, 1964); D. L. Gebhardt and C. E. Crump, *Joint Mobility Evaluation Manual for Entry Level Natural Gas Industrial Jobs* (Bethesda, Md.: Advanced Research Resources Organization, 1983); D. L. Gebhardt, D. C. Meyers, and E. A. Fleishman, "Development of a Job-Related Medical Evaluation System," *San Bernardino County Medical Standard News* 1 (1984): 1–2; D. C. Meyers, M. C. Jennings, and E. A. Fleishman, *Development of Job-Related Medical Standards and Physical Tests for Court Security Officers*, ARRO Final Report #3062/r81–3 (Bethesda, Md.: Advanced Research Resources Organization, 1981).

45. Olian, "New Approaches to Employment Screening," in *Readings in Personnel and Human Resource Management*, 3d ed., 206–16.

46. Office of Technology and Assessment, *The Role of Genetic Testing in the Prevention of Occupational Disease* (Washington, D.C.: U.S. Government Printing Office, 1983); Z. Haranyi and R. Hutton, *Genetic Prophecy: Beyond the Double Helix* (New York: Bantam Books, 1981).

47. Fortune, "The Rules Over Medical Testing (Aug. 19, 1985); 22–32.

48. "Drug Testing: Conference Policy Pointers," *Bulletin to Management*, 7 Aug. 1986, pp. 261–62. For more information see B. Heshizer and J. P. Muczyk, "Drug Testing at the Workplace: Balancing Individual, Organizational and Societal Rights," *Labor Law Journal* (June 1988): 342–57; P. L. Hunsaker and C. M. Pavett, "Drug Abuse in the Brokerage Industry," *Personnel* (July 1988): 54–58; M. F. Masters, G. Ferris, and S. L. Ratcliff, "Practices and Attitudes of Substance Abuse Testing," *Personnel Administrator* (July 1988): 72–78; J. P. Muczyk and B. P. Heshizer, "Mandatory Drug Testing: Managing the Latest Pandora's Box," *Business Horizons* (Mar./Apr. 1988): 14; M. Rothman, "Random Drug Testing in the Workplace: Implications for Human Resource Management," *Business Horizons* (Mar./Apr. 1988): 23; W. H. Wagel, "A Drug-Screening Policy That Safeguards Employees' Rights," *Personnel* (Feb. 1988): 10–11.

49. "Hair Testing Making Headway," *Bulletin to Management*, 3 Mar. 1988, p. 66.

50. "The AIDS Epidemic and Business," *Business Week*, 23 Mar. 1987, p. 122; "AIDS Focus: Employee Rights and On-Site Education," *Bulletin to Management*, 10 Mar. 1988, p. 74.

51. B. Kleinmutz, "Lie Detectors Fail the Truth Test," *Harvard Business Review* 63 (1985): 36–42; S. Labato, "Business and the Law: New Rules Limit Lie Detectors' Use," *New York Times*, 28 Nov. 1988: p. 22; "Preemployment Polygraph Testing Restricted," *Bulletin to Management*, 30 June 1988, p. 201; L. Saxe, D. Dougherty, and T. Cross, "The Validity of Polygraph Testing," *American Psychologist* 40 (1985); 355–56.

52. T. F. O'Boyle, "More Honesty Tests used to Gauge Workers' Morale," *Wall Street Journal*, 11 July 1985, p. 27.

53. P. R. Sackett and M. M. Harris, "Honesty Testing for Personnel Selection: A Review and Critique," *Personnel Psychology* 37 (1984): 221–46.

54. For greater detail on multiple regression in selection decisions, see W. F. Cascio, *Applied Psychology in Personnel Management*, 2d ed. (Reston, Va.: Reston, 1982), 210. For a discussion of the multiple hurdles approach, see L. J. Cronbach and G. C. Gleser, *Psycho-*

logical Tests and Personnel Decisions, 2d ed. (Urbana, Il.: University of Illinois Press, 1965). For multiple cutoffs, see L. S. Buck, *Guide to the Setting of Appropriate Cutting Scores for Written Tests: A Summary of the Concerns and Procedures* (Washington, D.C.: U.S. Office of Personnel Management, 1977).

55. M. Bazerman, *Judgement in Management Decision Making* (New York: Wiley, 19); M. Bazerman, "Norms of Distributive Justice in Interest Arbitration," *Industrial Relations Review* 38 (1985): 558–70; Huber, Northcraft, and Neale, "Foibles and Fallacies in Organizational Staffing Decisions," in *Reading in Personnel and Human Resource Management*, 3d. ed., 193–205; P. Slovic, "Toward Understanding and Improving Decisions," in *Human Performance and Productivity*, ed. W. C. Howell and E. A. Fleishman (Hillsdale, N.J.: Erlbaum, 1982).

56. Rodgers, "Personnel Computing."

57. R. S. Schuler and I. C. MacMillan, "Gaining Competitive Advantage Through Human Resource Management Practices," *Human Resource Management* (Fall 1984): 246.

58. P. J. Dowling and R. S. Schuler, *International Dimensions of Human Resource Management* (Boston: PWS-Kent, 1990).

59. M. Jelinek and N. J. Adler, "Women: World-Class Managers for Global Competition," *Executive* (Feb. 1988): 11–20; S. J. Kobrin, "Expatriate Reduction and Strategic Control in American Multinational Corporations," *Human Resource Management* (Spring 1988): 63–74; M. E. Mendenhall, E. Dunbar, and G. R. Oddou, "Expatriate Selection, Training and Career-Pathing: A Review and Critique," *Human Resource Management* (Fall 1987): 331; R. I. Sutton and M. R. Louis, "How Selecting and Socializing Newcomers Influences Insiders," *Human Resource Management* (Fall 1987), 347; R. L. Tung, "Expatriate Assignments: Enhancing Success and Minimizing Failure," *Executive* (May 1987): 117–26; R. L. Tung, *The New Expatriates* (Cambridge, Mass.: Ballinger, 1988).

60. C. A. Bartlett and H. Yoshihara, "New Challenges for Japanese Multinationals: Is Organization Adaptation Their Achilles Heel?" *Human Resource Management* (Spring 1988): 19–44; S. J. Carroll, "Asian HRM Philosophies and Systems: Can They Meet Our Changing HRM Needs?" in *Readings in Personnel and Human Resource Management* (St. Paul: West, 1988) 3rd ed., 442–55; W. C. Egelhoff, *Organizing the Multinational Enterprise* (Cambridge, Mass.: Ballinger, 1988); C. Johnson, "Japanese-Style Management in America," *California Management Review* (Summer 1988): 34–45; I. Nonaka, "Self-Renewal of the Japanese Firm and the Human Resource Strategy," *Human Resource Management* (Spring 1988): 45–62.

61. B. Teriet, "Flexiyear Schedules in Germany," *Personnel Journal* (June 1982): 428–29.

62. Some, but not all, of the statues define *age* so as to limit the effect of this particular ground of discrimination. Such definitions normally have an upper limit at age sixty-five, but the lower limit varies from nineteen to forty-five. This section on human rights in Canada was prepared by Robert J. Kerr, Professor of Law, University of Windsor, for use in this book.

63. Canadian Human Rights Act, *Statutes of Canada* (1976–1977), chapter 33.

64. *Affirmative Action for Women*, vols. 1 and 2 (Canberra: Australian Government Publishing Service, 1984).

65. Ibid.

66. For a discussion of this issue, see B. J. Chapman, "Affirmative Action for Women: Economic Issues," *Australian Bulletin of Labor* 11 (1984): 30–38; C. Davis and J. Nieuwenhuysen, *Equal Work Opportunity in Australia: Anti-Discrimination Laws and the Wider Issues*, Monograph M75, Committee for Economic Development in Australia, 1984.

Appraising and Compensating

Performance Appraisal

Appraisals for Professionals: Review System Switch

A revamped performance appraisal system that awards salary increases based on individual achievement of job requirements, rather than on an overall comparison of workers' achievements, receives wide support from salaried workers at American Cyanamid Co. By restoring the pay-for-performance link, Cyanamid's revised review system has increased employee satisfaction with the appraisal process, while simplifying management's task of awarding salary increases.

Quota Quandary

Under the company's former appraisal process, reviews for salaried workers comprised three basic ratings awarded in a predetermined ratio. Typically, 20 percent of the salaried employees received "O" (outstanding) ratings, 40 percent "E" (excellent) ratings, and 40 percent "R" ratings (achieves expected results). Salary increases were awarded based on the ratings, with the highest raises going to employees qualifying as "outstanding." However, employees complained that the use of quotas forced competition among employees and did not reward individual high performance. Similarly, management maintained that the system created apathy, resentment, and a sense of futility among the lowest-rated employees.

Experiment in Reform

To remedy the ills of its performance reviews, Cyanamid implemented an experimen-tal appraisal system in 1984 for about one-half of its medical research division's 140 employees. The new system does not rely on quotas and uses instead three ratings: "good" for employees who perform to expected levels; "exceptional" for those who exceed job demands; and "unacceptable" for those failing to fulfill job requirements. Good ratings earn employees salary increases, exceptional ratings, an increase plus lump-sum bonus, and unacceptable ratings no increase.

Polls of all the employees in the division at one- and two-year intervals indicate that the new system represents a welcome improvement over the old. According to the last survey, conducted in 1986, 55 percent of the employees appraised under the new system feel that it provides clearly defined and job-relevant performance measures, compared with 21 percent of their colleagues under the old system. Further, 63 percent of those under the new system, versus 24 percent under the old, say that the progress review gives a fair appraisal of overall performance. Cyanamid has since implemented the revised appraisal program company-wide.

SOURCE: "Appraisals for Professionals: Review System Switch," *Bulletin to Management*, 19 May 1988, p. 154. Used by permission from The Bureau of National Affairs, copyright 1988.

The preceding "PHRM in the News" reflects the practice of linking performance appraisal with compensation. It also highlights the importance of having the right type of performance appraisal form to facilitate this linkage. Finally, it provides as illustration of how an organization goes about changing one of its PHRM activities.[1]

Although employees may learn about how well they are performing through informal means, such as favorable comments from co-workers or superiors,

performance appraisal is defined here as a formal, structured system of measuring, evaluating, and influencing an employee's job-related attributes, behaviors, and outcomes, as well as level of absenteeism, to discover how productive the employee is and whether he or she can perform as or more effectively in the future, so that the employee, the organization, and society all benefit.[2]

To account for all the factors that affect this formal, structured system of measuring and evaluating performance, the term **performance appraisal system (PAS)** is used. In essence, the performance appraisal system involves

- Conducting a job analysis to identify job duties and responsibilities for which criteria need to be developed
- Choosing an appropriate and valid performance appraisal method to assess job behaviors or outcomes
- Developing a process for conveying job expectations to incumbents prior to the appraisal period
- Establishing a feedback system relating to job performance
- Evaluating how well the performance appraisal system is doing in relation to its stated objectives

How well the performance appraisal system works depends on the organizational culture and the characteristics of the rater and the incumbent.

Because of the importance of the performance appraisal process, two chapters are devoted to the topic. This chapter focuses on *gathering* performance information; Chapter 7 focuses on *using* appraisal information, especially the interview.

PURPOSES AND IMPORTANCE OF PERFORMANCE APPRAISAL

As indicated in Chapter 1, productivity improvement is of concern to almost all organizations. Although the productivity of most organizations is a function of technological, capital, *and* human resources, many organizations have not sought to increase productivity through improving the performance of their human resources. This is unfortunate because employees generally work at only 40–60 percent of their capabilities, with the difference in productivity ratio as high as 3:1 for high versus low performance.

Employee performance, as discussed in Chapter 1, includes an employee's outcomes (e.g., quality and quantity of output), behavior (e.g., making a loan, showing up for work on time), and job-related attributes (e.g., cooperativeness, initiative, team playing). All these can be measured and evaluated in a variety of ways. However, the choice of appraisal process has a profound effect on how effective the evaluation is. For example, management by objective (MBO) systems lead to average productivity gains of more than 45 percent, increased employee satisfaction, and fewer employee grievances. The utility of using a comprehensive performance appraisal, feedback, and goal-setting program in a company of 500 employees has been estimated at *$5.3 million* for one year![3] In contrast, trait rating can lead to reductions in performance.

In addition to having an impact on productivity, an effectively designed performance appraisal form serves as a contract between the organization and the employee. This contract acts as a control and evaluation system, better enabling performance appraisal to serve the following purposes:

- *Management development*: Focuses on the future by identifying and preparing individuals for increased responsibility or by establishing remedial training programs
- *Performance measurement*: Emphasizes the past, trying to determine the relative value of employee performance; is useful for promotion, transfer, compensation, and layoff decisions
- *Feedback*: Outlines what performance is expected from employees
- *Human resource planning*: Audits management talent to evaluate the present supply of human resources for replacement planning
- *Research on legal compliance*: Helps to establish the validity of employment decisions made on the basis of performance-based information
- *Communication*: Provides a format for the dialogue between superior and subordinate and improves understanding of personal goals and concerns; can also increase the trust between the rater and the ratee[4]

RELATIONSHIPS INFLUENCING PERFORMANCE APPRAISAL

As Exhibit 6.1 shows, performance appraisal is associated with several aspects of other PHRM activities and the internal and external environments.

Relationships, Processes, and Procedures of Appraising Employee Performance

EXHIBIT 6.1

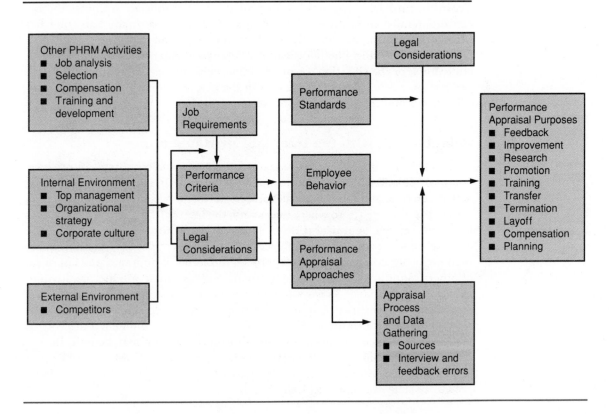

Relationships with Other PHRM Activities

Some of performance appraisal's most critical relationships are with job analysis, selection, compensation, and training and development.

Job Analysis.   The foundation of performance appraisal is job analysis. According to the *Uniform Guidelines of 1978*, a performance appraisal instrument should measure important aspects of performance. What is or is not important can be assessed only through job analysis. If a formal job analysis has not been conducted, courts may deny the validity of the appraisal system.[5]

Selection.   To help increase the likelihood that those selected from the job applicant pool will perform well on the job, organizations use validated selection tests, as discussed in Chapter 5. The empirical validation of a selection test is the correlation between test scores and performance scores. Therefore, having performance appraisal results is necessary because performance scores cannot be established without them. When performance appraisal is used in this way, it is particularly important that the appraisal forms be based on job analysis (*Albemarle Paper Company v. Moody*, 1975).

Compensation.   One purpose of performance appraisal is to motivate employees. One way in which performance appraisal can do this is by serving as a basis on which to distribute compensation. A valid appraisal of employee performance is necessary for an organization to provide contingent rewards (those based on performance).[6]

Training and Development.   To provide the appropriate training, the organization must know the employee's current level of performance and on what aspects of performance the employee is performing at an undesirable level. Also necessary is knowing whether the undesirable performance is caused by ability, motivation, or the situation. (A process that helps to determine the reasons for performance deficiencies is discussed in the next chapter.) To gain this knowledge, performance appraisal is necessary.

Relationships with the Internal Environment

Aspects of top management, organizational strategy, and corporate culture have important relationships with performance appraisal.[7] In addition to influencing how much time and attention is devoted to performance appraisal and keeping employees informed as to where they stand, the internal environment influences how performance appraisal is done. For example, if top management and the corporate culture emphasize employee participation, employees will be probably become involved in performance appraisal through self-appraisal and appraisal of others. Additionally, if top management decides to use product quality and employee performance as ways in which to gain competitive advantage for the organization, performance appraisal may be used to help shape organizational strategy. The organization's strategy, however, may also influence the way in which performance appraisal is done. Short-term criteria may be used in performance appraisal when an organization is pursuing a stable, extract profit strategy. Longer-term criteria may be used when an organization is pursuing a growth strategy, as shown in Exhibit 1.3.

Relationships with the External Environment

Because the intensity of domestic and international competition is making it more difficult, and yet more necessary, for organizations to survive, grow, and be profitable, organizations are seeking many ways to improve. Improving employee performance is among the most critical of these methods. Measuring employee performance and seeking reasons for any performance deficiencies can facilitate the process. Because this is the essence of gathering and using performance appraisal data, the entire performance appraisal system takes on greater importance in organizations. This will continue to happen in organizations as long as competition remains such a significant part of the external environment.

In addition to the relationships with other PHRM activities and the internal and external environments, performance appraisal can be viewed and analyzed as a system having several important processes and legal considerations.

LEGAL CONSIDERATIONS IN PERFORMANCE APPRAISAL

As Exhibit 6.1 illustrates, the organization must pay attention to legal considerations at two general points in the process of employee performance appraisal. Exhibit 6.2 summarizes the characteristics of legally defensible appraisal systems.[8]

Prescriptions for Legally Defensible Appraisal Systems

EXHIBIT 6.2

1. Job analysis to identify important duties and tasks should precede development of a performance appraisal system.
2. The performance appraisal system should be standardized and formal.
3. Specific performance standards should be communicated to employees in advance of the appraisal period.
4. Objective and uncontaminated data should be used whenever possible.
5. Ratings on traits such as dependability, drive, or attitude should be avoided or operationalized in behavioral terms.
6. Employees should be evaluated on specific work dimensions rather than on a single global or overall measure.
7. If work behaviors rather than outcomes are to be evaluated, evaluators should have ample opportunity to observe ratee performance.
8. To increase the reliability of ratings, more than one independent evaluator should be used whenever possible.
9. Behavioral documentation should be prepared for extreme ratings.
10. Employees should be given an opportunity to review their appraisals.
11. A formal system of appeal should be available for appraisal disagreements.
12. Raters should be trained to prevent discrimination and to evaluate performance consistently.

SOURCE: Adapted from H. J. Bernardin and W. F. Cascio, "Performance Appraisal and the Law," in *Readings in Personnel and Human Resource Management*, 3d ed., ed. R. S. Schuler, S. A. Youngblood, and V. Huber (St. Paul: West, 1988), 239.

Establishing Valid Performance Criteria and Standards

Developing performance appraisals that reflect critical job criteria (job components for performance appraisal) is necessary if the appraisals are to be considered valid. One U.S. Circuit Court of Appeals found in *Brito v. Zia Co.* (1973) that Zia Company violated Title VII when a disproportionate number of employees in a protected group were laid off because of low performance scores. The critical point was the fact that the performance scores were based on supervisors' best judgments and opinions, not on important components of job performance. When companies make performance-based decisions on the basis of appraisals, they are using the appraisals as employment tests; thus, they must be based on identifiable job-related criteria (*Stringfellow v. Monsanto Corp.*, 1970; *U.S.A v. City of Chicago*, 1978). The best way to determine whether the appraisal criteria are job related is to do a job analysis (*Albemarle Paper Co. v. Moody*, 1975).[9]

Once the appropriate performance criteria are determined, standards for acceptable behavior must be established. For example, if quantity of output is a critical job criterion, an appraisal form that asks supervisors for their general impressions of how personable and valuable an employee is may lead to an inappropriate appraisal; and if used for an employment decision, such an appraisal may lead to a *prima facie* case of disparate impact or illegal discrimination. Appraisal forms on which the rater indicates by a check mark his or her evaluation of such employee attributes as leadership, attitude toward people, and loyalty are often referred to as subjective forms.[10] In contrast, appraisal forms that require the evaluation of specifically defined behaviors and outcomes, such as level of output, level of specific goal attainment, and number of days absent, are often called objective forms.

Although the courts will allow a company to use a subjective form (*Roger v. International Paper Co.*, 1975), they generally frown on their use (*Oshiver v. Court of Common Pleas*, 1979; *Albemarle Paper Co. v. Moody*, 1975; *Baxter v. Savannah Sugar Refining Corp.*, 1974; and *Rowe v. General Motors*, 1972) because they may not produce fair or accurate evaluations. Consequently, the courts have found that when disparate impact is found, all PAS procedures, objective or subjective, must be shown to be job related (*Watson v. Fort Worth Bank and Trust*, 1988).

It is also important to communicate these expectations to incumbents in advance of the evaluating period. In *Donaldson v. Pillsbury Co.* (1977), a female employee who was dismissed was granted relief because she had never been shown her job description, which prohibited certain employee behaviors.

Civil Service Reform Act of 1978

The Civil Service Reform Act of 1978 (CSRA) includes guidelines regarding the way in which federal agencies communicate and develop performance criteria. While applicable only to federal agencies, it contains useful advice for any organization developing an appraisal system. With respect to performance appraisal, the act eliminated the former governmentwide requirement for the use of subjective, adjectival ratings of outstanding, satisfactory, and unsatisfactory and gave each federal agency considerable flexibility in developing its own performance appraisal system. The act requires agencies to do the following when establishing new appraisal systems:

- Encourage employee participation in establishing performance standards
- Set performance standards that permit accurate evaluation of job performance
- Provide periodic appraisals of job performance
- Use appraisal results as a basis for developing, rewarding, assigning, promoting, demoting, and retaining or separating employees

The act also requires that agencies communicate to employees their relevant performance standards and performance criteria.[11]

PERFORMANCE APPRAISAL AS A SYSTEM OF PROCESSES AND PROCEDURES

In establishing a performance appraisal system, decisions regarding *what* to measure should be made very early. Other important decisions center around the time period for the appraisal and the choice of raters.

Identifying Criteria

A valid performance appraisal system grows out of a comprehensive job analysis that identifies important job duties and tasks. Once duties and tasks are identified, performance criteria can be developed. Criteria are evaluative dimensions against which the incumbent's behaviors are measured. They are also performance expectations that the incumbent strives to attain. For example, if a bank decides that the criterion against which it will evaluate the assistant vice-president position described in Chapter 3 is a specific profit level resulting from market transactions, the assistant vice-president would (it is hoped) see this number as a goal and concentrate on meeting the criterion.[12]

Closeness to Organizational Goals.   Depending on the organization's strategy and its ability to measure performance, criteria can be developed that relate either to individual or group job behavior or outcomes or to overall organizational effectiveness. Consider the assistant vice-president job mentioned above. Behavioral criteria for this job may include "Phones arbitrageurs/traders within 10 minutes of order receipt." By comparison, outcome criteria refer to the product or output produced—for example, "Generates $5 million in sales each month." Organizational effectiveness involves an inferential leap; it entails aggregating individual and group outcomes in order to determine how well the organization is functioning. For example, an organizational effectiveness criterion for the bank at which the assistant vice-president works might relate to total profitability of the bank for a specific quarter.

Single or Multiple Criteria.   If coordinating market activities is the only job duty, then only criteria that relate to this single duty are needed. More often, however, jobs are multidimensional, composed of numerous different duties and related tasks. For the assistant vice-president job described in Chapter 3, the primary duty, "Coordinating market activities," is accompanied by other duties, such as "Stays abreast of current events" and "Closes out daily market activities." If job analysis identifies all these duties as important, all should be measured by the performance appraisal instrument.

If the form used to appraise employee performance lacks the job behaviors and results important and relevant to the job, the form is said to be **deficient.** If the form appraises anything either unimportant or irrelevant to the job, it is **contaminated.** Many performance appraisal forms actually used in organizations measure some employee attributes and behaviors that are unrelated to the employee's job. These forms are contaminated and are in many cases also deficient.[13]

Weighting of Criteria.   For jobs involving more than one duty, there is another decision to be made. How should these separate aspects of performance be combined into a composite score that will facilitate comparisons of incumbents? One way is to weight each criterion *equally*. The simplest, but most accurate approach is to use weights generated through job analysis. Individual weights can also be determined for each criterion, relative to its ability to *predict overall performance*. Multiple regression also can be utilized to determine appropriate weights for each job dimension.

Matching the Purpose to th

In addition to identifying appropriate criteria, consideration should be given to the time period for which performance is to be assessed. On average, most organizations require formal performance review sessions at six-month to one-year intervals. For some jobs, this may be an appropriate interval. For other jobs, performance should be evaluated more frequently. For example, a carpet layer's performance should be evaluated at the end of each one- or two-day job, rather than annually.

The evaluation period may also depend on the purpose of the appraisal. To meet communication and evaluation purposes, the focus should be on *current* employee performance during a *single* performance period. For promotion and training decisions, an examination of performance across multiple appraisal periods may be of use. If performance is steadily increasing or is consistently high, a promotion may be justified. If performance remains consistently low, then training may be necessary.

Choice of Raters

Sources of performance data include supervisors, peers, subordinates, self-appraisal, customers, and computer monitoring. While many of these can be used to gather data, the relevance of each source needs to be considered *prior* to choosing the rating method.

Appraisal by Superiors.   The superior is the immediate boss of the subordinate being evaluated. The assumption is that the superior knows the subordinate's job and performance better than anyone else. But appraisal by the superior has drawbacks. First, because the superior may have reward and punishment power, the subordinate may feel threatened. Second, evaluation is often a one-way process that makes the subordinate feel defensive. Thus, little coaching takes place; justification of actions prevails. Third, the superior may not have the necessary interpersonal skills to give good feedback. Fourth, the superior, by giving punishments, may alienate the subordinate.

Because of the potential liabilities, organizations may invite other people to share the appraisal process, even giving the subordinate greater input. Allowing other people to gather performance appraisal data creates a greater openness in the PAS, thus helping to enhance the quality of the superior-subordinate relationship.

Self-Appraisal.   The use of self-appraisal, particularly through subordinate participation in setting goals, was made popular as an important component of MBO. Subordinates who participate in the evaluation process may become more involved and committed to the goals. Subordinate participation may apparently also help clarify employees' roles and reduce role conflict.[14]

At this time, self-appraisals are effective tools for programs focusing on self-development, personal growth, and goal commitment. However, self-appraisals are also subject to systematic biases and distortions when used for evaluative purposes. Nevertheless, more employers adopt self-evaluation of job performance:

> "There is a clear trend toward self-evaluation," says Edward Morse of Hay Management Consultants' Dallas office. The idea is to get employees to participate in their job reviews and create more of a dialogue with the boss. Handleman Co. is testing an annual self-evaluation system with 30 managers. Employees first rate themselves on a form, then supervisors make ratings and the two evaluations are compared.
>
> Ryder Systems Inc. says, "Employees have greater expectations about (appraisals) being a two-way process." It is developing a program to help managers improve evaluation skills. Dennison Manufacturing Co. added sections to its appraisal forms to stimulate discussion of employee goals, projects and training.[15]

Peer Appraisal.   Peer appraisals appear to be useful predictors of subordinate performance. They are particularly useful when superiors lack access to some aspects of subordinates' performance. However, the validity of peer appraisals is reduced somewhat if the organizational reward system is based on performance and is highly competitive, and if the level of trust among subordinates is low. They are useful though when teamwork and participation are part of the organizational culture:

> Standard performance appraisals, conducted on an individual basis, do not contribute to the team building efforts that are such an important element in today's participative management style.
>
> Individual appraisals can, however, be supplemented with a periodic group appraisal process that yields a wealth of valuable information for the supervisor in a supportive coaching position, and provides a method for resolving those interpersonal conflicts that prevent groups from functioning as effective teams.[16]

Appraisal by Subordinates.   Perhaps many of you, particularly as students, have had the chance to evaluate an instructor. How useful do you think this evaluation process is? A significant advantage of appraisal by students is that many instructors are unaware of how their students perceive them. They may not realize that students fail to understand some of their instructions. The same is true in a work setting: subordinates' appraisals can make superiors more aware of their impact on their subordinates. Sometimes, however, subordinates

---

Managerial Assessment: View from Below

As a managerial assessment and development tool, subordinate appraisals are "one of the most practical and efficient methods for enhancing the quality" of an organization's managers, asserts H. John Bernardin, professor of management at Florida Atlantic University's College of Business and Public Administration. However, despite the unique information they can provide on managerial effectiveness, Bernardin says, subordinate appraisals "may be one of the best kept secrets on management assessment and development."

Reasons and Advantages

Subordinate appraisal systems work well for several reasons, Bernardin says. Because of their relationship to their managers, subordinates are in one of the best "observational" positions to provide valid information on management performance, he says. Moreover, information culled from a number of subordinate appraisals is likely to be more reliable than that provided by the observations of only one supervisor. In addition, the nature of sub-

ordinate appraisal systems complements the efforts to foster participative styles of management.

Subordinate appraisals offer a number of "major potential advantages" when properly implemented, Bernardin says. These include:

- Properly monitored, subordinates' observations can provide useful information that can help managers improve their performance in areas that may go unnoticed by higher-level employees. As opposed to appraisals from the top, which often dwell on production measures and other "hard output data," subordinate appraisals can provide valuable feedback on important—but less visible—practices such as guiding, coordinating, training, coaching, and motivating employees.
- Employees asked to appraise managerial behavior are much more apt to feel that they have a voice in the organization's decision-making processes.
- The appraisal process gives subordinates a channel through which they can feed pos-

continued

may evaluate their superiors solely on the basis of personality or whether they serve subordinates' needs rather than those of the organization. At times, subordinates may inflate the evaluation of the superiors, particularly if they feel threatened by them and have no anonymity. These disadvantages appear to be outweighed by the advantages described in the second "PHRM in the News."

Appraisal by Customers.   Another source of appraisal information comes from customers or clients of job incumbents. Appraisals by customers are appropriate in a variety of contexts. For example, a medical clinic in Billings, Montana, routinely has patients rate desk attendants and nursing personnel on such features as courtesy, promptness, and quality of care. Domino's Pizza hires mystery customers who order pizzas and then evaluate the performance of the telephone operator and delivery person. Doyle Ripley, owner of a carpeting firm in Utah, uses a customer checklist to monitor the on-site performance of carpet installers (see Exhibit 6.3). According to Doyle Ripley,

> When you've got installers out on jobs everywhere, it's impossible to check their work. The advantage of our appraisal instrument is that it educates customers regarding what to look for in a quality installation job. Simultaneously, it provides us with inexpensive performance feedback. From the in-

sible complaints or suggestions for change that their manager may have "mishandled or ignored altogether."

■ Better-skilled and more highly educated employees are attracted to organizations that encourage participative styles of management.

System Suggestions

While subordinate appraisals won't be much use if the information is not delivered honestly, Bernardin says, the level of honesty with which employees rate their managers is directly related to the level of confidence in which their remarks are held. To keep the system running smoothly and effectively, he suggests that:

■ The personnel or human resource department should maintain tight administrative control. This includes developing and field testing a "highly detailed plan for distribution and data collection," as well as testing the actual appraisal system.

■ Raters should be assured complete anonymity and confidentiality. Though rater confidence will increase as the organization gains more experience in administrating the program, at the outset the organization should avoid asking any questions that may allow raters to be identified. Having appraisals performed by groups of five or more also will "foster confidence in the anonymity of the system."

■ Subordinate appraisals should be part of a "multiple rater system" in which information provided by subordinates is considered in conjunction with feedback from other sources. A job analysis that outlines the parts of a manager's job can help in deciding which tasks are appropriate for subordinates to assess.

■ Subordinates should rate specific behavioral tasks rather than psychological traits such as judgment, attitude, dependability, and initiative.

■ All the parties involved should discuss the information gathered. The appraised manager's supervisor should provide feedback within four weeks after the appraisal is conducted. Sessions between the superior manager and the raters will clarify the results of the appraisal, and managers should be trained by the personnel department to discuss the results with their subordinates.

■ The personnel department should carefully monitor the system when the data is used for personnel decisions, making sure, for example, that the appraisal system does not adversely affect minority groups.

SOURCE: "Policy Guide," *Bulletin to Management*, 2 October 1986, p. 332. Reprinted by permission from *Bulletin to Management* copyright 1986 by The Bureau of National Affairs, Inc., Washington, D.C.

staller's perspective, the system works well because any problems can be resolved immediately without being recalled back to the job.

To encourage customers to return the surveys, Ripley holds a monthly drawing for free carpet shampooing. Installers with the highest ratings are recognized monetarily and praised verbally.

Computer Monitoring.   A more recent trend in performance appraisal is the gathering of performance data by computers:

Advances in computer technology make it possible for employers to continuously collect and analyze information about work performance and equipment use. More and more managers are using this type of data to help plan workloads, reduce costs, and find new ways to organize work.[17]

Although this method may be fast and seemingly objective, it has raised a number of critical issues in the management and use of human resources. One of the most critical is the employee's right to privacy. But according to the U.S. Office of Technology Assessment:

EXHIBIT
6.3

Customer Evaluation Form

Name _____   Date _____
Address _____

Your business and satisfaction are important to us. To help ensure quality installation and service, we would appreciate your help in completing this postage paid evaluation form and returning it to our store. Each statement is intended to describe and point out things to look for in a quality installation. **This completed evaluation form will qualify you for our monthly drawing, good for two free rooms of carpet cleaning which can be used within one year from the date of this drawing.**

Please circle Y if the installer met the statement or N if the installer did not meet the statement.

1. Y N The installer consulted with the customer on the location of all seams and placed them in the most desired areas.

2. Y N All seams were located in closets or low traffic areas other than doorways.

3. Y N Seams are not visible.

4. Y N The seams feel secure.

5. Y N The installer installed carpet avoiding property damage (i.e., scratches or mars on baseboards, walls, or doors).

6. Y N The installer stretched the carpet tight enough to avoid all wrinkles, waves, and bubbles.

7. Y N The installer trimmed and tucked all carpet edges flush with walls and/or metal stripping.

8. Y N The installer cleaned up the entire area leaving no scraps.

9. Y N The installer went over the job with the customer and ensured satisfaction.

Additional
Comments: (Use the back of this form if necessary) _____
_____
_____
_____

For office use only:

SCORE _____
(Y = 3, N = 0)

Modified from a project report submitted by Doyle Riley, Steve Barfuss, Gregory Love, and John Paul. University of Utah, 1987

Computer-generated statistics form the basis for the work evaluations of up to six million office workers, mostly in clerical occupations or jobs whose duties are largely repetitive. Similarly, some employers are using "service observations"—the practice of listening in on telephone conversations between employees and customers—to ensure that customers receive correct and courteous service.[18]

PERFORMANCE APPRAISAL APPROACHES

It should be emphasized that rating forms should not be equated with rating systems. The development of a rating form comes only after systematic job analysis, the identification of criteria and appropriate raters, and decisions about the timing of appraisals. While direct output measures of performance are available for some jobs, by far the most widely used performance measurement systems are judgmental. The simplest classifications are the norm-referenced, behavioral, and output formats, each of which is supplemented by essays.

Norm-Referenced Appraisals

For many types of PHRM decisions, the fundamental question often is, Who is the best performer in the group? or Who should be retained, given that we have to cut our work force? or Who should be assigned a specific task? For these types of decisions, norm-referenced performance formats are appropriate.

Straight Ranking.   In **straight ranking**, the superior lists the incumbents in order, from best to worst, usually on the basis of overall performance. Incumbents can also be ranked with regard to their performance of specific duties. Rankings such as these are appropriate only in small organizations. As the number of incumbents increases, it becomes difficult to discern differences in the performance of incumbents—particularly average incumbents. Alternative ranking can help.

Alternative Ranking.   The first step in **alternative ranking** is to put the best subordinate at the head of the list and the worst subordinate at the bottom. The superior then selects the best and worst from the remaining subordinates; the best is placed second on the list, the worst next to last. The superior continues to choose the best and worst until all subordinates are ranked. The middle position on the list is the last to be filled by this method.

Paired Comparisons.   The **paired comparison approach** involves comparing each incumbent to every other incumbent, two at a time, on a single standard to determine who is "better." A rank order of the individuals can be obtained by counting the number of times each individual is selected as the better of a pair. An advantage of this approach over traditional ratings is that it overcomes the problem of an "evaluation set." That is, it forces the rater to compare the performance of each incumbent to all other incumbents, one by one.

Several potential problems exist with paired comparisons. If the number of incumbents is large, the number of comparisons may be unmanageable. [There are $N[(N-1)/2]$ total comparisons, where N is the number of individuals. Thus, for 25 incumbents, there are 300 comparisons if only overall performance is evaluated.] Intransitivity in judgment is another problem. It occurs if incumbent A is rated better than B, and B is rated better than C, but C is rated better than A.

A problem with all three methods discussed so far is that each person is assigned a unique rank. This suggests that no two subordinates perform exactly alike. Although this may be true, many supervisors believe that some incumbents perform so similarly that individual differences cannot be discerned.

Forced Distribution Method.   The fourth method, **forced distribution**, was designed to overcome this complaint and to incorporate several factors or dimensions (rather than a single factor) into the ranking of subordinates. The term **forced distribution** is used because the superior must assign only a certain proportion of subordinates to each of several categories on each factor. A common forced distribution scale may be divided into five categories, with a fixed percentage of all subordinates in the group falling within each of these categories. Typically, the distribution follows a normal distribution; for example,

	Lowest 10%	Next 20%	Middle 40%	Next 20%	Highest 10%
Number of Employees	5	10	20	10	5

A problem with this method is that a group of subordinates may not conform to the fixed percentage. All four comparative methods assume that good and bad performers are in all groups. You may know from experience, however, of situations in which all the people in a group perform identically. If you encountered such a situation, how would you evaluate these people?[19]

Concerns with Norm-Referenced Methods. Regardless of the approach, all norm-referenced methods are based on the assumption that performance is best captured or measured by one criterion—overall performance. Because this single criterion is a global measure and is not anchored in any objective index, such as units sold, the results can be influenced by ratee subjectivity. As a consequence, the rankings lack behavioral specificity and may be subject to legal challenge.[20] Peer comparisons were used in the *Watkins v. Scott Paper Co.* (1976), *Albemarle Paper Co. v. Moody* (1975), and *Brito v. Zia Co.* (1973) cases. The courts ruled against the companies in all three decisions, saying that the comparisons were not based on objective performance criteria (or that the companies failed to establish that they were).

Another critical problem facing the rater is that no information regarding the absolute level of performance is available. Because these methods yield ordinal rather than interval data, managers do not know whether the best performer in a group is actually outstanding, average, or poor or whether two individuals with adjacent ranks are quite similar or quite different. Using such information for promotion decisions may be inappropriate because an average performer could be ranked high in a low-performing group but low in comparison to high performers.

Behavioral Approaches

With norm-referenced methods of evaluation, the supervisor is forced to evaluate each incumbent in relation to other incumbents. In contrast, the behavioral approach allows supervisors to evaluate each incumbent's performance independently in relation to behavioral criteria.

Graphic Rating Scales.   The **graphic rating scale** is the most widely used form of performance evaluation. Introduced in the 1920s, graphic rating scales were touted as useful because direct output measures were not needed and the rater was free to make as fine a discrimination as desired. The scales as originally developed and as used today consist of trait labels and unbroken lines with various numbers positioned along the line and sometimes with below descriptive adjectives.

As shown in Exhibit 6.4, graphic rating scales vary considerably in terms of the clarity with which the trait or performance dimension is delineated, the number of rating categories, and the specificity of the anchors associated with rating categories. Some graphic scales include only numbers and transmit only information about directionality (scales A and B). Others include adjectives or verbal descriptors as scale anchors (scales D and E). These scales vary in the specificity of the anchors and their information regarding what is to be rated and what type of performance is valued.

Scales A through D require the rater to define the dimension. This obviously leads to different interpretations by different raters. While scale E does a better job of defining work quality, it still provides latitude for disagreement. Scale F, on the other hand, is problematic in a different way; although it provides the most extensive definition of work quality, it provides no guidance regarding scale anchors. A second concern is that raters must consider more than one aspect of performance quality. If one rater focuses on the amount of work produced and another focuses on work flow, an incumbent may receive vastly different ratings from each rater.

Samples of Graphic Rating Scale Formats

EXHIBIT
6.4

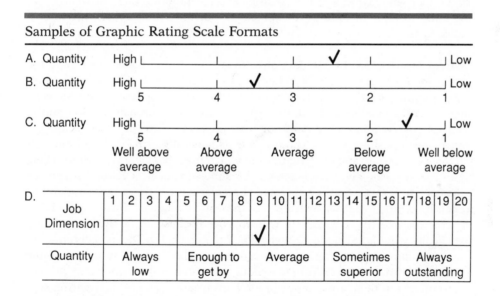

A. Quantity   High |_____|____|_____|__✓__|_____| Low

B. Quantity   High |_____|____✓__|____|_____|_____| Low
                    5   4   3   2   1

C. Quantity   High |_____|____|_____|____|__✓__| Low
                    5   4   3   2   1
               Well above Above   Average Below   Well below
               average   average   average average

D.

Job Dimension	1	2	3	4	5	6	7	8	9	10	11	12	13	14	15	16	17	18	19	20
									✓											
Quantity	Always low			Enough to get by			Average			Sometimes superior			Always outstanding				

E. **Quantity of Work** is the amount of work an individual does in a workday.

		X		
Does not meet minimum requirements	Does just enough to get by	Volume of work is satisfactory	Industrious; does more than is required	Superior work production record

F. **Quantity** In rating work quantity, give careful consideration to such items as amount of work produced in terms of the specific job, employee's application to the job, effect of employee on the general flow of work, and skill in handling special assignments. For *supervisors*, work quantity also includes skill in getting work out. Poor, 1–6; Average, 7–18; Good, 19–25
Score   **18**

Graphic forms are used extensively because they are relatively easy to develop, permit quantitative results that allow comparisons across ratees and departments, and include several dimensions or criteria of performance. But because the rater has complete control in the use of the forms, they are subject to several types of error, including leniency, strictness, central tendency, and halo (discussed later).[21]

In addition to their potential for errors, graphic forms are criticized because they can't be used for developmental purposes (i.e., they fail to tell a subordinate how to improve and are not useful for the subordinate's career developmental needs). Consequently, organizations often modify the graphic form and add space for short essays, so that the appraisal results can be used for developmental as well as evaluative purposes. Exhibit 6.5 shows an example of how one company focused on development.

Even when essays supplement the graphic rating form, the results vary in their length and detail and are still subject to errors. Consequently, comparisons of ratees within a department or across departments in a company are difficult. Furthermore, the essay form provides only qualitative data. Thus, these appraisals are not easily used in making zero-sum decisions (e.g., salary increases, promotions, and layoffs). This also applies to several other qualitative forms of appraisal, however, including critical incidents, behavioral checklists, and forced-choice forms.

Critical Incidents.   Dissatisfaction with graphic rating scales has lead to the development of other types of behavior rating scales. The most systematic of these approaches relies on **critical incidents** to replace ambiguous graphic scale anchors. At its most basic level, the critical incidents approach requires supervisors to observe and record behaviors that are particularly effective or ineffective in accomplishing jobs.[22] These incidents generally provide descriptions of the ratee's behaviors and the situations in which these behaviors occurred. Then, when the superior gives feedback to the subordinate, it is based on specific behaviors rather than on such personal characteristics or traits as dependability, forcefulness, and loyalty. This feature of the critical incidents form can increase the chances that the subordinate will improve because he or she learns more specifically what is expected. Drawbacks of the critical incidents technique include the following: (1) keeping records on each subordinate is time consuming for the superior, (2) the technique is nonquantitative, (3) the incidents are not differentiated in their importance to job performance, and (4) comparing subordinates is difficult because the incidents recorded for each one can be quite different.

Behaviorally Anchored Rating Scales.   A major breakthrough in utilizing critical incidents to evaluate incumbent performance was the development of **behaviorally anchored rating scales** (BARS). These scales were developed to provide results that subordinates could use to improve performance. They were also designed to allow superiors to be more comfortable in giving feedback. The development of a BARS generally corresponds to the first steps in the critical incidents method of job analysis (i.e., collecting incidents describing competent, average, and incompetent behavior for each job category). These incidents are then grouped into broad overall categories or dimensions of performance (e.g., administrative ability, interpersonal skill). Each dimension serves as one criterion in evaluating subordinates. Using these categories, another group of in-

EXHIBIT
6.5

Some Narrative Additions to Graphic Rating Scale Form

Give examples of effective behavior.

_____

Give examples of ineffective behavior.

_____

What steps have been taken or will be taken to modify weak points?

_____

Does the incumbent's job description need revising? No _____ Yes _____ Explain.
How promotable is the employee?
Ready Now _____ Ready in one year _____ Limited to this job _____
If promotable, what additional training and development are needed for the individual
    to be ready for promotion? Please describe.

_____

Supervisor's comments:

_____

Incumbent's comments:

_____

Signing this appraisal does not denote agreement with the ratings, only that the
    incumbent has read the appraisal.

_____   _____
Incumbent's Signature   Date

_____   _____
Supervisor's Signature   Date

_____

dividuals lists the critical incidents pertinent to each category. Exhibit 6.6 shows
an example of one such criterion or category—transacting loans—and the critical incidents listed as pertinent to it.[23] This exhibit also shows the next step:
the assignment of a numerical value (weight) to each incident in relation to its
contribution to the criterion.

Armed with a set of criteria with behaviorally anchored and weighted choices,
the superiors rate their subordinates with a form that is relatively unambiguous
in meaning, understandable, justifiable, and relatively easy to use. Yet the form
has its limitations. Because most BARS forms use a limited number of performance criteria (e.g., seven), many of the critical incidents generated in the job
analysis stage may not be used. Thus, the raters may not find appropriate cat-

EXHIBIT
6.6

Sample Behaviorally Anchored Rating Scale
for One Dimension of the Work Performance of
Corporate Loan Assistant

Transacting Loans

	10	Credit reports are always completed without error.
Prepares follow-up documentation in a timely manner.	9	
	8	Provides services desired but not asked for by customers.
Customers praise the help of the assistant.	7	
	6	Assists customers with loan applications.
Develops loan documentation accurately.	5	
	4	Prepares credit reports without having to be told.
Provides information to customers, even if not asked.	3	
	2	Fails to help other banks participating in loans.
Loan applicants complain about the loan interview.	1	

egories to describe the behaviors—the critical incidents—of their subordinates.[24] Similarly, even if the relevant incidents are observed, they may not be worded in exactly the same way on the dimension; the rater may thus be unable to match the observed behaviors with the dimension and anchors.

Another concern with BARS is that it is possible for an incumbent simultaneously to display behavior associated with high and low performance. For example, the corporate loan assistant could prepare follow-up documentation in a timely manner and also receive complaints from loan applicants about rudeness and inappropriate questioning. In a situation such as this, it is difficult for the rater to determine whether the rating should be high or low.

Mixed Standard Scales. **Mixed standard rating scales** were developed to eliminate some of the problems associated with BARS. Like BARS, critical incidents underscore the development of these scales. The format consists of sets of three statements that describe high, medium, and low levels of performance for a specific performance dimension. These items have been scaled using a process similar to that employed in the development of the BARS scales. The behavioral examples for each dimension are arranged randomly on the rating sheet. Unlike BARS, in which scale values are known, no values are attached to the behavioral incidents. Instead, the rater makes one of three responses to each example.

A score on each performance dimension is calculated on the basis of the pattern of results. Exhibit 6.7 shows an example of a mixed standard scale (MSS)

Mixed Standard Scale for Grocery Store Checkers

EXHIBIT
6.7

Name _____   Rater _____
Store _____   Date _____

Mark each of the following statements in one of three ways:
"+" Indicates the checker performs *better* than this statement
"0" Indicates the checker is *exactly like* this statement
"−" Indicates the checker performs *worse* than this statement

_____ 1. Arrives late for work for one shift per week
_____ 2. Averages twenty-three items per minute while checking
_____ 3. When closing, is out of balance in the register by more than $5.00 two times during appraisal period
_____ 4. Half of the time, takes breaks for longer than ten minutes or takes more than the authorized number of breaks
_____ 5. Asks other checkers the prices of unmarked items or sends a runner to check on items
_____ 6. When business is slow, hangs around check stand talking to other checkers, rather than cleaning
_____ 7. Arrives late to work once a month
_____ 8. Sales per hour equal $750 on Saturdays
_____ 9. Closes sales by saying thank you to the customer
_____ 10. When business is slow, cleans the check stand, helps with light stocking, or performs other tasks
_____ 11. Greets more than half of the customers by their names
_____ 12. When closing, is out of balance in the register by more than $5.00 five times during appraisal period
_____ 13. Averages eighteen items per minute while checking
_____ 14. Smiles and greets customers with a nonpersonalized greeting
_____ 15. Sales per hour equal $800 on Saturdays
_____ 16. Arrives late for work two shifts per week
_____ 17. Takes one ten-minute break every four hours but postpones a break 80 percent of the time when the store is busy
_____ 18. When business is slow, remains in and cleans check stand
_____ 19. Asks customers the prices of unmarked items and sends them back to look up the price
_____ 20. Takes allotted ten-minute breaks every four hours, regardless of the store business, and doesn't yield on this
_____ 21. When closing, is out of balance in the register by more than $5.00 ten times during appraisal period
_____ 22. Averages thirty-six items per minute while checking
_____ 23. More than half the time, forgets to thank the customer
_____ 24. Knows the prices of 90 percent of items, including sales and updates
_____ 25. Sales per hour equal $650 on Saturdays
_____ 26. Fails to greet at least half of the customers
_____ 27. When closing a sale, uses the customer's name and says, "Thank you for shopping at Dan's."

Adapted from a classroom project prepared by Ann Lewis.

developed to evaluate the performance of grocery store checkers. For this example, items 1, 6, and 10 form a dimension triad relating to checking accuracy. Items 3, 7, and 8 refer to knowledge of prices.[25]

The advantage of the MSS format is that the rater is not dealing with numbers. Consequently, some of the most common errors associated with rating are overcome. Additionally, analysis of rater response patterns can identify raters whose use of the scales is haphazard. A drawback of mixed standard scales is that scale values are not known. Consequently, developmental information is lost. Still, once developed, MSSs are relatively easy to use.

Behavioral Observation Scales.   A more recent development in behavioral scales is called the **behavioral observation scale** (BOS). Like the behavioral methods already discussed, these scales are derived from critical incidents of job behavior. BOS scales differ, however, in that job experts are *not* asked what level of performance they illustrate. Instead, job experts are asked to indicate the *frequency* with which job incumbents engage in the behaviors. Scores are obtained for each behavior by assigning a numerical value to the frequency judgment. For example, a score of 2 may be assigned if it is almost always observed. These scores can be summed to get an overall rating. Alternatively, scale items relating to a particular performance dimension can be summed and then multiplied by an importance weight. Behavioral items are eliminated if the observed frequency is too high or too low. In either case, the item does not discriminate well between high and low performers.

Exhibit 6.8 includes examples of effective and ineffective job behaviors and the resulting BOS scales. Note that the examples of ineffective performance are reverse-scored.

The advantages of BOS include the following: (1) it is based on a systematic job analysis; (2) its items and behavioral anchors are clearly stated; (3) in contrast to many other methods, it allows participation of employees in the development of the dimensions (through the identification of critical incidents in the job analysis), which facilitates understanding and acceptance; (4) it is useful for performance feedback and improvement because specific goals can be tied to numerical scores (ratings) on the relevant behavioral anchor (critical incident) for the relevant performance criterion or dimension; and (5) BOS appears to satisfy the *Uniform Guidelines* in terms of validity (relevance) and reliability.

The limitations of BOS are connected with some of its advantages, especially the time and cost for its development as compared with forms such as the conventional rating. Furthermore, several dimensions that are essentially behaviors may miss the real essence of many jobs, especially managerial and highly routinized jobs in which the job's essence may be the actual outputs produced, regardless of the behaviors used to obtain them. When these conditions exist, some argue that a better method is one that is goal oriented or that appraises performance against output measures. Additionally, BOS, more than other types of behavioral scales, requires that the rater be able to observe incumbent performance. If the span of control is large, this may be an impossible task for the supervisor.[26]

Output Approaches

While BARS, MSS, forced choice, and BOS focus on job behaviors or processes, output-based appraisals focus on job products as the primary criteria. There

Sample BOS Items for Corporate Loan
Assistant, Illustrating Both Effective and
Ineffective Performance

EXHIBIT
6.8

Effective Performance

1. The corporate loan assistant prepares credit reports accurately.

Almost Never				Almost Always
1	2	3	4	5

2. The corporate loan assistant is friendly when interviewing loan applicants.

Almost Never				Almost Always
1	2	3	4	5

3. The corporate loan assistant is effective when interviewing job applicants.

Almost Never				Almost Always
1	2	3	4	5

Ineffective Performance

1. The corporate loan assistant fails to prepare follow-up documentation.

Almost Never				Almost Always
1	2	3	4	5

2. The corporate loan assistant does not help customers with loan applications.

Almost Never				Almost Always
1	2	3	4	5

3. The corporate loan assistant needs to be told to prepare credit reports.

Almost Never				Almost Always
1	2	3	4	5

NOTE: On an actual form, the items would neither be grouped nor identified as effective and ineffective performance.

are four variants of output-based formats: (1) management by objectives; (2) performance standards; (3) the direct index measure; and (4) accomplishments records.

Management by Objectives. **Management by objectives** (MBO) is probably the most popular method used to evaluate managers. Its popularity apparently results from its identification with commonly held personal values, especially the philosophy that rewarding people for what they accomplish is important. MBO is also popular because it can inspire greater individual-or-ganizational goal congruence and reduce the likelihood that managers will be working on things unrelated to the objectives and purposes of the organization (goal displacement).[27]

Management by objective systems are premised on the assumption that an organization's objectives for a specific time period should cascade down through the organization. Once goals are established for the organization, they are distributed to divisions or responsibility centers and eventually individual employees. Central to this approach is the issue of goal congruence. An individual's goals must be in harmony with those of the department and organization.

If an MBO system is to be effective, several issues must be considered prior to its establishment. First, management must clearly be committed to the process. Without management commitment and a shared vision, productivity gains from the system are minimal. When management is committed and there is a cascade of goals from the top down, productivity gains *average* more than 45 percent. Additionally, there is a substantial reduction (more than 20 percent) in supervisory complaints. Second, MBO systems involve a large time investment. On average, it takes about two years after implementation for MBO systems to work effectively. Third, strategic planning is needed to ensure that organizational objectives filter down to divisions or responsibility centers and finally to individual employees.[28]

If and when objectives for departments have been agreed on, it is possible to set goals for individual managers. In some organizations, supervisors and managers work together to establish goals; in others, supervisors establish goals for their managers. Goals can refer to desired outcomes to be achieved, means (activities) for achieving the outcomes, or both. Goals also may relate to *routine* activities that comprise day-to-day duties or to the identification and solution of *problems* that hamper individual and organizational effectiveness; they may be innovative or have special purposes.

Effective objectives include the following characteristics:

- *Specificity*. Objectives must identify how well the behavior must be performed or how high the output must be to be considered acceptable. Specificity reduces variability in performance and in ratings.
- *Timeliness*. Objectives must identify the deadline for completion of the task or the attainment of the output level.
- *Conditions*. Any qualifications associated with attaining the objective (e.g., whether the production schedule is adhered to) need to be pointed out because many factors beyond the control of the incumbent may hamper goal attainment.
- *Prioritization*. Incumbents need to understand which objectives are most important. Supervisors and incumbents can weight them, or weights can be derived from the job description.
- *Consequences*. Objectives must specify the consequences of attaining or not attaining the specified level of performance.
- *Goal congruence*. For managers performing similar jobs, it is important to assign comparable goals.

After the establishment of appropriate goals for the upcoming performance period, the manager and supervisor need to delineate an appropriate strategy for goal attainment. Experienced and high-performing managers can develop their strategy; the freedom to perform the job in the way they think best is reinforcing in and of itself. However, for less experienced or low-performing incumbents, the supervisor may need to intervene. Clearly delineating how the goal is to be attained reduces ambiguity, and goal attainment is more likely. Strategy development includes outlining the steps necessary to attain the objective. Additionally, it is important to identify any constraints that may block the attainment of the objective. Finally, it is important to specify the responsibilities of the incumbent and those of the supervisor.

In implementing an MBO system, supervisors should bear in mind that the objectives are *only* guideposts that *facilitate two-way communication*. If the objective cannot reasonably be met or if obstacles prevent goal attainment, the supervisor should be open to discussions about revising the goals. In this way, objectives facilitate communication, rather than blocking it.

At the conclusion of the performance period, the next step is to compare actual performance to the agreed-on objectives. Here, it is important to develop an *appropriate* scoring algorithm. Because managers do not synthesize multi-dimensional data well, *each* objective should be scored *separately*. Scoring algorithms can be either simple (indicating whether the objective was or was not met) or complex (signaling how far above or below the objective actual performance was). After evaluation, the supervisor and the manager *jointly* explore the reasons why goals were not attained or were exceeded. This step helps determine training needs and development potential.

The final step is to decide on new goals and possible new strategies for goals not previously attained. At this point, subordinate and superior involvement in goal setting may change. Subordinates who successfully reach the established goals may be allowed to participate more in the goal-setting process the next time.

Although the use of goals in evaluating managers is effective in motivating their performance, capturing all the important dimensions of a job in terms of output is not always possible. How the job is done (i.e., job behaviors) may be as critical as the outcomes. For example, it may be detrimental to an organization if a manager meets a personal selling goal by unethical or illegal means. But even if output measures accurately describe the job, the concern still exists to establish goals that are of equal difficulty for all managers and that are *sufficiently difficult* to be challenging. Also, from the top down, a rigorous effort should be made to assure that there is a satisfactory balance between long- and short-term objectives. At Alcan, a manufacturing facility, they compensate for the ramifications of including longer-term objectives in an individual's annual performance evaluation by limiting attainment of objectives to 50 percent of a person's annual rating. The other half depends on how the person has carried out his or her principal accountabilities or has performed overall.[29]

Performance Standards Approach.   While similar to MBO, the **performance standards** approach uses more direct measures of performance and is usually applied to nonmanagerial employees. Standards, like objectives, need to be specific, time bound, conditional, prioritized, and congruent with organizational objectives. Compared to objectives, there are generally more standards, and each is more detailed. Exhibit 6.9 includes some performance standards for a plumber. This particular format specifies the average expected behavior, as well as the level of performance that would be considered exceptional. Notice that each standard is rated separately and multiplied by an importance weight. Scored in this manner, performance standards are compensatory in that high performance in one area can counteract deficiencies in other

EXHIBIT
6.9

Some Performance Standards for a Plumber

Duty	Meets Standard When (Score as 1)	Exceeds Standard When (Score as 2)	Performance Attained	Pts. Weight	Total
1. Complete job assignments	Averages five routine drain-cleaning jobs per day	Averages seven or more drain-cleaning jobs per day	Performed an average of six routine jobs per day	1 × 30%	30
2. Operates equipment in a safe manner	Wears required safety equipment (boots, gloves, safety belts) to prevent injury when handling drain-cleaning agents on four of five jobs	Always wear required safety equipment (boots, gloves, safety belts) to prevent job injury from cleaning agents	Wore safety equipment on all jobs that were spot-checked	2 × 10%	20
3. Diagnoses the problem at the job site	Recall reports indicate at least an 80% accuracy rate in diagnosing problems on first visit	Recall reports indicate a 90% accuracy rate in diagnosing problems on the first visit	Only 42 recalls out of 720 jobs during the six-month period	2 × 30%	60
4. Completes paperwork in a timely manner	Job reports are turned in the day of the job 80% of the time	Job reports are turned in the day of the job 90% of the time	Reports not filed in a timely manner; 30% of reports filed the next day or later	0 × 10%	00
5. Completes paperwork accurately	Less than 5 addition errors per 100 reports	Less than 2 addition errors per 100 reports	Numerous typographical errors; math errors made in more than 10% of reports	0 × 10%	00

Some Performance Standards for a Plumber (continued)   **EXHIBIT**
6.9

Duty	Meets Standard When (Score as 1)	Exceeds Standard When (Score as 2)	Performance Attained	Pts. Weight	Total
6. Maintains good customer relations	Telephone survey of 25% of customers shows that 80% of customers rated plumber as "good" in customer relations	Telephone survey of 25% of customers shows that 80% of customers rated the plumber as "very good" or "excellent" in customer relations; no dissatisfied customers	90% of customers rated the plumber as "good," 5% were dissatisfied, and 5% rated as outstanding	1 × 10%	10

Unacceptable: 80% or below the standards
Satisfactory: 81% to 120% of standards
Outstanding: 121% or more of standards

Total 120 points
Overall Performance Is Highly Satisfactory

SOURCE: Modified from a project report submitted by Linda Smith, Deridra Lacy, Lori Rosendahl, and Abutalib Kaba, University of Utah, 1987.

areas. When only one level of performance that meets the standard is specified, low performance cannot be compensated for in other areas; the system becomes noncompensatory.

The major advantage of performance standards is that they provide clear, unambiguous direction to incumbents regarding desired job outcomes. When exceptional performance is also specified, these scales can motivate the average as well as the exceptional employee. A recent study found that when standards were specific, extraneous factors such as the ratee's prior evaluation, the order of evaluation, and the current salary level did not affect judgment. When standards were vague, these items biased performance ratings.[30]

The disadvantages of these work standards are that they require time, money, and cooperation to develop. As with MBO, the essence of job performance may not be captured entirely by set standards. Consequently, important job behaviors may be ignored in the evaluation process. And although set standards may provide clear direction to the employees and the goals may be motivating, they may also induce undesirable competition among employees to attain their standards. If this competition does not lead to undesirable consequences, and if the employees want to participate in the standard-and-goal-setting process, this method can be highly motivating.

Direct Index Approach.   The **direct index** approach differs from the other approaches primarily in how performance is measured. This approach measures subordinate performance by objective, impersonal criteria, such as productivity, absenteeism, and turnover. For example, a manager's performance may be evaluated by the number of the manager's employees who quit or by the employees' absenteeism rate. For nonmanagers, measures of productivity may be more appropriate. These measures of productivity can be broken into measures of quality and measures of quantity. Quality measures include scrap rates, customer complaints, and number of defective units or parts produced. Quantity measures include units of output per hour, new customer orders, and sales volume. Exhibit 6.10 provides some examples of direct indexes for some jobs.

EXHIBIT 6.10	Examples of Direct Indexes of Performance
Salesperson	Dollar volume of sales over a fixed period Type of sales Sales renewels Number of new customers Delinquent accounts collected Net sales/months in territory Penetration of the market
Manager	Number of employee grievances Division profits Division growth Cost reductions Unit turnover Absenteeism Unit safety record Timeliness in completing appraisals Employee satisfaction with supervisor Division productivity Minorities hired
Police officer	Number of arrests for felony offenses Number of shots fired in the line of duty Number of complaints Clearance rates Average response time Number of letters of commendation
Scientist	Number of patents Number of grants Number of technical articles Number of society memberships Number of solo-authored manuscripts
Computer scientist	Number of coding signoffs Response time for requests Number of lines of code written Bytes of compiled code
Administrative assistant	Number of letters prepared Word processing speed Number of word processing packages known Number of errors in filing Number of jobs returned for reprocessing Number of calls screened

Accomplishment Records.   A relatively new type of output-based appraisal is called an **accomplishment record.** It is suitable for professionals who claim "my record speaks for itself" or who claim they can't write standards for their job because every day is different. With this approach, professionals describe their achievements relative to appropriate job dimensions on an accomplishment record form. The professional's supervisor verifies the accuracy of the accomplishments. Then a team of outside experts evaluates the accomplishments to determine their overall value. While time consuming and potentially costly because outside evaluators are used, this approach has been shown to be predictive of job success for lawyers. It also has face validity because professionals believe it is appropriate and valid. Exhibit 6.11 shows an example of an accomplishment rating for using knowledge. (This accomplishment was rated as 4.5 on a 6.0 scale.[31])

BIASES ASSOCIATED WITH PERFORMANCE JUDGMENT AND APPROACHES TO APPRAISAL TRAINING

Despite the prevalence of performance appraisal systems, many people are dissatisfied with them. This disillusionment centers on the vulnerability of these measures to intentional as well as unforeseen bias on the part of the rater. The

---

Accomplishment Record for Using Knowledge

EXHIBIT 6.11

Using Knowledge

Interpreting and synthesizing information to form legal strategies, approaches, lines of argument, etc.; developing new configurations of knowledge, innovative approaches, solutions, strategies, etc.; selecting the proper legal theory; using appropriate lines of argument, weighing alternatives, and drawing sound conclusions.

Time Period: 1989
General statement of what you accomplished:
I developed three new legal theories which could be used to justify jurisdiction in areas previously thought to be foreclosed as a result of a Supreme Court decision on EEOQ.

Description of exactly what you did:
I located and analyzed every judicial opinion discussing the "fair employment" jurisdiction, and demonstrated that sound legal arguments could be developed to support firm's action.

Awards or formal recognition:
The CEO sent me a note thanking me for my efforts.

The information was verified by: Ima Worker, Director
Rating 4.5

Adapted from: L. Hugh, "Development of the Accomplishment Record Method of Selecting and Promoting Professionals," *Journal of Applied Psychology* 69 (1984): 135–46. Copyright 1984 by the American Psychological Association.

rating process is made more complex because it requires the condensation and analysis of large amounts of information. First, incumbent behavior or outcomes must be observed. This information must then be aggregated and stored in the rater's short-term memory. Because of long appraisal periods, information must be condensed further and stored in long-term memory. When a judgment needs to be made, information relevant to the category to be rated must be retrieved from memory and a comparison made between observed behaviors and the rater's standards. Finally, a rating must be made based on aggregated data retrieved from memory and any additional information the rater intentionally or unintentionally chooses to include. Ratings at this point may be revised depending on the reaction of the incumbent or higher-level managers. Unfortunately, raters' memories are quite fallible. Consequently, they fall prey to a variety of rating errors, including deviations between the "true" rating an employee deserves and the actual rating assigned.[32]

Ratee and Rater Characteristics

The characteristics of ratee and rater can inappropriately affect judgments.

Ratee Characteristics.   As one might expect, the actual level of performance attained by a ratee has the *most* influence on performance ratings. However, other ratee characteristics also directly affect performance ratings, particularly when performance criteria are not precise. The gender of the ratee and the "gender" of the job interact, so that males receive higher ratings than females in male-dominated jobs but equivalent evaluations in traditionally female jobs. Due to **perceptual congruence,** ratees tend to receive higher ratings from same-race raters. Also, managers often associate job tenure with job competency. As a result, they tend to give higher ratings to senior employees. The exception is in government merit systems, where less senior employees receive higher ratings to advance them up the merit pay system. Age and education level tend not to affect ratings.

Rater Characteristics.   Characteristics of the rater exert a more subtle and indirect influence on performance judgments. Limited data suggest that female raters are more lenient than male raters. When performance standards are used, female raters also tend to give more extreme ratings to high and low performers than male raters do. For the average performer, gender of the rater doesn't make a difference.

Younger and less experienced raters and raters who have received low evaluations themselves rate more strictly than older, more experienced, and/or high-performing raters do. Contrary to popular belief, supervisors who have previously held the job in question rate accurately. The personality of the rater may also affect judgment accuracy. Self-confidence, low anxiety, intelligence, social skills and insight, and emotional stability tend to be associated with better judgments. Finally, the quality, not the quantity, of interaction between a rater and a ratee affects ratings positively.[33]

Rating Errors

When criteria are not clearly specified and there are no incentives associated with rating accuracy, a variety of errors may occur during the rating process.

Halo and Horn.   Performance on a single dimension may be so outstanding or so important that it overshadows performance of other tasks. Consequently, a rater will often evaluate the incumbent similarly on all dimensions of performance. This effect is called a **halo effect.** The opposite of a halo error is a **horn error,** when negative performance in one dimension supersedes any positive performance.[34]

Leniency.   A second common and often intentional rating error is called **leniency.** In order to avoid conflict, a manager rates all employees in a particular work group higher than they should be rated objectively. This is particularly likely when there are no organizational sanctions against high ratings, when rewards are not part of a fixed and limited pot, and when dimensional ratings are not required.

Strictness.   At an opposite extreme is the error of **strictness** in which ratees are given unfavorable ratings, regardless of performance level. Inexperienced raters who are unfamiliar with environmental constraints on performance, raters with low self-esteem, and raters who have received a low rating are most likely to rate strictly. Rating training that includes reversal of supervisor-incumbent roles and confidence building will reduce this error.

   Halo, horn, leniency, and strictness errors can be minimized further by establishing specific criteria for all performance dimensions, requiring raters to rate each performance dimension separately, and then summing these ratings to attain an overall rating. Additionally, raters should receive normative information about their rating patterns.

Central Tendency.   Rather than using extremes in ratings, there is a tendency on the part of some raters to evaluate all ratees as average, even when performance actually varies. This bias is referred to as the **error of central tendency.** Raters with large spans of control and little opportunity to observe behavior are likely to rate the majority of incumbents in the middle of the scale rather than too high or too low. This is a "play it safe" strategy. Central tendency may also be the byproduct of the rating method. The forced distribution format *requires* that most employees be rated average.

Primary and Recency.   As noted earlier, the typical appraisal period (six months to a year) is far too long for any rater adequately to retain in memory all performance-relevant information. As a cognitive shortcut, raters may fall prey to **primacy** and **recency** effects. As explained in Chapter 5, raters may use initial information to categorize a ratee as either a good or a bad performer. Subsequently, information that supports the initial judgments is amassed, and unconfirming information is ignored. Because special attention is paid to information initially collected, this bias is referred to as the **primary bias.**

   Conversely, a rater may not pay attention to employee performance throughout the appraisal period. As the appraisal interview draws near, the rater searches for information cues about the value of performance. Unfortunately, only recent behaviors or outputs are salient. As a result, recent events are weighted more heavily than they should be. Called the **recency of events error,** this bias can have serious consequences for a ratee who performs well for six months or a year but then makes a serious or costly error in the last week or two before he or she is evaluated. Incumbents and managers can minimize these two errors by keeping ongoing behavioral or critical incident files in which good and poor behaviors and outputs are recorded. While time consuming to compile, these files ensure that information for the entire appraisal period is incorporated into judgments.

Contrast Effects.   If criteria are not clear or ranking systems are used, **contrast effects** will occur. When compared to weak employees, an average employee will appear outstanding; when evaluated against outstanding employees, an average employee will be perceived as a low performer. Again, the solution is to have specific performance criteria established *prior* to the evaluation period. Then any employee with adequate performance receives an acceptable rating.

Escalation of Commitment.   This costly error results when managers are unable to cut their losses. Consider a situation in which you personally hired a new middle-level manager. Although you expected excellent performance, early reports suggest that she is not performing as expected. Should you fire her? After all, you can't afford to "carry" a low performer. On the other hand, you have invested in her training, and she may just be learning the ropes. Research indicates that if you made the initial hiring decision, you are likely to *escalate your commitment* and invest in her a bit longer. You may even go so far as to provide her with additional training so that she can succeed. On the other hand, if you did not make the initial decision, your investment is lower, and you are more likely to recommend immediate termination. According to decision experts, when faced with negative feedback about a prior decision, the decision maker feels the need to reaffirm the wisdom of having invested time and money. Further commitment of resources somehow justifies the initial decision.[35] This bias is alleviated by setting limits on involvement and commitment in advance.

Anchoring and Adjustment.   Past decisions affect current performance ratings in yet another way. Recall that when ratings are used for performance or pay decisions, they should be based on current performance. Unfortunately, prior performance information often anchors judgments about current performance, and adjustments away from that value will be insufficient. The tendency to use prior information inappropriately to make current judgments is referred to as the **anchoring and adjustment bias.** This bias can be controlled by limiting access to prior rating information and by having clear, concise performance standards and performance output data available to judge current performance.

Self-Fulfilling Prophecy.   The anchoring and adjustment bias may also partially account for the phenomenon of **self-fulfilling prophecies:** candidates evaluated positively tend to perform better in the future than those initially evaluated low do. Such judgments have been shown to affect supervisor-incumbent interactions. High performers receive more and more positive feedback and believe in their ability more than low performers do. Consequently, they perform better and/or receive higher evaluations.[36]

Rater Training to Minimize Bias

Even the most valid and reliable appraisal forms may not be effective when so many extraneous factors impinge on the process. But as noted above, many of these errors can be minimized if the following steps are taken:

- Each performance dimension addresses a single job activity, rather than a group of activities.
- Overall ratings are not used. Instead, ratings are made on a dimension-by-dimension basis and summed to determine the overall rating.
- The rater can observe the behavior of the ratee on a regular basis while the job is being accomplished.
- Terms like *average* are not used on a rating scale because different raters have various reactions to such terms.
- The rater does not have to evaluate large groups of employees.
- Raters are trained to avoid such errors as leniency, strictness, halo, central tendency, and recency of events.
- Raters are trained to share a common frame of reference.[37]

In addition to the above suggestions, rating accuracy can be improved through careful training that focuses on improving the observation skills of raters and providing feedback and coaching. **Frame-of-reference training** is also useful. A comprehensive frame-of-reference training program might include the following steps:

1. Raters are given a job description and instructed to identify appropriate criteria for evaluating the job.
2. When agreement is reached, raters view a tape of an employee performing a job.
3. Independently, they evaluate the videotaped employee's performance, using the organization's appraisal system.
4. The ratings are compared to each other and to those of job experts.
5. With a trainer as a facilitator, the raters present the rationales for their ratings and challenge the rationales of other raters.
6. The trainer then helps raters to reach consensus regarding the value of specific job behaviors and overall performance.
7. A new videotape is shown, followed by independent ratings.
8. The process continues until consensus is achieved.[38]

Organizations that cannot afford to develop videotapes or that use MBO performance standards can accomplish similar results using written performance profiles instead of videotapes of behavior.

ASSESSING APPRAISAL SYSTEM EFFECTIVENESS

Although the appraisal form or method is just one component of performance appraisal, the performance appraisal system often centers on that form. Attention is therefore often focused on assessing the available appraisal forms to enable organizations to choose the best one. This chapter discusses appraisal form assessment, and a discussion of PAS assessment appears in the next chapter.[39]

Criteria for Assessment

Determining the best appraisal form prompts a question: what criteria or criterion of assessment is the appraisal form going to use? The criteria include the purposes of performance appraisal—namely, evaluation and development—but an effective appraisal form should also be free from error, be reliable and valid, and allow comparisons across subordinates and departments in an organization. Each of these goals can be used as a criterion. Each form should also be evaluated in terms of its influence on the superior-subordinate relationship. Does the form encourage superiors to watch their subordinates to collect valid data for evaluation and developmental purposes? Does it facilitate the appraisal interview? (Appraisal review is discussed in Chapter 7.) All these criteria must be counterbalanced by one other major criterion: economics. The costs of developing and implementing a form must be compared against its benefits or how well it does on the other criteria. The costs and benefits of all forms should be compared to arrive at an estimate of the utility of each form. This is described in more detail in Chapter 16.[40]

Which Form Is Best?

Research on the question of which form is best is limited. It does, however, reinforce the necessity of first identifying the purposes the organization wants to serve with performance appraisal. Each form can then be assessed in relation to the following criteria:

- *Developmental usefulness:* motivates subordinates to do well, provides feedback, and aids in human resource planning and career development
- *Evaluational usefulness:* is used in promotion, discharge, layoff, pay, and transfer decisions and, therefore, must provide the ability to make comparisons across subordinates and departments
- *Economic:* can be assessed in terms of cost for development, implementation, and use
- *Freedom from error:* reduces halo, leniency, and central tendency and is reliable and valid
- *Interpersonal:* allows superiors to gather useful and valid appraisal data that facilitate the appraisal interview
- *Practicality:* can be developed or implemented with ease
- *User acceptance:* is accepted by users as being reliable, valid, and useful

Exhibit 6.12 shows an assessment of appraisal forms in relation to each of these criteria.

SUMMARY

Human variability is a fact of life, especially of organizational life. From a PHRM point of view, organizations attempt to *select* and *control* individual variability. Chapter 5 addressed how selection and placement decisions enable organizations to staff positions for effective performance. This chapter and the next discuss how organizations control performance variability through the performance appraisal system.

Performance appraisal is not a single act or a particular form used to evaluate job behavior. Rather, it is a system or a set of processes and procedures that evolve over time. A performance appraisal system is premised on the beliefs that individuals will vary in performance over time and that individuals can

Evaluation of Performance Appraisal Forms   **EXHIBIT 6.12**

Criteria for Evaluation	Norm-Referenced Approaches				Behavioral Approaches					Output-Based Approaches			
	Straight Ranking	Forced Distribution	Alternative Ranking	Paired Comparison	Graphic	Critical Incidents	BARS	Mixed Standards	BOS	MBO	Work Standards	Accomplishment	Direct Output
Developmental usefulness	1	1	1	1	1	2	2	2	2	3	2	3	1
Evaluative usefulness	3	2	3	3	2	1	2	3	2	3	3	3	3
Economic	3	3	3	3	3	2	1	1	1	1	1	1	3
Freedom from error	1	3	2	1	1	1	2	2	2	2	2	2	2
Interpersonal	1	2	1	1	1	2	3		3	2	2	2	2
Practicality	2	2	2	2	1	2	2	2	2	2	3	2	3
User acceptance	1	1	1	1	1	2	3	1	2	2	2	3	2

NOTE: 1 = low level; 2 = medium level; 3 = high level

exert some influence over their performance. Thus, an effective performance appraisal system must generally serve two purposes: (1) an evaluative role to let people know where they stand and (2) a developmental role to provide specific information and direction so individuals can change (improve) their performance. Performance appraisal is therefore linked to other important human resource functions such as compensation, promotion decisions, human resource planning, development and training, and validation of selection systems for legal compliance.

Because performance appraisal is linked to so many other human resource functions, it is important to understand why performance appraisal data are gathered, as well as how this information is used. Legal considerations have also heightened the need for organizations to review this process. Special emphasis is placed on the need for job analysis as a means of developing job-related performance criteria. In general, the more subjective the performance appraisal approach, the more vulnerable the performance appraisal system to legal challenge. Although various approaches to performance appraisal exist, they can be classified into four broad categories: norm-referenced, behavioral, output-based, and direct index. The choice of the best approach is really a function of several criteria: the purpose of the performance appraisal system (evaluation versus development), the costs of development and implementation of the system, the degree to which rater errors are minimized, and user acceptance of the system.

Despite the most well-laid plans for a performance appraisal system, human resource professionals are often frustrated by the failure of line managers to apply and use the performance appraisal system consistently. A number of obstacles can contribute to rater resistance to a performance appraisal system: raters may not have the opportunity to observe subordinates' performance, raters may not have performance standards, raters as human judges are prone to errors, and raters may view performance appraisal as a conflict-producing activity and therefore avoid it. For these reasons and others, it is important to examine not only why and how performance appraisal data are gathered but also, as the next chapter explores, how they are used.

DISCUSSION QUESTIONS

1. How can performance appraisal forms be developed so that supervisory errors in performance appraisal can be minimized?

2. Why does employee performance vary even after employees have successfully passed rigorous organizational selection and placement procedures? How can a performance appraisal system address this performance variability?

3. Assume the identity of each of the following persons: a subordinate, a superior, a personnel professional. Then answer this question: What purpose can a performance appraisal system serve for you? Are the purposes served by the PAS for each of these three people congruent or conflicting? Explain.

4. Why is job analysis essential for the development of a performance appraisal system?

5. Managers often complain that a performance appraisal system puts them in a bind. On the one hand, they are supposed to give the subordinate feedback to help improve future performance; on the other hand, they are supposed to use the PAS to allocate rewards (pay raises or promotions). How would you respond to this complaint?

6. What are the three major approaches to performance appraisal? Can you give an example of each approach?

7. What is BARS? BOS? Mixed standard? What advantages are offered by each of these performance appraisal approaches? What disadvantages?

8. Performance appraisal approaches often differ based on whether behavior or the results of behavior are evaluated. Can you cite examples from organizations with which you are familiar in which one approach might be preferred over the other? Explain why.

9. Teachers often complain that students should not be used to evaluate teacher performance. Argue the position that students should be used. What potential rater errors are students likely to commit? How can these be minimized? Are the rater errors that students might commit similar to the type of rater errors that teachers might commit when evaluating student performance?

10. For legal considerations, a well-developed performance appraisal system can provide measurable criteria of job success, which can then be used as a test to validate selection procedures. Under what circumstances could the criterion—in this instance, the performance appraisal—be an actual test, or a predictor of future job success? How would you validate this test?

CASE STUDY

Assessing Performance of Couriers at PAP

The Pacific Association of Pathologists, Inc. (PAP), is a regional medical laboratory founded in 1987 as a for-profit pathology laboratory. Since its inception, PAP has secured contracts with five of six hospitals in the Seattle area and has expanded its scope to the western United States. By centralizing laboratory operations, using the latest in computerized assessment, and achieving quick turnaround, PAP has gained economies of scale. As a result, PAP has grown to four times its original size and now has 321 employees.

One of PAP's major problems when moving from traditional hospital environments to a regional service was the need to transport specimens from draw sites to the central operation. To meet this need, PAP employs couriers who are responsible for picking up and transporting specimens and other items between PAP and its clients. The courier position is an entry-level position requiring little education or training. The position does require the ability to meet rigid deadlines and a safe driving record.

Since incorporation, the demand for couriers has increased six times: couriers now number thirty, compared to the original five hired in 1987. Unfortunately, turnover has been equally high. It is not uncommon for a courier not to show up for a shift. PAP has also fired ten couriers for poor performance over the past three years. Because pickups have to occur on schedule, PAP has had to rely upon overtime, with some couriers working over sixty hours a week. The inconsistency in service has resulted in PAP's losing one of its hospital contracts. Additional complaints about slow service, rudeness, and lack of knowledge on the part of couriers have filtered in from private physicians and veterinarians served by PAP.

Because PAP's competitive advantage lies in its ability to provide quick, efficient, off-size laboratory services, Kyra Burns, personnel and human resource manager, has targeted courier services as one of her first priorities. Since being hired two months ago, she has rewritten and standardized the courier's job descriptions (see Exhibit 1). Next she plans to tackle PAP's performance appraisal system (see Exhibit 2). However, corporate officers are resisting her plans. The following comment is typical of management's view: "It's a low-skill 'dime-

a-dozen' position. All the couriers do is drive, and if they don't work out, the company can simply replace them."

Kyra had found out that courier overtime has cost PAP $100,000 this past year, or about 25 percent of total payroll for couriers. The selection of new couriers has taken more than 250 hours of time and has cost more than $50,000. The problem of improving courier performance is exasperating because 70 percent of the couriers' time is spent driving to and from PAP—out of the supervisor's sight. Therefore, it is difficult to get a clear picture on what is actually going on at client sites. Another potential problem is that the couriers report to more than one supervisor. Besides the immediate courier supervisor, couriers also report to the administrative technologist over the Courier Department and to a medical doctor who coordinates medical services.

At the heart of the performance problem is PAP's current performance appraisal system. As Exhibit 2 shows, the instrument includes ratings in six categories (quality, quantity, timeliness, attendance, responsibility, and cooperation). Some of the complaints from supervisors are that feedback is not specific to the employee's job and that many of the levels on the behavioral checklist are not mutually exclusive. Thus, supervisors are forced to check two of the behavioral scores within one area. For example, when evaluating responsibility, raters sometimes are forced to check two areas: (1) reluctant at times to accept delegated responsibility and (2) self-starter who seeks out more effective ways to achieve results or seeks additional responsibilities.

There are also problems with rater bias. For the twenty out of thirty couriers who were rated during the last performance appraisal period, the average score was 3.8, which is significantly above the expected average level of 3.0. No couriers received a score lower than 2.0. While high scores may have been justified in some cases, high scores were given even to employees who the managers wanted to fire. This made it difficult to justify firing individuals for performance deficiencies. However, when compared to the average score for all employees at PAP, couriers received *lower* individual scores than

Position Description

Title: Courier

Position Summary:

Under the direction of lead courier/dispatcher, administrative technologist, and medical supervisor, provides timely and efficient transport of specimens, slides, mail supplies, and company personnel to and from PAP and its affiliated clients. Acts as a liaison in a public relations capacity by providing clients with needed information and handling customer complaints.

Supervision Received:

Lead courier dispatcher. When asked, takes direction from medical supervisor and administrative technologist.

Supervision Given:

None

Duties:

1. Drives to and from PAP and it's clients.
2. Locates the appropriate pick-up and/or receiving areas.
3. Picks up, sorts, and properly packages items for transport.
4. Delivers items to the appropriate receiving area.
5. Adjusts time schedule and driving routes to accommodate state pickups.
6. Creates a favorable public relations environment.
7. Properly handles and delivers interdepartmental mail.
8. Maintains equipment such as coolers, radios, and automobiles in working condition. Reports problems within one hour.
9. Keeps an accurate daily log of activities such as dispatch time, arrival time, breaks, and lunch.
10. Handles cash for COD pick-ups and makes change for petty cash.

Skills and Abilities:

Ability to: (1) closely follow a prescribed time schedule; (2) drive safely and effectively in heavy traffic and in poor road conditions; (3) determine and follow the quickest route between designated contact points; (4) make independent decisions about scheduling; (5) handle client relations when presented with conflicting client demands; (6) read, write, and speak English; and (7) lift and carry packages and boxes weighing up to 50 pounds.

Requirements:

21 years of age or older
Good driving record as shown by a current motor vehicle record
Class C driver's license
Good visual acuity
Willing to handle or be exposed to blood, urine, feces, tissue, and other samples from humans and animals
Willing to work overtime as required

Employee Performance Appraisal Form

EXHIBIT
2

EMPLOYEE NAME: _____ DATE: _____

DEPARTMENT: __Couriers_____ POSITION: __Lead Courier_____

RATING FACTORS	LIST COMMENTS, STRENGTHS, AREAS FOR IMPROVEMENT
Quality of Work refers to accuracy and margin of error: _____ 1. Makes errors frequently and repeatedly. _____ 2. Often makes errors. _____ 3. Accurate; makes occasional errors. _____ 4. Accurate; rarely makes errors. _____ 5. Is exacting and precise.	
Quantity of Work refers to amount of production or results: _____ 1. Usually does not complete workload as assigned. _____ 2. Often accomplishes part of a task; others must help. _____ 3. Handles workload as assigned. _____ 4. Turns out more work than requested. _____ 5. Handles unusually large volume of work.	
Timeliness refers to completion of task, within time allowed: _____ 1. Duties not completed on time. _____ 2. Often late in completing tasks. _____ 3. Tasks completed on time. _____ 4. Tasks usually completed in advance of deadlines. _____ 5. Completes all tasks always in advance of time frames.	
Attendance and Punctuality refers to adhering to work schedule as assigned: _____ 1. Takes longer or more frequent breaks than most; usually tardy or absent. _____ 2. Takes longer or more frequent breaks than most; often tardy or absent (comment). _____ 3. Usually assures that breaks do not cause inconvenience; normally not tardy or absent. _____ 4. Makes a point of being on the job and on time. _____ 5. Extremely conscientious about attendance and punctuality.	
Responsibility refers to completing assignments and projects: _____ 1. Usually does not assume responsibility for completing assignments. _____ 2. Reluctant at times to accept delegated responsibility. _____ 3. Accepts and discharges delegated duties willingly. _____ 4. Accepts additional responsibility. _____ 5. "Self-starter" who seeks out more effective ways to achieve results or seeks additional responsibilities.	

EXHIBIT 2   Employee Performance Appraisal Form (continued)

RATING FACTORS	LIST COMMENTS, STRENGTHS, AREAS FOR IMPROVEMENT
Cooperation with others refers to working and communicating with supervisors and co-workers: ——— 1. Has difficulty working with others, is usually unwilling to perform assignments, and rarely assists others. ——— 2. Sometimes has difficulty working with others and often complains when given assignments. ——— 3. Usually is agreeable and obliging; generally helps out when requested. ——— 4. Works well with others, welcomes assignments, and is quick to offer assistance. ——— 5. An outstanding teamworker; always assists others and continually encourages cooperation by setting an excellent example.	

Performance Summary (include strong areas and areas for future emphasis in improving performance or developing additional job skills):

Employee Comments/Concerns:

Signatures: Reviewed by Personnel Director _____ **Date:** _____

       Employee _____ **Date:** _____

       Supervisor _____ **Date:** _____

---

did all other employees (average of 4.1). Couriers who receive a high rating on one dimension tend to receive high ratings on all others. To make matters worse, the PHRM budget is limited, with little money available for revising the performance appraisal system or for training raters.

Armed with this gloomy report, Kyra sat at her desk, pondering where she should go from here.

Case Questions

1. What rating biases are associated with the current appraisal format?

2. Will changing the appraisal format alleviate the problems with courier performance? Why or why not?

3. Assuming the current appraisal system needs to be changed, what type of rating format would you recommend using to assess the performance of couriers?

4. Who should evaluate the performance of couriers?

5. What can be done to increase the commitment of PAP managers to performance appraisal?

6. Discuss the relationships among selection, appraisal, and training and their implications for improving the performance of couriers.

Modified from a project report by Kyle Steadman, Robyn Sutton, and Von Madsen, University of Utah, 1986.

NOTES

1. H. J. Bernardin and L. A. Klatt, "Managerial Appraisal Systems: Has Practice Caught Up to the State of the Art?" *Personnel Administrator* (Nov. 1985): 79–86; S. J. Carroll, Jr., and C. E. Schneier, *Performance Appraisal and Review (PAR) Systems* (Glenview, Ill.: Scott, Foresman, 1982); A. DeNisi and K. J. Williams, "Cognitive Approaches to Performance Appraisal," in *Readings in Personnel and Human Resource Management*, ed. G. Ferris and K. M. Rowland (Greenwich, Conn.: JAI Press, 1988): 109–56; R. I. Henderson, *Performance Appraisal* (Reston, Va.: Reston, 1984); K. N. Wexley and R. Klimoski, "Performance Appraisal: An Update," in *Research in Personnel and Human Resources Management*, 2d ed., ed. K. M. Rowland and G. D. Ferris (Greenwich, Conn.: JAI Press, 1984).

2. Carroll and Schneier, *Performance Appraisal*, 2-3; M. J. Kavanagh, "Evaluating Performance," in *Personnel Management*, ed. K. M. Rowland and G. R. Ferris (Boston: Allyn & Bacon, 1982), 187–225.

3. P. M. Podsakoff, M. L. Williams, and W. E. Scott, "Myths of Employee Selection," in *Readings in Personnel and Human Resource Management*, ed. R. S. Schuler, S. A. Youngblood, and V. L. Huber (St. Paul: West, 1988), 178–92.

4. For other descriptions of these purposes, see M. Beer, "Performance Appraisal: Dilemmas and Possibilities," *Organizational Dynamics* (Winter 1981): 24–36; Carroll and Schneier, *Performance Appraisal*; and L. L. Cummings and D. P. Schwab, *Performance in Organizations: Determinants and Appraisal* (Glenview, Ill.: Scott, Foresman, 1973).

5. J. A. Buford, Jr., B. B. Burkhalter, and J. T. Jacobs, "Assessment: Link Job Descriptions to Performance Appraisals," *Personnel Journal* (June 1988): 132–40.

6. D. B. Gehrman, "Beyond Today's Compensation and Performance Appraisal Systems," *Personnel Administrator* (March 1984): 21–33; G. P. Latham, L. L. Cummings, and T. R. Mitchell, "Behavioral Strategies to Improve Productivity," *Organizational Dynamics* (Winter 1981): 4–23; E. E. Lawler, A. M. Mohrman, Jr., and S. M. Resnick, "Performance Appraisal Revisited," *Organizational Dynamics* (Summer 1984): 20–42; J. McAdams, "Compensation: Performance-Based Reward Systems: Toward a Common-Fate Environment," *Personnel Journal* (June 1988): 103–11; P. J. Stonich, "The Performance Measurement and Reward System: Critical to Strategic Management," *Organizational Dynamics* (Winter 1984): 45–57.

7. J. Greenberg, "Determinants of Perceived Fairness of Performance Evaluations," *Journal of Applied Psychology* (May 1986): 340; R. Serpa, "Why Many Organizations—Despite Good Intentions—Often Fail to Give Employees Fair and Useful Performance Reviews," *Management Review* (July 1984): 41–46; C. A. Smith, D. W. Organ, and J. P. Near, "Organizational Citizenship Behavior: Its Nature and Antecedents," *Journal of Applied Psychology* (Nov. 1983): 653–63.

8. For a good review of the legal impact of court decisions on performance appraisal, see *FEP Guidelines*, no. 210(1) 1983; and M. H. Schuster and C. S. Miller, "Performance Appraisal and the Age Discrimination in Employment Act," *Personnel Administrator* (Mar. 1984): 48–57. See also H. J. Bernardin and W. F. Cascio, "Performance Appraisal and the Law," in *Readings in Personnel and Human Resource Management*, 3d ed., ed. R. S. Schuler, S. A. Youngblood, and V. L. Huber (St. Paul: West, 1988).

9. Bernardin and Cascio, "Performance Appraisal and the Law," in *Readings in Personnel and Human Resource Management*, 3d ed.; R. Giles and C. Landauer, "Setting Specific Standards for Appraising Creative Staffs," *Personnel Administrator* (Mar. 1984): 35–47; C. J. Hobson and F. W. Gibson, "Policy Capturing as an Approach to Understanding and Improving Performance Appraisal: A Review of the Literature," *Academy of Management Review* (Oct. 1983): 640–49; C. J. Hobson and F. W. Gibson, "Capturing Supervisor Rating Policies: A Way to Improve Performance Appraisal Effectiveness," *Personnel Administrator* (Mar. 1984): 59–68; J. S. Kane, "Measure for Measure in Performance Appraisal," *Computers in Personnel* (Fall 1987): 31–39.

10. *Wade v. Mississippi Cooperative Extension Service* (1974). *Brito v. Zia Co.*, 478 F.2d. 1200 (1973) 10th Circuit Court; *Albemarle Paper Co. v. Moody*, U.S. Supreme Court nos. 74-389 and 74-428, 10 FEP Cases 1181 (1975); *Rowe v. General Motors Corp.*, 457 F.2d 358 (1972); *Hill v. Western Electric Co.*, no. 75-375-A, 12 FEP Cases 1175 (E.D. Va. 1976); *Watkins v. Scott Paper Co.*, no. 74-1001, 12 FEP Cases 1191 (5th Cir. 1976).

11. *Manager's Handbook: A Handbook for Federal Managers* (Washington, D.C.: U.S. Office of Personnel Management, Office of Public Affairs, 1979); R. G. Pajer, "Performance Appraisal: A New Era for Federal Government Managers," *Personnel Administrator* (Mar. 1984): 81–89.

12. F. J. Landy and J. L. Farr, *The Measurement of Work Performance: Methods, Theory and Applications* (New York: Academic Press, 1983); P. C. Smith, "Behaviors, Results and Organizational Effectiveness: The Problem of Criteria," in *Handbook of Industrial Psychology*, ed. M. D. Dunnette (Chicago: Rand McNally, 1976).

13. G. V. Barrett and M. C. Kernan, "Performance Appraisal and Terminations: A Review of Court Decisions Since *Brito v. Zia* with Implications for Personnel Practices," *Personnel Journal* (Autumn 1987): 489; Carroll and Schneier, *Performance Appraisal*; Cummings and Schwab, *Performance in Organizations*.

14. H. J. Bernardin and J. Abbott, "Predicting (and Preventing) Differences between Self and Supervisory Appraisals," *Personnel Administrator* (June 1985): 151–57; J. S. Kim, "Effect of Behavior Plus Outcome Goal Setting and Feedback on Employee Satisfaction and

Performance," *Academy of Management Journal* (Mar. 1984): 139–48; G. P. Latham and T. P. Steele, "The Motivational Effects of Participation Versus Goal Setting on Performance," *Academy of Management Journal* (Sept. 1983): 406–17; R. S. Schuler, "A Role and Expectancy Perception Model of Participation in Decision Making," *Academy of Management Journal* (June 1980): 338.

15. *Wall Street Journal*, 25 June 1985, p. 1. Reprinted by permission of *The Wall Street Journal*, ©Dow Jones & Company, Inc., 1985. All Rights Reserved.

16. P. Lanza, "Team Appraisals," *Personnel Journal* (Mar. 1985): 50. See also J. D. Coombe, "Peer Review: The Emerging Successful Application," *Employee Relations Law Journal* (Spring 1984): 659–71; J. S. Kane and E. E. Lawler III, "Methods of Peer Assessment," *Psychological Bulletin* 3 (1978): 555–86; G. M. McEvoy, P. F. Buller, and S. R. Roghaar, "A Jury of One's Peers," *Personnel Administrator* (May 1988): 94–98; and L. Reibstein, "More Firms Use Peer Review Panel to Resolve Employees' Grievances," *Wall Street Journal*, (3 December 1986), p. 25.

17. "Electronic Monitoring: Employee Rights Invaded?" *Bulletin to Management*, 8 Oct. 1987, pp. 322–327.

18. Ibid., 322–327.

19. Landy and Farr, *The Measurement of Work Performance*.

20. W. F. Cascio and H. J. Bernardin, "Implications of Performance Appraisal Litigation for Personnel Decisions," *Personnel Psychology* 34 (1981): 211-26.

21. R. Jacobs and S. W. J. Kozlowski, "A Closer Look at Halo Error in Performance Ratings," *Academy of Management Journal* (Mar. 1985): 201-12; L. M. King, J. E. Hunter, and F. L. Schmidt, "Halo in a Multi-Dimensional Forced Choice Performance Evaluation Scale," *Journal of Applied Psychology* 65 (1980): 507–16.

22. J. C. Flanagan, "The Critical Incident Technique," *Psychological Bulletin* 51 (1954): 327–58.

23. In some forms of BARS, the anchors are stated as expected behaviors (e.g., the person could be expected to develop loan documentation accurately). When expected behaviors are included, the BARS form is more appropriately labeled BES—a Behavioral Expectation Scale. For further discussion, see F. J. Landy and J. L. Farr, "Performance Rating," *Psychological Bulletin* (Jan. 1980): 72–107; K. R. Murphy and J. I. Constans, "Behavioral Anchors as a Source of Bias in Rating," *Journal of Applied Psychology* (Nov. 1987): 573; and S. Zedeck, "Behavioral Based Performance Appraisals," *Aging and Work* 4 (1981): 89–100.

24. G. Latham and K. Wexley, *Improving Productivity Through Performance Appraisal* (Reading, Mass.: Addison-Wesley, 1981).

25. H. J. Bernardin and R. W. Beatty, *Performance Appraisal: Assessing Human Behavior at Work* (Boston: Kent, 1984); Landy and Farr, *The Measurement of Work Performance*.

26. G. Latham and K. Wexley, "Behavioral Observation Scales for Performance Appraisal Purposes," *Personnel Psychology* 30 (1977): 255–68; Latham and Wex-

ley, *Improving Productivity*, 63. M. Loar, S. Mohrman, and J. R. Stock, "Development of a Behaviorally Based Performance Appraisal System," *Personnel Psychology* (Spring 1982): 75–88. For a less supportive view of BOS, see J. S. Kane and H. J. Bernardin, "Behavioral Observation Scales and the Evaluation of Performance Appraisal Effectiveness," *Personnel Psychology* 35 (1982): 635–42; and K. R. Murphy, C. Martin, and M. Garcia, "Do Behavioral Observation Scales Measure Observation?" *Journal of Applied Psychology* 67 (1982): 562–67.

27. D. C. Anderson, C. R. Crowell, M. Doman, and G. S. Howard, "Performance Posting, Goal Setting and Activity-Contingent Praise as Applied to a University Hockey Team," *Journal of Applied Psychology* (Feb. 1988): 87; M. Erez and R. Arad, "Participative Goal-Setting: Social, Motivational, and Cognitive Factors," *Journal of Applied Psychology* (Nov. 1986): 591; J. R. Hollenbeck and H. J. Klein, "Goal Commitment and the Goal-Setting Process: Problems, Prospects, and Proposals for Future Research," *Journal of Applied Psychology* (May 1987): 212; J. R. Hollenbeck and C. R. Williams, "Goal Importance, Self-Focus, and the Goal-Setting Process," *Journal of Applied Psychology* (May 1987): 204; J. S. Kane and K. A. Freeman, "MBO and Performance Appraisal: A Mixture That's Not a Solution, Part 1," *Personnel* (Dec. 1986): 26–36; J. S. Kane and K. A. Freeman, "MBO and Performance Appraisal: A Mixture That's Not a Solution, Part 2," *Personnel* (Feb. 1987): 26–32; T. Matsui, T. Kakuyama, and M. L. U. Onglatco, "Effects of Goals and Feedback on Performance in Groups," *Journal of Applied Psychology* (Aug. 1987): 407; C. E. Shalley, G. R. Oldham, and J. F. Porac, "Effects of Goal Difficulty, Goal-Setting Method, and Expected External Evaluation on Intrinsic Motivation," *Academy of Management Journal* (Sept. 1987): 553; R. E. Wood, A. J. Mento, and E. A. Locke, "Task Complexity as a Moderator of Goal Effects: A Meta-Analysis," *Journal of Applied Psychology* (Aug. 1987): 416.

28. R. C. Rodgers and J. E. Hunter, "The Cumulative Evidence," working paper, University of Texas at Austin, 1983.

29. R. A. Gentles, "Alcan's Integration of Management Techniques Raises Their Effectiveness," *Management Review, AMA Forum* (Apr. 1984): 31.

30. L. Baird, *Managing Performance* (New York: Wiley, 1986); J. J. Carlyle and T. F. Ellison, "Developing Performance Standards," in *Performance Appraisal: Assessing Human Behavior at Work*. ed. H. J. Bernardin and R. W. Beatty (Boston: Kent, 1984); 343–47; E. A. Locke, "Toward a Theory of Task Motivation and Incentives," *Organizational Behavior and Human Performance* 3 (1968): 157–89; V. L. Huber, "A Comparison of the Effects of Specific and General Performance Standards on Performance Judgments," *Decision Sciences* (in press).

31. L. Hugh, "Development of the Accomplishment Record Method of Selecting and Promoting Professionals," *Journal of Applied Psychology* 69 (1984): 135–46.

32. DeNisi and Williams, *"Cognitive Approaches to Performance Appraisal,"* in *Readings in Personnel and Human Resource Management,* 109–56. D. R. Ilgen and J. M. Feldman, "Performance Appraisal: A Process Focus," in *Research in Organizational Behavior,* ed. B. Staw and L. Cummings (Greenwich, Conn.: JAI Press, 1983), 141–97.

33. Bernardin and Beatty, *Performance Appraisal;* Landy and Farr, *The Measurement of Work Performance;* G. B. Northcraft, V. L. Huber, and M. A. Neale, "Sex Effects in Performance-Related Judgments," *Human Performance* (1988): 1–14; V. L. Huber, M. A. Neale, and G. B. Northcraft, "Judgment by Heuristics: Effects of Ratee and Rater Characteristics and Performance Standards on Performance-Related Judgments," *Organizational Behavior and Human Decision Processes* (Oct. 1987): 149–69.

34. M. H. Bazerman, R. I. Beekun, and F. D. Schoorman, "Performance Evaluation in a Dynamic Context: A Laboratory Study of the Impact of a Prior Commitment to the Ratee," *Journal of Applied Psychology* (Dec. 1982): 873–76; B. E. Becker and R. L. Cardy, "Influence of Halo Error on Appraisal Effectiveness: A Conceptual and Empirical Reconsideration," *Journal of Applied Psychology* (Nov. 1986): 662; R. L. Cardy and G. H. Dobbins, "Affect and Appraisal Accuracy: Liking as an Integral Dimension in Evaluating Performance," *Journal of Applied Psychology* (Nov. 1986): 672; W. H. Cooper, "Internal Homogeneity, Descriptiveness, and Halo: Resurrecting Some Answers and Questions about the Structure of Job Performance Rating Categories." *Personnel Psychology* (Autumn 1983): 489–502; M. E. Heilman and M. H. Stopeck, "Being Attractive, Advantage or Disadvantage: Performance-Based Evaluations and Recommended Personnel Actions as a Function of Appearance, Sex, and Job Type," *Organizational Behavior and Human Decision Processes* 35 (1985): 202–15; R. L. Heneman and K. N. Wexley, "The Effects of Time Delay in Rating and Amount of Information Observed on Performance Rating Accuracy," *Academy of Management Journal* (Dec. 1983): 677–86; K. Kraiger and J. K. Ford, "A Meta-Analysis of Ratee Race Effects in Performance Ratings," *Journal of Applied Psychology* (Feb. 1985): 56–65; C. E. Lance and D. J. Woehr, "Statistical Control of Halo: Clarification from Two Cognitive Models of the Performance Appraisal Process," *Journal of Applied Psychology* (Nov. 1986): 679; K. N. Wexley and E. D. Pulakos, "The Effects of Perceptual Congruence and Sex on Subordinates: Performance Appraisals of Their Managers," *Academy of Management Journal* (Dec. 1983): 666–76.

35. G. Northcraft and G. Wolf, "Dollars, Sense and Sunk Costs: A Life Cycle Model of Resource Allocation," *Academy of Management Review* 9 (1984): 225–34.

36. M. Bazerman, *Judgment in Managerial Decision Making* (New York: Wiley, 1986); Bazerman, Beekun, and Schoorman, "Performance Evaluation in a Dynamic Context," 873–76; Huber, "Comparison of the Effects of Specific and General Performance Standards"; G. B. Northcraft, M. A. Neale, and V. L. Huber, "The Effects of Cognitive Bias and Social Influence on Human Resources Management Decisions," in *Research in Personnel and Human Resource Management,* ed. G. Ferris and K. M. Rowland (Greenwich, Conn.: JAI Press, 1988), 157–89; Northcraft and Wolf, "Dollars, Sense, and Sunk Costs," 225–34.

37. R. L. Dipboye, "Some Neglected Variables in Research on Discrimination in Appraisals," *Academy of Management Review* (Jan. 1985): 118–25; M. R. Edwards and J. R. Sproull, "Rating the Raters Improves Performance Appraisals," *Personnel Administrator* (Aug. 1983): 77–82; J. L. Gibson, J. J. Ivancevich, and J. H. Donnelly, *Organizations: Behavior, Structure, Processes,* 3d ed. (Dallas: Business Publications, 1979), 361; B. R. Nathan and R. A. Alexander, "The Role of Inferential Accuracy in Performance Rating," *Academy of Management Review* (Jan. 1985): 109–17; R. M. McIntyre, D. E. Smith, and C. E. Hassett, "Accuracy of Performance Ratings as Affected by Rater Training and Perceived Purpose of Rating," *Journal of Applied Psychology* (Feb. 1984): 147–56.

38. Henderson, *Performance Appraisal.*

39. Bernardin and Beatty, *Performance Appraisal.* W. F. Cascio, *Applied Psychology in Personnel Management,* 3d ed. (Reston, Va.: Reston, 1988; F. J. Landy and D. A. Trumbo, *Psychology of Work Behavior,* rev. ed. (Homewood, Ill.: Dorsey, 1980).

40. "Appraising the Performance Appraisal," *Business Week,* 19 May 1980, pp. 153–54; W. J. Birch, "Performance Appraisal: One Company's Experience," *Personnel Journal* (June 1981): 456–60; J. Farh, J. D. Werbel and A. G. Bedeian, "An Empirical Investigation of Self-Appraisal-Based Performance Evaluation," *Personnel Journal* (Spring 1988): 141; P. C. Grant, "How to Manage Employee Job Performance," *Personnel Administrator* (Aug. 1981): 59–65; B. McAfee and B. Green, "Selecting a Performance Appraisal Method," *Personnel Administrator* (June 1977): 61–64; M. E. Schick, "The Refined Performance Evaluation Monitoring System: Best of Both Worlds," *Personnel Journal* (Jan. 1980): 47–50; E. Yager, "A Critique of Performance Appraisal Systems," *Personnel Journal* (Feb. 1981): 129–33.

41. Adapted from a case report prepared by Kyle Steadman, Robyn Sutton, and Von Madsen, University of Utah, 1987.

Utilizing the Performance Appraisal

Performance Appraisal: Manager as Judge and Jury

Why are performance reviews a part of the management system of most organizations? And why do we review the performance of our subordinates? I posed both questions to a group of middle managers and got the following responses:

- To assess the subordinate's work
- To improve performance
- To motivate
- To provide feedback to a subordinate
- To justify raises
- To reward performance
- To provide discipline
- To provide work direction
- To reinforce the company culture

Next, I asked the group to imagine themselves to be a supervisor giving a review to a subordinate, and asked them what their feelings were. Some of the answers:

- Pride
- Anger
- Anxiety
- Discomfort
- Guilt
- Empathy/concern
- Embarrassment
- Frustration

Finally, I asked the same group to think back to some of the performance reviews they had received and asked what, if anything, was wrong with them. Their answers were quick and many:

- Review comments too general
- Mixed messages (inconsistent with rating or dollar raise)
- No indication of how to improve
- Negatives avoided
- Supervisor didn't know my work
- Only recent performance considered
- Surprises

This should tell you that giving performance reviews is a very complicated and difficult business and that we, managers, don't do an especially good job at it.

The fact is that giving such reviews is the single most important form of task-relevant feedback we as supervisors can provide. It is how we assess our subordinates' level of performance and how we deliver that assessment to them individually. It is also how we allocate the rewards—promotions, dollars, stock options, or whatever we may use. As we saw earlier, the review will influence a subordinate's performance—positively or negatively—for a long time, which makes the appraisal one of the manager's highest-leverage activities. In short, the review is an extremely powerful mechanism, and it is little wonder that opinions and feelings about it are strong and diverse.

But what is its fundamental purpose? Though all of the responses given to my questions are correct, there is one that is more important than any of the others: it is to improve the subordinate's performance. The review is usually dedicated to two things: first, the skill level of the subordinate, to determine what skills are missing and to find ways to remedy that lack; and second, to intensify the subordinate's motivation in order to get him on a higher performance curve for the same skill level.

SOURCE: A. S. Grove, *High Output Management* (New York: Random House, 1983), 181–83. Used by permission.

INHERENT CONFLICTS IN
PERFORMANCE APPRAISAL

Performance appraisal touches on one of the most emotionally charged activities in business life—the assessment of a person's contribution and ability. The signals a person receives about this assessment have a strong impact on self-esteem and on subsequent performance. Unfortunately, performance appraisals draw poor reviews from employees, employers, and experts alike: about 30 percent of employees believe that their performance appraisals weren't effective, says a poll by Opinion Research Corp. of Princeton, N.J.[1]

Managers seem equally disgruntled over the appraisal process. In a recent survey, there was generally agreement among managers that a performance appraisal should serve as a basis for determining pay increases, developing team players, and improving performance, but that it often fell short of these goals. In fact, only 10 percent of all managers believe that production increases as a result of the appraisal process! On the negative side, the majority of appraisers saw little or no practical value in conducting performance appraisals. Whether the feedback they gave was positive or negative, supervisors felt that at best the status quo was maintained; at worst, the outcome of giving negative feedback was perceived as so adverse that managers preferred not to conduct appraisals at all. This reaction was typical because the study found that positive appraisals and negative consequences (confrontations, "bad mouthing," more meetings and memorandums) are assured after negative appraisals. The study concluded that managers also feared the organizational consequences of "making waves" with their subordinates.[2]

Perceptual Focus

Another reason that performance appraisals are problematic is that supervisors and incumbents view the process from different perspectives. For the incumbent, the perceptual focus is outward, keying on the environmental factors (the supervisor, lack of supplies, co-workers) that impinge on his or her performance. The perceptual focus of the supervisor is on the incumbent and his or her motivation and ability. These differences in perceptual focus are called **actor and observer differences** and can lead to conflict when it comes to identifying the causes of poor or good performance. This perceptual problem is accentuated by the tendency to account for performance in a *self-serving* manner. In order to protect one's ego, an incumbent is likely to attribute the causes of poor performance to external factors (difficult task, unclear instructions, lack of necessary equipment) and attribute successful performance to one's motivation and ability. Supervisors may respond similarly.

The ramifications of actor-observer differences in appraisal were uncovered in a recent study. Incumbents and their supervisors universally agreed on the causes of job success and failure. However, when it came to the incumbent's job, there was absolutely *no* agreement on the causes of good *or* poor performance.[3] They leave the appraisal interview wondering what went wrong and why their views diverge so greatly.

High Performers All

One key reason that performance appraisal is viewed negatively centers on the self-evaluation of incumbents. The overwhelming majority of incumbents believe they perform better than 75 percent of their peers. Thus, when confronted with information suggesting they performed adequately, but not outstandingly, subordinates don't perceive the evaluation as fair or the rewards equivalent to their contributions. As a result, organizational committment and job satisfaction drop and remain low for as long as a year after evaluation.

While one would expect positive feedback to increase job satisfaction, this doesn't occur either. Because employees believe their performance is high, the receipt of positive feedback merely maintains their current level of satisfaction and commitment. Thus, no matter what a supervisor does, the best he or she can accomplish is to maintain the status quo.

Conflict in Goals

Goal conflict may also be the problem. From organizatinal and individual goals come three sets of conflicts. One is between the organization's evaluative and developmental goals. When pursuing the evaluative goal, superiors have to make judgments affecting their subordinates' careers and immediate rewards. Communicating these judgments can lead to the creation of an adversarial, low-trust relationship between superior and subordinate. This in turn precludes the superior from performing a problem-solving, helper role that is essential if the organization wants to serve the developmental goal.

A second set of conflicts arises from the various goals of the individuals who are being evaluated. On the one hand, these individuals want valid feedback that gives them information about how to improve and where they stand in the organization. On the other hand, they want to verify their self-image and obtain valued rewards. In essence, the goals of individuals imply a necessity to be open (to give valid feedback for improvement), yet to be protective (to maintain a positive self-image and obtain rewards).

The third set of conflicts arises between the individual's goals and those of the organization. One conflict is between the organization's evaluation goal and the individual's goal of obtaining rewards. Another conflict is between the organization's developmental goal and the individual's goal of maintaining self-image.[4] Exhibit 7.1 shows the nature of these conflicts.

Consequences of Inherent Conflicts

Among the several consequences of the inherent conflicts just described are ambivalence, avoidance, defensiveness, and resistance. Some of these consequences and the inherent conflicts are implicit in the discussion of the contextual impact on performance appraisal data gathering, particularly that of the superior-subordinate relationship discussed in Chapter 6.

Ambivalence is a consequence for both superiors and subordinates. Superiors are ambivalent because they must act as judge and jury in telling subordinates where they stand, both because the organization demands it and because the subordinates want it. Yet they are uncertain about their judgments and how the subordinates will react to negative feedback. This feeling is intensified when superiors are not trained in giving feedback. Subordinates are equally ambivalent because they want honest feedback, yet they also want to receive rewards and maintain their self-image (that is, they really want only positive feedback). Additionally, if they are open with their superiors in identifying undeveloped potential, they risk the chance that the superiors may use this to evaluate them unfavorably.

EXHIBIT
7.1

Conflicts in Performance Appraisal

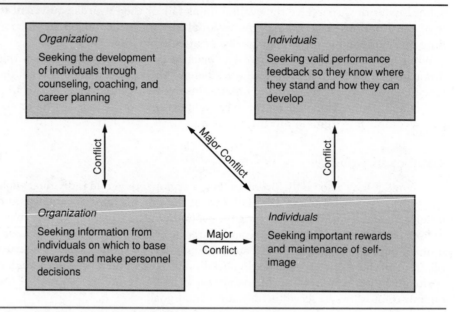

SOURCE: M. Beer, "Performance Appraisal: Dilemmas and Possibilities," *Organizational Dynamics* (Winter 1981) (New York: AMACOM, a division of American Management Association), 27.

A consequence of this joint ambivalence is avoidance. This process has given rise to the phenomenon of **vanishing performance appraisal**.[5] When this occurs, subordinates may report that they never received negative feedback despite superiors' reports that they gave it.

Defensiveness

Subordinates and superiors also become defensive in performance appraisals. The subordinate becomes defensive in responding to negative feedback that threatens self-image and the chances for gaining rewards. A study at General Electric made the following discoveries:

- Criticism has a negative effect on goal achievement.
- Praise has little effect one way or another.
- The average subordinate reacts defensively to criticism during the appraisal interview.
- Defensiveness resulting from critical appraisal produces inferior performance.
- The disruptive effect of repeated criticism on subsequent performance is greater among those who already have low self-esteem.[6]

Accordingly, subordinates attempt to blame others for their performance, challenge the appraisal form, and demand that their superiors justify their appraisals.

A majority of employees believe their bosses botch appraisals of their work, if they give reviews at all. Psychological Associates Inc. of St. Louis, surveying 4,000 employees at 190 companies recently, found that 70% believed review sessions hadn't given them a clear picture of what was expected of them on the job, or where they could advance in the company. Only half said their bosses helped them set job objectives, and only one in five said reviews were followed up during the ensuing year.[7]

Initially at least, subordinates are not inclined to apologize for their behavior and seek ways to improve; in fact, they resist superiors' efforts to engage in problem solving. Consequently, superiors spend most of their time trying to defend their appraisals and resisting subordinates' efforts to have their appraisals altered.

Overall, the appraisal process is uncomfortable for both participants, especially when poor performance and negative feedback are involved:

> "It's a tough job, the equivalent of walking up to a person and saying, 'Here's what I think of your baby,'" says Robert Lefton, president of Psychological Associates, a consulting company that has provided training on how to give reviews to over 100 large companies. "It requires knowing how to handle fear and anger and a gamut of other emotions, which a lot of managers aren't comfortable with," he adds.
>
> Increasingly managers must do a better job of appraising employees—not only to help employees mature but to increase productivity and company loyalty. Comprehensive performance reviews also reduce the chances that a fired employee who has been warned of unsatisfactory performance will sue the company.[8]

Even if good performance is involved, however, superiors still have to make evaluation decisions, and somebody may still end up looking like a poor performer. Because appraisals are uncomfortable, yet necessary, seeking ways to make the process better is important. Possible ways to improve the process involve the design of the appraisal system and the characteristics of the performance appraisal interview.

DESIGNING APPRAISALS FOR MAXIMUM RESULTS

Several features can be incorporated into the design of the appraisal process to minimize appraisal conflicts and maximize perceptual congruence.[9]

Use Appropriate Performance Data

The first step in reducing conflict and perceptual difference is to utilize performance data that focus on specific behaviors or goals. As noted previously, these performance expectations need to be communicated at the beginning of the appraisal period.

Performance data that focus on personal attributes or characteristcs are likely to prompt more defensiveness because they are more difficult for the superior to justify and because more of the subordinate's self-image is at stake. As Marilyn Moats Kennedy, managing partner of Career Strategies, a management consulting company in Wilmette, Ill., says,

> It's important to critique the behavior of an employee, not the employee himself.
> If you bark, "You have a bad attitude," to your receptionist, for example, you'll likely find yourself facing a very defensive employee. You'll probably get

better results if you say, "When someone steps up to your desk, I'd like them to get the distinct impression that you're delighted to see them."[10]

As shown in Chapter 6, superiors can facilitate specific performance feedback through their selection and use of the appropriate appraisal forms. Specifically, if superiors want to use performance data on behaviors, a critical incident form or a BOS method would facilitate using this data on goals. Using these appraisal forms allows supervisors to manage *what* subordinates are doing, as well as *how* they are doing.

Separate Past, Current, and Potential Performance Appraisals

It also is important to separate the evaluation of present performance from that of potential performance. Current performance of subordinates may have little to do with their performance potential, yet supervisors may unconsciously incorporate evaluations of performance potential into evaluations of current performance. Conversely, they may incorporate past performance into the evaluation of present performance. In either event, the appraisal of current performance is inappropriately an amalgamation of past, current, and/or potential performance.

As a result, the appraisal is likely to be viewed as unfair. Consider people with high potential. They may receive a lower evaluation than do their peers who are performing at an equivalent level because their supervisors have higher expectations of them. Conversely, adequate performers with low potential may be evaluated adversely simply because they don't have high potential. In the former case the appraisal is unfair to the high-potential employee because performance standards are raised. The latter appraisal is just as unfair to subordinates who may not be interested in being promoted, yet who perform adequately in their current job.

Part of the solution is to use **job-specific criteria** to evaluate current job performance and then to conduct a separate appraisal relating to potential. As discussed in the last chapter, the criteria for each need to be based on job analysis. Separating the two processes allows supervisors to avoid appraising the potential performance of incumbents who are not interested in promotion. And for those who are interested, volunteering to participate in an assessment center or other promotional process cues management that an incumbent is interested in moving up in the organization. In fact, one study of assessment centers found that participation, rather than the evaluation rating received, was the single most important determinant of who did or did not get promoted. By separating the evaluations of current and potential performance and by allowing incumbents to self-nominate, individual differences are recognized and incorporated into the appraisal process.[11]

Ensure Procedural and Distributive Fairness

To minimize the emotion-charged atmosphere that surrounds the performance appraisal process, managers also need to take steps to ensure that the process is perceived as fair and equitable. Performance appraisal procedures are viewed as fair to the extent that there is

- *Consistency.* Performance standards are applied consistently to all incumbents. Allowances are not made for workers with special problems, nor are high performers expected to carry more than their own weight.
- *Familiarity.* The use of diaries to record worker outputs, frequent observation of performance, and management by "wandering around" increase a supervisor's job knowledge and consequently create the impression that the manager and the appraisal are fair.
- *Solicitation of input.* Information regarding performance standards, as well as strategies to attain them, needs to be solicited *prior* to evaluation. More importantly, this information should not be solicited unless it is incorporated.
- *Opportunity to challenge rebut the evaluation.* Consistent with the problem-solving interview to be discussed in the next section, incumbents need to be able to challenge or rebut evaluations.

It is also important to ensure that outputs of the appraisal process are distributed fairly. For example, ratings need to be based on the levels of performance attained, and recommendations for salary increases and promotions need to be based on these ratings.[12]

Empower Incumbents

Part of the difficulty in managing the appraisal process is collecting and maintaining information on all incumbents. As the span of control increases in size, this task grows to unmanageable levels. One way to resolve this problem, while simultaneously increasing perceptions of fairness, is to shift the responsibility for performance record keeping to the incumbent. To carry out this process, incumbents first need training in writing performance standards and in collecting and documenting performance information. In addition, the two-way communication process discussed above needs to operate effectively, so that incumbents feel free to renegotiate performance standards that have become obsolete or unattainable due to constraints.

Delegating responsibility offers incumbents several advantages in terms of performance planning, goal setting, and record keeping. First, incumbents are no longer passive participants, reacting to supervisor directives. Second, because it is now their responsibility to identify performance hurdles and bring them to the attention of their manager, defensiveness is reduced. Third, the supervisor is free to *manage and coach* rather than police. Finally, the incumbent feels *ownership* of the process.

Provide an Appropriate Degree of Participation

Recently, many companies have viewed worker participation as *the* performance elixir. It was felt, and still is by some managers, that allowing workers the opportunity to set or participate in the development of their own goals will result in higher commitment and consequently better performance. Research, however, has shown that participation in and of itself does *not* lead to higher levels of performance.

More important than the method is that specific performance standards are developed and an explanation provided for their existence. Participation is useful only if it helps incumbents identify an appropriate strategy to attain performance. That is, as long as performance standards are specific, time bound, job relevant, and communicated, motivated incumbents will perform well.[13]

Use Reciprocal Appraisals

To encourage openness in the performance appraisal and to improve superior-subordinate relationships, subordinates can be allowed to engage in appraisal of their superiors as well as of themselves. Upward appraisal can help put into better balance, if not equalize, the power of the superior vis-a-vis that of the subordinate. Such a balance is useful in reducing the authoritarian character of the superior-subordinate relationship, which contributes most to defensiveness and avoidance in the performance appraisal process.[14]

Organizations and superiors facilitate the upward appraisal process by providing forms for subordinates to use and by engaging in other human resource policies and procedures that indicate openness—e.g., allowing employees to participate in deciding their own pay increases (Chapter 8) or in analyzing their own jobs (Chapter 3). Furthering this openness and the power equalization approach in performance appraisal is a policy of self-appraisal. Self-appraisal is likely to result in more information for the superior, a more realistic appraisal of the subordinate's performance, and a greater acceptance of the final appraisal by subordinates and superiors.

THE PERFORMANCE
APPRAISAL INTERVIEW

To further enhance the effectiveness of the performance appraisal, several considerations should be made regarding the actual performance appraisal interview.

Before the Interview

As emphasized throughout Chapters 6 and 7, performance appraisal is an ongoing process of which the interview is only one component. Prior to the interview, a supervisor needs to prepare.

Schedule in Advance.   A week or two prior to the scheduled performance review, the rater should *personally* notify the ratee of the time, date, and place of interview. Having a secretary schedule the interview increases the likelihood that the purpose and content of the session will be misunderstood. Sending a formal notice builds unneeded formality into the process and immediately shrouds the interview in ambiguity and mistrust. In setting up the interview, agreement should be reached regarding its purpose and content. For example, will the incumbent have an opportunity to evaluate the performance of the supervisor, or will the evaluation be one way? It is also useful, although possibly inconvenient, to select and use a neutral location, so that neither the supervisor nor the incumbent has a power advantage. Still, the session will be more constructive if both parties have time to do their homework.

Self-Review.   If subordinates are empowered, advance notice will give them sufficient time to update their performance records and do a self-review. In situations in which employees formally review their own performance, comparisons of self-ratings with ratings by the supervisor can actually be made by each party prior to the session and then used for subsequent discussion in the interview.

Gather Relevant Information.   In preparing for the interview, the rater and ratee must gather all information that has any bearing on the discussions. Here, critical incident files or behavior diaries can be reviewed. It is also important to review the employee's job description. An agenda can be developed to allow the ratee to study it and make additions or deletions.[15]

Types of Interviews

Initiating and carrying out an effective interview session require both coaching and counseling skills. Additionally, a supervisor needs to be able to listen and reflect back what his or her subordinates are saying with regard to performance, its causes, and its outcome.

Tell and Sell.   The **tell-and-sell or directive interview** lets subordinates know how well they are doing and sells them on the merits of setting specific goals for improvement (if needed). This efficient interview is also effective in improving performance, especially for subordinates with little desire for participation.[16] It may be most appropriate in providing evaluation; however, subordinates may become frustrated in trying to convince their superiors to listen to justifications for their performance levels.

Tell and Listen.   This approach follows no rigid format but requires that the rater have question-asking and listening skills. The **tell-and-listen interview** provides subordinates with the chance to participate and establish a dialogue with their superiors. Its purpose is to communicate the supervisor's perceptions of subordinates' strengths and weaknesses and to let subordinates respond to those perceptions. Supervisors summarize and paraphrase subordinates' responses but generally fail to establish goals for performance improvement. Consequently, subordinates may feel better, but their performance may not change.

Problem-Solving.   Because of the weaknesses of the approaches described above, it is better for the rater to view the appraisal interview as a **problem-solving** strategy. Here, an active and open dialogue is established between superior and subordinate. Perceptions are shared, and solutions to problems or differences are presented, discussed, and sought. Goals for improvement are also established mutually by superior and subordinate. Because this type of interview is generally more difficult for most superiors to do, prior training in problem solving is usually necessary and beneficial.

Mixed Interview.   A desirable approach is to use the tell-and-sell interview for evaluation and the problem-solving interview for development. Separate interviews for each purpose, however, may not be feasible. When corporate policies, time, and expectations prevent separation of purposes, a single interview must accomplish both purposes. Thus, in reality, supervisors need to be adaptive during the appraisal interview. They need the skills to conduct the tell-and-sell and the problem-solving interviews and to make the transition from one to the other. In this single interview, the subordinate may start out listening as the superior provides an appraisal of performance but then take a more active role in determining what and how performance improvements can be made (problem solving), concluding with agreed-on goals for improvement.[17]

Effective Feedback

Whether negative or positive, feedback is not always easy to provide.[18] Fortunately, several characteristics of effective feedback have been determined. First, effective feedback is **specific** rather than general. Telling someone that he or she is dominating is probably not as useful as saying, "Just now you were not listening to what I said, but I felt I either had to agree with your arguments or face attack from you."

Second, effective feedback is **focused on behavior** rather than on the person. Referring to what a person does is more important than referring to what that person seems to be. A superior might say that a person talked more than anyone else at a meeting rather than that he or she is a loud-mouth. The former allows for the possibility of change; the latter implies a fixed personality trait.

Effective feedback also **takes the receiver's needs into account.** Feedback can be destructive when it serves only the evaluator's needs and fails to consider the needs of the person on the receiving end. It should be given to help, not to hurt. Too often, feedback makes the evaluator feel better or allows him or her to belittle the receiver.

Effective feedback is **directed toward behavior that the receiver can change.** Frustration only increases when people are reminded of shortcomings or physical characteristics they can do nothing about. At an extreme, workers may experience **learned helplessness,** in which they give up trying to perform well because they know of no way to perform adequately.

Feedback is most effective when it is **solicited** rather than imposed. To get the most benefit, receivers should formulate questions for the evaluator to answer and actively seek feedback.

Effective feedback involves **sharing information** rather than giving advice. In this way, receivers are free to decide for themselves on the changes to make in accordance with their own needs.

Effective feedback is **well timed.** In general, immediate feedback is most useful—depending on the person's readiness to hear it, the support available from others, and so on.

Effective feedback also involves the **amount of information the receiver can use** rather than the amount the evaluator would like to give. Overloading a person with feedback reduces the possibility that he or she will use it effectively. An evaluator who gives more feedback than can be used is most likely satisfying a personal need rather than helping the other person.

Effective feedback concerns **what is said or done and how—not why.** Telling people what their motivations or intentions are tends to alienate them and contributes to a climate of resentment, suspicion, and distrust; it does not contribute to learning or development. Assuming knowledge of why a person says or does something is dangerous. If evaluators are uncertain of receivers' motives or intent, the uncertainty itself is feedback and should be revealed.

Finally, effective feedback is **checked** to ensure clear communication. One way is to have the receiver try to rephrase the feedback, to see if it corresponds to what the evaluator had in mind. No matter what the intent, feedback is often threatening and thus subject to considerable distortion or misinterpretation.

Interview Follow-Up

Even with the most useful feedback, follow-up is essential to ensure that the behavioral contract negotiated during the interview is fulfilled. Because changing behavior is hard work, there is a tendency for supervisors, as well as incumbents, to put the agreement on the back burner. Consequently, a supervisor may wish to verify that the incumbent knows what is expected, has a strategy to perform as desired, and realizes the consequences of good or bad behavior.

Additionally, it is important to immediately reinforce any new behavior on the job that matches desired objectives. If there is a delay in reinforcement, it is less likely that new behavior will become a habit. Reinforcement can be as simple as a pat on the back or a compliment (That was nice work, George) or as tangible as a note placed in the employee's file indicating performance improvement.

DIAGNOSING PERFORMANCE

While the interview provides a mechanism by which performance information can be exchanged, it is only one component of an effective behavioral change process. That is, for performance appraisal processes to work well, the information on which the interview is based must be accurate. This means that performance gaps need to be identified as soon as possible and the cause of the deficiency accurately pinpointed. There are three ways to identify deficiencies.

Identifying Performance Gaps

As discussed in Chapter 6, employee job performance is appraised in terms of behaviors, outcomes, and goals. These serve not only to determine performance but also to identify peformance gaps. To do so, however, they are used somewhat differently. For example, goals can be used to identify performance deficiencies by determining how well an employee does in relation to the goals set. If an employee had a performance goal of reducing the scrap rate by 10 percent but reduced it by only 5 percent, a performance gap exists. The discrepancy between actual and set goals can thus be used to spot performance gaps. This method is valid if the goals are not contradictory and can be quantified in measureable terms, and if the subordinate's performance can be measured in the terms in which the goals are set.[19]

Exhibit 7.2 includes a checklist of other symptoms associated with performance problems. While the checklist does not identify the causes of the performance discrepancies, more than one "yes" indicates a need to probe deeper. In addition to comparing performance to relevant standards, the performance levels of incumbents, units, or departments can be compared with one another. For example, organizations with several divisions often measure the overall performance of each division by comparing it with that of all other divisions. The divisions ranked at the bottom then are identified as problem areas because they have performance gaps. Whether ranking individuals or units, identifying

EXHIBIT
7.2

Checklist for Identifying Performance Problems

Read each question. If you are thinking "yes" in response to a question, place a check mark next to that item. If not, leave it blank.

Do Peers Complain That
_____ 1. She is not treating them fairly?
_____ 2. He is not carrying his own weight?
_____ 3. She is rude?
_____ 4. He is agrumentative and confrontal?
_____ 5. She is all talk and no action?

Do Customers
_____ 1. Always ask for someone else to help them?
_____ 2. Complain about her attitude?
_____ 3. Complain that he has made promises to them that he's never fulfilled?
_____ 4. Say she is bad-mouthing you, the organization, or its products?
_____ 5. Complain that he is too pushy?

Do You
_____ 1. Find it difficult to get your own work done because you spend so much time with him on his problems and mistakes?
_____ 2. Worry about what she will say to customers and clients?
_____ 3. Check his work often because you are afraid of mistakes?
_____ 4. Do work yourself that you should have delegated to her?
_____ 5. Assign work to others because they can do it faster or better than he can?
_____ 6. Hear about her mistakes from your boss or others?
_____ 7. Sometimes find out that he has lied to you or stretched the truth?
_____ 8. Seldom think of her when you're deciding who should get an important assignment?

Does He/She
_____ 1. Infrequently complete assignments on time?
_____ 2. Often show up to work late or not at all?
_____ 3. Always have an excuse for poor performance?
_____ 4. Wait to be assigned additional work rather than asking for more work when an assignment is completed?
_____ 5. Rarely complete assigments in the way you want?
_____ 6. Ignore suggestions for improvement?

performance gaps by means of comparisons prevents an effective diagnosis of the cause of the perforamnce gaps.

Finally, gaps can be identified by comparisons over time. For example, a manager who sold one thousand record albums last month but only eight hundred this month appears to have a performance gap. Although performance has declined, does this gap represent a deficiency that should be or can be corrected? The month in which one thousand albums were sold may have fallen during the peak buying season. During the month in which only eight hundred albums were sold, the employee may have had to attend an important conference vital to longer-run record sales.

Regardless of the method used to discover if a performance deficiency exists, once detected, managers want to remove it. If they hope to improve their employees' performance, however, they must begin by examining the causes underlying any actual gaps.

Identifying Causes of Performance Deficiencies

To uncover the reasons for performance deficiences, a number of questions can be asked, based on a model of the determinants of employee behavior in organizations.[20] This model enables the personnel manager to diagnose performance deficiencies and correct them in a systematic way. In general, the model says that employees perform well if the following determinants are present:

- Ability
- Interest in doing the job
- Opportunity to grow and advance
- Clearly defined goals
- Certainty about what is expected
- Feedback on how well they are doing
- Rewards for performing well
- Punishments for performing poorly
- Power to get resources to do the job[21]

Exhibit 7.3 shows these determinants and the specific questions to ask in pinpointing the causes of performance deficiences. Negative responses indicate that the item is probably a cause. Based on a series of such responses, the likely causes of a performance deficiency can be established.

Attributional Processes

The process that people use to explain their behavior and that of others is called the **attribution process.** Individuals attribute their and others' behavior to various causes. Understanding the attributional processes that individuals use facilitates predicting what causes and responses managers are likely to attach to the performance deficiencies they see in their subordinates.

In relation to performance, managers attribute causes of subordinates' deficiencies to either the subordinates **(internal attribution)** or the subordinates' environment **(external attribution).** Internal attributions include low effort (motivation) and low ability, and external attributions include task interference, bad luck, lack of organizational rewards, and poor supervision. Managers are more likely to make internal attributions to the extent that the incumbent (1) does not perform poorly on other tasks (high directiveness), (2) performs poorly when other incumbents perform well on the same task **(low consensus),** and (3) has performed poorly on the same task in the past **(high consistency).** Managers are also likely to focus on motivation over ability if an incumbent has performed the task adequately in the past but isn't performing adequately now.

A major hurdle in identifying the causes of performance deficiencies is **actor-observed differences.** Whereas a supervisor focuses on incumbent characteristics that block the attainment of objectives, the incumbent concentrates on environmental factors that obstruct goal attainment. This difference in perceptual focus is problematic because if an incumbent believes that the cause of the performance deficiency lies elsewhere (difficult task, poor supervision, lack of information), he or she will not respond favorably to strategies designed to

Diagnosing the Causes of Performance Deficiences

Check those factors affecting an individual's performance or behavior that apply to the situation you are analyzing.

		Yes	No
I.	*Knowledge, Skills, and Abilities*		
A.	Does the incumbent have the skill to perform as expected?	____	____
B.	Has the incumbent performed as expected before?	____	____
C.	Does the incumbent believe he or she has the ability to perform as desired?	____	____
D.	Does the incumbent have the interest to perform as desired?	____	____
II.	*Goals for the Incumbent*		
A.	Were goals communicated to the incumbent prior to the performance period?	____	____
B.	Are the goals specific?	____	____
C.	Are the goals difficult but attainable?	____	____
III.	*Uncertainty for the Incumbent*		
A.	Has desired performance been clearly specified?	____	____
B.	Have rewards or consequences for good or bad performance been specified?	____	____
C.	Is the incumbent clear about his or her level of authority?	____	____
IV.	*Feedback to the Incumbent*		
A.	Does the incumbent know when he or she has performed correctly or incorrectly?	____	____
B.	Is the feedback diagnostic so the incumbent can perform better in the future?	____	____
C.	Is there a delay between performance and the receipt of the feedback?	____	____
D.	Can performance feedback be easily interpreted?	____	____
V.	*Consequences to the Incumbent*		
A.	Is performing as expected punishing?	____	____
B.	Is nonperformance more rewarding?	____	____
C.	Does performing as desired matter?	____	____
D.	Are there positive consequences for performing as desired?	____	____
VI.	*Power for the Incumbent*		
A.	Can the incumbent mobilize the resources to get the job done?	____	____
B.	Does the incumbent have the tools and equipment to perform as desired?	____	____

SOURCE: This format is based on R.F. Mager and P. Pipe, *Analyzing Performance Problems, or "You Really Oughta Wanna"* (Belmont, Calif.: Fearon Pitman, 1970).

improve his or her ability (training programs) or motivation. Conversely, if a supervisor has tunnel vision about the cause of the deficiency, the real problem may not be identified. As a result, the incumbent may be placed in an elaborate, costly, and unnecessary training program when all he or she needed was clearer instructions or performance feedback.[22]

STRATEGIES FOR
IMPROVING PERFORMANCE

When performance deficiencies are found, companies can do many things to improve employees' performance.

Positive Reinforcement Systems

The **positive reinforcement system** lets employees know how well they are meeting specific goals and rewards improvements with praise and recognition. In the sense that no money is involved, it is a unique incentive system. This approach to improvement encourages desirable job behaviors by establishing behavioral criteria and setting up reward systems contingent on achieving them.[23] Implementing this strategy requires developing accurate behavioral measures of performance. This can be done by using the critical incidents technique of job analysis (described in Chapter 3) to identify critical effective and ineffective performance behaviors. If the organization already uses a behaviorally based performance appraisal form, such as BARS and BOS, this can be used instead. (Using behavioral criteria should help eliminate many rating errors and improve the validity of the appraisals.)

Once these behavioral criteria are established, subordinates should be made aware of them. Next, goals should be established for each behavioral dimension and rewards specified for goal attainment. To obtain maximum benefit from the goal-setting process, the goals should be relatively difficult to achieve, specific, clear, and acceptable to subordinates.

As with all incentive systems, a basic premise of positive reinforcement is that behavior can be understood and modified by its consequences. That is, performance is elicited because of the consequence of getting rewards. In this case, the consequences of behaving well are not monetary rewards, but this need not be the case all the time. Examples of different monetary rewards to reduce absenteeism are described in the second "PHRM in the News."

Another program of rewards used specifically to reduce absenteeism is called **earned time.** This is a new approach to the way paid absence is accumulated and used. Under earned time, employees have more choice and responsibility in the way they use their paid time off. Accumulating earned time depends on each employee's preferences. Rather than dividing benefits into specific numbers of days for vacation, personal leave, sick leave, and short-term disability, the earned time approach lumps these days into one package. These days can be used for a variety of purposes, and unused days can result in a cash payment at the time of voluntary termination. Earned time is available for use as soon as it is "earned" on the job and, in effect, is "no-fault absence."[24]

The priniciple behind the program is that the number of earned-time days for which an employee may receive a cash payment is less than the previous total of sick, vacation, jury, and all other benefit days. For example, the combined total may be divided by two, three, or four to get the earned time. This time is then available for employees to use without having to meet special requirements. The program's prime advantages are (1) a reduction in unplanned absences, (2) a reduction in employee-supervisor conflict over legitimacy of absences and individual responsibility, and (3) flexibility to suit individual priorities.

Strategies for Improving Job Attendance

First-line supervisors are the key to any attendance improvement program, asserts John V. Schappi, BNA's vice president for human resources. In his book, *Improving Job Attendance*, Schappi outlines the role of first-line supervisors in communicating and enforcing attendance policies, and describes available enforcement options, including incentive programs that reward good attendance and a system of progressive discipline for chronic absenteeism.

First-Line Opportunities

Both the interview and orientation process provide first-line supervisors an opportunity to stress attendance issues, Schappi maintains. As part of the interview, Schappi suggests, first-line supervisors should assess the work ethic of potential new-hires by asking about their past attendance habits and conducting thorough reference checks that include questions about attendance records. At orientation, supervisors should emphasize the importance of good attendance in employees' future evaluations and explain the company's policy on monitoring attendance and disciplining those who are excessively or inexcusably absent, Schappi says.

During the course of employment, supervisors should record each worker's absences and their reasons, and watch for patterns of absenteeism. Each time an absence occurs, the supervisor should review the employee's entire attendance record to facilitate early detection of potential problem employees. For example, employees who are often absent before or after scheduled days off might be targeted for counseling, Schappi suggests. Supervisors also should review attendance records monthly, noting frequency, causes, and patterns of absence; tardiness record; total time absent over

a representative period; and compliance with call-in policies.

The Carrot . . .

Rewarding employees is one strategy for encouraging good attendance, according to Schappi. Rewards and incentives for good job attendance can be either tangible or intangible, he notes, adding that "the system's success depends on the type and frequency of the reward and the way it is communicated and granted." In particular, Schappi stresses, employees must know precisely what is expected of them and what the rewards will be for meeting those expectations.

Among tangible rewards, says Schappi, are:

- Cash awards or paid leave for perfect attendance,
- Bonuses for unused sick leave,
- Profit-sharing plans that offer greater financial gain for employees with better attendance,
- Retirement benefit plans in which unused sick leave goes toward extra benefits or is paid in a lump sum at retirement, and
- Lotteries in which employees are eligible for monthly prizes, with the number of prizes dependent on the group's overall attendance record.

Recognition for good attendance also can take the form of intangible rewards. These can include posting an honor roll of employees with perfect attendance on the bulletin board or in the company newsletter, holding a year-end recognition ceremony, or issuing monthly or annual commendations to employees with the best attendance records.

SOURCE: "Strategies for Improving Job Attendance," *Bulletin to Management*, 10 March 1988, p. 80. Used by permission of The Bureau of National Affairs, copyright 1988.

Positive Discipline Programs

Some organizations improve peformance through the use of **positive discipline or nonpunitive discipline.**[25] The essential aspects of a positive discipline program include the following:

> When disciplinary discussions have failed to produce the desired changes, management places the individual on a one-day, "decision-making leave." The company pays the employee for a day to demonstrate the organization's desire to see him or her remain a member of the organization and to eliminate the resentment and hostility the punitive actions usually produce. But tenure with the organization is conditional on the individual's decision to solve the immediate problem and make a "total performance commitment" to good performance on the job. The employee is instructed to return on the day following the leave with a decision either to change and stay or to quit and find more satisfying work elsewhere.[26]

Tampa Electric Company adopted a positive discipline program in 1981.

> The decline in absenteeism alone resulted in sizable financial savings for the company. Sick time usage in maintenance and production operations dropped from an average of 66.7 hours in 1977 to 36.6 hours in 1983. In one operating department, the average use of sick time per employee dropped from 58.8 hours to 19.5 hours per year in five years. Based on a 1983 average wage rate of $11.78 per hour, this reduction in sick time use saved the company $439,404, or 1.38% of the 1983 payroll—the equivalent of having 18 additional people on the job.[27]

Employee Assistance Programs

Employee assistance programs (EAPs) are specifically designed to assist employees with chronic personal problems that hinder their job performance and attendance. EAPs are often used with employees who are alcoholics or who have severe domestic problems. Because the job may be partly responsible for these problems, some employers are taking the lead in establishing EAPs to help affected workers.[28]

A company that establishes an employee assistance program generally thinks that it has a responsibility toward employees and that employees should be given a chance to correct any undesirable job behavior. Helping alcoholic employees also makes good economic sense because 25 percent of each alcoholic's salary is the average cost to the employer as a result of absenteeism, reduced productivity, accidents in the work place, and use of the company medical plan. Furthermore, an estimated 65 to 80 percent of those who receive treatment for chemical dependency return to the work force and do what their supervisors consider a satisfactory job. Nevertheless, employees must also help themselves. If they fail to participate in an EAP or to recover through other means, employers may have no choice but to terminate them. The philosophy of most EAPs is to help individuals help themselves within a context of fairness, yet firmness.

While EAPs that provide assistance with alcohol and drug abuse are most common, organizations have also established EAPs to help employees cope with marital/family problems, mental disorders, financial problems, stress, eating disorders, weight control, and smoking cessation and to provide dependent care programs, bereavement counseling, and AIDS support group meetings.

To be successful, an employee assistance program should possess the following attributes:

- Top management backing
- Union or employee support
- Confidentiality
- Easy access
- Trained supervisors
- Trained union steward, if in a union setting
- Insurance
- Availability of numerous services for assistance and referral
- Skilled professional leadership
- Systems for monitoring, assessing, and revising

Even though EAPs are designed to provide valuable assistance to employees, many employees in need fail to use the programs unless faced with the alternative of being fired. When so confronted, however, the success rate of those attending EAPs is high. The results can mean substantial gains in employee job performance and reductions in absenteeism. For example,

> Employees experienced an increase in work productivity and a decrease in lost work time, health insurance claims, and accidents after participating in the employee assistance plan at Detroit Edison Co. . .
>
> For the 67 employees receiving EAP treatment, the total number of lost work days dropped 29 percent, from 476 days before treatment to 341 days following treatment, the study reports. The study also finds that after EAP participation:
>
> - Combined lost work time was reduced by 18 percent—from 117 instances to 97 instances.
> - The cost of health insurance claims declined 26 percent—from a total $36,472 to $27,122.
> - Work suspensions dropped from five to three; written warnings decreased from eight to seven; and the number of job-related accidents went from seven to three.[29]

Employee Counseling

To change the habits of chronically absent employees, McGraw Edison has devised an innovative counseling program that stresses problem-solving and goal-setting techniques. This individual approach focuses on the "5 to 10 percent of the work force" that has a history of absenteeism. Before beginning the actual counseling with individual employees, supervisors take the following steps:

- Identify the consistently worst offenders. Make a list of all employees who have a record of repeated absences, regardless of the "presumed legitimacy or the underlying reasons" for missing work.
- Centralize the absenteeism data. Records and information should be accumulated, analyzed, and maintained in one central location.
- Collect long-term data. Absenteeism records on individuals should be kept for a sufficiently long period to show that a clear pattern exists.

Once the decision is made to meet with the employee, supervisors should do the following:

- Examine the attendance record with the employee.
- Be sure the employee is aware of the severity of the problem, as well as the organization's attendance standards.
- Prepare a brief, accurate memo at the session's end, outlining the problem, noting the reasons given by the employee, and specifying whether or not the employee responded with a desire to improve.

If the first session does not produce a significant change, a second counseling session should be scheduled. Participants in this session should include the worker's supervisor, the employee, a union representative (if applicable), and higher management officials. An upper-level manager should be present to ensure that due process protection (Chapter 14) is provided for the employee. Results of the second counseling session should also be documented.

If the employee shows no improvement after the second session, another session can be held, which should also include an upper-level manager. At this stage, responsibility for the "decision to meet the expected standard of attendance and continuity of employment" should be placed directly on the employee. To dramatize the importance and seriousness of the situation, the employee might be allowed to take off a day with pay to decide whether he or she wishes to resign or to commit to a long-term program of positive improvement. If no sign of improvement is shown after this step, discharging the employee may be necessary.

Negative Behavioral Strategies

While most employees want to conduct themselves in a manner that is acceptable to the organization and their fellow employees, problems of absenteeism, poor work performance, and rule violation do arise. When informal discussions or coaching fails to neutralize these dysfunctional behaviors, formal disciplinary action is needed. The objective of punishment is to decrease the frequency of an undesirable behavior. Punishments can include material consequences, such as a cut in pay, a disciplinary layoff without pay, a demotion, or, ultimately, termination. More common punishments are interpersonal and include oral reprimands and nonverbal cues, such as frowns, grunts, and aggressive body language.[30]

Punishment is commonly used by many organizations because of its ability to achieve relatively immediate results. Additionally, punishment is reinforcing to supervisors in that they feel they have taken action. Discipline (i.e. punishment) is an effective management tool for the following reasons:

- Discipline alerts the marginal employee that his or her low performance is unacceptable and that a change in behavior is warranted.
- Discipline has vicarious reinforcing power. When one person is punished, it signals other employees regarding expected performance and behavioral conduct.
- If the discipline is viewed as appropriate by other employees, it may increase their motivation, morale, and performance.

Punishment works when other strategies fail to produce the desired results.[31] A recent study in a retail store showed that managers who used the organization's disciplinary system more frequently than their peers did had higher departmental performance ratings.[32] One reason is that employees in the high-performing groups relied on one another to learn appropriate behavior. As a result, they modeled the behaviors of successful peers and imposed group norms on low-performing employees.

One caution is in order. Punishment may appear effective when it is not. Consider the following example. A word processing supervisor decides to examine whether punishment is more effective than positive reinforcement. To test this, she praises a subordinate each time individual performance is better than that of 80 percent of the work group members. She keeps accurate performance records and is surprised to find out that on average, performance of her subordinates *dropped* following the praise.

Is this a correct solution? Unfortunately, the logic is faulty because the manager has failed to consider regression to the mean. That is, low performers tend to regress up (perform better) and high performers tend to regress down (perform worse) toward the mean. Consequently, with or without praise or punishment, low performers on average will improve, and high performers on average will get worse. This often-ignored bias is referred to as **regression to the mean** and limits the ability to predict the future from the past.[33]

Punishment can also have undesirable side effects. For example, an employee reprimanded for low performance may become defensive and angry toward the supervisor and the organization. As recent news reports attest, this anger may result in sabotage (destroying equipment, passing trade secrets) or retaliation (shooting the supervisor). Second, punishment frequently leads to only the short-term suppression of the undesirable behavior, rather than its elimination. Another concern is that control of the undesirable behavior becomes contingent on the presence of the punishing agent. When the manager is not present, the behavior is likely to be displayed. Finally, the employee may not perceive the punishment as unpleasant. For example, an organization with a progressive disciplinary procedure may send an employee home without pay for being late one too many times. If this occurs at the beginning of the fishing season, the employee may relish the excuse not to go to work.

The negative effects of punishment can be reduced by incorporating several principles, including the following:

- Provide ample and clear warning. Many organizations have clearly defined disciplinary steps. For example, the first offense might elicit an oral warning; the second offense, a written warning; the third offense, a disciplinary layoff; the fourth offense, discharge.
- Administer the discipline as quickly as possible. If a long time elapses between the ineffective behavior and the discipline, the employee may not know what the discipline is for.
- Administer the same discipline for the same behavior for everyone everytime. Discipline has to be administered fairly and consistently.
- Administer the discipline impersonally. Discipline should be based on a specific behavior, not a specific person.

Because the immediate supervisor or manager plays the integral role in administering discipline, the personnel and human resource department and the organization should do the following to increase the discipline's effectiveness:

- Allow managers and supervisors to help select their own employees.
- Educate managers and supervisors about the organization's disciplinary policies and train them to administer the policies.

■ Set up standards that are equitable to employees and that managers and supervisors can easily and consistently implement.

Taking these steps not only reduces the likely negative effects generally associated with discipline but also helps ensure that employee rights are respected (discussed further in Chapter 14). This is further ensured with the establishment of fair work rules and work policies that are consistently applied and enforced.

To be effective, work rules and policies must be reasonably related to appropriate management goals and should also be effectively communicated. The rules and policies promulgated and enforced must not result in unfair adverse impact on any group of employees protected by fair employment laws, and they cannot violate several other acts and court decisions defining employee rights to job security. Furthermore, these rules and policies should embrace the notion of progressive discipline and respect due process. In other words, the rules and policies (1) must apply equally to all employees, regardless of race, religion, national origin, sex, age, or disability; (2) must be clearly stated; (3) must be enforced objectively; and (4) should reflect the information necessary to prove equal application and enforcement of work rules. When administered accordingly, discipline may be an effective strategy to improve performance.

When Nothing Else Works

Helping incumbents—especially the problem ones—to improve their work performance is a tough job. It is easy to get frustrated and to wonder if you are just spinning your wheels. Even when we want our efforts to work, they sometimes don't. Still, when you conclude that "nothing works," you are really saying that it is no longer worth your time and energy to help the employee improve. This conclusion should not be made in haste because the organization has already invested a great deal of time and money in the selection and training of its employees. However, some situations may require more drastic steps if

■ Performance actually gets worse.
■ There is a little change in the problem behavior—but not enough.
■ There is no change in the problem behavior.
■ Drastic changes in behavior occur immediately, but improvements don't last.

If, after repeated warnings and counseling, performance does not improve, then four last recourses are available.

Transferring.   Sometimes there is just not a good match between an employee and a job. If, however, the employee has useful skills and abilities, it may be beneficial to transfer him or her. Transferring is appropriate if the employee's skill deficiency would have little or no impact on the new position. The concern with transfers is that there must be a job available for which the problem employee is qualified.

Restructuring.   Some jobs are particulary unpleasant or onerous. For these positions, the solution may be redesigning the job, rather than replacing the employee. It may also make sense to redesign a position to take advantage of an employee's special strengths. If an employee has extraordinary technical expertise, it may be advantageous to utilize this expertise, rather than having the employee perform routine maintenance tasks.

Firing.   While PHRM policies vary across organizations and industries, firing is generally warranted for dishonesty, habitual absenteeism, substance abuse, and insubordination, including flat refusals to do certain things requested and consistently low productivity that cannot be corrected through training. Unfortunately, firing, even for legitimate reasons, is unpleasant. In addition to the administrative hassles, documentation, and paperwork involved, supervisors often feel guilty about being the "bad guy." And the thought of sitting down with an employee and delivering the bad news makes most supervisors anxious. As a result, they continue to put off the firing and justify it by saying that they won't be able to find a "better" replacement. Still, when one considers the consequences of errors, drunkenness, or "being high" on the job, firing may be cost effective. Employee rights regarding firing will be discussed in Chapter 14.

Neutralizing.   Neutralizing a problem employee involves restructuring that employee's job in such a way that his or her areas of needed improvement have as little impact as possible. Because group morale may suffer when an ineffective employee is given special treatment, *neutralizing should be avoided* whenever possible. However, it is a fact of organizational life that neutralizing may be practical when the firing process is time consuming and cumbersome or when an employee is close to retiring. In neutralizing the employee, a manager shouldn't harass the employee, hoping that he or she will quit or transfer, but instead should assign the employee noncritical tasks in which he or she can be productive.[34]

To help ensure the effectiveness of programs to improve performance, performance gaps and their potential causes should first be identified. Then alternative programs can be selected and their relative utility or effectiveness assessed. This assessment requires determining the costs of the program and the value of its benefits, including assessing the cost of the current performance gap and the extent to which the program can reduce it. In general, this paradigm for assessing performance improvement programs is also applicable to assessing the entire performance appraisal system.

TRENDS IN PERFORMANCE APPRAISAL AND PERFORMANCE IMPROVEMENT

As mentioned earlier in this chapter, when subordinates are empowered and responsible for their own behavior, the management of performance becomes easier. An extension of this philosophy is self-management, which requires employees to manage their own behavior. Other significant trends include the assessment of the performance management system and the linkage of performance appraisal processes to the strategic plan.

Self-Management

Self-management is a relatively new approach to resolving performance discrepancies. It teaches people to exercise control over their own behavior. Self-management begins by having people assess their *own* problems and set specific (but individual) hard goals in relation to those problems. Once goals are set, the employees discuss ways in which the environment facilitates or hinders goal attainment. The challenge here is to develop strategies that eliminate blocks to performance success. Put another way, self-management teaches people to observe their own behavior, compare their outputs to their goals, and administer their own reinforcement to sustain goal commitment and performance.[35]

The power of self-management in organizations is only beginning to be recognized. In a recent study, twenty unionized government employees with habitual attendance problems identified and learned to overcome personal obstacles to job attendance. During eight thirty-minute, one-on-one sessions they identified the reasons for using sick leave (legitimate illness, medical appointment, job stress, job boredom, difficulties with co-workers, alcohol and drug issues, family problems, transportation difficulties, and employee rights). After identifying problem behaviors, the employees identified the conditions that elicited and maintained the problem behavior and, more importantly, identified specific coping strategies. This completed the self-assessment phase of the program.

Next, distinct goals to increase attendance by a specified amount over a specified period of time were set. These were coupled with the development of individual day-by-day strategies to attain the long-term goal. The employees were then taught to record their own attendance, the reason for missing work, and the steps that were to be followed to get to work. Finally, they identified powerful rewards (e.g., self-praise, purchase of a gift) and punishers (clean the oven, do the laundry) that could be self-administered. The employees practicing self-management attended work 13 percent more (fifty-five hours in twelve weeks) than did other employees with similar past attendance problems. A follow-up study showed that the improvement in attendance persisted for over a year.[36]

While self-management has been proved effective in the management of attendance problems, its usefulness in resolving other performance problems remains to be seen. On a societal level, it has possibilities for helping the homeless, and welfare recipients, return to the work force. It also seems that self-management could be used to improve supervisory skills, safety equipment usage, and other types of dysfunctional behavior.

Assessment of PAS Success

Either as part of a complete organization assessment or as an independent effort, organizations are increasingly evaluating the effectiveness of their PAS. Such assessments can be brief, with five or six questions, or detailed, with more than two hundred questions. Budget limitations, time constraints, and situational practicalities dictate the depth of this analysis. However, when possible, the following questions should be answered in an assessment of a PAS:

- What purpose does the organization want its performance appraisal system to serve?
- Do the appraisal forms really elicit the information to serve these purposes? Are these forms compatible with the jobs for which they are being used (i.e., are they job related)? Are the forms based on behaviors or outcomes that might be included in a critical incidents job analysis?
- Are the appraisal forms designed to minimize errors and ensure consistency? As discussed previously, some superiors commit errors in their appraisals of subordinates. For example, two employees may perform identically, but one employee's superior may commit a strictness error, and the other employee's superior may commit a leniency error. This will cause one of the employees

to appear to be far less competent than the other. These errors are common in organizations using rating forms. If the organization is to treat all its employees fairly, it must try to reduce these errors, perhaps by monitoring the lack of consistency in the way in which superiors complete appraisal forms.[37]

- Are the processes of the appraisal effective? For example, are the appraisal interviews done effectively? Are goals established? Are they developed jointly? Do superiors and subordinates accept the appraisal process?
- Are superiors rewarded for correctly evaluating and developing their employees? Are they trained in giving feedback, setting goals, and using problem-solving techniques? Are they trained to spot performance deficiencies and correctly identify the causes?
- Are superiors relatively free from task interference in doing performance appraisal?
- Are the appraisals being implemented correctly? What procedures have been set up to ensure that the appraisals are being done correctly? What supporting materials are available to aid superiors in appraising their subordinates?
- Do methods exist for reviewing and evaluating the effectiveness of the total system? Are there goals and objectives for the system? Are there systematic procedures for gathering data to measure how well the goals and objectives are being met?[38]

By addressing these questions and taking corrective action where necessary, an organization's PAS is more likely to serve its purposes and the broader organizational human resource goals of productivity, quality of work life, and legal compliance. For an organization just beginning to implement a PAS, the implications of all these questions should be understood and incorporated into the initial PAS design.[39]

Strategic Involvement of Performance Appraisal

Organizations are increasingly using performance appraisal to gain competitive advantage. For example, at GTE performance appraisals are viewed as one of the most important tools in the management arsenal. According to former GTE chairman Theodore F. Brophy, the GTE appraisal system complements the emergent strategic planning emphasis in all areas of the corporation. The appraisal reviews assist executives in clarifying and articulating objectives and expectations for themselves and their employees. They give GTE a realistic assessment of its strengths, weaknesses, and future requirements. As such, the company is now able to better utilize its human resources than at any time in the past.[40]

Establishing the linkage between performance appraisal and an organization's strategy is not easy. Decisions must be made regarding how tight and complete the linkage will be. For example, will appraisal practices be standardized across organizational units, or will each unit be free to develop its own appraisal system? Standardization allows comparisons across units but may not provide the flexibility needed in large, diverse organizations.

Another issue is the security of the information. Questions need to be answered regarding who will have access to performance-related information and how that information will be stored (in a centralized system or in individual files). As will be discussed in the next chapter, another choice revolves around the linkage between appraisal results and organizational rewards. While these are only a few of the decisions that need to be made about performance appraisal processes, they exemplify the depth of probing needed to link appraisal processes to a corporation's strategic plan.

SUMMARY

Ineffective employee performance, whether anyone wants to admit it or not, plagues all organizations at least some of the time. For a performance appraisal system to be effective, it must not only permit the gathering of performance appraisal data; it must also enable the manager to *use* this information. Organizations that have developed an effective performance appraisal system, therefore, directly influence productivity, quality of work life, and legal compliance through the gathering and use of performance appraisal data.

Because of the dual appraisal purposes of evaluation and development, conflicts are inevitable. These conflicts, if unaddressed, will cripple the effectiveness of any performance appraisal system. Recognition of their sources, however, suggests how performance feedback can be given to reduce them. From a design perspective, an effective performance appraisal system can avoid inherent conflicts by (1) separating evaluation from development, (2) focusing on behavior rather than on subjective traits, (3) distinguishing evaluation of current performance from future performance, and (4) using multiple appraisals to improve reliability and validity.

If managers are to effectively improve their employees' performance, they must learn how to conduct a performance appraisal interview. Feedback can be given through a tell-and-sell, tell-and-listen, problem-solving, or mixed approach to the interview. Whereas Chapter 6 emphasized the content of performance appraisal, this chapter considered the process of giving performance feedback.

Although numerous motivation theories exist to explain human performance in organizations, a single diagnostic framework has been provided to help you, the appraiser, get at the "root cause" of the performance problem. Using this framework to understand performance gaps forms a basis for choosing different strategies to improve performance. From a developmental perspective, strategies that involve participation and job clarification encourage self-directed improvement. Ultimately, problem employees may require outside assistance through counseling or EAPs. Control of behavior can also be achieved by linking rewards to behavior or using group or organizational norms (as suggested by the discussion of socialization in Chapter 12). In some cases it may be necessary to neutralize the negative behavior or in extreme cases to fire the employee. But these strategies should be used only when all else fails. Because all organizations experience performance problems, it is crucial that the performance appraisal system—the process of gathering and feeding back appraisal data—function to improve individual performance. Performance assessment also plays a vital role in other key personnel functions, particlarly compensation and training, topics explored in the chapters ahead.

DISCUSSION QUESTIONS

1. Suppose you have decided that an employee is not working out and must be fired. What performance appraisal approach would you want to use to support this decision? Why?

2. An observer of the performance appraisal process once commented that when it comes to appraisal, all organizations experience a "shortage of bastards." What do you suppose this comment means? Does this comment relate to the types of inherent conflict associated with the PAS? Explain.

3. What considerations are there in designing an effective performance appraisal system?

4. With what causes are performance deficiencies associated, and what are the respective strategies used to correct those performance deficits?

5. What are the critical issues in determining the utility of a specific performance appraisal system?

6. Assume you are supervising a group of employees that fall into one of three categories: (1) an effective performer with lots of potential for advancement, (2) an effective performer who lacks motivation or ability (or both) for potential advancement, and (3) a currently ineffective performer. It is performance appraisal time, and you must plan interviews with subordinates from each of these three categories. How will your interviews differ? How will they be similar?

7. Assume you are a professor counseling a student with a grade complaint. Describe how you would conduct this session, using (1) the tell-and-sell approach, (2) the tell-and-listen approach, and (3) the problem-solving approach. As a professor, which would you feel most comfortable using? Why? As a student, which would you prefer? Why?

8. If subjective, trait-oriented approaches are legally vulnerable, why do you suppose organizations persist in using them?

9. What are the advantages of self-management for the organization? For the individual?

10. Discuss the ramifications of neutralizing employees' performance.

CASE STUDY

Evaluating the Performance of Nurses Aides at Sleepy Manor

Sleepy Manor is a privately owned long-term health care facility the primary objective of which is to create an atmosphere for its residents that adds life to their years, not just years to their lives. The staff of Sleepy Manor consists of fifty employees in addition to the administrator and general manager. Sleepy Manor also contracts with a local physician, physical therapist, and nurse consultant for special services. Sleepy Manor has adequate facilities for fifty residents and provides around-the-clock care.

Staff work three eight-hour shifts and some four-hour shifts depending on the mix of nurses aides and LPNs. One LPN is scheduled during each shift with six nurses aides during the daytime and three during the evening shifts. Nursing staff and nurses aides rotate regularly so aides do not report directly to any one nurse. Director of Nursing Marilyn Gest makes all job assignments and is responsible for selecting, training, and appraising all nurses and nurses aides. Presently, there are ten nurses and twenty-five nurses aides.

Employees are evaluated at the end of six months and once a year thereafter. Performance appraisal is done for feedback and employee development purposes only. However, occasionaly low ratings have been used to justify terminating an employee. Pay raises are indirectly linked to appraisal results. Input from performance appraisal is one of the factors used by the owner of the nursing home, Fred Sweet, to determine raises. It isn't, however, the only factor. Fred has been known to give a pret-

ty girl a little extra in her paycheck to keep her happy. Need also seems to be a factor. The more in need employees are, the more likely they are to get a pay raise. These practices have undermined the effectiveness of Sleepy Manor's performance appraisal system. As it is, performance appraisal generally is viewed as a big joke by all employees at Sleepy Manor.

As shown in Exhibit 1, employees are rated on ten dimensions (responsibility, independence,

---

Sleepy Manor Nursing Home Performance Appraisal Form	EXHIBIT 1

Name_____   Date_____

Score each factor using the following key:
1—poor, 2—below average, 3—average, 4—above average, 5—excellent

_____ 1. *Responsibility.* Identifies and takes appropriate nursing measures to meet the physical and emotional needs of the patient.
_____ 2. *Independence.* Works independently, but will request assistance if needed.
_____ 3. *Punctuality.* Is punctual and reports to work on time. Returns from lunch and breaks within allotted time.
_____ 4. *Self-starter.* Completes assignments. Is a self-starter.
_____ 5. *Teamwork.* Assists others when asked and offers independently to help. Is liked by peers.
_____ 6. *Enthusiasm.* Shows interest in the patients and the job. Never bad-mouths the company in front of patients or their familiies.
_____ 7. *Absenteeism.* Has no more than three call-ins during a six-month period. Calls in at least two hours before the shift starts.
_____ 8. *Organization.* Organizes work responsibilities carefully. Sets priorities. Does what is told when told once.
_____ 9. *Judgment.* Has good judgment.
_____ 10. *Personal appearance.* Always dresses in proper uniform. Uniform and hair are neat. Shoes are polished.

Overall Evaluation_____

Employee Comments:

Employee Strengths:

Employee Weakneses:

Supervisory Comments:

Employee's Signature   Supervisor's Signature   Date

punctuality, self-starting ability, teamwork, enthusiasm, absenteeism, organization, judgment, and
personal appearance). Traditionally, Marilyn has
had each employee rate his or her own performance *prior* to the annual review. She does the
same thing independently. Then they get together
and discuss the results. Generally, employees are
quite honest about their own abilities. In fact, they
usually rate themselves lower than Marilyn does.
This has always made her job easy. That is until
today.

Today she is meeting with Theresa Sawyer, a new
employee, to go over her six-month evaluation. As
usual, she had Theresa complete the appraisal independently. The results were surprising. Whereas
Marilyn felt Theresa was performing satisfactory
in most areas, she definitely felt Theresa needed to
work on punctuality. On three occasions in the last
two weeks, Marilyn had had to find Theresa and
tell her to get back to her work station after her
lunch or rest break. She would usually find Theresa
talking to Charlie Hill, a jolly 85-year-old in Ward
D. Theresa and Charlie seemed to have formed a
special attachment to one another. While Charlie
was a sweet guy, he was one of twenty patients
assigned to Theresa. And Theresa was spending far
too much time with him and neglecting other patients. Marilyn also felt that Theresa, dress was
unprofessional. There were always buttons missing
from her uniform.

Marilyn wasn't sure she knew how to address
these issues in the appraisal interview. As a result
of all this, Marilyn gave Theresa an overall rating
of 2 (see Exhibit 2), leaving plenty of room for her
to develop her skills in the future. While her appraisal ratings were low, Marilyn didn't want to fire
Theresa. The nursing home was short of nurses
aides, and this one at least showed up to work each
day. Still, she wasn't sure what to do next.

Case Questions

1. What type of appraisal instrument is currently being used by Sleepy Manor? Is it a good appraisal device to meet the organization's objectives? Why or why not?
2. What types of rating errors are Theresa and Marilyn committing? What could be done to reduce these errors?
3. Why do you think the ratings by Theresa and Marilyn differ so drastically?
4. How would you approach the appraisal interview if you were Marilyn?
5. How would you go about improving Theresa's performance in the critical areas?
6. What would you recommend to improve the appraisal system at Sleepy Manor?

EXHIBIT 2 Comparison of Theresa's and Marilyn's Ratings

Dimension	Theresa's Ratings	Marilyn's Ratings
1. Responsibility	5	3
2. Independence	4	2
3. Punctuality	5	1
4. Self-starter	5	2
5. Teamwork	4	1
6. Enthusiasm	4	2
7. Absenteeism	4	3
8. Organization	4	3
9. Judgment	5	3
10. Personal appearance	5	0

NOTES

1. *Wall Street Journal*, 28 Aug. 1984, p. 1. Reprinted by permission of *The Wall Street Journal*, © Dow Jones & Company, Inc., 1984. All Rights Reserved.

2. N. Napier and G. Latham, "Outcome Expectancies of People Who Conduct Appraisals," *Personnel Psychology* 39 (1986): 827–39.

3. V. Huber, P. Podsakoff, and W. Todor, "An Investigation of Biasing Facts in the Attributions of Subordinates and Their Supervisors," *Journal of Business Research* 14 (1986): 83–97.

4. M. Beer, "Performance Appraisal: Dilemmas and Possibilities," *Organizational Dynamics* (Winter 1981): 26; A. Zander, "Research on Self-Esteem, Feedback and Threats to Self-Esteem," in *Performance Appraisals: Effects on Employees and Their Performance*, ed. A. Zander (New York: Foundation for Research in Human Behavior, 1963).

5. D. T. Hall, *Careers in Organizations* (Glenview, Ill.: Scott, Foresman, 1976).

6. H. H. Meyer, E. Kay, and J. R. P. French, Jr., "Split Roles in Performance Appraisal," *Harvard Business Review* (Jan./Feb. 1965): 125.

7. W. Weitzel, "How to Improve Performance Through Successful Appraisals," *Personnel* (Oct. 1987): 18–23.

8. C. Hymowitz, "Bosses; Don't Be Nasty (and other tips for reviewing worker performance);" *Wall Street Journal* 17 Jan. 1985, p. 35.

9. Catalenello and J. A. Hooper, "Managerial Appraisal," *Personnel Administrator* (Sept. 1981): 75–81; T. Rendero, "Consensus," *Personnel* (Nov./Dec. 1980): 4–12; R. S. Schuler, "Taking the Pain Out of the Performance Appraisal Interview," *Supervisory Management* (Aug. 1981): 8–13; K. S. Teel, "Performance Appraisals: Current Trends, Persistent Progress," *Personnel Journal* (Apr. 1980): 296–301; "Training Managers to Rate Their Employees," *Business Week*, 17 Mar. 1980, pp. 178–79; K. N. Wexley, "Performance Appraisal and Feedback," in *Organizational Behavior*, ed. S. Kerr (Columbus, Ohio: Grid, 1979), 241–62.

10. C. Hymowitz, "Bosses: Don't Be Nasty (and other tips for reviewing worker performance);" *Wall Street Journal* (17 January, 1985): 35

11. Separating the reviews of past and future performance is described by Beer, "Performance Appraisal," and by S. J. Carroll and C. E. Schneier, *Performance Appraisal and Review Systems* (Glenview, Ill.: Scott, Foresman, 1982). For a presentation on why separate appraisal is not used for development and evaluation, see E. E. Lawler III, A. M. Mohrman, Jr., and S. M. Resnick, "Performance Appraisal Revisited," *Organizational Dynamics* (Summer 1984): 20–42.

12. J. Greenberg, "The Distributive Justice of Organizational Performance Evaluation," in *Research in Negotiations in Organizations*, eds. M. Bazerman, R. Lewicki, and B. Sheppard (Greenwich, Conn.: JAI Press, 1986), 25–41; J. Greenberg, "Using Diaries to Promote Procedural Justice in Performance Appraisal," *Social Justice Review* (1987): 20–37.

13. G. Latham, M. Erez, and E. Locke, "Resolving Scientific Disputes by the Joint Design of Crucial Experiments by the Antagonists: Applicaiton to the Erez-Latham Dispute Regarding Participation in Goal Setting," *Journal of Applied Psychology* 73 (1988): 753–72; G. Latham, T. Mitchell, and D. Dossett, "Importance of Participative Goal Setting and Anticipated Rewards on Goal Difficulty and Job Performance," *Journal of Applied Psychology* 63 (1979): 163–71.

14. J. S. Russel and D. L. Goode, "An Analysis of Managers' Reactions to Their Own Performance Appraisal Feedback," *Journal of Applied Psychology* (Feb. 1988): 63; F. L. Schmidt, J. E. Hunter, A. N. Outerbridge, and S. Goff, "Joint Relation of Experience and Ability with Job Performance: Test of Three Hypotheses," *Journal of Applied Psychology* (Feb. 1988): 46.

15. For a discussion of these characteristics for an effective appraisal interview, see Beer, "Performance Appraisal," 34–35; *Bulletin to Management*, 18 Oct. 1984, 2, 7; and P. Wylie and M. Grothe, *Problem Employees: How to Improve Their Performance* (Belmont, Calif.: Pitman Learning, 1981).

16. G. P. Latham and L. M. Saari, "The Importance of Supportive Relationships in Goal Setting," *Journal of Applied Psychology* 64 (1979): 163–68.

17. Carroll and Schneier, *Performance Appraisal*, 160–89; G. P. Latham and K. N. Wexley, *Increasing Productivity Through Performance Appraisal* (Reading, Mass.: Addison-Wesley, 1981) 152–54; N. R. F. Maier, *The Appraisal Interview* (New York: Wiley, 1958).

18. D. R. Ilgen, C. D. Fisher, and M. S. Taylor, "Consequences of Individual Feedback on Behavior in Organizations," *Journal of Applied Psychology* 64 (1979): 349–71; D. R. Ilgen and C. F. Moore, "Types and Choices of Performance Feedback," *Journal of Applied Psychology* (Aug. 1987): 401; B. L. Davis and M. K. Mount, "Design and Use of Performance Appraisal Feedback System," *Personnel Administrator* (Mar. 1984): 91–107; B. C. Florin-Thuma and J. W. Boudreau, "Performance Feedback Utility in Managerial Decision Processes," *Personnel Journal* (Winter 1987): 693; T. R. Mitchell, M. Rothman, and R. C. Liden, "Effects of Normative Information on Task Performance," *Journal of Applied Psychology* (Feb. 1985): 66–71; J. L. Pearce and L. W. Porter, "Employee Responses to Formal Performance Appraisal Feedback," *Journal of Applied Psychology* (May 1986): 211.

19. G. P. Latham, L. L. Cummings, and T. R. Mitchell, "Behavioral Strategies to Improve Productivity," *Organizational Dynamics* (Winter 1981): 4–23; J. C. Naylor and D. R. Ilgen, "Goalsetting: A Theoretical Analysis in Motivational Technology," in *Research in Organizational Behavior*, vol. 6, ed. B. M. Staw and L. L. Cummings (Greenwich, Conn.: JAI Press, 1984), 95–140; S. E. Jackson and R. S. Schuler, "A Meta-Analysis and Conceptual Critique of Research on Role Ambiguity and Role Conflict in Work Settings," *Organizational Behavior and Human Decision Processes*

36 (1985): 16–78; M. E. Kanfer and F. H. Kanfer, "The Role of Goal Acceptance in Goal Setting and Task Performance," *Academy of Management Review* (July 1983): 454–63.

20. This section is adapted in part from R. F. Mager and P. Pipe, *Analyzing Performance Problems or "You Really Oughta Wanna"* (Belmont, Calif.: Fearon Pitman, 1970).

21. R. D. Arvey, G. A. Davis, and S. M. Nelson, "Use of Discipline in an Organization: A Field Study," *Journal of Applied Psychology* (Aug. 1984): 448–60; J. Brockner and J. Guare, "Improving the Performance of Low Self-Esteem Individuals: An Attributional Approach," *Academy of Management Journal* (Dec. 1983): 642–56; D. N. Campbell, R. L. Fleming, and R. C. Grote, "Discipline Without Punishment at Last," *Harvard Business Review* (July/Aug. 1985): 162–78; D. Cameron, "The When, Why, and How of Discipline," *Personnel Journal* (July 1984): 37–39; D. R. Ilgen and J. M. Feldman, "Performance Appraisal: A Process Focus," in *Research in Organizational Behavior*, vol. 5, ed. B. M. Staw and L. L. Cummings (Greenwich, Conn.: JAI Press, 1983); R. C. Liden and T. R. Mitchell, "Reactions to Feedback: The Role of Attributions," *Academy of Management Journal* (June 1985): 291–304; T. R. Mitchell, S. G. Green, and R. E. Wood, "An Attributional Model of Leadership and the Poor Performing Subordinate: Development and Validation," in *Research in Organizational Behavior*, vol. 3, ed. L. L. Cummings and B. M. Staw (Greenwich, Conn.: JAI Press, 1981); D. Tjosvold, "The Effects of Attribution and Social Context on Superiors' Influence and Interaction with Low Performing Subordinates," *Personnel Psychology* (Summer 1985): 361–76.

22. Huber, Podsakoff, and Tudor, "An Investigation of Biasing Factors."

23. R. M. O'Brien, A. M. Dickson, and M. P. Rosow, *Industrial Behavior Modification: A Management Handbook* (New York: Pergamon Press, 1982).

24. Note, however, that many programs to control absenteeism are not effective: see D. W. Markham and S. Markham, "Absenteeism Control Methods: A Survey of Practices and Results," *Personnel Administrator* (June 1982): 79. See also the reply to this article: M. Geller, *Personnel Administrator* (Spet. 1982): 8, 10. For a general discussion, see D. R. Dalton and C. Enz, "New Directions in the Management of Employee Absenteeism: Attention to Policy and Culture," in *Readings in Personnel and Human Resource Management*, 3d ed., R. S. Schuler, S. A. Youngblood, and V. L. Huber (St. Paul: West, 1988) 357–66; G. Johns, "The Great Escape," *Psychology Today* (Oct. 1987): 30–33; F. E. Kuzmits, "What to Do About Long-Term Absenteeism," *Psychology Today* (Oct. 1986): 93–101; M. Moore, "Components of Absenteeism Control Programs," in *Readings in Personnel and Human Resource Management*, 3d ed., ed. R. S. Schuler, S. A. Youngblood, and V. L. Huber (St. Paul: West, 1988), 367–76; "Troubled Workers: Turnaround Tactics," *Bulletin to Management*, 3 Mar. 1988, p. 72.

25. L. S. Mosher, "Preventing Poor Past Practices from Becoming Future Policies," *Personnel Administrator* (Mar. 1978): 19–20; W. R. Flynn and W. F. Stratton, "Managing Problem Employees," *Human Resource Management* (Summer 1981): 31.

26. D. A. Nadler and E. E. Lawler, "Motivation—A Diagnostic Approach," in *Perspectives on Behavior in Organizations*, ed. J. R. Hackman, E. E. Lawler, and L. W. Porter (New York: McGraw-Hill, 1977).

27. Campbell, Fleming, and Grote, "Discipline Without Punishment—At Last," 170.

28. E. J. Busch, Jr., "Developing an Employee Assistance Program," *Personnel Journal* (Sept. 1981): 708–11; M. Douglass and D. Douglass, "Time Theft," *Personnel Administrator* (Sept. 1981): 13; H. J. Featherston and R. J. Bednarek, "A Positive Demonstration of Concern for Employees," *Personnel Administrator* (Sept. 1981): 43–47; R. C. Ford and F. S. McLaughlin, "Employee Assistance Programs: A Descriptive Survey of ASPA Members," *Personnel Administrator* (Sept. 1981): 29–35; R. T. Hellan and W. J. Campbell, "Contracting for AEP Sevices," *Personnel Administrator* (Sept. 1981): 49–51; R. W. Hollman, "Beyond Contemporary Employee Assistance Programs," *Personnel Administrator* (Sept. 1981): 37–41; D. Masi and S. J. Freidland, "EAP Actions and Options," *Personnel Journal* (June 1988): 61–67.

29. "Productivity and Performance: EAP-Improved," *Bulletin to Management*, 23 July 1987, p. 1.

30. For an excellent discussion of the application of discipline in organizations, see R. D. Arvey and J. M. Ivancevich, "Punishment in Organizations: A Review, Propositions, and Research Suggestions," *Academy of Management Review* 5 (1980): 123–32.

31. Wylie and Grothe, *Problem Employees*.

32. C. O'Reilly and B. Weitz, "Managing Marginal Employees: The Use of Warnings and Dismissals," *Administrative Science Quarterly* 25 (1980): 467–84.

33. M. Bazerman, *Judgement in Managerial Decision Making* (New York: Wiley, 1986); V. Huber, "Managerial Applications of Decision Theory Concepts and Heuristics," *Organizational Behavior Teaching Review* 10 (1986): 1–24; D. Kahneman and A. Tversky, "On the Psychology of Prediction," *Psychology Review* 80 (1973): 237–51; G. Northcraft, M. Neale, and V. Huber, "The Effects of Cognitive Bias and Social Influence on Human Resource Management Decisions," in *Research in Personnel and Human Resource Management*, ed. G. Ferris and K. M. Rowland (Greenwich, Conn.: JAI Press, 1988).

34. Wylie and Grothe. *Problem Employees*.

35. C. Frayne and G. Latham, "Application of Social Learning Theory to Employee Self-Management of Attendance," *Journal of Applied Psychology* 72 (1987): 387–92; F. Kanfer, "Self Management Methods," in *Helping People Change: A Textbook of Methods*, ed. P. Karoly and A. Goldstein (New York: Pergamon Press, 1980); 334–89; P. Karoly and F. Kanfer, *Self Management and Behavior Change: From Theory to Practice* (New York: Pergamon Press, 1986).

36. Frayne and Latham, Application of Social Learning Theory.

37. H. J. Bernardin and R. W. Beatty, *Performance Appraisal: Assessing Human Behavior at Work* (Boston: Kent, 1984); R. I. Henderson, *Performance Appraisal* (Reston, Va.: Reston, 1984).

38. Beer, "Performance Appraisal": Carroll and Schneier, *Performance Appraisal*; M. Kavanagh, "Evaluating Performance" in *Personnel Management*, ed. K. M. Rowland and G. Ferris (Boston: Allyn & Bacon, 1982), 187–226.

39. R. I. Lazar, "Performance Appraisal: What Does the Future Hold?" *Personnel Administrator* (July 1980): 69–73; A. M. Morrison and M. E. Kranz, "The Shape of Performance Appraisal in the Coming Decade," *Personnel* (July/Aug. 1981): 12–22.

40. C. G. Banks and K. R. Murphy, "Toward Narrowing the Research-Practice Gap in Performance Appraisal," *Personnel Psychology* (Summer 1985): 335–46; R. S. Schuler and I. C. MacMillan, "Gaining Competitive Advantage Through Human Resource Management Practices," *Human Resource Management* (Autumn 1984): 248–62; R. L. Taylor and R. A. Zawacki, "Trends in Performance Appraisal: Guidelines for Managers," *Personnel Administrator* (Mar. 1984): 71–79.

Total Compensation

Compensation and Benefits: Future Focus

Productivity Pointers

Productivity improvement programs focus on generating increased outputs from proportionately smaller resources, the report explains. Such programs can be used to set standards that aid in defining performance expectations and providing financial incentives for outstanding performance.

The various types of productivity improvement programs successfully used by employers include:

- *Gainsharing*—Most effective in companies where quantitative levels of production can be used to measure business success, these plans reward eligible employees on a unit-wide basis for performance exceeding established standards.
- *Profit sharing*—Employers increasingly are adopting systems in which cash payments are made based on a company's profit or performance. These plans, the report notes, work best in settings in which teamwork is required.
- *Group incentives*—Similar to gainsharing plans, group incentives make payouts based on small group, rather than large unit, performance.
- *Knowledge- or skill-based pay*—Systems that base pay on the number of jobs an employee can perform or the level of skill used at a particular time work well in environments organized around work teams rather than single job classifications.
- *Extended long-term incentives*—Once restricted to top management, these plans provide incentive payments to lower organizational levels for achievement of multi-year performance goals.

Cost Control Concerns

Employers are being forced to reassess their compensation practices in light of a cost-conscious business environment in which traditional reward methods, such as promotions, no longer can be counted on to motivate employees, the report says. Cost control efforts, which focus on maintaining levels of output from reduced resources, can take a variety of forms, including:

- *Lump-sum merit increases*—Eligible employees receive a one-time payment in lieu of all, or part of, a base salary increase. Lump-sum increases usually are awarded to workers performing above a fully acceptable level and do not become part of their base salary.
- *Two-tier pay*—New hires are paid at a lower rate (as much as 50 percent lower) than current employees in similar jobs.
- *Differential market pricing/competitive positioning*—An organization's compensation strategy is determined on a unit-by-unit basis and is targeted to specific competitive markets, with premiums placed on units critical to company success. In such a system, the prime consideration is a unit's relative contribution rather than internal equity.
- *Flexible staffing*—A core group of full-time employees is maintained to meet expected business volume, and nonpermanent staff (i.e., temporary, part-time, and contract personnel) are used to meet peak business demands. Another flexible approach is to try to develop employees' specializations for several types or areas of work.

SOURCE: "Compensation and Benefits: Future Focus," *Bulletin to Management*, 4 Feb. 1988, p. 40. Used with permission by *Bulletin to Management*, copyright 1988.

The preceding "PHRM in the News" illustrates two significant points about total compensation in organizations. One is that increased international competition has forced organizations to become more cost and productivity conscious. Improved methods of compensation are recognized as an effective way to reduce costs and increase productivity. These methods include lump-sum increases, skill-based pay, long-term incentives, and health care cost management. The second significant point is that organizations are now beginning to use compensation to help drive their strategies. They have come to recognize that compensation not only can retain, attract, and motivate employees but also can enhance organizational competitiveness, survival, and profitability.

Other issues in total compensation are important: How are wages really determined? How do we know when people are paid fairly? How do we decide the wage rate for a given individual? Also to be considered are the legal issues surrounding total compensation, particularly regarding pay for different jobs. Chapters 8–10 address important issues in compensating employees.

EXHIBIT 8.1   Components of Total Compensation

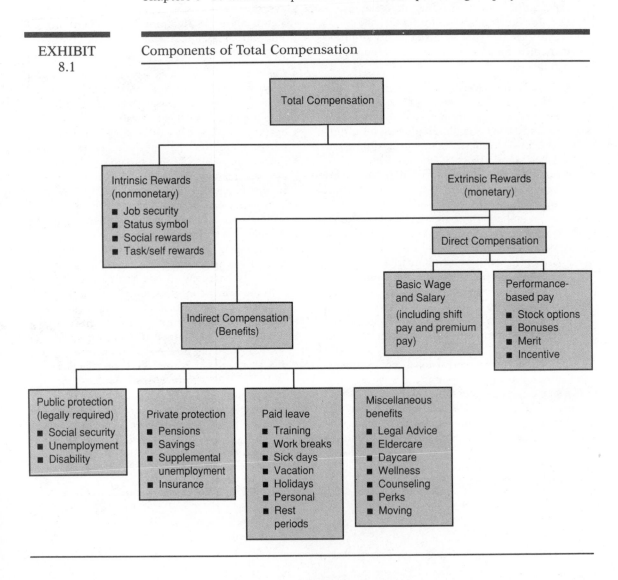

WHAT IS TOTAL COMPENSATION?

Total compensation involves the assessment of employee contributions in order to distribute fairly and equitably direct and indirect organizational rewards in exchange for that performance. As Exhibit 8.1 shows, extrinsic rewards can be categorized as direct or indirect compensation. **Direct compensation** includes an employee's **base salary** and **performance-based pay. Indirect compensation** consists of federal- and state-mandated protection programs, private protection programs, paid leave, and miscellaneous benefits. These will be discussed in Chapter 10. In addition to financial rewards, an organization may offer intrinsic rewards relating to job status and security. These can include anything from office size, location, and number of windows to formal awards and wall plaques. Social and self-administered rewards are less tangible. Friendly greetings, praise, pats on the back, and social gatherings are common social rewards. Self-administered recognition and praise, job autonomy, variety, and feedback are all self-administered rewards that can make a difference.[1]

PURPOSES AND IMPORTANCE OF TOTAL COMPENSATION

Total compensation is important because of several major purposes it can serve:

- *To attract potential job applicants.* In conjunction with the organization's recruitment and selection efforts, the total compensation program can help assure that pay is sufficient to attract the right people at the right time for the right jobs.
- *To retain good employees.* Unless the total compensation program is perceived as internally equitable and externally competitive, good employees (those the organization wants to retain) are likely to leave.
- *To gain a competitive edge.* Total compensation can be a significant cost of doing business. Depending on the industry, labor costs range from 10 to 80 percent of total costs. To gain a competitive advantage, an organization may choose to relocate to areas where labor is cheaper or to automate. In 1989, the average hourly compensation rate was approximately $14.50.[2]
- *To motivate employees.* While nonmonetary awards may influence an employee's motivation, performance-based pay has been shown to be the *most* effective motivator. Still, because of individual differences and preferences, organizations must determine the correct blend of monetary and nonmonetary rewards.[3]
- *To administer pay within legal regulations.* Because several legal regulations are relevant to total compensation, organizations must be aware of them and avoid violating them in their pay programs.
- *To facilitate organizational strategic objectives.* The organization may want to create a rewarding and competitive climate, or it may want to be an attractive place to work, so that it can attract the best applicants. Total compensation can attain these objectives and can also further other organizational objectives, such as rapid growth, survival, and innovation, as implied in the initial "PHRM in the News."[4]

■ *To reinforce and define structure.* The compensation system of an organization can help define the organization's structure, status hierarchy, and degree to which people in technical positions can influence those in line positions.

Obviously, these objectives are interrelated. When employees are motivated, the organization is more likely to achieve its strategic objectives. When pay is based on the value of the job, the organization is more likely to attract, motivate, and retain its employees. Nonmonetary rewards become more important in attaining the above objectives as monetary rewards decrease.

RELATIONSHIPS INFLUENCING TOTAL COMPENSATION

No other PHRM activity has more relationships with other PHRM activities and the internal and external environments than total compensation does. Exhibit 8.2 illustrates these relationships, along with the administrative issues and processes in total compensation.

Relationships with the Internal Environment

As the initial "PHRM in the News" describes, total compensation is increasingly being influenced by factors within the organization. Three characteristics of the internal environment—the organization's culture, strategy, and stage of development—affect and are affected by an organization's compensation practices.

Corporate Culture.   Organizations differ in the values, norms, and expectations that make up their culture. An organization's compensation system is an important signal of what is valued by an organization. For example, in a hierarchy-based reward system, qualitative criteria, which are subjectively weighted and evaluated by a supervisor, are used to allocate rewards. As a result, a **clan-type culture** emerges in which loyalty is exchanged for the organization's long-term commitment to the individual. In this culture, members share a sense of pride in the "fraternal network."

By comparison, when rewards are objectively and explicitly linked to performance, a **market culture** evolves. In this culture, the relationship between the individual and the organization is contractual with obligations specified in advance. The market culture is not designed to generate loyalty, cooperation, or a sense of belonging. Members do not feel constrained by norms, values, or allegiance to accepted ways of doing things. The market culture does, however, generate personal initiative, a strong sense of ownership, and responsibility.

Because these cultures influence employee values, attitudes, and styles, as well as behavior, an organization must be systematic in matching its compensation practices with its desired culture.[5]

Organizational Strategy.   Compensation can be integral to an organization's strategic plan. For example, a manufacturer of technology-based products developed a new strategic vision of itself as a leader in new technologies. Because accomplishing this goal could have proved disruptive to the current business (located on the East Coast), the company decided to acquire small entrepreneurial companies in the Sun Belt. The parent company quickly realized that

Relationships, Administrative Issues, and Processes of
Total Compensation

EXHIBIT
8.2

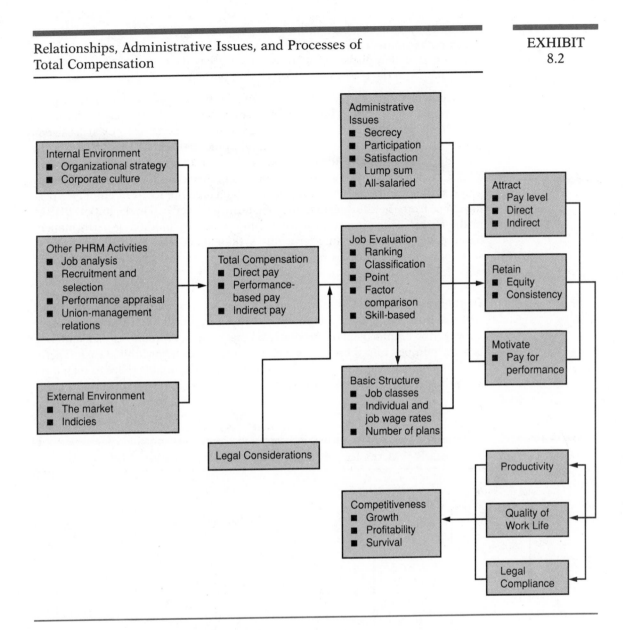

these smaller companies required different management styles and a different
pay system. Consequently, the general managers' base salary at these small
companies is lower when compared to managers' salaries at the parent company,
but the potential size of their annual bonus is four times greater.[6]

Large banks now employ people not only in regular commercial banking functions but also in managing investments, in handling corporate mergers and
acquisitions, on bond and currency trading, and in support functions like data
processing. To a degree each of these areas has its own unique character. Facing
so much diversity, the banks are having to abandon the effort to have only a
single compensation system. A money center bank now is likely to have at least
five distinguishable systems: one providing salary alone, another hourly pay,

a third pay by work accomplished, a fourth stressing commissions, and a fifth combining limited salary with potentially large bonuses. Employees of the bank earn widely disparate amounts of money, based partly on their functions and partly on the pay system in which they participate.[7]

An organization may also have a human resource policy that has a direct impact on compensation. For example, it may decide to be the pay leader in an area. If the planning activity identifies shortages of personnel, or at least potential shortages, the compensation level could be adjusted to attract more individuals. Or it may decide to pay below the market (area) average but provide a large package of indirect compensation to increase company loyalty and employees retention rates. Or is may decide to change the focus of employee performance from the short term to the long term, as described in the initial "PHRM in the News." This change in focus is often made by modifying performance-based pay plans so that long-term rather than short-term criteria are used. In sum, pay systems need to be designed to reinforce the strategies adopted by organizations.

Organizational Life Cycle.   Compensation programs also must be congruent with the firm's stage of development, as shown in Exhibit 8.3. During the *start-up* stage the emphasis is on product and market development. Because money is being pumped into these endeavors, the organization has limited cash. Therefore, base pay and benefits are often low, but the potential is there to reap lofty incentives should the product take off. The compensation mixture is quite dif-

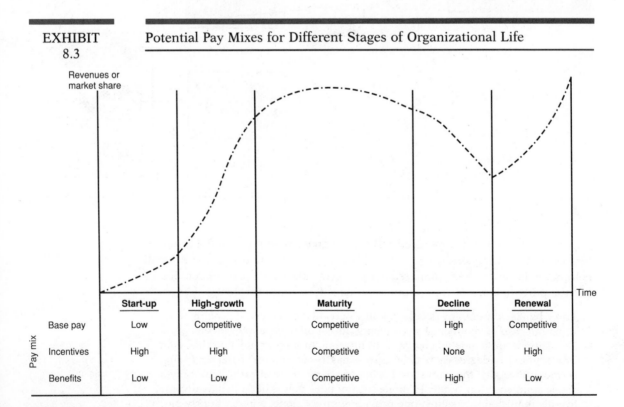

EXHIBIT 8.3   Potential Pay Mixes for Different Stages of Organizational Life

Pay mix	Start-up	High-growth	Maturity	Decline	Renewal
Base pay	Low	Competitive	Competitive	High	Competitive
Incentives	High	High	Competitive	None	High
Benefits	Low	Low	Competitive	High	Low

SOURCE: Modified from G. Milkovich and J. Newman, *Compensation* (Plano, Tex.: BPI, 1988). 2d.

ferent when a firm has matured. Here, base pay and benefits are usually high and competitive, but the need for incentives is low. By the time of decline, there is no need for incentives, but the demand for high base pay and incentives still exists.[8]

Relationships with the External Environment

Marginal revenue product theory in labor economics indicates that the value of a person's labor is equal to what someone is willing to pay for it. In setting rates of pay, organizations rely on wage surveys developed by public agencies (Bureau of Labor Statistics) and companies (e.g., Hay; Towers, Perrin, Foster & Crosby; Hewitt). A number of market factors influence these rates of pay.

The Market.   Organizations often utilize wage and salary surveys to determine prevalent rates of pay. The surveys are used to ascertain wage rates for comparable work in other sections of the industry, as well as wages paid in the locality or the relevant labor market. As was demonstrated in Chapter 4, these data vary depending on how the labor market is defined. For example, a senior compensation analyst earning an annual salary of $32,346 could be expected to receive higher or lower salaries in different geographic areas.

Salaries also vary depending on job specialization. In 1989, starting salaries for college graduates with a bachelor's degree varied from a low of $17,735 in education to a high of $29,706 in petroleum engineering.[9] When markets become "tight" or "loose," these salaries may escalate or decline, respectively.

Although many organizations use wage survey results to help set pay levels for jobs, they should be aware that paying what the market will bear—e.g., paying women and minorities less because they are willing to accept less—is no excuse for wage discrimination (*Marshall v. Georgia Southwestern College*, 1981). Nonetheless, paying one employee more than another for the same job is not necessarily illegal if market conditions differ for the two employees. Organizations also need to be concerned over the issue of price fixing. If organizations exchange market data on their own and set pay rates based on this information, the organizations may be charged with price fixing and collusion.

Market data can be used directly or indirectly to set rates of pay. Indirectly, rates of pay for benchmark jobs are used to establish pay rates for all other jobs. Alternatively, a job evaluation study of existing jobs can be conducted first. Then internal rates of pay are compared to existing rates of pay.

Indicies.   In addition to the market wage levels, other criteria for wage determinations are labor market conditions (the number of people out of work and looking for work), traditions and past history of the organization's wage structure, indices of productivity, company profit figures or turnover data, and the Consumer Price Index and the Urban Workers' Family Budget figures, both of which help to determine cost-of-living increases.[10]

Relationships with Other PHRM Activities

In addition to being affected by the internal and external environments, compensation practices are integrally linked to other PHRM activities.

Job Analysis.   To determine the relative worth of jobs, it is important to know what the content of each job is. As discussed in Chapter 3, job analysis is the process by which job content is examined. When used for compensation purposes, job analysis differs in that job information is needed that relates to compensable factors rather than duties and tasks. At a minimum, this includes the skill, effort, responsibility, and working conditions of the job.

Recruitment and Selection.   Employees differ in the value they put on pay. To attract and retain even the best applicants, maximum pay levels (i.e., the most competitive) need not be offered. Individuals choose jobs on the basis of several factors, including the location of the organization, its reputation as a place to work, what friends think of the company, and the nature of the job that pays the most. Individuals often take the job that satisfies or does as well as possible across all these factors. Research does indicate that organizations must meet an applicant's **reservation wage,** the lowest pay rate he or she is willing to accept.

Performance Appraisal.   Without the ability to measure performance (based on attributes, behaviors, or outcomes) in a reliable and valid way (see Chapter 6), linking such an important reward as pay to performance appraisal results may lead to diminished motivation and lowered performance. (Conditions appropriate for performance-based pay are discussed in Chapter 9.) Where promotions are available, the performance evaluation system can have added significance to the extent that promotion is a reward for performance.[11]

Union-Management Relations.   Unions and employee associations have had a major impact on wage structures, wage levels, and individual wage determinations, regardless of whether specific organizations organized. Although unions generally do not conduct job evaluation programs, in many instances they do help design, negotiate, or modify company programs. Even if union interests are not completely served in the job evaluation process, they can be served at the bargaining table.

LEGAL CONSIDERATIONS IN
TOTAL COMPENSATION

As with many PHRM activities, several state and federal laws and court decisions are important legal considerations in total compensation.

Davis-Bacon and Walsh-Healey Acts

The federal government has imposed several laws influencing the level of wages that employers may pay, pay structures, and individual wage determinations. The first federal law to protect the amount of pay employees received for their work was the Davis-Bacon Act of 1931, which requires organizations holding construction contracts with federal agencies to pay laborers and mechanics the *prevailing wages of the locality* in which the work is performed. The Walsh-Healey Public Contracts Act of 1936 extended the Davis-Bacon Act to include all federal contracts exceeding $10,000 and specified that pay levels conform to the industry minimum rather than the area minimum, as specified in Davis-Bacon. This has since been modified so that the area minimum can be used to establish pay levels. The Walsh-Healey Act also established overtime pay at one-and-one-half times the hourly rate. These wage provisions, however, do not include administrative, professional, office, custodial, and maintenance employees or beginners and disabled persons.

Wage Deduction Laws

Three federal laws influence how much employers may deduct from employee paychecks. The Copeland Act of 1934 authorized the secretary of labor to regulate wage deductions by contractors and subcontractors doing work financed in whole or in part by a federal contract. Essentially, the Copeland Act was aimed at illegal deductions. Protection against a more severe threat from an employer with federal contracts was provided in the Anti-Kickback Law of 1948. The Federal Wage Garnishment Law of 1970 also protects employees against deductions to pay for indebtedness. It provides that only 25 percent of one's disposable weekly earnings or thirty times the minimum wage, whichever is less, can be deducted for repayment of indebtedness.

Fair Labor Standards Act

Partially because the coverage of Davis-Bacon and Walsh-Healey were limited to employees on construction projects, the Fair Labor Standards Act of 1938 (FLSA or the Wage and Hour Law) was enacted. The FLSA set minimum wages, maximum hours, child labor standards, and overtime pay provisions for all workers except domestic and government employees. However, a recent Supreme Court decision extended the coverage of the FLSA to include state and local government employees *(Garcia v. San Antonio Metropolitan Transit Authority,* 1985).

Minimum Wage.   The minimum wage began at 25 cents an hour and had reached to $3.35 by 1981. Still, subminimum wages are permitted for learners in semiskilled occupations, apprentices, handicapped persons working in sheltered workshops, and employees who receive more than $30 per month in tips (up to 40 percent of the minimum requirement may be covered by tips). While not part of the FLSA, states have also adopted minimum wage legislation for employees who are exempt from the FLSA. Alaska and Washington currently have minimum wages higher than the federal requirement. The lowest minimum wage of $.50 per hour is paid in Puerto Rico.

Child Labor.   In order to prevent abuses regarding children, the FLSA also prohibits anyone under the age of 18 from working in hazardous occupations. For nonhazardous positions, the minimum age ranges from 14 to 16 depending on the type of work to be performed and whether or not the employer is the employee's parent.

Overtime.   The overtime provision of the FLSA establishes who is to be paid overtime for work and who is not. Most employees covered by the FLSA must be paid time and a half for all work exceeding forty hours per week. These are called **nonexempt employees.** Several groups of individuals are exempt from both overtime and minimum wage provisions. These **exempt employees** include employees of firms not involved in interstate commerce, employees in seasonal industries, and outside salespeople. Three other employee groups—

executives, administrators, and professionals—are also exempt from overtime pay and minimum wage laws in most organizations. Trainee managers and assistant managers, however, are considered nonexempt and should thus be paid overtime.[12]

To be exempt, professionals must spend 80 percent of their work hours

■ Doing work requiring knowledge acquired through specialized, prolonged training;
■ Exercising discretion or judgment; and
■ Doing work that is primarily intellectual and nonroutine.

The criteria for exempt status as an executive include spending at least 80 percent of work time

■ Undertaking management duties;
■ Supervising two or more employees;
■ Controlling or greatly influencing hiring, firing, and promotion decisions; and
■ Exercising discretion.

In both cases, a comprehensive job analysis is necessary to determine whether or not a job is exempt.

Equal Pay.   This fourth provision of the FLSA was added as an amendment in 1963. Called the Equal Pay Act, this amendment prohibits an employer from discriminating

> between employees on the basis of sex by paying wages to employees . . . at a rate less than the rate at which he pays wages to employees of the opposite sex . . . for equal work on jobs the performance of which requires equal skill, effort and responsibility, and which are performed under similar working conditions.[13]

To establish a *prima facie* case of wage discrimination, the plaintiff needs to prove that a disparity in pay exists for males and females performing substantially equal, but not necessarily identical or comparable, jobs. To determine this, the skill, effort, responsiblity, and working conditions required by each job need to be assessed through careful job analysis. In making this judgment, job content rather than the window dressing of a job title should be examined. If jobs are found to be substantially equal, wages for the lower-paying job must be raised to match those of the higher-paying position. Freezing or lowering the pay rate of the higher-paid job is unacceptable.

However, the existence and use of the following can provide a legal defense to unequal pay for equal work charges (1) seniority system, (2) merit system, (3) system that measures earnings or quality of production, or (4) any additional factor other than sex. As noted earlier, to establish a *prima facie* case, the plaintiff must prove that a disparity in pay exists for employees in equal jobs. If the employer can show the existence of one or more of the four exceptions, however, the differential may be found to be jusitified. Drawing on a recent case law, Exhibit 8.4 contains suggestions on operationalizing the Equal Pay Act.

Title VII of the Civil Rights Act

The Equal Pay Act provides legal coverage only for *equal pay for equal work.* Only when men and women are performing jobs requiring equivalent skills,

---

| Enforcement of Fair Labor Standards Act and Equal Pay Act Provisions | EXHIBIT 8.4 |

1. Conduct a *systematic job analysis* to identify skill, effort, responsibility, and working conditions of jobs.
2. Use an *established job evaluation system* to determine whether jobs are similar. Remember, they need to be substantially equal and not identical or comparable.
3. *Examine job content, not job titles*. Titles may be biased (e.g., beautician or barber; orderly or nurse's aide).
4. *Examine total compensation* including fringe benefits *and* direct pay.
5. *Exempt employees are not exempt from equal pay stature*. Those performing substantially equal work need to be paid the same rates of pay.
6. Pay trainees different rates of pay only if the *training program is bona fide*.
7. If a violation is found, *raise the pay of the lower-paid job*. Do not lower the pay of the higher-paid job.
8. *Keep records* including job descriptions, job evaluation, minimum wage information, overtime, and hours of employment.
9. *Don't hide behind a union contract*. If a violation is found, the employer, not the union, foots the bill because the employer pays the wages.
10. Remember, *males and females can sue* under the Equal Pay Act. Minorities cannot.

---

effort, and responsibility are they entitled to identical pay (unless there are differences in performance, seniority, or other conditions). Title VII of the Civil Rights Act of 1964, however, provides broader legal coverage for pay discrimination:

> Addressing the interrelationship between the Equal Pay Act and Title VII, [the] EEOC observes that while both laws prohibit sex-based wage discrimination, Title VII's prohibitions are broader. In cases where a complainant meets the jurisdictional requirements of both laws, the rules say, "any violation of the Equal Pay Act is also a violation of Title VII." But since Title VII covers types of wage discrimination not actionable under the EPA, "an act or practice of an employer or labor organization that is not a violation of EPA may nevertheless be a violation of Title VII," according to the rules.
>
> If an employer violates both EPA and Title VII, the complainant may recover under both laws for the same period of time, as long as the individual "does not receive duplicative relief for the same wrong," according to the regulations. Relief will be computed, the rules say, "to give each individual the highest benefit which entitlement under either statute would provide (e.g., liquidated damages may be available under the EPA, but not under Title VII)."[14]

Comparable Worth

Because comparable worth, or pay equity, is a significant compensation issue, it deserves a separate discussion. The heart of the comparable worth theory is the contention that while the "true worth" of jobs may be similar, some jobs (often held by women) are paid at a lower rate than others (often held by men). The resulting differences in pay that are disproportionate to the differences in the true worth of jobs, therefore, amount to wage discrimination. Consequently, legal protection should be provided in these cases, according to the comparable worth advocates.[15]

Two cases involving comparable worth are *Gunther v. County of Washington* (1981) and *AFSCME v. State of Washington* (1985). In *Gunther,* the U. S. Supreme Court ruled that women prison guards suffered pay discrimination not because they were being paid less than male prison guards doing the same work but because they were being paid at a rate lower than male guards based on the prison's job evaluation results. That is, the job evaluation results indicated that the two guard jobs were different (they were given different point values), but in relation to their separate evaluations, the women were being paid at a lower percentage rate of their job evaluation value than the men were. The women were being paid at approximately 70 percent of their value, while the men were being paid at approximately 90 percent of theirs.[16]

In *State of Washington,* a U.S. district court ruled that the state had systematically paid jobs dominated by females less than the value indicated by the results of job evaluation. The consulting firm of Willis and Associates had conducted a job evaluation study in the early 1970s, but the state did not entirely follow the results in setting the final wage rates of females and males. In 1985, however, a U.S. court of appeals overturned the district court decision, saying, among other things, that although the state was free to implement a comparable worth program, it could not be forced "to eliminate an economic inequality that it did not create." Subsequently, the employees' unions and the state negotiated a settlement based on the state's original plan.

Although several state and local governments and unions have passed comparable worth or pay equity legislation, comparable worth plans have made few inroads in the private sector:

> Standard Oil of Indiana monitors its job-evaluation procedures but insists that "we do have pay equity." Wells Fargo & Co. says that "we haven't had any pay-related problems." Ralston-Purina tries to keep "abreast of the issue." But San Francisco's Amfac Inc., a diversified concern, hires a pay consultant to make sure that the "french-fry cooker in Portland is paid the same as a sugar-cane worker in Hawaii."
>
> The concept booms in the public sector. More than 30 states are doing job studies or adjusting salaries of mostly female jobs to align them with comparable jobs held by men. But corporations "are looking at it with a jaundiced eye. It would be a horrendous task," says a New York recruiter.
>
> It's controversial: A Deere & Co. spokesman says "we'd prefer not to be involved in a discussion of that issue."[17]

Internationally, comparable worth is an idea that has been around for some time.

> With all the sound and fury about comparable worth—the idea that men and women should get paid the same for work of equal value even if their jobs are different—it's easy to get the impression that the idea is both recent and uniquely American. But the truth is, it's neither.
>
> The International Labor Organization, the Geneva-based U.N. specialized agency the U.S. joined in 1934, adopted an international convention on comparable worth almost 35 years ago. And what the ILO's experience shows is that while comparable worth may have helped reduce the gap between male and female wages in some countries that have tried it, it hasn't eliminated that gap. But neither has it led to the major economic or bureaucratic headaches that its critics prophesy.
>
> In 1951 the ILO adopted Convention No. 100 requiring "equal remuneration for men and women workers for work of equal value." Governments that ratify

the convention must promote "objective appraisal of jobs" whenever that would help assure equal pay for different jobs having equal value.

Since its adoption, more than 100 governments—but not . . . the U.S.—have ratified the convention. These include most of the nations of Western Europe, Canada, Australia, New Zealand, Japan, virtually all of the Soviet bloc, and more than 70 developing countries.[18]

DETERMINING THE RELATIVE WORTH OF JOBS

Job evaluation emphasizes a systematic, rational assessment of jobs to establish internal equity among the different jobs in an organization. While the amount paid for a job can be based on a manger's impression of what the job is worth or on what the external market is paying, more formal methods are often used. Choosing among these methods depends on several factors:

- *Legal and social background.* The choice of job evaluation methods may be limited by collective bargaining arrangements or by what is legally acceptable.
- *Organizational structure.* In small firms, simple systems such as ranking may be appropriate. However, in a multiplant enterprise, plans may be more complex.
- *Management style.* Mangement style can vary from autocratic to democratic. This style will primarily affect the scope of worker participation in the design and application of a job evaluation scheme.
- *Labor-management relations.* No job evaluation scheme can succeed unless the workers accept it. Indeed, the results of many a job evaluation program have been totally rejected because of union opposition. To prevent this, organizations may choose a plan that provides for participation.
- *Cost in time and money.* Job evaluation, like other PHRM activities, costs time and money. There is up-front cost in developing a tailor-made plan. Canned programs may also be costly in terms of dollar cost and user acceptance. Usually job evaluation takes between 6 and 12 months for firms employing more than 500 employees.[19]

The establishment of a job evaluation system involves several major decisions. They include (1) deciding whether to use a single plan or multiple plan, (2) choosing an appropriate job evaluation approach, and (3) establishing a pay structure.

Single Plan Veruse Multiple Plans

An initial decision that needs to be made is whether one or multiple job evaluation plans should be used to evaluate jobs in an organization. Traditionally, job evaluation plans have varied depending on the job family (e.g., clerical, skilled craft, professional). This approach is premised on the assumption that the work content of various job families is too diverse to be captured by one plan. For example, manufacturing jobs may vary in terms of working conditions and physical effort, while professional jobs may not differ in terms of these compensable factors. Proponents of multiple plans contend that these are necessary to capture the unique job characteristics of job families.

Proponents of comparable worth and pay equity advocate a single pay plan. Their argument is premised on the assumption that there are universal compensable factors that relate to *all* jobs. Only when jobs are evaluated using the same criteria can the relative value of *all* jobs be determined. When separate plans are used, it is much easier to discriminate against specific classes of jobs (e.g., clerical versus skilled). To prevent this, universal factors need to be utilized. The Hay Plan and Arthur Young's Decision Banding Method (DBM) are "canned" job evaluation systems with universal factors. Both will be discussed in detail in the next section. It is also possible, but difficult, to develop firm-specific job evaluation systems with universal factors. Some companies, such as Control Data and Hewlett-Packard, use a set of core factors and another set of factors unique to particular occupational groups.

Choosing a Job Evaluation Method

Job evaluation methods differ in several respects. Some methods evaluate the whole job, while others evaluate jobs using compensable factors. Job evaluation approaches also vary with regard to the type of output produced. For example, the factor comparison method evaluates jobs directly in dollar worth, while the point evaluation system requires conversion of points to dollars. Five of the most frequently utilized job evaluation systems will be discussed. Additionally, a new approach to job evaluation, skill-based pay, will be examined.

Ranking Method.   The least specific job evaluation method is **ranking.** One approach to ranking relies on the market value of each job. Alternatively, jobs can be ranked on the basis of such factors as difficulty, criticality to organizational success, and skill required.

This method is convenient when there are only a few jobs to evaluate and when one peson is familiar with them all. As the number of jobs increases and the likelihood of one individual knowing all jobs declines, detailed job analysis information becomes more important, and ranking is often done by committee. Especially when a large number of jobs are to be ranked, key or benchmark jobs are used for comparison.

One difficulty in the ranking method is that all jobs are forced to be different from each other. Making fine distinctions between similar jobs is often difficult, and thus disagreements arise.

Job Classification Method.   The **job classification method** is similar to the ranking method, except that classes or grades are established and the jobs are then placed into the classes. Jobs are usually evaluated on the basis of the whole job, often using one factor such as difficulty or an intuitive summary of factors. Again, job analysis information is useful in the classification, and benchmark jobs are frequently established for each class. Within each class or grade, there is no further ranking of the jobs.

Although many organizations use job classification, the largest is the U.S. government, which has eighteen distinct classifications from GS 1 to GS 18 (GS means "general schedule"). The top three classifications are referred to as super grades. GS 11 and above usually denote general management and highly specialized jobs, while GS 5 to GS 10 are assigned to management trainees and lower-level management positions, and GS 1 to GS 4 are for clerical and non-supervisory personnel.

A particular advantage of the job classification method is that it can be applied to a large number and a wide variety of jobs. As the number and variety of jobs in an organization increase, however, the classification of jobs tend to become more subjective. This is particularly true when an organization has a large number of plant or office locations, and thus jobs with the same title may differ in content. Because evaluating each job separately is difficult in such cases, the job title becomes a more important guide to job classification than job content is.

A major disadvantage of this method is that the basis of the job evaluations is either one factor or an intuitive summary of many factors. The problem with using one factor, such as difficulty (skill), is that it may not be important on all jobs. Some jobs may require a great deal of skill, but others may require a great deal of responsibility. Does this mean that jobs requiring much responsibility should be placed in a lower classification than jobs requiring much skill are? Not necessarily. Perhaps both factors could be considered together. Thus, each factor becomes a compensable factor, valued by the organization, and jobs would be evaluated and classified on the basis of both factors. However, "this balancing of the compensable factors to determine the relative equality of jobs often causes misunderstandings with the employees and the labor leaders."[20] To deal with this disadvantage, many organizations use more quantifiable methods of evaluation.

Factor Comparison Method.   Approximately 10 percent of employers evaluate jobs using the **factor comparison** approach. This method to job evaluation represents a significant change from ranking and classification because compensable factors are utilized to determine job worth. Second, the system systematically links external market rates of pay with internal, work-related compensable factors.

The factor comparison method of job evaluation consists of several steps:

1. *Select compensable factors.* While any number of compensable factors can be used, mental requirements, skill, and physical and working conditions are universally used.
2. *Conduct job analysis.* Once the compensable factors are chosen, jobs should be evaluated in relation to the compensable factors and job specifications that relate to each factor written.
3. *Pick benchmark jobs.* Benchmark jobs serve as reference points and, consequently, should be chosen with care. The content of benchmark jobs should be well known and stable, with consistent pay rates in the external market. Benchmark jobs should also cover the entire range of jobs being evaluated.
4. *Allocate benchmark wages across factors.* Using a compensation committee, wage rates for each job are allocated to each compensable factor. As shown in Exhibit 8.5, the $12.00 salary for drill press operator equals $3.00 for skill, $3.00 for effort, $4.00 for responsibility, and $2.00 for working conditions.
5. *Slot nonbenchmark jobs.* Other jobs are then slotted into each factor scale based on the amount of pay assigned to each factor. In doing this, jobs are compared against each benchmark job to determine whether they are of greater or lesser value.

The "price" or wage rates for the benchmark jobs are determined by the market. Although this is a quick method by which to set wage rates, it has the potential to perpetuate traditional pay differentials between jobs because the wage rates for other jobs are determined against these jobs. Because the process

EXHIBIT
8.5

Factor Comparison Ratings for Benchmark Positions in a Small Batch Manufacturing Facility

Pay/ Hour	Skill	Effort	Responsi- bility	Working Conditions
$5.25	Parts Insp.			
5.00				
4.75				
4.50	Crane Opr.			Com. Labor
4.25		Com. Labor	Crane Opr.	
4.00			Drill/Press	
3.75		Crane Opr.		
3.50		Parts Insp.	Parts Insp.	
3.25		Riveter		
3.00	Drill/Press	Drill/Press		Watchman
2.75		Watchman		Crane Opr.
2.50				
2.25	Riveter			Riveter
2.00				Drill/Press
1.75			Watchman	
1.50				Parts Insp.
1.25	Watchman		Riveter	
1.00	Com. Labor		Com. Labor	
.75				
.50				
.25				

of determining the rates of other jobs is in the hands of the wage and salary analyst, it can be subjective, furthering the potential for wage discrimination.[21] As such, it has come under attack from the job comparability advocates as fostering pay discrimination. Another concern is that the relationship among jobs may change as external rates of pay shift for benchmark jobs.

In spite of these limitations, the factor comparison method of job evaluation is a definite improvement over ranking and classification. Additionally, it has been found to be acceptable to management, unions, and rank-and-file employees. Because jobs are ranked directly in terms of dollar value, internal equity and external equity are integrally linked.

Point Rating Method.   The most widely used method of job evaluation is the **point rating** or **point factor method,** which consists of assigning point values for previously determined compensable factors and adding them to arrive at a total. As with the factor comparison method, compensable factors play the central role in the point system. Factors are weighted relative to their importance. A job's total point value is the sum of the numerical values for each degree of each compensable factor that the job possesses. This total value determines the location of the job in the pay structure. The point evaluation system detailed in Exhibit 8.6 has six compensable factors. Five factors are used to evaluate all jobs; supervisory jobs are evaluated on one additional dimension. As shown, problem solving is weighted heaviest (260/1000 points), while working conditions is the least important (50/1000 points). The factors also differ in the number and point value of degrees associated with them.

Compensable Factor	First Degree	Second Degree	Third Degree	Fourth Degree	Fifth Degree
1. Job knowledge	50	100	150	200	
2. Problem solving	50	100	150	205	260
3. Impact	60	120	180	240	
4. Working conditions	10	30	50		
5. Supervison needed	25	50	75	100	
6. Supervison given	30	60	90	120	150

Sample Point Evaluation System

EXHIBIT 8.6

Once factors are identified and weighted, scale anchors reflecting the different degrees within each factor are developed. Exhibit 8.7 shows the degree statements developed by a broadcast company to describe problem solving. In establishing factor scales, an organization may choose to use an existing system or to develop compensable factors that are organization-specific. In either event, they need to be written in clear language. Once the basic system is set up, each job is rated on all compensable factors. The more points assigned to a job, the more valuable it is to the organization.

The point rating method has several advantages:

1. The point rating plan is widely used throughout industry, permitting comparisons on a similar basis with other firms.
2. The point rating plan is relatively simple to understand and is the simplest of the quantitative methods of job evaluation.
3. A well-conceived point rating plan has considerable stability: it is applicable to a wide range of jobs over an extended period of time. The greatest assets here are consistency, uniformity, and widespread use throughout industry.
4. The point rating method is a definitive approach, requiring several separate and distinct judgment decisions.[22]

The limitations of the point rating method are few, but an especially critical one is the assumption that all jobs can be described with the same factors. Many organizations avoid this limitation by developing separate point rating methods for different groups of employees. Exhibit 8.6 shows six compensable factors used by one organization to evaluate the jobs in supervisory, nonsupervisory, and clerical categories. Exhibit 8.7 also shows a description of what is associated, by degree and points, with one of the factors (complexity and judgment), and sets forth the specifications for the degrees or levels within that factor. Some factors are more important than others, as shown by the different point values. For example, the second degree of practical experience is worth four times as much as the second degree of job conditions. Each job is evaluated only on its compensable factors. The personnel and human resource department determines which degree of a factor is appropriate for the job. Then, the points assigned to each degree of each factor are totaled. Levels of compensation are determined on the basis of the point totals. The description provided on complexity and judgment is similar to that written on all of the compensable factors.

As with other job evaluation plans, the point factor method incorporates the potential subjectivity of the job analyst. As such it has the potential for wage discrimination. Bias or subjectivity can enter (1) in the selection of the com-

EXHIBIT
8.7

Compensable Factor and Related Degree Statements

2. Problem solving:
This factor examines the types of problems dealt with in your job. Indicate the one level that is most representative of the majority of your job responsibilities.

Degree 1: Actions are performed in a set order per written or verbal instruction. Problems are referred to supervisor.

Degree 2: Solves routine problems and makes various choices regarding the order in which the work is performed within standard practices. May obtain information from varied sources.

Degree 3: Solves varied problems that require general knowledge of company policies and procedures applicable within area of responsibility. Decisions made based on a choice from established alternatives. Expected to act within standards and established procedures.

Degree 4: Requires analytical judgment, initiative, or innovation in dealing with complex problems or situations. Evaluation not easy because there is little precedent or information may be incomplete.

Degree 5: Plans, delegates, coordinates, and/or implements complex tasks involving new or constantly changing problems or situations. Involves the orgination of new technologies or policies for programs or projects. Actions limited only by company policies and budgets.

pensable factors, (2) in the assignment of relative weights (degrees) to factors, and (3) in the assignment of degrees to the jobs being evaluated. At stake here are equal pay and job comparability. To make sure its point factor evaluation system is free from potential bias and is implemented as objectively as possible, an organization may solicit the input of the job incumbent, the supervisor, and job evaluation experts, as well as staff of its personnel department.[23]

Hay Guide Chart-Profile Method.   One of the most widely used job evaluation systems in the world combines the best characteristics of the point evaluation and factor comparison methods of job evaluation. Used by more than 5,000 employers worldwide (130 of the 500 largest U.S. corporations), **the Hay Guide Chart-Profile** is particularly popular for evaluating executive, managerial, and professional positions, but is also widely used for many others, including technical, clerical, and manufacturing positions.

Operationally, the Hay system relies on three primary compensable factors—problem solving, know-how, and accountability (see Exhibit 8.8 for definitions). Point values are determined for each job, using the three factors and their subfactors. Additionally, jobs are compared to one another on the basis of each factor. The former approach parallels traditional point evaluation processes, and the latter parallels factor comparison methods.

According to Hay Associates, a major advantage of its system centers on its wide acceptance. Because organizations worldwide use the system, Hay can provide clients with comparative pay data by industry or locale. Another advantage of the system is that it has been legally challenged and found acceptable by the courts.

Still, the Hay Guide Chart-Profile Method, like any "canned" or standardized system, may not reflect an organization's true values. Thus, an organization needs to consider whether its job problem solving, know-how, and accountability are truely congruent with its values. It is also difficult to explain to employees

Hay Compensable Factors

EXHIBIT
8.8

Mental Activity (Problem Solving)	Know-How	Accountability
The amount of original, self-starting thought required by the job for analysis, evaluation, creation, reasoning, and arriving at conclusions	The sum total of all knowledge and skills, however acquired, needed for satisfactory job performance (evaluates the job, not the person)	The measured effect of the job on company goals
Mental Activity has two dimensions:	Know-How has three dimensions:	Accountability has three dimensions:
■ The degree of freedom with which the thinking process is used to achieve job objectives without the guidance of standards, precedents, or direction from others ■ The type of mental activity involved; the complexity, abstractness, or originality of thought required	■ The amount of practical, specialized, or technical knowledge required ■ Breadth of management, or the ability to make many activities and functions work well together; the job of company president, for example, has greater breadth than that of a department supervisor ■ Requirement for skill in motivating people	■ Freedom to act, or relative presence of personal or procedural control and guidance; determined by answering the question, How much freedom has the job holder to act independently?—for example, a plant manager has more freedom than a supervisor under his or her control ■ Dollar magnitude, a measure of the sales, budget, dollar value of purchases, value added, or any other significant annual dollar figure related to the job. ■ Impact of the job on dollar magnitude, a determination of whether the job has a primary effect on end results or has instead a sharing, contributory, or remote effect
Mental Activity is expressed as a percentage of Know-How for the obvious reason that people think with what they know. The percentage judged to be correct for a job is applied to the Know-How point value; the result is the point value given to Mental Activity.	Using a chart, a number can be assigned to the level of Know-How needed in a job. This number—or point value— indicates the relative importance of Know-How in the job being evaluated.	Accountability is given a point value independent of the other two factors.

NOTE: The total evaluation of any job is arrived at by adding the points (not shown here) for Mental Activity, Know-How, and Accountability.

why one job receives a certain number of points and another job receives a different number. Finally, implementation of the Hay system may also not be financially feasible for small organizations.

Decision Banding Method.   A second "canned" job evaluation process that is widely used is Arthur Young's **Decision Banding Method** (DBM). This ap-

EXHIBIT
8.9

Arthur Young's Single-Factor Decision Banding Approach

A Defined	B Operational	C Process	D Interpretive	E Programming	F Policy

		NC	C	NC	C	NC	C	NC	C	NC	C

1 2 3 4 5 6 7 8 9 10 11 12 13 14 15 16 17 18 19 20 21 22 23 24 25 26 27

Pay Grades

NC = Noncoordinating

C = Coordinating

proach measures the amount of decision-making discretion an employee has in a job. As shown in Exhibit 8.9, DBM classifies jobs into six decision categories (defined, operational, process, interpretive, programming, and policy). Using task statements obtained through job analysis, each job is placed in the decision band associated with the highest level of decision making required for the job. Jobs are then classified as either coordinating (C) the work of others at the same decision band or noncoordinating (NC). Jobs are further categorized into subgrades based on the number, frequency, and diversity of decisions at the highest band. This division yields 27 pay grades. If warranted by the labor market or working conditions, a pay differential may be added on top of base pay. Such adjustments are temporary and should be removed once the market stabilizes or the working conditions are improved.

Critics of DBM contend that jobs are not unidimensional and that one factor cannot adequately represent the entire domain of jobs. Advocates counter that DBM is composed of component parts that are consistent with the most commonly used factors in other job evaluation systems. Because of its simplicity, DBM is easy to explain to managers and employees. The critical decision then is whether DBM or any other job evaluation system reflects the values of the organization.

Skill-Based Evaluation.   Whereas the first five job evaluation plans "pay for the job," **skill-based evaluation** is based on the idea of "paying for the person." As such, this type of evaluation is concerned with employee skills and with developing training programs to facilitate employee skill acquisition.[24] This type of evaluation is also called "pay for knowledge."

Skill-based evaluation plans are based on a starting rate given to all new employees. After coming on board, employees are advanced one pay grade for each job they learn. Jobs can be trained in any order and at any price. Members of each employee's team ensure that the jobs are learned correctly, and they decide when the employee has mastered a job. Employees reach the top pay grade in the plant after learning all jobs.

The idea of paying for the person, or at least the person-job combination rather than just the job, is not new. Many professional organizations, such as universities, law offices, and research and development labs, have been doing this for a long time. What is new, however, is paying for the person (as determined by skills possessed) in blue-collar jobs. Skill-based evaluation is used for blue-collar jobs at Honeywell, Westinghouse, and TRW. According to a manager at TRW, "the more you know, the more you make."[25] At these companies all new employees receive the same starting rate and are advanced one pay grade for each job they learn.

Establishing the Wage Structure

Whatever method is used to determine the worth of jobs, the next step is to develop a wage structure. The wage structure is the order of pay rates for jobs in the organization. For the pay structure to be equitable, rates of pay must be internally consistent *and* comparable to those in the external market. Achieving both objectives involves several steps including (1) developing the internal pay structure, (2) conducting a pay survey to relate the internal structure to the external market, (3) setting the wage policy, and (4) deciding on pay ranges.

Developing the Internal Structure.   Once the internal value of jobs is determined, it is useful to examine the resulting job hierarchy. In doing this, job points for each job are plotted against current salary. Exhibit 8.10 shows the job structure for an organization with 100 different jobs and approximately 200 incumbents. The scatter diagram includes one point for *each* incumbent. Males and females have been identified separately so the potential for gender-based pay differences can be investigated. The point values of jobs in this organization range from 331 points to 1,066 points. Monthly salaries range from $945 to $2,900 a month.

The firm's current corporate pay line can be determined in one of three ways. First, the scatter diagram can be "eye-balled," and a line drawn approximately midway through the cluster of points. Alternatively, a line connecting the pay rate of the highest-valued job to that of the lowest-valued job can be drawn. While these approaches are good approximations, simple regression provides a more accurate judgment. For the organization detailed in Exhibit 8.10, the pay policy regression equation is

$$\text{Salary} = \$315 + \$2 \text{ (points)}$$

This equation predicts that a job worth 500 points, should be paid $1,315 a month [$315 + $2(500)]; a job worth 700 points should be paid $1,715 [$315 + $2(700)] on average.

Conducting a Wage Survey.   As discussed earlier, the market, along with other factors, can influence the wage rates established by the organization. The market exerts this influence when the organization conducts wage and salary surveys.

"Market pricing," the use of pay survey data to determine prevailing wage rates in the labor market, is the method most frequently used by employers to evaluate a job's worth or assign jobs to a salary range or level, according to an American Compensation Association survey of 1,415 firms. Virtually all the firms responding to ACA's study of salary management practices have established a formal method for evaluating jobs or assigning them to salary ranges or levels. More than 50 percent of these firms reported using the market-pricing method, either alone or in combination with another method of determining pay.[26]

EXHIBIT
8.10

Corporate Pay Line Compared to External Market Pay Line

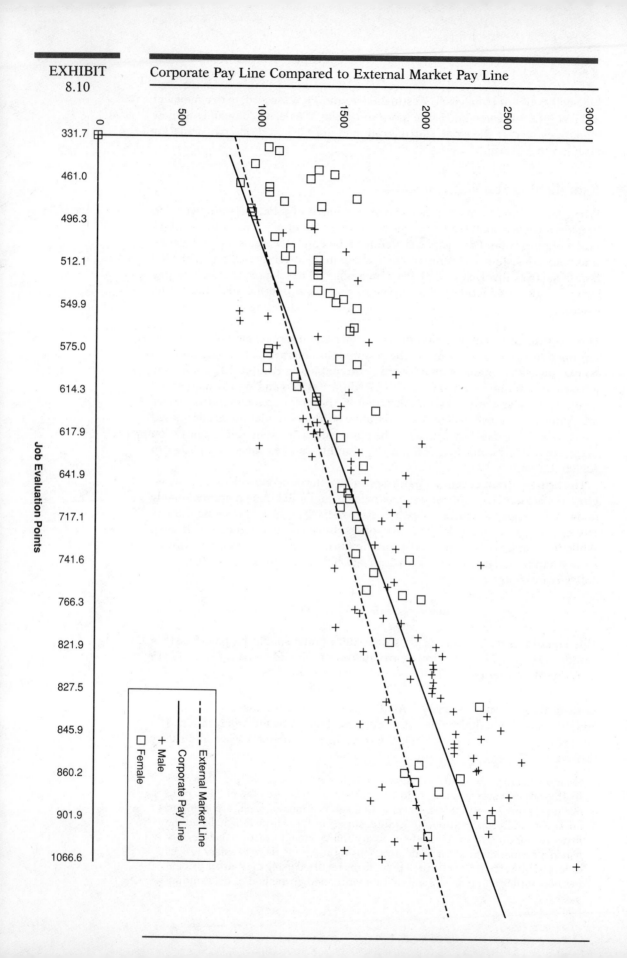

In conducting a wage survey, an organization first needs to select appropriate benchmark jobs. Benchmark jobs should have relatively stable job content and supply and demand. They should also represent the entire job structure under study and, if at all possible, all funtions, as well as minorities and female employees. The point in using benchmark jobs is to anchor the comparisons in the external market with descriptions of similar work in the organization. For the study detailed above, twenty benchmark jobs were selected.

Wage surveys can be used to develop compensation levels, wage structures, and even payment plans (the amount and kind of direct and indirect compensation). Whereas job evaluation helps ensure internal equity, wage surveys provide information to help ensure external equity. Both type of equity are important if an organization is to be successful in attracting, retaining, and motivating employees. In addition, survey results can also be used to indicate compensation philosophies of competing organizations. For example, a large electronics company may have a policy of paying 15 percent above the market rate (the average of all rates for essentially the same job in an area); a large service organization may choose to pay the market rate; a large bank may decide to pay 5 percent less than the market rate.

Most organizations use wage surveys extensively. Separate surveys are published for different occupational groupings; thus, many larger organizations subscribe to several surveys. For example, there are surveys for clerical workers, professional workers, managers, and executives. Separate surveys are conducted not only because such wide differences exist in skill levels but also because labor markets are so different. An organization surveying clerical workers may need to survey companies only within a ten-mile radius, whereas a survey of managerial salaries may cover the entire country.[27]

Once the survey data are collected, the organization must decide how to use them. The organization needs to decide whether to use only the average wage and salary levels from all the companies in the survey to determine its own wage and salary levels or whether to weight the wage and salary levels of companies by the number of employees.[28] The organization must also decide if it is going to use the wage and salary ranges from all the companies to determine its own wage and salary ranges. After deciding on the wage and salary information it wants, an external market pay policy line is determined by calculating the relationship between job points and market pay for the benchmark jobs.

Exhibit 8.10 includes the external pay policy line for company described earlier. Because the survey data were two years old, they had to be updated. An examination of the data showed that pay rates increased approximately 3 percent each year. Because the data were two years old, survey data were multipled by 1.06 percent to approximate current pay rates. Again, the "eyeball" technique, a comparison of external pay for the highest- and lowest-paid jobs, or simple regression can be used to develop an external pay policy line. Using the point values already calculated for the benchmark jobs, but plugging in external, rather than internal, salary rates, the following external pay line regression equation was developed:

$$\text{External pay} = \$630 + \$1.42 \text{ (points)}$$

This equation predicts that a job worth 300 points should be paid $1,066 a month [$630 + $1.42(300)]. A job worth 700 points should be paid $1,624 [$630 + $1.42(700)]. Notice that for jobs with low values, rates of pay in the external market are *higher* than what the company is currently paying. For higher-valued jobs, the firm is paying *too much* relative to the external market. In other organizations, the opposite effect may be found. It is also possible that a firm can pay consistently *below* or *above* the market rate of pay for *all* jobs.

Deciding on a Pay Policy.   With information in hand regarding the internal pay structure and its relationship to the external market, an organization has data sufficient to decide on its pay policy line. Some of the factors that influence the choice of a pay policy include

- Pay rates paid by major competitors
- Employee unrest
- Firm's profits or losses
- Surplus or shortage of qualified workers
- Stage of firm development (start-up, growth, mature, decline)
- Strength of union demands
- Organizational culture[29]

Regardless of the potency of these factors, there are three prevalent pay-level policies. The rationale behind a **lead policy** is to maximize the ability to attract and retain quality employees and to minimize employee dissatisfaction with pay. A lead policy signals employees that they are valued by the firm. However, a concern is whether the additional pay actually attracts and retains the *best* or merely the *most* applicants. It is also uncertain how much a firm needs to lead others to gain a distinct competitive advantage. Finally, there is a tendency for pay rates of other firms to escalate and eventually match the leader's rate of pay.

By far the most common approach is to **pay with the competition.** While this approach does not give an employer a competitive advantage, it does ensure that the firm is not at a disadvantage. One way to maximize a match policy is to implement annual pay adjustments prior to major recruiting periods. By doing so, the organization essentially leads the market for the first half of the year and lags the market during the last half of the year.

The final approach is a **lag policy.** This approach may hinder a firm's ability to attract potential employees unless other factors (job security, benefits, locale, job content) compensate for the low pay.[30]

Regarding the effectiveness of these strategies, there is little evidence to recommend one policy over another. The most important step is translating the policy into practice.

Developing a Grade Structure.   Once the firm's pay policy line has been set, a pay grade structure can be developed. Exhibit 8.11 shows the pay grade structure for the organization described earlier.

The boxes shown are associated with a range of job evaluation points (the job class) and a range of pay (the pay grade).[31] In essence, these **pay grades** are the job classes. Consequently, several different jobs may be within one box, but they are similar in terms of job evaluation points, if not in content. The boxes may be the same size or vary in height but generally ascend from left to right. This reflects increased job worth and the association of higher pay levels (shown on the vertical axis) with more valued jobs. The pay levels are established using market information (to help ensure external equity).

Proposed Pay Grades for an Organization

EXHIBIT
8.11

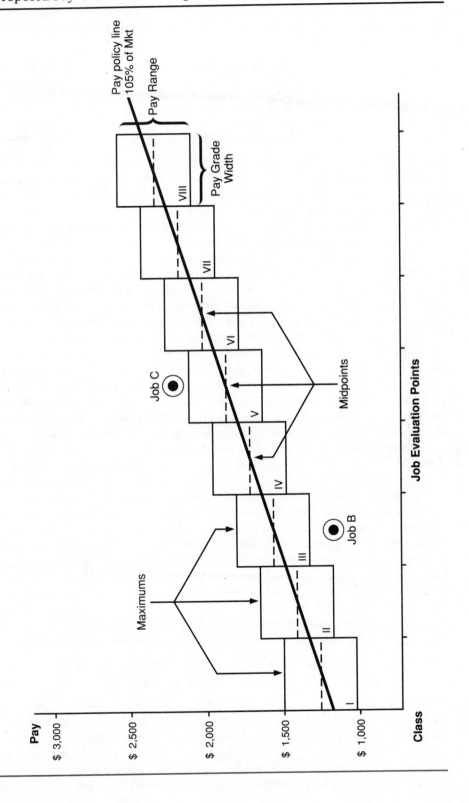

In establishing pay ranges, the corporate pay line generally serves as the pay grade midpoint. Pay grade maximums and minimums are generally set at a percentage above and below that amount. The difference between the two is the pay range. Some common ranges above and below pay grade midpoint include

■ Nonexempt:	Laborers and trades	Up to 25%
■ Nonexempt:	Clerical, technical, paraprofessional	15–49%
■ Exempt:	First-level management Professionals	30–50%
■ Exempt:	Middle and senior management	40–100%

For the company described earlier, the pay range for grade I is $1,100 a month to $1,500 a month; the midpoint of this range is $1,144 a month. This represents a 12 percent spread. For pay grade VII the minimum pay is $2,000 a month and the maximum is $2,800, a spread of 20 percent.

The choice of ranges can become critical. Adjacent pay grades should have some, but not too much, overlap. When there is too much overlap, the pay structure is said to be **compressed,** with pay differentials too small to reflect true differences in job values. When there is little or no overlap between adjacent pay grades, the organization overrewards individuals at the low end of the pay grade and assumes they are more valued than more senior employees in the lower pay grade. Ideally, organizations like to have the average salary of employees in a pay grade equal to the midpoint. If the average is higher than the midpoint, employees might no longer be able to receive significant salary increases without being promoted. This effect is often referred to as **topping out.** That is, the only time an employee at the top of a pay grade receives a salary increase is when the *entire* pay structure is adjusted to be consistent with the market or when cost-of-living increases are given. Because these adjustments are automatic, there is no incentive for the employee to perform well.

Occasionally, jobs are found that fall outside the established pay grades (Jobs B and C in Exhibit 8.11). When a job falls *below* the established pay grade (Job B in pay guide III), it is *blue circled,* and usually a wage adjustment (sweetener) is made to bring the job within the established pay grade. Sometimes, though, a job will be overpaid (Job C in pay grade V). One means of dealing with this is to *red circle* the job. That is, as long as the current incumbent remains in the job, the pay rate remains unchanged. But when the incumbent leaves the job, the rate will be adjusted downward to put the job back in the established grade. Sometimes the entire salary structure has to be adjusted upward to bring jobs within established pay grades, thereby moving the midpoints up for all pay grades.

To determine how management is actually paying employees relative to the pay line midpoint, managers often rely upon an index called a **compa-ratio:**

$$\text{Compa-ratio} = \frac{\text{Average rate of pay for employees in pay class}}{\text{Range midpoint}}$$

A compa-ratio of less than 1.00 means that, on average, employees in the pay grade are being paid below the midpoint. Translated, this means that managers are paying below the intended policy. One valid reason may be that employees are newly hired or poor performers. Alternatively, employees could be promoted so rapidly that they don't reach the upper half of the pay range. A compa-ratio greater than 1.00 means the organization is paying more than the stated policy.

ISSUES IN WAGE AND SALARY ADMINISTRATION

Among the several contemporary issues in wage and salary administration four are of particular importance: (1) To what extent should employees be able to participate in choosing their forms of pay and in settling their own wages? (2) What are the advantages and disadvantages of pay secrecy? (3) What is needed for employees to be satisfied with their pay? (4) Should all employees be salaried? More administration issues are addressed in Chapters 9 and 10.

Participation Policies

Job evaluation judgments, like other PHRM decisions, can be made by a variety of raters including compensation professionals, managers, and job incumbents. An important decision is who should be involved in the development of a job evaluation system and in the determination of job worth.

Traditionally, compensation professionals and managers had the most involvement in the design of compensation systems. Recently, however, there has been an emphasis on employee involvement in job evaluation. For example, 64 percent of all labor agreements require incumbent involvement. Employee participation in job evaluation also is a key feature of what is called "new pay." New pay gives employees ownership over their work outcomes. For example, the Polaroid Corporation, having established its policy of openness, involves employees in making salary decisions. Employees are also involved in the job evaluation process to get a broad understanding of the process by which job value is established.[32]

One of the most common ways of increasing involvement is to establish a job evaluation committee composed of management, nonmanagement, and union representatives. Individuals on such a committee should be knowledgeable about a wide range of jobs. It may also be useful to co-op antagonists. By involving representatives from all areas, communication is improved, and the likelihood that the organization's values are reflected in the job evaluation system is increased. The involvement of multiple parties does, however, increase the potential for conflict. For example, managers may try to distort job evaluation ratings of a favorite or superstar employee, so that pay can exceed the maximum permitted for a job of that value. Conversely, compensation professionals will want to preserve pay equity at all costs. However, managers and employees are less likely to accept the results of a job evaluation study when they were not consulted.

Bonneville International, a broadcast group, had incumbents update their job descriptions and their supervisors sign off on the descriptions. Using the job description as a common frame of reference, supervisors and incumbents *independently* completed the firm's point evaluation instrument. Next, the ratings for the two groups were compared. When rating differences were found, the supervisor met with incumbent(s) to reach a consensus on the point value of the job. Because incumbents were personally involved, there were *no* job classification appeals, and the system was perceived as procedurally fair. These results indicate that employee participation is well worth the additional time involved.

In addition to involving employees in the development of a job evauation system and the determination of job worth, a newer method of employee participation is allowing employees to set their own wage rates. One way of doing this is to let employees vote on who should get a raise. At Romac, a pipe-fitting plant in Seattle, Washington, employees request their pay raises by completing a form that includes information about their current pay level, previous raise, raise requested, and reasons why they think a raise is deserved. The employee then "goes on board." His or her name, hourly wage, and photograph are posted for six consecutive working days. The employees then vote, and the majority rules. Although top-level managers can't vote, they can veto a raise. This, however, hasn't happened yet because management has learned that employees can responsibly set their own wages if they trust management and have a sufficient understanding of the "cost of doing business."[33]

Pay Secrecy

According to organizational etiquette, asking others their salaries is generally considered gauche. In a study of E. I. du Pont de Nemours, all employees were asked if the company should disclose more payroll information, so that everyone would know everyone else's pay. Only 18 percent voted for an open pay system. Managers also favor pay secrecy because it makes their lives easier. Without knowledge of pay differentials, employees are less likely to confront their supervisor about inequitable pay. Consequently, managers do not have to defend or justify their actions.

Despite these common perceptions, there are several reasons *for* open communication about pay practices. First, there is research that indicates that employees misperceive the pay levels of other employees. They tend to overestimate the pay of those with lower-level jobs and to underestimate the pay of those with higher-level jobs. Because pay differentials are designed to motivate employees to seek promotion, this misperception may be detrimental to employee motivation. After all, why should an employee in training gain experience and accept greater responsibility for meager increases?

A second, more practical reason for an open pay policy is that considerable resources have been devoted to developing a fair and equitable system. For managers and employees to gain an accurate view of the system, they must be informed.

Finally, and potentially most important, pay is a powerful motivator only when its linkage to performance is explicitly stated and known to employees. For an employee to perform well, he or she must know what performance is desired, what the reward will be for performing well, and what the consequence is for performing poorly. The potency of pay as a motivator is increased through a process called **vicarious reinforcement** or **observational learning**. Observing a peer being rewarded or punished is instructional to other employees who observe the consequences of specific behaviors. Vicarious reinforcement only works, however, when pay is not a secret.

Regarding what should be communicated, many employers specify the range for an incumbent's job and other jobs in a typical career path. In addition to ranges, some organizations detail the typical increases associated with low, average, and top performance. A concern in communicating the latter is that the organization may not be able to maintain the same pay schedule in the future. If increases are lower in subsequent years, some employees may be dissatisfied. Still, if it is made clear that the size of the bonus pool is contingent on the profitability of the organization, this problem can be avoided.[34]

Satisfaction with Pay

If organizations want to minimize absenteeism and turnover through compensation, they must make sure that employees are satisfied with their pay. Because satisfaction with pay and motivation to perform are not necessarily highly related, organizations must know the determinants of pay satisfaction. With this knowledge, organizations can develop pay practices more likely to result in satisfaction with pay. Three major determinants of satisfaction with pay are pay fairness, pay level, and pay administration practices.[35]

Pay Fairness. Pay fairness refers to what people believe they deserve to be paid in relation to what others deserve to be paid. The tendency is for people to determine what they and others deserve to be paid by comparing what they give to the organization with what they get out of the organization. In comparing themselves with others, people may decide whether they are being paid fairly. If they regard this comparison as fair or equitable, they are more likely to be satisfied. If they see this comparison as unfair, they are likely to be dissatisfied.

Fairness can also be increased by providing "voice" and due process to employees. Thus, it is important for organizations to establish formal appeals procedures. These appeals procedures vary in the degree of formality and in how independent the process is from traditional lines of authority. Union contracts often prescribe a formal system in which complaints are first filed with the immediate supervisor. If a satisfactory resolution is not attained, the appeal moves forward to a higher level of management. IBM has an open-door policy in which employees are free to write to *any* manager, including the CEO. Each letter is answered personally.

Pay Level. Pay level is an important determinant of the perceived amount of pay satisfaction. People use this perception and compare it with what they believe they should receive. The result of the comparison is satisfaction with pay if the "should" level of pay equals the actual level of pay. Pay dissatisfaction results if the actual level is less than the "should" level.

Increasingly, pay-level satisfaction is being related to differences in pay levels for employees at different levels in the organization. Not revealed in the average hourly total compensation figure of $14.50 cited earlier is the range by organizational level of employees. The range data show that the average hourly total compensation for all managers was $25.00, and for nonmanagerial service workers it was $7.25. Illustrating greater disparity are the salaries of the most highly paid individuals in the United States. For example, Charles Lazarus, CEO of Toys 'R' Us, earned more than $60 million in 1987.[36] While this was an unusually high compensation, the average pay differential between the highest and lowest paid employees in large U.S. organizations is about 20:1. This is caused in large part by the relatively high level of total CEO compensation. According to Exhibit 8.12, the total compensation for U.S. CEOs is substantially greater than it is for CEOs in other countries. Reflections on these differences are presented in the "International PHRM in the News."

Pay Administration Practices. What does the preceding discussion suggest for pay administration practices? First, if the employer is to attract new employees and keep them satisfied with their pay, the wages and salaries offered

PHRM IN THE NEWS

Abroad, It's Another World

And how much do CEOs make outside the U.S.? Less, generally much less. But as business globalizes, the discrepencies may soon start to narrow.

The CEO of a billion-dollar-a-year U.S. corporation makes $983,000 on average, including all forms of direct pay—salary, bonus, and incentives—according to a survey conducted for Fortune by TPF&C, a New York–based benefits and compensation consulting firm. The chieftain of a French company of comparable size comes in a distant second with $577,000, followed by his Swiss counterpart at $468,000, a typical West German at $403,000, a British boss at $342,000, and the Japanese CEO at just $330,000. All pay totals were converted into dollars at current exchange rates.

The major element of the disparity is performance incentives, such as stock options. CEOs outside the U.S. don't get many. Such incentives constitute 60% of total cash compensation for chief executives of the biggest U.S. companies, according to TPF&C, but in West Germany and Japan they add only about 12%. Even in those rare years when performance incentives don't kick in, U.S. chiefs remain the superchiefs. In a recent study, the Wyatt Co., an employee benefits and compensation consulting firm, looked just at base pay and normal bonuses and found that Japanese and German chief executives net only about 65% of what their well-heeled American brethren take home, after the effects of higher taxes and costs of living in those countries are figured in. Elsewhere the headman's buying power is even worse.

Certain perquisites offered outside the U.S. balance the scales a bit. The U.S. is the only one of 20 major countries surveyed by TPF&C where a car (often with a driver) is not usually provided to the CEO of a $100-million-a-year company. And in many countries with confiscatory tax policies, companies offer tax-favored perks such as club memberships, augmented pensions, and entertainment and housing allowances.

But, says Michael Emig, a principal with Wyatt Co., "the order of magnitude of these perks is nothing compared with how much wealth U.S. executives can accumulate over a period of time."

Americans hold a distinctive view of the CEO's relation to the rest of a company's employees. Most European and Japanese managers feel an organization suffers when the CEO receives an astronomical multiple of the typical employee's check. A recent study found that a European CEO's pay was generally six to eight times that of an entry-level professional. In the U.S. the ratio was 14. "There's more of a consensus approach to managing in a country like Germany," says Brian Brooks, an international compensation consultant with TPF&C. "When you put workers on the board, as they often do, that creates pressure to keep executive pay down."

The American obsession with superstars also helps drive up the chief's pay. Says TPF&C's David Swinford: "In Europe and Japan they still reward longevity and loyalty by promoting from within, whereas we find a home-run hitter and pay to get him as a free agent." Adds Lance Berger of Philadelphia's Hay Group: "Each time a CEO changes jobs, it cranks the whole market up a notch."

That constant cranking in the U.S. is starting to ratchet up pay around the world. The market for CEOs, along with everything else, is becoming increasingly international, and it is not unusual these days for the CEO of a big, recently acquired American subsidiary of a European or Japanese company to be making up to twice as much as his boss overseas. That may be one reason Britain's Lord Hanson, chairman and CEO of the acquisitive Hanson PLC, recently wrote in his company's annual report that "British executives of multinationals should receive "global" (read "U.S.") pay rates. Lord Hanson's board practices what he preaches. His pay last year was nearly £ 1.3 million ($2.4 million), enough to place him well up in America's major leagues.

SOURCE: D. Kirkpatrick, "Abroad, It's Another World," *Fortune*, 6 June 1988, p. 78. Used with permission from *Fortune*, copyright 1988.

Average Total Cash Compensation of CEOs as a Percentage of U.S. Total Cash Compensation Operations with $100 Million in Annual Sales

EXHIBIT
8.12

Country	%
Argentina	36%
Australia	37
Belgium	52
Brazil	42
Canada	57
France	46
Hong Kong	34
Italy	42
Japan	50
Mexico	48
Netherlands	47
Singapore	48
Spain	38
Sweden	37
Switzerland	71
United Kingdom	38
United States	100
Venezuela	52
West Germany	54

SOURCE: *Worldwide Total Remuneration* (New York: TPF&C, 1985). Reprinted with the permission of Towers Perrin.

---

should approximate the wages and salaries paid to other employees in comparable organizations (i.e., external equity must exist).[37]

Second, the pricing of jobs can enhance pay satisfaction when it is perceived as embodying a philosophy of equal work or equal pay for jobs of comparable worth. The determination of equal pay for equal work can be aided by sound job evaluations. But the worth of jobs must be evaluated according to the factors considered most important by the employees and the organization (so that internal equity exists).

Third, pay-for-performance systems must be accompanied by a method for accurately measuring the performance of employees and must be open enough so employees can clearly see the performance-pay relationship.[38] This is discussed further in Chapter 9.

Fourth, compensation rates and pay structures should be continually reviewed and updated if necessary. Over time the content of a job may increase or decrease, thus distorting the relationship between its true worth and its job-evaluated worth.

A final pay administration practice involves maintenance of trust and consistency. Employees must perceive that the organization is looking out for their interests as well as its own. Without trust and consistency, pay satisfaction is low, and pay becomes a target for complaints regardless of the real issues.

All-Salaried Work Force

Although some evidence indicates that all employees prefer to be salaried rather than paid on an hourly basis, most organizations distinguish their employees by method of pay. That is, salary status is usually reserved (along with a parking space) for management, and nonmanagement employees (except clerical workers) are usually paid on an hourly basis.

Still, some organizations put all their employees on salary. IBM has had an all-salaried work force since the 1930s. Eaton Corporation is using the all-salary concept in its newer plants, along with throwing out the time clocks. Some employees may abuse being on salary (for example, they can come in late or miss a day and still be paid). Alternatively, companies may take advantage of individuals paid on salary and not pay them overtime, even when legally mandated to do so.

Research is sparse regarding the effectiveness of an all-salaried work force. Anecdotal evidence does suggest that labor costs are lower when employees are salaried. Other testimonials claim that by treating employees a mature, responsible individuals, the climate of an organization is improved. Whether these reported benefits are organizational myths or realities remains to be seen. What really matters is whether the organization's compensation system stimulates a climate of respect, trust, and confidence.[39]

TRENDS IN STRATEGIC COMPENSATION

Compensation is a dynamic, challenging, and exciting PHRM activity. It is also a valuable activity for positively influencing the bottom line of organizations, as illustrated by the following description of two trends in compensation. Chapters 9 and 10 provide further descriptions of compensation trends.

Assessing Total Compensation

The effectiveness of total compensation should be assessed against a program's objectives:

- Attract potentially qualified employees
- Motivate employees
- Retain qualified employees
- Administer pay within legal constraints
- Facilitate organizational strategic objectives
- Reinforce and define structure

To achieve these purposes, employees generally need to be satisfied with their pay. This means that the organization's pay levels should be extremely competitive, that employees should perceive internal pay equity, and that the compensation program should be properly administered.[40] It also means that compensation practices must adhere to the various state and federal wage and hour laws. It suggests that the notion of comparable worth should be considered in pay administration practices. Consequently, an organization's total compensation can be assessed by comparing its pay levels with those of other organizations, by analyzing the validity of its job evaluation method, by measuring employee perceptions of pay equity and performance-pay linkages, and by determining individual pay levels within jobs and across jobs. By doing these activities, the strategic objectives of an organization may be facilitated.

Because attracting, motivating, and retaining employees are worthy purposes of total compensation and can facilitate organizational objectives, attaining them at a lower rather than higher cost of total compensation can also facilitate an organization's strategic objectives. This can be done by replacing nondeductible pay expenditures (e.g., expensive perquisites such as cars and club memberships) with deductible pay expenditures, such as contributions to employee stock ownership plans. This replacement must be done with consideration for the differential impact of alternative pay expenditures on attracting, motivating, and retaining employees. These differentials being relatively minimal, replacing nondeductible forms of compensations with deductible forms can increase the effectiveness of the total compensation dollar.

Total compensation is composed of base pay, performance-based pay, and indirect pay, so the assessment here of total compensation represents only the first part of the total assessment. Chapters 9 and 10 cover the other two parts necessary for total assessment.

Strategic Involvement of Total Compensation

Lincoln Electric is a leader in small motors and arc welders and has a compensation system tied to the company's profits. This system has resulted in the average Lincoln worker making up to $44,000 a year. In addition to having the high motivation to produce, Lincoln workers rarely quit. Their turnover rate is less than 1 percent. The result of Lincoln's compensation system is a cost-efficiency competitive advantage that allows it to price its products below competitors with equal, if not better, quality. Other companies also use their compensation systems strategically. For example, TRW and the Hewlett-Packard Company use compensation to drive their search for innovative products and services.

At Hewlett-Packard, entrepreneurial behavior is stimulated in its project leaders by tying more rewards to their success. Successful project leaders are being given banquets, stock options, and personal computers. At TRW, units or teams are given credit for sales generated in another department in return for helping that department. TRW fosters innovation by stimulating interdependence through its compensation practices. These companies get what they pay for: a steady stream of product and service improvements and enhancements that help them stand alone among their competitors,—hence, a strong competitive advantage.

SUMMARY

Many pay-related issues are of concern to personnel and human resource managers and others in organizations. One particular issue is comparable worth and its impact on organizations. The notion of comparable worth is that the true value of a job should be used in determining compensation rates. Proponents of comparable worth maintain that compensation rates of jobs presently reflect that men occupy certain jobs and women occupy others. Attaining comparable worth would significantly raise compensation rates and costs but would probably help remove previous wage discrimination. It would also involve some changes in the job evaluation procedures of many organizations.

Although determining a job's true worth is an important concept in comparable worth, it is difficult to measure or determine precisely. True worth can be determined only with great difficulty; using sound job evaluation procedures can enable an organization to move in that direction. Sound procedures, such as a point factor system, involve (1) using a single set of factors (i.e., just one evaluation system or plan) rather than one for the clerical staff, one for the blue-collar workers, and yet another for the supervisory group; (2) selecting factors that reflect the working environment and the organization's objectives; (3) developing factors and relative weights free of bias; (4) eliminating as much as possible the subjective measurement error in evaluating positions; (5) eliminating bias in the evaluation committee that reviews job evaluation results on jobs; and (6) sustaining an updated system to ensure that factors or evaluations do not become outdated.

Even if true worth is determined precisely, jobs must still be priced. Although job evaluation procedures are important in establishing true worth, they are more relevant to establishing relative job prices than absolute job prices. To help establish absolute job prices, organizations often use market survey data, especially for those jobs that have identical or nearly identical counterparts in the marketplace. Doing market surveys to directly price jobs that are not found in other organizations should be done with caution. It involves subjectivity and therefore is open to potential wage discrimination charges. Organizations should be careful not to use market rates to perpetuate wage differentials that are obviously discriminatory. Fair evaluations should be conducted to help reduce that likelihood.

In establishing wages, organizations can rely on job evaluations and market surveys and can use inputs from the employees themselves. Apparently, employees can responsibly set their own wages. In the few companies that have tried it, employees have set their own wages without management's having to alter the procedures or change decisions. The method is most successful, however, in organizations in which employees and management have mutual trust and employees are provided with information to help them understand the financial status of the company.

Establishing wages and determining which job evaluation method to use, though important, are only two components of compensation. Other components include selecting the best performance-based pay plan and obtaining benefit from indirect compensation. These and other important components of compensation are discussed in Chapters 9 and 10.

DISCUSSION QUESTIONS

1. How can the true worth of jobs be determined?
2. How does an organization determine whether jobs are exempt under the FLSA?
3. What are the basic wage issues that any job evaluation system must address?
4. What is the importance of pay grades? How are they established?
5. Why might an organization want to involve employees in the development of a compensation system? Why wouldn't they?

6. What are the components of an effective compensation communication program?
7. What is comparable worth, and why would an organization want to establish such a strategy? Why wouldn't it?

CASE STUDY

Planned Parenthood of Midwest City

Mary Johnson, executive director of Planned Parenthood of Midwest City (PPMC), sat at her desk sifting through miscellaneous compensation and budget documents. A major agenda item at the next PPMC board meeting was salary recommendations for the coming year. "This just isn't going to do the job," she thought as she looked at the old salary scale. "It really needs to be revised."

The present salary scale had been adopted by the board four years previously. While designed to last a number of years, inflationary pressures had rendered it useless. Cost-of-living adjustments had moved some employees right off the scale, and the gap between lower- and higher-paid employees appeared to be widening. "In spite of our efforts to keep pace with inflation, Ann, Ellen, and Kathryn still feel underpaid," she thought. "I think it's time to revamp the whole system."

PPMC is a private, non profit organization which provides educational, counseling, and clinical services to the community. Located in a small university town, PPMC employs nine full- and part-time employees. Numerous volunteers also provide services to the agency without pay. Funding for PPMC comes from multiple sources: the federal government (48 percent), local sources and patient fees (45 percent), and other sources (7 percent). Last year's annual budget was $213,755. A slight increase (5–7 percent) in funding is projected for the coming year, assuming federal funding is authorized by Congress. Mary Johnson has been with PPMC for ten years and has served as the executive director the past nine years.

Mary began organizing the relevant documents she had gathered. Taking a file folder from her drawer, she organized the documents as follows: First was a list of present employees, their position, years of service, present pay level, and hours of work (see Exhibit 1). Next she added a copy of the organization chart (see Exhibit 2) and summarized job descriptions in the file. "I want the pay system to be perceived as equitable by employees," she thought. "Pay levels should reflect varying levels of job responsibilities and skills, as well as reporting relationships."

PPMC Employee Summary (Fiscal Year 1989)

EXHIBIT
1

Name[1]	Position	Years PPMC	Years Position	FTE*	Salary
Mary Johnson	Executive Director	10	9	.8	$18,843
Peter Martin	Administrative Director	10	9	.6	9,427
Ann Mitchell	Clinic Manager	14	3	1.0	12,570
Sarah Watson	Education Director	4	3	1.0	13,750
Janet Smith	Nurse Practitioner	1	1	1.0	21,969
Rick Winters	County Coordinator	8	2	.5	5,864
Ellen Peters	Clinical Asst. II	3	3	1.04	11,345
Kathryn Woo	Clinical Asst. I	10	5	1.0	10,837

* 1 FTE = 35 hours/week

1. Note medical director is excluded from the plan.

EXHIBIT
2

PPMC Organization Chart

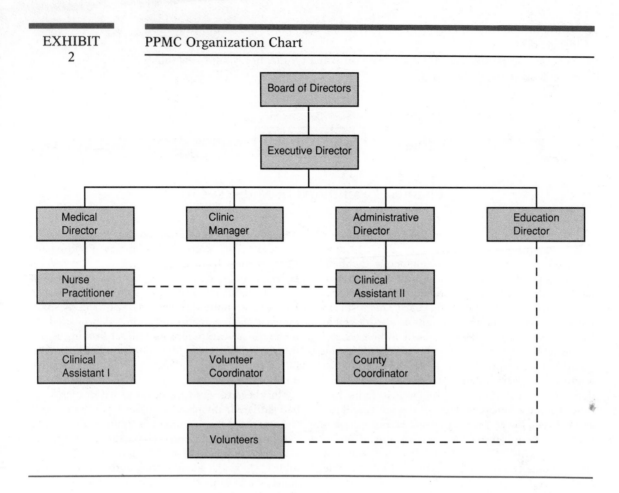

The next item she placed in the folder was a salary survey reflecting pay ranges of other planned parenthood clinics in the region (see Exhibit 3). While the job titles in the survey didn't match those used at PPMC in all cases, Mary felt it was useful to compare pay levels at PPMC with other clinics whenever possible.

"One thing I don't have in my life," Mary mused, "is comparative wage information from other organizations in Midwest City that employ personnel in positions similar to ours. Perhaps the state employment service has that information. I'll have to get it from somewhere. I want our salaries to be sufficient and fair. Yet, as a nonprofit organization, I don't feel we should pay the highest wages in the community."

Other desired outcomes began to flow into Mary's mind: "I want the system to be objective and systematic. I want it to be flexible and adjustable from year to year." Mary liked the idea of pay ranges, allowing her flexibility in accounting for experience and years of service when determining specific pay levels. Ranges played a vital role in her ability to project salary costs one or two years into the future. "If possible, I'd also like to be able to reward team productivity. We've had some success with productivity bonuses in the past."

"In developing a pay plan," reasoned Mary, "I want to make sure it fits with our other personnel policies." All employees at PPMC are paid on a salaried basis and work 35 hours a week. PPMC has a fairly liberal fringe benefits package and has received awards for its innovative personnel policies.

"Another criteria," thought Mary, "is that the pay system must meet federal and state wage and salary guidelines. "Finally," she thought, "I don't want anyone to receive a pay cut as a result of changing the system, yet the cost of the system should not exceed budget projections."

By Steve Hanks, Utah State Univ.
and Gaylen Chandler, Univ. of Utah

Planned Parenthood Regional Salary Survey[1]

EXHIBIT
3

Position	Average Low Salary[2] (Range)[4]	Average Current Salary[3] (Range)	Average High Salary[2] (Range)	Average Years in Position (Range)
Executive Director	$18,240 ($17,600–$19,800)	$21,673 ($17,722–$24,750)	$25,961 ($19,800–$30,800)	3.04 years (.58–9 years)
Director of Administration/ Fiscal	$13,868 ($13,750–$13,985)	$16,693 ($15,711–$17,674)	$19,575 ($18,150–$21,000)	7.50 years (5–9 years)
Clinic Director	$13,875 ($11,000–$18,150)	$18,250 ($12,570–$25,967)	$19,640 ($15,400–$26,530)	3.38 years (2–6 years)
Educator	$11,825 ($11,000–$13,300)	$14,453 ($12,584–$16,170)	$17,372 ($16,245–$19,925)	3 years (1–6 years)
Nurse Practitioner	$18,168 ($16,020–$20,020)	$20,979 ($18,280–$23,140)	$24,060 ($22,000–$25,740)	3.5 years (1–10 years)
All-Purpose Person[5]	$9,090 ($8,000–$10,810)	$10,831 ($8,500–$12,575)	$13,059 ($10,000–$16,240)	4.44 years (.33–10 years)
Records Clerk[6]	$9,075 ($8,800–$9,350)	$11,297 ($11,100–$11,350)	$13,200 ($12,700–$13,400)	2.13 years (1.25–3 years)
Secretary[6]	$8,980 ($8,580–$9,350)	$11,125 ($9,650–$12,600)	$12,526 ($10,725–$13,650)	.61 years (.08–1.25 years)

[1]Salary survey data taken from eight planned parenthood clinics in the Midwest region, having total annual budgets under $275,000. Survey data is based on a thirty-five hour workweek. The County Coordinator position was not included in the regional salary survey, so no regional data are available.

[2]Average Low and Average High Salaries summarize the low and high points on the pay scale for each position.

[3]Average Current Salary is the average reported salary for current job incumbents.

[4]Range is the statistical range of responses in each category.

[5]Job descriptions of PPMC's Clinical Assistant I and the All-Purpose Person position surveyed above are similar.

[6]PPMC's Clinical Assistant II position involves 50 percent records Clerk duties and 50 percent secretarial duties.

Case Questions

1. What should be the objectives of Planned Parenthood's compensation program?
2. What are the advantages and disadvantages of using market rates to set the pay for all PPMC employees?
3. Discuss the merits of using a job classification versus a point system to determine the worth of the PPMC's jobs.
4. Are there legitimate reasons for the three employees to be dissatisfied? Why or why not?
5. What strategies are available to Mary to alleviate the pay dissatisfaction of PPMC's three employees?
6. How should Mary go about developing a fair and equitable compensation system for Planned Parenthood?
7. What salary adjustments, if any, do you recommend if PPMC is to be competitive with other agencies? Justify your answers.

NOTES

1. E. E. Lawler III, *Pay and Organizational Development* (Reading, Mass.: Addison-Wesley, 1981); E. E. Lawler III, "The Strategic Design of Reward Systems," in *Readings in Personnel and Human Resource Management*, 2d ed., R. S. Schuler and S. A. Youngblood (St. Paul: West, 1984); G. T. Milkovich and J. M. Newman, *Compensation*, 2d ed. (Homewood, Ill: Richard D. Irwin, 1989).

2. *Bulletin to Management*, 21 Jan. 1988, p. 21.

3. C. Alderfer, *Existence, Relatedness, and Growth* (New York: Free Press, 1972); J. Campbell and R. Pritchard, "Motivation Theory in Industrial and Organizational Psychology," in *Handbook of Industrial and Organizational Psychology*, ed. M. Dunnette (Chicago: Rand McNally, 1976); W. H. Griggs and S. Manning, "Money Isn't the Best Tool for Motivating Technical Professionals," *Personnel Administrator* (June 1985): 63–78; V. Vroom, *Work and Motivation* (New York: Wiley, 1964).

4. D. B. Balkin, "Compensation Strategy for Firms in Emerging and Rapidly Growing Industries," *Human Resource Planning* 11, No. 3 (1988): 207–14; S. J. Carroll, "Business Strategies and Compensation Systems" in *New Perspectives on Compensation*, ed. D. B. Balkin and L. R. Gomez-Mejia (Englewood Cliffs, N.J.: Prentice-Hall, 1987), 343–55; S. J. Carroll, "Handling the Need for Consistency and the Need for Contingency in the Management of Compensation," *Human Resource Planning* 11, No. 3 (1988): 191–96; L. R. Gomez-Mejia and T. M. Welbourne, "Compensation Strategy: An Overview and Future Steps," *Human Resource Planning* 11, No. 3 (1988): 173–90; R. I. Henderson and H. W. Risher, "Influencing Organizational Strategy through Compensation Leadership," in *New Perspectives on Compensation*, ed. D. B. Balkin and L. R. Gomez-Mejia (Englewood Cliffs, N.J.: Prentice-Hall, 1987), 331–42; E. F. Hufnagal, "Developing Strategic Compensation Plans," *Human Resource Management* (Spring 1987): 93–108; J. L. Kerr, "Strategic Control through Performance Appraisal and Rewards," *Human Resource Planning* 11 No 3. (1988): 215–24; J. E. McCann, "Rewarding and Supporting Strategic Planning," in New Perspectives on Compensation, ed. D. B. Bolkin and L. R. Gomez-Mejia (Englewood Cliffs, N.J.: Prentice-Hall, 1987), 356–363; J. P. Muczyk, "The Strategic Role of Compensation," *Human Resource Planning* 11, No. 3 (1988): 225–40; J. M. Newman, "Selecting Incentive Plans to Complement Organizational Strategy," in *New Perspectives on Compensation*, ed. D. B. Balkin and L. R. Gomez-Mejia (Englewood Cliffs, N.J.: Prentice-Hall, 1987), 214–24; J. M. Newman, "Compensation Strategy in Declining Industries," *Human Resource Planning* 11, No. 3 (1988): 197–206; R. M. Steers and G. R. Ungson, "Strategic Issues in Executive Compensation Decisions," in *New Perspectives on Compensation*, ed. D. B. Balkin and L. R. Gomez-Mejia (Englewood Cliffs, N.J.: Prentice-Hall, 1987), 294–308.

5. J. Kerr and J. W. Slocum, Jr., "Managing Corporate Culture through Reward Systems," *Executive* (May 1987): 99–108; J. Kerr and J. Slocum, Jr., "Linking Reward Systems and Organizational Cultures," in *Readings in Personnel and Human Resource Management*, 3d ed., ed. R. S. Schuler, S. A. Youngblood, and V. Huber (St. Paul: West, 1988), 297–311; S. E. Markham, "Pay-for-Performance Dilemma Revisited: Empirical Example of the Importance of Group Effects," *Journal of Applied Psychology* (May 1988): 172–80; R. D. Prtichard, S. D. Jones, P. L. Roth, K. K. Stuebing, and S. E. Ekeberg, "Effects of Group Feedback, Goal Setting, and Incentives on Organizational Productivity," *Journal of Applied Psychology* (May 1988): 206–337.

6. D. B. Balkin and L.R. Gomez-Mejia, "Compensation Practices in High Technology Industries," *Personnel Administrator* (June 1985): 111–23; D. B. Balkin and L. R. Gomez-Mejia, "Entrepreneurial Compensation," in *Readings in Personnel and Human Resource Management*, 3d ed., ed. R. S. Schuler, S. A. Youngblood, and V. L. Huber (St. Paul: West, 1988); R. J. Greene and R. G. Roberts, "Strategic Integration of Compensation and Benefits," *Personnel Administrator* (May 1983): 79–86; Lawler, "Strategic Design of Reward Systems"; J. Schuster, *Management Compensation in High Technology Companies* (Lexington, Mass.: Lexington Books, 1984); P. Stonich, "The Performance Measurement and Reward System: Critical to Strategic Management," *Organizational Dynamics* (Winter 1984): 45–57.

7. D. Q. Mills, *The New Competitors* (New York: Wiley, 1985), 121.

8. T. Wils and L. R. Dyer, "Relating Business Strategy to Human Resource Strategy: Some Preliminary Evidence," presented at the 44th Annual Meeting of Management Meeting, August 1984, Boston.

9. *CPC Salary Survey* (College Placement Council, NY, 1989).

10. D. W. Belcher and T. J. Atchison, *Compensation Administration*, 2d (Englewood Cliffs, N.J.: Prentice-Hall, 1987); Lawler, *Pay and Organizational Development*; G. Milkovich and J. Newman, *Compensation* (Plano, Tex.: BPI, 1987).

11. D. B. Balkin and L. R. Gomez-Mejia, "The Strategic Use of Short-Term and Long-Term Incentives in the High-Technology Industry," in *New Perspectives on Compensation*, ed. D. B. Balkin and L. R. Gomez-Mejia (Englewood Cliffs, N.J.: Prentice-Hall, 1987), 237–46; T. R. Hinkin, P. M. Podsakoff, and C. A. Schriesheim, "The Mediation of Performance-Contingent Compensation by Supervisors in Work Organizations: A Reinforcement Perspective," in *New Perspectives on Compensation*, ed. D. B. Balkin and L. R. Gomez-Mejia (Englewood Cliffs, N.J.: Prentice-Hall, 1987), 196–210; H. H. Meyer, "How Can We Implement A Pay-for-Performance Policy Successfully?" in *New Perspectives on Compensation*, ed. D.

B. Balkin and L. R. Gomez-Mejia (Englewood Cliffs, N.J.: Prentice-Hall, 1987), 169–78.

12. G. Ameci, "Overtime Pay: Avoiding FLSA Violations," *Personnel Administrator* (Feb. 1987): 117–18; H. L. Angle and J. L. Perry, "Dual Commitment and Labor-Management Relationship Climates," *Academy of Management Journal* (Mar. 1986): 31–52; R. M. Pattison, "Fine Tuning Wage and Hour Practices," *Personnel Journal* (Sept. 1987): 166–69; H. Stout, "Propping Up Payments at the Bottom," *New York Times*, 24 Jan. 1988, 4.

13. *FEP Guidelines*, Jan. 1985, p. 2. This copyrighted material is reprinted with permission of the Bureau of Business Practice, Waterford, CT 06386.

14. "Final Equal Pay Interpretations Issued by EEOC," *Fair Employment Practices*, 4 Sept. 1986, p. 108.

15. D. Elizur, *Systematic Job Evaluation and Comparable Worth* (Brookfield, Vt.: Gower, 1987).

16. E. R. Auster, "Wage Difference between Men and Women: Performance Appraisal Ratings vs. Salary Allocation as the Locus of Bias," *Human Resource Management* (Summer 1987): 157–68; Balkin and Gomez-Mejia, "Entrepreneurial Compensation," in *Readings in Personnel and Human Resource Management*, 3d ed., 291–96; T. J. Bergmann, "Conducting an 'Equal Pay for Equal Work' Audit," in *New Perspectives on Compensation*, ed. D. B. Balkin and L. R. Gomez-Mejia (Englewood Cliffs, N.J.: Prentice-Hall, 1987), 80–89; "Earning Gap between Men and Women Continues to Narrow," *Fair Employment Practices*, 3 Mar. 1988, p. 27; K. Judd and L. R. Gomez-Mejia, "Comparable Worth: A Sensible Way to End Pay Discrimination or the Lonniest Idea Since Looney Tunes?" in *New Perspectives on Compensation*, ed. D. B. Balkin and L. R. Gomez-Mejia (Englewood Cliffs, N.J.: Prentice-Hall, 1987), 61–79; Kerr and Slocum, "Linking Reward Systems and Organizational Cultures," in *Readings in Personnel and Human Resource Management*, 3d ed., 297–308; J. Ledvinka, "The Legal Status of Comparable Worth," in *New Perspectives on Compensation*, ed. D. B. Balkin and L. R. Gomez-Mejia (Englewood Cliffs, N.J.: Prentice-Hall, 1987), 51–60; J. Newman, "Rewards in Organizations," in *Readings in Personnel and Human Resource Management*, 3d ed., ed. R. S. Schuler, S. A. Youngblood, and V. L. Huber (St. Paul: West, 1988), 267–74; T. H. Patten, "Comparable Worth Issues Today and Tomorrow," in *Readings in Personnel and Human Resource Management*, 3d ed., ed. R. S. Schuler, S. A. Youngblood, and V. L. Huber (St. Paul: West, 1988) 248–55; B. Southward, K. Murphy, W. E. Barlow, and D. D. Hatch, "Manager's Newsfront," *Personnel Journal* (Nov. 1987): 24–32.

17. *Wall Street Journal*, 16 Apr. 1985, p. 1. Reprinted by permission of *The Wall Street Journal*, © Dow Jones & Company, Inc., 1985. All Rights Reserved.

18. T. Linsenmayer, "Comparable Worth Abroad: Mixed Evidence," *Wall Street Journal*, 27 May 1986, p. 26.

19. Milkovich and Newman, *Compensation*. 2nd ed.

20. R. Snelgar, "The Comparability of Job Evaluation Methods in Supplying Approximately Similar Classifications in Rating One Job Series," *Personnel Psychology* (Summer 1983): 371–80.

21. Judd and Gomez-Mejia, *New Perspective on Compensation*.

22. Milkovich and Newman, *Compensation*, 2nd ed.

23. D. Doverspike, "An Internal Bias Analysis of a Job Evaluation Instrument," *Journal of Applied Psychology* (Nov. 1984): 648–50; S. L. Fraser, S. F. Cronshaw, and R. A. Alexander, "Generalizability Analysis of a Point Method Job Evaluation Instrument: A Field Study," *Journal of Applied Psychology* (Nov. 1984): 643–47.

24. Lawler, *Pay and Organizational Development*; H. Tosi and L. Tosi, "Knowledge Based Pay: Some Propositions and Guides to Effective Use," *Organizational Dynamics* (Winter 1986): 52–64.

25. "Usual Pay Plans," *Wall Street Journal*, 22 May 1984, p. 1.

26. *Bulletin to Management*, 14 Jan. 1988, p. 10.

27. The types of surveys that organizatons use in helping to establish wage rates include several published by associations and consulting firms, such as Hewitt and Associates, Hay Associates, Handy Associates, and Towers, Perrin, Forster, and Crosby. The use of survey pay data has antitrust implications. For a discussion, see G. D. Fisher, "Salary Surveys—An Antitrust Perspective," *Personnel Administrator* (Apr. 1985): 87–97, 154. See also M. Camuso, "Keep Competitive with the Right Salary Survey," *Personnel Journal* (Oct. 1985): 86–92; J. Pfeffer and A. Davis-Blake, "Understanding Organizational Wage Structures: A Resource Dependence Approach," *Academy of Management Journal* (Sept. 1987): 437–55.

28. Pay data from surveys can be analyzed by mathematical or statistical processes, such as histograms, scattergrams, sample variances and standard deviations, least squares, standard error of estimate, correlation coefficients, and coefficients of determination and multiple regression. For a description of these, see any basic compensation text, such as Belcher and Atchison, *Compensation Administration*, or J. D. Dunn and F. M. Rachel, *Wage and Salary Administration: Total Compensation Systems* (New York, McGraw-Hill, 1971).

29. Milkovich and Newman, *Compensation*, 2d ed.

30. Belcher and Atchison, *Compensation Administration*; J. Franklin, "For Technical Professionals: Pay for Skills and Pay for Performance," *Personnel* (May 1988): 20–28; J. C. Kail, "Compensating Scientists and Engineers," in *New Perspectives on Compensation*, ed. D. B. Balkin and L. R. Gomez-Mejia (Englewood Cliffs, N.J.: Prentice-Hall, 1987), 278—81; G. T. Milkovich, "Compensation Systems in High-Technology Companies," in *New Perspectives on Compensation*, ed. D. B. Balkin and L. R. Gomez-Mejia (Englewood Cliffs, N.J.: Prentice-Hall, 1987), 269–77; Milkovich and Newman, *Compensation* 2d ed.; C. F. Schultz, Compensating the Sales Professional, " in *New Perspectives on Compensation*, ed. D. B. Balkin and L. R. Gomez-Mejia (Englewood Cliffs, N.J.: Prentice-Hall, 1987), 250–57.

31. R. Henderson, *Compensation Management* (Reston, Va.: Reston Publishing, 1985).

32. M. Zippo, "Roundup," *Personnel* (May/June 1981): 43–50.

33. M. Zippo, "Roundup," *Personnel* (Sept./Oct. 1980): 43–45.

34. Lawler, *Pay and Organizational Development*.

35. V. Scarpello, V. Huber, and R. J. Vanderberg, "Compensation Satisfaction: Its Measurement and Dimensionality," *Journal of Applied Psychology* (May 1988): 163–71.

36. J. A. Byrne, "The $60 Million Chairman," *Business Week*, 16 May 1988, p. 42; R. Moss Kanter, "The Attack on Pay," *Harvard Business Review* (Mar./Apr. 1987): 60–67; "Who Made the Most and Why," *Business Week*, 2 May 1988, pp. 50–148.

37. L. Dyer, D. P. Schwab, and J. A. Fossum, "Impacts of Pay on Employee Behaviors and Attitudes: An Update," *Personnel Administrator* (Jan. 1978): 56.

38. Dyer, Schwab, and Fossum, "Impacts of Pay"; T. R. Mitchell, "Motivational Strategies," in *Personnel Management*, ed. K. M. Rowland and G. R. Ferris (Boston: Allyn & Bacon, 1982), 263–300.

39. Lawler, *Pay and Organizational Development*.

40. A "properly administered" compensation program implies several qualities of total compensation, including that the job evaluation process is valid, pay structures are fairly and objectively derived, pay is administered in a nondiscriminatory way, compensation policies are communicated so as to be understood, administrative costs are contained, it has sufficient motivational value, and it is supported by top management. For a discussion of these, see R. E. Azevedo and J. M. Beaton, "Costing the Pay Package: A Realistic Approach," in *New Perspectives on Compensation*, ed. D. B. Balkin and L. R. Gomez-Mejia (Englewood Cliffs, N.J.: Prentice-Hall, 1987), 143–50; S. B. Henrici, "A Tool for Salary Administrators: Standard Salary Accounting," *Personnel* (Sept./Oct. 1980): 14–23; and J. C. Horn, "Bigger Pay for Better Work," *Psychology Today* (July 1987): 54–57.

CHAPTER

9

Performance-based Pay Systems

Clarified Carrots

In the hurry-up, competitive world of overnight delivery, who needs incentive plans that are too complicated to communicate to employees? "Thats why Airborne Express (Seattle, WA) studied its incentive pay plans last year, and that's why the newly-streamlined programs are now being communicated with clarity," said Dick Goodwin, vice president of HR for the overnight delivery and international freight forwarding company . . .

"Because the competition is so keen and because the services offered among competitors are so similar, the company as a whole has always believed in the concept of incentive pay for people who can have a significant impact on the bottom line. Each employee must understand the corporate goals and how the goals relate to his or her job.

"But, our incentive plans needed revamping, so we studied them with the assistance of a consulting firm . . .

"No one was surprised to learn that employees were confused by the existing incentive plans. . . .

"In addition to a general confusion about the objectives of the incentive programs, the employees didn't understand how their incentive payments were calculated—and most important, they didn't even know why they did or did not receive a quarterly incentive check. We set out to change that.

"The new incentive packages for each position are directly linked to corporate goals:

- growth
- profitability
- service
- cost control and
- productivity

"In addition to tying performance to corporate objectives, another goal was to design the plans for each position with optimum clarity and simplicity. Measurement is easy in our business—and we established simple formulae for shipment volume and revenue . . .

"A popular feature in the new plans is the elimination of all caps on incentives earnings. This seemed to give a psychological boost to the kind of people we like.

"We tend to attract young, aggressive managers at Airborne and we encourage internal competition to the point of publicly ranking peers on sales volume and revenue performance.

"Once the recommendations for the new incentive plans were accepted by management, we still had a communications job in front of us, and were intent on doing it right since communication had been part of the employees' confusion about the old plans.

"The compensation director and I first wrote detailed descriptions of the incentive programs for each position covered in a lengthy source document intended for headquarters staff and senior field management.

"Then, for six key positions such as account managers, sales reps and district operations managers, we have written or are in the process of writing customized booklets of 10 or 15 pages, written in the first person.

"These booklets are concisely written, while containing all the needed information on how a given position's incentive program works. They even include a worksheet, formulae and tables with formulae already calculated for them, to take out any mystery about the plans.

"In addition to the written communications, which have included many more documents to instruct managers, my staff and I will be visiting each of the 10 regional meetings to make certain the plans are fully comprehended."

SOURCE: "Clarified Carrots," *HR Reporter* (May 1987): 2-3. Used with permission from *HR Reporter*, copyright 1987.

T he preceding "PHRM in the News" illustrates several important aspects of performance-based pay. One is that organizations such as Airborne Express see it as a necessity for survival in a highly competitive business.[1] Second there is a need to keep performance-based pay plans simple and understandable. Another is that incentive compensation must be linked to important organizational goals. Plans also need to be customized because employees have different jobs and are motivated by different factors. A final aspect of performance-based pay is that properly designed it is an effective way to motivate employees and improve organizational profitablity.[2]

TYPES OF PERFORMANCE-BASED PAY SYSTEMS

Performance-based pay systems relate pay to performance in one of two ways. **Incentive pay plans**, such as the one at Airborne Express, measure performance output of individuals, groups, or organizations *directly*. Performance-based pay accounts for a *major* portion of the individual's compensation. For example, salespersons may be assured a small base salary, but the majority of their compensation is earned through commissions.[3] By contrast, **merit pay plans** generally rely on indirect measures of performance (ratings or rankings). Because the measure of performance is indirect, merit pay plans only affect a *small percentage* of an individual's total compensation. Despite the limitations of performance appraisal, merit pay plans are by far the most prevalent type of performance-based pay. Various types of performance-based pay plans are identified in Exhibit 9.1.

PURPOSES AND IMPORTANCE OF PERFORMANCE-BASED PAY

Money is one of the *most* powerful *motivators* available to a manager because it is valued directly as a reward and because it facilitates the purchase of items that are valued. Its potential to motivate is unquestionable. Consider the effect of a twenty-five-cent reward at Creole Foods of Opelousas, Louisiana. When Alex Chachere took over as president in 1981, he found a lethargic work forced content to ship fewer than 3,500 cases per month, far below the company's potential. So he devised a bonus plan. Every month that shipments topped 7,000

Performance-Based Pay Systems

Merit Pay Plans	Incentive Pay Plans	
	Individual	*Group*
■ Traditional	■ Piecework plan	
■ Lump-sum bonus	■ Standard hour plan	■ Scanlon plan
	■ Measured day plan	■ Customized plans
	■ Sales incentive plan	■ Improshare
	■ Suggestion systems	■ Profit-sharing plans
		■ Games/awards

EXHIBIT 9.1

cases, workers would divide up an additional twenty-five-cents per case. If the cost of sales stayed under 50 percent, they would get another dime. Chachere expected them to reach these targets in a year or so. The first month they shipped about 8,000 cases. Last year, the company's twenty-eight employees averaged 30,000 cases per month, and Chachere paid $77,000 in bonuses. "That's a lot of money," he admits. "But the day we discontinue the bonuses is the day I quit."[4]

As the initial "PHRM in the News" illustrates, pay is also important because it enhances organizational survival and competitiveness. One in every fifteen companies among three-hundred surveyed by the Hay Group, a management consulting group, granted bonuses in lieu of salary increases last year. For example, a spokesperson for Cleveland's Parker Hannifin Corp. stated that now that quarterly bonuses are tied to performance, "You can't say 'The company's doing well, so I'll coast.'"

Similarly, American Greeting Corp. says that even its cost-of-living increases are now tied to merit, and bonuses are based on each unit's results. About 2,500 executives at Aetna Life & Casualty Co. vie for bonuses under a new "Superior Pay for Superior Performance" program. Bank of America increased by 29 percent the number of managers whose salary depends in part on performance. Hewlett-Packard Co. and Bechtel Group Inc. base all salary increases on merit.[5]

Performance-based pay systems are also useful in promoting teamwork and participation. For example, when incentives are based on the performance of the group, people pitch in more often to help one another. Similarly, when employees share profit savings equally with management, productivity, work quality, and attendance improve. Additionally, there are fewer employee complaints.

Performance-based pay systems, however, have some disadvantages. One is that they take time to administer; typically, employees have to work exceptionally hard to earn large incentive bonuses, and occasional conflicts can arise from not rewarding certain behaviors. These advantages and disadvantages of performance-based pay apply only when the appropriate conditions exist for its implementation. When these conditions do not exist, the disadvantages far outweigh the advantages. These conditions, critical in determining when to use performance-based pay, are described later in this chapter. Also important to consider are the relationships influencing performance-based pay.

RELATIONSHIPS INFLUENCING PERFORMANCE-BASED PAY

Although most of the key relationships of performance-based pay are described in Chapter 8, three relationships with other PHRM activities, are highlighted here.

Relationships with Other PHRM Activities

Performance Appraisal.   Nine out of ten managers believe that paying good performers more than mediocre performers makes sense. Good pay and larger increases help retain employees, and good performers are the ones managers most want to keep. Additionally, it is widely believed that an employee who is rewarded for good performance will be encouraged to continue performing well.

Although most managers would agree that the best way to allocate scarce payroll dollars is to provide significant rewards to their top performers, most would admit reluctantly in private that they really do not end up paying their top performers much differently than they do the rest. Two principal reasons emerge:

1. The typical pay system does not provide enough leeway to reward the really good performers without unfairly penalizing the satisfactory but unexceptional workers who also must be retained and kept motivated.
2. Managers are not comfortable with basing large pay distinctions on the often-hazy performance information that they are able to develop.[6]

It is the second point that is of particular relevance here. Conventional performance appraisal forms described in Chapter 6 have the potential for numerous errors and subjectivity. Because these forms are most common in organizations, many managers are uncomfortable basing performance-based pay decisions on this information.

Training and Development.   Managers must be trained to be aware of the effects of contingent (performance-based) rewards on performance, to observe employee performance accurately, and to provide employees with feedback as quickly as possible after the desired behavior, via pay, praise, and other rewards. In addition, employees must be trained to be able to perform as expected.

The Union-Management Relationship.   Because wages are a bargainable issue, whether an organization has a performance-based pay system may depend on a union's desires. Further, because unions have traditionally opposed performance-based pay systems, organizations must convince the union of the benefits of these pay systems. Once shown the benefits and even the necessities of such pay systems, some unions seem willing to cooperate and help implement these systems.

Organizational Culture

Pay-for-performance programs are not appropriate for all organizations. In fact, they are more prevalent in industries in which labor accounts for a large proportion of the total costs of production and the market is extremely cost competitive. Incentive programs also seem to be more prevalent in organizations with slowly advancing technologies and when the potential for production bottlenecks is high. By rewarding team performance, management can get workers to pitch in and help alleviate bottlenecks.

Organizational cultures that promote risk taking, rather than stability and growth through tried and true methods, encourage the use of performance-based pay systems. Entrepreneurial behavior is stimulated through incentive systems that encourage individual drive and initiative. For performance-based pay systems to work, employee-management trust must be maintained at a high level. Exhibit 9.2 details some questions regarding organizational culture that should be asked prior to implementing a performance-based pay system.[7]

EXHIBIT
9.2

Ten Questions to Answer Before Implementing a
Performance-Based Pay System

1. Is pay valued by employees?
2. What is the objective(s) of the performance-based pay system?
3. Are the values of the organization conducive to a performance-based pay system?
4. What steps will be taken to ensure that employees and management are committed to the system?
5. Can performance be accurately measured? If not, what type of an appraisal system will be used?
6. How frequently will performance be measured or evaluated?
7. What level of aggregation (individual, group, organization) will be used to distribute rewards?
8. How will pay be tied to performance (e.g., merit increase, bonus, commission, incentive)?
9. Does the organization have sufficient financial resources to make performance-based pay meaningful?
10. What steps will be taken to control and monitor the system?

LEGAL CONSIDERATIONS IN PERFORMANCE-BASED PAY

As indicated in Chapter 8, Title VII of the Civil Rights Act of 1964 applies not only to selection decisions but also to pay decisions. A supervisor may be charged with unlawful discrimination by an employee (in a protected group) who believes that a pay raise was denied on the basis of factors unrelated to performance. Raises not related to performance, however, can be given legally. Defensible factors (when they are equally applied to all employees) include the following.

- Performance
- Position in salary range
- Time since last increase
- Size of last increase
- Pay relationships within the company or department
- Pay levels of jobs in other companies
- Salaries of newly hired employees
- Budgetary limits

What is critical is that the same rules of the game are used to give raises fairly and consistently to all employees. The same is true for incentive pay plans.

Tax laws are also important considerations in performance-based pay, particularly where frequent use is made of stocks and stock options to reward executives for performance. Compensation for executives is often designed with the tax laws in mind. For example, the tax rules and regulations of incentive stock option (ISO) plans are defined and described by the Economic Recovery Tax Act of 1981 (ERTA) (discussed in Chapter 10). The level of executive compensation is also subject to legal considerations. For example, the Internal Revenue Service (IRS) can claim that executives are paid in excess of what they are worth and that their pay must be reduced. Excessive pay, referred to by the IRS as "unreasonable compensation," is illegal because the federal government receives more money when a company's profits are paid as dividends than it does when they are distributed as wages, and is therefore losing tax dollars. Another form of executive compensation that can be regarded as incentive compensation is the "golden parachute." Because it is really a benefit, it is described in Chapter 10.

   In general, incentive pay plans appear to have substantially more motivational value, but merit pay plans remain much more frequent because they tend to be easier to set up and administer. Whereas essentially one type of merit plan exists, there is a wide variety of incentive plans. The range of both types is shown in Exhibit 9.1.

MERIT PAY PLANS

While incentive pay plans have substantially more motivational power, **merit pay plans** are more common because they are easier to set up and administer and because hard output data are not available for most jobs. In merit pay plans, guidelines must be established for determining the size of merit pay raises, the timing of reward distribution, and the relationship between merit pay increments and one's place in the salary range.

Merit Pay Guidelines

Exhibit 9.3 presents typical merit pay plan. As shown, the size of the pay increment depends on the individual's position (employee's salary/midpoint of salary range) in the salary range.[8] Although the percentage of the merit increase is greater in the lower quartiles, the absolute size of the increase is often larger in the higher quartiles. Therefore, the compensation manager must carefully monitor line managers to ensure that they don't push employees to the top of pay ranges to get employees more money. This problem, most prevalent when managers are not directly responsible for managing merit increase funds, can be controlled by making managers accountable for salary increases.

Sample Merit Pay Plan

EXHIBIT 9.3

Performance Rating	Current Position in Salary Range			
	First Quartile	Second Quartile	Third Quartile	Fourth Quartile
Truly outstanding	13–14% increase	11–12% increase	9–10% increase	6–8% increase
Above average	11–12% increase	9–10% increase	7–8% increase	6% increase or less
Good	9–10% increase	7–8% increase	6% increase or less	delay increase
Satisfactory	6–8% increase	6% increase or less	delay increase	no increase
Unsatisfactory	no increase	no increase	no increase	no increase

Merit Versus Cost-of-Living Adjustments

In addition to merit increases, many organizations grant nonperformance **cost-of-living adjustments** (COLAs). While the actual cost of living differs for each of us, COLAs are generally tied to changes in the consumer price index (CPI), a measure of the changes in prices for a hypothetical market basket of goods and services. The present index compares current prices to the base period of 1967. For example, a CPI of 400 indicates that it cost $400 to buy the same goods and services that cost $100 in 1967. The CPI is of interest because a one-percent increase can trigger increases of more than $2 billion in pay budgets, social security payments, and pensions.[9]

While unions pushed and won COLAs in the 1970s and early 1980s, management is now pushing back.[10] The current trend is away from COLAs and toward performance-based pay for several reasons. First, the more the CPI increases, the more the organization must pay. In times of high inflation, COLAs can be so large that they subsume the *entire* salary increase pool. This means there will be little or no money available for merit raises. Second, once granted, COLA increases become a permanent payroll expense. Third, there appears to be no relationship between COLA and employee performance. Thus, employers who grant such increases endure sunk costs with little return on their investment.

Performance Bonuses

With increased emphasis on cost-effective PHRM practices, firms are questioning the traditional practice of granting annual salary or merit increases. Consider an employee who performs outstandingly one year and is given a 15 percent merit pay increase. The next year, for whatever reason, the employee may not perform as well, or even adequately. While subsequent performance may decrease, the original salary increase is a permanent cost for the organization. Merit increases administered in this way may also demotivate other employees because the employee who had performed well previously may have a higher base pay rate than the employee who is currently performing well. As a result, the low performer may receive a larger increase than the better-performing employee whose base pay is lower.

To rectify this situation, firms such as B. F. Goodrich, Timex, and Westinghouse are replacing merit increases with one-time, semianuual, or quarterly performance bonuses. These bonuses may be distributed in one lump sum or in the traditional way (divided into parts and added to each paycheck). Bonuses are also popular in competitive high-technology firms. A recent survey showed that 7 percent of managerial, professional, and technical employees were eligible for bonuses in large high-tech firms. In smaller high-tech firms with sales less than $1 billion, almost half of all technical employees receive bonuses. These may be tied to meeting product development deadlines or based on the profitablility of product lines.[11] Lump-sum bonuses are also working their way into union contracts. The Bureau of National Affairs reported that lump-sum increases were included in 33 percent of all nonconstruction contracts settled in 1986, up from 19 percent the previous year. Common forms of bonuses in union contracts include a flat amount, a percentage of the preceding year's pay, and a specified dollar amount multiplied by the number of hours worked.[12]

There are several advantages of bonuses over salary increases. First, the bonuses increase the meaning of pay. The lump-sum payment of $5,000 is more striking than a before-tax increase of $100 a week. A wise employee can leverage the value of the bonus further by investing it carefully. This is not possible when increases are spread throughout the year. Second, bonuses maximize the relationship between pay and performance. Unlike permanent salary increases, an employee must perform above average year in and year out to continue receiving bonuses. A major constraint with this, as well as any performance-based pay system, is measurement. If subjective appraisal criteria are used, the fairness of the system will be undermined, and the motivational potential of the bonus will be lost. However, this is probably a constraint only on traditional merit pay systems.

Occasionally, traditional merit pay and lump-sum plans are combined. For example, reasoning that excellence is the standard, not the exception, a broadcast firm set its pay policy line at 105 percent of the external market. Pay grade minimums were also established so entry-level trainees with no experience could be paid less. Merit increases were awarded until the employee's base salary reached the pay grade midpoint. Then annual salary increases were replaced with an annual performance bonus for all excellent or above average employees. Depending on the employee's base salary, these bonuses ranged from $1,000 to $5,000.

INCENTIVE PAY PLANS

While individual incentive programs are the oldest, organizational incentive plans such as Improshare are among the newest forms of performance-based pay. Incentive plans can best be classified according to the level at which they are applied: individual or group.

Individual-Level Incentive Plans

Individual incentives remain the most popular form of incentive plan. In this type of plan, each person's output is measured, and subsequent rewards are based on their *individual* output. The utilization of incentive plans varies with the type of job. Although very few office workers work under incentive plans, the textile, clothing, cigar, and steel industries rely extensively on individual incentive systems.

While a variety of individual incentive plans exist, they differ in terms of the method of rate determination. When the work cycle is short, units of production generally serve as the method of rate determination. For longer-cycle jobs, the standard is typically based on the time required to complete a unit. Individual incentive systems also vary with regard to the constancy with which pay is a function of production level. One option is to pay a consistent amount at *all* production levels (e.g., twenty-five cents per carton). Alternatively, pay may vary as a function of production level. For example, employees may be paid twenty-five cents a carton up to 1,000 units a day. When this threshold is passed, the incentive rises to twenty-seven cents a carton.

Individual incentive plans also share a common job analysis foundation. As discussed in Chapter 3, time and motion studies are often employed to determine how wages are tied to output. The challenge is to identify a "normal" rate of production.[13]

Piecework Plan.   **Piecework** is the most common type of incentive pay plan. In this plan, employees are guaranteed a standard pay rate for each unit of output. Under the **straight piecework plan,** employees are guaranteed a standard pay rate for each unit of production. For example, if the base pay of a job is $40 per day and the employee can produce at a normal rate twenty units a day, the piece rate may be established at $2 per unit. The incentive pay rate is based on the standard output and the base wage rate. The "normal" rate is more than what the time-and-motion studies indicate but is supposed to represent 100-percent efficiency. The final rate also reflects the bargaining power of the employees, economic conditions of the organization and community, and what the competition is paying.

In a **differential piece rate plan,** there is more than one rate of pay for the same job. This plan can be operationalized in different ways. The **Taylor Dif-**

PHRM IN THE NEWS

Right From the Start

Many experts argue that, given the pressures in today's economy, compensation plans quickly lose their punch. So a lot of managers are continually tinkering—a bonus for teamwork, say, one year and for quality the next. Consultants love it—it keeps them employed. But the irony is that some of the best incentive plans haven't been touched in decades. Just ask the folks at The Lincoln Electric Co.

Lincoln Electric, in Cleveland, is a 93-year-old manufacturer of welding machines and motors—a company that might seem to be an unlikely candidate for survival, let alone success. Its biggest customers have been in such cyclical markets as oil, steel, and construction, and during the downturns, Lincoln, like other machinery-makers, has taken some licks. But, its managers argue, it has remained solvent—and keeps bouncing back—because of its approach to managing and rewarding people.

Lincoln Electric's system has been in place since 1934, and the basic idea is as straightforward as can be: the company pays individuals on the basis of what they produce. Nearly all of Lincoln's 1,800 production employees—all nonunion—receive no base salary at all. Their earnings are based on their individual output and on bonuses from the company's profits. (Lincoln's professional people, such as engineers, are on salary, although most also participate in the bonus plan.). . . And lest employees worry about working themselves right out of a job, the company has a long-standing policy of no layoffs.

For more than 50 years, the combination of pay by output, bonus, and job security has worked like a charm. Lincoln's employees produce an average of two to three times what their counterparts produce at competitive plants, including those in Japan. Hard workers who don't mind overtime have been known in a good year to gross more than $80,000, with bonus. Not everyone does that well, says Donald F. Hastings, a 35-year company veteran who is now president, but the philosophy has always been that top performers should not be constrained. "We think it's very important to give people the fruits of their efforts," Hastings says.

Overall, Lincoln is a no-frills company: there is no dental insurance, no paid holidays—not even sick days. (Employees do get paid vacations.) The main facility looks as though it's out of the 1950s, with two-tone green walls, no windows, and no air-conditioning. Still, the company has gathered an almost cultlike following. . .

The basic element is paying people for their output, known as piecework. It requires understanding—and, so far as possible, measuring—every production sequence. Lincoln itself has documented thousands of discrete funtions that go into making its line of products. Different jobs have different piecework ratings (and pay scales), based on such qualities as degree of skill and responsibility required. . .

The piecework method doesn't guarantee that everyone produces as much as is humanly pos-

ferential Plan consists of a higher rate of pay for work completed in a set time period. When production time per unit is greater than the established time, the rate of pay is lower. Merrill Lynch, one of the largest stock brokerage firms in the county, instituted a commission plan similar to Taylor's plan. Sales personnel having higher sales volume receive higher rates of commission than do sales personnel with lower volume.

Merrick's Multiple-Wage Plan operates in the same way, except three piece rates are established. Workers receive a 10-percent bonus when they reach 83 percent of standard and an additional 10-percent bonus when they achieve the standard.

The success of any piece rate system depends on more than just paying individuals for more work. Its success is dependent on how employees are treated and the level of employment security provided. These ideas are captured in the "PHRM in the News" feature on Lincoln Electric.

---

sible. Not everybody arrives at 5 a.m., for example, to get things organized for the day. But some do; the beauty of the system is that people have a choice. To maintain credibility, management resists the temptation to revise ratings every time an employee does well. In fact, the only time piecework ratings are adjusted, says Richard Sabo, assistant to the CEO, is when there's a bona fide change in technology. And even then, employees have the right to challenge the new rates.

Piecework sets the overall tone. It also reduces the need for constant supervision, Sabo says. But it's really just the beginning of the Lincoln system. For more than 50 years, everyone, except the top three managers, has taken part in Lincoln's bonus plan, with payments based on the performance of both the company and the individual. Technically, whether to pay an annual bonus is left to the discretion of the board of directors, but the fact is that Lincoln has never missed a year.

The company goes to great lengths to see that the bonuses aren't arbitrary. Every six months, each person in the company, including those on salary, is evaluated in four distinct areas: output; quality; dependability; and idea generation and cooperation. Supervisors are required to rank employees and to grade them. The average score is set at 100, with some scores as low as 60 and others as high as 140. Each score is reviewed by three or four layers of management before it's final.

How well do employees do? In a good year, a top performer can more than double earnings with the bonus. And even in bad years, the bonus often exceeds 50% of an individual's other pay. The average bonus in 1987 was $18,773, or about 70% of other earnings. Over the past decade, Lincoln has handed out checks totaling about $421 million—more than 12% of revenues. Why so much? Because, thanks to the system, there's more money to play with, Hastings says—and because the system's future depends on it. "Our goal is to make the bonus checks significant enough to make a difference to people."

Clearly, money can be a great motivator. But the managers doubt that employees would be so dedicated if it weren't for the company's long-standing commitment to maintaining employment. Anyone who's been working at Lincoln for more than two years is virtually guaranteed a job somewhere in the company. The guarantee does two things: it assures the employees that they won't be done in by their own efficiency, and it protects them in downturns. Technically, the company pledges that it will give workers at least six months' notice before laying anyone off, but the last layoff was at least 30 years ago. . .

To be sure, Lincoln's work environment is not modeled after a company picnic. During busy periods people are expected to work extra shifts and weekends, and, unlike a lot of companies of its kind, there's no seniority. People are producing all day long, and competing with their peers for bonus money. Tough as it is, it seems to work. Turnover rates are high—around 25%—during the first three months or so, as people learn that nothing is given away. But after that, most employees stay longer than 30 years. . .

SOURCE: B. G. Posner, "Right from the Start," *INC.* (Aug. 1988): 95–96. Used with permission from *INC.*, copyright 1988.

Standard Hour Plan.   The **standard hour plan** is the second most common incentive plan. It is essentially a piecework plan, except that standards are denominated in time per unit of output rather than money per unit of output. Tasks are broken down by the amount of time it takes to complete them. This can be determined by historical records, time-and-motion studies, or a combination of both. The time to perform each task then becomes a "standard."

Consider a standard time of 2 hours and a rate of pay of $12 an hour. If a worker completes six units in an eight-hour day, the worker would receive 6 X $24 or $144. This is substantially more than the standard rate of pay for eight hours of $96.

Rewarding Indirect Labor.   While individual piece rate systems work well for direct labor personnel, it is more difficult to reward personnel who support and make possible the productivity improvements of the direct laborer. The problem is that these workers often assist a number of direct laborers. They may sort, feed, and prepare raw materials or remove and inspect finished materials. One approach is to provide the same percentage of increase above normal as is earned by the *average* direct laborer.

Suggestion Systems.   **Suggestion systems** reward employees for money-saving or money-producing ideas and are used extensively. They are perhaps unique in that they attempt to increase the number of good ideas rather than direct output. Yet they are similar to other plans in that the rewards are monetary. Approximately 80 percent of the nation's five hundred largest corporations have suggestion systems.[14]

Suggestion systems are important because they can bestow substantial sums of money. Some organizations allow employees as much as 30 percent of the first year's savings. New York City–based Con Edison has a cap of $15,000 per suggestion. In 1987, more than $150,000 was awarded to 176 employees for their suggestions. Several of those employees received the maximum benefit of $15,000.

Suggestion systems generally do not have a favorable reputation, however, because individual awards are too small. Also, employees sometimes never learn the results of their ideas, and companies often save more than the individual receives. To solve this problem Con Edison publishes regular bulletins about employee suggestions. They have also reduced the turnaround time (three to six months versus a year in most companies).

Group-Level Incentive Plans

As organizations become more complex, a growing number of jobs become interdependent in terms of sequencing of actions or joint effort. In either case, the measurement of individual performance is often impossible. **Group-level incentives** offer a viable option. These plans distribute incentives on the basis of profits earned or cost savings against estimated costs.

There are several prerequisites to the effective administration of group incentives:

■ Group or organizational performance measures must exist.
■ Group members must believe they can affect performance outcomes.
■ Organizational culture must be congruent with team problem solving and participation.

When these conditions do not exist, the benefits of group incentive plans may be undermined. The operation of group incentives is also influenced by a variety of factors, the most common of which are detailed in Exhibit 9.4

Cost-Reduction Plans

While a variety of cost-reduction programs exist, the Scanlon Plan developed in the late 1930s is among the oldest. It relies on a ratio between labor costs and sales value of production as the measure for judging business performance. A newer approach, which focuses on an engineering-based productivity measurement, is called Improshare (IMproved PROductivity through SHARing). These two appraches, as well as customized plans, are discussed below.

Scanlon Plan.   The **Scanlon Plan** exemplifies a philosophy of management that emphasizes employee-employer participation *and* sharing in operations and profitability. Used in union and nonunion environments, the Scanlon plan requires good management, mutual respect, and trust on the part of management and labor. Research indicates that Scanlon plans are effective about half the time they are used and work best in small companies (500 employees or less). Productivity gains range from 0 to 65 percent, with an average gain of 20 percent.

At the heart of a Scanlon plan is the ratio between total labor costs and the sales value of production. While the ratio is affected by the factors listed in Exhibit 9.4, labor costs generally total between 35 and 45 percent of total sales. It is important to note that a small reduction in labor costs (1–2 percent) can produce a large improvement in the profitability of an organization (10–20 percent).

The size of the performance bonus is contingent on the reduction in costs below the preset level. Consider an expected monthly payroll of $1.5 million and an actual payroll of only $1.2 million. The bonus pool would be $300,000. Normally, one-fourth of the cost savings is retained in an escrow account to cover expenses when the ratio becomes too high. The remainder is shared between employees (75 percent) and the employer (25 percent).

Scanlon plans utilize **production and screening committees.** The production committees operate in each organizational department. Their objective is to develop suggestions to increase productivity, improve quality, and reduce

---

Variables That Influence the Effectiveness of Incentive Programs

1. New machinery or other technological changes
2. Changes in methods, procedures, or processes
3. Changes in the product mix
4. Availability, cost, and quality of raw materials
5. Inventory policies and backlog
6. Delivery procedures
7. Sales price of products or services
8. Financing and funding patterns
9. Labor costs including overtime, hourly rates, subcontracts

**EXHIBIT
9.4**

SOURCE: Modifed from R. Henderson, *Compensation Management: Rewarding Performance*, 4th ed. (Reston, Va.: Reston, 1985).

waste. The screening committee includes members of management and worker representatives and reviews suggestions and devises implementation plans.[15]

Improshare.   Developed in the mid-1970s by Mitchell Fein, Improshare uses easy-to-obtain past production records to establish base performance standards. Any savings arising from production of the agreed-on output in fewer than the expected number of hours are shared by the firm and the employees. As a percentage of pay, Scanlon plans average 5-percent payouts, whereas Impro-share plans provide 10 percent.

Three controls in the Improshare plan permit changes in the measurement standards. The maximum employee gainshare is 30 percent of base wages. Gains above this amount are "banked" and added to the next payout that is below 30 percent. If production continues to be high, management can buy back the gain over 160 percent. Consider an employee who earns $10 an hour and worked 2,500 hours. If the gain for the year rests at 180 percent, employees receive 50 percent of the difference between 160 percent and 180 percent, or $2,500:

$$20\% \text{ (buyback)} \times 50\% \text{ (division)} \times \$10 \text{ (hourly rate)}$$
$$\times\ 2,500 \text{ (hours worked)} = \$2,500$$

The base for future calculations would be increased by

$$1.8/1.6\ =\ 1.125$$

When new technology leads to production gains, employees reap 20 percent of the profits.[16]

Customized Plans.   Although Scanlon and Improshare programs are popular, 43 percent of all gainsharing plans are customized. The majority of these plans have been designed to increase productivity and product quality.

An example of a customized plan is the Sharing Helps Accumulate Rewards for Efficiencies (SHARE) program at St. Luke's Hospital. Begun in 1979, the plan now covers approximately 3,000 employees in all departments of the 680-bed hospital. In 1986, the plan generated $2.5 million in savings. Half of this amount ($1.25 million) was distributed in the form of bonuses to employees. Fifty percent was distributed equally to all hospital employees; the remainder was distributed to employees in the departments that achieved the cost savings.

According to Randall House, SHARE coordinator, in addition to the more obvious benefits, the program has resulted in improved attendance rates, better recruitment, and improved communication and cost awareness at all levels of the organization. Pivotal to the program are management support, positive reinforcement for creative ideas, sound performance standards, and ongoing communication. Performance standards are derived from expense data, past production statistics, and past man-hour information, which have been adjusted for inflation and product mix.[17]

Profit-Sharing Plans

Introduced first in the Gallatin glassworks factory in New Geneva, Pennsylvania, in 1794, approximately 430,000 **profit-sharing plans** now exist in American businesses. As defined by the Council of Profit Sharing, these plans include any program under which an employer pays or makes available to regular employees special current or deferred sums based on the profits of business in addition to their regular pay.[18]

Profit-sharing plans fall into three categories. **Current distribution plans** provide for between 14 and 33 percent of profits to be distributed quarterly or annually to employees. **Deferred plans** are the fastest-growing type of plan due to tax advantages. Earnings are placed in an escrow fund for distribution on retirement, termination, death, or disability. About 20 percent of firms with profit-sharing programs have **combined plans.** Here, a portion of profits is distributed immediately to employees, with the remaining amount set aside in a designated account.

Like cost-reduction plans, profit-sharing plans are designed to pay out incentives when the organization is most able to afford them. They differ in that employee involvement is not an important component of the plan. The motivational potential of deferred plans is also questionable because employees are unlikely to see the relationship between their performance and the profitability of the firm. Profit-sharing plans are easy to administer and do not require elaborate cost accounting systems to calculate incentives.[19]

Games and Awards

As competition increases, companies are turning to novel ways to motivate employees. Domino's Pizza spends a million dollars holding its "Distribution Olympics." Top employees from across the country are identified, flown to the national headquarters, and paid to spend three days playing job-related games. Winners of the games garner substantial cash prizes. Accordng to a Domino's spokesperson, the games encourage employees to hone their job skills and produce a better product. They also enhance Domino's fundamental belief that the contribution of every employee matters.[20]

Other companies are using on-the-job lotteries as a way to spark high productivity. Employees with performance above a specified threshold participate in the lottery.[21] Even better than games and awards for motivating employees are apartments and cars. As described in the "International PHRM in the News," such incentives are being offered in Russia to employees who perform well.

COMPENSATION FOR SPECIAL GROUPS

The performance-based systems described so far share an important characteristic: they are usually applied to employees who are covered by the Fair Labor Standards Act (FLSA). There are other groups, however, for which there are special compensation concerns. This section will discuss the special compensation concerns of sales personnel, executives, and foreign service personnel.

Sales Personnel

Because a large part of a salesperson's job is unsupervised, performance-based compensation programs are useful in directing sales activities. Still, only 20 percent of all sales personnel are paid by straight incentives. The remaining plans use a combination of salary and individual or group incentives.

Straight Salary.   Approximately 30 percent of all sales personnel are paid a straight salary. This is appropriate when the major function of the salesperson is providing customer service or prospecting new accounts under low success conditions. Straight salary plans are also appropriate for jobs demanding high technical expertise but little ability to close sales. Consider the job of a product engineer for a software publishing house. Duties of this job might include developing and executing sales and product training programs, participating in trade shows, promoting new products, and meeting with distributors to encourage them to push product lines. In such jobs, a high salary to attract technically competent individuals is more critical than incentives to close the sale are.

The straight salary program has several advantages. From the salesperson's viewpoint, it takes the ambiguity out of the salary process. It is also simpler to

INTERNATIONAL
PHRM IN THE NEWS

For Workers, a New Profit System

SUMY, U.S.S.R. — As a showplace of Mikhail S. Gorbachev's economic program, the Frunze machinery-manufacturing complex here is not much to look at. Five aging factory buildings and a research institute sprawl across this neatly groomed city in the eastern Ukraine.

But within this nondescript complex, Mr. Gorbachev's economic advisers say, they think they have seen the future of Communism. It goes by the suspiciously un-Marxist-sounding name of "profit."

At the Frunze plant, which makes pumps, compressors and other equipment for the chemical and oil and gas industries, the managers' success and the workers' comfortable life style ride in large part on their ability to be efficient and innovative.

"We work for profit, and it feeds us," said Aleksandr N. Dyachenko, the plant manager. Officials here say this businesslike philosophy has displaced the more cynical Soviet blue-collar aphorism, "We pretend to work, and they pretend to pay us."

Model for Other Plants

After two years as a closely watched experiment, the Frunze plant is now to become the model for industrial enterprises around the country. Soviet officials say they hope to apply the same methods to farms.

The change, under the Gorbachevian rubric of "self-financing," is one of the maneuvers in the battle to make workers more productive.

The Frunze plant has long been the economic mainstay in this pleasant city of 270,000 people, where the central park has a Disney-style children's castle and thousands of rose-bushes wait under the winter snow.

Two years ago it was one of two plants—the other was the Togliatti auto plant—to test self-financing. Under this system, the plant pays half its profits into the treasury as a tax, and keeps the rest to spend as it sees fit on bonuses, worker housing or more modern equipment.

"Three years ago, when we needed money for worker housing, we asked the ministry for it," said Vladimir P. Moskalenko, deputy plant manager. "Now the workers know we have to earn this money by producing more, to get higher profits."

Guaranteed Basic Wage

The workers have a guaranteed basic wage, but those who perform well can increase their pay by as much as 40 percent. Many earn more than 400 rubles ($610 a month) compared with an average wage in Soviet industry of 215 rubles ($330).

Those who hold up production by drunkenness or laziness are docked bonuses and ben-

administer, and if nonsales functions (e.g., paperwork, customer support) are important, salaried sales personnel are more willing to perform these functions. The drawback is that straight salaries reduce the connection between performance and pay.

Straight Commission.   In theory, a commission is simply a percentage of the sales price of the product. The exact percentage depends on the product being sold, industry practices, the organization's economic conditions, and special pricing during sales promotions. When establishing a sales commission program, the following questions need to be answered:

- What criteria will be used to measure performance?
- Are territories equivalent in sales potential?
- Will commission rates vary by product or vary depending on sales level?

---

efits by fellow workers, who are organized in self-governing brigades.

Many of the innovations in pay that have been tested at the Frunze plant are to be applied throughout Soviet industry under a new system of wages and salaries.

With its profits, the Frunze plant has put up enough high-rise housing so that a new worker can now count on a relatively spacious, subsidized apartment within three years. Elsewhere the wait can be 10 years.

"I have a good car, a good apartment, everything," said Igor V. Tereshchenko, a machinist, in an interview at his routing machine in a shop that makes pumps. "Those who work honestly live well here."

Organized into Brigades

The 20,000 workers are organized into a set of interlocking brigades. Mr. Tereshchenko, the machinist, for example, is part of a seven-member team that runs a cluster of grinding and routing machines producing rotors for gas pumps. The brigade shares responsiblity for producing the assigned number of parts each month, and getting them past the more rigourous system of quality control that has been introduced under the Gorbachev administration.

Foremen receive their bonuses based not on the number of parts produced, but on how well they orchestrate the various brigades so that all components come together at the same time in a finished product.

The plant has advantages that may make its success hard to emulate.

It was a flourishing enterprise even before the experiment, thanks in part to the fact it is the only supplier of critical oil and gas pipeline equipment. The demand for its products rose after the United States imposed an embargo on sales of equipment after Soviet forces joined the conflict in Afghanistan in 1979.

Given Imported Equipment

Although plant officials say they have not received favored treatment in the allocation of supplies, the Government has dipped into its scarce reserves of hard currency to buy West German and Italian machine tools for the plant. Mr. Moskalenko said that beginning this year, the plant could buy imported equipment only with the money it earned by selling its products abroad.

Last year, Vladimir M. Lukyanenko, a former plant manager who later became head of the Compressor Design Institute, was made Minister for Chemical and Petroleum Machinery to oversee the spread of self-financing throughout the industry. He is well placed to help cut the red tape that normally entangles plant managers when they try to get raw materials delivered on time.

Mr. Moskalenko contends that Moscow should give priority in delivering supplies to those enterprises paying with their own profits, but that it has not always done so.

SOURCE: B. Keller, "For Workers, a New Profit System," *New York Times*, 4 Mar. 1987, p. D2. Used by permission from *The New York Times*, copyright 1987.

- Will there be a cap on earnings?
- Will credit for a sale be given at the point of sale, on delivery, or on receipt of payment?
- What will be the timing of commission payments (monthly, quarterly)?

Once these questions are answered, a program can be set up. The success of commission-only plans rests directly on the salesperson. The more sales, the greater the earnings; no sales, no income.

The power of such incentives can be so high that it elicits unintended behaviors. Churning among stockbrokers is one example. As long as investment brokers are paid on straight commission, the potential exists for brokers to excessively trade accounts in an effort to generate fees without regard to the customers' financial needs and investment objectives. Commission-only plans also make it difficult to direct the efforts of salespersons toward activities (such as paperwork) that do not have an immediate influence on obtaining additional sales.

Combined Plans. Because of these concerns, more than half of all sales compensation plans combine base salary and incentives. In setting up a combined plan, the critical question is, What percentage of total compensation should be salary, and what percentage should be commission? The answer to this question depends on the availability of sales criteria (sales volume, units sold, product mix, retention of accounts, number of new accounts) and the number of nonsales duties in the job. Commonly, these plans are based on an 80/20 salary to commission mix. However, organizations wishing to push sales over customer service functions may utilize different ratios (60/40 or even 50/50).

The commission portion of the sales compensation can be established in one of two ways. The simplest uses a commission combined with a **draw.** The salesperson receives a specific salary including a draw each payday. Then the total commission due that salesperson is calculated quarterly or monthly. The amount taken as a draw is deducted, with the salesperson receiving the remainder. Alternatively, **bonuses** can be given when sales reach a specific level.[22]

Sales plans often include contests to direct sales activities to certain products or outcomes. Vacations, as well as goods such as golf clubs, are common rewards. These contests provide very visible rewards. Records of who is winning can be placed on the bulletin board and in company newsletters. By observing a peer receiving the contest reward, other sales personnel are encouraged to perform similarly. This process, called **vicarious reinforcement,** can have a potent effect on performance.

Executive Compensation

Annual Bonuses. **Annual bonuses** ranging from 20 to 45 percent of base salary are the most prevalent nonsalary compensation device used by companies to reward their executives, according to a Conference Board survey of 580 large U.S. firms. Annual bonus plans are nearly universal in energy (97 percent), manufacturing (92 percent), service firms (92 percent), and banking (81 percent) but less prevalent in public utilities. Because base salaries are considerably lower in companies with bonus plans, bonuses provide a strong incentive for executives to perform well in the short run. However, they do not work well in the following types of organizations: (1) companies with tight control of stock ownership, (2) not-for-profit institutions, and (3) firms operating in regulated industries.[23]

Stock Options.   The next most frequently used method of rewarding executives is **stock options.** Approximately 75 percent of energy, manufacturing, and insurance firms provide such plans. A stock option is an opportunity for a manager to buy organization stock at a later date but at a price established when the option is granted. The awarding of stock options is premised on the assumption that managers will work harder to increase their performance and the performance of the firm if they share in the firm's long-run profits. This focus on long-term incentives reflects a growing preference on the part of boards of directors for long-term achievement over short-run profits. Stock option plans, however, lose their motivational power during downturns in the market. Following the 1987 stock market drop, many firms redesigned their entire stock option programs to reflect the lower value of corporate stock, only to have the market rebound the next year to its former level.[24]

Following passage of the Economic Recovery Tax Act of 1981, most companies with stock option plans began to offer **incentive stock options** . When exercised, an executive pays only 20-percent capital gains on the first $100,000 of appreciated valued. While this is far less than the previous 50-percent tax rate, these programs still require a large cash investment. Consequently, some companies are experimenting with **stock appreciate rights** (SAR) which allow executives to realize the capital gains of stock options without requiring the purchase of stocks.

Expatriate Compensation

What most international compensation programs attempt to do is *keep the employee whole*. That means compensation of the U.S. expatriate (Expat) must be sufficient to ensure that the employee maintains the standard of living that she or he would have if occupying a similar position in the United States. Maintaining equity for Expat while serving in a foreign country typically translates into a three-component compensation package.

Base salary.   The base salary of a Expat should be the same as that of a comparable employee working in the United States. Using the same job evaluation plan for domestic and foreign employees assumes that job responsibilities are roughly comparable. Even when they differ, the home corporation's job evaluation system can be used to determine job worth.

Equalization Premiums.   Under the Economic Recovery Tax Act of 1981, the need to provide **tax equalization allowances** has been diluted but not eliminated. The $95,000 exclusion on foreign earned income allows many Expats to escape U.S. income tax, but they still are liable for heavy foreign taxes. Because equalization and housing premiums are considered income, major U.S. firms also provide **tax protection programs.** These programs provide for the payment of foreign taxes and the payment of U.S. taxes on monies paid as cost-of-living, housing, and overseas premiums.

Allowances are provided to compensate the expatriate for differences between U.S. housing costs and comparable foreign housing costs. Many organizations also pay for foreign language training for expatriates and their families. If public schools are inadequate, an allowance for private school education is also needed.[25]

Earlier in this chapter we indicated that COLAs were on the decline in the United States. The exception lies in the area of international compensation for several reasons. First, high-quality goods are often not readily available in foreign locations. Second, the expatriate earns income in U.S. dollars but spends money in the host country, using the currency of that country. With the devaluation of the dollar, adjustments need to be made. The underlying principle in all these adjustments is that there should be no positive or negative impact on base salaries. Otherwise, decisions on foreign assignments would be based on inequities, rather than on the nature of the assignment.

Incentives.   The final component of expatriate compensation includes a premium for accepting a foreign assignment. Despite the adjustments listed above, a foreign assignment still requires less supervision (a plus or a minus), unfamiliar customs that may restrict how the employee and his or her family members behave, a different language, and possibly sole representation of the company. Depending on the nature of these hardships, companies may provide a foreign service premium (usually 10–20 percent of base salary).

Host and Third-Country Nationals

Developing an equitable compensation package for host country nationals (HCNs) and third-country nationals (TCNs) is a very real challenge. The problem centers on determining what standard should be used to set wages. If the job performed is used for making this judgment, HCNs, TCNs, and Expats should receive the same base pay. If, however, the concept of "keeping the worker whole" is applied, pay will vary as a function of home country economics.

Traditionally, companies have favored the home country balance sheet approach. This approach has been cost effective because wages in the host country are usually lower than in the United States, and the U.S. dollar has been relatively strong. Still, if the differentials between groups are known, employees may rightly become dissatisfied. To resolve this problem, firms either adopt a pay secrecy policy or structure the Expat job as a short-term consulting position, training HCNs and TCNs to run the operation.[26]

OBSTACLES TO THE EFFECTIVENESS OF PERFORMANCE-BASED PAY SYSTEM EFFECTIVENESS

Although performance-based pay systems are capable of substantially improving productivity, many obstacles in their design and implementation may suppress their potential effectiveness. However, organizations can identify these obstacles and remove them. The following discussion of the obstacles pertains equally to both merit pay and incentive pay.

The many obstacles in the design and implementation of performance-based pay systems can be grouped into three general categories: (1) difficulties in specifying and measuring job performance, (2) problems in identifying valued rewards (pay being one of many rewards), and (3) difficulties in linking rewards to job performance.[27]

Activities prerequisite to rewarding job performance are specifying what job performance is, determining the relationships between levels of job performance and rewards, and accurately measuring job performance. These activities are often difficult because of the changing nature of work, its multidimensional nature, technological developments, lack of supervisory training, and the manager's value system.

A second set of obstacles applies to monetary and nonmonetary rewards. These obstacles highlight the importance and value of using rewards other than pay to reward desired behaviors. Rewards other than pay may have more motivational value, especially for employees whose pay increments may be largely consumed by increased taxes.[28] Managers must learn which rewards are most valued by employees and contingently administer on a timely basis those that are most reinforcing. This process is filled with potential problems.

The third set of obstacles involves the difficulties in linking rewards to job performance. The causes of these difficulties include the creation of inappropriate contingencies, the use of an inaccurate performance appraisal measure, and existing employee opposition. Employee opposition is often a major obstacle to successful implementation of performance-based pay, especially incentive plans, yet perceptions that employees may have about incentives plans are usually inaccurate (e.g., incentive plans can result in work speedups or can work you out of a job). Incentive plans appear to work best and overcome these obstacles when

- The plan is clearly communicated.
- The plan is understood, and bonuses are easy to calculate.
- The employees have a hand in establishing and administering the plan.
- The employees believe they are being treated fairly.
- The employees have an avenue of appeal if they believe they are being treated unfairly.
- The employees believe they can trust the company; therefore, they believe they have job security.
- The bonuses are awarded as soon as possible after the desired performance.

Unfortunately, meeting all these conditions is difficult for many organizations.

TRENDS IN PERFORMANCE-BASED PAY

Because Chapter 8 discussed the trends in strategic involvement, only the trends associated with assessing performance-based pay and computer technology are discussed here.

Assessing Performance-Based Pay Systems

Regardless of organizational conditions and considerations, performance-based pay systems can be assessed on the basis of three criteria: (1) the relationship between performance and pay—that is, the time between performance and the administration of the pay (the actual time and the time as perceived by employees),[29] (2) how well the plan minimizes the perceived negative consequences of good performance, and (3) whether the plan contributes to the perception that rewards other than pay (such as cooperation and recognition) also stem from good performance.[30] The more the plan minimizes the perceived negative consequences, and the more it contributes to the perception that other good rewards are also tied to performance, the more motivating it is likely to be.

Exhibit 9.5 uses three objective measures to determine the level of job performance to be rewarded: sales or units made (productivity), cost effectiveness or savings below budget, and traditional supervisor ratings. As discussed in Chapter 6, more objective measures tend to clarify what is rewarded and what is not. This may produce more keen competition with other workers, result in more social ostracism, and lead workers to perceive that good job performance may reduce the work available to them.[31]

The overall evaluation of plans suggests that when compared with individual-level incentive plans, department and organizationwide incentive plans are not as effective in relating individual performance to pay, but they do result in fewer negative side effects (the exception is with intergroup competition) and additional benefits besides pay, such as esteem, respect, and social acceptance from other employees.

Computer Technology

Much of the time spent in compensation planning is lost to pencil pushing and number crunching, not planning. Computer technology can accommodate per-

EXHIBIT 9.5   Effectiveness of Performance-Based Pay Systems

	Type of Plan	Performance Measure	Tie Pay to Performance	Minimize Negative Side Effects	Tie Other Rewards to Performance
Merit	Individual	Productivity	+2	0	0
		Cost effectiveness	+1	0	0
		Superiors' rating	+1	0	+1
	Department	Productivity	+1	0	+1
		Cost effectiveness	+1	0	+1
		Superiors' rating	+1	0	+1
	Organization wide	Productivity	+1	0	+1
		Cost effectiveness	+1	0	+1
		Profit	0	0	+1
Incentive	Individual	Productivity	+3	−2	0
		Cost effectiveness	+2	−1	0
		Superiors' rating	+2	−1	+1
	Department	Productivity	+2	0	+1
		Cost effectiveness	+2	0	+1
		Superiors' rating	+2	0	+1
	Organization wide	Productivity	+2	0	+1
		Cost effectiveness	+2	0	+1
		Profit	+1	0	+1

formance-based pay planning and administration in the following ways. First, administration may be conducted by establishing a merit pay plan grid on a computer system. The computer can be programmed to post the appropriate percentage increases. Second, budget planning is facilitated simply by manipulating the percentage values on the grid, automatically changing each individual's pay. As in total compensation, performance-based planning may be considered by department, by position, or in other meaningful ways. In addition, these values may be equally useful to top management. Because time is a cost to the organization, the ability to analyze this information with a minimal time investment represents a substantial cost efficiency.[32]

Computer technology facilitates the management and manipulation of data that can be used to formulate projections concerning salary structure proposals, compra-ratios, compensation cost/amount of revenue generated ratios, total cost of selected configurations of benefits packages, and the cost of compensation in the future under different rates of inflation. These calculations may be made on an individual employee, group, or overall organizational basis. Selected information may be further extracted to make summary reports and projections for areas other than the personnel department, such as a budget sheet for the comptroller.

Computer technology can also be applied to compensation planning by analyzing the various monetary components that make up compensation. These include, for example, base salary, performance-based salary, seniority bonus, performance bonus, profit sharing, and cost of benefits.

SUMMARY

Performance-based pay systems continue to attract the attention of many personnel and human resource managers, and line managers continue to ask whether pay can be used as a motivator with their employees. The success of many incentive plans indicates that pay can motivate job performance, although many problems can arise because of the many issues associated with the implementation of performance-based pay system.

Despite the potential motivational value of performance-based pay systems, the majority of organizations continue to choose essentially nonperformance-based plans. Some organizations believe that performance-based pay systems are not possible because of the lack of appropriate conditions or because of the cost. However, if organizations can measure performance, and if everyone thinks the system is fair and tied to the objectives of the organization, paying for performance should increase profitability.

Which performance-based pay plan to use must be determined by several factors, such as the level at which job performance can accurately be measured (individual, department, or organization) for given individuals, the extent of cooperation needed between departments, and the level of trust between management and nonmanagement. However, there may be limits on a specific organization's decision to use performance-based pay, which may include management's desire to have performance-based pay, management's commitment to take the time to design and implement one or several systems, the extent to which employees influence the output, the extent to which a good performance appraisal system exists, the existence of a union, and the degree of trust in the organization. Whether the organization is public or private influences the decision, too. Generally, only private organizations utilize incentive systems. Both types, however, can and do use merit pay systems.

A final major consideration is the extent to which employees will understand and accept the plan.

Compensation programs for some employee groups (sales personnel, executives, and overseas employees) demand special consideration. Sales staff compensation requires decisions about the ratio of salary to commission. The relationship between bonus and base salary affects the motivational potential of executive jobs. Overseas compensation entails the development of compensation programs for U.S. expatriates and for host and third-country nationals. The challenge here is balancing employee equity against external equity.

DISCUSSION QUESTIONS

1. What conditions are necessary for effective performance-based pay systems (i.e., systems that enhance the organization's strategic goals)?
2. What obstacles are there in specifying and measuring job performance?
3. How can an organization determine whether merit pay is administered accurately across all employees or across all its units and divisions?
4. Describe a performance-based pay system that you have directly experienced. Did the system work? If not, why not?
5. Under what conditions would you expect a perforamnce-based pay system to have the greatest likelihood of success?
6. Debate the following assertion: If selection and placement decisions are done effectively, individual performance should not vary by a great deal; therefore, a performance-based pay system is not needed.
7. What are the challenges in setting up an international compensation program?
8. How would a compensation program for a sales manager differ from that for sales personnel directly under her? Explain why.
9. Assume you are the manager of a small job shop that employs machinists in drilling, punch press, and grinding positions. Bottlenecks have been a concern in production. Design a compensation program to address this problem.
10. Debate the issue that performance incentives, bonuses, and games treat employees like children.

CASE STUDY

Productivity, Compensation, and Layoffs at St. Luke's Hospital[33]

St. Luke's Hospital, located in a large southern city, is a 295-bed community hospital offering a full line of health care services. These services range from maternity to hospice care and vary in complexity from simple surgery to advanced cardiac care. The hospital is supported by an associated system of health care centers. These centers include physician-staffed clinics, emergency rooms, an industrial accident clinic, and two urgent care clinics. They are designed to act as entry points to the health care system for those individuals who do not have a regular physician or access to regular health care.

While St. Luke's is part of a nationwide corporation of health care facilities, corporate control is minimal. Individual hospitals have a high degree of autonomy. The CEOs of the individual hospitals are all members of the Catholic religious order. As a result, St. Luke's traditionally has been run with an "iron hand" by the sister in charge. While innovative in the use of new technology, a conservative approach to employee relations has prevailed at St. Luke's. Attempts to unionize nursing personnel have been blocked, but there have been a number of close calls, with the last vote barely losing despite the hospital's competitive base pay structure.

The main competitors to St. Luke's include the flagship hospital of the Southwest Health Care Association, Providence Hospital, and the University Medical Center. Both are located a short distance from St. Luke's. Due to deregulation, a variety of special care facilities for ambulatory, adult and juvenile mental health, and alcoholism problems have sprung up in the community over the last four years. These have divided the market further.

This increase in competition has occurred at the same time as changes in the way providers are being paid have occured. Third-party payers, both public and private, have realized that the least cost-efficient method of health care is an extended hospital stay. Consequently, the length of stay for a patient has dropped from a national average of approximately 6 days to 4.5 days.

At St. Luke's, the *number* of patients admitted to the hospital has remained at former levels. However, the average length of stay has decreased from 5.7 days to 4.0 days in two years. Because the majority of services are provided during the first two days of a patient's stay, the cost of the patient's stay has not declined at the same rate as the revenue from that stay has. As a result, a series of low-profile layoffs in selected revenue areas, such as radiology and physical therapy, occurred in 1989. In general, these were accomplished through retirements and layoffs of temporary and part-time personnel.

Because the downturn in the length of patient stays appears permanent, St. Luke's administration faces a serious financial problem. To remain competitive it appears the hospital will need to cut 10 percent of its labor budget of 1,400 FTEs by July 1990.

Unfortunately, the reductions in staffing that have already occurred have generated morale problems throughout the hospital. As one nurse summed up the current situation, "You can't get blood out of a turnip. We can't provide quality care and be expected to handle bigger and bigger patient loads. We're tired of not being involved in decisions that affect us. Nobody knows how or why the prior cuts were made. They just were made, and now we're expected to live with them."

The problem is expected to get worse because the new cuts will affect departments that have not traditionally felt the impact of staffing problems. And there are rumors that union organizers are back on the scene. As Tom Lee, director of administrative services, sees it, beyond the 10 percent staffing cut, the hospital faces the problem of generating further increases in productivity without causing further deterioration of relationships with the staff. These increases in productivity will have to come in all departments, including those that already are at a bare minimum or will be after the 10-percent reduction. As Tom sat at his desk, he puzzled over how he was going to pull it all off.

By Robert McDonough,
Fidelity Investment

Case Questions

1. Describe the culture at St. Luke's Hospital.
2. Summarize the major problems at St. Luke's Hospital.
3. If the work force needs to be cut 10 percent, how should it be done?
4. What could Tom do to improve employee morale?
5. Is keeping out the union a worthy objective? Why or why not?
6. Would a performance-based pay system work at St. Luke's? If so, what kind?

NOTES

1. P. M. Podsakoff, C. N. Greene, and J. M. McFillen, "Obstacles to the Effective Use of Reward Systems," in *Readings in Personnel and Human Resource Management*, 3d ed., ed. R. S. Schuler, S. A. Youngblood, and V. L. Huber (St. Paul: West, 1988).

2. For a description of the one hundred best companies, see R. Levering, M. Moskowitz, and M. Katz, *The 100 Best Companies to Work for in America* (Reading, Mass.: Addison-Wesley, 1984).

3. E. E. Lawler III, "Pay for Performance: A Motivational Analysis," in *Readings in Personnel and Human Resource Management*, 2d ed., ed. R. S. Schuler and S. A. Youngblood (St. Paul: West, 1984).

4. "Compensation: Growth Bonuses," *INC.* (Feb. 1988): 100.

5. G. Milkovich and J. Newman, *Compensation* (Plano, Tex.: 2nd Edition BPI, 1987). D.Q. Mills, *The New Competitors* (New York: Wiley, 1985).

6. L. C. Cumming, "Linking Pay to Performance," *Personnel Administrator* (May 1988): 47–52; T. Rollins, "Pay for Performance: Is It Worth the Trouble?" *Personnel Administrator* (May 1988): 42–46.

7. D. B. Balkin and L. Gomez-Mejia, "Entrepreneurial Compensation," in *Readings in Personnel and Human Resource Management*, 3d ed., ed. R. S. Schuler, S. A. Youngblood, and V. L. Huber (St. Paul: West, 1988), 291–97; J. Kerr and J. W. Slocum, Jr., "Linking Reward Systems and Organizational Culture," in *Readings in Personnel and Human Resource Management*, 3d ed., ed. R. S. Schuler, S. A. Youngblood, and V. L. Huber (St. Paul: West, 1988), 297–308.

8. E. E. Lawler III, "Paying for Performance: Future Directions," in *New Perspectives on Compensation*, ed. D. B. Balkin and L. R. Gomez-Mejia (Englewood Cliffs, N. J.: Prentice-Hall, 1987); 162–69; J. L. Pearce, "Why Merit Pay Doesn't Work: Implications from Organization Theory," in *New Perspectives on Compensation*, ed. D. B. Balkin and L. R. Gomez-Mejia (Englewood Cliffs, N. J.: Prentice-Hall, 1987), 169–78.

9. D. W. Belcher and T. J. Atchison, *Compensation Administration*, 2d ed. (Englewood Cliffs, N. J.: Prentice-Hall, 1977); R. I. Henderson, *Compensation Management: Rewarding Performance*, 4th ed. (Reston, V. A.: Reston, 1985); Milkovich and Newman, *Compensation*.

10. C. R. Deitsch and D. A. Dilts, "The COLA Clause: An Employer Bargaining Weapon?" *Personnel Journal* (Mar. 1982): 220–23.

11. A. Bernstein, "How'd You Like a Big Fat Bonus—And No Raise?" *Business Week*, 3 Nov. 1986, pp. 30–31; G. S. Crystal, "Executive Compensation: Challenges in the Year Ahead," *Personnel* (Jan. 1988): 33–36; E. E. Lawler III, "Gainsharing," in *New Perspectives on Compensation*, ed. D. B. Balkin and L. R. Gomez-Mejia (Englewood Cliffs, N. J.: Prentice-Hall, 1987), 225–30; S. L. Minken, "Does Lump-Sum Pay Merit Attention?" *Personnel Journal* (June 1988): 77–83; "Number of Lump-Sum Bonuses Escalating," *Bulletin to Management*, 9 Apr. 1987, p. 113; L. Uchitelle, "Bo-

nuses Replace Wage Rises and Workers Are the Losers," *New York Times*, 26 June 1987, pp. 1, 31.

12. "Incentive Pay: Popularity Booms," *Bulletin to Management*, 18 Oct. 1984, p. 8.

13. Belcher and Atchison, *Compensation Administration*, 2d ed. Henderson, *Compensation Management*, 4th ed.; Milkovich and Newman, *Compensation*.

14. A. W. Bergerson, "Employee Suggestion Plan Still Going Strong at Kodak," *Supervisory Management* (May 1977): 32–33; V. G. Reuter, "A New Look at Suggestion Systems," *Journal of Systems Management* (Jan. 1976): 6–15; M. A. Tather, "Turning Ideas into Gold," *Management Review* (Mar. 1975): 4–10.

15. H. DePree, *Business as Unusual* (Zealand, Mich.: Herman Miller, 1986); A. J. Geare, "Productivity from Scanlon-Type Plans," *Academy of Management Review* (July 1976): 99–108; Henderson, *Compensation Management*, 4th ed.; B. E. Moore and T. L. Ross, *The Scanlon Way to Improved Productivity: A Practical Guide* (New York: Wiley, 1978); R. J. Schulhof, "Five Years with a Scanlon Plan," *Personnel Administrator* (June 1979): 55–63; L. S. Tyler and B. Fisher, "The Scanlon Concept: A Philosophy as Much as a System," *Personnel Administrator* (July 1983): 33–37.

16. "Gain-Sharing Plan Pointers," *Bulletin to Management*, 16 Apr. 1987, p. 128; J. C. Horn, "Bigger Pay for Better Work," *Psychology Today* (July 1987): 54–57; M. Magnus, "Vulcan Materials' Plant-Wide Bonuses Build Productivity," *Personnel Journal* (Sept. 1987): 103–4; C. S. Miller and M. H. Schuster, "Gainsharing Plans: A Comparative Analysis," *Organizational Dynamics* (Summer 1987): 44–67; T. L. Ross, R. A. Ross, and L. Hatcher, "Communication: The Multiple Benefits of Gainsharing," *Personnel Journal* (Oct. 1986): 14–25; R. C. Scott, "Test Your Gain Sharing Potential," *Personnel Journal* (May 1988): 82–84; B. W. Thomas and M. H. Olson, "Gain Sharing: The Design Guarantees Success," *Personnel Journal* (May 1988): 73–79.

17. "Productivity and Compensation: Houston Conference Highlights," *Bulletin to Management*, 20 Nov. 1986: p–1

18. Henderson, *Compensation Management*, 4th ed.

19. Bureau of National Affairs, "Incentive Pay Schemes Seen as a Result of Economic Employee Relation Change," *BNA Daily Report*, 9 Oct. 1984, p. 1; G. W. Florkowski, "The Organizational Impact of Profit Sharing," *Academy of Management Review* (Oct. 1987): 622–36; Milkovich and Newman, *Compensation*.

20. A. Halcrow, "A Gold Medal Boost to Morale at Domino's Pizza," *Personnel Journal* (Aug. 1987): 23–26.

21. K. M. Evans, "On-the-Job Lotteries: A Low-Cost Incentive That Sparks Higher Productivity," *Personnel* (Apr. 1988): 20–26; W. S. Humphrey, *Managing for Innovation: Leading Technical People* (Englewood Cliffs, N. J.: Prentice-Hall, 1987), 128–33; M. Magnus, "First Interstate Banks on Compensation Redesign to Beat Competition," *Personnel Journal* (Sept. 1987), 106–8.

22. C. F. Schultz, "Compensating the Sales Professional," in *New Perspectives on Compensation,* ed. D. B. Balkin and L. R. Gomez-Mejia (Englewood Cliffs, N. J.: Prentice-Hall, 1987), 250–58; J. O. Steinbrink, *Sales Force Compensation: Dartnel's 22nd Biennial Survey* (Chicago: Dartnell Corp., 1984), 47.

23. "Executive Compensation: A Look at Incentives," *Bulletin to Management,* 16 June 1988, pp. 185–86; also see J. R. Deckop, "Top Executive Compensation and the Pay-for-Performance Issue," in *New Perspectives on Compensation,* ed. D. B. Balkin and L. R. Gomez-Mejia (Englewood Cliffs, N. J.: Prentice-Hall, 1987), 285–93; G. R. Ungson, "Strategic Issues in Executive Compensation Decisions," in *New Perspectives on Compensation,* ed. D. B. Balkin and L. R. Gomez-Mejia (Englewood Cliffs, N. J.: Prentice-Hall, 1987), 294–308.

24. G. S. Crystal, "Handling Underwater Stock Option Grants," *Personnel* (Feb. 1988): 12–15; M. A. Mazer, "Benefits: Are Stock Option Plans Still Viable?" *Personnel Journal* (July 1988): 48–50.

25. Belcher and Atchison, *Compensation Administration,* 2d ed.; Milkovich and Newman, *Compensation;* A. V. Phatak, R. Chandram, and R. A. Ajayi, "International Executive Compensation," in *New Perspectives on Compensation,* ed D. B. Balkin and L. R. Gomez-Mejia (Englewood Cliffs, N. J.: Prentice-Hall, 1987), 315–27.

26. Henderson, *Compensation Management,* 4th ed.

27. These have been identified and discussed by Podsakoff, Greene, and McFillen, "Obstacles to Effective Use of Reward Systems." See also R. I. Henderson, "Designing a Reward System for Today's Employee," *Business Horizons* (July/Sept. 1982): 2–12.

28. This is particularly true for individuals in high tax brackets. When taxes are significant, individuals may prefer the same size (in dollar value equivalence) reward as an indirect benefit (e.g., the use of a car, club membership, and other possibilities listed in Chapter 10). See also K. E. Foster, "Does Executive Pay Make Sense?" *Business Horizons* (Sept./Oct. 1981): 47–58; "Pay at the Top Mirrors Inflation," *Business Week,* 11 May 1981, pp. 58–59; "Surge in Executive Job Contracts," *Dunn's Business Month* (Oct. 1981): 86–88; and D. B. Thompson, "Are CEOs Worth What They're Paid?" *Industry Week,* 4 May 1981, pp. 65–74.

29. J. G. Goodale and N. M. Mouser, "Developing and Auditing a Merit Pay System," *Personnel Journal* (May 1981): 391–97; J. D. McMillan and V. C. Williams, "The Elements of Effective Salary Administration Programs," *Personnel Journal* (Nov. 1982): 832–38; T. A. Mahoney, "Compensating for Work," in *Personnel Management,* ed. K. N. Rowland and G. R. Ferris (Boston: Allyn & Bacon, 1982), 227–62.

30. E. E. Lawler III, *Pay and Organizational Development* (Reading, Mass.: Addison-Wesley, 1981); N. B. Winstanley, "Are Merit Increases Really Effective?" *Personnel Administrator* (Apr. 1982): 37–41.

31. S. R. Collings, "Incentive Programs: Pros and Cons," *Personnel Journal* (July 1981): 571–75; R. B. Goettinger, "Compensation and Benefits," *Personnel Journal* (Nov. 1981): 840–42. For a case study illustration of merit pay assessment issues, see S. C. Freedman, "Performance-Based Pay: A Convenience Store Case Study," *Personnel Journal* (July 1985): 30–34; and J. R. Terborg and G. R. Ungson, "Group Administered Bonus Pay and Retail Store Performance: A Two-Year Study of Management Compensation," *Journal of Retailing* (Spring 1985): 63–77.

32. W. H. Wagel, "A Software Link between Performance Appraisals and Merit Increases," *Personnel* (Mar. 1988): 10–14.

33. Robert McDonough.

CHAPTER 10

Indirect Compensation

Eldercare: Employers Taking Action

The "graying" of the U.S. population is forcing more and more employers to focus on ways to assist workers who are caring for elderly relatives. The most common type of employer-provided eldercare assistance is information and referral programs that help link up employees with community services that already exist. In addition, some companies are looking into other forms of eldercare, such as contributing to the cost of respite care and providing adult day care.

When You Care Enough

At Hallmark Cards in Kansas City, Mo., employees with caregiving responsibilities may be eligible to participate in a dependent care spending account plan that is included in the company's flexible benefits package, notes Marilyn King, the firm's manager of equal opportunity programs. Hallmark employees who have responsibilities for eldercare, child care, and care for disabled dependents also have access to a resource referral and information service, called Family Care Choices, King says. Hallmark contracts with Heart of America Family Services to provide the information, she explains, and has a telephone line employees can use to ask for information. Last year about 13 percent of the calls Heart of America received from Hallmark employees concerned eldercare. . .

The eldercare assistance program, which was launched in June 1986, requires continual marketing to ensure its success, according to King. Hallmark tries to heighten the program's visibility by mentioning it in the company's daily noon news, featuring it in articles in its quarterly magazine, and explaining it in a brochure that was mailed to every employee and is available in the employee relations office.

Reaching Out to Caregivers

An awareness of the growing need for—and problems in obtaining—eldercare led South-western Bell Telephone in St. Louis, Mo., to produce a multi-media informational program for the public, according to Jim Reddout, a benefit and health services manager for the firm. The program consists of informational audio and video tapes, and a manual that is geared to professionals working with caregivers and receivers. . .

Beyond Information

In a random survey of its employees, Remington Products in Bridgeport, Conn., found that 25 percent of the respondents were providing some level of care to elderly relatives, according to Michael Duda, the firm's vice-president for personnel. With the help of the University of Bridgeport Center for the Study of Aging, the company began sponsoring support groups that meet during the lunch hour and after work, Duda says.

The company also decided it should do something to give employees with caregiving responsibilities some free time "to enhance the quality of life," Duda says. The result is a policy under which Remington will pay half the cost of respite care in order to give an employee-caregiver some time off.

As early as 1981, Champion International in Stamford, Conn., saw that the problem of caring for aging relatives affects productivity and ultimately profitability, and began offering help for these problems through its employee assistance program. Champion's EAP allows for three visits to a licensed psychiatrist or psychologist to obtain help in dealing with problems associated with caring for elderly relatives. . . In addition, Champion has a dependent care program, under which employees can use pre-tax dollars to help pay for eldercare assistance. . .

SOURCE: "Eldercare: Employers Taking Action," *Bulletin to Management*, 25 Feb. 1988, p. 64. Used by permission from *Bulletin to Management*, copyright 1988.

T he preceding "PHRM in the News" highlights a significant trend in indirect compensation: the provision of elder care as a benefit for employees. Not only is the baby boom generation large, but also its members are in positions of power in organizations. This generation also has parents who, increasingly, are in need of care. Consequently, organizations are moving to provide this benefit, as well as other "new" benefits.

As with direct compensation, many employees are vitally concerned with indirect compensation. Aside from its high value, this is a form of compensation on which employees generally do not have to pay income taxes. But as the cost of indirect benefits grows in proportion to the total payroll cost, organizations are becoming more concerned about how they do or can provide benefits, what they must do to satisfy employees, and how they can keep the cost of these benefits down.[1]

WHAT IS INDIRECT COMPENSATION?

Indirect compensation includes

- Public protection
- Private protection
- Paid leave
- Miscellaneous benefits

Although several of these categories are mandated by federal and state governments and must therefore be administered within the boundaries of laws and regulations, many others are provided voluntarily by organizations[2] and vary with the organization.

PURPOSES AND IMPORTANCE OF INDIRECT COMPENSATION

As shown in Exhibit 10.1, the costs of indirect compensation average between 36.8 and 42 percent of total compensation costs. The magnitude of the percentage typically varies across industries. Indirect compensation tends to be greater on average in the manufacturing industries than it is in the nonmanufacturing industries, and greater for blue-collar workers than it is for white-collar and service workers. Benefits are also higher in mature companies, as compared to start-up companies.

Indirect compensation costs in private-sector organizations also differ from those of the federal government. Whereas the benefits received by federal employees used to be inferior to those received by private employees, the federal benefits package is now valued at approximately 5 percent more. The most significant difference is benefits between the two sectors is in retirement benefits. Federal retirement benefits total 28.2 percent of pay (only the employer's contributions), while private retirement benefits, including social security, total only 16.7 percent.[3] Regardless of salary level or sector of the economy, however, the cost of benefits to organizations is enormous.

There are several reasons why organizations pump so much money into benefits programs. They believe that benefits help

EXHIBIT
10.1

Employee Benefits as a Percentage of Payroll by Type of Benefit

Type	Overall	Manu-facturing	Nonmanu-facturing
1. *Legally Required Payments* Social security Unemployment compensation Workers' compensation	8.9%	8.7%	9.0
2. *Retirement and Savings* *Plan Payments* Defined pension plan Defined contribution plan	6.7	7.2	6.3
3. *Life Insurance and* *Death Benefits*	.5	.5	.5
4. *Medical Benefits* Hospital, medical premiums Short-term disability Long-term disability Dental insurance	8.3	10.2	6.7
5. *Paid Rest Periods* Lunch breaks Wash-up time Travel time	3.4	3.3	3.4
6. *Payment for Time Not Worked* Vacation Holidays Sick leave Parental leave	10.2	10.2	10.1
7. *Miscellaneous Benefits* Discount on goods and services Employee meals Education expenses	1.3	1.9	.8
Total Benefits	39.3	42.0	36.8

SOURCE: *Bulletin to Management Datagraph,* 4 Feb. 1988, p. 37. Used by permission from The Bureau of National Affairs, Inc. Copyright 1988.

- Attract good employees
- Increase employee morale
- Reduce turnover
- Increase job satisfaction
- Motivate employees
- Enhance the organization's image among employees and in the business community
- Make better use of compensation dollars

Unfortunately, there is ample research to demonstrate that these purposes are not being attained, largely because of inadequate communication. Another important reason why some of the purposes of indirect compensation are not being attained is that employees may regard compensation benefits not as rewards but as conditions (rights) of employment. They may also think of indirect benefits as safeguards against insecurity, provided by the organization as a social responsibility because they are not provided by society.[4]

Even when indirect compensation is regarded as a reward, its importance relative to other aspects of the organization (e.g., opportunity for advancement, salary, geographic location, job responsibilities, and prestige on the job) may be low.

RELATIONSHIPS INFLUENCING INDIRECT COMPENSATION

Although the many relationships of total compensation that are described in Chapter 8 are applicable here, highlighting a few that apply to indirect compensation is appropriate. The relationships between indirect compensation and other PHRM activities are particularly influential.

Relationships with Other PHRM Activities

Indirect compensation has important relationships with recruitment and selection, direct compensation, and safety and health.

Recruitment and Selection. Without providing benefits comparable to those offered by others in the same industry or same area, an organization may lose qualified individuals to other employers.

But just as an organization's recruitment and selection can be adversely affected by its indirect compensation, they can also be favorably affected. Organizations such as J. P. Morgan, TRW, and IBM are attractive to job candidates partly because of their indirect compensation. Their benefits packages are not only extensive but also flexible. Thus, employees can have what they want within broad parameters, and the employers can recruit and select from the most highly qualified job applicants.

Direct Compensation. Indirect compensation can have an immediate impact on direct compensation, especially when organizations strive to hold total payroll costs constant. In this situation, as organizations find themselves offering more indirect benefits (to be able to recruit and select effectively), they are forced to restrain the pressure to increase direct compensation. This in turn makes it more difficult for direct compensation to be used to attract, retain, and motivate employees.

Safety and Health. As the rates of safety and health in organizations decline, the level of worker compensation rates often increases. This in turn increases the cost of indirect compensation to organizations. In addition, even if indirect compensation costs do not increase, larger costs in damage suits against the employer could result, effectively increasing total compensation costs. This is explored further in the discussion of workers' compensation insurance.

LEGAL CONSIDERATIONS IN INDIRECT COMPENSATION

In 1929, indirect benefits were less than 5 percent of the cost of total compensation—a dramatic contrast to the average 35–40 percent today. The depression of the 1930s gave the necessary impetus for the beginning of the legal impact on indirect benefits. It prompted the passage of the Social Security Act and the Wagner Act. The Social Security Act, passed in 1935, provided old age, disability, survivors', and health benefits and was the basis for federal and state unemployment programs. The Wagner Act, or the National Labor Relations Act of 1935 (NLRA), helped ensure the growth of indirect benefits by strengthening the union movement in the United States (see Chapter 15). Both of these acts continue to play a significant role in the administration of benefits.

After World War II, the legal environment further stimulated indirect benefits. Two court cases helped to expand benefit coverage by declaring that pension and insurance provisions were bargainable issues in union and management relations. The right to bargain over pensions was decided in *Inland Steel v. National Labor Relations Board* (1948), and the right to bargain over insurance was decided in *W. W. Cross v. National Labor Relations Board* (1949). In the 1960s the legal environment became more complex with the passage of several acts by Congress.

Equal Pay Act

The Equal Pay Act, described in Chapter 8, mandates that employees who have identical jobs be paid equally, except for differences in seniority, merit, or other conditions unrelated to sex. Included in the term *paid equally* is direct as well as indirect compensation. For example, women and men on the same job, other factors being equal, must receive the same level of direct and indirect compensation. However, actuarial data indicate that women live approximately seven years longer than men. Therefore, on the average, women will receive a greater total level of retirement benefits than men. Is this equal indirect compensation? Would it be equal if women contributed more? In *Los Angeles Department of Water v. Manhart* (1981), the Supreme Court ruled against the department's policy of having female employees contribute more to their retirement than male employees did because women on the average live longer than men. In *Spirit v. Teachers Insurance and Annuity Association and College Retirement Equities Fund* (1982), the U.S. Court of Appeals for the Second Circuit ruled that retirement annuities must be equal, regardless of sex. More recently, however, the Supreme Court ruled that pension benefits paid out to males and females must be equal *(Arizona Governing Committee v. Norris,* 1983). Additional guarantees for equal pension benefit treatment of surviving spouses, male and female, are contained in the Retirement Equity Act of 1984.

Pregnancy Discrimination Act

Recently, questions have been raised about classifying pregnancy as a voluntary condition which should *not* be covered under disability plans. Based on the Pregnancy Discrimination Act of 1978,[5] a state appeals court in Michigan ruled that a labor contract between General Motors Corp. and the United Auto Workers that provided up to 52 weeks of sickness and accident benefits but only six weeks of pregnancy benefits was illegal. The 1978 law requires that pregnancy must result in the same benefits as any other disability. The U.S. Supreme Court has also ruled that benefits must be comparable for spouses. In *Newport News Shipbuilding and Dry Dock Co. v. EEOC* (1983), the Court said that health care programs for spouses which cover all disabilities except pregnancy are illegal.

Age Discrimination in Employment Act

Although the Social Security Act allows women to retire earlier than men (at age 62 as opposed to age 65), the U.S. Supreme Court, by refusing to hear a lower court ruling, affirmed the provisions of the Age Discrimination in Employment Act (ADEA) of 1967 making it illegal to require women to retire earlier than men. On the issue of mandatory retirement, neither men nor women can now be forced to retire if they are working for a private business with at least twenty persons on the payroll. Exceptions to this include top-level executives, who can be retired at age 70. These provisions are contained in a 1986 amendment to the ADEA, which took effect on January 1, 1987. Employees may still choose to retire at 65 and receive full benefits, however. Some members of Congress now seek to increase the age at which full social security benefits can start to 68. Although this has not been done yet, Congress has attempted to reduce some of the burden on social security through a provision in the Tax Equity and Fiscal Responsibility Act of 1982. According to that act, employers of twenty or more workers must include those between the ages of 65 and 69 in their group health plans unless the employees specifically choose Medicare, funded by social security, as their primary coverage. Nonetheless, employers may still freeze pension contributions and plans for employees at age 65.[6]

ERISA and Private Employees' Pensions

Building on the foundation laid by the Revenue Act of 1942, the Employees' Retirement Income Security Act (ERISA) was enacted in 1974 to protect employees covered by private pension programs. While ERISA does not require an employer to offer a pension fund, it is designed to protect the interests of workers covered by private retirement plans. Employees are eligible for private pension fund participation after one year of service or at age 25.[7]

Vesting.   Because of problems over ownership of pension funds, ERISA also established provisions regarding **vesting,** the time when employer contributions belong to the employee. There are three basic options:

1. Full vesting after 10 years of service
2. 25-percent vesting after five years, with 5-percent additional vesting until ten years of service, and then 10-percent vesting for years 10–15
3. 50-percent vesting when the employee has worked five years and age and service equal 45. Each additional year of service increases vesting by 10 percent.[8]

Funding.   Because companies in the past have used pension funds for operating expenses, ERISA also prohibits the use of *unfunded* pension programs. This type of fund relies on the good will of the employer to pay retirement benefits out of current operating funds when needed. Money paid into a pension fund has to be earmarked for retirees, whether paid in part by the employee as in **contributory programs** or solely by the employer as in **noncontributory programs.**

In a **defined benefit plan,** the actual benefits received on retirement vary by age and length of service of the employee. One concern with such plans is **overfunding,** having more money in the account than is needed to meet future funding requirements. Overfunding increases the likelihood of takeover bids because an acquiring company can terminate the pension program, retrieve the excess funding, and then start a new pension fund. To resolve this problem, organizations are reducing their contributions to defined benefit plans or switching to **defined contribution plans.** In the latter approach, each employee has a separate account to which individual and/or organizational contributions are added. Growth of investments directly benefits the employee. Consequently, there is no fiscal advantage to take over firms.[9]

Fiduciary Responsibility. With more than $400 billion invested in private pension accounts, ERISA contains a provision called the **"prudent man" rule,** which says that the investment decisions made with pension funds must be similar to those a prudent person would make. The Pension Benefit Guaranty Corporation (PBGC) also was formed to guarantee payment of vested benefits to employees covered by terminated pension plans.

Portability Provisions. Under ERISA, employers are not required to accommodate new or transferred employees who wish to deposit funds in their retirement plan. On a voluntary basis, employers can allow employees to transfer money to individual retirement accounts. When this occurs, the pension funds are said to be **portable.**

Because ERISA only covered single employer plans, the Multiemployer Pension Plan Amendment Act of 1980 was passed to broaden the definition of defined benefit plans to include multiemployer plans. If any employer withdraws from a multiemployer plan, they, rather than the employees, face liability for doing so and must reimburse employees for money lost.[10]

Tax Acts and the Internal Revenue Service

Congress has passed several tax acts that influence the administration or level of indirect compensation programs.

Economic Recovery Tax Act of 1981. A major provision of the Economic Recovery Tax Act (ERTA) is that employees can make tax-deductible contributions of up $2,000 to an employer-sponsored pension, profit-sharing, or savings account or to an individual retirement account (IRA). ERTA also makes it possible for employers to provide company stock to employees and pay for it with tax credits or to establish a payroll-based stock ownership plan (PAYSOP), which facilitates employee stock ownership of organizations.

Because of the attractiveness of these plans to organizations, 10 million employees have gained direct ownership of stock in their own companies. By the year 2000, 25 percent or more of all U.S. workers will own part or all of their companies. Despite the potential benefits of ESOPs, critics contend that organizations benefit at the expense of employees. Some of these issues are discussed in the second "PHRM in the News."[11]

Tax Equity and Fiscal Responsibility Act of 1982. The Tax Equity and Fiscal Responsibility Act (TEFRA) sharply cut the maximum benefit and contribution limits for qualified pension plans and set limits for loans from such plans. The maximum benefit now stands at $94,023, and the maximum employer contribution is $30,000. As an outgrowth of TEFRA, some organizations have established nonqualified pension plans for high-income employees. Contributions to these plans are taxable, while contributions to qualified plans are not.

Including Labor in the Division of Capital

"If we want this private property system of ours to succeed," Senator Russell B. Long of Louisiana warned a few years ago, "we simply must insure that as many Americans as possible have an opportunity to earn an ownership stake."

Mr. Long was advocating the Employee Stock Ownership Plan, a share-the-wealth idea that has swept the nation—and a device, some now think, that has already proliferated and mutated to excess.

The idea of encouraging workers to own stock in the boss's company, as a way of expanding their stake in the economic system, was the brainchild of Louis O. Kelso, a maverick lawyer and investment banker in San Francisco. He began promoting the notion in the mid-1950's; by 1974, Congress moved to enshrine the concept in the tax code, passing the first of almost a score of measures. In the past 15 years almost 9,000 companies have enrolled nearly nine million of their workers in them.

Although each plan is custom designed, there are three basic ways an ESOP, as the plans are called, obtains stock: as a contribution from the company, by purchase from the company, or from existing stockholders, such as a company's founders. Generally, a worker is allocated a special kind of share of the company's stock equal to, say, 15 percent of pay. That is roughly triple what the typical profit-sharing plan might provide.

. . .The National Center for Employee Ownership, a Washington-based organization. . . found that companies with Employee Stock Ownership Plans have grown 5 percent faster than those without them.

Keeping Control

But employee ownership is not necessarily the same thing as employee management. Indeed, many plans are created by relatively small companies whose aging founders or other family members seek to withdraw capital for estate planning or other reasons but do not want to give up control. Though the special stock the employees receive generally gives them the right to vote on major issues, such as merger or reorganization, they don't become full-fledged holders until they leave the company—so the workers do not help select board members or otherwise help management run things. "Through the ESOP, you can sell the company and still keep it," observes Robert A. Frisch, a Los Angeles–based consultant.

Tax Rulings.   Benefits also have been influenced by tax rulings. The popular **401(k) plan** received its name from the federal tax code. Also called a **cash-or-deferred arrangement** (CODAs), this plan can be structured in several ways. For example, an organization can permit employees to save or participate in employee stock ownership plans on a tax-deductible basis. The tax laws also permit employers to convert an existing thrift plan or establish a new plan using a CODA approach. This allows employees to make contributions on a pre-tax basis. When properly structured, CODAs also can provide a high level of benefits for the top-one-third-income employees.[12]

Deficit Reduction Act of 1984.   The Deficit Reduction Act, along with several IRS rulings, makes some benefits—particularly flexible spending plans—taxable. In one form, employees are given the choice between several nontaxable benefits in return for reduced pay. In another, money is set aside initially, and if employees don't use the benefits, they receive the money. In still another, no money

Some companies with stock plans do encourage worker participation, through such devices as "juries" of one's peers. But so, in a productivity-conscious period, do many companies without them. . . .

One of the most prominent critics is Joseph R. Blasi, a professor of management at California Polytechnic University's School of Business at San Luis Obispo. He strongly supports the concept, but maintains that to be effective stock ownership needs to be combined with profit-sharing and programs to give workers a greater role in day-to-day decisions. He argues . . . that the typical allocation of shares, according to salary, aggravates a "hierarchical" system. "In a number of cases," he says, "management uses it as a tool to entrench their own power.". . .

Organized labor has customarily opposed the theory of employee stock ownership, on the ground that the plans can make workers unnatural allies of management. But in practice, unions have embraced them because of the advantages that sale of stock to employees can give ailing enterprises, in raising capital for expansion and rewarding loyal employees— who may well be the only available buyer for a minority interest.

Remarkable Revivals

Some near-moribund companies have enjoyed remarkable revival, using such plans and the tax breaks that go with them. Weirton Steel in West Virginia, 100 percent worker-owned, was created when a plan was put in place at a National Steel Corporation plant that was to have been closed; it has been profitable in all 16 quarters of its existence. It remains to be seen, however, if the workers are willing to pay for needed plant refurbishment.

Large, publicly owned companies that have installed stock-ownership plans include Ashland Oil, Colt Industries, Dennison Manufacturing and the FMC Corporation. Avis, once a public company, became 100 percent worker-owned when such a plan was used to take it private; unions at Pan American World Airways have come to hold a stake of their distressed company in return for pay concessions.

Many states have passed laws encouraging the formation of stock plans. New York, in an ambitious effort, offers loans to employee groups seeking to buy plants marked for closure. And the President's Commission on Privatization recently proposed not only that the Postal Service turn to employee stock ownership to promote efficiency, but also that the Agency for International Development export the device "as a method of transferring state-owned enterprises to the private sector in developing countries."

SOURCE: R. D. Hershey, Jr., "Including Labor in the Division of Capital," *New York Times*, 24 Apr. 1988, p. 2. Used by permission from *The New York Times*, copyright 1988.

---

is set aside, but employees are reimbursed for some expenses. This arrangement is called **zero-balance reimbursement account.**

Consolidated Omnibus Budget Reconciliation Act.   Passed in 1985, the Consolidated Omnibus Budget Reconciliation Act (COBRA) assures that terminated or laid-off employees have the option to maintain health care insurance by personally paying the premiums. The option must also be extended to employees who lose their health benefits eligibility because their work hours have been reduced to the point at which they no longer are eligible for coverage.

Tax Reform Act of 1986.   This law has two provisions that affect indirect compensation. Essentially it caps at $7,313 the amount of tax-exempt deferred contributions employees can make to a deferred pay plan. Effective in January 1989, the act also put into force provisions to reduce the disparity of benefits provided high- and low-income employees. Three tests have been developed.

Under the **75-percent average benefit test,** average benefits to nonhighly compensated employees must be at least 75 percent of the average benefits provided highly compensated employees (top 20 percent). Additionally, at least 90 percent of nonhighly compensated employees must have benefits equal to at least 50 percent of the largest benefit available to any highly compensated employee **(90/50-percent availability test).** Finally, under the **50-percent availability test,** at least 50 percent of employees for whom a plan is available must be nonhighly compensated. The new tax law also limits individual contributions to IRAs for employees eligible to participate in corporate-sponsored pension funds.[13]

PROTECTION PROGRAMS

Protection programs are designed to assist the employee and his or her family if and when the employee's income (direct compensation) is terminated and to alleviate the burden of health care expenses. Protection programs required by federal and state government are referred to as public programs, and those voluntarily offered by organizations are called private programs. Typical private and public protection programs appear in Exhibit 10.2.

EXHIBIT 10.2

Protection Programs

Hazard	Private Plans	Public Plans
Retirement	■ Defined benefit pensions ■ Defined contribution pensions ■ Money purchase and thrift plans [401(k)s and ESOPs]	■ Social security old age benefits
Death	■ Group term life insurance (including accidental death and travel insurance) ■ Payouts from profit-sharing, pension, and/or thrift plans ■ Dependent survivors' benefits	■ Social security survivors' benefits ■ Workers' compensation
Disability	■ Short-term accident and sickness insurance ■ Long-term disability insurance	■ Workers' compensation ■ Social security disability benefits ■ State disability benefits
Unemployment	■ Supplemental unemployment benefits and/or severance pay	■ Unemployment benefits
Medical/dental expenses	■ Hospital/surgical insurance ■ Other medical insurance ■ Dental insurance	■ Workers' compensation ■ Medicare

SOURCE: Adapted from J. S. Sullivan, "Indirect Compensation: The Decade Ahead," *California Management Review* 15 (Winter 1972): 65.

Public Protection Programs

Public protection programs are the outgrowth of the Social Security Act of 1935. The act initially set up systems for retirement benefits, disability, and unemployment insurance. Health insurance, particularly Medicare, was added in 1966 to provide hospital insurance to almost everyone age 65 and older.

Social Security System.   Funding of the social security system is provided by equal contributions from the employer and employee under terms of the Federal Insurance Contribution Act (FICA). Initially, employee and employer paid 1 percent of the employee's income up to $3,000. Currently, they pay tax on the first $48,000 of the employee's income at a rate of 7.65 percent, or a maximum of $3,604.80 each. Although funding of the social security system was in doubt in 1983, recent reforms have diminished this concern.

The average social security benefit for a single person is $6,444, and for a married couple it is $11,052 per year, with adjustments routinely made for increases in the consumer price index. The maximum benefits from social security are now approximately $899 a month for a person who retired in 1988. Retired people age 65 to 69 can also earn $8,800 annually without sacrificing benefits; beneficiaries under age 65 can earn $6,480.[14]

Unemployment Compensation Benefits.   To control costs, the Social Security Act dictates that unemployment compensation programs be jointly administered through the federal and state governments. Because income levels vary from state to state, unemployment compensation also varies by state. With the exception of Alabama, Alaska, and New Jersey, only employers contribute to the unemployment fund. All profit-making organizations pay a tax on the first $7,000 to $10,000 of wages paid to each employee. The contribution rate for employers, however, varies according to the number of unemployed people drawing from the fund. Consequently, during periods of high unemployment, employers make larger contributions than they do during periods of stable employment.

To be eligible for benefits, and employee must

- Have worked a specified number of weeks (set by the state);
- Be able and available to work;
- Be actively looking for work;
- Not be unemployed due to a labor dispute (except in Rhode Island and New York);
- Not have been terminated for gross misconduct; and
- Not have terminated voluntarily.

The period of time an employee may receive benefits is a function of how long the employee had worked prior to termination, but the standard maximum is 26 weeks. Extended benefits of up to 13 weeks are provided during periods of high unemployment or when jobs are lost due to foreign competition. The level of benefits ranges from 50 to 70 percent of base salary up to a maximum weekly amount that varies by state (around $225). With the passage of the Tax Reform Act of 1986, unemployment compensation became *fully taxable,* making actual benefit levels much lower.[15]

Disability and Workers' Compensation Benefits.   Disability and workers' compensation benefits are administered at the state level and are fully financed by employers to assist workers who cannot work because of occupational injury or ailment. Workers' compensation benefits are provided for temporary and permanent disability, disfigurement, medical expenses, and medical rehabilitation; survival benefits are provided following fatal injuries. Specific terms and conditions vary by state.

Workers' compensation benefits are provided regardless of fault in an accident. Awards can consist of lump-sum monetary benefits (e.g., $10,000 for loss of an eye), the payment of medical benefits, or long-term payments tied to the worker's income level. Employers' contributions to the state programs are contingent on their accident rates.[16]

Because the costs of employee disabilities are so high, employers are turning to new cost-cutting rehabilitation programs to get employees back to work. For example, Sprague Electric Co. in Concord, New Hampshire, assembles a team consisting of the worker's supervisor, a rehabilitation counselor, and the firm's personnel and human resource manager. Using videotaped demonstrations of the employee's job and physician input, the team identifies components of the jobs the worker can still perform, as well as appropriate accommodations that need to be made.[17]

Medicare.   When Medicare became operational in 1966, benefits managers felt this program would be a cure-all, satisfying the health care needs of older Americans. Managers anticipated significant cost savings by coordinating private medical programs with Medicare. Unfortunately, this has not proved to be true. In the era of early retirements to reduce staffing levels, organizations have discovered that the assurance of continuing health coverage is a critical factor in an individual's decision to elect retirement. Because 80 percent of retirements occur before the age of 65 (the age for Medicare eligibility), there is a gap in health care coverage that must be subsumed by organizations. Medicare has progressively shifted cost responsibility to subscribers, and as a result, retirees over age 65 are demanding supplemental health benefits from their former employers.

With employers' liabilities for postretirement health benefits estimated in the trillions of dollars and expected to increase, the Financial Accounting Standards Board (FASB) is expected to specify in the next year or two that these liabilities must be included in corporate financial statements. Court challenges have also increased. At present, the issue of an employer's right to terminate or reduce benefits for those already retired is unresolved. Until a definitive decision is made, organizations are responding by avoiding promises of specific levels of benefits for future retirees.[18]

Private Protection Programs

Private protection programs are those programs offered by organizations but not required by law. They include benefits for health care, income after retirement, insurance against loss of life or limb, and occasionally supplemental unemployment benefits and guaranteed pay and work programs.

Retirement Benefits.   Half of the American work force is covered by **private pension programs.** While ERISA provides for several vesting options, in 80 percent of the plans, employees are vested after 10 years and must be 65 years old to collect full benefits. Most private pensions are noncontributory and consequently are completely funded by the employer. However, public employees contribute on average 7 percent of their wages to their retirement fund so pension benefits tend to be one-third greater for them than for private employees.

As noted earlier, the passage of ERISA and several tax acts has stimulated redesign in pension plans. Today's typical retirement benefit plans are "multisystem" plans which include worker-contribution-intensive plans, such as 401(k) and thrift plans; company stock plans, which increase the employer's capital, reduce costs, and guard against takeovers; and PAYSOPs, which provide tax credits to employers.

From 1982 to 1987, the number of employers sponsoring 401(k) plans increased 40 percent. More than three-fourths of employers also provide matching contributions. However, interest in these accounts may decline due to the Tax Reform Act of 1986, which restricts the amount of annual contributions, penalizes early withdrawals and sets deduction levels for high-income individuals. Conversely, the popularity of defined benefit plans has declined over the same period.[19]

Early retirement has also become a popular solution to job plateauing and staffing reduction demands. The service requirement for early retirement is usually 10 years, and the most prevalent minimum age is 55. On first blush, such a program appears cost effective. However, companies such as Polaroid and Kodak have discovered that it can remove talented employees. Consequently, early retirement programs msut be coupled with progressive employee development and planning programs.[20]

Insurance Benefits.   Because the cost is far below what employees would pay on their own, **life, health,** and **disability insurance** represents important benefits. Research indicates, however, that most employees *underestimate* the cost to the organization of these benefits.

Basic term life insurance represents the core of employer-provided insurance benefits. Because it is intended purely for protection and does not accumulate in value, it is relatively inexpensive. For managerial employees and about 40 percent of all other employees, benefits are equal to about two years' income.

Firms also provide **supplemental life insurance,** which is available to employees through group enrollment on a contributory basis. Because an employed group is rated as a better risk, premiums for this coverage are less than individual rates are. However, rates are not as low as those for basic term life insurance because it is assumed that a disproportionately large number of high-risk employees will opt for maximum coverage.

A final component of group survivor benefits is **accidental death insurance,** which is normally fully paid by the employer. These plans tend to have double indemnity clauses. However, some compensation managers question the logic and cost of this clause. They contend that there is a low probability of accidental death and that a person's need for life insurance seldom doubles if he or she dies in an accident. Because most firms offer insurance with the double indemnity, it is unlikely that they will eliminate such coverage completely, and the trend seems to be toward increasing this coverage.

As a result of rising health care costs, a different philosophy permeates private **health insurance programs.** While employers continue to provide some coverage, only half of all employers now provide full coverage. Instead, employers are shifting costs to employees through increased deductibles, contributions, and coinsurance payments. Organizations also are exploring different health care delivery options. For example, employees can choose among (1) a health maintenance organization, (2) preferred providers, and (3) a regular private medical plan, provided they pay a large cost for services. More than half of all employers now have hospital utilization programs which review the necessity and appropriateness of hospitalization prior to admission and/or during a stay.[21]

Trends in insurance benefits include **business travel accident insurance** which addresses the cause of death without considering survivor needs. Such insurance can protect an organization against public outcry should employees be killed while on company business. Such plans may limit coverage to travel to and from assigned destinations. Other insurance benefits include **group survivor income benefits insurance** and **group disability income insurance.** The former provides a regular income to the surviving spouse and dependents on death, and the latter guarantees income on employee disability.

Supplemental Unemployment Benefits.   A small number of organizations offer employees protection against loss of income and loss of work before retirement. These benefits are often negotiated by unions and are found most frequently in the automotive, steel, rubber, glass, ceramic, and women's garment industries. When these benefits are combined with unemployment compensation benefits, laid-off employees can receive as much as 95 percent of their average income. The size of these benefits makes it easier for senior employees to accept layoffs.

PAID LEAVE

Paid leave is not as complex to administer as benefits from protection programs, but it is the more costly, accounting for more than 10 percent of the total payroll. If absenteeism policies are not designed correctly, costs may escalate even further. The two major categories are time not worked *off* the job (holidays, vacations, sick days) and time not worked *on* the job (rest periods, wash-up, times, lunches).

Off the Job

The most common paid off-the-job components are vacations, sick leave, holidays, and personal days. The challenge in administering these benefits is to contain the costs of these programs while seeking better ways to package them.

Vacations.   Vacations are granted because employees need time to recuperate away from the physical and mental demands of work. It is also believed that vacation time is an appropriate reward for service and commitment to the organization. Recently, a small number of firms have granted sabbaticals to employees (similar to those in academia) which after a stated period of service can be used for self-improvement, community work, or teaching. Tandem Computers, which has been granting six-week sabbaticals plus normal vacation time at full pay, claims that in the short term such programs have a negative impact on productivity, but in the long term they enhance productivity.

Length of vacations tends to vary by industry, locale, company size, and profession. Some firms believe that longer vacations for more senior employees help to counterbalance salary compression problems. However, there are no hardcore data to suggest that employees view this as a fair exchange.

In setting up vacation programs, several issues need to be addressed: (1) Will vacation pay be based on scheduled hours or on hours actually worked? (2) Under what circumstances can an employee be paid in lieu of a vacation? (3) Can vacations be deferred, or will they be lost if not taken? (4) What pay rate applies if an employee works during a vacation? The trend is toward vacation banking, with employees able to roll over a specified period of unused vacation days into a savings investment plan.[22]

Holidays.   Employees in the United States average about ten paid holidays a year. However, the actual days vary by industry and locale. For example, in some southern states Jefferson Davis's and Robert E. Lee's birthdays are observed, in Utah there is Mormon Pioneer Day, and in Alaska there is Seward's Day.

Trends in union contract negotiations are to include floater holidays that meet employee preferences, as well as personal holidays in recognition of the employee's birthday. Conversely, other organizations are cutting back on the number of paid holidays because they are an investment with marginal return. Companies are also moving toward established holiday pay policies such as "In order to be eligible for holiday pay, an employee must perform work on the day before and the day after the holiday." Obviously these policies are intended to deter absenteeism.

Paid Absences.   On any given day, one million American workers who are otherwise employed will *not* attend work; they will be absent. In the United States the absenteeism rate ranges from 2 to 3 percent of total payroll. However, some organizations report absenteeism in excess of 20 percent. An estimated 400 million person days are lost each year as a result of employee absenteeism. This is almost 10 times the number of person days lost to strikes over a ten-year period.[23]

In comparison with other countries, the United States is midrange. Japan and Switzerland have lower absenteeism rates; Italy, Fance, and Sweden report substantially higher rates. The problem in Italy became so severe at one point that police began arresting some of the habitual absentees, charging them with fraud. The Soviet Union has adopted policies such that an employee who misses work without a good reason loses a day of vacation.[24]

What makes absenteeism so problematic is the cost of employee replacement It has been estimated that for every 1 percent change in the national absence rates, the gross national product goes down by $20 billion. Absenteeism at General Motors has been estimated to cost $1 billion annually.[25]

While there are numerous reasons why employees do not attend work (health, family problems, transportation difficulties), there is evidence that absences are proportional to the number of paid days off offered by an organization. That is, as the number of paid days off increases, the number of days of actual absence increases proportionally. As pay rates rise, absenteeism also increases, with employees potentially "buying" time off. Consequently, because of lax policies, many organizations unwittingly not only tolerate or accept absenteeism but actually reward it. Their policies make it easier to be absent than to come to work.[26]

Negative strategies to control absenteeism include disciplinary procedures against employees who are absent weekly, once every two weeks, without a physician's excuse, before or after a holiday, after payday, without calling in, or for personal business. Absences for these reasons are subject to employee discipline ranging from oral warnings for first offenses to discharge. Unfortunately, these policies appear to be generally ineffective in controlling absenteeism among habitual offenders.

Programs that reward attendance—cash prizes, bonuses, conversion of a proportion of unused absence days to vacation days—appear more promising. To prevent unscheduled absenteeism, organizations have also moved to personal days. The logic here is that employees must notify officials in advance that they will be absent. As discussed earlier, self-management programs for habitual offenders also offer some hope for controlling excessive absenteeism.

On the Job

Pay for time not worked on the job includes rest periods, the lunch period, wash-up time, and clothes-change and get-ready times. Together these are the fifth most expensive indirect compensation benefit.

Another benefit that is growing in popularity is paid time for physical fitness. This is clearly pay for time not worked, but organizations often offer it because of its on-the-job benefit—healthy workers.

MISCELLANEOUS BENEFITS

This third major category of indirect compensation is the most dynamic and thus the one most likely to change in upcoming years. New types of benefits include (1) elder care, (2) day care or child care, (3) wellness programs, and (4) employee services and perquisites.

Elder Care

The U.S. population 80 years old and older is expected to go from 5 million in 1980 to 23 million by the year 2040. It is estimated that nearly 12 percent of women who care for aging parents are forced to quit their jobs to do so—an added reason for companies facing labor shortages to worry about elder care.

Consider the program established by The Travelers Company in Hartford, Connecticut. To help employees manage the cost of providing care for dependents, Travelers has established a flexible spending account, which allows employees to deduct up to $5,000 per year in pretax dollars from their paycheck. The money is then used for health care or dependent care for children or elderly dependents. "Flextime also makes it easier for caregivers to schedule doctor appointments and run errands," Jim Davis, vice president for PHRM, states.[27]

Day Care/Child Care

More than 55 percent of all women work; 80 percent of these working women are of childbearing age, and 90 percent will become pregnant during their working lives. Recognizing that child care is a responsibility that is shared, more and more employers are providing child care assistance to their employees. In fact, a survey of 10,345 establishments employing 10 or more workers showed that 63 percent of the employers offer some benefits, schedule help, or services relating to child care. To meet child care obligations, organizations are also turning to part-time work schedules (35 percent), job sharing (16 percent), and work at home plans (8 percent).

Although child care benefits are expensive, they tend to attract a bigger pool of potential employees. Campbell Soup Company subsidizes 50 percent of child care fees at its on-site day care center. According to Gordon McGovern, Campbell president, "The center is enormously successful. We started hiring people we couldn't hire before because they were able to bring their children to the center.[28]

Wellness Programs

With increased awareness of the relationship between job stress and coronary heart disease and other physical and mental disabilities, organizations have become concerned with improving employee health. Research indicates that when people are in good health, they can deal with stress better and have fewer side effects. While the verdict is still out regarding the effectiveness of wellness programs, organizations are encouraging their employees to be physically fit and engage in exercise. Many provide on-site athletic facilities.[29]

To complement the physical exercise, companies are also establishing formal policies on smoking. In a recent study, half of all employers limit smoking in the work place through designated smoking and nonsmoking areas. One in five firms does not permit smoking at all.[30] Still other firms are paying employees who quit smoking. Some companies are also offering assistance to employees who are children of alcoholic parents.[31] Other types of counseling and assistance programs, discussed in Chapter 7, also serve to improve employee performance.

Employee Services and Perquisites

According to a recent survey, the growth in executive perquisites (perks) has continued in recent years. The most common perk is a company car (provided by 69 percent of all firms to some employees), special parking (54 percent), country club memberships (42 percent), and nonqualified deferred compensation programs (34 percent).

In an attempt to equalize benefits, companies now are extending benefits to rank-and-file employees. Common benefits include employee discounts, employer-sponsored scholarships for employees and their children, low cost loans, and company-leased vehicles.

While many of these services have been provided for years, a few benefits have been added recently. One in particular is housing subsidies. In response to the lack of affordable housing, companies such as Colgate-Palmolive are providing inclusive programs including mortgage assistance plans for all salaried workers. Colgate pays the full loan origination fee on loans up to $168,700 and any fee over 1 percent for larger loans. In high-cost real estate markets, this can save a buyer as much as $4,000.[32] Union Pacific Railroad and many other firms have provisions to buy employee homes that don't sell prior to transfer. These homes are then marketed to current employees at bargain rates.

Golden Parachutes.   A recent development in executive perks is the **golden parachute**. This arrangement generally provides financial protection for top corporate executives in the event of a change in control of the company. This protection is either in the form of guaranteed employment or severance pay on termination or resignation. The need for golden parachutes came about with the flurry of mergers and acquisitions in the early 1980s. Because mergers or acquisitions can financially help some companies and shareholders, the parachutes were devised to soften top-management resistance to takeover attempts. Thus, top managers who might be replaced as the result of a takeover would still be financially well off.

Golden Handcuffs. In contrast to the golden parachute that eases an executive's departure from an organization are the **golden handcuffs**. These handcuffs make it too costly for an executive to leave an organization. They include many types of compensation, but stock options and retirement packages are the major inducements. By leaving, the executive forfeits these financially attractive benefits. Wise use of golden handcuffs can help keep valued employees.[33]

ADMINISTRATIVE ISSUES IN INDIRECT COMPENSATION

Although organizations tend to view indirect compensation as a reward, recipients do not always see it that way. This causes organizations to become concerned with their package of indirect compensation benefits and how they are administered.

Determining the Benefits Package

The benefits package should be selected on the basis of what's good for the employee as well as for the employer. Knowing employee preferences can often help determine what benefits should be offered. For example, employees in one company indicated a strong preference for dental insurance over life insurance, even though dental insurance was only one-fourth the cost to the company. As workers get older, the desire for higher pension benefits steadily increases. This is also the case for employees with rising incomes. Employees with children prefer greater hospitalization benefits than do those without.[34]

Providing Benefit Flexibility

When employees can design their own benefits packages, both they and the company benefit. At least that's the experience at companies such as Ex-Cello, TRW, the Educational Testing Service (ETS), and Morgan Stanley.[35] At ETS, the company provides a core package of benefits to all employees, covering basic needs such as personal medical care, dental care, disability, vacation, and retirement. In addition, each individual can choose, cafeteria-style, from optional benefits or can increase those in the core package. Employees are allowed to change their packages once a year. At Morgan Stanley, about two-thirds of its eligible employees elected their own benefit package over the standard no-choice plan. The options themselves were developed by the employees, working in small discussion groups. That providing benefit flexibility is so effective is not surprising. What is surprising is that so few organizations provide such flexibility.

A recent benefits survey showed that workers want to choose how to pay for their benefits and would modify their benefits if given the opportunity. Among the most preferred benefits are preventive medical care, wellness programs, vision care, and deferred compensation plans. One-third of all employees would prefer expanded medical and dental benefits over other types of benefits.[36]

Communicating the Benefits Package

Considering that most benefits program objectives are not currently attained, assessment of communication effectiveness would probably produce unfavorable results. This may be partly due to the communication techniques used. Almost all organizations use impersonal, passive booklets and brochures to convey benefits information; only a few use more personal, active media, such as slide presentations and regular employee meetings. An especially good technique is one that communicates the total compensation components every day. This can be done through giving employees calendars. Each month of the calendar shows a company employee receiving a compensation benefit. For example, one month may feature a photo of an employee building a new home made possible through the company's incentive program and savings plan. Another month may feature the usefulness of the company's medical plan.

Through communicating the benefits package and providing employees with benefit flexibility, the positive image of indirect compensation can be increased. Hewitt Associates found that 72 percent of employees who understand their compensation program perceived it as fair, while only 36 percent of employees who did not understand the system said it was fair. Information about how to file claims and where to get services tend to bring more employees into the positive camp.[37]

TRENDS IN INDIRECT COMPENSATION

Major trends in indirect compensation focus on reducing indirect compensation costs. The trends of assessing indirect compensation plans and using computer technology to aid this assessment enable organizations to contain, if not reduce, indirect compensation costs.

Assessing Indirect Compensation

Listed at the beginning of this chapter are several purposes of indirect compensation. The impact of indirect compensation on these purposes is one way to measure the effectivenss of benefits package. An organization can also determine the dollar value of the costs of indirect compensation by measuring

- Total cost of benefits annually for all employees
- Cost per employee per year divided by the number of hours worked
- Percentage of payroll allocated to benefits divided by total payroll
- Cost per employee per hour divided by employee hours worked[38]

These costs can be compared with the corporate gains, such as reduced turnover, absenteeism, and enhanced company image. After the company has determined these cost/benefit ratios, it can also examine the internal cost to the company of all benefits and services by payroll classification, by division, by profit center, or for each benefit. This information helps monitor benefit costs and helps ensure some degree of uniformity in the costs across levels and divisions in the organization. Company average costs for the package as a whole and for each benefit per employee can also be compared to industry averages. Finally, the organization can examine how satisfied employees are with the organization's current program.[39]

The methods above focus on assessing the current benefits provided by an organization. It is also useful to explore the costs and benefits of alternative indirect compensation possibilities. Costs in this case involve those associated with the benefits themselves, as well as the administrative costs. The fact that employees usually choose the benefits they will use the most becomes important when considering flexible benefits programs.

Computer Technology and HRIS in Indirect Compensation

Computer technology can be applied to indirect compensation planning to analyze its various components. These include such items as health and medical benefits, vacation time, sick time, pensions, and profit sharing. The key here is planning. Given budgeted values for salary and bonuses, projections of spending and allocation may be determined with regard to budget restrictions. In addition, including information about actual benefit usage may reveal that a significant amount of money is being spent on one that is not widely used. Thus, personnel may maximize the value of limited funds by offering employees only the most relevant benefits.

With an HRIS and computer technology, an organization can more easily implement and administer a flexible or cafeteria-style benefit package. The computer can quickly cost out different benefit combinations that employees may select. As a consequence, equity can be more easily attained across employees. The costs of indirect compensation can be more strictly controlled and even reduced with compensation information in an HRIS.[40]

Strategic Involvement of Indirect Compensation

A trend in indirect compensation is to use it to gain competitive advantage for the organization. This ranges from using pension funds to fend off corporate takeovers to taking steps to engage in strategic planning for compensation.[41] According to Timothy L. Williams, director of human resource planning at Owens-Illinois in Toledo, Ohio, organizations can take several steps in strategic compensation planning.

First, employers should conduct an external survey to determine if their compensation programs are at a level that will attract and retain talented labor. Exit interviews with employees who have resigned are beneficial to determine if compensation or benefits affected their decisions to leave. It is important also to understand the financial advantages of different methods of financing benefits. Examining these issues will help an organization use its benefits packages strategically.

INTERNATIONAL COMPARISONS IN APPRAISING AND COMPENSATING

Japan and China's compensation and appraisal practices, which emphasize seniority, company loyalty, and dependability, contrast sharply with those in the

United States. In Australia, a powerful labor union movement and a centralized arbitration system have also produced compensation systems that differ from those in the United States. In Eastern European planned economies, wages are determined nationally.

The Netherlands

Job evaluation has been used in the Netherlands since the 1950s when the government introduced a national job evaluation plan as part of its postwar reconstruction of the economy. The orginal plan set the weights of compensable factors equal in all industries. If jobs were found to be of similar point value, they received identical wages, regardless of their contribution to the national economy.

Currently more than 80 percent of manual jobs and more than 40 percent of nonmanual jobs are evaluated using point ratings. However, there are more than 40 different point evaluation systems in use, which differ in factors, weights, and degrees.

The United Kingdom

Job evaluation has been widely used in the United Kingdom for many years. In fact, some novel approaches to job evaluation—time span of discretion and decision banding—were invented there. The Equal Pay Act of 1970, which put the burden on companies to prove that wage differentials were *not* due to gender, stimulated the growth of job evaluation. By 1980, more than 80 percent of British firms were using job evaluation to obtain a fair pay structure, establish a job hierarchy, and meet the obligations of the Equal Pay Act.

Planned Economy Countries

Job evaluation is an essential part of national wage policies or "tariff systems" in Eastern European planned economy countries. The tariff systems lay down the basic framework for job evaluation and classification, as well as set uniform wage rates for comparable work in different sectors of the economy. Grading of jobs is industry based but part of a national system designed to avoid unfair disparities in wages across industries. Within the limits provided by the national government, each branch of activity has some flexibility in setting wages through collective bargaining or administrative decisions.

While the choice of compensable factors varies by country, most rely on the universal factors of complexity, working conditions, and effort. Particular emphasis is given to the number, variety, and difficulty of work operations necessary to obtain an end product. From this analysis, judgments are made regarding the necessary worker skills required to complete the work process. For example, in the USSR, complexity of work and responsibility anchor the job-evaluated tariff system. Recently, the degree of mechanization has been added. The system is similar in Poland. In addition to complexity and responsibility, effort also is assessed. In Czechoslovakia, there are five primary compensable factors—theoretical training, practical training, responsibility, effort, and special requirements (managerial ability)—and occasionally risk of injury, complexity of organization of work, and employment relationships.[42]

Canada

In Canada, the sharpest contrasts with the United States concerning appraisal and compensation are found in indirect compensation, particularly pensions. Yet even these differences appear relatively minimal. For example, Canada has the Canada Pension Plan (CPP) and the Quebec Pension Plan in the province of Quebec, both of which are similar to the U.S. social security system. CPP is a mandatory plan for all employees except federal workers. Like the social security system, CPP pays retirement benefits, disability pensions, benefits for children of disabled contributors, orphans' benefits, and pension benefits to survivors' spouses. Canada also has private pension plans, although fewer than 40 percent of all employees are covered by these plans. The administration of these plans is governed by the Pension Benefits Act, which is less extensive in its regulation of private pension plans than is the U.S. Employees' Retirement Income Security Act.

Australia

In Australia, appraisal and compensation occur in the context of a powerful labor union movement which covers almost half of the work force and a long-established, centralized conciliation and arbitration system which plays a central role in national wage determination. These two factors together make appraisal and compensation practices in Australia very different from those in the United States.

The key institution in the Australian industrial relations system is the Australian Conciliation and Arbitration Commission (ACAC) which has its statutory basis in the Conciliation and Arbitration Act of 1904. In addition to settling industrial disputes, the ACAC has over time become the mechanism by which national wage policy is implemented.[43] ACAC and its permanent staff are legally independent of the government of the day but clearly must seriously consider the government's views. In April 1983 the Labor federal government signed an accord with the labor unions whereby the government supported the unions' request to the ACAC for quarterly national wage increases to match changes in the consumer price index in return for broad compliance with the government's macroeconomic strategy to reduce inflation and unemployment.[44]

In early 1987 the indexed wages system was replaced by a more flexible, two-tiered system of wage determination. The first tier of the new system provides for a maximum level of wage increases for all employees over a period, consistent with economic and social factors. The second tier of the system allows for enterprise-level bargaining between unions and employers through which wage increases can be negotiated in exchange for increased efficiency arrangements (e.g., agreements to introduce new technology, more flexible work practices, a reduction of demarcation disputes between unions, and changes in training/skill formation systems). These second-tier agreements must be ratified by the ACAC. For many companies and unions, this has been their first experience with enterprise-level bargaining without the facilitation of the ACAC.

Even with the introduction of a more flexible wage determination system, labor unions in Australia have tended to oppose individual performance appraisal.[45] The reality for most employers is that they must pay all workers performing a similar job the award rate determined by the ACAC, plus any over-award benefits that may have been negotiated between the employer and the unions. A traditional U.S.–style, individually oriented appraisal and compensation system only appears with managerial-level employees who are not covered by an industry award.

Japan

The Japanese are fond of saying there are three sacred treasures of the Imperial House. The first of these is lifetime employment. The second, which stems from lifetime employment, is the traditional seniority system, which determines not only wages but also the timing of promotions. Under this system, an employee rarely works under someone with less seniority in service length, assuming both have similar educational backgrounds. This system has its roots in the traditional *Oyabun-Kobun*, or parent-child relationship, which attaches great respect to the older or senior member of the family (company). The third treasure of the Imperial House is the enterprise (or company) union.

During the past several years much consideration has been given to the argument that if wages are paid on the basis of seniority only, then those who have more ability may not always work hard. Accordingly, the predominant method for determining wage increases is now one that incorporates both seniority and merit. The annual incremental rate for wage increases, which differs by enterprise, is generally about 2–4 percent. The amount of the increment is determined by a merit rating, seniority, job responsibility, and work requirements.

Initially, individual companies pay almost the same starting salary for new employees hired on graduation from either high school or college. After that, an employee's annual earnings increase according to the merit rating system. In addition, earnings will increase annually, even if an employee's job responsibilities remain unchanged, until the age of mandatory retirement, now commonly sixty years of age.

Japanese basic hourly wages are among the highest in the world. Starting about 1955, Japanese trade unions initiated a concerted, industrywide campaign known as the "spring offensive," during which many of the trade unions took simultaneous, instead of independent, actions in demanding wage hikes. Today, approximately 80 percent of the organized workers negotiate wage hikes in the spring. As a result, wage decisions in the major industries, such as steel, influence the outcomes of other industries. This has resulted in relatively standardized wage increase rates throughout Japanese industry.

A distinguishing feature of the Japanese wage system is the provision for a semiannual bonus or wage allowance, which is separate from the annual incremental rate. Usually paid without exception, even in times of recession, the bonus amount is closely related to both the general economy and the profitablity of the company. Generally, the equivalent of five to six months' salary is paid in bonuses at midsummer and at the end of the year.

In addition to basic salary, Japanese workers customarily receive compensation in the form of housing or a housing allowance, daily living support (including transportation, meals, and workers' uniforms), cultural and recreational benefits, and medical and health care.[46]

China

During Mao's tenure in China, the evaluation of individual performance and the use of performance-based pay systems were denounced as capitalistic and incompatible with communist ideology. Instead, job security was absolute, and compensation administration was egalitarian. To be eligible for a wage increase, a worker's political standing, attitude toward labor, experience, and achievements had to be appraised democratically by colleagues. Under strict guidelines, raises were allocated in such a manner as to be equivalent. By the time of the economic reforms in the 1980s, the lowest-paid workers earned approximately 35 yuan a month, and the highest-paid official, including the premier, earned only 450 yuan, a differential of only 12 times, which is far less than the differential in the United States.[47]

With the economic revolution, it was decided that an enterprise's performance should be directly linked to the amount of profits generated. This was particularly true in the free economic zones where capitalistic principles were encouraged. The mandated philosophy became "from each according to his ability, to each according to his work" and "more pay for more work, less pay for less work."

There is limited evidence that the Chinese have made this philosophical shift. In one recent study, the Chinese relied primarily on supervisory assessments or performance to allocate pay raises. Unfortunately, peer evaluations as well as individual needs were still considered when granting raises. In another study, performance was the most important determinant of performance appraisal ratings and pay decisions. Another recent study indicates employee performance is the most important determinant of performance ratings and pay raises among the Chinese *and* Americans. Consistent with new Chinese management, lower performance results in lower performance ratings *and* lower pay. However, remnants of the past Chinese regime and its values still persist. Chinese decision makers still consider dependability, loyalty to the enterprise, and job experience as important and tend to reward employees who display these behaviors. The bottom line in setting up ventures in China is to modify U.S. pay-for-performance systems, so that a portion of pay is based on loyalty and job seniority.[48]

SUMMARY

Unlike in the past, the growth in indirect compensation has been double that of direct compensation. This doubling has occurred despite the lack of evidence that indirect compensation helps to attain the purposes of total compensation. Money, job challenge, and opportunities for advancement appear to serve the purposes of compensation as much as, if not more than, pension benefits, disability provisions, and services, especially for employees aspiring to managerial careers.

This is not to say, however, that employees do not desire indirect benefits. Organizations are offering them at such a rapid rate in part because employees desire them. Unfortunately, the specific indirect benefits offered by an organization are not always valued by all employees, and all employees may not even know what benefits are offered. As a result, some organizations now solicit employee opinions about their preferences for compensation programs. Organizations are also becoming more concerned with the communication of their benefits programs. Current evidence suggests that employees' lack of awareness of the contents and value of their benefit programs may partially explain why the programs are not perceived more favorably.

These benefits do not come without costs. To ensure that an organization is getting the most from its indirect compensation, thorough assessments must be made of what the organization is doing, what other organizations are doing, and what employees prefer to see the organization doing. To improve the motivational value of indirect compensation, organizations should try to provide what employees want. As with direct compensation, employees apparently will continue to want more benefits like the ones they now have, as well as some they presently do not have. For example, employees want greater private retirement benefits, more health and insurance coverage, and more time off. Demands for dental coverage, eye care, and legal services will probably increase. Greater educational and career development opportunities are also likely to be demanded by employees.

Although the trend in many benefits is for more, the one benefit that may be the most important is job security. As the economy continues to shift and dislocate employees, and as international competition increases, job security will continue to take on even greater importance.

In providing indirect benefits, numerous federal and state laws must be taken into account and observed. Federal laws, such as the Pregnancy Discrimination Act, the Equal Pay Act, and the Multiemployer Pension Plan Act, have a significant influence on indirect compensation. Ignoring these federal laws and various state laws may result in fines and penalties, thus reducing the effectiveness of indirect compensation.

As more U.S. firms move into international markets, the need to understand international compensation and appraisal trends increases in importance. While practices in countries such as Britain and Canada are quite similar to those in the United States, the same cannot be said for Pacific Rim countries and the East European controlled economy countries. The former rely on seniority more than does the United States, and the latter have wage rates set by the government.

DISCUSSION QUESTIONS

1. How are unemployment benefits derived, and what is the status of unemployment compensation?
2. In what sense is indirect compensation "indirect"?
3. How has legislation shaped the total compensation package? How has legislation shifted the balance of direct to indirect compensation? What implications does this shift have for employee performance?
4. Distinguish between public and private protection programs, and give examples of each.
5. How have legislation and the changing nature of the work force created the tremendous social security benefit burden that most employers and workers confront when they witness the size of the FICA deduction from their paycheck?
6. How would you rationalize the benefit to the organization of providing a physical fitness facility and program for the work force? How would you assess and compare benefits and costs?

7. For each of the various forms of indirect compensation, describe what incentives the employer and the employee have for minimizing the cost of this benefit.
8. In theory, flexible benefit plans sound great. In practice, this may not be so. Describe the problems that could be encountered in administering a flexible benefit program.
9. What are the components of an effective benefits communication program?
10. What factors should be considered in establishing a compensation program in a foreign country?

CASE STUDY

You're Darned If You Do and Darned If You Don't

Sally Yuen, director of PHRM for Dough Pineapple's Maui cannery, returned to her office deep in thought. She'd just spent the last hour and half in a lengthy and somewhat heated discussion with cannery manager Danny Sackos regarding the latest turnover crisis among cannery employees. Shrugging her shoulders, Sally wondered if Sackos was right. Maybe the current turnover problem was her fault—well, the fault of her department, that is. According to Sackos, if she'd done a better job in selecting employees in the first place, Dough Pineapple (DP) would not be in the current mess. "You hired quitters," he argued, pointing to the high turnover among temporary *and* permanent full-time employees. But then Sally wondered if it really was her fault.

DP maintained a regular work force of 200 employees. Depending on the harvest, as many as 150 temporary employees were also employed. Temporary workers were paid higher base salaries than regular employees ($6.25 an hour). However, they were not eligible for any benefits, including vacation leave, day care, and sick leave. If they were sick, they had to take time off without pay. They also could not participate in DP's highly successful profit-sharing program and matching pension fund.

Full time, regular cannery workers were paid $5.00 an hour ($10,400 annually). While DP's hourly rate was below the industry average of $6.00 an hour ($12,480 annually), employees more than recouped this amount in performance bonuses. To date, they were the only cannery on the islands to have a state-of-the-art incentive pay program. In fact, they were the only cannery that shared organizational profits with employees at all.

Last year, employees received approximately $2,000 each. This amount was lower than usual due to a hurricane that destroyed almost all of one harvest. Since the program was implemented in 1986, bonuses had averaged $8,000 per employee. And this year they were expected to be back on target. Sally anticipated handing out bonuses in the range of $10,000 each. Employees had the option of taking the money in one lump sum, in quarterly installments, or in even distributions throughout the next year. According to company policy, employee bonuses would be announced at the semi-annual employee's meeting, which was to be held in six weeks.

Sally also was proud of DP's benefits. Employee benefits as a percentage of payroll averaged 30 percent in the industry. DP's percentage was 45 percent. All full-time employees with one year's seniority (tenured) were eligible to participate in DP's extensive benefit program, which included such innovations as an on-site day care center (Sally's brain child which took her two years to get approved) and an employee assistance program, including free legal assistance. The company also matched dollar for dollar employee contributions to a retirement fund and offered two college scholarships annually to employees' children. Sally was particularly proud of DP's fitness center which could be used by any "tenured" employees and their families. Swimming lessons were provided free of charge to family members.

Vacation days also were above the industry average. Employees with one to two years of seniority earned one-half day of paid vacation per month, three-fourths day per month with three to five years seniority, and one day per month with more than five years of service. Personal days accrued at the same rate for tenured employees. To prevent abuse, employees calling in absent before or after a holiday or after a payday are charged with an absence of 1.5 days. Employees with less than one year's service and temporary employees are not reimbursed for absences. The failure of any employee to call in to report an absence at least four hours before his or her shift starts is grounds for disciplinary procedures.

By having a core of permanent, tenured employees, DP is assured of having enough employees to meet average production demands. By paying temporary employees base salaries slightly above the labor market average, DP has traditionally had its pick of new employees. The system was cost effective because the salaries of temporary employees were only 18 percent over the base pay for cannery employees and well under the estimated hourly rate (with benefits) for permanent tenured employees (estimated at $7.98 an hour).

With all this going for DP, Sally wondered where things had gone wrong. Maybe Sackos was right, and she just hadn't picked the right kind of employees. Shaking her head in bewilderment, she had her assistant Mark George interview some employees to see what was going on. Additionally, he prepared a report on causes of turnover at DP (see Exhibit 1).

According to Mark, the following comments are representative of the feelings of full-time permanent employees:

■ "Sure, it's a great place to work, but I'm tired of those young kids walking in off the street and making more than I do."

■ "I know, I know, we're eligible to get bonuses, but they just can't make up for a weekly salary—at least not when you have three kids to support."

■ "I'm worry that things are going to be the same as last year. I hung in there and look what I got, a lousy $2,500. The bottom line is that I still made less than temporary employees and those at the other canneries. I don't like it one bit."

The following comments are typical of the views of permanent untenured workers (2 years seniority):

■ "I got really steamed last month when they docked my pay for being sick. I mean, I was really sick. I hadn't gone out with the girls or anything. I was down flat in bed with the flu. Why should I work hard here if I can't even get a lousy day off when I'm sick?"

■ "I've worked here seven months already, and I'm pulling my own weight around here. Know what I mean? Well, it doesn't seem right that I should be paid less than those part-timers."

Among temporary workers, the view was

■ "Yeah, we make a good rate of pay but that's not everything. My wife had to have a C-section last month. Without insurance, it cost me a bundle."

■ "I work just as hard as everyone else, so why shouldn't I have the same benefits. I'm getting up there in years. It'd be nice to have a little bit set aside."

In reading these comments, it seemed to Sally that she couldn't win for losing. Maybe the most current employee attitude survey would be of help. At least it was worth a try (see Exhibit 2). All she knew was that if they didn't come up with a strategy soon,

---

Turnover among Employees   EXHIBIT 1

Reason	Higher Pay	Better Benefits	Supervision	Moving	Better Job	Job Security	Fired
Group							
Permanent							
<1 year	40	22	1	2	3	1	2
1–2 years	10	0	3	3	2	4	1
>2 years	1	0	5	4	4	2	0
Temporary							
<6 months	10	45	4	3	10	17	3
6–12 months	12	23	1	0	2	32	2
>1 year	5	15	2	3	15	19	0

NOTE: An employee could list more than one reason for quitting.

EXHIBIT
2

Results of the Employee Attitude Survey

	Permanent			Temporary
	⟨1 year	1–2 years	⟩2 years	
Satisfaction with:				
1. Pay level	2.1	2.3	2.4	3.4
2. Pay system	1.5	2.4	3.2	3.3
3. Benefits	1.0	3.2	4.1	1.1
4. Supervision	3.4	4.1	3.7	3.3
5. Job	2.4	2.7	3.1	2.3
6. Co-workers	3.3	4.0	4.7	2.3
7. Work environment	3.4	4.1	3.6	2.7

NOTE: 1 = very dissatisfied, 5 = very satisfied.

DP would not meet its canning quotas, and the employee bonuses would be lost forever.

Case Questions

1. Do you agree with Sackos that selection procedures are flawed, causing the high turnover? Why or why not?

2. What does the employee attitude survey tell you that is helpful in understanding the turnover problem at DP?

3. What should Sally's bottom-line response be to resolve the current crisis?

NOTES

1. "Employee Benefit Costs," *Bulletin to Management Datagraph*, 4 Feb. 1988, pp. 36–37.
2. Employers, however, may still provide benefits not required by law, such as private pensions, that must still be administered within federal or state guidelines, as the ERISA does for private pensions. For extensive discussion here, see B. J. Coleman, *Primer on Employee Retirement Income Security Act* (Washington, D.C.: Bureau of National Affairs, 1985); and K. D. Gill, ed., *ERISA: The Law and the Code*, 1985 ed. (Washington, D.C.: Bureau of National Affairs, 1985).
3. Other differences between private and federal benefits include .5 percent of pay for life insurance in the private sector versus .3 percent in the federal; $1,045 health insurance value for the private sector versus $760 in the federal; 2,062 hours per year of work in the private sector versus 2,080 in the federal; and 360 hours per year of time off in the private sector versus 367 in the federal. These differences are reported in the *OPM Newsletter*, Aug./Sept. 1981.
4. T. J. Bergmann and M. A. Bergmann, "How Important Are Fringe Benefits to Employees?" *Personnel* (Dec. 1987): 59–64; R. M. McCaffery, *Employee Benefit Programs: A Total Compensation Perspective* (Boston: PWS–Kent, 1988).
5. The Pregnancy Discrimination Act (PDA) also has other provisions. For a description of them, see R. Trotter, S. R. Zacur, and W. Greenwood, "The Pregnancy Disability Amendment: What the Law Provides," pt. II, *Personnel Administrator* (Mar. 1982): 55–58. Congress enacted the PDA because the Supreme Court ruled in *General Electric Co. v. Gilbert* (1976) that pregnancy-related classifications (provisions) did not on their face constitute discrimination under Title VII. *Fair Employment Practices*, 6 Sept. 1984, pp. 1–8; *Fair Employment Report*, 22 Oct. 1984, p. 165; *Fair Employment Report*, 6 Mar. 1985, p. 37; J. S. Lublin, "Big Test Nears on Benefits for Pregnancy," *Wall Street Journal*, 3 Jan. 1983, pp. 25, 31; S. Wermiel, "Sex-Discrimination Suit May Force Big Changes in Retirement Benefits," *Wall Street Journal*, 10 Jan. 1983, p. 21.
6. G. Leshin, *EEO Law: Impact on Fringe Benefits* (Los Angeles: University of California, Institute of Industrial Relations, 1979), 45; H. Robertson, "The Social Security Fix," *Compensation Review* 3 (1983) : 63–70. "Social Security Taxes Too High, Kemp Says," *Buffalo News*, 26 Feb. 1986, p. 1.
7. B. J. Coleman, *Primer on Employee Retirement Income Security Act* (Washington, D.C.: The Bureau of National Affairs, Inc., 1985); "ERISA's Effects on Pen-

sion Plan Administration," *Bulletin to Management,* 9 Aug. 1984), pp. 1–2; K. D. Gill, ed., *ERISA: The Law and the Code,* 1985 ed. (Washington, D. C.: The Bureau of National Affairs, Inc., 1985).

8. McCaffery, *Employee Benefit Programs.*

9. "ERISA's Effects on Pension Plan Administration," 1–2; Coleman, *Primer on Employee Retirement Income Security Act;* Gill, ERISA.

10. D. S. Bowling III, "The Multiemployer Pension Plan Amendments Act of 1980," *Personnel Journal* (Jan. 1982): 18–20; J. A. LoCicero, "How to Cope with the Multiemployer Pension Plan Amendments Act of 1980," *Personnel Administrator* (May 1981): 51–54, 68; J. A. LoCicero, "Multiemployer Pension Plans: A Time Bomb for Employers?" *Personnel Journal* (Nov. 1980): 922–24, 932; P. T. Schultz and H. J. Golden, "Current Developments in Employee Benefits," *Employee Relations Law Journal* 6, no. 3 (1986): 494–97.

11. J. Case, "ESOPs: Dead or Alive?" *INC.* (June 1988): 94–100; "Congress Is Forming Battle Lines over ESOPs," *Business Week,* 8 Aug. 1988, 61–63; "A Hardheaded Takeover by McLouth's Hardhats," *Business Week,* 6 June 1988, pp. 90–92; P. Nulty, "What a Difference Owner-Bosses Make," *Fortune,* 25 Apr. 1988, pp. 97–104.

12. T. Brambley, "The 401(k) Solution to Retirement Planning," *Personnel Journal* (Dec. 1984): 66–67; E. J. Brennan, "Benefits and Liabilities of Deferred Compensation," *Personnel Journal* (June 1984): 26–28; C. Gould, "The New Math for Joining a 401(k) Plan," *New York Times,* 3 Jan. 1988, p. 9; U. Gupta, "Sifting through 401(k) Plans," *Venture* (May 1985): 34; G. E. Hagerty, "Should You Establish a Qualified Cash or Deferred Arrangement?" *Personnel Journal* (Feb. 1983): 110–14; "Pension Equity Bill Signed into Law," *Resource* (Sept. 1984): 1; "Section 401(k) Plans: Final and Proposed Rules Issued," *Bulletin to Management,* 11 Aug. 1988), pp. 249–50.

13. Employee Benefits, *Bulletin to Management,* 22 Mar. 1984, p. 8; "Integrating Human Resources and Payroll," *Bulletin to Management,* 21 July 1988, p. 232; J. N. Erlenborn, "New Standards and Nondiscrimination Rules for Benefit Plans Coordinated with ERISA Compliance," *Human Resource Management,* A.S.P.A. (Summer 1988): 1–7; "Executive Benefits Conference Highlights," *Bulletin to Management,* 9 June 1988, pp. 177–78; "Section 89 Nondiscrimination Tests: Does Your Plan Pass?" *Benefits* (Mar./Apr. 1988): 5.

14. "Changes in the Social Security Law," *Bulletin to Management Datagraph,* 14 Jan. 1988, p. 12; B. Keller, "Another Stab at Pension Reform," *New York Times,* 15 July 1984, p–1. R. C. Murphy and R. E. Wallace, "New Directions for the Social Security System," *Personnel Journal* (Feb. 1983): 138–41.

15. B. DeClark, "Cutting Unemployment Insurance Costs," *Personnel Journal* (Nov. 1983): 868–72; McCaffery, *Employee Benefit Programs;* B. S. Murphy, W. E. Barlow, and D. D. Hatch, "Unemployment Compensation and Religious Beliefs," *Personnel Journal* (June 1987): 36–43; L. Uchitelle, "Jobless Insurance System Aids

Reduced Number of Workers," *New York Times,* 26 July 1988, p. 1.

16. "Workers' Compensation: Total Disability Benefits," *Bulletin to Management Datagraph,* 19 May 1988, pp. 156–57.

17. "Injured Workers: Cost-Cutting Rehabilitation Option," *Bulletin to Management,* 15 Oct. 1987, pp. 330, 335.

18. McCaffery, *Employee Benefit Programs.*

19. "1987 Benefits Report from Hay/Huggins," *Bulletin to Management,* 2 June 1988, p. 176.

20. D. R. Godofsky, "Early Retirement Pensions: Penalty or Perk?" *Personnel Journal* (Aug. 1988): 69–79.

21. "1987 Benefits Report from Hay/Huggins," 176.

22. McCaffery, *Employee Benefit Programs.*

23. G. Latham and N. Napier, "Practical Ways to Increase Employee Attendance," in *Absenteeism: New Approaches to Understanding, Measuring and Managing Employee Absence,* ed. P. Goodman and R. Atkins (San Franciso: Jossey-Bass, 1984), 322–59; R. Steers and S. Rhodes, "Major Influences on Employee Attendance: A Process Model," *Journal of Applied Psychology* 63 (1978): 391–407.

24. D. Scott and S. Markham, "Absenteeism Control Methods: A Survey of Practices and Results," *Personnel Administrator* 27 (1982): 73–86.

25. C. R. Deitsch and D. A. Dilts, "Getting Absent Employees Back on the Job: The lose of General Motors," *Business Horizons* (Fall 1981): 52–58.

26. J. Chadwick-Jones, N. Nicholson, and C. Brown, *Social Psychology of Absenteeism* (New York: Praeger, 1982).

27. E. D. Lee, "Firms Begin Support for Workers Who Look After Elderly Relatives," *Wall Street Journal,* 6 July 1987, p. 15; Also see M. Magnus, "Eldercare: Corporate Awareness, But Little Action," *Personnel Journal* (June 1988): 19–23; "The Graying of America Spawns a New Crisis," *Business Week,* 17 Aug. 1987, pp. 60–62; W. H. Wagel, "Eldercare Assistance for Employees at The Travelers," *Personnel* (Oct. 1987): 4–6.

28. T. A. Campbell and D. E. Campbell, "71% of Employers Say They Could Be Part of the Child Care Solution," *Personnel Journal* (Apr. 1988): 84–86; "Child Care: Benefit of the Future?" *Bulletin to Management Datagraph,* 11 Aug. 1988, p. 252; "The Corporate Cradle: Employers Offer Child-Care Aid," *Bulletin to Management Datagraph,* 17 Mar. 1988, p. 84; "Employee Benefit Costs," *Bulletin to Management Datagraph,* 4 Feb. 1988, p. 36; "Employers and Child Care: The Human Resource Professional's View," *1988 Child Care Survey Report of the American Society for Personnel Administration.* (Alexandria, Virg. ASPA, 1988); "Employers Offer Aid on Child Care," *New York Times,* 17 Jan. 1988, p. 5; J. Fraze, "Parental Leave Measure Reintroduced in Senate," *Resource* (July 1988): 1, 5; T. Gohtsubo, Y. Hashimoto, J. Manogue, M. Steelman, and K. Yokoyama, "A Case Study in Corporate Child Care," unpublished manuscript, New York University, 1988; E. K. LaFleur and W. B. Newsom, "Opportunities for Child Care," *Personnel Administrator*

(June 1988): 146–54; D. J. Petersen and D. Massen-gill, "Childcare Programs Benefit Employers, Too," *Personnel* (May 1988): 58–62; S. S. Schiffer, "The Piper Must Be Paid: Can Business Afford to Neglect Family Issues?" unpublished manuscript, 1988; E. L. Toomey and J. M. Connor, "Employee Sabbaticals: Who Benefits and Why," *Personnel* (Apr. 1988): 81–84; W. H. Wagel, "Help for Working Parents at Morgan," *Personnel* (November 1987): 4–6.

29. L. Abramson, "Boost to the Bottom Line," *Personnel Adminstrator* (July 1988): 36–39; A. D. Anderson, "In the Office: See How They Run," *New York Times,* 3 Jan. 1988, p. 13; G. Kramon, "The 'Wellness' Discount Plans," *New York Times,* 22 Sept. 1987, p. D2; R. P. Sloan and J. C. Gruman, "Does Wellness in the Workplace Work?" *Personnel Administrator* (July 1988): 42–48.

30. "ASPA–BNA Survey No. 51, Smoking in the Workplace: 1987 Update," *Bulletin to Management,* 26 Nov. 1987.

31. J. E. Brody, "For Children of Alcoholics, a Life of Fear, Humiliation and Broken Promises," *New York Times,* 26 Aug. 1987, p. C4.

32. D. C. Schwartz, "Business Can Attack Housing Costs," *Fortune,* 15 Aug. 1988, pp. 85–87.

33. A. Howard, "Who Reaches for the Golden Handshake?" *Academy of Management Review* (May 1988): 133–44; "Parachute Protections: Golden and Tin Increasing," *Bulletin to Management,* 22 Oct. 1987, pp. 338, 343.

34. K. P. Shapiro and J. A. Sherman, "Employee Attitudes Benefit Plan Designs," *Personnel Journal* (July 1987): 49–53.

35. C. A. Baker, "Flex Your Benefits," *Personnel Journal* (May 1988): 54–60; J. E. Burkholder, "Cafeteria-Style Benefits: No Free Lunch," *Personnel* (Nov. 1987): 13–16; "Flexible Benefit Plans Finding Acceptance," *Bulletin to Management,* 28 Apr. 1988, p. 136; "Flexible Comp Programs: Health Care Cost-Cutting Tool," *Bulletin to Management,* 12 Mar. 1987, p. 82; "Personnel Shop Talk," *Bulletin to Management,* 14 Jan. 1988, p. 10.

36. "Employees Would Change Benefits If Possible," *Bulletin to Management,* 15 Aug. 1985, pp. 1–2. Reprinted by permission from *Bulletin to Management,* copyright 1985, by The Bureau of National Affairs, Inc., Washington, D.C.

37. "Cost, Communication, and Compliance Concerns," *Bulletin to Management,* 21 Mar. 1985, p. 7; "Pay Off," *Wall Street Journal,* 8 July 1982, p. 1; R. Foltz, "Communiqué, *Personnel Administrator* (May 1981): 8; R. M. McCaffery, "Employee Benefits: Beyond the Fringe?" *Personnel Administrator* (May 1981): 26–30, 66; T. F. Casey, "One-to-One Communication of Employee Benefits," *Personnel Journal* (Aug. 1982): 572–74; "Employee Benefits: Attitudes and Reactions," *Bulletin to Management,* 11 Apr. 1985, p. 1.

38. R. B. Dunham and R. A. Formisano, "Designing and Evaluating Employee Benefit Systems," *Personnel Administrator* (Apr. 1982): 29–36.

39. M. Lerner, "Measuring Pay Costs in Your Organization against Pay in Other Organizations," *Personnel* (Aug. 1988): 70–73.

40. P. Farish, "Interactive Pension Data," *Personnel Administrator* (July 1985): 10–12; E. M. Fowler, "Employees, Benefits and Computers," *New York Times,* 16 Feb. 1988, p. 3; R. D. Huff, "The Impact of Cafeteria Benefits on the Human Resource Information System," *Personnel Journal* (Apr. 1983): 282–83; "IRS Benefit Regulations Call for Strict Record-Keeping," *Resource* (Feb. 1985): 1, 9; J. L. Krakauer, "Slash Health Care Costs with Claims Automation," *Personnel Journal* (Apr. 1985): 88–91; H. D. Spring, "Medical Benefit Plan Costs," *Personnel Administrator* (Dec. 1984): 64–72.

41. L. Asinof, "Excess Pension Assets Lure Corporate Raiders," *Wall Street Journal,* 11 Sept. 1985, p. 6; "Business Reduces Pension Funding to Cut Costs, Fend Off Takeovers," *Wall Street Journal,* 11 Oct. 1984, p. 35; P. F. Drucker, "Taming the Corporate Takeover," *Wall Street Journal,* 30 Oct. 1984, p. 30; R. J. Greene and R. G. Roberts, "Strategic Integration of Compensation and Benefits," *Personnel Administrator* (May 1983): 79–82; "Total Compensation Strategies," *Bulletin to Management,* 4 Oct. 1984, p. 8.

42. International Labour Organisation, *Job Evaluation* (Geneva: ILO, 1987).

43. For a detailed discussion of wage determination in Australia, see S. Deery and D. Plowman, *Australian Industrial Relations,* 2d ed. (Sydney: McGraw-Hill, 1985), chapter 11.

44. F. Bairstow, "The Trend toward Centralized Bargaining—A Patchwork Quilt of International Diversity," *Columbia Journal of World Business* 20, no. 1 (1985): 75–83.

45. M. Derber, "Reflections on Aspects of the Australian and American Systems of Industrial Relations," in *Perspectives on Australian Industrial Relations,* ed. W. A. Howard (Melbourne: Longman Cheshire, 1984).

46. M. S. O'Connor, *Report on Japanese Employee Relations Practices and Their Relationship to Worker Productivity,* a report prepared for the study mission to Japan, 8–23 November 1980. Her permission to reproduce this material is appreciated. Also see ——— , *Employment and Employment Policy* (Tokyo: Japan Institute of Labor, 1988).

47. R. L. Tung, "Patterns of Motivation in Chinese Industrial Enterprises," *Academy of Management Review* 6 (1981): 481–89; M. Warner, "Managing Human Resources in China: An Empirical Study," *Organizational Studies* 7 (1983): 353–66.

48. V. L. Huber, G. Northcraft, M. Neale, and Xiande Zao, "Comparison of Appraisal and Pay Decisions of Chinese and Americans: A Management Revolution in the Making?" paper presented at the Eastern Academy of Management's International Conference, Hong Kong, June, 1989); G. Northcraft, M. A. Neale, and V. L. Huber, "Behind the Great Wall: A Comparison of Pay Allocation Values of Americans and Chinese," paper presented at the 1987 National Meeting of the Adademy of Management, New Orleans.

Training and Development

PHRM IN THE NEWS

Making Dreams Come True

Walt Disney said that it takes people to make a dream come true—dreamers as well as doers—and he founded Disney University (Amaheim, CA) as a place for developing Disney people. When Disneyland was launched in 1955, its creator wanted customers to feel like invited guests. Disney believed in training staff people to have good guest relations practices—and Disney pioneered a highly successful concept.

Today, guest relations programs in service companies are common—and Disney is working to build on its experience to maintain its service edge. Disney University continues to play a key role in this process, with its focus on "cast members," Disney's term for employees who are expected to play their part, and play it well.

"Disney University serves multiple functions," Bill Ross, manager, Disney University, said. "HR planning and development, cast communications (internal publications, formal communication programs), cast activities (social, recreational, and interpersonal communication programs), and audio visual programs are all handled out of the University.

"Each Disneyland unit has a dotted line relationship to Disney U, so that we can provide centralized hr services, yet have a strong link to individual entities. At Disneyland, we have about 6,000 employees.

International Focus

"Putting together our PHRM planning group is one of our newest hr efforts. Within the last two years, we've computerized information on our salaried employee population so that we can submit the criteria for a particular position, and generate the names of candidates through the computer. This system has also allowed us to pinpoint some of our development needs.

"We've found this capability particularly helpful since we've launched Tokyo Disneyland and our Euro-Disney project.

"We relocated about 200 executives to Japan—some for short stays, some for long. Given the expanded scope of our operations, we need to know all we can about the talent we have to draw on.

"We've been focusing on our need to become more internationalized. We are undertaking extensive training of Japanese managers, and our managers in the U.S., so that we can better understand cultural issues. We know that we can cross cultural lines—but we want to understand the issues to enhance our chances for success. We have established an International Fellowship with that goal in mind.

"We've also worked on providing a support system for those who return to the U.S. after a tour abroad. We recognize them for their efforts, we listen to their descriptions of their experiences, and we review what took place here while they were gone. After all, they are not returning to the same organization that they left—things change. And the manager who has served abroad has changed, too.

"We make every effort to reinforce the whole fabric of the organization. For example, when EpcotCenter was launched in 1982, the dedication ceremonies were telecast here in Anaheim—and shared with all sites.

Guest Courtesy—Inside Disney

"We believe that, for our cast members to treat our guests in a friendly and helpful way, they themselves must be treated that way. We look at guest courtesy as something that must extend to those within the organization, too.

"When cast members join Disneyland, they are treated as VIP's—they are personally greeted, and everyone is on a first-name basis. We reinforce good guest relations through our orientation process, training, performance appraisal system, and we circulate guest compliments and complaints. Our biggest challenge is to stay in touch with the changing values of both our guests and our cast members.

continued

"We look at how our guests define service—both first-time visitors and repeat visitors. We look at the environment itself, since elements such as temperature have a definite effect on people's perceptions of their experience. We encourage those behind the scenes to be conscious of courtesy, too—for example, we have a campaign called "Put a Smile in your Voice" that emphasizes telephone courtesy. And for our Christmas party, cast members and their families come to the park—and management mans the park for that day. Cast members experience the park as a guest—and management experiences the cast members' jobs. There is a management program that focuses on guest courtesy, as well.

"We have a two-person team whose sole job is to evaluate the level of courtesy that exists in the organization. We poll guests daily, and circulate results.

"We show examples of good and bad guest relations in our training program, based on the information we gather. We teach cast members to understand outcomes—their goal is to focus on what they want the guests to experience. There are many ways to get to that goal—but the end result is what counts.

"Our training teaches them to enhance skills to initiate a relationship, to take the first step in approaching guests who might look puzzled or in need of help. In the service business, we are fortunate to get a second chance when something goes wrong: a guest may have an unfortunate experience in the ticketline, but a helpful interchange in a restaurant that helps compensate. We want to avoid the first mistake—but make sure we take advantage of all opportunities for a second chance."

SOURCE: "Making Dreams Come True," *HR Reporter* (Jan. 1987): 2–3. Used with permission from *HR Reporter*, copyright 1987.

THE preceding "PHRM in the News" illustrates several aspects of training and development. One is that companies such as Disneyland are strongly committed to training and developing their employees. A second is that commitment to training starts at the top of the organization, typically the founder or the chief executive officer. Another aspect is that training plays a critical role in the mission of the organization. At Disneyland customer service is key to its identity and success, and all its employees are trained to have good guest relation skills. A fourth aspect is the importance of training managers for international assignments, both when they go abroad and when they return.

Because training and development is so important and costly, organizations want to do it as effectively as possible. Effective training and development require awareness and use of many techniques and programs. This chapter discusses the importance and purposes of training and development, along with training techniques and programs that organizations can provide. Prior to these discussions, training and development is defined, and its several relationships are described.

WHAT IS TRAINING AND DEVELOPMENT?

Sometimes, training and development are distinguished and treated separately. When this is done, **training** usually refers to improving an employee's skills to do the *current job*, and **development** refers to improving an employee's knowledge for *jobs in the future*. Nonetheless, both are concerned with improving the employee's ability to perform. And because many programs offered by organizations help to improve both skills and knowledge for current and future jobs, training and development are treated together here.[1]

The need for training and development is determined by the employee's performance deficiency, computed as follows:

Standard or desired performance (present or future)
— Actual (present or potential) performance
= Training and development need[2]

Although this formula is simple, it may be difficult for an organization to determine exactly what performance is desired, especially in the future, and what level of performance employees are currently exhibiting or are likely to exhibit in the future. Nevertheless, organizations that engage in training and development attempt to make these estimates to increase the potential effectiveness of their training and development programs. This is becoming particularly true as the importance and purposes of training and development are recognized.

PURPOSES AND IMPORTANCE OF TRAINING AND DEVELOPMENT

As noted, a major purpose of training and development is to remove performance deficiencies, whether current or anticipated, that cause employees to perform at less than the desired level. Training and development thereby enables employees to be much more productive. Training for performance improvements is particularly important to organizations with stagnant or declining rates of productivity. It is also important to organizations that are rapidly incorporating new technologies and consequently increasing the likelihood of employee obsolescence. And it is becoming even more critical because of the nation's increasing illiteracy rate:

Adult illiteracy presents "staggering" problems for employers, observes Harold McGraw, Jr., chairman of the board of McGraw-Hill, Inc., and founder of the Business Council for Effective Literacy (BCEL), a national foundation dedicated to encouraging and assisting employer participation in literacy activities. Noting that an estimated 25 million adults are unable to read, write, or do simple arithmetic and that "at least another 50 million adults are so limited in their basic skills that they are only marginally competent to cope" with the requirements of everyday life, McGraw maintains that illiteracy represents a "tremendous" barrier to employers' ability to improve productivity and maintain a competitive edge.

Currently, McGraw says, an estimated 30 percent of unskilled jobs, 29 percent of semi-skilled jobs, and 11 percent of managerial positions are held by persons who are unable to fill out a job application, write a letter to a customer, read a warning label on a chemical container, or understand machine operating symbols. Such deficiencies, McGraw maintains, contribute to low productivity, absenteeism, workplace accidents, poor product quality, decreased profits, and a reduced pool of candidates for hire, promotion, or advancement. When you consider that as many as three-quarters of the unemployed population also is judged to have serious basic skills problems, then you begin to realize that illiteracy is more than a social problem—it's "a major economic problem for all of us," McGraw says.

While awareness of the magnitude of the illiteracy problem is growing, too few employers have become "wound up" about the "paramount importance" of literacy education in the workplace, McGraw asserts. On-the-job basic skills training is "a job that really needs doing," he insists, pointing out that if employers don't "do considerably more" to help plan, organize, manage, and fund literacy activities, both in and outside the workplace, they will have no foundation on which to build for the future. With the number of adult illiterates continuing to grow each year, further reducing the pool of workers able to do a job, employers must "get involved now," McGraw says.[3]

Another purpose of training and development that is especially relevant is that of making the current work force more flexible and adaptable in order to deal with new technologies. If an organization can increase the adaptability of its work force through training and development, it can increase the adaptability of the organization itself, thus increasing its potential for survival and profitability.

Training and development can also increase the level of commitment of employees to the organization and increase their perceptions that the organization is a good place to work. Increased commitment can result in less turnover and absenteeism, thus increasing an organization's productivity.[4] Increasingly recognized is that training and development can benefit society by enabling individuals to be productive and contributing members of organizations.

RELATIONSHIPS INFLUENCING TRAINING AND DEVELOPMENT

As Exhibit 11.1 shows, training and development activities are related to many of the PHRM activities discussed so far. It is also related to the internal environment.

Relationships with Other PHRM Activities

Training and development has critical relationships with human resource planning, job analysis, performance appraisal, recruitment and selection, and compensation.

Human Resource Planning.   As result of changing technology, organizations are finding it increasingly difficult to fill some of their human resource needs with already trained employees. Consequently, they are finding it necessary to do more of their own training to develop talent from within the organization. Human resource planning helps formalize this necessity and articulates management's concern for effectively utilizing its human resources now and in the future. Furthermore, human resource planning serves to integrate changing business needs with other PHRM activities.[5]

Job Analysis and Performance Appraisal.   Whereas planning establishes the general context within which training and development takes place, job analysis and performance appraisal help identify specific training and development needs. Performance appraisal may reveal a performance deficiency, and further analysis can then determine the specific training needed to remove the deficiency.[6]

Training and Development Processes, Procedures, and Relationships

EXHIBIT
11.1

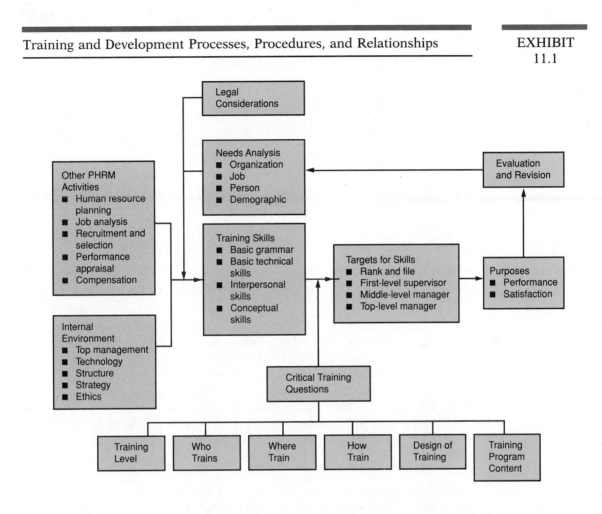

Recruitment and Selection.   If an organization can recruit trained individuals, this may save training and development costs. But when organizations do this for jobs above the entry level, they risk reducing the promotional rewards that could be used as incentives for their current employees. Consequently, many organizations have training and development programs for employees needing skills for both current and future jobs. Training and development then essentially becomes a way of life for employees. For example,

> service industry "superstar" companies conduct lifelong training, beginning during the selection process and continuing until an employee's retirement. For example, General Electric and IBM send supervisors to school regularly to reinforce skills and the company's service ethic. Characteristics of ongoing training programs at leading service firms include customer service standards which are clearly communicated to employees and supervisory training programs which are mandatory—at least one full week every year—and address such topics as performance management, human resource motivation, and effective supervision. Finally, training is provided to "behind-the-scenes" employees and stresses how their jobs affect customers indirectly.[7]

Compensation. The use of incentives is important not only for getting employees into training and development programs but also for maintaining the effects of these programs. For example, at Motorola:

> Quality is the No. 1 concern of everyone. It's a heavily promoted notion in the classes that employees attend.
>
> Even so, Motorola is finding that education alone won't precipitate reform without reworking incentives and hiring practices. So in exchange for meeting tough goals, such as cutting product-design time, Motorola now hands out incentive bonuses. Still, there is grumbling that its accounting system discourages cooperation among business units. One reason: Such programs often produce costs that show up on a manager's profit-loss statement—but their contribution to profits can be harder to pinpoint.[8]

Relationships with the Internal Environment

As the initial "PHRM in the News" suggested, the roles of top management and changing technology are important in training and development.

Top-Management Support. Management commitment to training and development in the United States lags behind that of other countries. According to A. William Wiggenhorn, vice-president and director of training for Motorola, Japanese electronics companies spend "three times as much money and time" on training as their American counterparts. While training is more expensive in the United States, he contends that U.S. companies must begin to invest "as much in the updating of people as they do in capital investments." Otherwise, the U.S. will never recoup productivity losses experienced in the 1970s and early 1980s.[9]

Changing Technology. One factor that is stimulating an emphasis on and commitment to training is technological change. The skills of today will not be sufficient for the future. Although this applies to both manufacturing and service industries, the pace of complex technological change is perhaps greatest in manufacturing. It is predicted that the

> next generation of manufacturing managers will need to know computer-aided design and computer-aided manufacturing (CAD/CAM), computer-integrated manufacturing (CIM), group technologies, flexible manufacturing, "just-in-time" inventory control, manufacturing resource planning (MRP), robotics, and a whole litany of other techniques and technologies in manufacturing.
>
> They're going to have to understand systems thinking, as more and more of the major corporations move toward the globalization of their manufacturing to achieve the competitive advantages of economies of scale, vertical integration, and offshore production.
>
> They'll have to develop different perspectives on managing a work force as the concepts of lifesyle employment, worker participation, and job enrichment extend further and further through the American enterprise system.
>
> Perhaps most importantly, they are going to have to have a well-developed understanding of corporate strategies, not only to find those organizations and subunits of organizations in which they will be most comfortable and successful, but also to be able to take an important role in determining and directing those strategies. The demands on manufacturing managers—on their skills, abilities, and training—are going up, but so too are their status and importance in manufacturing-based industries.[10]

With the pace of technology likely to accelerate, the most reasonable scenario is one in which organizations continually retrain current employees and recruit new employees with unique skills. Changing technology necessitates continual training program formulation and implementation and employees who are willing to adapt, to be reassigned to different jobs, and to be retrained.[11] For example, in the late 1980s, Kodak launched a major training initiative in which chemists participated in an intensive reeducation program to give them the engineering skills Kodak perceived would be needed to meet future demands. While Kodak could have hired trained engineers, it felt the training cycle would be shorter and the commitment of employees greater if retraining was provided.[12]

According to a recent study, this approach makes sense. Employers that invest the heaviest in employee learning also make the greatest effort to provide employment security in order to protect their investment.[13]

Strategy and Structure.   Not only do employees need a well-developed understanding of corporate strategies; they also need training and development to help them behave in ways consistent with those strategies. Consider IBM's move to a marketing-oriented strategy. The deployment of 21,500 employees from manufacturing, development, and administration into marketing and programming was coupled with massive training and development programs relating to corporate sales. Similarly, as organizations shift to high-quality or innovative strategies, they need to train their employees in new work methods such as statistical quality control and risk taking, respectively.

Additionally, organizations are finding it necessary to be able to adapt and respond quickly. This need is causing organizations to structure themselves to be lean, flexible, and adaptable. As the second "PHRM in the News" indicates, the consequences of this for management development are enormous.[14]

Business Ethics.   Recognizing the need for promoting moral excellence, many companies are providing training in ethical behavior. For example, Chemical Bank has included ethics discussions in its training programs since 1983. According to Karen Alphin, employee communications director, Chemical Bank's "Decision-Making and Corporate Values" program addresses issues that are of interest not just to bankers but also to ethical individuals. Convinced of the need for "a conversation about ethics," Polaroid Corporation set up a major internal conference in 1983 which brought philosophers, ethicists, and business professors to the compnay for lectures and discussions of ethical concepts.[15]

LEGAL CONSIDERATIONS IN TRAINING AND DEVELOPMENT

While there are numerous laws that affect PHRM practices, training and development activities are particularly affected by discrimination laws, the Fair Labor Standards Act, and the Occupational Safety and Health Act, each of which will be discussed below. Additional federal and state programs that help to defray costs for training specific groups will be discussed.

Discrimination Laws

As mentioned in Chapters 4 and 5, Title VII of the Civil Rights Act of 1964 and the Age Discrimination in Employment Act pertain to discrimination in many

Management Development Assumes New Importance

"There are no flexible organizations, only flexible people," an executive observed. Human resource staff are expected to guide and support company efforts in developing managers as leaders for the new flat, lean, and flexible environment. General Electric believes that teamwork, company-wide perspective, global insight, and customer orientation are critical attributes for its leaders. With fewer managers and fewer management levels, management capabilities are more important. Providing challenging and broadening experiences is the key to developing flexible managers. However, in flat and lean organizations, job rotation and mobility are difficult because there are fewer managers—and increased time pressures and demands. . . .

In response, companies are emphasizing flexible careers, fostering individual growth and learning through changing on-the-job experiences, assignments under different managers, and special projects. They are seeking to leverage training and education to address critical needs rather than curricula or career steps. . . .

. . .Traditionally, classroom-type programs have concentrated on building knowledge, awareness, and basic individual skills relevant to management tasks. They have not always reached the managers who need the development the most; neither have they always been regarded as uniformly successful in changing behaviors. To address these concerns, many companies are now redesigning programs to support directly company strategies for change and to focus on specific issues, skills, and behaviors.

The urgency of keeping management abreast of changes in a company, its industry, and its markets makes management development a priority in rapidly changing businesses. The human resource function has a primary responsibility to guide managers into assignments and job duties which will provide the most challenging developmental experiences for managers. Similarly, they are responsible for customizing educational and training programs so they are attuned to changing needs and yield the greatest possible benefit.

Managers in large, complex organizations that are changing rapidly recognize the need for a balance between entrepreneurship and formal, disciplined management. Interest in innovation, creativity, initiative, and competitiveness reflect widespread acceptance of the need for change, but in the context of maintaining the management coordination necessary in complex organizations. Managing flexibility requires maintenance of a creative tension between order and chaos. Flexible companies seek enough latitude for business units to thrive in their marketplaces as entrepreneurial businesses, yet enough discipline to achieve the necessary benefits of large-scale integration and management value added in a highly-competitive global marketplace.

SOURCE: J. W. Walker, "Managing Human Resources in Flat, Lean and Flexible Organizations: Trends for the 1990's," *Human Resource Planning* 11, no. 2 (1988): 125–32. Used with permission from The Human Resource Planning Society, copyright 1988.

aspects of the employment process. Discriminatory practices in training and development decisions are no exception. For example, an employee or job applicant who feels he or she has been denied access to a training program can establish a *prima facie* case of discrimination under either the disparate impact or the disparate treatment theory of recovery.[16]

Consider the woman who charged that her employer discriminated against her and all other female employees by closing special management training programs to women. The Eleventh Court of Appeals held that the woman could establish a *prima facie* case of sex discrimination through "statistical data indicating a disparity between the overall percentage of female employees and the percentage of females in better paid managerial positions" (*Reed v. Lockheed Aircraft Corp.*, 1987).[17] The ban on discrimination in employment and training opportunities extends to on-the-job training, one-day job orientations or introductions to new equipment, affirmative action, and formal apprenticeship training programs.[18]

Admission to formal training programs can be limited to those under a certain age as long as those excluded are not women or minorities who have previously been denied training opportunities. However, an applicant cannot be eliminated from a selection pool because he or she lacks a skill that can be mastered in eight hours or less of training. Another legal mandate is that if training test scores are used to select job candidates, they should be used only to screen out applicants, rather than to rank them (*Washington v. Davis*, 1976; *Ensley Branch NAACP v. Seibels*, 1980). Thus, it is important to determine what skills an individual needs to perform a job, whether training can remove any deficiency, and how much time will be necessary to complete the program.

Fair Labor Standards Act

The Fair Labor Standards Act (FLSA), which was discussed in depth in Chapters 8 and 9, specifies that time spent in activities considered an integral part of an employee's job must be compensated. Training time must be compensated, *except* when

- Attendance is voluntary.
- Training takes place outside of regular work hours.
- Training is not directly related to the employee's job.
- An employee doesn't conduct any production work during the training.

The FLSA does permit payment of subminimum wages (if approved by the Wage and Hour Division of the U.S. Department of Labor) to learners in semiskilled occupations, apprentices in skilled occupations, and handicapped individuals working in sheltered training workshops.

Occupational Safety and Health Act

No law has stimulated greater demand for training than the Occupational Safety and Health Act of 1970 and the subsequent Hazard Communication Standard of 1986 (to be discussed in depth in Chapter 13). According to the Occupational Safety and Health Administration (OSHA), safety training is required to

1. Orient employees to safety rules, penalties for unsafe behavior, and incentives for good safety records.
2. Teach safe work procedures.
3. Provide instruction in how to uncover or identify safety hazards.

The Hazard Communication Standard of 1986 requires that employers provide workers with information *and* training on hazardous chemicals in their work place when they are assigned to a job or when new hazardous chemicals are introduced into the work area. According to the standard, training should include instruction on what the standard states, how to determine the presence of chemicals in the work place, how to protect against exposure to chemicals, and how chemicals should be handled.

OSHA also dictates that training programs and sites be free from hazards. On first blush, this provision may not appear relevant to training. However, many types of training do entail risk (driving motor vehicles, operating machinery, dealing with hazardous substances). Still other types of training (wilderness survival programs, sensitivity training) intentionally subject trainees to physical challenges (falling from cliffs while rappelling, electrolyte imbalances, dehydration) or mental challenges (stress, anxiety) in order to open them up to new ways of problem solving, build confidence, or promote teamwork. Two questions remain unanswered about such programs. First, what liability, if any, does an organization have when it requires employees to enroll in such programs? Second, can an organization reduce its liability by informing participants about the risks in advance or by contracting with a third party to conduct the training? Consequently, training that occurs during work hours or that is demanded outside of work hours generally requires compensation and adherance to safety procedures.[19]

Federal and State Support

A final legal consideration in training and development is federal and state governmental support. This support can enable organizations to defray some training costs and receive already trained employees. It can also enable employees to obtain training and jobs. Currently, support from the federal government is funneled through block grants to states and through the Office of Federal Contract Compliance Programs under provisions in the Job Training Partnership Act of 1982. Under that act, grants are provided to states that in turn use the money to train economically disadvantaged youths and adults, as well as workers whose jobs have been eliminated. In addition, money is to be provided for training individuals to overcome sex stereotyping in occupations traditionally thought to be for the other sex.

The federal government also supports training by providing funds to 460 private industry councils. These councils are composed primarily of business people who help determine what training programs should be offered and disburse funds to those who provide that training. Determining what training and development programs should be offered is therefore critical. In general, however, it begins with determining training and development needs.[20]

DETERMINING TRAINING AND DEVELOPMENT NEEDS

Training can be conducted for a variety of reasons. In some organizations, attendance at an executive training program is a reward for past performance. In other organizations, participation in a training program is an organizational ritual which signals to the employee who is promoted and the members of his or her former work group that a switch in stature has occurred (a rank-and-file employee is now a manager). However, most often training is conducted to rectify skill deficiencies and provide employees with job-specific skills.[21]

A first step in establishing a viable training program is assessment, which determines the training and development needs of the organization. While less than one-third of all U.S. companies currently conduct formal needs assessment, its importance cannot be emphasized enough.[22] Without determining the need for training, there is no guarantee that the right training is being provided for the right trainees. This process is detailed in Exhibit 11.2.

Organizational Needs Analysis

Conducting an **organizational needs analysis** is the first step in effective needs assessment. It begins with an examination of the short and long term objectives of the organization and the trends that are likely to affect these objectives. According to one expert, attaining organizational objectives should be the ultimate concern of any training and development effort. Organizational needs

Model for an Instructional System   EXHIBIT 11.2

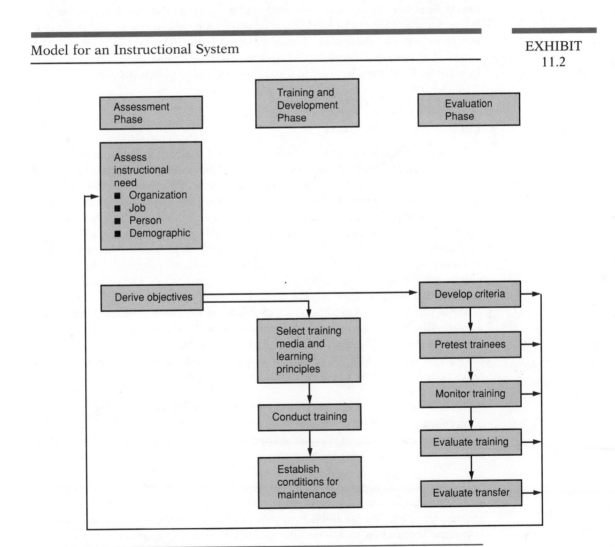

SOURCE: Adapted from I. Goldstein, *Training: Program Development and Evaluation*, 8. Copyright © 1974 Wadsworth, Inc. Reprinted by permission of the publisher, Brooks/Cole Publishing Company, Monterey, Calif.

Note: Many other models for instructional systems are used in the military, in business, and in education. Some of the components of this model were suggested by these other systems.

analysis also can include a human resource analysis, analyses of efficiency indices, and an assessment of the organizational climate.[23]

This analysis should translate the organization's objectives into an accurate estimate of the demand for human resources. Efficiency indices, including cost of labor, quantity of output, quality of output, waste, and equipment use and repairs, can provide useful information. The organization can determine standards for these indices and then analyze them to evaluate the general effectiveness of training programs and to locate training and development needs in departments.

Job Needs Analysis

The content of present or anticipated jobs should be examined through **job needs analysis.** Using such job analysis, information on the tasks to be performed in each job (information contained in job descriptions), the skills necessary to perform those tasks (from job qualifications), and the minimum acceptable standards (gleaned from perfromance appraisal) are gathered. This information can then be used to ensure that training programs are job specific and useful.

Person Needs Analysis

After information about the necessary skills and their importance and the minimal acceptable standards of proficiency has been collected, the analysis shifts to the person. A **person needs analysis** can be accomplished in two different ways. Employee performance discrepancies may be identified either by comparing actual performance with the minimum acceptable standards of performance or by comparing an evaluation of employee proficiency on each required skill dimension with the proficiency level required for each skill. The first method is based on the actual, current job performance of an employee; therefore, it can be used to determine training needs for the current job. The second method, on the other hand, can be used to identify development needs for future jobs.[24]

In examining various methodologies for determining employee training needs, a continuing problem concerns the ambiguity of the word "need." Need can be an expression of preference or demand and not an observable discrepancy produced by a lack of skill. At this level, several different approaches can be used to identify the training needs of individuals.

Output Measures. Performance data (e.g., productivity, accidents, customer complaints), as well as peformance appraisal ratings, can provide evidence of performance deficiencies. Person analysis can also consist of work sampling and job knowledge tests that measure actual performance and knowledge.[25]

Self-Assessed Training Needs. The self-assessment of training needs is growing in popularity. A recent study of training practices in major U.S. firms showed that between 50 and 80 percent of all corporations allow managers to nominate themselves to attend short-term or company-sponsored training or education programs. Self-assessment can be as informal as posting a list of company-sponsored courses and asking who wants to attend or as formal as conducting surveys regarding training needs.[26] Exhibit 11.3 shows sample questions from a managerial self-assessment survey.

Sample Questions from a Self-Administered Training Needs Survey

EXHIBIT
11.3

Please indicate in the blanks the extent to which you have a training need in each specific area. Use the scale below.
To what extent do you need training in the following areas?

To no extent				To a very large extent
1	2	3	4	5

Basic Management Skills (organizing, planning, delegating, problem solving)

_____ 1. Setting goals and objectives
_____ 2. Developing realistic time schedules to meet work requirements
_____ 3. Identifying and weighing alternative solutions
_____ 4. Organizing work activities

Interpersonal Skills

_____ 1. Resolving interpersonal conflicts
_____ 2. Creating a development plan for employees
_____ 3. Identifying and understanding individual employee needs
_____ 4. Conducting performance appraisal reviews
_____ 5. Conducting a discipline interview

Administrative Skills

_____ 1. Maintaining equipment, tools, and safety controls
_____ 2. Understanding local agreements and shop rules
_____ 3. Preparing work flowcharts
_____ 4. Developing department budgets

Quality Control

_____ 1. Analyzing and interpreting statistical data
_____ 2. Constructing and analyzing charts, tables, and graphs
_____ 3. Using statistical software on the computer

SOURCE: Modified from J. K. Ford and R. A. Noe, "Self Assessed Training Needs: The Effects of Attitude toward Training, Mangerial Level and Function," *Personnel Psychology* 40 (1987): 40–53.

Self-assessment is premised on the assumption that employees, more than anyone else, are aware of their skill weaknesses and performance deficiencies. Therefore, they are in the best position to identify their own training needs. One drawback of self-assessment is that individuals who are fearful of revealing any weaknesses may not know or be willing to report accurately their training needs. Consequently, these individuals may not receive the education necessary to remain current in their fields. On the other hand, managers forced to attend programs that they believe they do not need or that do not meet their personal training needs are likely to become dissatisfied with training and lack the motivation to learn and transfer skills.

Attitude Surveys. Attitude surveys completed by a supervisor's subordinates and/or by customers also can provide information on training needs. For example, when one supervisor receives low scores regarding his or her fairness in treatment as compared to other supervisors in the organization, this may indicate that the supervisor needs training in that area.[27] Not only does this format provide information to management about service, but also results can be used to pinpoint employee deficiencies.

One concern with most attitude surveys is that they are not designed for diagnostic purposes. That is a low score may indicate a problem but seldom suggests how behavior should be changed. However, instruments can be designed that do provide specific feedback and can be used to establish training programs. An example is the Satisfaction with My Supervisor Scale (SWMSS) presented in Exhibit 11.4. This instrument assesses three types of skills required for effective supervision: technical, human relations, and administrative. Items are worded such that remedial training can be provided if deficiencies are found. Another advantage of surveys such as the SWMSS is that they can be administered before and after training. If positive changes are found, the results could be attributed to training.

Competency-Based Assessment.   A type of needs assessment growing in popularity is **competency-based assessment.** This approach involves five major steps:

Step 1: *Develop Broad Compenency Categories.* The initial step is to develop a set of broad competency areas, i.e., to determine the critical skills that employees at a given level or job classification in the organization need to be most effective.

**EXHIBIT
11.4**

Satisfaction with My Supervisor (SWMSS) as a Training Dianostic Tool

Please indicate how satisfied you are with your supervisor. Use the following scale, and next to each item write the number that best represents your degree of satisfaction with that particular aspect of supervisory behavior.

Very dissatisfied				Very satisfied
1	2	3	4	5

_____ 1. The way supervisor listens when I have something important to say.
_____ 2. The way my supervisor sets clear work goals.
_____ 3. The way my supervisor treats me when I make a mistake.
_____ 4. My supervisor's fairness in appraising my job performance.
_____ 5. The way my supervisor is consistent in his/her behavior toward subordinates.
_____ 6. The way my supervisor helps me to get the job done.
_____ 7. The way my supervisor give me credit for my ideas.
_____ 8. The way my supervisor gives me clear instructions.
_____ 9. The way my supervisor informs me abut work changes ahead of time.
_____ 10. The way my supervisor follows through to get problems solved.
_____ 11. The way my supervisor understands the problems I might run into doing the job.
_____ 12. The way my supervisor shows concern for my career progress.
_____ 13. The way my supervisor backs me up with other management.
_____ 14. The frequency with which I get a pat on the back for doing a good job.
_____ 15. The technical competence of my supervisor.

Step 2: *Develop Specific Competencies*. Once broad categories are selected, the next step is to further define each and develop a list of more specific competencies.

Step 3: *Develop a Resource Guide and a Competency Rating Form*. The third step involves the development of resource guides or competency manuals that will aid employers and employees in developing skills.

Step 4: *Prepare a Developmental Plan for Each Employee*. Once each employee has been evaluated, the next step would be for the boss to work with each of his/her subordinates to develop a specific improvement plan.

Step 5: *Evaluate Employee Progress and Develop a New Plan*. Periodic assessment of an employee's progress skill development is essential.[28]

Demographic Needs Analysis

In addition to organizational, job, and person analyses, organizations also should conduct **demographic studies** to determine the training needs of specific populations of workers.[29] For example, Frito Lay conducted a special assessment to determine the training needs of women and minorities in its sales force. According to Dave Knibbe, Frito Lay management development director, the needs assessment was critical to see if there were ways in which the organization could facilitate more rapid career advancement for these employees.

Research indicates that different groups have different training needs. For example, first-line supervisors need more technical training (record keeping, written communications), while mid-level managers rate PHRM courses as most important for meeting their needs, and upper-level managers rate conceptual courses (goal setting, planning skills) as critical to their development.[30] In a study of male and female managers, male managers were found to need training in listening, verbal skills, nonverbal communication, empathy, and sensitivity; women managers, on the other hand, needed training in assertiveness, confidence building, public speaking, and dealing with male peers and subordinates.[31]

SETTING UP TRAINING AND DEVELOPMENT PROGRAMS

Successful implementation of training and development programs depends on selecting the right programs for the right people under the right conditions.

Who Participates in Training?

Once a training need has been established, a decision must be made regarding *who* will be trained. This is because for most programs, only one target audience is in attendance, and the training program is designed to address only one topic.[32]

Also important here is the decision as to *how many* employees are to be trained simultaneously. If only one or two employees are to be trained, then on-the-job approaches such as coaching are generally cost effective. If large numbers of individuals need to be trained in a short period of time, then programmed instruction may be the most viable option.

Who Conducts the Training?

Training and development programs may be taught by one of several people, including

- The supervisor
- A co-worker, such as a lead worker or a buddy
- An internal or external subject area expert
- The employee

Which of these people is selected to teach often depends on where the program is held and which skill(s) is being taught. For example, basic job skills are usually taught by the immediate job supervisor or a co-worker, whereas a basic organizational orientation is usually handled by a member of the PHRM staff. Interpersonal skills and conceptual, integrative skills for management are usually taught by university professors or consultants. However, technical skills may be taught by either internal or external subject matter experts.

A concern with using immediate supervisors or co-workers as trainers is that while they may perform adequately, they may not be able to instruct anyone in proper work procedures. It is also possible that they will teach workers their own shortcuts rather than correct procedures. On the other hand, immediate supervisors or co-workers may be more knowledgeable than anyone else about work procedures. If co-workers or managers are to be used as trainers, they should receive training in how to train and be given sufficient time on the job to work with trainees.[33]

Subject area experts may have specific knowledge but may not be familiar with procedures in a specific organizational culture. As a result, they may be respected for their expertise but mistrusted because they are not a member of the work group. Still, if no one in the immediate work environment possesses the knowledge needed, or if large numbers of individuals need to be trained, the only option may be to hire experts.

Self-paced instruction is also an option. Learning at one's own pace is both an advantage and a disadvantage of self-paced instruction. Trainees benefit because they learn at a speed that maximizes retention. However, if there are no incentives for the trainee to complete the instruction in a specified period of time, training may be placed on a back burner.

What Types of Skills Are to Be Acquired?

In addition to using appropriate training techniques, the training program must have content congruent with the types of skills being taught. In general, skills fall into three broad areas; as discussed below.

Basic Skills.   As noted in Chapter 2, organizations are increasingly concerned about illiteracy. Consequently, it is estimated that training programs designed to correct basic skill deficiencies in grammar, mathematics, safety, reading, listening, and writing will increase in the 1990s. For example,

> Ask most business executives how they would like to improve their reading on the job, and they will probably answer, "I would like to read faster. I can't keep up with all the reading material that comes across my desk." Employers. . . ., such as Scott Paper Company, Providence National Bank, Western Electric Company, and Getty Oil, have appreciated this need and have implemented [reading] programs for their employees.[34]

Training that expands or maintains the technical expertise of employees is a subset of basic job skills training. Due to rapid changes in technology and the implementation of automated office, industrial, and managerial systems, technological updating and skill building have become a major thrust in training to keep technical skills current.[35]

Interpersonal Skills. Skills in communications, human relationships, performance appraisal, leadership, and negotiations are increasingly in demand. In fact, this type of training tops the list of training needs for first- and middle-level managers. The development of interpersonal skills is also important for those employees who interface with the public (e.g., receptionist, sales associates).[36]

Conceptual Integrative Skills. Strategic and operational planning, organization design, and policy skills are needed by organizational planners, as well as by top management. Adapting to complex and changing environments is often a part of top- and middle-management responsibilities, and conceptual training helps such employees to make new associations. It is at the heart of today's emphasis on creativity and intrapreneurship.

Where Is the Training Conducted?

Decisions also need to be made regarding where the training will take place. This decision may be constrained by the type of learning that is to occur (basic, interpersonal, or conceptual), as well as by cost and time considerations. Exhibit 11.5 summarizes the various approaches to training according to the locale of the training.

On-the-Job. A frequently used alternative is to train workers on the job. **On-the-job training** (OJT) occurs when an employee is taught a new job under the direct supervision of an experienced worker or trainer. The trainee is expected to learn the job by observing the experienced employee and by working with the actual materials, personnel, and/or machinery that comprise the job. The experienced employee/trainer is expected to provide a favorable role model and to take time from regular job responsibilities to provide job-related instruction and guidance.

One advantage of OJT is that transfer of training is high. That is, because trainees learn job skills in the environment in which they will actually work, they will be more apt to apply these skills on the job. Assuming the trainer works in the same area, the trainee receives immediate feedback about performance. However, such on-site training is appropriate only when a small number of individuals need to be trained and when the consequence of error is low. The quality of the training also hinges on the skill of the manager or lead employee conducting the training.[37]

The disadvantages of on-the-job training can be minimized by making the training program as systematic and complete as possible. **Job instruction training (JIT)** represents such a systematic technique. JIT was developed "to provide a guide for giving on-the-job skill training to white- and blue-collar employees as well as technicians."[38] Because JIT is a technique rather than a program, it can be adapted to training efforts for all employees in off-the-job as well as on-the-job programs.

JIT consists of four steps: (1) careful selection and preparation of the trainer and the trainee for the learning experience to follow; (2) a full explanation and demonstration by the trainer of the job to be done by the trainee; (3) a trial on-

EXHIBIT
11.5

A Summary of the Advantages and Disadvantages of On-the-Job, On-Site, and Off-the-Job Training Programs

	Advantages	Disadvantages
On-the-job		
Job instruction training	Facilitates transfer of learning	Interferes with performance
	No need for separate facilities	Damages equipment
Apprenticeship	No interference with real job performance	Takes a long time
		Expensive
	Provides extensive training	May not be related to job
Internships or assistantships	Facilitates transfer of learning	Not really a full job
	Gives exposure to real job	Learning is vicarious
Job rotation	Exposure to many jobs	No sense of full responsibility
	Real learning	Too short a stay in a job
Supervisory assistance	Informal	Effectiveness rests with supervisor
	Integrated into job	
	Inexpensive	Not all supervisors may do it
On-Site But Not On-the Job		
Programmed instruction	Provides for individualized learning and feedback	Time-consuming to develop
	Faster learning	Cost effective only for large groups
Videotapes	Conveys consistent information to employees in diverse locations.	Costly to develop
	More portable than film	Don't provide for individual feedback
Videodisks	Stores more information than tapes	Extremely costly to develop
	Allows for fast forward	Courseware is limited
	Portable	
Interactive	Training draws on more senses	Costly to develop and implement
	Self-paced learning and feedback	Requires diverse staff to develop
Telecom- munications training	Provides for latest insights and knowledge	Costly and difficult to set up
	Speeds up communications	Not feasible for small firms
	Standardized	
Off-the-Job		
Formal courses	Inexpensive for many	Require verbal skills
	No interference with job	Inhibit transfer of learning
Simulation	Helps transfer	Can't always duplicate real situations exactly
	Creates lifelike situations	
Role playing	Good for interpersonal skills	Can't create real situations exactly-still playing
	Gives insights into others	
Sensitivity training	Good for self-awareness	May not transfer to job
	Gives insights into others	May not relate to job

the-job performance by the trainee; and (4) a thorough feedback session between the trainer and the trainee to discuss the trainee's performance and the job requirements.[39]

Another method for minimizing the disadvantages of on-the-job training is combining it with off-the-job training. Apprenticeship training, internships, and assistantships are programs based on this combination. **Apprenticeship training** is mandatory for admission to many of the skilled trades, such as plumbing, electronics, and carpentry. These programs are formally defined by the U.S. Department of Labor's Bureau of Apprenticeship and Training and involve a written agreement "providing for not less than 4,000 hours of reasonably continuous employment. . .and supplemented by a recommended minimum of 144 hours per year of related classroom instruction." The Equal Employment Opportunity Commission (EEOC) does not prevent the nation's 48,000 skilled trade (apprentice) training programs from excluding anyone age forty to seventy because apprenticeship programs are part of the educational system aimed at youth.[40] To be most effective, the on- and off-the-job components of the apprenticeship program must be well integrated and appropriately planned and must recognize individual differences.

Somewhat less formalized and extensive than apprenticeship training are the internship and assistantship programs. **Internships** are often part of an agreement between schools and colleges and local organizations.[41] As with apprenticeship training, individuals in these programs earn while they learn, but at a rate that is less than that paid to full-time employees or master crafts workers. The internships, however, function as a source not only of training but also of realistic exposure to job and organizational conditions. **Assistantships** involve full-time employment and expose an individual to a wide range of jobs. However, because the individual only assists other workers, the learning experience is often vicarious. This disadvantage is eliminated by programs of job or position rotation and multiple management.

Job rotation programs are used to train and expose employees to a variety of jobs and decision-making situations. Although **job rotation** provides employee exposure, the extent of training and long-run benefits it provides may be overstated. This is because the employees are not in a single job for a long enough period to learn very much and are not motivated to work hard because they know that they will move on in the near future. As a personal career planning strategy, you may want to avoid job rotation and opt instead for job assignments that are more fixed but that provide a greater challenge.

The final and most informal program of training and development is **supervisory assistance or mentoring**.[42] This method of training is a regular part of the supervisor's job. It includes day-to-day coaching, counseling, and monitoring of workers on how to do the job and how to get along in the organization. The effectiveness of coaching, counseling, and monitoring as a technique for training and development depends in part on whether the supervisor creates feelings of mutual confidence, provides opportunities for growth to employees, and effectively delegates tasks. Mentoring programs, in which an established employee guides the development of a less-experienced worker or "protege," can increase employees' skills, achievement, and understanding of the organization:

> At NCR Corp., proteges are usually chosen from among high-potential employees in middle or entry-level management, says James E. McElwain, vice president for personnel resources. Each executive is encouraged to select two

people to mentor, and must decide how to develop the relationships, McElwain notes. Executives counsel their proteges on how to advance and network in the company, and sometimes offer personal advice, he says.[43]

On-Site But Not On-the-Job.   Another option is to conduct the training at the work site but not on the job. On-site training is appropriate for required after-hours training programs and for training programs in which contact needs to be maintained with work units but OJT would be too distracting or harmful. On-site training is also appropriate for voluntary after-hours training programs and for programs that update employees' skills while allowing them to attend to their regular duties.

For example, when a major Northeast grocery store chain switched to computerized scanners, it faced the problem of training thousands of checkers spread out across three states. The cost of training them off site was prohibitive. Yet management also was fearful about training employees on the job, lest their ineptness in learning to use the scanners would offend customers. To solve the problem, the grocery chain developed a mobile training van that included a vestibule model of the latest scanning equipment. Checkers were trained on site but off the job in the mobile unit. Once the basic skill of scanning was mastered, employees returned to the store, and the trainer remained on site as a resource person. According to one store manager, the program was effective because employees could be trained rapidly and efficiently. Yet because the training was not conducted on the job, no customers were lost due to checker errors or slowness.

New technologies have rapidly increased the options available to organizations that want to provide on site training. **Programmed instruction** (PI) is one of the oldest on-site training methods. Here, the instructional material is broken down into frames. Each frame represents a small component of the entire subject to be learned, and each frame must be learned successfully before going on to the next one.

An advantage of PI is that large numbers of employees can be trained simultaneously, with the learner free to explore the material at his or her own pace. Additionally, PI includes immediate and individualized feedback. The down side is that programming computers for PI is involved and time consuming. While the development of several authoring systems in the 1980s eased the burden of developing PI modules, instruction still must be carefully planned. It is estimated that one hour of programmed instruction requires 50 hours of development work. Consequently, this approach is effective only if "canned" programs (e.g., word and data base tutorials) are used or if large numbers of employees are to be trained so that development costs for an original program can be justified.

Videotaped presentations can be used on site or off site and have generally replaced films as the visual medium of choice for organizational training. At its most basic level, video training includes taped instruction that can be stopped and started at any point in time. Because videotapes are less expensive than traditional training films, their use has increased rapidly in recent years. In fact, it is estimated that organizations will spend $7 billion on video-based education in 1990.

An advantage of videotape is that instruction can be standardized. For example, Pizza Hut faced the burden of training 10,000 employees in various locales on such matters as competing with Domino's Pizza in the home delivery market, new products (e.g., pan pizza), safe driving, and customer service. Professionally prepared video presentations were mailed out to its individual locations, and the training was then provided on site to each shift of workers. Cost savings over traditional off-site or on-site training were substantial.

Organizations with large budgets for training are replacing videotapes with **videodisks.** A videodisk relies on a laser beam instead of a needle to pick up images and project them on a television screen. While more expensive to produce than simple videotape programs, videodisks provide higher-quality images, quicker starts and stops, and greater durability than tapes do. Because disks are much smaller than tapes, they are also easier to transport and utilize. The newness of videodisk technology and the lack of standardized courseware make these systems cost ineffective for small companies. Still corporations such as NCR and Kodak are relying on videodisks for training in business, computer logic, mechanics, and new technology. For example, Kodak uses videodisks to keep its scientists and engineers updated on technological advances.[44]

Interactive video training (IVT) combines the best features of PI with the best attributes of videotape and/or videodisk instruction. Interaction video programs present a short video and narrative presentation (via tape or disk) and then require the trainee to respond to it. Usually, the video program is attached to a personal computer, and the learner responds to video cues by using the keyboard or by touching the screen. This sequence—packaged program, learner response, and more programmed instruction—provides for individualized learning.

Interactive video has been used by a variety of organizations. Kodak developed an IVT system to train office personnel in the use of a new word processing system. The Kodak system relied on two computer screens. On one screen a model demonstrated how to use the software package (via videodisk); written instructions, as well as the trainee's word processing output, was displayed on the adjacent screen. Support staff could complete their training on site. If portions were forgotten, that segment could be repeated merely by walking over to the on-site training center and calling up the module of concern.

Interactive video training also has been used to train 400,000 General Motors workers in occupational health and safety procedures and Dow Chemical employees in how to deal with petrochemical hazards. Electrical workers have learned how to solve complex wiring problems by tracing patterns on touch-sensitive screens. The U.S. Army has found interactive video so effective that it installed 48,000 IVT units at army bases and developed more than 5,000 hours of course work by 1989.[45]

One of the more elaborate IVT programs was developed by the American Heart Association to teach cardiopulmonary resuscitation (CPR). The IVT program includes a demonstration via a computer of correctly performed CPR. After observing the model and receiving verbal and written instructions, the trainee is asked to perform the same manipulations on a "computerized" dummy. Computer sensors inside the dummy record the location, intensity, and frequency of pressure applied. Consequently, rapid and accurate computer-generated feedback can be provided. In particular, the computer is programmed to provide instructions on how to perform better (e.g., apply more pressure to the left, lighter strokes, more rapid strokes). While development costs were high, CPR training time is cut in half by use of the IVT program.[46]

On the down side, development and equipment costs associated with IVT are high. Hardware alone can cost between $6,000 and $12,000, and master videodisk costs between $2,000 and $5,000. For sophisticated programs, more than 500 hours can be spent on developing one hour of interactive video training, with costs running as high as $150,000. A sizable and diverse staff is also needed to make IVT work. Instruction designers, script writers, programmers, video producers, and subject experts are all needed. Still IVT offers fast, effective training. And it is expected that as its popularity increases, development and hardware costs should drop, making IVT more affordable to small organizations.

Another innovation for on-site training involves **telecommunications training,** using video satellite networks. In 1987, the Public Broadcasting System (PBS) entered the field of satellite training with the establishment of the National Narrowcast System (NNS). Produced in cooperation with the American Society for Training and Development (ASTD), the network offers more than five hours of daily programming via microwave to subscribing businesses, public agencies, and colleges and universities. Contractors are free to tape programs for six months to one year, and the system has nine training tracks targeted for specific groups (e.g., sales, supervision, computer literacy, effective communications).

The major advantage of telecommunications training is its potential for speeding up communications within large corporations. A cost study conducted by Kodak estimates that a new product training program beamed via satellite to three cities costs $20,000. However, Kodak also estimates that it would cost five to six times that amount to send engineers and managers on the road to do the same training. More important, six weeks of training time was saved, which is invaluable in a competitive industry.[47]

Off-the-Job.   When the consequence of error is high, it is usually more appropriate to conduct training off the job. For example, most airline passengers would readily agree that it is preferable to train pilots in flight simulators, rather than having them apprentice in the cockpit of a plane. Similarly, it is usually useful to have a bus driver practice on an obstacle course before taking to the roads with a full load of school children.

Off-the-job training is also appropriate when complex skills need to be mastered or when there is need to focus on specific interpersonal skills that might not be apparent in the normal work environment. For example, it is difficult to build a cohesive work team when members of management are constantly interrupted by telephone calls and subordinate inquires. Yet team building is likely to occur during a management retreat when there is time to focus on establishing relationships.

The costs of off-the-job training are, however, high. There also is concern over transfer of knowledge to the work place. As research has shown, the more dissimilar the training environment is from the actual work environment, the more likely it is that trainees will *not* be able to apply knowledge learned to their jobs. For example, the transfer of knowledge problem is minimal for **vestibule training,** in which trainees work in an environment that is comparable to the actual work environment. However, it may be difficult to apply skills learned during a wilderness survival program or on float trip down the Colorado River to a job because the training environment is dissimilar to the actual work environment.

The **formal course method** of training and development can be accomplished either by oneself—using programmed instruction, computer-assisted instruction, reading, and correspondence courses—or by others—as in formal classroom courses and lectures. Although many training programs use the lecture method because it efficiently and simultaneously conveys large amounts of information to large groups of people, it does have several drawbacks:

- It perpetuates the authority structure of traditional organizations and hinders performance because the learning process is not self-controlled.
- Except in the area of cognitive knowledge and conceptual principles, there is probably limited transfer of the actual skills and abilities required to do the job.
- The high verbal and symbolic requirements of the lecture method may be threatening to people with low verbal or symbolic experience or aptitude.
- The lecture method does not permit individualized training based on individual differences in ability, interests, and personality.

Because of these drawbacks, the lecture method is often complemented by other training methods.

Simulation, a training and development technique that presents participants with situations that are similar to actual job conditions, is used for both managers and nonmanagers.[48] A common technique for nonmanagers is the **vestibule method,** which simulates the environment of the individual's actual job. Because the environment is not real, it is generally less hectic and safer than the actual environment; as a consequence, the potential exists for adjustment difficulties in going from the simulated training environment to the actual environment. However, the arguments for using the simulated environment are compelling: it reduces the possibility of customer dissatisfaction that can result from on-the-job training; it can reduce the frustration of the trainee; and it may save the organization a great deal of money because fewer training accidents occur. Even though these arguments may seem compelling, not all organizations, even in the same industry, see the situation the same way. Some banks, for example, train their tellers on the job, whereas others train them in a simulated bank environment.

An increasingly popular simulation technique for managers is the **assessment center method.** This is discussed in Chapter 5 as a device for selecting managers. Assessment centers are also especially useful for identifying potential training needs. Whether used for training or selection, they appear to be a valid way to make employment decisions.[49] In fact, certain aspects of the assessment center, such as the management games and in-basket exercises, are excellent for training and do not have to be confined to these programs.

Regardless of where they are used, **management or business games** almost always entail various degrees of competition between teams or trainees. In contrast, the **in-basket exercise** is more solitary. The trainee sits at a desk and works through a pile of papers found in the in-basket of a typical manager, prioritizing, recommending solutions to problems, and taking any necessary action in response to the contents.[50]

Although the in-basket exercise tends to be an enjoyable and challenging exercise, the extent to which it improves a manager's ability depends in part on what takes place after the exercise. The analysis of what happened and what should have happened in both the business games and the in-basket exercise, when done by upper-level managers in the organization, should help trainees learn how to perform like managers. The opportunity for improvement may be drastically reduced if the trainees are left to decide what to transfer from the game or exercise to the job.

Whereas the simulation exercises may be useful for developing conceptual and problem-solving skills, two types of **human relations** or process-oriented training are used by organizations. **Role playing** and **sensitivity training** develop managers' interpersonal insights—awareness of self and of others—for changing attitudes and for practice in human relations skills, such as leadership or the interview.

Role playing generally focuses on emotional (that is, human relations) issues rather than on factual ones. The essence of role playing is to create a realistic situation, as in the case discussion method, and then have the trainees assume the parts of specific personalities in the situation. The usefulness of role playing depends heavily on the extent to which the trainees get into the parts they are playing. If you have done any role playing, you know how difficult this can be and how much easier it is to do what amounts to simply reading the part. But when the trainee does get into the role, the result is a greater sensitivity to the feelings and insights that are presented by the role.

Another method of training and development is **sensitivity training.** Individuals in an unstructured group exchange thoughts and feelings on the "here and now" rather than the "there and then." Although the experience of being in a sensitivity group often gives individuals insight into how and why they and others feel and act the way they do, critics claim that these results may not be beneficial because they are not directly transferable to the job.[51]

Other methods organizations use to increase employees' feelings about the here and now and their own self-esteem include programs that involve physical feats of strength, endurance, and cooperation. These can be done on wilderness trips to the woods or mountains or even the water.

Everyone goes overboard during strategic planning meetings of the Meridian Group. But that doesn't bother Harvey Kinzelberg, 43, chairman of the $250-million-a-year Illinois computer-leasing firm, the nation's third largest. On the contrary, he requires it. Twice a year Kinzelberg charters a boat in the Caribbean, puts his top executives aboard, and leads them in a five-day brainstorming session cum scuba-diving expedition. . .As often as three times a day, the company's managers pause from strategizing, strap on air tanks and face masks, and go for a plunge in the briny.

Kinzelberg claims the downward bound excursions focus his executives' attention on business by eliminating the . . .distractions of the office. More important, he says, they foster team spirit. . ."In the potentially life-threatening environment underwater," he explains, "you realize that you depend on everyone else in the company not just for your livelihood in business but for your life as well."

Excursions in the deep also provide the benefits of a different perspective, says Kinzelberg. . .After spearing and killing a large barracuda, as he did on a recent dive, Kinzelberg finds that the sharks he faces in business seem like small fry.[52]

MAXIMIZING TRAINEE LEARNING

Even when the training technique is appropriate, learning may not take place if the training is not structured to facilitate learning. Exhibit 11.6 details learning factors that affect the success of training. As shown, prior to training, the environment must be made ready for learning to occur. During training, steps need to be taken to increase self-efficacy and retention of knowledge. After

Learning Principles to Increase the Effectiveness of Training

EXHIBIT
11.6

Setting the Stage for Learning
  1. Provide clear task instructions.
  2. Model appropriate behavior.

Increasing Learning during Training
  1. Provide for active participation.
  2. Increase self-efficacy.
  3. Match training techniques to trainees' self-efficacy.
  4. Provide opportunities for enactive mastery.
  5. Ensure specific, timely, diagnostic, and practical feedback.
  6. Provide opportunities for trainees to practice new behaviors.

Maintaining Performance after Training
  1. Develop learning points to assist in knowledge retention.
  2. Set specific goals.
  3. Identify appropriate reinforcers.
  4. Train significant others in how to reinforce behavior.
  5. Teach trainees self-management skills.

training, the work environment must be monitored to ensure that what was learned is retained.

Setting the Stage for Learning

Prior to launching a training program, a trainer or manager needs to consider how information will be presented. Additionally, attention should focus on the beliefs of trainees regarding task-specific competencies.

Clarity of Instructions.   Research has demonstrated that learning will not occur unless task instructions are clear and precise. As noted when discussing performance standards (Chapters 6 and 7), an employee must know what is expected in order to perform as desired. Giving clear instructions includes establishing appropriate behavioral expectations. As with performance standards (see Chapter 6), statements of training expectations should be specific, and conditions under which performance is or is not expected (e.g., Given receipt of information) should be identified, along with the behavior to be demonstrated.

   To set the stage for desired performance, it is also useful to specify up front what the reward will be for performing as desired. A trainee is more likely to be motivated if he or she knows that successful performance can lead to positive reinforcement (promotion, pay raise, recognition) or can block the administration of negative reinforcement (e.g., supervisory, criticism, firing).[53]

Use of Behavioral Models.   Even when instructions are clear, desired behavior still may not occur if the trainee does not know how to perform as desired. This problem can be overcome through **behavioral modeling.** Behavioral modeling is a visual demonstration of desired behavior. The model can be a supervisor, co-worker, or subject area expert, and the demonstration can be live or videotaped. The important thing is to show employees what needs to be done *prior* to their performance.[54]

Care is needed in choosing an appropriate behavioral model. If the model makes the task look too simple, trainees may lose confidence or quit the first time they encounter a difficulty. Thus, models should show not only how to achieve desired outcomes but also how to overcome performance obstacles.

Increasing Learning during Training

While employees should be responsible for their own learning, several factors make learning easier for adults.

Active Participation.   Individuals perform better if they are actively involved in the learning process. Participation may be direct (hands on) or indirect (role-plays and simulations). The important point is to hook the trainee on learning. Through active participation, trainees stay more alert and are more likely to be confident.

Self-Efficacy.   Even with modeling, learning may not occur if people judge themselves low in self-efficacy. **Self-efficacy** is defined as a trainee's beliefs about a task-specific ability. If individuals dwell on their personal deficiencies relative to the task, potential difficulties may seem more formidable than they really are. On the other hand, people who have a strong sense of self-efficacy are more likely to be motivated to overcome obstacles.

The choice of an appropriate training method is critical to self-efficacy. In a recent study, a group of trainees was taught how to use computer spreadsheets. People low in self-efficacy performed better when one-on-one tutorials were conducted; individuals with high self-efficacy (they believed they could easily learn how to use spreadsheets) performed better when appropriate behavior was merely modeled. Consequently, before choosing training techniques, the level of self-efficacy for each trainees should be determined.[55]

Enactive Mastery.   Self-efficacy increases when experiences fail to validate fears and when skills acquired allow for mastery of once-threatening situations. This process is called **enactive mastery.** To facilitate task mastery, trainers should arrange the subject matter so that trainees experience success. While this may be easy when tasks are simple, it can be quite difficult when tasks are complex.

Solutions include segmenting the task, shaping behavior, and/or setting proximal goals. Task segmentation involves breaking a complex task into smaller or simpler components. For some jobs (e.g., laboratory technician), the components (e.g., drawing blood, culturing a specimen, running a blood chemistry machine) can be taught individually and in any order. In others, segments must be taught sequentially because Task B builds upon Task A and Task C builds upon Task B (e.g., using mathematics, driving a car, conducting an effective interview.)[56]

Shaping includes rewarding closer and closer approximations to desired behavior. For example, in teaching managers how to conduct a selection interview, trainees can be reinforced for making eye contact and for developing situational questions.

The setting of proximal or intermediary goals also increases mastery perceptions. Consider a software developer with an overall objective of developing a new word processing package. Proximal goals might include meeting a project specifications deadline, developing algorithms for fonts by a set deadline, developing an algorithm for formatting paragraphs, and so on. These proximal goals all lead to the attainment of the distal or overall objective.[57]

Plenty of Feedback.   In order for individuals to master new concepts and acquire new skills, they must receive accurate diagnostic feedback about their performance. When feedback is not received or is inaccurate, the wrong behaviors may be practiced. While feedback can be provided by a supervisor, co-workers, customers, computers, or the individual performing the task, it must be specific, timely, behaviorally and not personally based, and practical. If a performance discrepancy exists, the feedback should also be diagnostic and include instructions or modeling of how to perform better.[58]

Practice, Practice, Practice.   While an individual may be able to perform as desired one time, the goal of training is to ensure that desired behavior occurs consistently. This is most likely to occur when trainees are able to practice and internalize standards of performance. As noted, practice of the wrong behaviors is detrimental. Therefore, practice must follow specific feedback.

It should be stressed that for some jobs, tasks must be **overlearned.** Over-learning includes the internalization of responses so that the trainee doesn't have to consciously think about behavior before responding. For example, if a plane is losing altitude rapidly, a pilot must know immediately how to respond. There isn't time to think about what should be done. The emergency routine must be second nature and internalized.

Maintaining Performance after Training

Once training has occured, the environment needs to be monitored to ensure that new behaviors will continue. Several steps can be taken to ensure that this does occur.

Development of Learning Points.   First, new skills or information is more likely to be retained when **learning points** are developed. Learning points summarize key behaviors—particularly those that are not obvious—and serve as cognitive cues back on the job. While learning points can be written by trainers, trainee-generated learning points—even if they are of lower quality—enhance recall and lead to better skill acquisition and retention.[59]

Reinforcement.   Learning new behaviors is difficult and threatening. To ensure that trainees continue to demonstrate the skill they have learned, behavior must be reinforced. **Reinforcement** can be positive (praise, financial rewards) or negative (if you perform as desired, I will quit screaming at you) but it must be performance contingent.[60]

Train Significant Others.   To ensure that reinforcers are appropriately administered, trainers must also train significant others to look for and reinforce desired changes. If a person labeled a troubled employee continues to be viewed as a problem employee, there is no incentive for the person to display new behavior. If, however, a supervisor or co-worker responds positively to the change in behavior, the frequency with which the new behavior will be displayed is likely to increase.

Set Specific Goals.   It is also useful to set specific goals for subsequent performance. These goals should be challenging but not so difficult as to be perceived as impossible. Without goals, people have little basis for judging how they are doing.[61]

Self-Reinforcement.   Because it is not always possible for significant others to reinforce an individual worker, a long-term objective should be to teach employees how to set their own goals and administer their own reinforcement. When people create self-incentives for their efforts, they are capable of making self-satisfaction contingent on their own performance. Obviously, the challenge here is to ensure that personal goals are congruent with organizational goals. As noted in previous chapters, this leads to self-management.[62]

Follow-up.   A final principle to remember is **follow-up.** Once a participant leaves the training program, the personnel and human resource manager should provide a means of follow-up to help ensure that the participant will do what was taught. All too often, participants who want to change their current behavior get back to work and slip into the old patterns. This in turn results in a significant loss of effectiveness of the training program. One approach to help prevent this from happening is the **contract plan.** Its simplicity is a key factor in its success. Each participant writes an informal agreement near the end of a training program, stating which aspects of the program he or she believes will have the most beneficial effect back on the job and then agreeing to apply those aspects. Each participant is also asked to choose another participant from the program to whom a copy of the contract is given and who agrees to check up on the participant's progress every few weeks.

Although incorporating these principles of learning is desirable, many training and development programs do not have them or are designed without consideration of individual differences, motivation, learning curves and plateaus, and reinforcement, feedback, and goal setting. Nevertheless, application of these principles of learning can increase the chances of successfully implementing a training and development program. Successful implementation also depends on selecting where the program is conducted.

ASSESSING TRAINING AND DEVELOPMENT PROGRAMS

The assessment of training and development programs is a necessary and useful activity, though in practice it is often not conducted. However, without an evaluation of results, it is impossible to tell if the training and development program met its objectives.

Assessment Criteria

Numerous ways of evaluating training and development programs have been proposed. Among the many options are changes in productivity, attitude survey results (covering, for example, satisfaction with supervisor, job satisfaction, stress, role conflict, and knowledge of work procedures), cost savings, benefit gains, and attitudes toward training.[63]

While different evaluation methods have been proposed through the years, most training experts agree that evaluation should include at least four components:

1. *Reaction to Training.* Did the trainess like the program? Was the instruction clear and helpful? Do they believe that they learned the material?
2. *Learning.* Did they acquire the knowledge and skills that were taught? Can they talk about things they couldn't talk about before? Can they demonstrate appropriate behaviors in training (role-play)?
3. *Behavior or Performance Change.* Can trainees now do things they couldn't do before (e.g., negotiate, conduct an appraisal interview)? Can they demonstrate new behaviors on the job? Is performance on the job better?
4. *Produce Results.* Were there tangible results in terms of productivity, cost savings, response time, quality, or quantity of job performance? Did the training program have utility?

The choice of criteria hinges on the level at which the training evaluation is to be conducted. For example, a short attitude survey could be used to assess the response of trainees to the course. However, such a survey would not provide information regarding learning, behavior, and results. In fact, when learning has been stressful or difficult, the trainees' reaction may even be negative.

If the objective is to assess what was learned, then paper-and-pencil tests can be used to determine knowledge acquisition. Additionally, it is possible to analyze the content of responses to such training exercises as in-basket tests, role-plays, or case analyses. While, this may indicate that learning has occured, it will not reveal whether learning has been transferred to the job.

To assess whether behavior or performance has changed, output measures, performance evaluation reports, and employee attitude surveys provide better information. For example, if employees report more positive attitudes toward supervisory communications *after* they complete an interpersonal skills program, it may be deduced (assuming other hypotheses can be ruled out) that the training resulted in behavioral change. Finally, bottom-line results might be assessed by examining work group or unit output measures or by conducting a utility analysis, which will be discussed in depth in Chapter 16.

Evaluation Designs

In addition to determining the appropriate criteria to evaluate the program, the personnel and human resource manager must select an **evaluation design.** Evaluation designs are important because they help the personnel manager determine if improvements have been made and if the training program caused the improvements. In addition to aiding in the evaluation of training programs, evaluation designs can (1) aid in evaluating any personnel and human resource program to improve productivity and the quality of work life, and (2) aid in evaluating the effectiveness of any personnel and human resource activity. Combining the data collection tools (i.e., organizational surveys) discussed in Chapter 16 with knowledge of evaluation designs can prove essential for PHRM in demonstrating its effectiveness, and that of any of its programs and activities, to the rest of the organization. Because the combination of data collection and evaluation design is vital for PHRM, evaluation design is discussed in more detail here. Review the assessment sections of all the other chapters to see how these evaluation designs might be used with data collection techniques to help measure personnel and human resource effectiveness.

The three major classes of evaluation designs are pre-experimental, quasi-experimental, and experimental.[64] Although each can be used to evaluate the effectiveness of a PHRM program, it is preferable to use the **experimental design,** which is the most rigorous. Evaluation using the experimental design allows the personnel and human resource manager to be more confident that

- A change has taken place—for example, that employee productivity has increased;
- The change is caused by the program or PHRM activity; and
- A similar change could be expected if the program were done again with other employees.

Because of many organizational constraints, however, the personnel manager is generally not able to use the experimental design and must settle for the moderately rigorous **quasi-experimental design.** Even when quasi-experimental designs are feasible, most evaluations that are done rely on the **pre-experimental design.** This design is used because it is easier and quicker. Unfortunately, this design is a poor one for most purposes. Exhibit 11.7 illustrates all three designs. This exhibit is also used to convey how programs can be evaluated using these designs and what is required. In Exhibit 11.7, X indicates that the program was administered. T_1 indicates that a measure of the variable against which the program is to be evaluated (e.g., productivity or the level of accidents) is taken. T_2 indicates that a second measure is taken on the same variable after training has occurred. Then the results of T_1 and T_2 are compared. Note that the two designs in the experimental class are different from those in the other two classes because all the individuals used in the evaluation are randomly assigned. Thus, if there are differences between T_1 and T_2, the personnel and human resource manager can be more confident that the changes were due to the program (X) and that the results can be repeated in future programs.

EXHIBIT 11.7	The Three Major Classes of Evaluation Designs Used to Help Determine Program Effectiveness

Pre-experimental	Quasi-experimental	Experimental
1. One-shot case study design 　　X　　　T_2	1. Time-series design 　$T_1T_2T_3$　X　$T_4T_5T_6$	1. Pretest/post-test control group design 　T_1　　X　　T_2 　T_1　　　　T_2
2. One-group pretest/ post-test design 　T_1　X　T_2	2. Nonequivalent control groups 　T_1　X　T_2 　T_1　　T_2	2. Solomon four-group design 　T_1　X　T_2 　T_1　　T_2 　　　X　T_2 　　　　T_2

SOURCE: Based on I. Goldstein, *Training: Program Development and Evaluation,* 2d ed. (Monterey, Calif.: Brooks/Cole Publishing Company, 1986), 157–167.

As indicated, although using the experimental design is desirable, many organizations find it difficult to randomly assign employees to training programs. Organizations generally want all employees in a section trained, not just a few who are randomly selected. Consequently, the pre-experimental design is more typical of the type of evaluations that organizations use.

TRENDS IN TRAINING AND DEVELOPMENT

As with other PHRM activities, two important trends are evident in training and development. One is the trend to establish company schools to provide specific education to employees. The other relates to the strategic importance of training and development.

Company Schools

Motorola dedicated its $10-million Galvin Center for Continuing Education in 1986. The facility contains 88,000 square feet of classrooms, individual instruction centers, an auditorium, lounges, dining facilities, and a fitness center. Affiliated with the National Technological Union, a consortium which teaches by satellite, Motorola offers courses leading to three master's degrees.

Like a growing number of corporations, Motorola is committed to company-based education. In fact, recent research suggests that 65 percent of all major firms offer some form of executive education. In 1985, there were eighteen corporate colleges which offered degrees, as well as course offerings leading to degrees at hundreds of other corporations.

Many firms are now affiliated with the National Technological Institute of Fort Collins, Colorado, which provides training for engineers via satellite transmission. Professionals from leading universities, such as Georgia Tech, Boston University, and MIT, teach classes at 24 cooperating colleges of engineering. The companies involved provide courses which come both live and on tape to suit the convenience of the students. Students interact with instructors via teleconferencing and electronic mail.

Trends in corporate training also include the development of corporate schools, the mainstay of which is education of employees and sometimes customers. McDonald's Hamburger University, which was begun in 1961, is among the oldest corporate universities. Started in a basement, the center now trains more than 2,500 students annually in the fine details of restaurant and franchise operations. General Electric, which has been an advocate of training and development for years, has an up-to-date facility in Croton-on-Hudson, New York, which it uses for divisional and group training. This is described more in the second "PHRM in the News." Citicorp operates its Citicorp Center complete with a university-size catalogue of courses for its managers, and General Motors Institute operates on a multimillion-dollar annual budget. Corporate schools have also been developed by such diverse firms as AT&T, Ford Motor Company, United Airlines, Chase Manhattan, Kodak, and Digital Equipment.

In summing up the future in corporate education, George Odiorne and Geary A. Rummler, two noted business educators, speculate that advanced and specialized training will be a way of life for the careerist of the future. While some company schools will concentrate on the operational mechanics of the business they operate, others will provide more general management education, even

Keeping New Managers on Track

First-time managers can benefit from training that allows them to practice supervisory tasks and assess their developmental needs, according to A. Nicholas Komanecky, program manager at General Electric's Management Development Institute, in Croton-on-Hudson, New York. At the heart of GE's New Managers program, Komanecky explains, is a six-day course that teaches the skills and knowledge new managers need, while steeping them in GE's corporate culture.

Training Risk-Takers

At GE, "management believes that continually challenging current practices, methods, procedures, and ideas is the way to keep the company competitive," Komanecky points out. Therefore, he notes, the company "encourages new managers to take initiative, take risks, and even challenge their managers." The training program focuses on developing such "activist" management skills, Komanecky says, outlining its three-step process:

- Initially, new managers receive a "starter kit." It includes audio-taped presentations by GE's

chairman and other experienced managers; booklets on GE systems, procedures, and supervisory situations that can arise; and a calendar containing useful tips for a manager's first months on the job.
- Between the sixth and twelfth months of the program, new managers become what GE considers "teachable," says Komanecky. During this time, they attend the six-day course.
- A communications skill-building exercise, based on behavioral-modeling concepts, caps the training program.

Skills for Leaders

Before the six-day course begins, trainees discuss their developmental needs with their managers. Other precourse work includes questionnaires on the trainees' management practices, which are completed by their peers and subordinates, and articles on corporate restructuring and the need to remain competitive.

A discussion of GE's key values—e.g., customer satisfaction, respect for others, and integrity—launches the course. Komanecky notes that the course addresses these less-technical

global education. Almost without exception, the two scholars predict, the charges for training will be paid for by the home organization of the trainees, making corporate education a business within a business.[65]

Strategic Involvement of Training and Development

Gaining Competitive Advantage.   Organizations can use their training and development activity to gain competitive advantage. For example,

> designing, manufacturing and operating increasingly complex high-technology systems demands advanced knowledge and hands-on expertise. That's why Siemens—one of the world's leading manufacturers of high-technology equipment—conducts a variety of training programs for many of its 27,000 employees, as well as for its customers, all across America.
> Siemens USA courses are designed to meet the special needs of customers and their markets. For example, on-the-job training for customers ensures that all the capabilities of the company's technolgically advanced systems are fully

topics throughout, and with them ties together the training's skill development modules.

Skills and knowledge-building, the second stage of the six-day course, teaches participants to:

- Create and lead competitive work teams;
- Communicate directly and effectively;
- Apply proven work-planning techniques in structuring tasks and manipulating work flow;
- Develop networks outside their immediate work unit;
- Coach and counsel;
- Apply corporate values to the workplace and marketplace; and
- Conduct performance appraisals and provide staff development.

Overall, the course emphasizes leadership, Komanecky maintains. For example, in one module, trainees discuss examples of leadership they have witnessed. Participants write a vision statement for implementing leadership qualities in their work units; six months later, the trainees use the statement to measure their progress. They also view a videotape of GE's chairman discussing leadership with management personnel.

In the final days of the course, practice in cooperative problem-solving brings into focus the material of the earlier program segments. The class divides into four teams; each ana-

lyzes different parts of a hypothetical problem and works to find a solution to the whole. The exercise reveals participants' teamwork strengths and pinpoints developmental weaknesses, Komanecky explains, adding that trainees also have time to examine their overall management proficiency and select areas for postcourse work.

Communication in the Real World

During the final communications skill-building phase, participants bring real management problems into the classroom for discussion and, if possible, resolution, notes Komanecky. Role plays on work-planning, performance appraisal, and career discussion provide participants with hands-on experience, and, in groups of three, trainees discuss coaching and counseling techniques and give each other feedback on personal development plans.

This part of the program stresses "building positive relationships and fostering open communication," Komanecky says. These interpersonal skills contribute to improved employee work attitudes and productivity, he adds, and help each trainee achieve managerial success.

SOURCE: "Keeping New Managers on Track," *Bulletin to Management*, 23 June 1988, p. 200. Used with permission from The Bureau of National Affairs, Inc., copyright 1988.

utilized, and all their benefits are full realized. Similarly, the special classes for Siemens engineering, manufacturing, service and administrative personnel are designed to sharpen skills, enhance professional knowledge, and improve service expertise and effectiveness.

Constant, specialized training is one of the ways Siemens is fullfilling their commitment to keep customers and employees ahead of the competition in a fiercely changing, tough and complex high-technology marketplace.[66]

Similarly, in the low-margin, highly competitive world of department-store sales,

Seattle-based Nordstrom has turned exacting standards of customer service into a billion-dollar annual business. The rapidly expanding chain, which has 46 stores in California, Washington, Oregon, Alaska, Montana and Utah, has drilled its staff incessantly with the venerable dogma that the customer is always right. Result: the chain's sales, 73% derived from women's retailing, passed the $1 billion mark for the first time in 1985 and reached an estimated $1.6 billion for 1986. Sales per square foot of space, a basic retail performance yardstick, is about double the average for the industry.

A major ingredient in Nordstrom's success is the quality of the salesclerks. They are paid about 20% better than those of competitors, and they are well trained and encouraged to do almost anything within reason to satisfy customers. In Seattle, a store salesclerk personally ironed a customer's newly bought shirt so that it would look fresher for an upcoming meeting. Thomas Skidmore, vice president of a Los Angeles–area real estate brokerage, tells of bringing back a squeaky pair of year-old shoes to a local Nordstrom outlet, hoping merely for repairs. Instead, he got a new pair of shoes free.[67]

Linking with Organizational Strategy.   As with other PHRM activities, the training and development menu also consists of many choices that link it with the organizational strategies. The first choice is the extent to which training and development focuses on the short-term versus the long-term needs of employees. To the extent that emphasis is given to the short term, there will be more training programs and fewer development programs.

Even though training may focus more on the shortrun, it can still be offered to improve an employee's skills, knowledge, and abilities to do his or her present job or to enable that employee to learn skills, knowledge, and abilities more relevant for other jobs in the organization. A similar distinction can also be made with development programs. The choice here is to provide training and development for a more narrow or a more broad application. To some degree, this choice is also influenced by whether the utilization of human resources focuses primarily on a company's need for improved quality of work life or for productivity. Although those improvements are not mutually exclusive, the primary emphasis constitutes a training and development choice.

Another critical choice is the degree to which the training and development activities are planned, formalized, and systematically linked to the other PHRM activites. At issue is how closely the training and development activities are linked with human resource planning, job analysis, recruitment, selection, performance appraisal, and compensation. Also at issue is whether these activities have been established proactively or merely in reaction to the short-term needs of the company.

Another choice is whether to deliver training and development with an individual or group orientation. Being a member of a cohortlike group can facilitate the socialization process as well as the training and development activities. Group membership can also buffer its individual members against the stress and time pressures in the company.

A final choice in training and development involves the extent of employee participation. For example, companies can allow employees to identify preferred career paths and goals. They can also allow employees to help identify their own training needs. This type of participation may better enable companies to spot training needs and performance deficiencies because employees may ordinarily attempt to hide this information from their supervisors.[68]

EXPATRIATE TRAINING AND DEVELOPMENT

The training and development of expatriates (U.S. citizens working abroad for a U.S. company) presents special problems. Management development of expatriates should take up where selection leaves off. Although only a few companies provide expatriate training, it is critical. The basic aspects of expatriate development include the following:

- Development of expatriates before, during, and after foreign assignments
- Orientation and training of expatriate families before, during, and after foreign assignments
- Development of the headquarters staff responsible for the planning, organization, and control of overseas operations[69]

This range of training is aimed at bringing about attitudinal and behavioral changes in the expatriates, their families, and the staff (here and abroad) responsible for the multinational operations.

By having such an extensive management development effort for expatriates, multinational companies can help increase the effectiveness of their expatriate managers. Such a program can also increase the likelihood of getting more domestic managers to apply for expatriate positions. To really make expatriate positions attractive, however, multinational companies must also offer commensurate salaries.[70] This in turn makes it expensive for these companies to have expatriate managers. For example, it would currently cost a company almost $200,000 a year to maintain an expatriate manager in Japan, whereas such a middle-level manager would earn about $60,000 at home. In addition to providing an attractive salary to expatriate managers, multinational companies also need to provide an attractive package of indirect compensation, including such things as 401(k) plans.[71]

Although the selection and development of expatriate managers is a large and expensive undertaking, doing this well can help multinational companies operate and compete more effectively abroad. And as the economies of nations become more interconnected, it becomes increasingly necessary for companies, especially those in the United States, to operate as multinational firms. Hence, the importance of expatriate development will continue to grow, for international as well as for national reasons.

SUMMARY

Rapidly changing technology, illiteracy, and foreign competition are putting pressure on organizations to train effectively. This requires careful attention to the three phases of training and development: assessment, program development and implementation, and evaluation. The four types of needs analysis (organizational, job, person, and demographic) discussed in this chapter are designed to systematically diagnose the short- and long-term human resource needs of an organization. When there is a difference between actual performance and desired performance, there is a training need.

In setting up a training program, there are legal considerations regarding rates of pay during training (FLSA), admission to the training programs (Civil Rights Act), content of the training program (OSHA), and degree of federal and state support for training. Following effective needs analysis, a training program must be designed and implemented. Decisions on who will be trained, who will train, and where the training will occur must be made before an appropriate training method can be selected. Cost considerations, coupled with the types of skills to be acquired (basic, interpersonal, or conceptual) and the location of the training (on-the-job, on-site, or off-the-job), have important effects on selection of an appropriate training method.

Regardless of the method chosen, the content of the training should be designed to maximize learning. Factors to consider include clear instructions, proper role models, active participation, feedback, and practice. These should be viewed in relationship to the trainees' self-efficacy or competency beliefs. It is also important to examine the work environment to ensure that new behaviors will be reinforced rather than punished.

The last major phase of training and development is the evaluation phase. Not only should the reaction to training be assessed, but also the degree of learning, the change in job behavior, and organizational outcomes should be examined against program objectives. Research design principles should guide the evaluation process.

Regarding the future of training and development, new technology in training is making it possible to train more individuals faster and more effectively. To provide the specialized training needed in today's technologically oriented environment, companies are establishing their own corporate schools.

DISCUSSION QUESTIONS

1. As a first-line supervisor, what indicators would you use to determine whether a low-performing subordinate was a selection mistake or merely in need of training?
2. Assume you have just been hired as a training specialist for a major corporation. How would you go about determining whether there was a need for training? How would your strategy differ if you were in a company with only 100 employees?
3. You have been asked to train managers in how to conduct an effective performance appraisal interview. What factors would you consider in designing the program?
4. What might be some objectives for the training program you are setting in response to question 3?
5. How could you evaluate whether your performance appraisal training program was effective?
6. When is off-the-job training preferable to on-the-job training? To on-site training? When is on-site training preferable to off-site and on-the-job training?
7. Why do organizations often overlook or lack proper methods to evaluate employee training and development programs?

CASE STUDY

Walton Memorial Hospital: Starting Up the Training Function

Dennis Springer sat at his desk looking at the notes he'd scrawled on a yellow legal pad. Today was his first day on the job. He marveled at his emotions: they seemed to vacillate between total exhilaration and stark terror. He could hardly believe he'd finally landed a job using his education, yet he wondered if he could accomplish what Walton management wanted him to do. As a matter of fact, he wasn't totally sure management knew what it wanted.

Dennis was the new training manager at Walton Memorial Hospital, a primary care hospital with 257 patient beds. Affiliated with the hospital were an on-site outpatient clinic and four small clinics located in outlying rural communities. The hospital and clinics combined to employ a work force of approximately 1,100 employees.

Dennis began his training at Oregon State University, where he completed a teaching degree. He then went to the University of Utah, where he studied human resource management, completing a master's degree. During his last year at the university, Dennis picked up an internship working part time for Linda McAlisster, training manager with the university's Personnel Office.

While Dennis had never really thought about a career in training, he found it fit well with his teaching background, and Linda was a wonderful mentor, involving him in all aspects of the training process. It is often difficult for new graduates to break into the training field. However, because of his hands-on experience at the university, Dennis had been successful in landing the position at Walton Memorial.

Medical inservice training for nursing personnel had been conducted at Walton Memorial for a number of years. However, management and general employee training represented a new endeavor. "I'm really excited about starting up my own program," thought Dennis. "It's nice not to be locked into someone else's system."

Dennis's most pressing challenge at present was determining where to begin. "I've learned that effective training must have a purpose and should focus on real training needs," he thought. "What should my major objectives be? What are the most pressing needs?" On the legal pad in front of him, he began to write down some of the things he'd learned about Walton Memorial during the selection process that resulted in his hiring.

Walton Memorial Hospital had a long and rich history, spanning over one hundred years. Its founder, Dr. Benjamin Walton, was a country doctor, known for his kindness and his "unusual gift" for healing. In the post–Civil War years, students came from as far away as Europe to study with Dr. Walton.

Management's decision to hire a training manager was triggered by events of the previous year. The health care industry was rapidly changing. Declining levels of Medicare reimbursement combined with rising health care costs to bring Walton Memorial its first financial crisis since the Great Depression. Just two weeks before Christmas, 135 employees had been laid off. Walton Memorial had always been a source of stable employment in the community, and many of those laid of felt betrayed by Walton management. Employee morale seemed to be at an all-time low.

Another factor impacting on Walton Memorial's financial condition was the erosion of its patient base by a small, private, doctor-owned hospital which was offering competitive services. This smaller hospital was viewed by many in the community as more personal and caring than Walton Memorial.

Shortly after the layoff, representatives of the Service Employees International Union began a campaign to organize a union at Memorial. In hearings before the National Labor Relations Board regarding which employees were eligible to join the union, it became apparent that many of Walton Memorial's first-line supervisors didn't perceive themselves as a part of the management team. The hospital's labor counsel advised management that if they wished to retain a nonunion work force, they should begin immediately to upgrade the skills of their first- and second-level supervisors. Effective managers at these levels can do much to quell union organizing efforts.

As to which problems demanded immediate attention, there were significant differences of opinion. The director of human resources felt poor employee morale was due to poor interpersonal skills on the part of management. Further, she was concerned that employees weren't being as helpful or as friendly to patients as they should be. The hospital administrator echoed these concerns. The lab director felt that the greatest problem was a lack of motivation on the part of hospital employees. Ms. DePuell, the director of nursing, had recently attended a seminar on the Managerial Grid and the Johari Window and wanted these topics taught to her people. The chief of staff, a physician, wanted training for those who transported patients between the nursing floors and outpatient areas of the hospital. "They're always getting lost," he complained. Finally, the director of hospital security had expressed concern that employees and supervisors were unfamiliar with fire and disaster procedures.

Dennis began to wonder if he would be able to meet this diverse set of expectations. Further, he wasn't sure that all these problems were really training problems and, if they were, which should be addressed first. "Well, I've got to start somewhere," thought Dennis. "The Executive Committee is expecting my training recommendations in four weeks!"

Case Questions

1. How should Dennis determine training needs for the hospital?
2. Is training the solution for morale problems? Why or why not?
3. What are the advantages and disadvantages with "canned" training programs such as the managerial grid and the Johari Window?

Steven H. Hanks
Utah State University

NOTES

1. G. P. Latham, "Human Resource Training and Development," *Annual Review of Psychology* 39 (1988): 545–82; "Policy Guide," *Bulletin to Management, 18 Dec. 1986, p. 420.*

2. M. L. Moore and P. Dutton, "Training Needs Analysis," *Academy of Management Review* (July 1978): 532–45.

3. "Overcoming the Illiteracy Barrier," *Bulletin to Management,* 16 Apr. 1987: pp. 3–4; For other resources see "Building a Better-Educated Workforce," *Bulletin to Management,* 24 Mar. 1988, p. 96; J. Fraze, "Common Sense' Key in U.S. War on Illiteracy," *Resource* (May 1988): 8; A. Halcrow, "Invest in the Future Work Force," *Personnel Journal* (May 1988): 14–15; R. Kuttner, "The U.S. Can't Compete without a Top-Notch Work Force," *Business Week,* 16 Feb. 1987: p. 20; L. S. Richman, "Tomorrow's Jobs: Plentiful, But. . .," *Fortune, 11 Apr. 1988, pp. 42–56;* "Workers Need 'Booster Shots of Knowledge,'" *Resource* (May 1988): 8–9.

4. For a description of the turnover and productivity relationships, see D. R. Dalton, "Absenteeism and Turnover: Measures of Personnel Effectiveness," in *Applied Readings in Personnel and Human Resource Management,* ed. R. S. Schuler, J. M. McFillen, and D. R. Dalton (St. Paul: West, 1981), 20–38; T. R. Horton, "Training: A Key to Productivity Growth," *Management Review* (Sept. 1983): 2–3.

5. A. O. Manzini, "Integrating Human Resource Planning and Development: The Unification of Strategic, Operational and Human Resource Planning Systems," *Human Resource Planning* 11, no. 2 (1988): 79–94; M. A. Sheppeck and C. A. Rhodes, "Management Development: Revised Thinking in Light of New Events of Strategic Importance," *Human Resource Planning 11, no. 2 (1988): 159–72.*

6. G. P. Latham, "Human Resource Training and Development."

7. "Customers for Keeps: Training Strategies," *Bulletin to Management,* 31 Mar. 1988, p. 104.

8. L. Therrien, "Motorola Sends Its Work force Back to School," *Business Week,* 6 June 1988, pp. 80–81. See also E. J. Metz, "Managing Change towad a Leading-Edge Information Culture," *Organizational Dynamics* (Autumn 1986): 28–40.

9. "American Workers Need More Training to Stay Competitive," *BNAC Communicator* 7, no. 4 (Winter 1987): 1, 17.

10. Reprinted, by permission of the publisher, from "The Next Elite: Manufacturing Supermanagers," by Jeanne Lynch and Dan Orne, MANAGEMENT REVIEW, April 1985, p. 49, © 1985 AMA Membership Publications Division, American Management Association, New York. All rights reserved.

11. D. Q. Mills, *The New Competitors* (New York: Free Press, 1985).

12. "Strategic Retraining and Job Security," *Bulletin to Management, 2 Apr. 1987, p. 106.*

13. "Building a Better-Educated Workforce," *Bulletin to Management;* P. Sellers, "How IBM Teaches Techies to Sell," *Fortune,* 6 June 1988, pp. 141–46; S. A. Stumpf and N. M. Hanrahan, "Designing Organizational Career Management Practices to Fit Strategic Management Objectives," in *Readings in Personnel and Human Resource Management* 2d ed., ed. R. S. Schuler and S. A. Youngblood (St. Paul: West, 1984), 326–48.

14. J. F. Bolt, "Tailor Executive Development to Strategy," *Harvard Business Review* (Nov. Dec. 1985): 168–76; "Integrating with the Business," *HR Reporter* (March 1987): 4.

15. "Ethics Exams: Focus for Too Few?" *Bulletin to Management,* 19 Feb. 1987, p. 64; R. W. Goodard, "Are You an Ethical Manager?" *Personnel Journal* (March 1988): 38–47; "Policy Guide," *Bulletin to Management, 18 Dec. 1986, p. 420;* "Values and Ethics," *HR Reporter* (March 1987): 3.

16. C. J. Bartlett, "Equal Opportunity Issues in Training," *Human Factors 20* (1978): 179–88; C. J. Bartlett, "Equal Opportunity Issues in Training," *Public Personnel Management* (Nov./Dec. 1979): 398–405; K. N. Wexley and G. P. Latham, *Developing and Training Human Resources in Organizations* (Glenview, Ill.: Scott, Foresman, 1981), 22–27.

17. "Apprenticeship and Training," *Fair Employment Practices* (No. 270, 1, 1987).

18. "Training for Promotion," *FEP Guidelines,* no. 224(3), 1984, pp. 1–8. For an excellent review of relevant court cases involving training and development, see J. S. Russell, "A Review of Fair Employment Cases in

the Field of Training," *Personnel Psychology* (Summer 1984): 261–78.

19. "Business Tackles Hard-Core Unemployment," *Business Week*, 20 Spet. 1982, pp. 86–88; "Job Training Bill Geared to Some Special Interests," *Fair Employment Report*, 6 Dec. 1982, p. 196.

20. Goldstein, *Training*, 1980; I. I. Goldstein, *Training: Program Development and Evaluation*, 2d ed. (Monterey, Calif.: Brooks/Cole, 1986); J. Laurie, "Diagnosis Before Prescription: Data Collection, Part I," *Personnel Journal* (July 1982): 494–98; W. McGehee and P. W. Thayer, *Training in Business and Industry* (New York: Wiley, 1961); S. D. Truskie, "Getting the Most from Management Development Programs," *Personnel Journal* (Jan. 1982): 66–68; J. W. Walker, "Training and Development," in *Human Resource Management in the 1980s*, ed. S. J. Carroll and R. S. Schuler (Washington, D.C.: Bureau of National Affairs, 1983).

21. T. J. Von der Embse, "Choosing a Management Development Program: A Decision Model," *Personnel Journal* (Oct. 1973): 908, McGehee and Thayer, *Training in Business and Industry*; M. L. Moore and P. Dutton, "Training Needs Analysis."

22. L. Saari, T. Johnson, S. McLaughlin, and D. Zimmerle, "A Survey of Management Training and Education Practices in U.S. Companies," *Personnel Psychology* 41 (1988): 731–45.

23. W. F. Joyce and J. W. Slocum, "Climates in Organizations," in *Organizational Behavior*, ed. S. Kerr (San Francisco: Grid, 1979); W. F. Joyce and J. Slocum, "Climate Discrepancy: Refining the Concepts of Psychological and Organizational Climates," *Human Relations* 35 (1982): 951–72; B. Schneider, "Organizational Climates: An Essay," *Personnel Psychology* 28 (1975): 447–79; B. Schneider, "Organizational Climates: Individual Preferences and Organizational Realities Revisited," *Journal of Applied Psychology* 60 (1975): 459–65; B. Schneider and A. E. Reichers, "On the Etiology of Climates," *Personnel Psychology* 36 (1983): 19–40.

24. Walker, "Training"; Goldstein, *Training*, 1986; Wexley and Latham, *Developing and Training*.

25. L. A. Berger, "A DEW Line for Training and Development: The Needs Analysis Survey," *Personnel Administrator* (Nov. 1976): 51–55.

26. R. B. McAfee and P. J. Champagne, "Employee Development: Discovering Who Needs What," *Personnel Administrator* (Feb. 1988): 92–93.

27. Latham, "Human Resource Training and Development."

28. E. L. Bernick, R. Kindley, and K. Petit, "The Structure of Training courses and the Effects of Hierarchy," *Public Personnel Journal* 13 (1984): 109–19.

29. C. Berryman-Fink, "Male and Female Managers' Views of the Communication Skills and Training Needs of Women in Management," *Public Personnel Management* 14 (1985): 307–14; Latham, "Human Resource Training and Development"; F. D. Tucker, "A Study of Training Needs of Older Workers: Implications for Human Resources Development Planning," *Public Personnel Management* 14 (1985): 85–95.

30. M. J. Kruger and G. D. May, "Two Techniques to Ensure That Training Programs Remain Effective," *Personnel Journal* (Oct. 1985): 70–75; E. E. Lawler III, "Education, Management Style, and Organizational Effectiveness," *Personnel Psychology* (Spring 1985): 1–17; M. London and S. Stumpf, "Individual and Organizational Career Development in Changing Times," in *Career Development in Organizations*, ed. D. T. Hahl (San Francisco: Jossey-Bass, 1986).

31. J. Main, "The Executive Yearn to Learn," *Fortune*, 3 May 1982, pp. 234–48; M. M. Starcevich and J. A. Sykes, "Internal Advanced Management Programs for Executive Development," *Personnel Administrator* (June 1982): 27–28.

32. T. Hornberger and R. Trueblood, "Misused and Underrated: Reading and Listening Skills," *Personnel Journal* (Oct. 1980): 809–12. Reprinted with the permission Personnel Journal, Costa Mesa, Calif. All rights reserved.

33. "AMA Designs Training Programs for Use on Personal Computers," *AMA Forum* (Dec. 1983): 29–30; W. C. Heck, "Computer-Based Training—The Choice Is Yours," *Personnel Administrator* (Feb. 1985): 39–46; V. L. Huber and G. Gray, "Channeling New Technology to Improve Training," *Personnel Administrator* (Feb. 1985): 49–57; G. Kearsley, *Computer-Based Training: A Guide to Selection and Implementation* (Reading, Mass.: Addison-Wesley, 1983); S. Schwade, "Is It Time to Consider Computer Based Training?" *Personnel Administrator* (Feb. 1985): 25–35.

34. "Training Bosses," *Time*, 7 June 1982, p. 61.

36. Goldstein, *Training, 1986.*

37. B. M. Bass and J. A. Vaughan, *Training in Industry: The Management of Learning* (Belmont, Calif.: Wadsworth, 1966), 88.

38. Goldstein, *Training*, 1986; P. S. Greenlaw and W. D. Biggs, *Modern Personnel Management* (Philadelphia: Saunders, 1979), 270–72.

39. Bureau of National Affairs, "Planning the Training Program," *Personnel Management*. BNA Policy and Practice Series, no. 41 (Washington, D.C.: Bureau of National Affairs, 1975), 205. See also Bass and Vaughan, *Training in Industry*, 89–90; and J. M. Geddes, "Germany Profits by Apprentice System," *Wall Street Journal*, 15 Sept. 1981, p. 33.

40. Bass and Vaughan, *Training in Industry*; Goldstein, *Training; 1986, D. T. Hall, *Careers in Organizations* (Santa Monica, Calif: Goodyear, 1976); J. R. Hinrichs, "Personnel Training," in *Handbook of Industrial and Organizational Psychology*, ed. M. D. Dunnette (Chicago: Rand McNally, 1976), 854.

41. T. Delone, "What Do Middle Managers Really Want from First-Line Supervisors?" *Supervisory Management* (Sept. 1977); 8–12; W. E. Sasser, Jr., and F. S. Leonard, "Let First Level Supervisors Do Their Job," *Harvard Business Review* (Mar./Apr. 1980): 113–21; L. R. Sheeran and D. Fenn, "The Mentor System," *INC.* (June 1987): 138–42; The Woodlands Group, "Management Development Roles: Coach, Sponsor, and Mentor," *Personnel Journal* (Nov. 1980): 918–21.

42. Kram, "Phases"; Baird and Kram, "Career Dynamics." See also R. W. Gooddard, "The Pygmalion Effect," *Personnel Journal* (June 1985): 10–16; J. Naisbitt, "Challenge for the 1980s: Retraining Managers," *Management Review* (Apr. 1985): 33–35; G. S. Odiorne, "Mentoring an American Management Innovation," *Personnel Administrator* (May 1985): 63–70.

43. S. Bartlett, "Our Intrepid Reporter Wheels and Deals Currencies" *Business Week*, 1 Feb. 1988, pp. 70–71; N. Madlin, "Computer-Based Training Comes of Age," *Personnel* (Nov. 1987): 64–65.

44. Huber, and Gray, "Channeling New Technology"; G. S. Odiorne and G. A. Rummler, *Training and Development: A Guide for Professionals* (Chicago: Commerce Clearing House, 1988); D. Torrence, "How Video Can Help," *Training and Development Journal* (Dec. 1985): 122–30.

45. Odiorne and Rummler, *Training and Development.*

46. Huber and Gray, "Channeling New Technology."

47. Odiorne and Rummler, *Training and Development.*

48. G. Waddell, "Simulations: Balancing the Pros and Cons," *Training and Development Journal* (Jan. 1982): 75–80.

49. For an excellent discussion of assessment centers, see V. R. Boehm, "Assessment Centers and Managemeent Development," in *Personnel Management*, ed. K. M. Rowland and G. Ferris (Boston: Allyn & Bacon, 1982), 327–62; R. B. Finkle, "Managerial Assessment Centers," in *Hankbook of Industrial and Organizational Psychology*, ed. M. D. Dunnette (Chicago: Rand McNally, 1976), 861–88.

50. S. Carey, "These Days More Managers Play Games, Some Made in Japan, as a Part of Training," *Wall Street Journal*, 7 Oct. 1982, p. 35.

51. J. P. Campbell, M. D. Dunnette, E. E. Lawler III, and K. E. Weick, Jr., *Managerial Behavior, Performance, and Effectiveness* (New York: McGraw-Hill, 1970); B. Mezoff, "Human Relations Training: The Tailored Approach," *Personnel* (Mar./Apr. 1981): 21–27.

52. "Downward Bound," *Fortune*, 15 Aug. 1988, p. 83.

53. V. L. Huber, "A comparison of Goal Setting and Pay as Learning Incentives," *Psychological Reports* 56, (1985): 223–35; V. L. Huber, "Interplay between Goal Setting and Promises of Pay-for-Performance on Individual and Group Performance: An Operant Interpretation," *Journal of Organizational Behavior Management* 7, no. 3/4 (1986): 45–64.

54. Latham, "Human Resource Training and Development."

55. A. Bandura, "Self efficacy mechanisms in human agency," *American Psychologist* 37 (1982): 122–47; A. Bandura, *Social Foundations of Thought and Action* (Englewood Cliffs, N.J.: Prentice-Hall, 1986): M. Gist, "Self efficacy: Implications for Organizational Behavior and Human Resource Management," *Academy of Management Review* 12 (1987): 472–85; M. Gist, C. Schwoerer, and B. Rosen, "Modeling Versus Nonmodeling: The Impact of Self Efficacy and Performance in Computer Training for Managers," *Personnel Psychology* (1989):; Latham, "Human Resource Training and Development."

56. Bandura, "Self efficacy mechanisms"; Bandura, *Social Foundations of Thought and Action.*

56. Huber, "Interplay between Goal Setting and Promises of Pay-for-Performance."

57. V. L. Huber, G. P. Latham, and E. A. Locke, "The Management of Impressions through Goal Setting," in *Impression Management in the Organization*, ed. R. A. Giacalone and P. Rosenfield (Hillsdale, N. J.: Erlhaun, 1989) D. R. Ilgen, C. D. Fisher, and M. S. Taylor, "Consequences of Individual Feedback on Behavior in Organizations," *Journal of Applied Psychology* 64 (1979): 349–71; E. A. Locke, "Effects of Knowledge of Results, Feedback in Relation to Standards, and Goals on Reaction-Time Performance," *American Journal of Psychology* 81 (1968): 566–75.

58. P. Hogan, M. Hakel, and P. Decker, "Effects of Trainee-Generated vs. Trainer-Provided Rule Codes on Generalization in Behavioral Modeling Training," *Journal of Applied Psychology* 71 (1986): 469–73.

59. W. Honig, *Operant Behavior* (New York: Appleton-Century-Crofts, 1966); Huber, "Interplay between Goal Setting and Promises of Pay-for-Performance"; J. S. Russel, K. Wexley, and J. Hunter, "Questioning the Effectiveness of Behavior Modeling Training in an Industrial Setting," *Personnel Psychology 34 (1984): 465–82.*

60. "A Comparison of Goal Setting and Pay"; Huber, E. Locke and G. Latham, *Goal Setting: A Motivational Technique That Works* (Englewood Cliffs, N. J.: Prentice-Hall, 1984).

61. C. Frayne and G. Latham, "The Application of Social Learning Theory to Employee Self-Management of Attendance," *Journal of Applied Psychology* 72 (1987): 387–92; Latham, "Human Resource Training and Development."

62. S. R. Siegel, "Improving the Effectiveness of Management Development Programs," *Personnel Journal* (Oct. 1981): 770–73.

63. For extensive description of training and development assessment, see M. J. Burke and R. R. Day, "A Cumulative Study of the Effectiveness of Managerial Training," *Journal of Applied Psychology* (1986): 232–45; "Cost-Effective Training Techniques," *Bulletin to Management* 21 Aug. 1986; p. 284; H. E. Fisher and R. Weinberg, "Make Training Accountable: Assess Its Impact," *Personnel Journal* (Jan. 1988): 73–75; J. Fitzenz, "Proving the Value of Training," *Personnel* (Mar. 1988): 17–23; J. K. Ford and S. P. Wroten, "Introducing New Methods for Conducting Training Evaluation and for Linking Training Evaluation to Program Redesign," *Personnel Psychology* (Winter 1984): 651–66; V. S. Kaman and J. D. Mohr, "Training Needs Assessment in the Eighties: Five Guideposts," *Personnel Administrator* (Oct. 1984): 47–53; D. L. Kirkpatrick, "Four Steps to Measuring Training Effectiveness," *Personnel Administrator* (Nov. 1983): 19–25; D. F. Russ-Eft and J. H. Zenger, "Common Mistakes in Evaluating Training Effectiveness," *Personnel Administrator* (Apr. 1985): 57–62; H. W. Smith and C. E. George, "Evaluating Internal Advanced Management Programs," *Personnel Administrator* (Aug. 1984): 118–

31; and W. G. Thomas, "Training and Development Do Make Better Managers!" *Personnel* (Jan. 1988): 52–53.

64. F. O. Hoffman, "A Responsive Training Department Cuts Costs," *Personnel Journal* (Feb. 1984): 48–53; D. L. Kirkpatrick, "Four Steps to Measuring Training Effectiveness"; H. W. Smith and C. E. George, "Evaluating Internal Advanced Management Programs"; S. B. Wehrenberg, "Evaluation of Training: Part I," *Personnel Journal* (Aug. 1983): 608–10; S. B. Wehrenberg, "Evaluation of Training: Part II," *Personnel Journal* (Sept. 1983): 698–702.

65. Odiorne and Rummler, *Training and Development*.

66. Used by permission of Siemens, Siemens, USA, New Brunwisk, New Jersey.

67. "Pul-eeze! Will Somebody Help Me?" *Time*, Feb. 1987, p. 49.

68. J. R. DeLuca, "Strategic Career Management in Non-Growing, Volatile Business Environments," *Human Resource Planning* 11, (1988): 49–62; J. Guyon, "Culture Class: GE's Management School Aims to Foster Unified Corporate Goals," *Wall Street Journal*, 10 Aug. 1987, p. 29; M. London, "Organizational Support for Employees' Career Motivation: A Guide to Human Resource Strategies in Changing Business Conditions," *Human Resource Planning* 11, no. 1 (1988): 23–32; S. A. Stumpf, "Choosing Career Management Practices to Support Your Business Strategy," *Human Resource Planning* 11, no. 1 (1988): 33–48.

69. A. Rahim, "A Model for Developing Key Expatriate Executives," *Personnel Journal* (Apr. 1983): 315.

70. C. G. Howard, "How Best to Integrate Expatriate Managers in the Domestic Organization," *Personnel Administrator* (July 1982): 27–33; A. Kupfer, "How to Be a Global Manager," *Fortune*, 14 Mar. 1988, pp. 52–58; M. E. Mendenhall, E. Dunbar, and G. R. Oddou, "Expatriate Selection, Training and Career-Pathing: A Review and Critique," *Human Resource Management* 26, no. 3 (Fall 1987): 331–45; F. Rice, "Should You Work for a Foreigner?" *Fortune*, 1 Aug. 1988, pp. 123–34; N. Shahzad, "The American Expatriate Manager," *Personnel Administrator* (July 1984): 23–28.

71. J. C. Roberts, "Section 401(k) and the Expatriate Employee," *Personnel Administrator* (July 1984): 18–21. For related issues, see R. L. Tung, *The New Expatriates* (Boston: Ballinger, 1988).

CHAPTER 12

Quality of Work Life and Productivity

Valuing People Produces Value

Steelcase Inc. (Grand Rapids, MI) has a history of valuing relationships: the company emphasizes serving the people groups in its world—customers, independent distributors, stockholders, vendors, employees and the community at large. And Steelcase's strategy of fostering mutual benefit has paid off—the company has experienced compounded annual growth of 10% or more each year. With 12,000 employees in the U.S. and Canada, Steelcase is now the largest producer of office environments.

The company is privately held by a small group of stockholders and is debt free—and not shy about reinvesting in new facilities, technology and human beings. . . .

In 1986, the company's profit sharing plan—which was started in the 1940's—paid out 72% of base pay to each employee. "I've been here since 1969, and the profit sharing plan has paid out at least 50% of base pay each year," Pearson said.

But Steelcase tries to encourage discontent. "We're always trying something new, trying to do something differently. Nobody ever said we had to be the biggest company—but we want to be the best," Paul A. Pearson, director of HRM development. "The atmosphere here is casual and informal—but intense."

In its search to apply people's skills in the best way, Steelcase recently undertook an Effectiveness Study, using management consultants A. T. Kearney. . . .

"Last year, we piloted a program that integrated the basic models into a profile on individuals, so that we have a good talent assessment. . . .

"Our whole purpose is to help answer the question: what does the organization need, what does the individual need, and how can we help the individual develop so that company and individual needs are met?

The Development Responsibility

"We take the position that human development is not totally a corporate responsibility. . . .

. . . We have a good support system in place for all employees—a tuition reimbursement program, extensive internal programs, many held right on our complex, seminars. We post jobs up to management positions, provide information about jobs (giving job descriptions, wage and salary information, and expectations for the job based on job models), and individual career counseling.

"We get about 40–50 applications for each position—last year, we filled about 1,500 positions by job posting in our salaried groups. This means that employees must be prepared to compete. We spend time helping supervisors learn to give constructive, meaningful feedback.

"In addition, we get about 35,000 unsolicited resumes each year. We have the public relations problem of insuring that we treat applicants well, and the hr problem of seeing that we select those candidates that we want. We've established an applicant tracking system to do so. Some problems are good to have."

"We formed a study team in Sept., 1986, composed of both Kearney and Steelcase staff. The Steelcase staff represented each of our major business groups. . . . We've analyzed what people do by developing a standardized instrument to measure the percent of time they spend on particular tasks. Then, we've looked at what other successful companies do, and compared them with our results.

"To identify our greatest opportunities for improvement, we formed Delphi groups. These groups reality-test ideas and findings. For example, we are addressing the issue of whether research and development should be a part of engineering or marketing, or whether sales and marketing should be combined or separate. We are looking at the impact of technology on how we do work.

"Early this year, we plan to provide feedback on the first phase of the study to 100% of our salaried people (about 500 salespeople were covered in a separate study). Then, we will hold
continued

individual meetings to cover organization and individual goals and objectives.

Integrated Systems Contribute

"Part of our effort to manage the culture revolves around our Leadership Program. Our research and experience indicate that leaders concentrate on doing the right things, while managers concentrate on doing things right. Organizations need both.

"We created a curriculum around Wilson Learning Company's Leadership Management

program. . . . Using the basic models provided by the Program, we created an assessment center that we use for development purposes (we use the assessment center as only one input on selection). At the assessment center, an individual may look at one aspect of leadership—such as determining goals—and go through some simulation and problem solving exercises. Then, we can put together a development plan specifically geared for that individual.

SOURCE: "Valuing People Produces Value," *HR Reporter* (July 1988): 6–7. Used with permission from *HR Reporter,* copyright 1988.

The preceding "PHRM in the News" highlights several issues. One is how companies continually seek to improve themselves. Another is the importance of employee participation in efforts to improve companies. A third is the variety of ways companies can gather information from their employees, e.g., Delphi groups. A fourth is the importance of managing the corporate culture and developing leadership skills. A final issue is the importance of identifying and serving the needs of the individuals and the organization. This example of Steelcase, however, represents just one company's way of improving itself.

Increasing U.S. productivity is a dilemma discussed in executive suites and by almost all personnel and human resource managers. Without increased productivity, the intense domestic and international competition will not allow any organization to survive. **Productivity** is defined here as measures or indicators of output of an individual, group, or organization in relation to (divided by) inputs or resources used by the individual, group, or organization to create outputs. Although units of output may be an appropriate measure to determine productivity in one organization, the measurement of each employee's performance against past efforts may be more appropriate in another. Whatever criterion is used, it must be (1) measurable in some way (e.g., by units of output, by valid performance appraisal results, by quality of output, or by comparisons of actual costs versus budgeted costs); (2) related to the goals of the organization (e.g., units and quality of output for a manufacturing firm and actual costs versus budgeted costs for a governmental agency); and (3) relevant to each job (e.g., units of output for a production worker and performance appraisal results for a white-collar knowledge worker).

Quality of work life (QWL), although quite different from the notion of productivity, is defined here as a process by which all members of the organization, through appropriate and open channels of communication, have some say in decisions that affect their jobs in particular and the work environment in general, resulting in greater job involvement and satisfaction and reduced levels of stress. In essence, QWL represents an organizational culture in which employees experience feelings of ownership, self-control, responsibility, and self-respect.[1] Generally in an organization characterized as having a high QWL, extensive participation, suggestions, questions, and criticism that might lead to any kind of improvement are encouraged and welcomed. In such a setting, creative discontent is viewed as a manifestation of constructive caring about the organization rather than destructive griping. Management encouragement of such feelings of involvement often leads to ideas and actions for upgrading operational effectiveness and efficiency, as well as environmental enhancement. Increased productivity, measured in work quality and quantity, is thus likely to result as a natural byproduct, as illustrated by the initial "PHRM in the News."[2]

PURPOSES AND IMPORTANCE OF QWL AND PRODUCTIVITY

The importance of QWL is reflected in the effects of its absence. Some people attribute part of the present productivity slowdown and decline in the quality of products in the United States to deficiencies in the quality of work life and to changes in the interests and preferences that employees consider important, as described in Chapter 2. People are demanding greater control and involvement in their jobs. They prefer not to be treated as cogs in a machine. When they are treated with respect and given a chance to voice their opinions and a greater degree of decision making, productivity improves, as indicated by the initial "PHRM in the News."

An equal if not greater level of attention is being paid to productivity because the level of productivity is generally a major factor in determining profitability or staying within budget. This is especially true now, with the current rate of productivity growth in the United States *less than* that in most other industrialized countries. If the United States increases its productivity, it should become more competitive in the international as well as national markets.[3]

Increasing productivity is also important because more Americans are realizing that their standard of living is *declining*. If the current trend continues, the present generation will live less well than the previous generation—a first-time occurrence in America. Interest in QWL and productivity usually focuses on changing aspects of the organization to improve:

- Employee satisfaction and, consequently, absenteeism and turnover
- Job involvement to increase employee understanding and commitment to their jobs
- Performance and, consequently, organizational profitability, competitiveness, and survival[4]

Programs for both QWL and productivity are critical for effective PHRM.

RELATIONSHIPS INFLUENCING QWL AND PRODUCTIVITY IMPROVEMENT

Relationships with Other PHRM Activities

Even when PHRM activities operate effectively, QWL and productivity improvement programs may or may not be needed as supplements. It is also possible to base QWL or productivity programs in other areas, such as pay plan programs. As shown in Exhibit 12.1 QWL and productivity programs are interrelated with other PHRM programs.

EXHIBIT
12.1
Relationships of and Programs for Quality of Work Life and
Productivity Improvements

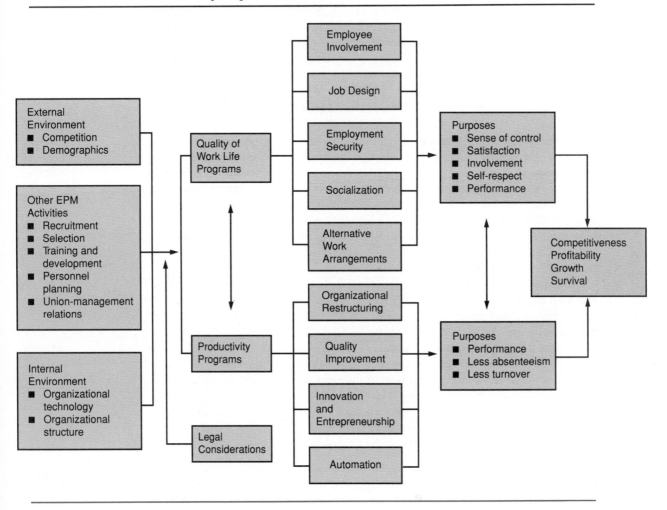

Training and Development.   For QWL programs to work effectively, managers may need to be taught the basics of participative management. Employees also need skill in self-management. Alternatively, if QWL programs reduce turnover and absenteeism, less training, particularly employee orientation, will be needed.[5]

Union-Management Relations.   The success of QWL programs also hinges on worker-management cooperation. Traditionally structured jobs may need to be redesigned, and in unionized environments, these modifications *must* be approved by the union. While some unions may favor innovations to save jobs, others do not care to be a party to improvement programs. For the latter group, involvement blurs the distinction between the roles of management and labor.[6]

Relationships with the Internal Environment

Although top management must be behind efforts to improve productivity and QWL, productivity and QWL programs are also affected by the technology and structure of the organization.

Organizational Technology.   The **technology** of an organization refers to the machines, methods, and materials that are used to produce the organization's product.

Although technology can strongly influence job design, organizations can sometimes choose the type of technology they want to use to make a product. For example, in the manufacture of automobiles, General Motors, Ford, and Chrysler have traditionally chosen to use the assembly line. This, however, is not the only way to make cars. Volvo in Sweden is an example in which a nonassembly-line method was adopted.[7] This switch in technologies represented more than a change in technology; it also represented a way of thinking about people as human resources. People no longer were thought of as replaceable parts but rather as irreplaceable components of the organization. In diagnosing the technology, one must consider its impact on job design, the variety of technologies that can be used in making a product, and the organization's philosophy about its human resources.

Organizational Structure.   Just as technology can limit efforts to improve productivity and QWL, so can organizational structure. This is particularly true for control structure in the organization. Because locating who is responsible for problems or errors is important, control structures often specify who is accountable, how things should be done, and from whom to get approval for doing something differently. Although this helps reduce the complexity of each job and the responsibility of each worker, the effect is to set up impersonal boundaries. The boundaries then become critical in the way people behave and what they will not do.

Changing control structures is just as difficult as changing technology. Yet both need to be changed to facilitate job design changes. Furthermore, particular types of job designs are unlikely to be adopted, given the philosophies of key decision makers. For example, if the top management or owners want to retain close control, or if they don't think employees can act responsibly, they will likely choose the scientific approach to job design rather than one of the contemporary approaches discussed later in this chapter.[8]

Relationships with the External Environment

Intense levels of domestic and international competition are forcing organizations to be more productive. As illustrated in the first "PHRM in the News," the more effective management of human resources is seen as a way to help organizations improve their productivity. Because of the nature of work force demographics, many of the efforts to better manage human resources use some form of employee involvement or participation.[9] This is consistent with the preferences of many individuals in the 25- to 54-year-old age group for greater involvement and a greater say in work place decisions.

LEGAL CONSIDERATIONS IN QWL AND PRODUCTIVITY

In establishing QWL programs, organizations must operate within the parameters of the Wagner Act of 1935. This law states that a **labor organization** is an "organization of any kind or any agency or employee representative committee or plan in which employees participate or which exists for the purpose, in whole or in part, of dealing with employers" regarding working conditions and terms. Organizations that interfere with the formation or administration of labor organizations or that contribute financially to their support can be charged with unfair labor practices.

While the courts traditionally have interpreted the Wagner Act strictly, recent National Labor Relation decisions have been more liberal and have recognized that not all employee committees constitute a "labor organization" (*General Foods Corp.*, 1977; *Sparks Nugget*, 1977). Based on rulings to date, it appears that employers can establish QWL programs involving committees, worker cooperation, and communication, providing the committee

- Does not serve as a bargaining agent for employees;
- Is composed predominately of employee, not management, representatives who choose to voluntarily participate;
- Is designed to serve limited roles; and
- Cannot be traced to a union-organizing drive.

In unionized environments, the establishment of programs to improve productivity and QWL can and should be bargained over with the union.

QWL IMPROVEMENT PROGRAMS

Programs for QWL improvements include (1) quality circles (QC), (2) job design, (3) job security and full employment and (4) alternative work arrangements. All these programs share an orientation of concern and respect for employees.

Quality Circles

Since Honeywell and Lockheed first introduced quality circles in the United States, more and more corporations have developed similar programs. Among the 1,500–2,000 companies running more than 2,500 circles are Bethlehem Steel, Westinghouse, Ford, Solar Turbine, Hughes Aircraft, General Electric, Boeing, Martin Marietta, RCA, Control Data, and General Motors. While the success of quality circles in Japan initially stimulated interest in quality circles, they are now popular in the United States for several other reasons:

1. *The programs are accessible.* The fact that a wealth of consultants can provide a "turn key" product for a fixed price is appealing.
2. *Quality circles are manageable.* Management can control the number of employees participating and the cost of the programs.
3. *They preserve management authority.* First-line supervisors generally facilitate circle discussion, and top management has the final decision-making authority.
4. *They are a fad.* The ranks of QC adopters are somewhat swollen by faddists who like to experiment with new ideas.

5. *They are good for public relations.* Ford Motor Company is just one of many firms to get good mileage out of press coverage of their QC program.[10]

A quality circle consists of seven to ten people from the same work area who meet regularly to define, analyze, and solve quality and related problems in their area.[11] Because membership is strictly voluntary, unions have not opposed the introduction of QCs.[12] To reinforce the existing organizational authority pattern, the first-line supervisor usually runs the team meeting and serves as a facilitator. During the initial group meeting, QC members are trained in problem-solving techniques, including brainstorming, cause-and-effect analysis, histograms, control charts, and scatter diagrams.

A few spectacular cases demonstrate that QC programs can benefit companies enormously. At GM's Packard Electric plant in Warren, Ohio, worker-management suggestions regarding the construction of four factories resulted in a $13.5-million cost reduction and a $4.5-million inventory reduction. Injury, grievance, and absenteeism rates were the lowest in the industry. Prior to implementing QCs, GM's Tarrytown, New York, plant represented everything bad about union-management relations (sabotage, resentment, contentiousness). Once union members became involved, absenteeism dropped from 7 to 2.5 percent; grievances fell from 2,000 to only 30. Bethlehem Steel's Los Angeles works reduced operating costs by $225,000 over two months following QC recommendations for reducing production downtime. Anecdotal evidence suggests that QC programs also increase communication and enhance satisfaction, teamwork, and group cohesion. Together, these results suggest that employees themselves may be the key to productivity gains.[13]

Despite their potential for productivity gains, QCs have not been an unmitigated success. Even in Japan, it is estimated that more than a third of all circles contribute nothing to their organizations. QC success often hinges on several factors:

■ *Avoiding overexpectations.* A QC is not a panacea. It can help identify problems and solutions. However, ideas generated by the group may be no better than those of the best member. And it can't be assumed that because it worked in Japan, the technology is transferable. The two cultures are quite different. The Japanese have traditionally used small work groups with norms and shared worker dependency which result in long-term relationships with peers. Americans are accustomed to financial inducements and put their personal interests ahead of group well-being.[14]
■ *Selecting group members carefully.* Participation should be voluntary, with members selected because of their technical expertise and internalization of organizational norms.
■ *Providing organizational support.* Organizations must be committed to nurturing and maintaining the groups and be ready to *act* on viable ideas. A recent study of two QC programs in government facilities showed that circles also must be given sufficient time to develop operating procedures.[15]
■ *Defining what the organization wants.* Objectives must be clearly communicated to QC members. Because QCs focus on solving operations problems, members must have the expertise and experience to make a substantive contribution. They also must have the communication skills to present their ideas and the political savvy to understand political ramifications of their suggestions.

Consequently, care needs to be taken in establishing and setting objectives for quality circles.

Job Design Approaches

Jobs can be designed in many different ways, four of which are discussed here. Other methods of designing jobs are essentially combinations of these four major approaches.

Scientific.   Under the **scientific approach,** job analysts (typically industrial engineers) take special pains to design jobs so that the tasks performed by employees do not exceed their abilities. The jobs designed by scientific management often result in the work's being partitioned into small, simple segments. These tasks lend themselves well to motion and time studies and to incentive pay systems, each for the purpose of obtaining high productivity. The scientific approach to job design still is an important part of many present organizational structures described in Chapter 2.[16]

Through meticulous human engineering and close scrutiny of its 152,000 employees, United Parcel Service (UPS) has grown highly profitable, despite stiff competition. According to Larry P. Breakiron, the company's senior vice-president of engineering, "Our ability to manage labor and hold it accountable is the key to our success."[17] In other words, in the business where "a package is a package," UPS succeeds as a result of its work standard/simplification method. This method has been the key to gains in efficiency and productivity since the privately held company was founded in 1907. As early as the 1920s UPS engineers cut away the sides of UPS trucks to show how the drivers performed. The engineers then made changes in techniques to enhance worker efficiency.

Time and motion studies also enable the company to closely monitor the performance of the workers. At UPS, more than 1,000 industrial engineers use time study to set standards for a variety of closely supervised tasks. In return, the UPS drivers, all of whom are Teamsters, earn wages of approximately $15 per hour—a dollar or so more than the drivers at other companies. Because of the company's success, they also offer job security to those employees who perform at acceptable levels.

Individual Contemporary.   Concerned over the human costs associated with the scientific approach, organizations began searching for alternative job design approaches. Following on the heels of Herzberg, Hackman and Oldham developed their job characteristics model. As shown in Exhibit 12.2, five positive personal and work outcomes—high motivation, high-quality work performance, increased satisfaction, low absenteeism, and low turnover—result when an employee works in an environment in which work is meaningful, there is knowledge of results, and there is responsibility for work outcomes.

According to these researchers, these three critical psychological states evolve from five core dimensions: (1) skill variety (the degree to which tasks are performed that require different abilities and skills); (2) job identity (the degree to which a whole and identifiable piece of work with a visible outcome is produced); (3) job significance (the degree to which the job has substantial importance); (4) autonomy (the degree of freedom and discretion allowed in work scheduling and procedures); and (5) feedback (the amount of direct and clear information obtained about performance effectiveness). When people value feelings of accomplishment and growth, enriching jobs can lead to positive outcomes.[18]

Several different strategies can be used to stimulate core job characteristics. For example, **job rotation** doesn't change the nature of a specific job, but it

EXHIBIT
12.2

The Impact of the Core Job Characteristics on
Employee Psychological States

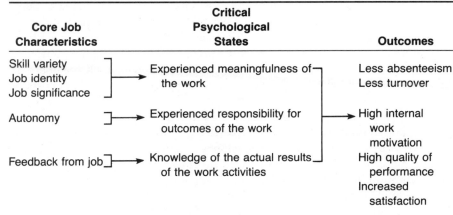

Core Job Characteristics	Critical Psychological States	Outcomes
Skill variety Job identity Job significance	Experienced meaningfulness of the work	Less absenteeism Less turnover
Autonomy	Experienced responsibility for outcomes of the work	High internal work motivation
Feedback from job	Knowledge of the actual results of the work activities	High quality of performance Increased satisfaction

SOURCE: Adapted from J. R. Hackman and G. R. Oldham, *Work Redesign,* © 1980, Addison-Wesley Publishing Company, Inc., Reading, Mass. Pg. 77, figure 4.2. Reprinted with permission.

does increase the number of duties an employee performs over time. This increases task variety and also may boost job identity and scope of purpose because the employee is performing several jobs.

Job enlargement is the opposite of the scientific approach, which seeks to reduce the number of duties. It has the potential of increasing skill variety. Task identity can also be improved when the employee completes a whole and identifiable piece of work.

Horizontal loading involves adding more duties with the same types of task characteristics; **vertical loading** means creating a job with duties that have many different characteristics. The former approach may increase skill variety, but it is also likely to foster resentment because the employee is expected to do more of the same. Vertical loading is more promising because it closes the gaps between planning, doing, and controlling the work. As a result, it affects job autonomy, skill variety, and possibly feedback.

Client relationships can be established by placing quality control closer to the worker and providing summaries of performance to workers. When this occurs, task significance, skill variety, and feedback are increased. For example, Exhibit Systems of Salt Lake City designs industrial displays for trade shows. Its manufacturing team goes to trade shows and sets up displays; thus, any problems are directed to the workers—not to an intermediary or the account manager.

Finally, organizations can open communication channels by placing quality closer to the worker and by providing summaries to workers. Emery Air Freight improved performance substantially by having employees mark a checklist each time they used appropriate containers.

Team Contemporary. Whereas the individual contemporary and scientific approaches design jobs for individuals, the **team contemporary approach** designs jobs for teams of individuals. The final designs generally show a concern for the social needs of individuals as well as the constraints of the technology.

Here, teams of workers often rotate jobs and may follow the product they are working on to the last step in the process. If the product is large—for example, an automobile—teams may be designed around sections of the final car. Each group then completes only a section and passes its subproduct to the next team. In the team contemporary design, each worker learns to handle several duties, many requiring different skills. Thus, they can satisfy preferences for achievement and task accomplishment and some preferences for social interaction.

When faced with decisions, teams generally try to involve all members. If their decisions and behaviors result in greater output, all team members share the dollar benefits.

Some recent manufacturing innovations draw from this approach for their success. For example, **cellular manufacturing** rearranges the traditional job shop layout by clustering different machines together and gives work teams a "whole" piece of work to complete. **Zero inventory systems** are premised on the assumption that rather than allowing inventory to build up in queues, production should stop until the bottleneck or work problem is solved. Workers pitch in to solve the problem, rather than waiting for solutions.

Ergonomics.   Ergonomics is concerned with trying to design and shape jobs to fit the physical abilities and characteristics of individuals so they can perform the jobs. The **ergonomic approach** is being used to redesign jobs to accommodate women, as well as handicapped individuals. Often this serves equal employment opportunity and affirmative action objectives. This approach is even helping to serve as an alternative to retirement. Studies have shown that when jobs are designed along ergonomic principles, worker productivity is greater.

In a recent study done by the National Institute for Occupational Safety and Health (NIOSH), two groups of employees working under an incentive pay system were compared. The group working on jobs designed according to ergonomic principles was 25 percent more productive than the group working on the jobs designed without these principles. NIOSH, along with several unions, is also actively involved in redesigning jobs using ergonomic principles to help reduce the incidence and severity of **carpal tunnel syndrome,** which is characterized by numbness, tingling, soreness, and weakness in the hands and wrists. It is caused or aggravated by jobs requiring repetitive hand motions, such as those used by meat cutters. Jobs are being successfully redesigned using ergonomic principles to eliminate these motions by companies such as Armco, Inc., and Hanes Corporation.[19]

Which Design to Use?   Exhibit 12.3 shows some of the advantages and disadvantages to consider in selecting a job design. The decision of which job design to implement is a complex one and includes the following steps:

1. Recognize a need for a change and gather prechange data for evaluation.
2. Determine that task redesign is the appropriate change.
3. Diagnose the organization, work flow, group processes, and individual needs.
4. Determine how, when, and where to change jobs.
5. Provide for training and support if necessary.
6. Make the job changes.
7. Evaluate the change by comparing postchange data with prechange data.[20]

A Summary of Some of the Advantages and Disadvantages of the Four Job Design Approaches

EXHIBIT
12.3

Approach	Advantages	Disadvantages
Scientific	Ensures predictability Provides clarity Fits abilities of many people Can be efficient and productive	May be boring May result in absenteeism, sabotage, and turnover
Individual contemporary	Satisfies needs for responsibility, growth, and knowledge of results Provides growth opportunity Reduces boredom Increases quality and morale Lowers turnover	Some people prefer routine and predictability May need to pay more because more skills needed Hard to enrich some jobs Not everyone wants to rotate
Team contemporary	Provides social interaction Provides variety Facilitates social support Reduces absenteeism problem	People may not want interaction Requires training in interpersonal skills Group no better than weakest member
Ergonomics	Accommodates jobs to people Breaks down physical barriers Makes more jobs accessible to more people	May be costly to redesign some jobs Structural characteristics of the organization may make job change impossible

Employment Security

Employment security is another option. For example,

> Sony Corporation has had a plant in San Diego for many years. Several years ago the company encountered a sudden decline in sales. Soon the San Diego plant was piling up inventory, and then had to begin reducing production. Where were costs to be cut?
>
> The American managers of the plant requested permission from headquarters in Japan to begin work force reductions. They received a refusal. They renewed the request, pointing out that sales were way down and that significant losses would soon appear on the bottom line. To this, Akio Morita, the founder of Sony, replied, "Think of the opportunity." "What opportunity?" the American managers persisted. "We are going to be drowning in red ink." "Think of the opportunity," Morita repeated. Then he explained. "If we keep the American work force with us through these difficult times, then they will understand that we are really committed to them. And they will be committed to us."
>
> There was no layoff. The company absorbed losses for a while until business recovered. In the next few years the San Diego plant performed very well, in some instances even outperforming the company's plants in Japan—the first foreign facility of Sony to do so.[21]

Other organizations, small as well as large, have also considered the opportunity from offering employment security. Managers know layoffs are expensive.

The costs of layoffs include lower employee involvement and loyalty, severance pay, higher unemployment compensation taxes, continuation of health and other benefits for a period after the layoff, legal and administrative expenses, and the expense of rehiring and training workers when recalled. In addition to these, companies face the costs of lower productivity and the lack of ability to compete in world markets.

Still, offering employment security is probably unwise if an organization is already overstaffed or pursuing a strategy of liquidation or divestment. As several major computer firms found out in the 1980s, full employment or job security provisions are easy to maintain during periods of growth but difficult to endure during economic downturns.

A solution is to have a core of full-time employees with job guarantees. This core work force can be augmented by **contingent** or **buffer employees.** According to Audrey Freedman, an economist with the Conference Board, one out of every four workers today is actually a contingent worker. They include freelancers and contract workers, temporary office and accounting personnel, and part-timers. Because the size of the work force can be quickly reduced or increased to match business needs, the deployment of buffer employees increases staffing flexibility. And because contingent workers receive no pensions, vacations, or holiday pay and there is no obligation to train them, they also cost less. This situation is applauded by business strategists concerned with costs because it reduces labor costs per unit of output enormously.[22]

Alternative Work Arrangements

This may be the decade in which Americans free themselves from the tyranny of the time clock. Already more than 10 million workers have taken advantage of several types of **alternative work arrangements.** Far from representing a decline in the work ethic, alternative work arrangements seem to strengthen it by reducing the stresses caused by the conflicts among job demands, family needs, leisure values, and educational needs. Thus, organizations can expect to reduce absenteeism and turnover by offering alternatives to their standard work arrangements.[23]

Standard Work Schedules.   Since the end of World War I, shift work systems have become more prevalent in industrialized countries. Currently about 20 percent of all industrial workers in Europe and the United States are on shift work schedules. The percentage of employees on part-time schedules has also increased steadily—from approximately 15 percent in 1954 to 23 percent today. All these standard work schedules have advantages and disadvantages, as Exhibit 12.4 shows. Initially, employees may select a given schedule, but after that, the days of the week (five) and the hours of the day (eight) are generally fixed. Because employee preferences and interests change over time, what had once been an appropriate work schedule may no longer be so. If alternative arrangements are not provided, the employee may leave the organization. Furthermore, the organization may have a difficult time attracting similar types of employees.[24] As a result, more organizations have learned that it pays to give employees a choice between nonstandard and standard schedules.

Flextime Schedules.   The flextime schedule is popular with organizations because it decreases absenteeism, increases employee morale, fosters better

Advantages and Disadvantages of Standard Work Schedules

EXHIBIT
12.4

Type of Schedule	Advantages	Disadvantages
Regular	Allows for standardization, predictability, and ease of administration; consistent application for all employees	Does not fit needs of all employees; not always consistent with preferences of customers
Shift	More effective use of plant and equipment; allows continuous operation and weekend work	Can be stressful, especially if rotating shifts; lower satisfaction and performance
Overtime	Permits more efficient utilization of existing work force; cheaper than alternatives; allows flexibility	Job performance may decline; may not be satisfying and may contribute to employee fatigue
Part-time	Allows scheduling flexibility to the organization, enabling it to staff at peak and unusual times; cheaper than full-time employees	Applicable to only a limited number of jobs; increases cost of training; no promotion opportunities

SOURCE: From "Part-Time and Temporary Employees," ASPA–BNA Survey 25, *Bulletin to Management*, 5 Dec. 1974, p. 5. Reprinted by permission from *Bulletin to Management*, copyright 1974 by The Bureau of National Affairs, Inc., Washington, D.C.

labor-management relations, and encourages a high level of employee participation in decision making, self-control, and discretion. Simply stated, fl**extime** is a schedule that gives employees a daily choice in the timing of work and nonwork activities. Consideration is given to **band width,** or maximum length of the workday. This band (often ranging between ten and sixteen hours) is divided into core time and flexible time. **Core time** is when the employee *has to work;* **flexible time** allows the employee the freedom to choose the remaining work time.

Among the advantages of flextime is its ability to generally increase employee productivity. It also allows organizations to accommodate employee preferences, some of which may be legally protected, such as reasonable religious obligations. On the other hand, flextime forces the supervisor to do more planning, makes communications sometimes difficult between employees (especially with different schedules), and complicates record keeping of employees' hours. Furthermore, most flextime schedules still require employees to work five days a week.

Compressed Work Weeks. An option for employees who want to work fewer than five days is the **compressed work week.** By extending the workday beyond the standard eight hours, employees generally need to work only three to four days to equal a standard forty-hour week.[25] For example, at two General Tire and Rubber plants, some employees work only two twelve-hour shifts each weekend and yet are considered full-time employees. Compressed work weeks are becoming especially popular for certain occupations, such as nursing.

At the same time, compressed work weeks permit an organization to make better use of its equipment and decrease turnover and absenteeism. Scheduling and legal problems may accompany such arrangements, but legal exceptions can be made, and scheduling can become a joint negotiation process between supervisor and employees.

Permanent Part-Time Work and Job Sharing.   Traditionally, part-time work has meant filling positions that lasted only for a short time, such as those in retail stores during holiday periods. Now some organizations have designated **permanent part-time (PPT)** positions. A permanent part-time work schedule may be a shortened daily schedule (e.g., from 1:00 to 5:00 P.M.) or an odd-hour shift (e.g., between 5:00 and 9:00 P.M.). Organizations can also use PPT schedules to fill in the remainder of a day composed of two ten-hour shifts (representing a compressed work week).[26]

Job sharing is a particular type of part-time work. In job sharing, two people divide the responsibility for a regular full-time job. Both may work half the job, or one could work more hours than the other. Part-time workers generally receive little or no indirect compensation, but workers on permanent part-time and job-sharing schedules often do.

Both PPT positions and job sharing provide staffing flexibility that can expand or contract to meet actual demands, using employees who are at least as productive, if not more so, than regular full-time employees. Individuals benefit from being able to enjoy permanent work with less than a full-time commitment to the company.

Industrial and Electronic Cottages.   Increasingly, individuals are working at home. Scientific personnel can work at home when they have computer terminals linked to the mainframe at their regular office or plant. In essence, the employee's home becomes an **electronic cottage.** Individuals may also take work home that involves assembly, such as small toys, circuit boards, or art objects. After a batch is done, the worker takes it to the regular plant and turns it in for more parts. In this example, the home becomes an **industrial cottage.**[27]

One drawback, however, is the difficulty of protecting the health and safety of the employee at home. Another is ensuring that workers are still paid a fair wage for their work. State and federal laws can also restrict home work. For example, a federal law prohibits commercial knitting at home. These restrictions must be dealt with carefully if such expanding cottages are to remain a viable option.

PROGRAMS FOR PRODUCTIVITY IMPROVEMENTS

As with QWL, productivity improvements can represent the results of a wide range of programs. For example, Citizens and Southern National Bank in Georgia completely turned around its operations with a new top management that emphasized a hard-nosed management by objectives program.[28]

A less frequently used approach to improving productivity was Intel's "work more hours" solution. Intel Corporation, based in Santa Clara, California, asked its 5,100 professional managers to work fifty hours a week instead of forty for the same pay. Intel's purpose in using this solution was to increase the pace at which new money-making products were produced.[29]

In addition to these examples, other programs to improve productivity include (1) organizational restructuring, (2) quality improvement, (3) innovation and intrapreneurship, and (4) automation.

Organizational Restructuring

Faced with intense competition and a rapidly changing environment, organizations are responding by restructuring themselves. Although this restructuring is done in a variety of ways, two ways involving PHRM are downsizing and decentralizing.

Downsizing. **Downsizing,** or the act of eliminating employees by permanent layoffs, cutbacks, attrition, early retirement, and termination, is proving an effective way of improving productivity. In essence, downsizing is done to make organizations "lean and mean." It hits service industries as well as manufacturing. According to W. James Fish, Ford Motor Company's personnel planning manager, "We're looking at a total restructuring of American business and it appears as if middle management is one of the hardest hit areas on cost-cutting efforts."[30]

> The reasons for the ever-tightening grip on executives are as diverse as the companies involved. For companies plagued by financial problems, it's an obvious way to save money. And it's easy, too, since middle managers rarely enjoy the job protection afforded by unions at the blue-collar level or the employment contracts enjoyed by top management. In addition, administrative jobs have little direct impact on output, making them more dispensable than manufacturing positions.[31]

Decentralizing. Although downsizing is done because it is easy, saves money quickly, and improves productivity, it can also stimulate the remaining employees. This last benefit occurs when the downsizing results in decentralized authority and decision making. By **decentralizing,** organizations move decision making farther down the organization. This enhances employee involvement in the company and improves productivity. Quality is also improved, especially when accompanied by training programs. These aspects of decentralizing are illustrated in the "PHRM in the News" on Burlington.

Visually the results of downsizing efforts and decentralizing activities are depicted in Exhibit 12.5. This exhibit shows the traditional pyramid-shaped organization going to a rectangle in the future.

Quality Improvement

At Xerox, CEO David Kearns defines quality as "being right the first time, every time."[32] The implications for managing people are significant. The "total quality approach" at Corning Glass Works is about people, according to James Houghton, Corning CEO. At Corning, good ideas for product improvement often come from employees. In order to carry through on their ideas, Corning workers form short-lived "corrective action teams" to solve specific problems:

PHRM IN THE NEWS

Burlington Weaves Decision Making Throughout The Organization

In the past 10 years, Burlington Industries has made major business changes and faced highly competitive and critical times. To survive and to succeed, it has sold off some of its businesses, reduced the number of employees, spent more than $2 billion in improved and better equipment, upgraded employees' skills, consolidated plants and decentralized.

To make these changes work, Burlington has had to involve its employees to make them understand the changes and to communicate the reasons behind the changes.

Ten years ago, says Michaels, the company had between 65,000–70,000 employees. "Now we're just under 40,000," he says. The textile industry has been the victim of a tremendous amount of import products. As a result, Burlington has been sorting its markets, adjusting production capabilities and staffing, selling off some of its businesses and identifying the appropriate markets to be in.

And to be able to respond to new product developments and changes more rapidly, the organization is changing to give Burlington's divisions more autonomy.

Markets are changing rapidly these days, he explains, and "in our business the life of a product is not as long as it once was. We're hopeful the technology available combined with decision making on an operating level will help divisions identify market needs more quickly and act on them more quickly," explains Michaels.

"I truly believe these moves are good for the times. Now seems to be a time to decentralize, to allow people to have the freedom to make plans and decisions, to succeed, fail or survive" on their own.

"We are working toward work teams, quality circles, participative management . . . or whatever you want to call it. We have several hundred quality circles and work teams" in operation, and they are the focus of additional training and communications efforts.

To make these changes work, says Michaels, employees have to be made aware of the production goals and the work schedules, and they have to develop a commitment to new projects, such as Burlington's "just-in-time" production concept.

"We're trying to move products as fast as we can" based on customer demand and to reduce inventory, says Michaels. That is part of the rationale behind the "just-in-time" production concept: The product is delivered "just in time."

A production program like this requires "an awful lot of customer linkage" and training says Michaels. To stress the concept, "customer linkage is a concept heard every day in our operations along with high quality standards," he adds.

"A lot of our managers are going through training programs on quality engineering and quality requirements.

"Our management is very conscious of the importance of training and development," says Michaels, "and we have a very extensive personnel development program."

SOURCE: M. Magnus, "Personnel Policies in Partnership with Profit," *Personnel Journal* (Sept. 1987): 104–5. Reprinted with the permission of PERSONNEL JOURNAL, Costa Mesa, CA., all rights reserved.

Employees [also] give their supervisors written "method improvement requests," which differ from ideas tossed into the traditional suggestion box in that they get a prompt formal review so the employees aren't left wondering about their fate. In the company's Erwin Ceramics plant, a maintenance employee suggested substituting one flexible tin mold for an array of fixed molds that shape the wet ceramic product baked into catalytic converters for auto exhausts.[33]

At Corning, then, quality improvement involves getting employees committed to quality and continual improvement. While policy statements emphasizing

---

Evolving Shape of the Corporate Organization

EXHIBIT
12.5

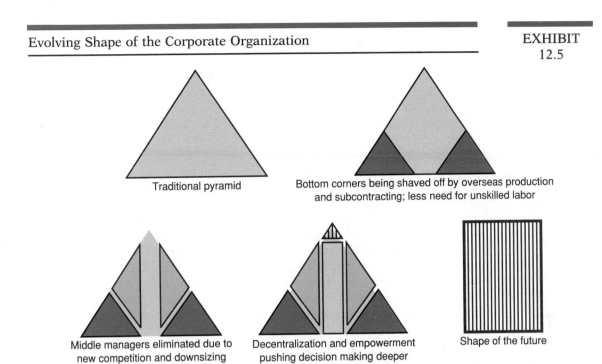

Traditional pyramid

Bottom corners being shaved off by overseas production and subcontracting; less need for unskilled labor

Middle managers eliminated due to new competition and downsizing

Decentralization and empowerment pushing decision making deeper into the organization

Shape of the future

SOURCE: J. Coates, "An Environmental Scan: Projecting Future Human Resource Trends," *Human Resource Planning* 10, no. 4 (1987): 232. Used with permission.

---

the "total quality approach" are valuable, they are also followed up with specific PHRM practices. At Corning and elsewhere, feedback systems are in place, teamwork is permitted and facilitated, decision making and responsibility are a part of everyone's job description, and job classifications are flexible.

Quality improvement often means changing the processes of production in ways that require workers to be more involved and to be more flexible. As the nature of the jobs change, so must job classification systems. At Brunswick's Mercury Marine Division, the number of job classifications was reduced from 126 to 12. This has permitted greater flexibility in the use of production processes and the employees. In the Marine Division today, machine operators inspect their work and do preventive maintenance in addition to running the machines. It is because of human resource practices such as these that people have become committed to the firm and hence are willing to give more.

Because quality improvement typically involves greater employee commitment and utilization, fewer employees are needed to produce the same level of output. For example, L. L. Bean's sales have increased tenfold while the number of employees has risen only fivefold.[34] Thanks to a quality improvement program and a cooperative work force, Toyota is producing 3.5 million vehicles a year with 25,000 production workers—the same number of workers it took to produce 1 million vehicles in 1966. Not only are Toyota workers more productive, but also rejects for poor quality are fewer. This further reduces the need for employees.[35]

Ford Motor Company, which has become a leader in quality improvement programs, follows the principles of W. Edwards Deming. The fourteen points listed below guide Ford's programs:

- Create consistency and continuity of purpose.
- Refuse to allow commonly accepted level of delay for mistakes, defective material, defective workmanship.
- Eliminate the need for and dependence upon mass inspection.
- Reduce the number of suppliers. Buy on statistical evidence, not price.
- Search continually for problems in the system and seek ways to improve it.
- Institute modern methods of training, using statistics.
- Focus supervision on helping people to do a better job. Provide the tools and techniques for people to have pride of workmanship.
- Eliminate fear. Encourage two-way communication.
- Break down barriers between departments. Encourage problem solving through teamwork.
- Eliminate the use of numerical goals, slogans, posters for the workforce.
- Use statistical methods for continuing improvement of quality and productivity and eliminate all standards prescribing numerical quotas.
- Remove barriers to pride of workmanship.
- Institute a vigorous program of education and training to keep people abreast of new developments in methods, materials, and technologies.
- Clearly define management's permanent commitment to quality and productivity.[36]

Innovation and Intrapreneurship

Innovation can originate as an official and deliberate decision at the highest level of management or as a spontaneous creation of lower-level employees who take the initiative to solve a program in new ways.[37] For example, 3M has developed a formal policy that allows employees to "bootleg" 15 percent of their time to work on their own projects.[38]

Because these innovations are occurring within existing organizations, companies are referring to them as **intrapreneurship.** According to a report by Ameritech, the Midwest regional telephone company of AT&T, intrapreneurs added $2 million to Ohio Bell's net income. Employees submit their ideas to reduce expenses, bring in new revenues, or develop new lines of business as part of the Ohio subsidiary's "Enter-Prize" program.

In a recent Dow Chemical corporate report, CEO Frank Popoff said management's job is to liberate people to think intrapreneurially. This can be facilitated by creating a climate in which people can be "change-oriented," with decision making at the lowest level.[39]

Some organizations have been utilizing PHRM practices to stimulate intrapreneurial behavior. Essentially, PHRM practices are linked with a corporate intrapreneurial strategy. For example, Frost, a small manufacturer of overhead conveyer trolleys used in the automobile industry, combined automation and PHRM practices to implement an innovative program. Employee identification was increased by giving each employee ten shares of closely held corporate stock and calling them "shareholder-employees." Shared ownership can be further increased through stock purchases deposited to a 401(k) plan. By having their future depend on firm profitability, Frost hopes employees will acquire a long-term perspective.

Frost's compensation package also was restructured to strike a balance between employee concern for results—i.e., productivity—and the process by which goods get manufactured. The company instituted a quarterly bonus based on companywide productivity and established a "celebration fund" that managers can tap at their discretion to reward significant employee contributions. While most rewards are as simple as a lunch with Chad Frost, the owner, or, at most, a weekend for an employee and spouse at the local Marriott Hotel, they have proved to be motivational.

Frost encourages cooperative behavior in a number of other ways as well. Most of the offices are without doors. Chad Frost's "office," for example, is simply a large, open area at the end of a hallway, which allows employees easy access. Major executive perks, including reserved parking spaces, have been eliminated.

Frost encourages employees to broaden their skills by paying for extensive training programs, both at the company and at local colleges. But Frost goes even further, indentifying the development of additional skills as advancement in its own right. This is partly out of necessity because Frost has compressed its previous eleven levels of hierarchy into just four, in order to speed decision making.[40]

Automation

It is estimated that more than 45 million U.S. jobs will have been modified by automation by the year 2000. Because automation is so prevalent and important, managers must understand how to implement it. These changes will affect job content, recruitment selection, performance appraisal, and training.

Factory Automation.   U.S. manufacturers are finally in a position to leap into total automation and they are now beginning to do so. Although the United States currently lags behind Japan and Germany in automation use, many executives predict this will change in the late 1990. "We are gathering momentum in the U.S. today, and as that momentum builds we are going to make quantum leaps in factory automation," according to Joseph Tulkoff, director of manufacturing technology for Lockheed-Georgia Company.[41]

Accompanying the increase of factory automation is increased use of robots. Annual sales of robots are expected to be twenty thousand units by the end of the century, compared with the current rate of five thousand units. Estimates are that by 1995, robots will displace about 4.3 percent of the work force. Although most employees are expected to remain with their current employers, substantial retraining will be required. The costs of this training will be offset by lower labor costs, enhanced product quality, fewer defects, and a better flow of materials.[42]

Office Automation.   While the media have devoted attention to office automation and its effects on clerical workers, the biggest gains will come from office automation for managers and professionals. Booz, Allen, and Hamilton predicts that U.S. companies can increase their productivity by 15 percent and save up to $125 billion annually by

- using automated calendars, tickler files, and other forms of equipment that replace the handwritten lists made by business people to keep track of their time and that of others.
- Using word and image processors that allow managers and professionals to better review and edit their work. Personal computers could reduce the time these individuals spend in making decisions and analyzing data, and audi-

Change at Ford: Bottoms Up

"There's nothing glamorous about changing an organization. It takes a strong resolution to change, and persistence. . . . You just have to walk down the road, and stick with it. We've been consciously trying to change—and to apply the lessons we've learned about change management—for about eight years now—and it's every bit as difficult every step of the way. . . .

"At Ford, we've gone through three progressive stages of change during the past eight years. Toward the end of each stage, pressure within the organization mounted to create the setting for the next stage of change. It would have been impossible to grow past each stage if the company hadn't positively responded to this internal pressure.

Stage 1: Quality Improvement/Plant Level

"During the first stage, we focussed on how to create and improve quality. We concentrated at the plant level, working with plant managers and union leadership, and sharing information with employees about business objectives. We were learning to focus our organization on an issue—and quality was the issue.

"After two to three years, it was clear that more people needed to be included in the quality effort—above the plant level—or progress made at the plant level would be stymied, and people would become frustrated. These pressures created the second stage.

Stage II: Intermediate Level

"At the intermediate or division level, changes increased in speed. More education was involved, often derived from Japanese management techniques and 'excellent' companies. Study groups and task forces were the primary vehicles we used to introduce change at this level.

"Again, it became clear that, for change to continue spreading throughout the organization, the next-highest level of management would need to become involved.

Stage II: Senior-Most Management Level

"By the time our senior-most management level became involved, we realized an important lesson: *that* everyone *must take responsibility for change—that a piece of a problem is in everybody, and everybody has to act and not wait for others to become perfect. At the same time, in taking responsibility for change, each individual must recognize limitations, and the need for help from higher levels of management or other parts of the organization.*

"At the senior level, one task force recognized the combination of high people skills and high quality could put us at a tremendous competitive advantage. Management began placing great emphasis on encouraging continual challenges and acquiring new skills and perspectives. We set out to create an executive development center.

"A high-level study group, composed primarily of vice presidents who commanded large parts of the organization plus myself, was chartered to answer the question: 'How can we learn from the best? What should we do to avoid pitfalls in providing this challenge and new skills for our managers?' We took some risk in forming this group, because we didn't just pick those who were sympathetic—we chose those who could kill the idea of a development center.

"When the study group was finished, they had seen for themselves the value of having executive development—and had literally planned an 'ideal' center. The group recommended establishing the center to Ford's Policy and Strategy Committee, and an advisory board was formed to help launch the effort. The advisory board is still in existence—it provides feedback and helps keep us honest."

SOURCE: "Change at Ford: Bottoms Up," *HR Reporter* (Feb. 1987): 3. Used with permission from *HR Reporter*, copyright 1987.

ovisual conferences could replace the face-to-face meeting—and eliminate the accompanying travel time.

■ Installing retrieval-of-information services and electronic mail (the latter a broad term encompassing facsimile, keyboard, and speech or voice-activated mail) that could increase productivity and help connect other types of automated tools with each other.[43]

Managing the Change Process

The quality of work life and productivity programs described in this chapter involve important changes for most organizations. According to Linda Ackerman, president of Linda Ackerman Inc. in Oakland, California, managing change is one of the cutting-edge areas for managers today. "Most employees are traumatized by complex change. Management has the obligation to guide the change and minimize its effects on employees."

On an individual level, employees resist change for a variety of reasons including habit and fear of the unknown. There may also be economic reasons why employees resist change. In addition, the past offers security. When life become difficult, it's easy to think about a happier time, even when the old ways no longer lead to desired outcomes.[44]

Change may be resisted by organizations that have limited resources or fixed investments that make change prohibitively expensive. Change may also topple existing organizational and power structures. Finally, interorganizational agreements with unions may constrain change.

Among factors that seem to ease the stress associated with change is employee communication. Some organizations have installed "hot lines" so employees can get immediate responses to their questions. Participation and involvement in implementing the change tends to lower resistance. An example of how Ford Motor Company facilitated change is described in the "PHRM in the News." Finally, some organizations are attempting to select employees who are adaptable and flexible in their thinking.[45]

TRENDS IN QWL AND PRODUCTIVITY IMPROVEMENT

Two major trends are described here: assessing improvement programs and using computer technology and HRIS to improve QWL and productivity. Issues associated with strategic involvement and choices are the essence of this entire chapter.

Assessing Improvement Programs

As Exhibit 12.1 shows, the programs aimed at improving QWL and productivity have several intended purposes. Although the two sets of programs have different purposes, QWL programs can also bring about the intended purposes of the productivity programs. Consequently, QWL programs can be assessed by how well they attain all the purposes listed in Exhibit 12.1.

QWL Programs. As with the other PHRM activities discussed, assessing the benefits of QWL programs solely on the basis of dollars and cents is almost impossible. For example, what dollar value would be gained by increasing employee satisfaction or self-control by 10 percent? It may be difficult to say, but the question is, Do all QWL programs have to be justified on the basis of dollars and cents? Or can they be justified solely on the basis of increasing self-control, satisfaction, involvement, and self-respect (essentially all employee benefits)?[46] The answer is the latter. For example, Kroger Corporation in Cincinnati, Ohio, implemented a team development program in seven stores and assessed its effectiveness by attitude surveys measuring employee commitment, involvement, and interest in the success of its stores. The program was considered a success in relation to these benefits alone, although the company could have easily assessed the program in terms of costs as well as benefits.

Productivity Programs.   The process of assessing productivity programs is less complex because outcomes are much more measurable. For example, productivity programs can be assessed on the basis of individual job performance, absenteeism, and turnover. Productivity programs can also be assessed at the organizational level on the basis of profitability, competitiveness, and survival measures.[47] The difficulty appears to lie gaining acceptance for the idea that productivity *will* be measured, rather than that it *can* be measured. Once the organization accepts the fact that productivity can be assessed, productivity measures can be established in white-collar as well as blue-collar jobs, and the effects of productivity improvement programs can be assessed.

Computer Technology and HRIS in Improving QWL and Productivity

Computer technology can affect quality of work life in two ways. One way is to gather and store information that can be used to improve working conditions. This is tied to the use of organizational surveys described in Chapter 16. Another way is to measure and monitor the work environment of employees. Jobs can be designed around and with the benefit of computer technology. Computerized operations tell employees when to do particular operations and can be programmed to prescribe how the operations will be done.[48]

Current information in an HRIS can be helpful in trying to improve productivity. Data on performance, absenteeism, and turnover can be part of an HRIS and be used to measure levels of productivity in different areas of the organization. This information can also be used to determine if programs to improve productivity are successful.

INTERNATIONAL COMPARISONS

In contrast to companies in the United States, Japanese companies appear to offer far more extensive training for their employees. This also appears to be the case in Germany, particularly with regard to apprenticeship training and job redesign. In Sweden, Volvo's quality of work life programs have led to changes in the technology for assembling cars.

Japan

According to a 1983 study of vocational training in Japan, 80.4 percent of all business enterprises conduct in-company job training. Broken down according to employee classification, job training is made available to new regular employees in 75.5 percent of all companies and to new nonregular employees in 52.7 percent of them.

If firms are classified according to the size, it becomes evident that training increases with organizational size. Every firm with more than five thousand employees provides its own training. Vocational training in small to medium-sized companies depends to a greater extent on cooperative centers established through the effort of the government's employment promotion agency, aided by prefectural, municipal, and town agencies.

The in-company form of training is looked on as the key to each company's productivity and managerial control. Regular employees generally have academic training but few, if any, vocational skills. The company views training as a means of orienting the employee to its needs, and it is not unusual for a new employee to have anywhere from one to six months' training before being integrated into the work force. Supplemental training usually continues throughout the first three years of an employee's career, with additional training provided as needed.

Descriptions of training programs generally reveal a greater emphasis on the company as a whole—on its role in society (including the community, the nation, and the world), its relationship to the competition, and its marketing goals and objectives. In short, training constantly seeks to develop the individual as a fully rounded worker who can not only see the whole picture but also respond to it. The payoffs of this philosophy are substantial, as described in the "International PHRM in the News."

Actual job training teaches workers to apply skills to a variety of situations, thereby permitting worker rotations. All blue-collar workers are expected to be *multiskilled* within four to five years after joining the company. Many believe that this orientation toward skills enrichment and labor mobility is a crucial factor in the rapid growth of the Japanese economy.

The Japanese also differ substantially in the way they train today's college graduate to become tomorrow's manager. The two major aspects of this training are preemployment education, or socialization and training given before the first day on the job, and initial managerial education. This training has the following general aims:

- To educate new graduates regarding discipline and the transition from student to company life
- To teach professionalism and the significance and meaning of work
- To provide background information about the company and to familiarize employees with distinctive management trends, rules, and etiquette
- To cultivate a spirit of harmony and teamwork among employees[49]

Preemployment education consists of communications between the company and the future employees who are still in school. Future employees are frequently sent a directory of all new recruits, an employee handbook, a booklet on health and nutrition, and even words of encouragement from senior employees. Many companies provide an opportunity for future employees to get to know one another by holding meetings that

> afford an opportunity . . . to learn the company song, to meet senior employees who are graduates of the same university, to visit the factories and see exhibitions of the company's products, and to become familiar with the company's various departments and divisions.[50]

INTERNATIONAL
PHRM IN THE NEWS

How Japan Inc. Profits From Low Labor Turnover

Japan's so-called lifetime employment system isn't simply a cultural phenomenon, report economists Jacob Mincer and Yoshio Higuchi in a new National Bureau of Economic Research working paper. They find that Japanese manufacturing workers tend to receive more intensive and continuous on-the-job training than their U.S. counterparts—training that ultimately results in faster wage and earnings growth.

Mincer and Higuchi note that in both Japan and the U.S., labor turnover tends to be slower and wage hikes faster in industries that post speedy productivity growth. But in Japan, productivity growth and adaptation to technological change have been far more rapid, requiring constant training and retraining. For Japanese workers, that has meant greater job involvement, faster wage hikes, and enhanced loyalty to employers.

If this thesis is correct, American workers in Japanese-owned plants should develop similarly strong company ties, particularly since the Japanese currently spend about $1,000 more per U.S. worker for training and recruitment than do comparable U.S. companies. In fact, Mincer and Higuchi find that in recent years, U.S. workers in Japanese plants have enjoyed annual wage increases of about 3.3%—closer to the Japanese rate of 4.2% than to the average U.S. rate of 1.4%. Similarly, their monthly turnover rate of 1.7% is closer to Japan's 0.9% than the U.S.'s 3.5%. In short, Japan's legendary low worker turnover seems directly related to the willingness of companies to make an investment in human capital that pays off for employers and employees alike.

SOURCE: "How Japan Inc. Profits from Low Labor Turnover," *Business Week*, 7 Dec. 1987, 24. Used by permission of *Business Week*, copyright 1987.

Initial managerial education involves starting from the ground up, especially in the area of production. For example, the current president of Matsushita Electric Works spent his first six months carrying and shifting goods in the company's storage area. During orientation and the work experience program, new employees live together in company residences and learn social rules, etiquette, human relations, and punctuality—all considered necessary for an effective manager.

An important aspect of this training and development is the evaluation of how well the new employees have done. Mitsubishi and Isetan, for example, administer a quiz, which the recruits must pass, on the knowledge essential for handling the companies' products.

Germany

Germany is the world's largest exporting nation, and its economy is based on providing high-priced, high-quality goods. German executives say a key factor in their industrial success is a sophisticated work force. "You need highly qualified people when you produce high-quality goods," says Hans-Peter Kassai, chief economist with Daimler-Benz.[51]

A relatively unique feature of training and developing employees in Germany is an extensive and successful apprenticeship system. The three-and-a-half-year apprenticeship program gives employees wide expertise on many machines. The program costs about $15,000 per apprentice, and each year West German companies spend about $20 billion on their programs. Apprenticeship training for almost a half million German students begins at age fifteen when compulsory schooling ends. At that point, youths select one of several programs. By comparison, in the United States, many machine operators receive just a week or two of training.

Even though these apprenticeship programs are costly, German firms believe they pay off because workers end up being more loyal and more willing to stay. Once the apprentices are taken on as permanent employees, they often stay for years, giving a stability and maturity to the work force that many countries lack.

Jobs may also be designed differently in Germany. For example, many German workers perform in "work islands" where they can avoid boredom by rotating jobs, socializing, and working in cycles of up to twenty minutes rather than a few seconds. In assembling electronics products, automobiles, and appliances, the Germans appear to be well ahead of other countries in modifying or reducing the conventional assembly line and its simple, repetitive jobs. This enlightened position in alternative job design utilization is a product of the work humanization movement in Germany, initially funded by the German government in 1974 and maintained by the cooperative relationship between labor and management. Many companies also furnish their own funds for work design innovation projects.

Although each company's project may result in different types of job design, common emphasis is placed on enlarging assembly jobs by adding more complex tasks. One goal is to increase the job cycle to over one and one-half minutes, the point below which employees have been found to become dissatisfied with the job. As a consequence of the experiments in various companies, three major ways are being used to modify the traditional assembly line and its jobs. In **group assembly,** workers rotate jobs as they follow the product from the first to the last step in the assembly process. This is the notion of the "work island," where workers have the opportunity to socialize and are tied together by a group incentive pay plan. With **individual work stations,** work is done by the individual in a cycle time of ten to fifteen minutes. During this time, the worker assembles a major subcomponent of the total product (for example, an electric motor for a washing machine). Finally, **assembly lines** are being modified to make work easier and lighter. Where the assembly line cannot be easily replaced, as in automotive assembly, the line has been altered so that the worker stands on platforms moving at the same speed as the car.[52]

Sweden

The Volvo quality of work life projects have been implemented in several plants in Sweden, but the most famous is at Volvo's new assembly plant in the city of Kalmar. This plant, in operation since 1972, uses work teams instead of the traditional assembly line and allows employees to design and organize their own work. The plant was built in response to employees' job hopping, absenteeism, apathetic attitudes, and antagonism and an extremely low level of unemployment in Sweden.

Volvo's quality of work life project made substantial improvements by changing the technology for assembling cars. Although changing the technology of an organization is not easy or inexpensive, Volvo proved that it can be done successfully. In fact, changing the technology may be the only way to satisfy the needs and values of employees. As P. G. Gyllenhammar of Volvo reported in the *Harvard Business Review:*

> When we started thinking about reorganizing the way we worked, the first bottleneck seemed to be production and technology. We couldn't really reorganize the work to suit the people unless we also changed the technology that chained people to the assembly line.[53]

Now car assembly is done in work groups of about twenty people. The change in technology has been accompanied by a new climate of cooperation, partnership, and participation and an improved physical working environment.

Employee participation through councils and committees resulted in increased employee involvement and further improvements in the work itself. This participation is implemented in accordance with a 1977 Swedish law calling for full consultation with employees and full participation by their representatives in decision making from board level to the shop floor.

A quality of work life project has also been instituted at Volvo's major plant in Torslanda. Here, participation and autonomous groups are the two dominant techniques, rather than just participation, as at Kalmar. This is mostly because Torslanda has a large-scale assembly line and employs eight thousand workers, compared with six hundred at Kalmar.

A technique used in both plants at the discretion of the workers is **job rotation.** This is done within the relatively autonomous work groups. Today approximately 70 percent of the assembly workers engage in job rotation. Again, P. G. Gyllenhammar of Volvo observes: "There will always be a few people, however, especially older ones, who don't want to change (jobs) at all." This recognition and acceptance of employee differences is an important factor in the long-run success of quality of work life projects in general.[54]

SUMMARY

Faced with increasing international competition, U.S. companies are confronted with a productivity crisis of major proportions. Changing social and individual values have created a similar crisis in quality of work life. Some U.S. companies are responding to these crises by implementing programs for productivity and QWL improvements. Other companies have avoided these crises because they have had productivity and QWL programs for many years. In some cases, faced with crises or not, organizations are engaging in new productivity and QWL programs as they are developed.

This chapter examines only a few of many programs being used by U.S. companies to improve productivity and QWL. Among the many things that can be done to increase productivity, some may not work as well as others in all organizations. A diagnosis must be done to determine what is needed. Once this diagnosis is accomplished, an organization can choose from among several programs, many directly related to their PHRM activities. For example, the total compensation system could be changed to be more performance based. Wholesale adoption of programs because they are popular is not likely to result in success. Regardless of the particular program, employee involvement in program design or implementation (or both) enhances the program's success. Getting such involvement generally implies that the organization shares relevant information with the employees.

Just as many programs can be used to improve QWL. Indeed, some suggest that much of the productivity crisis would be solved if QWL were improved. But many reasons account for the current productivity crisis, including the way managers are rewarded and promoted, the decline in research and development, and the proportionately larger segment of the U.S. economy not producing goods and services. The increasing age of the capital equipment in the United States and increased international competition are also important in understanding our current productivity crisis.

Although the programs presented in this chapter can improve QWL and productivity, they represent only one major way to improve organizations. Another major way is by designing and implementing programs to improve the health and safety of employees. The importance of and need for such programs, as well as possible programs to implement, are described in the next chapter.

DISCUSSION QUESTIONS

1. What are the important factors in considering the effectiveness or utility of increased participation in decision making?
2. What are the essential characteristics of any quality circle effort?
3. Why are the benefits of QWL programs more difficult to ascertain than are the benefits associated with productivity programs—if indeed they are?
4. How would you distinguish QWL from productivity issues? How are the two issues related?
5. Some evidence suggests that the quality of your work experience affects your behaviors and attitudes off the job. Can you think of an example to illustrate this? What implications does this phenomenon have for PHRM?
6. Given what you know about the PHRM functions related to selection and placement, job analysis, training and development, and performance appraisal, explain how doing these functions poorly will detract from QWL.
7. How are job enrichment programs different from job enlargement programs of job design?
8. Automation of office systems since the advent of microcomputers has resulted in some companies permitting employees (e.g., computer programmers) to work at home. What are some advantages to this arrangement? Disadvantages? How would you overcome these disadvantages?
9. Describe in your own words what quality circles, survey feedback programs, and organizational restructuring efforts are. What do these programs have in common? What makes them distinctive?

CASE STUDY

Reach Out and Touch Big Brother

The year 1984 has come and gone, and so have many jobs in the telecommunications industry. In perhaps no other field has the impact of technology had such a significant effect on the jobs of so many workers. Mitch Fields, for example, still remembers that tragic day in November 1963 when President Kennedy was assassinated while Mitch was pulling the afternoon shift as a switchman for Midwest Telephone Company (MTC). As Mitch described it, it sounded like thirty locomotives hammering their way through a twenty-by-thirty-foot room filled with walls of mechanical switches putting phone calls through to their destination. Today that room of switches has been replaced by a microchip. Mitch himself has undergone extensive training to operate a computer console used to monitor and diagnose switching problems.

The job of operator has changed from sitting in long rows operating equipment attached to walls of jacks and cords to individual workstations that look like command centers out of a Star Trek spaceship. In addition, the competitive environment of telephone services has changed dramatically because of deregulation and competition from other phone companies offering similar services. The new thrust now is to shift operator performance from being not just fast and friendly but profitable as well, by marketing the company ("Thank you for using MTC.") and selling high-profit-margin services ("Is there someone else you would like to talk to? The person-to-person rate is only additional for the first minute.").

The operator's job at MTC remains unchanged in two respects: operators will talk to nearly six hundred people in a typical day, some of whom are still abusive. Operator job performance is monitored by *both* supervisors and, yes, the computer. Technological innovation has enabled MTC to monitor each operator by computer to produce statistics on numbers of calls handled per shift, speed of the call, and amount of revenue generated by the calls. In addition to computer monitoring, supervisors may also listen in on operators to ensure that proper operator protocol is followed. For example, customers are never told they dialed the "wrong" number, obscene calls are routed to supervisors, and one learns to say "hold the line" or "one moment, please" instead of "hang on."

Meeting performance standards based on these criteria does not typically lead to large rewards. A beginning operator usually earns about $10,000 a year working swing shifts that may begin at 8:30 A.M., noon, 2:00 P.M., 4:30 P.M., 8:30 P.M., or 2:00 A.M. Only the highest-rated operators have the opportunity to be transferred, be promoted, or receive educational benefits.

Steve Buckley, training and development manager for MTC, knows that to change the fast and friendly MTC operator of the past to one who is fast, friendly, and profitable as well is going to be a real challenge. Steve hasn't figured out yet how to get the operators to conclude each transaction by saying "Thank you for using MTC." A recent clandestine supervisor survey revealed that fewer than 20 percent of the operators were using the requested reply. Steve is also being pressured by the local union leaders that represent the telephone operators to reduce the job stress brought on by the high volume of people transactions and the constant, computer-assisted surveillance. One thing is for sure, however: Steve must implement a plan for improvement, or big brother will be calling him.

Case Questions

1. How are QWL and productivity issues related at MTC?
2. Describe how technological changes at MTC have influenced both productivity and QWL.
3. What personnel activities are potential tools for encouraging productivity improvements at MTC? Which would you give priority for making the change?
4. Suggest some approaches Steve Buckley could take to improve QWL for the operators. For each approach describe the potential risks as well as the advantages.

NOTES

1. J. R. Hackman and J. L. Suttle, *Improving Life at Work* (Santa Monica, Calif.: Goodyear, 1977); D. A. Nadler and E. E. Lawler III, "Quality of Work Life: Perspectives and Directing," *Organizational Dynamics* (Winter 1983): 20–30; J. Rosow, "Quality of Work Life Issues for the 1980's," *Training and Development Journal* (Mar. 1981): 33–37.
2. G. Gallup, Jr., *Forecast 2000: George Gallup, Jr., Predicts the Future of America* (New York: William Morrow, 1984); M. Maccoby, *Why Work: Leading the New Generation* (New York: Simon & Schuster, 1988); G. P.

Shea and R. A. Guzzo, "Group Effectiveness: What Really Matters?" *Sloan Management Review* 28, no. 3 (Spring 1987): 25–32.
3. W. List, "When Workers and Managers Act as a Team," *Report on Business* (October 1985): 60–67; D. Q. Mills, *The New Competitors* (New York: Free Press, 1985).
4. R. R. Blake and J. S. Mouton, "Increasing Productivity through Behavioral Science," *Personnel* (May/June 1981): 59–67; D. S. Cohen, "Why Quality of Work Life Doesn't Always Mean Quality," *Training/HRD* (Oct. 1981): 54–60.

5. L. M. Apcar, "Middle Managers and Supervisors Resist Moves to More Participating Management," *Wall Street Journal*, 16 Sept. 1985, p. 27; "Participative Management: Recipe for Success," *Bulletin to Management*, 30 May 1985, p. 1; L. A. Schlesinger and B. Oshry, "Quality of Work Life and the Manager: Muddle in the Middle," *Organizational Dynamics* (Summer 1984): 4–14.

6. Bureau of National Affairs, "74 Daily Labor Report," 16 Apr. 1982. See also R. P. Hummel, "Behind Quality Management: What Workers and a Few Philosophers Have Always Known and How It Adds Up to Excellence in Production," *Organizational Dynamics* (Summer 1987): 71–82; C. S. Miller and M. H. Schuster, "Gainsharing Plans: A Comparative Analysis," *Organizational Dynamics* (Summer 1987): 44–70; and J. P. Swann, Jr., "The Most Effective Employee Committees Are Probably Illegal," *Personnel Journal* (Nov. 1984): 91–92.

7. B. Jonsson and A. G. Lank, "Volvo: A Report on the Workshop on Production Technology and Quality of Work Life," *Human Resource Management* (Winter 1985): 455–66; H. F. Kolodny and B. Dresner, "Linking Arrangements and New Work Designs," *Organizational Dynamics* (Winter 1986): 33–51.

8. R. Griffin, *Task Design—An Integrative Approach* (Glenview, Ill.: Scott, Foresman, 1982); J. C. Latack, "Coping with Job Stress: Measures and Future Directions for Scale Development," *Journal of Applied Psychology* 71, no. 3 (Aug. 1986): 377–85.

9. B. Garson, *The Electronic Sweatshop* (New York: Simon & Schuster, 1988).

10. C. N. Greene and T. A. Matherly, "Quality Circles: A Need for Caution and Evaluation of Alternatives," in *Readings in Personnel and Human Resource Management*, 3d ed., ed. R. S. Schuler, S. A. Youngblood, and V. L. Huber (St. Paul: West, 1988), 509–18.

11. G. Ferris and J. A. Wagner III, "Quality Circles in the United States: A Conceptual Reevaluation," *Journal of Applied Behavioral Sciences* 21 (1985): 156–67; R. W. Griffin, "Consequences of Quality Circles in an Industrial Setting: A Longitudinal Assessment," *Academy of Management Journal* 31, no. 2 (June 1988): 338–58. E. E. Lawler III and S. A. Mohrman, "Quality Circles: After the Honeymoon," *Organizational Dynamics* (Spring 1987): 42–55.

12. L. Friedman and R. J. Harvey, "Factors of Union Commitment: The Case for a Lower Dimensionality," *Journal of Applied Psychology* 71, no. 3 (Aug. 1986): 371–76.

13. G. J. Gooduz, Jr., "What Is a Quality Circle?" *BNAC Communicator* (Winter 1982): 3; D. Hage, "Goal Is Improving Work Place," *Minneapolis Star*, 19 Nov. 1981, p. 1C; R. Wood, "Productivity: Quality Circles for Supermarket," *New York Times*, 15 Apr. 1982, p. F19.

14. Ferris and Wagner, "Quality Circles in the United States."

15. R. Steel, A. Mento, B. Dilla, N. Ovalle, and R. Lloyd, "Factors Influencing the Success and Failure of Two Quality Circle Programs," *Journal of Management* 11 (1985): 99–119.

16. R. Ford, *Motivation through Work Itself* (New York: American Management Association, 1969); Garson, *The Electronic Sweatshop*.

17. Machalaba, "United Parcel Service Gets Deliveries Done by Driving Its Workers," *Wall Street Journal*, 22 Apr. 1986, pp. 1, 23.

18. M. A. Campion and P. W. Thayer, "Development and Field Evaluation of an Interdisciplinary Measure of Job Design," *Journal of Applied Psychology* (Feb. 1985): 29–43; Y. Fried and G. Ferris, "The Dimensionality of Job Characteristics: Some Neglected Issues," *Journal of Applied Psychology* 71, no. 3 (Aug. 1986): 419–26. J. R. Hackman, G. R. Oldham, R. Janson, and K. Purdy, "A New Strategy for Job Enrichment," *California Management Review* (Summer 1975): 57–71; J. R. Hackman, J. L. Pearce, and J. C. Wolfe, "Effects of Changes in Job Characteristics on Work Attitudes and Behaviors: A Naturally Occurring Quasi-Experiment," *Organizational Behavior and Human Performance* 21 (1978): 289–304; J. Thomas and R. Griffin, "The Social Information Processing Model of Task Design: A Review of the Literature," *Academy of Management Review* (Oct. 1983): 672–82.

19. "Ergonomics Training Eases Man-Machine Interface," *Management Review* (Oct. 1984): 55.

20. J. A. Aldag and A. P. Brief, *Task Design and Employee Motivation* (Glenview, Ill.: Scott, Foresman, 1979); Griffin, *Task Design*; R. E. Kopelman, "Job Redesign and Productivity: A Review of the Evidence," *National Productivity Review* (Summer 1985): 237–55; B. Schneider, A. Reichers, and T. M. Mitchell, "A Note on Some Relationships between the Aptitude Requirements and Reward Attributes of Tasks," *Academy of Management Journal* 25 (1982): 567–74.

21. Mills, *The New Competitors*, 69–70. "Employment Security News and Views," *Bulletin to Management*, 1 Aug. 1985, p. 40. For additional views on employment security, see Mills, *The New Competitors*; and S. Weinig, "Guaranteed Lifetime Employment Pays Off Employee Commitment," *AMA Forum* (Aug. 1984): 29, 34.

23. J. A. Breaugh, "The Twelve-Hour Work Day: Differing Employee Reactions," *Personnel Psychology* (Summer 1983): 277–91; S. E. Jackson, S. Zedeck, and E. Summers, "Family Life Disruptions: Impact of Job-Induced Functional and Emotional Interference," *Academy of Management Journal* (Sept. 1985): 574–86; G. L. Staines and J. H. Pleck, "Nonstandard Work Schedules and Family Life," *Journal of Applied Psychology* (Aug. 1984): 509–14.

24. S. A. Coltrin and B. Barendse, "Is Your Organization a Good Candidate for Flextime?" *Personnel Journal* (Sept. 1981): 712–15; L. F. Copperman, F. D. Keast, and D. G. Montgomery, "Old Workers and Part-Time Work Schedules," *Personnel Administrator* (Oct. 1981): 35–38; T. E. Curry, Jr., and D. N. Haerer, "The Positive Impact of Flextime on Employee Relations," *Personnel Administrator* (Feb. 1981): 62–66; P. Farish, "PAIR Potpourri," *Personnel Administrator* (June 1981): 10; D. J. Petersen, "Flextime in the United States: The Lessons of Experience," *Personnel* (Jan/Feb. 1980): 21–31; D. Stetson, "Work Innovation Improving Morale,"

New York Times, 20 Sept. 1981, p. 53; "Why Flextime Is Spreading," *Business Week*, 23 Feb. 1981, pp. 455–60.

25. A. R. Cohen and H. Gadon, *Alternative Work Schedules: Integrating Individual and Organizational Needs* (Reading, Mass.: Addison-Wesley, 1978); R. B. Dunham and J. L. Pierce, "The Design and Evaluation of Alternative Work Schedules," *Personnel Administrator* (Apr. 1983): 67–75; J. C. Latack and L. W. Foster, "Implementation of Compressed Work Schedules: Participation and Job Redesign as Critical Factors for Employee Acceptance," *Personnel Psychology* (Spring 1985): 75–89.

26. S. J. Mahlin, "Peak-Time Pay for Part-Time Work," *Personnel Journal* (Nov. 1984): 60–65; S. R. Sacco, "Are In-House Temporaries Really an Option?" *Personnel Administrator* (May 1985): 20–24.

27. D. Kroll, "Telecommuting: A Revealing Peek Inside Some of Industry's First Electronic Cottages," *Management Review* (Nov. 1984): 18–23.

28. "How One Troubled Bank Turned Itself Around," *Business Week*, 24 Aug. 1981, pp. 117–22.

29. D. P. Garino, "Some Companies Try Fewer Bosses to Cut Costs, Decentralize Power," *Wall Street Journal*, 10 Apr. 1981, sec. 2; and "Intel's 125% Solution," *Business Week*, 9 Nov. 1981, p. 50. See also "The Rise of the Productivity Manager," *Dunn's Review* (Jan. 1981): 64, 65, 69.

30. "Middle Managers Are Still Sitting Ducks," *Business Week*, 16 Sept. 1985, p. 54.

31. "Middle Managers Are Still Sitting Ducks," *Business Week*, 16 Sept. 1985, p. 28. See also A. B. Fisher, "The Downside of Downsizing," *Fortune*, 23 May 1988, pp. 42–52; R. E. Nelson, "Common Sense Staff Reduction," *Personnel Journal* (Aug. 1988): 50–57; and R. M. Tomasko, "The Right Way to Shrink a Company," *New York Times*, 10 Jan. 1988, p. 3.

32. Z. Schiller, "Quality" *Business Week*, 8 June 1987, p. 132.

33. M. McComas, "Cutting Costs without Killing the Business," *Fortune*, 13 Oct. 1986, p. 76.

34. S. E. Prokesch, "Bean Meshes Man, Machine," *New York Times*, 23 Dec. 1985, pp. 19, 21.

35. D. K. Denton, "Quality Is Pepsi's Challenge," *Personnel Journal* (June 1988): 143–47; G. E. Forward (Interviewed by A. M. Kantrow), "Wide-Open Management at Chaparral Steel," *Harvard Business Review* (May/June 1986): 96–102; S. Goldstein, R. Howe, and D. Gaeddert, "Rockwell's Approach to Improving Quality," *Personnel Journal* (July 1988): 44–47; R. S. Schuler and S. E. Jackson, "Linking Competitive Strategies with Human Resource Management Practices," *Academy of Management Executive* 1, no. 3 (Aug. 1987): 207–19.

36. W. E. Deming, *Quality, Productivity and Competitive Position* (Cambridge, Mass.: MIT Center for Advanced Engineering Study, 1982).

37. R. M. Kanter, "Supporting Innovation and Venture Development in Established Companies," *Journal of Business Venturing* (Winter 1985): 47–60.

38. H. DePree, *Business as Unusual*, (Zeeland, Mich.: Herman Miller, 1986); K. Labich, "The Innovators," *Fortune*, 6 June 1988, pp. 50–64.

39. E. M. Fowler, "Productive Ideas from Employees," *New York Times*, 25 Aug. 1987, p. 21.

40. S. P. Galante, "Frost Inc. Technological Renewal and Human Resource Management: A Case Study," *Human Resource Planning* 10, no. 1 (1987): 57–67.

41. M. Kanabayashi, "A March of the Robots, Japan's Machines Race Ahead of America's," *Wall Street Journal*, 24 Nov. 1981, p. 1.

42. D. Leonard-Barton and W. A. Kraus, "Implementing New Technology," *Harvard Business Review* (Nov./Dec. 1985): 102–10; J. G. Miller and T. E. Vollman, "The Hidden Factory," *Harvard Business Review* (Sept./Oct. 1985): 142–50; "The Productivity," *Business Week*, 6 June 1988, pp. 100–13; "Robots Create Changes in the Work Force," *Ann Arbor Business-to-Business* (Oct. 1985): 9.

43. T. Rendero, "Want to Boost Managerial Productivity and Cut Costs? Try Automation," *Personnel* (Mar./Apr. 1981) © 1981 by AMACOM, a division of American Management Associations, pp. 39–40. Reprinted by permission of the publisher. See also the entire Sept. 1984 issue of *Personnel Administrator;* and D. L. Tarbania, "Automation in the Office: Users Expand Its Role at All Levels," *AMA Forum* (Nov. 1984): 29–30.

44. "Effective Strategies for Managing Change," *Bulletin to Management*, 14 July 1988, p. 3.

45. B. Arogyaswamy and C. M. Byles, "Organizational Culture: Internal and External Fits," *Journal of Management* 13, no. 4 (Winter 1987): J. J. Sherwood, "Creating Work Cultures with Competitive Advantage," *Organizational Dynamics* (Winter 1988): 4–27.

46. N. M. Tichy and M. A. Devanna, *The Transformational Leader* (New York: Wiley, 1986).

47. However, for an example of how QWL programs can be evaluated in dollars and cents, see P. H. Mirvis and E. E. Lawler III, "Measuring the Financial Impact of Employee Attitudes," *Journal of Applied Psychology* 62 (1977): 1–8. See also Chapter 16 of this textbook; J. W. Boudreau, "Effects of Employee Flows on Utility Analysis of Human Resource Productivity Improvement Programs," *Journal of Applied Psychology* (Aug. 1983): 396–406; J. W. Boudreau, "Economic Considerations in Estimating the Utility of Human Resource Productivity Improvement Programs," *Personnel Psychology* (Autumn 1983): 551–65; C. R. Day, Jr., "Solving the Mystery of Productivity Measurement," *Industry Week*, 26 Jan. 1981, pp. 61–66; and J. W. Forrester, "More Productivity Will Not Solve Our Problems," *Business and Society Review* (Spring 1981): 10–19.

48. Garson, *The Electronic Sweatshop*.

49. "The Japanese Manager Meets the American Worker," *Business Week*, 20 Aug. 1984, pp. 128–29; J. Main, "The Trouble with Managing Japanese-Style," *Fortune*, 2 Apr. 1984, pp. 50–56; R. Novotny, "Working for the Japanese," *Personnel Administrator* (Feb. 1984): 15–19; H. Tanaka, "The Japanese Method of Prepar-

ing Today's Graduate to Become Tomorrow's Manager," *Personnel Journal* (Feb. 1980): 109–10.

50. R. R. Rehder, "Education and Training: Have the Japanese Beaten Us Again?" *Personnel Journal* (Jan. 1983): 42.

51. S. Greenhouse, "An Unstoppable Export Machine," *New York Times*, 6 Oct. 1988, p. D7.

52. This is based on the description by J. M. Geddes, "Germany Profits by Apprentice System," *Wall Street Journal*, 15 Sept. 1981, p. 22.

53. P. G. Gyllenhammar, "How Volvo Adapts Work to People," *Harvard Business Review* (July/Aug. 1977): 106.

54. Ibid.

Occupational Safety and Health

Stress on the Job

It's not just the frequency of stress that's increasing; it's the duration. At a time when mergers and acquisitions are rampant, executives must handle many tasks at once—on shorter deadlines. Atlanta therapist Geneva Rowe believes the pace of modern decision making has become so rapid that managers don't have enough time to decompress or recharge. "Twenty-five years ago, we had more intermittent stress," Rowe says. "We had a chance to bounce back before we encountered another crisis. Today, we have chronic, unremitting stress. Our bodies have eroded."

Stress is also eroding the bottom line. The toll on corporations runs from hobbled productivity to absenteeism and spiraling medical costs. While exact figures are hard to come by, some experts put the overall cost to the economy as high as $150 billion a year—almost the size of the federal deficit. Dr. Kenneth R. Pelletier, a specialist in executive health at the University of California, San Francisco, notes that many large corporations spend more than $200 million a year on medical benefits for their employees. The surgeon general's most recent report, meanwhile, indicates that two-thirds of all illnesses before the age of 65 are preventable. Compared with treating stress, Pelletier says, attempting to prevent it would be "relatively speaking, low cost."

SOURCE: "Stress on the Job," *Newsweek*, 25 Apr. 1988, pp. 40–41. Used with permission from *Newsweek*, copyright 1988.

THIS "PHRM in the News" illustrates that occupational stress is a significant health concern in today's organizations. It also indicates that there can be severe consequences of occupational stress. As a result, organizations are moving to treat it and its symptoms. Because of its growing importance, stress, along with many other aspects of health and safety in organizations, is discussed throughout this chapter.[1]

Occupational safety and health refers to the physiological, physical, and sociopsychological conditions of an organization's work force resulting from the work environment. An organization that is effective from an occupational safety and health perspective will have fewer employees suffering from harmful physiological, physical, or sociopsychological conditions than will an organization that is less effective.[2]

Hazardous physiological and physical conditions, the essence of occupational diseases and accidents, include loss of life or limb, cardiovascular diseases, various forms of cancer, emphysema, and arthritis. This set of conditions also includes leukemia, white lung disease, brown lung disease, black lung disease, sterility, central nervous system damage, and chronic bronchitis.

Hazardous sociopsychological conditions, the essence of occupational stress and a low quality of work life, are dissatisfaction, apathy, withdrawal, projection, tunnel vision, forgetfulness, inner confusion about roles or duties, mistrust of others, vacillation in decision making, inattentiveness, irritability, procrastination, and a tendency to become distraught over trifles. Safety and health should be the concern of everyone in the organization. However, strong support and extensive communication by top management are essential if safety and health programs are to succeed.[3]

PURPOSES AND IMPORTANCE OF IMPROVING OCCUPATIONAL SAFETY AND HEALTH

The purposes of improving safety and health are to reduce the costs resulting from the harmful conditions described above and to make the work environment better for employees.

Costs

Each year in the United States an average of as many as 3,750 deaths and 6,000,000 lesser injuries occur in occupational accidents. At the same time, as many as 400,000 new incidences of occupational disease occur, and as many as 100,000 workers die as a result of such diseases. The National Safety Council conservatively estimates that the annual cost is $30 bilion for occupational accidents and about $25 billion for occupational diseases.

In addition, enormous costs are associated with organizational stress. For example, alcoholism, often the result of drinking to cope with job pressures, costs organizations more than $65 billion annually. A total of $20 billion is attributed to lost productivity, with 5 percent of the labor force purported to have an alcohol problem. Drug use in the work place is equally problematic. Cost estimates run up to $35 billion annually for lost productivity, accidents, and rehabilitation due to drug addiction. While more difficult to quantify, workers' feelings of job dissatisfaction and lack of meaning and purpose are also symptomatic of stress and poor-quality work life.[4]

Benefits

Eliminating harmful conditions in organizations can be very beneficial. Fewer incidences of accidents and diseases, a reduced level of occupational stress, and improved QWL result in (1) more productivity due to fewer lost workdays for absenteeism, (2) more efficiency from workers who are more involved with their jobs, (3) reduced medical and insurance costs, (4) lower workers' compensation rates and direct payments because far fewer claims are filed, (5) greater flexibility and adaptability in the work force as a result of increased participation and feelings of ownership resulting from QWL projects, and (6) better selection ratios because of the increased attractiveness of the organization as a place to work. As a consequence of all these factors, companies can increase their profits substantially.[5]

RELATIONSHIPS INFLUENCING OCCUPATIONAL SAFETY AND HEALTH

Because the costs and benefits of occupational safety and health are so enormous, organizations are concerned about trying to make improvements in this area. A variety of factors facilitate or impinge on this goal.

Relationships with Other PHRM Activities

Exhibit 13.1 provides a summary of the many relationships that safety and health activities have with other PHRM activities.

Recruitment and Selection.   To the extent that an organization can provide a safe, healthy, and comfortable work environment, it may increase its success in staffing. When organizations have high rates of accidents, particularly fatal ones, they need to recruit more employees. However, if organizations develop reputations for being unsafe places to work, they will find it more difficult to recruit and select qualified employees.

Job Redesign.   As described in Chapter 12, the ways in which jobs are physically designed have an important impact on people's performance. Ergonomics problems stemming from a failure to properly match people and jobs also have an impact on work place accidents.

   According to Roger Stephens, ergonomist with the Occupational Safety and Health Administration (OSHA), by applying ergonomic principles to job design, employers can balance workers' physical capabilities with job demands, thus

Aspects and Relationships of Safety and Health in Organizations   EXHIBIT
13.1

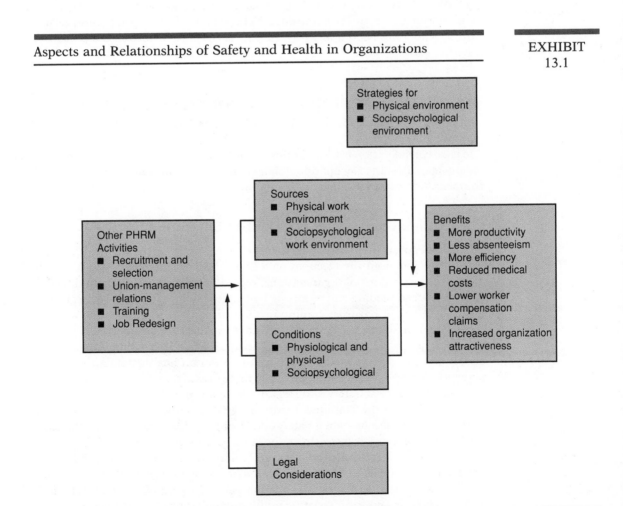

helping to prevent "broken workers," reduce disability claims, and improve employee relations. Noting that he is the only ergonomist on OSHA's staff, Stephens stresses that employers must carry out this mission themselves because OSHA "will never be able to force job redesign or even lead the way."[6] Matching the physical abilities of individuals with those required by the job may mean redesigning the job. This option is described later in the chapter.

Training.   For employees to perform their jobs safely, they may need specialized training. This may include how to deal with toxic substances, enforce correct safety procedures, or use protective devices. In fact, OSHA's Hazard Communication Standard which went into effect in 1986 requires that employees be trained prior to job assignment and retrained any time a new hazard is introduced into the work environment.

Union-Management Relations.   Occupational safety and health is a major concern of unions. Many union contracts have some type of safety provisions, including the right to refuse unsafe work, a union-employer pledge of cooperation in the development and operation of safety and health programs, the right to grieve unsafe work, the right to discipline employees for violating safety rules, regulation of crew size, the posting of safety rules, and the right of inspection by a joint or union safety committee.[7] The sanctity of the union contract regarding safety has been upheld by the courts (*Irvin H. Whitehouse & Sons Co. v. NLRB*, 1981).

LEGAL CONSIDERATIONS OF OCCUPATIONAL SAFETY AND HEALTH

The legal considerations of occupational safety and health can divided into three major categories: the Occupational Safety and Health Administration, workers' compensation programs, and the common law doctrine of torts.

Occupational Safety and Health Administration

The federal government's main response to the issue of safety and health in the work place has been the Occupational Safety and Health Act of 1970, which prescribes inspections of organizations, regardless of size, for safety and health hazards; record keeping and reporting by employers; investigations of accidents and allegations of hazards; communication of hazards to employees; and establishment of standards. Although this act was well intentioned, it was soon perceived as emphasizing minor safety matters while overlooking major ones and, even more vital, as failing to focus attention on health standards.[8] These perceptions developed around one of the three organizations established by the act: the Occupational Safety and Health Administration (OSHA). The other two organizations are the National Institute of Occupational Safety and Health (NIOSH) and the Occupational Safety and Health Review Commission (OSHRC). OSHRC reviews appeals by organizations that have received citations from OSHA inspectors for alleged safety and health violations. In addition to conducting research, NIOSH aids in the dissemination of occupational health information.

OSHA is responsible for establishing and enforcing occupational safety and health standards and for inspecting and issuing citations to organizations that violate these standards. According to *Marshall v. Barlow's, Inc.* (1978), however, employers are not required to let OSHA inspectors enter their premises unless they have search warrants. Access to an organization's health and safety records also requires a search warrant (*Taft Broadcasting*, 1988).

In *Taft*, an employee had complained to OSHA that workplace conditions had caused him eye and respiratory problems. Without presenting a search warrant or subpoena, an OSHA compliance officer asked the employer for its log of occupational illnesses and injuries for the previous three years so that he could review them for hygienic and environmental problems. The employer refused access and was cited for failing to produce the records. The Occupational Safety and Health Review Commission invalidated the citation, finding unconstitutional a federal law that requires employers to surrender their injury and illness logs upon request.[9]

In *Chamber of Commerce v. OSHA*, the U.S. Court of Appeals for the District of Columbia Circuit struck down the walk-around pay requirement. The requirement had made it mandatory for companies to pay the wages of employees during the time they spent accompanying an OSHA inspector on the tour of the work site.

Record Keeping.   Organizations are required to keep safety and health records so that OSHA can compile accurate statistics on work injuries and illnesses.[10] Exhibit 13.2 shows OSHA's guidelines for determining what must be recorded.

Falsification of records or failure to keep adequate records can result in some rather substantial fines. For example,

Nearly $2.6 million was levied against IBP, Inc., for more than 1,000 alleged willful violations of injury and illness recordkeeping requirements. OSHA also charges the company with failure to provide a copy of its injury and illness records to the United Food and Commercial Workers Union. The proposed fine caps an investigation that began in January at IBP's Dakota City, Neb., meatpacking plant. OSHA's attention was drawn to the plant when UFCW, which represents 2,800 employees there, charged that IBP was keeping fraudulent records in an attempt to mask high injury rates at the facility. OSHA Administrator John Pendergrass calls the alleged violations "the worst example of underreporting of injuries and illnesses" ever encountered by the agency. Among the injuries that the company failed to record, according to the citation, were knife cuts, concussions, burns, and fractures.[11]

Communicating Health and Safety Information.   In addition to keeping records, the Access to Employee Exposure and Medical Records (AEEMR) regulation of 1980 requires organizations to show or give to employees, their designated representatives, and OSHA their on-the-job medical records of measurements of employee exposure to toxic substances. The employee's right to know has been further strengthened by the Hazard Communication Standard that went into effect in 1986.[12] Under this standard, employers are required to provide workers with information and training on hazardous chemicals in their work area at the time of their initial assignment and whenever a new hazard is introduced. According to OSHA, effective communication should include instructions for employees on the following:

■ The standard's requirements and operations in the work place that use hazardous chemicals

EXHIBIT
13.2

OSHA Guidelines for Recording Cases

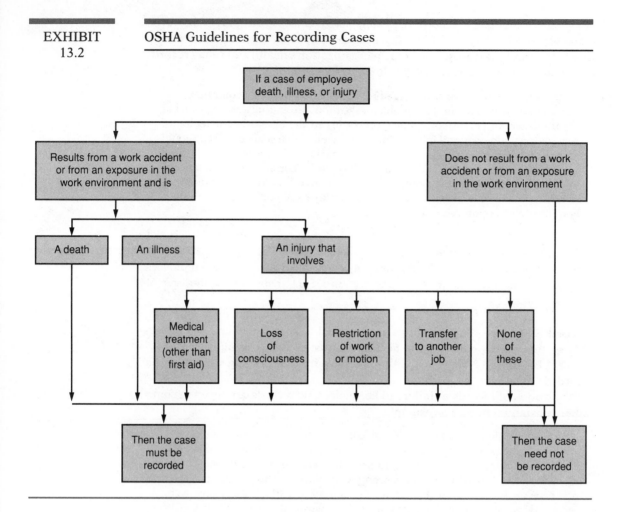

■ Proper procedures for determining the presence of chemicals and detecting
hazardous releases
■ Protective measures and equipment that should be used
■ Location of the written hazard communication program[13]

Meanwhile, some state laws require companies to label chemicals and identify
their potential health threats.[14]

Establishing Standards.   Previously, OSHA could tell companies that they
had to make a work environment absolutely free of any risk from employee
exposure. Now, however, OSHA has the burden of making a threshold assessment that an existing exposure level poses **significant risks** to employee health
before it can force companies to adhere to a more stringent **no-risk standard**
(*Industrial Union Department, AFL-CIO v. American Petroleum Institute*, 1980).
This decision is also referred to as the **benzene standard.** However, if significant
risks from exposure are shown to exist, OSHA can demand compliance, regardless of the costs (*United Steelworkers of America, AFL-CIO v. Marshall*, 1980).[15]
Whereas OSHA was established to provide workers protection against accidents
and diseases, workers' compensation was established to provide financial aid
for those unable to work because of accidents and diseases.

Workers' Compensation Programs

For years, workers' compensation awards were granted only to workers unable to work because of physical injury or damage (i.e., due to accidents and diseases). Since 1955, however, court decisions have either caused or enticed fifteen states to allow workers' compensation payments in job-related cases of anxiety, depression, and mental disorders.[16] In that year, the Texas Supreme Court charted this new direction in workers' compensation claims by stating that an employee who became terrified, highly anxious, and unable to work because of a job-related accident had a compensable claim, even though he had no physical injury (*Bailey v. American General Insurance Company*, 1955). In a more recent case (*James v. State Accident Insurance Fund*, 1980), an Oregon court ruled in favor of a worker's claim for compensation for inability to work due to job stress resulting from conflicting work assignments.

Although coverage for worker injury caused by the physical and sociopsychological environment may be consistent with the intention of workers' compensation, inclusion of nonphysical or mental injury claims is putting financial strains on workers' compensation funds in many states. Workers also are going outside the state-run workers' compensation programs that provide only limited disability income, to seek much larger settlements by suing employers.

Common Law Doctrine of Torts

Employees can obtain damage awards by suing employers; however, the employee must demonstrate that the employer engaged in reckless or intentional infliction designed to degrade or humiliate. Although cases of such a type have been successfully brought against employers (*Alcorn v. Ambro Engineering*, 1970; *Contereras v. Crown Zellerbach Corporation*, 1977), they appear to be the exception. Nevertheless, with these precedents established, additional cases against employers are likely. This is particularly true for cases charging sexual harassment, described in the next chapter.

It is important for organizations to keep all these legal considerations in mind when deciding on strategies to locate and improve conditions affecting safety and health.

HAZARDS TO OCCUPATIONAL SAFETY AND HEALTH

As Exhibit 13.3 shows, occupational diseases and accidents can pose physical threats to employees' health. While sociopsychological hazards can arise through job-related stress and low quality of work life, interventions have traditionally focused on only the physical environment. Increasingly, however, organizations are recognizing that job-related stress also may be hazardous.

Factors Affecting Occupational Accidents

Certain organizations, and even certain departments within the same organization, have higher **occupational accident** rates than others. Several factors explain this difference.

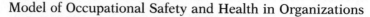

EXHIBIT
13.3

Model of Occupational Safety and Health in Organizations

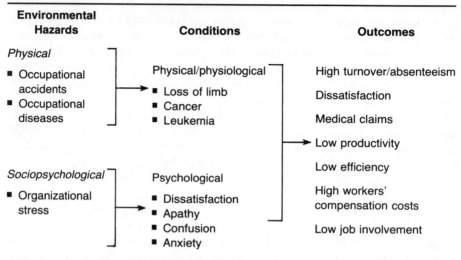

Organizational Qualities.   Accident rates vary substantially by industry. For example, firms in the construction and manufacturing industries have higher incidence rates than firms in services, finance, insurance, and real estate do. Small and large organizations (those with fewer than one hundred employees and more than one thousand, respectively) have lower incidence rates than medium-sized organizations do. This may be because supervisors in small organizations are better able to detect safety hazards and prevent accidents than those in medium-sized organizations are. And larger organizations have more resources to hire staff specialists who can devote all their efforts to safety and accidents.

Safety Programs.   Organizations that have no safety programs generally have higher injury costs than similar companies that have implemented safety programs do. The effectiveness of safety programs is affected by the industry, organizational size and culture, and management support. As a result, some organizations in the same industry may have higher injury costs than others. For example, DuPont's accident rate is 28 times lower than that of the chemical industry as a whole; officials attribute this to their safety program.

The Unsafe Employee.   Even with environmental engineering and explicit programs, accident rates are affected by the behavior of the person, the degree of hazard in the work environment, pure chance, and the badly informed, ambivalent, or frightened employee. The second "PHRM in the News" illustrates the latter source.

The degree to which people contribute to accidents is often regarded as an indicator of proneness to accidents. While not stable traits, certain psychological and physical characteristics make some people more susceptible to accidents than others. For example, employees who are *emotionally low* have more accidents than those who are *emotionally high* do; employees who have fewer accidents are more optimistic, trusting, and concerned for others than those who have had more accidents are.[18] Employees under *greater stress* are likely to have

PHRM IN THE NEWS

Workers Are Often a Hazard to Themselves

After 12 years working in a Florida battery recycling plant, George Mount has lead coursing through his bloodstream. Doctors have told him that, at age thirty-two, he has serious kidney damage from exposure to the poison.

But when the Federal Occupational Safety and Health Administration ordered him moved to a safer job, Mount did more than resist; he volunteered to participate in a controversial experiment that would have kept him near the vats of molten lead. "Sure, I'm worried about my health," Mount said. "But what am I supposed to do? Just give up everything I worked for and put into that company?"

That attitude is not unique. Advocates of workplace safety sometimes find their toughest enemy is not a malevolent employer or lax regulatory agency, but an ambivalent, frightened, or badly informed work force. Dorothy Nelkin, a Cornell University sociologist . . . said workers often feel confused and powerless when confronted with the issue. They are easily reassured by company experts, she said, especially if the experts suggest that costly safety measures could mean layoffs.

. . . Sheldon W. Samuels, safety director for the Industrial Unions Department of the A.F.L.–C.I.O., noted, . . . that where risks are long term, workers are tempted to gamble.

"Workers know the chances they won't get cancer or lung disease are greater that the chances of getting it," he explained. "They say it's not going to happen to me, and in most cases, that's true." That is why many health experts prefer more expensive engineering controls such as ventilation systems, which automatically clean an area, to apparatus such as respirators, which must be worn to be effective.

The lesson seems to be that employee education is at least as important as government regulation when it comes to workplace safety. Yet, Congress and the Reagan Administration have cut OSHA's safety training grants from $13.9 million in 1981 to $6.8 million—and at a time when economic uncertainty and tech-

nological complexity have made employees particularly ambivalent about safety measures.

[Consider] George [Mount]. When a checkup found that the level of lead in his blood exceeded Federal standards, OSHA rules required that he be moved from his job supervising lead refining vats to a risk-free area. The non-union employer, Gulf Coast Lead, said it considered Mount indispensable. Apparently, so did Mount, who was the company's strongest ally when it sought its waiver. OSHA acceded to the exemption and helped design an experiment whereby Mount would wear a respirator. The experiment began in April. It was canceled a month later when a medical examination detected his kidney condition.

Mount now does chores at a company-owned apartment complex, a job he considers menial. It also lacks the pay bonuses to which he is accustomed. He may return to his old job if his blood lead count drops below Federal standards.

Meanwhile, Mount said, he resents the company for putting him at risk, OSHA for upsetting his life, and both for keeping him in the dark about the risks of lead and the ramifications of his kidney ailment.

In another case, an experiment proposed by Dan River involves the theory that a bacterium growing in cotton, and not cotton dust, causes byssinosis, or brown lung disease. Instead of installing $7.5 million worth of ventilating equipment in one of its Virginia textile mills, as required by Federal safety rules, the company wants workers to wear respiratory masks.

With OSHA's blessing, Virginia officials have granted the company a temporary waiver, permitting blood tests on about twenty workers. The state will soon decide whether to allow the respirator experiment.

The Dan River proposal has met with protests from scientists, national union officials and newspaper editorials, but silence from Local 248 of the United Textile Workers of Amer-

continued

ica. The U.T.W.A. is a small union with a reputation for timidity. In Danville, where Dan River is the dominant employer, few of the 6,500 company employees pay union dues. It came as no surprise, then, that when the company proposed the byssinosis experiment, the union accepted assurances that workers would not be endangered. Only under prodding from state and national union officials has it expressed some misgivings. Kim Meeks, the local's business agent, said the several hundred affected workers have also been silent. "The key to this thing is they haven't been explained to and don't know what this is all about," Meeks said. Be-

sides, "these people have been pretty much subject to the proposition that, well, if we get too much static here we'll just close this little plant up."

Meeks said that if workers at the textile plant did complain, it would very likely be about wearing the heavy respirators. And that, according to Meeks, is why Dan River officials have been "as liberal as they can be" about not forcing workers to wear the devices.

SOURCE: B. Keller, "Workers Are Often a Hazard to Themselves," *New York Times*, 8 July 1984, p. 0.2. Copyright © 1984/85 by The New York Times Company. Reprinted by permission.

more accidents than those under *less stress* are, and those with *better vision* have fewer accidents than those with *poorer vision* do. *Older workers* are less likely to be hurt than *younger workers* are.[19] People who are quicker in recognizing differences in visual patterns than in making muscular manipulations are less likely to have accidents than those who are faster in muscular manipulations are. Psychological conditions—hostility, emotional immaturity, neuroticism—may also be related to accident proneness. Still, none of these characteristics is related to accidents in *all* work environments.

Factors Affecting Occupational Diseases

The potential sources of work-related diseases are as distressingly varied as the ways they affect the human organism are. Through the work of several federal agencies, the following work place hazards have been detected: arsenic, asbestos, benzene, bickloromethylether, coal dust, coke-oven emissions, cotton dust, lead, radiation, and vinyl chloride. Workers likely to be exposed to these types of hazards include chemical and oil refinery workers, miners, textile workers, steelworkers, lead smelters, medical technicians, painters, shoemakers, and plastics industry workers. The long-term consequences linked to these hazards include thyroid, liver, lung, brain, and kidney cancer; white, brown, and black lung diseases; leukemia; bronchitis; emphysema; lymphoma; aplastic anemia; central nervous system damage; and reproductive disorders (for example, sterility, genetic damage, abortions, and birth defects). Continued research will no doubt uncover additional hazards that firms will want to diagnose and remedy for the future well-being of their work forces.[20]

Categories of Occupational Diseases.   "Chronic bronchitis and emphysema are the fastest growing diseases in the country, doubling every five years since World War II, and [they] account for the second highest number of disabilities, under Social Security."[21] Cancer, however, tends to receive the most attention because it is a leading cause of death in the United States (second after heart disease). Many of the known causes of cancer are physical and chemical agents in the environment. And because physical and chemical agents are theoretically more controllable than human behavior, OSHA places emphasis on eliminating them from the work place.

While cancer and respiratory diseases are of major concern, OSHA requires that all diseases in the following categories be reported:

1. Skin diseases and disorders
2. Dust diseases of the lungs
3. Respiratory conditions due to toxic agents
4. Poisoning (systematic effects of toxic materials)
5. Disorders due to physical agents
6. Disorders associated with repeated trauma
7. Other occupational illnesses

Occupational Groups at Risk.   Miners, construction and transportation workers, and blue-collar and lower-level supervisory personnel in manufacturing industries experience the bulk of occupational disease and injury. The least safe occupations are firefighting, mining, and law enforcement. Large numbers of petrochemical and oil refinery workers, dye users, textile workers, plastic industry workers, painters, and industrial chemical workers are also particularly susceptible to some of the ten most dangerous health hazards. Interestingly, skin diseases are the most common of all reported occupational diseases, the group most affected being leather workers.

Occupational diseases are not exclusive to the blue-collar workers and manufacturing industries. The "cushy office job" has evolved into a veritable nightmare of physical and psychological ills for white-collar workers in the growing service industries. Among the common ailments are varicose veins, bad backs, deteriorating eyesight, migraine headaches, hypertension, coronary heart disorders, and respiratory and digestive problems. The causes of these ailments in an office environment include too much noise, uncomfortable chairs, chemically treated paper, and office equipment such as video display terminals.[22]

Sources of Organizational Stress

A variety of factors can cause stress on the job. However, the most prevalent include organizational change, work pace, work overload, the physical environment, and job burnout. In addition, there are several employee-specific factors that cause stress.

Employee Stressors.   Referred to as the four S's, supervision, salary, job security, and safety often cause individual-specific stress.

The two major stressors that employees associate with the supervisor are petty work rules and relentless pressure for more production. Both deny workers fulfillment of their needs to control the work situation and to be recognized and accepted.

Salary is a stressor when it is perceived as being given unfairly. Many blue-collar workers believe that they are underpaid relative to their white-collar counterparts in the office. Teachers think they are underpaid relative to people with similar education who work in private industry.[23]

Employees experience stress when they are unsure whether they will have their jobs the next week, the next month, or even the next day. For many employees, lack of job security is even more stressful than jobs that are unsafe. With a lack of job security, employees are always in a state of uncertainty.[24]

Organizational Change.   Changes in organizational structure, job assignments, technology, and reporting relationships, as well as downsizings, mergers, and takeovers, are common in today's work world. Unfortunately, all these changes—even when they are for the better—are stressful. The reason is that change often is accompanied by uncertainty and often occurs without advance warning. Even the rumors that precede change can cause stress as people speculate about whether and how the change will affect them. As a result, many employees suffer stress symptoms.[25]

Work Pace.   Work pacing, particularly who or what controls the pace of the work, is a potential stressor in organizations. Machine pacing gives control over the speed of the operation and the work output to something other than the individual. Workers on machine-paced jobs reportedly feel exhausted at the end of the shift and are unable to relax soon after work because of increased adrenaline secretion on the job. In a study of twenty-three white- and blue-collar occupations, assembly workers reported the highest level of severe stress symptoms.

Jobs that entail unplanned interruptions also are stressful. For example, broadcast engineers must be able to make exacting repairs on telecommunication equipment at a moment's notice. If that is not bad enough, they make the repairs knowing that the station is losing viewers and money each second they are off the air. This type of work is far more stressful than work that involves planned cycles of peak activity with planned downtime in between.[26]

Work Overload.   Although some employees complain about not having enough to do, others have far too much.[27] Some have so much to do that their workload exceeds their abilities and capacities.

> Employees in high-stress jobs should be compensated for stress-related disabilities, according to the Rhode Island Supreme Court.
> The high court has ruled that the *Pawtucket Evening Times* must compensate the widow of one of its sports writers who died after covering a football game in 1978. He died of a cerebral hemorrhage. The widow of Edward Mulcahey sued the paper, saying job stress aggravated his high blood pressure and diabetes because of the odd hours he worked and the deadlines he was under.[28]

Physical Environment.   Although office automation (discussed in Chapter 12) is a way to improve productivity, it has its stress-related drawbacks. One aspect of office automation with a specific stress-related drawback is the video display terminal (VDT). While findings are not complete, countries such a Sweden and Norway have taken more steps to deal with VDTs than has the United States. Other aspects of the work environment associated with stress are crowding, lack of privacy, and lack of ability to change aspects of the environment (e.g., to move the desk or chairs or even to hang pictures in a work area in an effort to personalize it).[29]

Job Burnout.   A special type of organizational stress is called **job burnout**. This stress condition happens when people work in situations in which they have little control over the quality of their performance but feel personally responsible for their success or lack of it. People most susceptible to burnout include police officers, nurses, social workers, and teachers. When people begin to show burnout, they reveal three symptoms: (1) emotional exhaustion, (2) depersonalization, and (3) a sense of low personal accomplishment. Because this condition benefits neither the individual nor the organization, many programs have been designed to help people deal with burnout.[30]

STRATEGIES TO IMPROVE OCCUPATIONAL SAFETY AND HEALTH

Once the cause of stress is identified, strategies can be developed for eliminating or reducing it (see Exhibit 13.4). To determine if the strategy was effective, organizations can compare the incidence, severity, and frequency of illnesses and accidents before and after the intervention. Methods to establish safety and health rates will be described first, and then strategies for improving accident and disease conditions will be presented.

Safety and Health Rates

OSHA requires organizations to maintain records of the incidence of accidents and disease. Some organizations also record the frequency and severity of each.

Incidence Rate.   The most explicit index of industrial safety is the **incidence rate**. It is calculated by the following formula:

$$\text{Incidence rate} = \frac{\text{Number of recordable injuries and illnesses} \times 1 \text{ million}}{\text{Number of employee exposure hours}}$$

Suppose an organization had 10 recorded injuries and illnesses and 500 employees. To calculate the number of exposure hours, it would multiply the number of employees by 40 hours and by 50 work weeks: $500 \times 40 \times 50 = 1$ million. Thus, in this case the incidence rate would be 10.

Severity Rate.   Strategies will vary depending on whether an organization is experiencing numerous minor safety problems or one or two major problems.

Summary of Sources and Strategies for Occupational Safety and Health

EXHIBIT
13.4

Physical Work Environment

Occupational accidents	Redesigning the work environment
	Setting goals and objectives
	Establishing safety committees
	Training
	Providing financial incentives
Occupational diseases	Measuring the work environment
	Setting goals and objectives

Sociopsychological Work Environment

Organizational stress	Establishing organizational stress programs
	Establishing individual stress strategies

Sources *strategies* *strategies*

The **severity rate** reflects the hours actually lost due to injury or illness. It recognizes that not all injuries and illnesses are equal. Four categories of injuries and illnesses have been established: deaths, permanent total disabilities, permanent partial disabilities, and temporary total disabilities. OSHA assigned each category a specific number of hours to be charged against an organization. The severity rate is calculated by this formula:

$$\text{Severity rate} = \frac{\text{Total hours charged} \times 1 \text{ million}}{\text{Number of employee hours worked}}$$

An organization with the same number of injuries and illnesses as another but with more deaths would have a higher severity rate. However, because OSHA decided the assignment of hours charged for each type of accident and illness was arbitrary, it dropped the idea of using a severity rate.

Frequency Rate.   While similar to the incidence rate, the **frequency rate** reflects the number of injuries and illnesses per million hours worked rather than per year.[31] It is calculated by

$$\text{Frequency rate} = \frac{\text{Number of disabling injuries} \times 1 \text{ million}}{\text{Number of employee hours worked}}$$

Strategies to Control Accidents

Designing the work environment to make accidents difficult is perhaps the best way to prevent accidents and increase safety. Among the safety features that can be designed into the physical environment are guards on machines, handrails in stairways, safety goggles and helmets, warning lights, self-correcting mechanisms, and automatic shutoffs. The extent to which these features will actually reduce accidents depends on employee acceptance and use. For example, eye injuries will be reduced by the availability of safety goggles only if employees wear the goggles correctly. If employees are involved in the decision to make some physical change to improve safety, they are more likely to accept the decision than if they are not part of the decision-making process.

Ergonomics.   Another way of improving safety is to make the job itself more comfortable and less fatiguing through ergonomics. **Ergonomics** considers changes in the job environment in conjunction with the physical and physiological capabilities and limitations of the employees.[32]

In an effort to reduce the number of back injuries, Ford Motor Company redesigns workstations and tasks that may be causing musculoskeletal problems for workers. For instance, lifting devices are being introduced on the assembly line to reduce back strain, and walking and working surfaces are being studied to see if floor mats can reduce body fatigue. Videotapes that feature Ford employees performing their jobs both before and after ergonomic redesign are used in training.[33]

Safety Committee.   Another strategy for accident prevention is the use of **safety committee,** composed of employee representatives. The personnel department can serve as a facilitator of the process, assisting in the collection of accident-related information.

The personnel department can also be instrumental by assisting the super-visors in their training efforts and by implementing safety motivation programs, such as contests and communications. Many organizations display signs indi-cating the number of days or hours worked without an accident or posters that read "Safety First." In safety contests, prizes or awards are given to individuals or departments with the best safety record. These programs seem to work best when employees are already safety conscious and when physical conditions of the work environment provide no extreme safety hazards.[34] By way of example,

> Augurias G. Manomaitis, safety director for the Nashua Corporation in Na-shua, N.H., cites his company's "safety work order system" as an example of a safety incentive program that works. Under the system, any employee can make out a safety work order that ensures prompt corrective action on any procedure or equipment believed to be hazardous. The goal at each of the locations is to make that facility the safest in the corporation, Manomaitis says. The reward—or incentive—is to win the charity safety award—a two-part reward for completion of 30 consecutive workdays without a lost-time injury. Employees who work at the plant winning the award can name a local charity to receive a $500 donation and also receive free coffee, soft drinks, and pastries for a 24-hour period.[35]

Behavior Modification.   Reinforcing behaviors that reduce the likelihood of accidents can be highly successful. Reinforcers can range from nonmonetary reinforcers, such as feedback, to activity reinforcers, such as time off, to material reinforcers, such as company-purchased doughnuts during the coffee break, to financial rewards for attaining desired levels of safety. The behavioral approach relies on measuring performance before and after the intervention, specifying and communicating the desired performance to employees, monitoring perfor-mance at unannounced intervals several times a week, and reinforcing desired behavior several times a week with performance feedback.

Exhibit 13.5 shows the before and after results for a behavior modification program to increase safe behavior in two food processing plants. Behavior was monitored for twenty-five weeks—before, during, and after a safety training programs. Slides were used to illustrate safe and unsafe behavior. Employees also were given data on the percentage of safe behaviors in their departments. A goal of 90-percent safe behaviors was established. Supervisors were trained to give positive reinforcement when they observed safe behavior. As shown, following the intervention, the incidence of safe behavior increased substan-tially—from an average of 70 percent to more than 95 percent in the wrapping department and from 78 percent to more than 95 percent in the make-up de-partment. One year after the program, the incidence of lost-time injuries per million hours worked was less than 10, a substantial decline from the preceding year's rate of 53.8.[36]

Management by Objectives Programs.   Behavior modification programs are often linked successfully to management by objectives programs that deal with occupational health. The seven basic steps of these programs are as follows:

1. Identify hazards and obtain information about the frequency of accidents.
2. Based on this information, evaluate the severity and risk of the hazards.
3. Formulate and implement programs to control, prevent, or reduce the pos-sibility of accidents.

EXHIBIT
13.5

Results of a Behavioral Safety Program Introduced in Two Food
Manufacturing Departments.

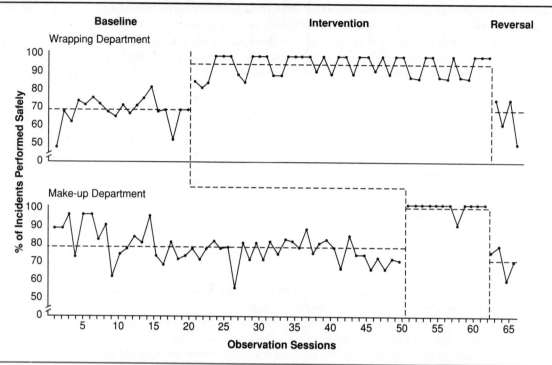

SOURCE: J. Komaki, K. D. Barwick, and L. R. Scott, "A Behavioral Approach to Occupational Safety: Pinpointing and Reinforcing Safe Performance in a Food Manufacturing Plant," *Journal of Applied Psychology*, 63 (1978): 434–445. Copyright 1978 by American Psychological Association. Reprinted by permission.

4. Set specific, difficult, but attainable goals regarding the reduction of accidents or safety problems.
5. Consistently monitor results.
6. Provide positive feedback for correct safety procedures.
7. Monitor and evaluate the program against the goals.[37]

Strategies to Reduce Occupational Diseases

More costly and harmful to organizations and employees than occupational accidents are occupational diseases. Because the causal relationship between the physical environment and occupational diseases is often far more subtle, developing strategies to reduce their incidence is generally more difficult.[38]

Record Keeping. At a minimum, OSHA requires that organizations measure the chemicals in the work environment and keep records on these measurements. Their records must also include precise information about ailments and exposures. Such information must be kept for as long a period as is associated with the incubation period of the specific disease—even as long as forty years. If the organization is sold, the new owner must assume responsibility for storing the old records and continuing to gather the required data. If the organization goes out of business, the administrative director of OSHA must be informed of the whereabouts of the records.

Monitoring Exposure.   While the obvious approach to controlling occupational illnesses is to rid the work place of chemical agents or toxins, an alternative approach is to monitor exposure to hazardous substances. For example, the nuclear industry recruits hundreds of "jumpers" who fix the aging innards of the nation's nuclear generating stations. The atmosphere is so radioactive that jumpers can only stay in about 10 minutes before they "burn out." Their exposure has to be closely monitored to ensure that it does not exceed more than 5,000 millirems (roughly 250 chest x-rays) annually.

Unfortunately, jumpers get rewarded for absorbing the maximum rather than a safe limit of radiation on any given job. Rather than twelve hours of pay for their ten minutes of work, jumpers get a bonus of several hundred dollars each time they "burn out" between jobs. Even with monitoring, it is estimated that 3 to 8 of 10,000 jumpers eventually will die as a result of the exposure.[39]

In addition to monitoring for radioactivity, some organizations now monitor genetic changes due to exposure to carcinogens (e.g., benzene, arsenic, ether, and vinyl chloride). Samples of blood are obtained from employees at fixed intervals in order to determine whether there has been damage to chromosomes. If damage has occurred, the employee is placed in a different job.

Genetic Screening.   **Genetic screening** is the most extreme, and consequently the most controversial, approach to controlling occupational disease. As discussed in Chapter 5, the genetic makeup of individuals makes them more or less predisposed to specific occupational diseases. By genetically screening out individuals who are susceptible to certain ailments, organizations lower their vulnerability to workers' compensation claims and problems. Opponents of genetic screening contend that genetic screening measures one's predisposition to disease, not the actual presence of disease; therefore, such testing violates an individual's rights.[40]

Assistance Programs.   Other organizations are helping employees cope with occupational ailments. For example, Burlington Industries has undertaken a joint program with the Arthritis Foundation and the University of North Carolina School of Medicine to assist employees with arthritis. In an average year, arthritis sufferers lose 27 million working days and receive over $1 billion in disability payments (about 15 percent of all social security disability payments are made to them).[41]

Strategies to Improve the Sociopsychological Work Environment

Increasingly organizations are offering training programs designed to help employees deal with work-related stress. For example, J. P. Morgan offers stress management programs as part of a larger supervisory and management development curriculum. Offered to supervisors, professional staff, and officers, these courses are designed to introduce supervisory and management material, specific technical supervisory/management information skills, and a developmental program designed to give experienced nonofficer managers and professionals some perspective on their roles within the bank. The emphasis here is on providing workers with concrete information to reduce the ambiguity associated with fast-paced changing work roles.[42]

TRENDS IN OCCUPATIONAL SAFETY AND HEALTH

There appear to be two major trends in the area of occupational health and safety.

Occupational Health Policies

As scientific knowledge accumulates and liabilities for health hazards rise, more and more organizations are developing policy statements regarding occupational hazards. These policy statements grow out of concern that organizations should be proactive in dealing with occupational hazards. For example, Dow Chemical's policy states that "No employee, male or female, will knowingly be exposed to hazardous levels of materials known to cause cancer or genetic mutations in humans." The policy also states that women capable of reproduction will not be allowed to work in any areas involving exposure to materials that can be harmful to a fetus.

Because of the newness of these policies, they have been subject to few legal tests. To date, courts have struck down fetal protection policies as discriminatory—unless the company provides strong scientific evidence that exposure can be harmful to the fetus.[43]

What makes the situation more complex is that many workers are reluctant to leave jobs to avoid occupational exposure unless they are guaranteed that their income will not suffer. Some workers have gone so far as to have themselves sterilized to protect their jobs. The policies of AT&T and Digital Equipment seem more humane. They provide income protection for pregnant production workers who might be exposed to the toxic gases and liquids used to etch microscopic circuits onto silicon wafers. Other companies are obtaining signed, voluntary consent agreements from employees who choose to continue working on hazardous jobs. While these statements can absolve employers from punitive damages in civil court, they do not alleviate liability under workers' compensation laws and suits for compensatory damages.

Wellness Programs

Corporations increasingly are focusing on keeping employees healthy rather than on helping them get well. They are investing in wellness programs at record rates:

> Their offerings range from the cheap and simple, like free raisins for morning snacks and scales in the bathrooms, to the expensive and technological, like corporate gymnasiums and computerized health-risk analyses. There are classes for quitting smoking, losing weight, eating better, exercising and managing stress. There are seatbelt and drug-awareness campaigns, and tests for high blood pressure or diabetes.
>
> Part of the reason is spiraling costs of hospitalization, and of health insurance. "The bottom line for business is that it's been losing money on health

care," said Benno Isaacs, a spokesman for the Health Insurance Association of America.

Studies indicate that about half of worksites with more than 50 employees offer some form of wellness program. This year I.B.M., one of the leaders in worksite health care, sponsored 1,800 wellness-oriented programs.[44]

Such programs appear to be paying off. A four-year study of 15,000 Control Data employees showed that employees who participate in limited exercise spend 114 percent more on health insurance claims than co-workers who exercise more do. Smokers and obese workers also had higher medical claims. Control Data, which has had its "Stay Well" program in place since the early 1980s, now markets their program to other organizations, such as Philip Morris and the National Basketball Association.[45]

INTERNATIONAL HEALTH AND SAFETY ISSUES

As consciousness of health and well-being has risen worldwide, pressures to improve health care in work environments have increased in some countries. In others, however, the trend is to ignore health hazards. By having lax safety standards, developing countries can lure large multinational firms to their shores.

Closer Monitoring of Foreign Firms

Following the leakage of lethal methyl isocyanate gas at Union Carbide's pesticide plant in Bhopal, India, that killed more than two thousand persons, India has formed committees in every state to identify potential hazards in factories. While foreign investments and technology are still welcome, the government now insists on knowing more about the potential as well as actual risks involved. New regulations in India require environmental impact studies for all new plants.

By comparison, some countries have had workers' compensation programs and monitoring systems for years. For example, in 1972 New Zealand introduced a no-fault insurance program which covers job injuries. Finland passed an accident insurance act, making it possible to compensate for muscular pain and tendonitis caused by one's work, that same year. In 1977, Sweden passed a law requiring employers to modify the work environment to meet the physical and psychological makeup of workers.

The response to health hazards has been quite different in Mexico. A disaster which killed more than five hundred people and wounded thousands at Pemex, a state-owned gas monopoly in Mexico, has had no noticeable effect on regulations. As one critic contends, "The Mexican government is loathe to crack down on the problem because that would focus attention on the real culprit—the Mexican government itself." The situation is similar in other developing countries. These countries are often so desperate for economic development that they will accept any industry—even those that have the potential for significant harm.[46]

Repetitive Strain Injury In Australia

A computer-related health epidemic known as **repetitive strain injury** (RSI) is widespread in Australia and threatens to drown the country's workers' compensation system. RSI is a label given to a variety of painful, debilitating conditions believed to be caused by rapid, repetitive movements of the hands or arms. RSI appears most often in work involving rapid repetitive movements, such as those associated with operating keyboards, cutting meat, or soldering circuits. It has also been found among such diverse groups as professional tennis players, journalists, court reporters, telephone operators, dog groomers, assembly line workers, welders, and machinists.

One form of RSI that is particularly traumatic is **carpal tunnel syndrome**—a nerve blockage that occurs at the base of the palm of the hand between the thumb and little finger where the carpal ligament stretches between the two muscle groups. With excessive use, the ligament tightens and depresses the nerve into the carpal bones. The result is severe, sharp pain in the wrist that makes gripping impossible as described in Chapter 12.

In the United States, these clinical problems occur in less than 1 percent of the population. In contrast, it is estimated that half of all office workers in Australia suffer from some form of RSI. The Australian problem is exacerbated because a record number of workers' compensation claims (up more than 200 percent) and suits have been filed. In 1984, more than two billion Australian dollars were spent by private insurance programs to settle RSI claims. Additionally, labor-management disputes over RSI have skyrocketed.

There are several potential causes of RSI. Some researchers speculate that technological changes are responsible. When typewriters were used, there were breaks to insert paper, change margins, and adjust the platen. Now files are accessed through the computer rather than from filing cabinets. Employees don't even need to leave their workstations to hand in completed work. This can be accomplished through computer networks and electronic mail systems. Thus, there is no letup in the *pace* of work.

Ergonomists contend the problem is due to poorly designed equipment and tools. In response, the Australian Public Service Association has established detailed workstation design principles. Some of the standards include footrests for short operators; identical viewing distance for screen, source document, and keyboard; a 38-degree angle of viewing; a 90-degree screen angle; and fully adjustable height and knee clearance of computer tables. But still the frequency of RSI is increasing.

An alternative explanation is that repetitive, unrelieved work is part of otherwise unchallenging, dead-end, boring, and monotonous jobs. Therefore, it may be that people aren't getting sick from *doing* the job but from *having* a boring, colorless, dull job. It also seems possible that RSI is best understood as a labor relations and political issue, a form of economic and political resistance to conditions of work and society on the part of unions and feminists in Australia but not elsewhere. While researchers can't agree on the cause, what is known is that RSI is costing the Australian government and firms billions of dollars annually.[47]

SUMMARY

The health of employees in organizations will become increasingly important in the years ahead. Employers are becoming more aware of the cost of ill health and the benefits of having a healthy work force. The federal government, through OSHA, is also making it more necessary for employers to be concerned with employee health. The government's current concern is primarily with employee health as related to occupational accidents and diseases, both aspects of the physical environment. However, organizations can choose to become involved in programs dealing with employee health and the workers' sociopsychological environment as well. If organizations choose not to become involved with improving the sociopsychological environment, the government may prescribe mandatory regulations. Thus, it pays for organizations to be concerned with both aspects of the work environment now. Effective programs for both environments can significantly improve both employee health and the effectiveness of the organization.

When adoption of programs for improvement is being considered, employee involvement is important. As with many quality of work life programs being implemented in organizations, employee involvement in improving safety and health is not only a good idea but also one likely to be desired by the employees. Many things can be done to make work environments better. But it is important to distinguish two types of environments: the physical and the sociopsychological. Each is different and has its own unique subparts. Although some improvement strategies may work well for one part of the work environment, they will not work in other parts. Again, a careful diagnosis is required before programs are selected and implemented.

Assuming that a careful diagnosis indicates the need for a stress management program, the challenge is in deciding which program or strategy to select from the many organizational and individual stress management strategies currently available. Programs such as time management or physical exercise could be set up so employees could help themselves cope, or the organization could alter the conditions within the organization that are associated with stress. The latter requires a diagnosis of what is happening, where, and to whom before deciding how to proceed. Because so many possible sources of stress exist, and because not all people react the same way to them, implementing individual stress management strategies may be more efficient. However, if many people are suffering similar stress symptoms in a specific part of the organization, an organizational strategy is more appropriate.

Information regarding many aspects of safety and health is insufficient—either because it does not exist (e.g., knowledge of causes and effect) or because organizations are unwilling to gather or provide it. From a legal as well as humane viewpoint, it is in the best interests of organizations to seek and provide more information so that more effective strategies for improving safety and health can be developed and implemented. Failure to do so may result in costly legal settlements against organizations or further governmental regulation of work place safety and health. These comments apply equally to the next chapter on employee rights.

DISCUSSION QUESTIONS

1. In what ways can an organization prevent occupational accidents?
2. How can physical work environment strategies and sociopsychological work environment strategies be assessed?
3. The United States prides itself on freedom, democracy, and free labor markets. If this is true, why not make employees responsible for health and

safety? In other words, employers who offer riskier employment will simply pay workers more for bearing the risk (a wage premium), and the workers can in turn buy more insurance coverage to cover this risk. Discuss the advantages and disadvantages of this approach.

4. Who is responsible for work place safety and health? The employer? The employee? The federal government? Judges and juries? Explain.

5. How are physical hazards distinct from sociopsychological hazards? What implications does this have for programs to deal with these hazards?

6. Is there such a thing as an unsafe worker? Assuming that accident-prone workers exist, how can effective personnel functions address this problem?

7. Is accident proneness a reliable trait? If not, does that mean that organizations cannot control it? Explain.

8. What incentives does OSHA provide the employer for promoting work place safety? Explain.

9. How might a company's strategy to prevent occupational accidents differ from a program to prevent occupational disease? In what ways might the programs be similar?

10. Distinguish the "no-risk" from the "significant risk" standard.

CASE STUDY

Does Our Government Really Protect Us?

B erea, Kentucky, is a small community of thirty thousand people located in the rolling hills of eastern Kentucky. Berea College is a small liberal arts college well known for its student crafts industry. The industry provides employment for students, many of whom are from Appalachian families who cannot afford to send their children to school. Nearby, the Army maintains the Blue Grass Depot, affectionately known as the "Bunny Farm" because of the rabbits once housed in the igloo-shaped huts that dotted the rolling hills. The rabbits are gone now, replaced by machine monitors that run continuously to detect any leaks in the seventy thousand lethal M-55 nerve-gas rockets that have been stockpiled here since 1960.

Recently, a citizens group has begun an aggressive lobbying campaign with both the Pentagon and the local depot to have the nerve gas removed. Over a relatively short period of six years the local citizens, through a succession of mishaps and sometimes mysterious events, have come to distrust the management of the depot and to question the wisdom of the depot's continued operations.

The local citizens have learned, for example, that the wooden crates donated by the depot as scrap wood to anyone willing to haul them away had been treated with PCP, a chemical giving off cancer-inducing dioxin when burned. A local doctor reported his own study of what he termed a "high incidence" of leukemia in the county surrounding Berea. Such happenings, coupled with recent reports of cattle mysteriously dying in pastures surrounding the depot, had brought the local citizenry precariously close to hysteria.

The incident that mobilized the group to action was the Army's routine disposal of smoke pots designed for making battlefield smoke screens during World War II. The depot had fallen behind its incinerating schedule for disposing of the smoke pots, and in late summer it scheduled a massive burning of the pots. Unfortunately, the incineration coincided with a temperature inversion (common to this area of the country) which resulted in a thick cloud blanketing the entire area, including nearby Interstate 45. Traffic had to be halted, and fifty people were taken to local hospitals with complaints of nausea, stinging eyes, and respiratory problems.

At first the depot denied any knowledge or responsibility for the smoke cloud. Officials at the depot later stated that they did not want to "inflame" (no pun intended) already strained relations between the depot and the community. Local officials, however, soon learned of the depot's role in the smoke cloud and of local doctors' frustrations when seeking clues for treatment of the rash of victims.

Sally Hopkins has recently reported to the Blue Grass Depot as the new public affairs officer. Her primary assignment is to help repair community relations. Scarcely settled into her job, she has just discovered that the path ahead will be filled with more obstacles: nerve-gas machine monitors have malfunctioned, and some of the missiles are beginning to leak small amounts of gas.

Case Questions

1. What protection do citizens have from actions of their own government?
2. What risks does the depot pose to the local community? How can these risks be minimized?
3. How would you attempt to assess whether the risks posed by the depot are too great? Do you think these risks would be any less great if a private sector firm were responsible for the safekeeping of the nerve gas?
4. As Sally Hopkins, what specific actions would you take to improve community relations?

NOTES

1. A. Miller, K. Springen, J. Gorgon, B. Cohn, L. Drew, and T. Barrett, "Stress on the Job," *Newsweek*, 25 Apr. 1988, p. 25; S. Swooplop, R. Rhein, Jr., and J. Weber, "Stress: The Test Americans Are Failing," *Business Week*, 18 Apr. 1988, p. 75; L. Vallarosa, "Stressed-Out," *American Banker*, 19 Oct. 1987, p. 38.
2. R. S. Schuler, "Occupational Health in Organizations: Strategies for Personnel Effectiveness," *Personnel Administrator* (Jan. 1982): 47–56; R. S. Schuler, "Occupational Health in Organizations: A Measure of Personnel Effectiveness," in *Readings in Personnel and Human Resource Management*, 2d ed., ed. R. S. Schuler and S. A. Youngblood (St. Paul: West, 1984).
3. See the entire April 1983 and October 1985 issues of the *Personnel Administrator*. See also A. Bennett, "Is Your Job Making You Sick?" *Wall Street Journal*, 22 Apr. 1988, IR–28R. L. Falkenberg, "Employee Fitness Programs," *Academy of Management Review* (June 1987): 514; J. Quick and D. Quick, *Organizational Stress and Preventive Management* (New York: McGraw-Hill, 1984): 20.
4. J. Olian, "New Approaches to Employment Screening," in *Readings in Personnel and Human Resource Management*, 3d ed., ed. R. S. Schuler, S. A. Youngblood, and V. L. Huber (St. Paul: West, 1988), 206–16.
5. T. A. Beehr and R. S. Schuler, "Stress in Organizations," in *Personnel Management*, ed. K. M. Rowland and G. Ferris (Boston: Allyn & Bacon, 1982); A. P. Brief, R. S. Schuler, and M. Van Sell, *Managing Job Stress* (Boston: Little, Brown, 1980); R. S. Schuler and S. E. Jackson, "Managing Stress through PHRM Practices: An Uncertainty Interpretation," in *Research in Personnel and Human Resources Management*, vol. 4, ed. K. M. Rowland and G. Ferris (Greenwich, Conn.: JAI Press, 1986); D. S. Thelan, D. Ledgerwood, and C. F. Walters, "Health and Safety in the Workplace:

A New Challenge for Business Schools," *Personnel Administrator* (Oct. 1985): 37–46.
6. M. Mallory and H. Bradford, "An Invisible Workplace Hazard Gets Harder to Ignore," *Business Week*, 30 Jan. 1989, pp. 92–93.
7. "Principles for Worker Safety and Comfort," *Bulletin to Management*, 5 June 1986, p. 189.
8. *The Occupational Safety and Health Act*, Public Law 91–596, 29 Dec. 1970, and *The Occupational Safety and Health Act*, publication no. 149 (Washington D.C.: American Federation of Labor and Congress of Industrial Organizations), Sept. 1971. See also "Has OSHA Become Too Much of a Pussycat?" *Business Week*, 11 Mar. 1985, pp. 82G–82J; M. Hayes, "What Can You Do When OSHA Calls?" *Personnel Administrator* (Nov. 1982): 65–66.
9. "Warrant Needed to Inspect Injury/Illness Records," *Bulletin to Management*, 7 July 1988, p. 210.
10. B. Meier, "Use of Right-to-Know Rules Is Increasing Public's Scrutiny of Chemical Companies," *Wall Street Journal*, 23 May 1985, p. 10; "OSHA's Final Labelling Standard," *Bulletin to Management*, 1 Dec. 1983, p. 1; P. A. Susser, "The OSHA Standard and State "Right-to-Know" Laws: The Preemption Battle Continues," *Employee Relations Law Journal* (Spring 1985): 615–34.
11. "OSHA Action: AIDS, Health Care and Record Fine," *Bulletin to Management*, 30 July 1987, p. 241. See also "On the Safety and Health Scene," *Bulletin to Management*, 2 Apr. 1987, p. 105.
12. B. Meir, "Use of Right-to-Know Rules"; M. G. Miner, "Legal Concerns Facing Human Resources Managers: An Overview," in *Readings in Personnel and Human Resource Management*, 3d ed., ed. R. S. Schuler, S. A. Youngblood, and V. L. Huber (St. Paul: West, 1988); "OSHA's Final Labelling Standard," *Bulletin to Management*; P. A. Susser, "Update on Hazard Com-

munication," *Personnel Administrator* (Oct. 1985): 57–61.

13. "Hazard Communication Training: Compliance Cues," *Bulletin to Management*, 13 Mar. 1986, p. 81.

14. F. Allen, "Battle Building over "Right to Know" Laws Regarding Toxic Items Used by Workers," *Wall Street Journal*, 3 Jan. 1983; J. B. Dubeck and P. A. Susser, "Hazard Communications: New Disclosure Burdens on Management," *Personnel Administrator* (May 1984): 79–83; "State Right-to-Know Laws: Toxic Substances," *Bulletin to Management*, 22 Nov. 1984, pp. 4–5; "Worker Right to Know," *Chemical Work*, 18 Apr. 1984, pp. 38–44; W. E. Stead and J. G. Stead, "OSHA's Cancer Prevention Policy: Where Did It Come From and Where Is It Going?" *Personnel Journal* (Jan. 1983): 54–60.

15. "From the Editor," *Employee Relations Law Journal* (1981): 361–63; L. Greenhouse, "Court Goes Its Own Way on Key Regulatory Cases," *New York Times*, 21 June 1981; R. H. Sand, "Current Developments in OSHA," *Employee Relations Law Journal* (1981): 484–93.

16. J. M. Ivancevich, M. T. Matteson, and E. P. Richards III, "Who's Liable for Stress on the Job?" *Harvard Business Review* (Mar./Apr. 1985): 60–70.

17. "Safety Sense," *Personnel Administrator* (Jan. 1983): 73.

18. "Rates of Production and Emotional State," *Personnel Journal* (Apr. 1982): 355–64; B. Keller, "Workers Are Often a Hazard to Themselves," *New York Times*, 8 July 1984: 1.

19. A. Halcrow, "Safety: Seeing Is Believing," *Personnel Journal* (Aug. 1988): 22–24; N. Root, "Injuries at Work Are Fewer among Older Employees," *Monthly Labor Review* (Mar. 1981): 30–34.

20. K. Noble, "For OSHA, Balance Is Hard to Find," *New York Times*, 10 Jan. 1988, p. E5; "Occupational Injuries and Illnesses," *Bulletin to Management Datagraph*, 17 Dec. 1987, p. 404.

21. M. Corn, "An Inside View of OSHA Compliance," *Personnel Administrator* (Nov. 1979): 39–44.

22. Ashford, "The Nature and Dimension," p. 48; C. L. Wang, "Occupational Skin Disease Continues to Plague Industry," *Monthly Labor Review* (Feb. 1979): 17–22.

23. A. Freedman, "Cigarette Smoking Is Growing Hazardous to Careers in Business," *Wall Street Journal*, 23 Apr. 1987, p. 1; C. Lemaistre, "Nobody Is Safe If a Smoker Is Around," *New York Times*, 4 Jan. 1987, sec. 3, p. 2.

24. J. Hyatt, "Hazardous Effects of VDT Legislation," *INC.* (Mar. 1985): 27; K. R. Pelletier, "The Hidden Hazards of the Modern Office," *New York Times*, 8 Sept. 1985, p. F3; R. Sutton and A. Rafaeli, "Characteristics of Work Stations as Potential Occupational Stressors," *Academy of Management Journal* 30, no. 2 (June 1987): 260–76; "VDT Study: Safety Charges, Design Changes," *Bulletin to Management*, 21 July 1983, p. 27; W. L. Weis, "No Smoking," *Personnel Journal* (Sept. 1984): 53–58.

25. M. Fusilier, D. Ganster, and B. Mayes, "Effects of Social Support, Role Stress, and Locus of Control on

Health," *Journal of Management* 13, no. 3 (Fall 1987): 517–28; S. E. Jackson, R. S. Schuler, and D. J. Vredenburgh, "Managing Stress in Turbulent Times," in *Occupational Stress and Organizational Effectiveness*, ed. A. Riley, S. Zaccaro, and R. Rosen (New York: Praeger, 1986); R. Wolfe, D. Ulrich, and D. Parker, "Employee Health Management Programs Review, Critique, and Research Agenda," *Journal of Management* 13, no. 4 (Winter 1987): 603–16.

26. E. E. Lawler III, *Pay and Organizational Development* (Reading, Mass.: Addison-Wesley, 1981); A. B. Shostak, *Blue Collar Stress* (Reading, Mass.: Addison-Wesley, 1980).

27. M. Frankenhaeuser and B. Gardell, "Underload and Overload in Working Life: Outline of a Multidisciplinary Approach," *Journal of Human Stress* 2 (1976): 35–45; M. Pesci, "Stress Management: Separating Myth from Reality," *Personnel Administrator* (Jan. 1982): 57–67; But even if individuals are under heavy work loads and stress, they may not necessarily want to eliminate them. See R. Richlefs, "Many Executives Complain of Stress, But Few Want Less-Pressured Jobs," *Wall Street Journal*, 29 Sept. 1982, p. 35.

28. "Deadline Pressures Aggravate Stress: Court Orders Money for Widow," *Resource* (May 1985): 1.

29. For extensive discussion of office space and physical design issues, see L. Altman, "Some Who Use VDT's Miscarried, Study Says," *New York Times*, 5 June 1988, p. 22; "Reproductive Hazards—How Employers Are Responding," *Fair Employment Practices*, 29 Oct. 1987, p. 132; R. S. Schuler, L. R. Ritzman, and V. Davis, "Merging Prescriptive and Behavioral Approaches for Office Layout," *Production and Inventory Management Journal* 3 (1981): 131–42.

30. B. Dumaine, "Cool Cures for Burnout," *Fortune*, 20 June 1988, pp. 78–84; S. E. Jackson and R. S. Schuler, "Preventing Employee Burnout," *Personnel* (Mar./Apr. 1983): 58–68.

31. H. J. Hilaski, "Understanding Statistics on Occupational Illnesses," *Monthly Labor Review* (Mar. 1981): 25–29; R. A. Reber, J. A. Wallin, and J. S. Chhokar, "Reducing Industrial Accidents: A Behavioral Experiment," *Industrial Relations* (Winter 1984): 119–25.

32. Corn, "An Inside View," 42; C. G. Drury, "Most Workplace Accidents Are the Result of Ergonomic Problems," *Bulletin to Management*, 23 Dec. 1982, pp. 1–2; V. Reinhart, "Ergonomic Studies Improving Life on the Job," *Job Safety and Health* (Dec. 1975): 16–21.

33. "National ASPA Conference Highlights," *Bulletin to Management*, 28 July 1988, p. 239.

34. A. Czernek and G. Clark, "Incentives for Safety," *Job Safety and Health* (Oct. 1973): 7–11; D. Hampton, "Contests Have Side Effects, Too," *California Management Review* 12 (1970): 86–94; "New OSHA Tack," *Personnel Administrator* (June 1981): 12.

35. "Safety Tips from the Pros," *Bulletin to Management*, 16 May 1985, p. 1.

36. J. Komaki, K. D. Barwick, and L. Scott, "Pinpointing and Reinforcing Safe Performance in a Food Manufacturing Plant," *Journal of Applied Psychology* 63 (1978): 434–45.

37. H. M. Taylor, "Occupational Health Management-by-Objectives." *Personnel* (Jan./Feb. 1980): 58–64.

38. "Dubious Tactics in the War on Cancer," *Business Week*, 14 June 1976, p. 76.

39. M. Williams, "Ten Minutes Work for 12 Hours Pay? What's the Catch?" *Wall Street Journal*, 12 Oct. 1983, p. 19.

40. J. Olian, "New Approaches to Employment Screening, "in *Readings in Personnel and Human Resource Management*, 3d ed., ed. R. S. Schuler, S. A. Youngblood, and V. L. Huber (St. Paul: West, 1988), 206–16.

41. R. E. Dedmon and M. K. Kubiak, "The Medical Director's Role in Industry, *Personnel Administrator*, (Sept. 1981): 59–67.

42. R. W. Driver and R. A. Ratliff, "Employers' Perceptions of Benefits Accrued from Physical Fitness Programs," *Personnel Administrator* (Aug. 1982): 21–26; Jackson and Schuler, "Preventing Employee Burnout"; M. T. Matteson and J. M. Ivancevich, "The How, What, and Why of Stress Management Training," *Personnel Journal* (Oct. 1982): 768–74.

43. B. Meier, "Companies Wrestle with Threats to Workers' Reproductive Health," *Wall Street Journal*, 5 Feb. 1987, p. 25. Also see,

44. M. F. Davis, "Worksite Health Promotion," *Personnel Administrator* (Dec. 1984): 45–50; W. Hartman and J. Cozzetto, "Wellness in the Workplace," *Personnel Administrator* (Aug. 1984): 108–17; J. J. Hoffman, Jr., and C. J. Hobson, "Physical Fitness and Employee Effectiveness," *Personnel Administrator* (Apr. 1984): 101–13; N. Kondrasuk, "Corporate Physical Fitness Programs: The Role of the Personnel Department," *Personnel Administrator* (Dec. 1984): 75–80; S. Salmans, "A Fitness Center for Professionals," *New York Times*, 3 Jan. 1985, p. D5; J. Hirsch, "What's New in 'Wellness' Programs," *New York Times*, 5 Oct. 1986, p. F19; J. Olian, "Employee Wellness: Managerial, Governmental and Legal Reactions in the U.S. and Internationally," paper presented at the Conference on International Personnel and Human Resource Management, Dec. 1987, Singapore.

45. F. B. James, "Study Lays Groundwork for Tying Health Costs to Workers' Behavior," *Wall Street Journal*, 14 Apr. 1987, p. 37.

46. "Foreign Firms Feel the Impact of Bhopal Most," *Wall Street Journal*, 26 Nov. 1986, p. 24; P. R. Balgopal, C. Ramanathan, and M. Patchner, "Employee Assistance Programs: A Cross-Cultural Perspective," paper presented at the Conference on International Personnel and Human Resource Management, Dec. 1987, Singapore.

47. S. Kiesler and T. Finholt, "The Mystery of RSI," *American Psychologist* (Dec. 1988): 1004–15.

Employee Rights

Charges and Discharges

When it comes to protecting yourself against lawsuits from your employees, generally the best practice is to treat them decently and fairly. Still, that's not an absolute guarantee, particularly when the issue is termination, a difficult and painful experience all around. . . .

In most cases, of course, you and your employees are free to establish and end working relationships to best suit your needs. But times are changing, and to protect your company, you should at least be aware of recent legal trends.

Traditionally, the most common contract between U.S. employers and employees, whether oral, written, or implied, established an at-will relationship. The employee was free to quit at any time, and the employer could fire at any time, for any or no reason and without obligation for severance pay or any other benefits. . . .

Today, most of the work force are still at-will employees, but court decisions and statutes from 43 states have put new limits on what their employers can do. Now, lawsuits from fired at-will employees, far from being dropped, are increasingly being decided against employers. For example, in recent years, close to 70% of California's wrongful-discharge cases were decided against employers.

While the decisions and statutes governing at-will employment vary from state to state, the new underlying assumption is that such employees may gain at least limited rights to job security. The decisions fall into a few broad legal categories: good faith and fair dealing; the public interest; and implied contracts.

Good Faith and Fair Dealing

Many judges don't require specific promises of job security, oral or written, to uphold the claims of a fired employee. Instead, they have ruled that at-will employment contracts contain implied promises to deal fairly and in good faith, as does every other commercial contract.

Perhaps the most notorious breaches of good faith and fair dealing are the horror stories we've all heard about employees who work years for a company and then are fired just months before their pensions are vested. But most cases are far less dramatic. For you as an employer, the thing to remember about good faith and fair dealing is this: you can't enter into a bargain with employees and then prevent them from getting what they bargained for, whether pensions, sales commissions, warnings of poor performance, vacation days, stock options—whatever. And the bargain need not be in writing.

Even employers with legitimate concerns about employee performance may run afoul of a court-imposed requirement of dealing fairly and in good faith with at-will employees. American Airlines, for example, dismissed Lawrence M. Cleary, an at-will employee, for three instances of misconduct: leaving his work station without permission, harassing another employee, and stealing. But it acted contrary to its expressed policy of giving employees an impartial hearing before dismissal. When Cleary sued to get his job back, the court, noting his 18 years of apparently satisfactory service and American's dismissal policy, said this combination created a right to job security and told the company it had to give Cleary a chance to prove, in court, that he was fired without good reason. Every business contract, the court ruled, implies a promise to deal fairly and in good faith. American had led Cleary to expect that impartial hearing, so he should have received it.

Restrictions in the Public Interest

Your prerogative to fire at-will employees is limited by a number of public policy considerations. . . . Federal and most state antidiscrimination laws, for example, say you can't fire someone for filing a discrimination complaint.

continued

Many states also have statutes that make it illegal to fire employees because their wages are garnisheed, because they refuse to work under conditions they believe unsafe, insist on time off to vote, or demand to be paid at the minimum wage. In many states you aren't permitted to fire employees for exercising the right to file a workers' compensation claim, say, or promote a union, or ask for information about hazards in the workplace. While these rights may seem undeniable, a surprising number of employees are fired for exercising them. And when they sue, they often win. Now, many courts go beyond the statutes and find that a vaguer concept of public policy or the public interest can prevent employers from dismissing at-will employees even when there is no specific statute prohibiting it.

In an Oregon case, for example, jury duty was the issue. Vickie Nees, a clerk at Hocks Laboratories, was called for jury duty. Her boss gave her a letter addressed to the court asking that she be excused. Nees wanted to serve, however, and ignored his request. Soon after she was seated on the jury, her boss fired her. And although she was an at-will employee, Nees sued Hocks. She claimed that the company had fired her only becuase she wanted to serve as a juror, not because her work was poor, as it claimed. . . . The jury awarded her $3,000 in punitive damages and $650 in compensatory damages. Although an appellate court reversed the punitive damages award because the Nees case created new law, the judge indicated that punitive damages could be available in the future. . . .

Not surprisingly, the courts also have ruled that an employee can't be fired for refusing to do something that is clearly illegal—such as committing perjury, or fixing prices as part of a marketing strategy.

The best general guide when it comes to issues of public interest is to rely on your business judgment and sense of community ethics.

Implied Contracts

Many employers believe that they have an at-will employment policy but lose wrongful-discharge cases in court because their *practices* have created unintended obligations—what the courts consider implied contracts. As you've no doubt read, these unintended obligations often are spelled out in personnel manuals or other management communications.

In a case that Blue Cross & Blue Shield of Michigan lost, Charles Toussaint was told during an initial interview that his job would be secure if he performed adequately. When Toussaint pressed the interviewer to find out just how secure his job would be, the interviewer told him that as long as his work was OK, he would never have to look for a job again. In fact, the interviewer said, he couldn't remember Blue Cross ever firing anyone. Five years later, Blue Cross fired Toussaint. He successfully sued, and the company appealed, arguing that Toussaint had no written contract and could be fired at any time. Michigan's highest court ruled that the promises Blue Cross made during the interview created an enforceable oral contract and upheld the decision.

The other side of the coin, however, is that well-thought-out personnel manuals and other employee communications can protect you rather than create unintended commitments. In a case brought by an employee of Sears, Roebuck & Co., for example, the company's employment contract and personnel manual became key issues. The contract contained a clear statement that the company reserved the right to dismiss an employee at any time, without any reason. The personnel manual specified that employees could be dismissed for such reasons as disorderly conduct, excessive tardiness, and damaging company property, then went on to say the company wasn't limited to these reasons. Thus, the court ruled, Sears had explicitly reserved its right to fire at will.

If you, too, value maximum flexibility in hiring and firing, you'll want to maintain at-will employment relationships—within the limits allowed by statutes and court decisions. You're probably safest to incorporate a clear policy statement in your employment contracts or employee handbooks. The law doesn't require any such written statement for at-will employees, but as the Sears case suggests, it can short-circuit litigation that might otherwise be costly. You might also consider using written employment contracts of only a year's duration, which must be renewed to remain effective.

SOURCE: M. Manley, "Charges and Discharges," *INC.* (March 1988): 124–28. Used with permission from *INC.*, copyright 1988.

T HIS "PHRM in the News" feature illustrates two major issues in PHRM. One is the predominance of employees who can be fired at will, and the other is the growing emphasis on employee rights. Some managers view employee rights as a way in which employees can second-guess management's decisions and begin to take control of the organization. Other managers and many employees view employee rights as a way to help ensure that management decisions are made on a sound, justifiable basis and that employees are protected from arbitrary and vindictive management actions.

Employee rights are regarded here as those rights that employees desire regarding the security of their jobs and the treatment administered by their employers while on the job, regardless of whether or not those rights are protected by law or collective bargaining agreements.

Other important employee rights not described in the "PHRM in the News" include (1) the right to privacy, (2) the right to know about work place hazards, (3) the right to work in an environment free of sexual harassment, (4) the right to be assisted in correcting ineffective performance, and (5) the right to plant/office closing notification and outplacement assistance.[1]

PURPOSES AND IMPORTANCE OF EMPLOYEE RIGHTS

Treating employees fairly and with respect is important to organizations. Violation of legally protected employee rights (e.g., the right to not be discriminated against in employment decisions) can result in severe penalties and fines.

For example, in one age discrimination case, U.S. Judge Robert Merhige, Jr., declared that the Liggett and Myers Cigarette Company illegally dismissed 107 white-collar workers over the age of forty. The court ordered ten years of back pay, benefits, and raises. Because the firings were intentional, the actual awards were double the pay determination. As a result of the Toussaint case described in "PHRM in the News," Blue Cross/Blue Shield paid $72,000 as a settlement.[2]

Not respecting employee rights can also be costly because of the increased difficulty in attracting and retaining good employees. Once an organization gets a reputation as an unfair employer, it is difficult to overcome. As a result, recruiting efforts are stymied.

RELATIONSHIPS INFLUENCING EMPLOYEE RIGHTS

As Exhibit 14.1 shows, the area of employee rights has extensive relationships with other PHRM activities and the internal environment.

Relationships with Other PHRM Activities

The most important relationships between PHRM activities and employee rights are those involving union-management relations, training and development, and performance appraisal.

Union-Management Relations. Where unions exist, employee job security rights are generally protected by the union-management contract. Because less

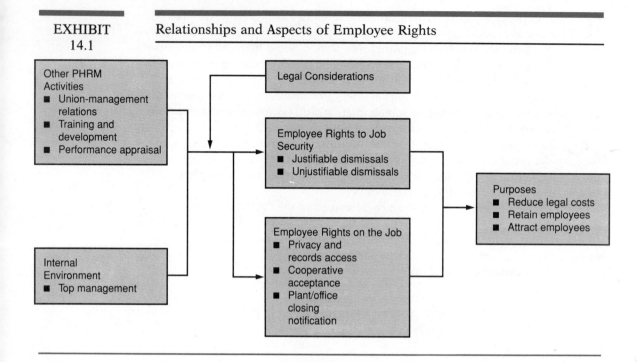

EXHIBIT 14.1   Relationships and Aspects of Employee Rights

than 20 percent of the labor force is unionized, many workers are left without this protection. However, as more cases similar to the Blue Cross/Blue Shield case are settled, the protection afforded the union-management contract becomes relatively less protective. Nevertheless, if job security becomes a major issue, it may stimulate organizing activity, as suggested in Chapter 15.

Training and Development.   Supervisors are more likely to unjustifiably dismiss employees and commit sexual harassment offenses if they have not received effective training on these issues. A frequently suggested approach to the issue of sexual harassment is to develop an organizational policy on it and train all the supervisors and managers in avoiding sexual harassment.[3] Training is also an often overlooked alternative to dismissal. Yet for the employee who suffers from a skill deficiency but who has the ability to perform the job, it may be the most cost-effective option.

Performance Appraisal.   A ground for dismissal (in addition to the termination-at-will doctrine) that supervisors frequently use is poor employee performance. When asked by the court to show evidence of such, however, supervisors are often unable to produce it. Records of employee performance are either inaccurately maintained or inaccurately used. Sometimes employees are never made aware that they are performing inadequately or never given a chance to respond to charges of poor performance or to improve (lack of due process). As more suits against unjustifiable dismissal are won by employees, organizations are likely to intensify efforts to train supervisors and managers in good appraisal practices, to maintain accurate PHRM records, and to establish grievance procedures to ensure due process protection.[4]

Relationships with the Internal Environment

Top management shares some of the responsibility for employee rights because they set policy, with input from PHRM, on the treatment of human resources. Although flexibility may be limited in deciding whether or not to respect the legal rights of employees, there is flexibility in deciding whether or not to respect the "humane" rights of employees. Top management's policy regarding these rights is important in shaping some of the PHRM activities and the way the organization's human resources are treated—above and beyond the way they "must" be treated.

LEGAL CONSIDERATIONS IN
EMPLOYEE RIGHTS

Because the entire activity of employee rights is filled with legal considerations, this section is much larger than those in previous chapters. This section is followed by suggested PHRM strategies to facilitate employer recognition of all the employee rights discussed in this chapter.

Employee Rights to Job Security

Over the years, the major limit on employee rights to job security has been the employer's right to terminate employees for any reason. This right is known as the **termination-at-will rule** (also referred to as the **employment-at-will rule**). The termination-at-will rule, which was developed in the United States over 100 years ago, was explained by one Tennessee court in 1884 in this way: "All may dismiss their employee(s) at will, be they many or few, for good cause, for no cause, or even for cause morally wrong without being thereby guilty of legal wrong" (*Payne v. Western & A.R.R. Co.*, 1884).

Limitations on Termination.   Although employers have relied on the termination-at-will rule over the years, it is proving to be less of a legally justifiable defense today because of several recent statutes (Title VII of the Civil Rights Act of 1964, the Age Discrimination in Employment Act of 1967, and the Rehabilitation Act of 1973) which have been discussed elsewhere.[5]

The National Labor Relations Act of 1935 prohibits discharge for union-organizing activities or for asserting rights under a union contract, even if the employee in question had a record of poor performance (*NLRB v. Transportation Management*, 1983).[6] When employees are represented by a union, the union contract replaces the termination-at-will doctrine and specifies the conditions under which an employee can be fired.

Such court decisions as the *Board of Regents of State Colleges v. Roth* (1972) protect workers from discharge when due process has not been given the employee. Various state acts, such as Montana's Maternity Leave Act which prohibits employers from terminating female employees because of pregnancy, also limit the employer's rights.

In summary, discharge is not a legitimate action under any circumstances for the following employee actions:

- Whistleblowing (e.g., opposing and publicizing employer policies or practices that violate laws such as the antitrust, consumer protection, or environmental protection laws)[7]
- Garnishment for any one indebtedness
- Complaining or testifying about equal pay or wage/hour law violations
- Complaining or testifying about safety hazards and/or refusing an assignment because of the belief that the assignment is dangerous
- Engaging in union activities, provided there is no violence or unlawful behavior
- Engaging in concerted activity to protest wages, working conditions, or safety hazards
- Filing a workers' compensation claim
- Filing unfair labor practice charges with the NLRB or a state agency
- Filing discrimination charges with the Equal Employment Opportunity Commission (EEOC) or a state or municipal fair employment agency
- Cooperating in the investigation of a charge
- Reporting Occupational Safety and Health Administration (OSHA) violations[8]

Permissible Termination.   Although termination for good cause has not been an explicitly accepted doctrine for nonunion organizations, the decisions that courts are rendering suggest the safest (legal) grounds for discharge include the following:

- Incompetence in performance that does not respond to training or to accommodation
- Gross or repeated insubordination
- Too many unexcused absences
- Repeated lateness
- Verbal abuse
- Physical violence
- Falsification of records
- Drunkenness on the job
- Theft[9]

Firing or discharge, even under one of the prior nine conditions, should be the last step in a progressive discipline system such as the one presented in Chapter 7.[10] Furthermore, all evidence and material relevant to each step and even any decision to discharge an employee should be documented.

Even though an employer may have the right to fire an employee, the employer may be requested to show evidence indicating that none of the protections against termination at will or for good cause was violated.

Employee Rights on the Job

Rights to Privacy and Access to Employment Records.   Recently, several lawsuits have been brought against organizations for invasion of privacy rights. The encompassing law is the Privacy Act of 1974 which applies only to federal agencies. It pertains to the verification of references in selection and employment decisions. This act allows individuals to determine which records pertaining to them are collected, used, and maintained; to review and amend such records; to prevent unspecified use of such records; and to bring civil suit for damages against those intentionally violating the rights specified in the act.

The second federal privacy law is the Fair Credit and Reporting Act, which permits job applicants to know the nature and content of the credit file on them that is obtained by the organization. The third law is the Family Education Rights and Privacy Act, or the Buckley Amendment. This allows students to inspect their educational records and prevents educational institutitons from supplying information without students' consent. If students do not provide this consent, potential employers are prevented from learning of their educational record. The fourth law is the Freedom of Information Act, which also pertains only to federal agencies. This act allows individuals to see all the material an agency uses in its decision-making processes.

While the four laws detailed above apply primarily to federal agencies, several states (e.g., California, Connecticut, Maine, Michigan, Oregon, and Pennsylvania) have enacted laws that give employees access to their personnel files and define what information employees are entitled and not entitled to see, as well as where, when, and under what circumstances the employees may see their files.[11]

As employee's right to privacy has recently been extended to include the right not to be subjected to a polygraph test as a condition of employment (Employment Polygraph Protection Act of 1988). As illustrated in the second "PHRM in the News," court rulings are also being applied in the area of drug testing (*O'Connor v. Ortega*, 1987).

Right to Cooperative Acceptance.   The right of employees to be treated fairly and with respect, regardless of race, sex, national origin, physical disability, age, or religion, while *on the job* (as well as in obtaining a job and maintaining job security) is called **cooperative acceptance.** Not only do employees have the right *not* to be discriminated against in employment practices and decisions, but also they have the right to be free of sexual harassment.

The 1980 EEOC guidelines state that **sexual harassment** is a form of sex discrimination. According to the guidelines, verbal and physical conduct of a sexual nature is harassment under the following conditions:

- Submission to such conduct is either explicitly or implicitly made a term or condition of an individual's employment.
- Submission to or rejection of such conduct by an individual is used as the basis for employment decisions affecting such individuals.
- Such conduct has the purpose of effect of substantially interfering with an individual's work performance or creating an intimidating, hostile, or offensive working environment.[12]

A recent U.S. Supreme Court decision illustrates why employers should be especially concerned about the issue of sexual harassment (*Meritor Savings v. Vinson*, 1986). A bank teller charged that her supervisor intimidated her into engaging in a sexual liaison. The bank claimed that if, in fact, she had a sexual affair with her supervisor, she submitted voluntarily to his advances, and he never conditioned employment benefits on her particpation in the affair. But the Supreme Court rejected those arguments. Even if the teller wasn't forced to participate in the alleged sexual liaison, the Court ruled that she could still make a case if she could show that those advances were "unwelcome." And though there was no evidence that her supervisor conditioned tangible job benefits on her participation in the alleged liaison, she could still sue by demonstrating that his conduct created an "intimidating, hostile, or offensive working environment."[13]

PHRM IN THE NEWS

Ex-Employee Wins Drug-Test Case

SAN FRANCISCO, Oct. 30—A computer programmer who was dismissed from her job with the Southern Pacific Transportation Company for refusing to participate in a random drug test of employees was awarded $485,000 in damages today by a jury here.

The jury found that Southern Pacific had wrongfully discharged the employee, Barbara Luck, who had challenged the drug test on the basis of personal privacy. It also found Southern Pacific guilty of breaching its duty of good faith and fair dealing and of intentional infliction of emotional harm.

Kay Lucas-Wallace, one of the San Francisco lawyers representing Mrs. Luck, said the verdict "means that employers must consider the appropriateness of testing individual employees." . . .

A First For Private Sector

While numerous lawsuits have been brought by public employees challenging drug testing requirements for police officers, customs service agents and teachers, the trial here was one of the few private-sector cases in the country. . . .

California, like a dozen or so other states, has a constitutional provision guaranteeing individuals the right to privacy. This provision elevated the issue to a constitutional standard, requiring that a "compelling interest" be shown to allow the intrusion on the personal privacy of an employee.

Before the case went to the jury, San Francisco Superior Court Judge Maxine M. Chesney ruled that Southern Pacific's basic drug testing program was constitutional because it served a compelling interest in protecting the public safety.

Question For The Jury

The question remaining for the jury was whether an employee performing duties like Mrs. Luck's needed to be included in drug testing in order to achieve the safe operation of the train system.

. . . In closing arguments on Thursday, Mark S. Rudy, . . . representing Mrs. Luck, told the jury that "there was no basis at all" for including his client in the drug test. "She did not operate a train," Mr. Rudy said. "She was not involved with safety."

Southern Pacific's Argument

Robert S. Bogason, a lawyer for Southern Pacific, argued that because a portion of her job dealt with programs for replacement of defective rails, there was a safety factor involved.

The case arose when Mrs. Luck, who had worked for Southern Pacific for six years, came to work on July 11, 1985, and without prior notice was asked to sign a form consenting to a drug test and provide a urine sample for testing. She refused on grounds of privacy and was the only one of nearly 500 employees to do so. She was terminated a week later.

Southern Pacific subsequently halted its random drug testing program when San Francisco passed a city ordinance in November 1985 banning mandatory testing except when an employer had reason to believe that an employee is impaired because of drug use.

SOURCE: Katherine Bishop, *New York Times*, 31 Oct. 1987 P.D.I. Copyright © 1987 by The New York Times Company. Reprinted by permission.

Rights to Plant/Office Closing Notification.   The employee's **right to plant/ office closing or relocation** was assured with the passage of the Plant Closing Act of 1988. This law requires that employers give sixty days prenotification of plant closings and relocations. While notification must be given, the Supreme Court has ruled that a corporate decision to close a particular location or even a product line is not a subject that must be negotiated in advance with a union—provided the closing is for economic reasons, and not union busting (*First National Maintenance v. NLRB*, 1981).[14]

STRATEGIES FOR JOB SECURITY

While the establishment and maintenance of viable PHRM programs is one way to ensure that employees are treated humanely and fairly, there are several specific strategies that may explicitly recognize employee rights.

Communicate Expectations and Prohibitions

Although ignorance is generally no excuse in nonemployment settings, it *is* in employment settings. Employees may be disciplined only for conduct not in accordance with what they know or reasonably understand is prohibited or required (*Patterson v. American Tobacco Co.*, 1976, 1978; *Sledge v. J. P. Stevens & Co.*, 1978; *Donaldson v. Pillsbury Co.*, 1977). Employers must therefore ensure that performance expectations are conveyed to employees along with information about what is prohibited. Employers can do this by requiring written policy statements, job descriptions, and performance criteria. Written standards should also exist for promotions (*Robinson v. Union Carbide Corp.*, 1976; *Rowe v. General Motors Corp.*, 1972).

Establish Due Process Procedures

Not only must performance expectations be communicated to employees *prior* to performance, but also employees must be informed of the consequences for nonperformance. Several strategies assure procedural fairness.

Consistent Rules.   If the employer discharges one employee for five unexcused absences, then another employee with five unexcused absences must also be discharged (*McDonald v. Sante Fe Trail Transportation Co.*, 1976). Periodic training for supervisors can help ensure that discharge policies are communicated and administered the same way by all supervisors.

Grievance Procedures and Due Process.   Grievance procedures not only should be established to ensure due process for employees but also should be administered consistently and fairly.[15] For example, evidence should be available to employee and employer, and both parties should have the right to call witnesses and refuse to testify against themselves. Furthermore, these grievance procedures should be clearly stated as company policy and communicated to the employees. Increasingly organizations are using peer review panels to review employee grievances and appeals.

> At Adolph Coors a peer review system is "one of the most effective tools for resolving employee relations problems, especially in nonunion settings," according to Edward Cruth and Barbara Stuver, employee relations representatives. Not only does such a system give employees the chance to be heard by management and co-workers, Cruth and Stuver point out, it also helps prevent costly, time-consuming litigation.
>
> The peer review system works well and produces desired results, Cruth and Stuver stress. Since implementation of the system 13 years ago, the number

of disciplinary actions that have been appealed has increased steadily—from a low of less than 10 appeals per year in the years 1975–1977, to an average of 100 appeals per year in 1986. Significantly, Cruth and Stuver point out, almost all the disciplinary actions have been upheld on review. Of 80 complaints heard by an appeal board in 1986, 37 were upheld, 32 were modified, nine were reversed, and two were pending. As of June 1, 1987, 28 appeals had been heard. Of these, 21 were upheld, two were modified, three were overturned, and two were pending.[16]

Establish a Progressive Discipline Procedure

In addition to setting up a procedure to ensure due process, it is important to establish procedures for disciplining employees. Such systems include several steps.

An **oral warning** should be given first and then documented with a note in the employee's file which specifies the time, date, and nature of the warning. Having a disciplinary procedure spelled out in writing and having all relevant information in the personnel file are important when building a case for disciplinary discharge.

Issuing a **written warning** is the next step in the process. Not only should the employee be warned that behavior is unacceptable, but also correct procedures should be specified. All information should be documented and added to the employee's file.

Next, comes **suspension,** which can be as short as part of a day or as long as several months without pay. The length of the suspension depends on the seriousness of the offense and precedent in the company for similar offenses. Alternatively, some organizations are replacing the traditional unpaid suspension with a paid timeout for the employee to rethink his or her commitment to the company. Companies employing this approach claim it shows greater respect for the employee.

A **disciplinary transfer or demotion** may take the pressure off a situation that might explode into violence or one in which personality conflicts are part of the problem. Demotion may also be a reasonable answer to problems of incompetence or an alternative to layoff for economic reasons. As noted in Chapter 7, some performance problems may be due to skill mismatching, rather than complete incompetence. Therefore, a different job may be the answer.

Discharge is the last resort and should be used only when all else has failed. It might be a reasonable immediate response to violence, theft, or falsification of records. Regardless of the cause, firing can be extremely painful for all concerned.

Even after taking all these steps, termination may still be necessary. The termination interview should be *brief;* normally, a ten- to fifteen-minute meeting is sufficient. A longer meeting increases the opportunity for the company representative (in this case, you) to make a mistake—and some mistakes can be costly.

It is best to conduct the termination meeting *in that person's office* or in some office other than your own. If conducted in your own office, you may be trapped into a lengthy harangue by a disgruntled individual who is using the meeting to vent . . . hostility, anger, and frustration. Many individuals hear very little after they understand they have lost their job. This is understandable as they begin to think of their future, or/and the anxiety and stress of having no job.

There also is a strong concern about their family, especially if the individual is the chief wage earner in the family.

Have a written description of benefits and/or salary continuation ready, if applicable. Also include information on how the individual is to be paid.

It is a good idea to *role play* with someone before you actually do the termination. It is even better if you can videotape the role-play(s). Practice can help iron out the bugs and the discomfort and make easier and less cumbersome the actual termination meeting.[17]

STRATEGIES FOR EMPLOYEE RIGHTS ON THE JOB

To protect employee rights on the job, employers must develop effective policies, procedures, and programs with regard to privacy and records access, cooperative acceptance (particularly sexual harassment), and plant or office closings.

Privacy and Record Access Rights

While not required legally, many companies such as General Foods and Chase Manhattan Bank are moving ahead on their own to establish policies and rules governing employee privacy and access rights.[18]

Establish Access Policies.   While a few years ago, only a handful of employers had policies, today more than 50 percent of all major companies have written policies regarding the privacy of personnel records. In addition, more than 85 percent provide employees access to records containing information about themselves.

General Foods' privacy policy includes the following points:

- Employees who want to examine their personnel files must give the company advance notice and may review their files only during regular business hours in the presence of a management representative. Before employees are allowed to examine their personnel files, the company removes any information dealing with co-workers or the firm's activities or plans in such areas as investigations, litigation, and personnel or salary planning.
- Because release of employee medical records can lead to problems, such as worker's misinterpretation of health records, GF allows company physicians to make oral reports to workers and send written reports to their doctors. Medical information is regarded as confidential and is not released to a third party, except when an employee files an insurance claim.
- The company will release information in compliance with a subpoena without contesting the subpoena, but will advise the employee that the information was released, unless prohibited by law from doing so.
- When information is to be released within the company for reasons outside normal requirements, the employee is notified and given a chance to object to the release. For example, the United Givers Fund, a charity campaign within GF, requested payroll records showing charitable contributions. Before the information was supplied to the fund, workers were notified and given the option of keeping their payroll records confidential.[19]

Preemployment Screening.   Privacy concerns are also influencing preemployment screening and drug testing. While policies regarding the release of information may be established by top management, it is often beneficial to involve employees in developing procedures.

At Ceiba-Geigy Corporation, focus groups were formed to solicit employee opinions on drug problems. As a result, the company decided the following:

- to take an educational thrust to our program. We want supervisors and employees to recognize drug problems, and know what to do about them.
- to encourage employees and their families to ask for help when they need it—before there are problems. Our Employee Assistance Program is available to them on a confidential basis.
- to establish a positive tone program—not a punitive one. We offer a rehabilitation program through our Employee Assistance Program.
- to test when there [is] an accident or behavior indications. . . .
- to take a top-down approach to training, so everyone in management would learn how to handle abuse situations—both for alcohol and for drugs.
- to provide uniform training materials for each division, so there are consistent messages throughout the company.[20]

Rights to Cooperative Acceptance

Although many issues are associated with employee rights to cooperative acceptance, sexual harassment and smoking bans have recently become prominent concerns for many employees and employers.

Sexual Harassment.   Because sexual harassment creates an offensive and hostile work environment, many employers are developing strategies to curb sexual harassment. And because the employer is liable for sexual harassment, except where it can be shown that the organization took immediate and appropriate corrective action (when the offending individual is guilty), a company must have an *explicit* policy forbidding sexual harassment.

Additionally, a grievance system should be established which details how complaints will be handled and what the consequences are for harassment when proved. Once these procedures are in place, employees as well as managers need training regarding sexual harassment and the company's grievance system.[21] Another useful check is to establish a policy that all discharges must be reviewed by a senior corporate officer or review board.

Smoking Regulations.   Increasingly, employers are establishing bans against smoking—on the job and even during breaks and lunch time. One study estimated that each smoker costs an employer $1,000 per year in higher absenteeism, in health, life, and fire insurance, and in reduced productivity due to "smoking rituals." Employers who resist smoking controls also face increasing risks of legal action—including handicap discrimination claims from "smoke sensitive" employees and charges that the employers are avoiding their legal obligation to provide a safe environment. The latter complaints are likely to increase due to recent reports linking passive smoking—the breathing of cigarette smoke from others—to cancer and other life-threatening diseases.[22]

There is also mounting pressure to *not* impose smoking bans. Smoking controls (e.g., smoke outside) which force employees to leave their work to take smoking breaks cost organizations more than $850 per smoker. There is also the possibility that smoking controls may stimulate handicap claims by "addicted" smokers and possibly racial discrimination charges because black men are more likely to smoke than white men.[23]

In an attempt to resolve existing conflicts, many employers have implemented one or more of the following policies:

1. Allow smoking during lunch and on breaks.
2. Stagger the break times of smokers and nonsmokers.
3. Install more effective ventilation systems.
4. Designate specific areas for smoking.
5. Institute and encourage participation in smoking cessation programs.

While more expensive and administratively problematic than a total ban on smoking, these policies involve less legal risk.

Layoffs and Plant Closing Notification

With the passage of the Plant Closing Act in 1988, employers are obligated to notify employees in advance of a closing of a plant. However, layoffs that are temporary in nature or downsizings that are permanent but do not require complete shutdowns do not require advance notification. Regardless of the cause, the loss of a job can be traumatic for employees. To minimize the difficulty of this transition, organizations are pursuing several different strategies.[24]

Job Sharing.   Rather than terminating employees, some companies have initiated job sharing programs. Job sharing involves reducing each employee's work week and pay. This helps the company cut labor costs and may actually lead to higher overall productivity because each employee is working more concentrated hours. One major disadvantage is that expenses per employee may not decrease proportionately because benefits are usually a function of the number of employees, not the number of hours worked or the amount of pay. While few studies have investigated the payoffs of job sharing, Motorola found that job sharing, rather than layoffs, saved an average of $1,868 per employee or almost $1 million overall in one plant.[25]

Early Retirement Windows.   While retirement essentially cannot be required, organizations are exploring early retirement for selected employees as a possible option to layoffs. Key to successfully implementing an early retirement programs are understanding the needs of targeted employees and providing incentives that meet those needs. Incentives may include pension payments before and after age sixty-two when social security payments start and company-paid health and life insurance. Alternatively, a company may maintain its current retirement program but lower the qualifying age. This increases the pool of potential retirees.

In setting up an early retirement program, an organization needs to answer the following questions:

- Who will be eligible?
- What incentives will be offered?
- How will early retirement benefits be calculated?
- What effect, if any, will incentives have on regular retirement benefits?
- What is the election period for participation?
- What source of funds will finance the early retirement obligations?

One study found that annual costs of early retirement programs range from $1,000 to $300,000, with an average cost of $50,000. By comparison, first-year cost savings averaged $7.3 million.

Early retirement programs vary in terms of their success. An IBM plan was designed in 1986 to eliminate four thousand jobs. By the first quarter of 1987, more than twelve thousand IBM employees had taken advantage of the program. Blue Cross and Blue Shield of Chicago had 41 percent of its eligible employees leave under a plan offering health, dental, life, vision, and accident insurance. International Telephone and Telegraph was less successful. Its early retirement program failed to achieve its 50-percent reduction goal. Consequently, the company resorted to layoffs.[26]

Outplacement Assistance.   When early retirement and job sharing won't work or fail to reduce staffs sufficiently, organizations have no choice but to move to layoffs. However, humane employers are providing outplacement assistance to ease the strain of involuntary termination.

Outplacement help ranges from offering job retraining to preparing résumés or providing job search information and secretarial and administrative support. In 1986 the cost of outplacement assistance ranged from a low of $44 to a high of $50,000 per employee, with the average being $3,138.[27]

Severance Pay.   Organizations can also ease the transition by providing severance pay based on seniority. For example, employees can be given one week's salary for one to four years of service, two weeks' salary for five to eight years of service, and three weeks salary for over eight years of service. Severance pay becomes particularly critical for upper-level positions. One study found that for every $10,000 in salary, the job search takes an additional month.

Continuation of Benefits.   The Bureau of National Affairs found that 80 percent of all firms continue health care benefits after plant closings. However, only half continue the benefits for more than five months—even when a new job has not been found.

TRENDS IN EMPLOYEE RIGHTS

The major trend in employee rights is in computer technology and it is likely to provoke a great deal of interest and legal activity on the part of employees and employers.

Computer Technology and Employee Rights

With computers and an HRIS, personnel and human resource departments can generate confidential personnel information in a variety of formats in a short time. Thus, many copies of confidential information may exist at any one time, increasing the likelihood that some may be misplaced or even stolen.

As a result, **file security** is of concern. Today's HRIS systems include access protectors which limit who can read or write to a file, and they may be designed to allow a single person or a group of individuals access or no access. While these systems reduce the threat of file invasion, most designers of "secure" systems build in backdoor entries. If these are discovered by an unauthorized user, he or she may gain access to the program.

Computer technology is also being used to ensure that employee policies are implemented fairly. **Expert systems** such as those developed HumanTek, a San Francisco software company, guide managers with employee problems to solutions. By asking a series of questions, the computer steers the manager to organizational policies and precedents that relate to the specific performance problem. Some of the more sophisticated programs even give managers advice. According to Walter Ratcliff, HRIS consultant, expert systems will be the best friend of tomorrow's manager. Rather than flipping through a personnel manual, a supervisor will turn on his or her computer for advice.

SUMMARY

Although many employers claim that essentially all their rights have been taken away, they still retain the right to terminate workers for poor performance, excessive absenteeism, unsafe conduct, and generally poor organizational citizenship. However, employers must maintain accurate records of these events for their employees and inform the employees of where they stand. To be safe, employers should also have a grievance process for employees to ensure that due process is respected. These practices are particularly useful in discharge situations that involve members of groups protected by Title VII, ADEA, the Rehabilitation Act, or the Vietnam Era Veterans Act.

Today, keeping objective and orderly personnel and human resource files is more important than ever. They are critical evidence that employers have treated their employees fairly and with respect and have not violated any laws. Without these, organizations may get caught on the short end of a lawsuit. Although several federal laws influence record keeping, they are primarily directed at public employers. Many private employers, however, are moving on their own initiative to give their employees the right to access their personnel files and to prohibit the file information from being given to others without their consent. In addition, employers are casting out of their personnel files any non-job-related information and ending hiring practices that solicit that type of information.

Many employers are now giving their employees advance notification consistent with the Plant Closing Act. In addition to giving such notification, employers are implementing outplacement assistance programs. These offer employees retraining for new jobs, counseling and aid in finding new jobs or in getting transfers, severance pay, and even retention bonuses for those who stay until closing time. Closing a facility with notification and with outplacement assistance seems to produce positive results for the organization and minimize the negative effects for the employees.

Finally, in the area of employee rights to cooperative acceptance, employers must prevent sexual harassment. This can be done with top-management support, grievance procedures, verification procedures, training for all employees, and performance appraisal and compensation policies that reward those who practice antiharassment behavior and punish those who do not. Where appropriate, developing policies to prevent harassment in cooperation with the union is also useful. Union cooperation, however, should be sought on many issues. The beneifts of doing so can be substantial, as discussed in the next chapter.

DISCUSSION QUESTIONS

1. Identify and discuss the four federal laws that have an impact on employee rights to privacy and access of employee records.

2. What is the bottom line in protection offered to employees concerning plant closing/relocation?

3. What is the termination-at-will doctrine? Why do you suppose courts in the late 1880s were more willing to uphold the doctrine than courts are today?

4. How would you distinguish a just from an unjust dismissal? Is this distinction easier to make for lower-level jobs than for upper-level or managerial jobs? Explain.

5. The industrial, occupational, and demographic composition of the labor force has shifted over the past twenty years. How might these specific shifts coincide with the heightened interest in employee rights in the 1980s?

6. Due process has been interpreted as the duty to inform an employee of a charge, solicit employee input, and provide the employee with feedback in regard to the employment decision. How can a grievance procedure ensure this type of due process for an employee accused of sexual harassment? How can the grievance procedure protect the victim of the alleged harassment?

7. Develop counterarguments for the following arguments in support of the termination-at-will doctrine:

   a. If the employee can quit for any reason, the employer can fire for any reason.

   b. Because of business cycles, employers must have flexibility to expand and contract their work force.

   c. Discharged employees are always free to find other employment.

   d. Employers have incentives not to unjustly discharge employees; therefore, their power to terminate should not be restricted.

8. What do you suppose are the most common reasons for termination decisions? How can PHRM prevent these causes of termination?

9. What potential employee rights violations could occur with an automated HRIS? How could you protect against these violations?

10. What kinds of behaviors might constitute sexual harassment? How does an organization prevent those types of behaviors from occurring?

CASE STUDY

Bill Davenport

Background

For over three years, Bellweather Corporation and Helist Corporation had been courting each other regarding a possible merger. Both manufacturing companies produced various types of customized pumps for use in the processing industry. By merging two small companies with annual sales of $30 million each, a stronger company could emerge with greater potential for capturing a larger share of the market and for reducing operating expenses.

In 1989 the sudden death of Helist's owner/founder made the possibility of a merger an actuality. The president of Bellweather would assume the responsibilities of chief executive officer of Helist/Bellweather Corporation within a few months.

Bill Davenport

One of the first problems facing the president was the assignment of senior management responsibility. Bill Davenport, age 51, had joined Bellweather in 1975 as director of manufacturing when it was a struggling $3 million family business. He was a hard-working, loyal employee. Back in 1975, he was excellent at supervising the twenty-five operators who reported to him. As the manufacturing operation expanded, however, Bill was promoted to vice-president of manufacturing and was responsible for the work of 150 operators and 4 foremen. Bill was the type of person who liked having direct contact with operators, and there were complaints by foremen that Bill did not let them supervise. Production always seemed to be late, and Bill did little coordinated planning for the future.

As long as Bellweather was a relatively small company, his deficits as a manager did not outweigh the fact that he was a loyal employee who had contributed to past success. While the president had expressed some concern to Bill in 1985, Bill had not changed his ways. There is no formal management performance appraisal system at Bellweather, and Bill always received a salary increase which was average relative to that given to other vice-presidents. The president decided that Bill was not capable of adequately running the expanded manufacturing operation. Thus, the vice-president of manufacturing at Helist would be named as vice-president of manufacturing for Helist/Bellweather.

The president knew that Bill would be upset at not getting the senior manufacturing job. He wondered if Bill was aware that the president was coming to the conclusion that Bill was not suited to *any* senior management position in the new company.

As the president saw it, he had the following three options:

Option #1: Fire Bill, although this seemed like cruel punishment for a hard-working and loyal employee.

Option #2: Keep Bill in his present position with the title of assistant vice-president of manufacturing, but remove all real authority from him and give it to the new vice-president.

Option #3: Demote Bill to a lower level of management more suitable to his talents.

Option #4: Provide management training for Bill so that he will function more effectively.

Case Questions

1. Evaluate the options other than dismissal for dealing with Bill Davenport's situation.
2. Assume that after evaluation of the alternatives, you decide on dismissal.
   a. How will you handle the dismissal interview? Come up with a plan for the interview, and state what you will say to Bill. Anticipate his questions and reactions, and estimate how long the interview should last.
   b. What are your worst fears concerning Bill's reaction to your decision?
   c. What assistance will you provide, if any, following the dismissal interview?
   d. What repercussions might this have within the organization?
3. What is your bottom-line recommendation regarding Bill? Why?

Janina Latach,
Ohio State University

NOTES

1. "Beyond Unions," *Business Week*, 8 July 1985, pp. 72–77; "The Growing Costs of Firing Non-Union Workers," *Business Week*, 6 Apr. 1981, pp. 95–98; L. Ingrassia, "Non-Union Workers Are Gaining Status, But So Far the Talk Outweighs the Action," *Wall Street Journal*, 24 July 1980, p. 42; A. F. Westin and A. G. Feliu, *Resolving Employment Disputes without Litigation* (Washington, D.C.: Bureau of National Affairs, 1988).

2. For a description of these cases, see *Fair Employment Report*, 11 Oct. 1982, p. 165; *Fair Employment Report*, 8 Nov. 1982, p. 178.

3. G. E. Biles, "A Program Guide for Preventing Sexual Harassment in the Workplace," *Personnel Administrator* (June 1981): 49–56.

4. S. Brigg, "The Grievance Procedure and Organizational Health," *Personnel Journal* (June 1981): 471–74; "Dispute-Resolution Options: Ombudsmen and Arbitration," *Fair Employment Practices*, 23 Feb. 1984, pp. 3–4; J. P. Swann, Jr., "Formal Grievance Procedures in Non-Union Plants," *Personnel Administrator* (Aug. 1981): 66–70.

5. W. M. Bulkeley, "Nuns vs. the Bishop: Teachers' Dismissal Winds Up in Court," *Wall Street Journal*, 13 Sept. 1982, p. 1; E. L. Harrison, "Legal Restrictions on the Employers' Authority to Discipline," *Personnel Journal* (Feb. 1982): 136–46; W. L. Wall, "Firms See Aid on Avoiding Employee Suits," *Wall Street Journal*, 28 July 1982, p. 23; T. H. Williams, "Employment-at-Will," *Personnel Journal* (June 1985): 73–77; S. A.

Youngblood and L. Bierman, "Due Process and Employment-at-Will: A Legal and Behavioral Analysis," in *Research in Personnel and Human Resource Management*, vol. 3, ed. K. Rowland and G. Ferris (Greenwich, Conn.: JAI Press, 1985), 185–230. See also A. T. Oliver, Jr., "The Disappearing Right to Terminate Employees at Will," *Personnel Journal* (Dec. 1982): 910–17; according to Oliver, two recent court decisions in California (*Cleary v. American Airlines, Inc.*, 1980; *Pugh v. See's Candies*, 1981) appear to have all but ended termination at will in that state.

6. B. B. Durling, "Retaliation: A Misunderstood Form of Employment Discrimination," *Personnel Journal* (July 1981): 555–58.

7. "Armor for Whistle-Blowers," *Business Week*, 6 July 1981, pp. 97–98; W. F. Westin, "Michigan's Law to Protect Whistle Blowers," *Wall Street Journal*, 13 Apr. 1981, p. 1.

8. For further description of related cases and issues, see "Another View of Employment-at-Will," *Bulletin to Management*, 12 Sept. 1985, p. 88; "Employment-at-Will Evolves," *Bulletin to Management*, 5 Apr. 1984, pp. 1–2; *Holien v. Sears Roebuck*, 1984; B. Keller, "Of Hearth and Home and the Right to Work" *New York Times*, 11 Nov. 1984, p. 8E; "Mandatory Retirement," *FEP Guidelines*, no. 225(H), 1984; B. S. Murphy, W. E. Barlow, and D. D. Hatch, "Constructive Discharge under Title VII," *Personnel Journal* (Feb. 1985): 17; *Yancey v. State Personnel Board*, 1985.

9. "Firing," *FEP Guidelines*, no. 241(8), 1985, p. 3. See also "Discrimination Denied," *Bulletin to Management*, 13 June 1985, p. 3.

10. However, if a union-management contract exists, an arbitrator may not uphold firing if based on false application information. J. N. Drazin, "Firing over False Applications," *Personnel Journal* (June 1981): 433. See also D. L. Beacon and A. Gomez III, "How to Prevent Wrongful Termination Lawsuits," *Personnel* (Feb. 1988): 70–72; D. A. Bradshaw and B. C. Stikker, "Wrongful Termination: Keeping the Right to Fire At-Will," *Personnel Journal* (Sept. 1986): 45–47; B. S. Murphy, W. E. Barlow, and D. Hatch, "Constructive Discharge," *Personnel Journal* (Oct. 1986): 30–31; "RIFS, Exit Incentives, and the ADEA," *FEP Guidelines*, no. 273(4); "Wrongful Discharge," *FEP Guidelines*, no. 275(6).

11. For suggested courses of action, see *Employee Access to Records* (Englewood Cliffs, N.J.: Prentice-Hall, 1984); see also R. J. Nobile, "Employee Searches in the Workplace: Developing a Realistic Search Policy," *Personnel Administrator* (May 1985): 89–98; and J. C. O'Meara, "The Emerging Law of Employees' Right to Privacy," *Personnel Administrator* (June 1985): 159–65; D. Bennett-Alexander, "Sexual Harassment in the Office," *Personnel Administrator* (June 1988): 174–88; S. R. Mendelsohn and K. K. Morrison, "Testing Applicants for Alcohol and Drug Abuse," *Personnel* (Aug. 1988): 57–60; J. Pereira, "Women Allege Sexist Atmosphere in Offices Constitutes Harassment," *Wall Street Journal*, 10 Feb. 1988, sec. 2, p. 23; and I. M. Shepard and R. L. Duston, *Workplace Privacy* (Washington, D.C.: Bureau of National Affairs, 1988).

12. C. K. Behrens, "Co-Worker Sexual Harassment: The Employer's Liability," *Personnel Journal* (May 1984): 12–14; "New Ruling on Sexual Harassment," *Management Review* (June 1985): 5; "Participation Bars Protest," *Fair Employment Practices*," 12 Jan. 1984, p. 1; R. E. Quinn and P. L. Lees, "Attraction and Harassment: Dynamics of Sexual Politics in the Workplace," *Organizational Dynamics* (Autumn 1984): 35–46; "Retaliation," *FEP Guidelines*, no. 237(4), 1985; S. Seymour, "The Case of the Mismanaged Ms.," *Harvard Business Review* (Nov./Dec. 1987): 77–87; "Sexual Harassment," *FEP Guidelines*, no. 238(5), 1985; "Sexual Harassment: Prevention Is the Key," *Fair Employment Practices*, 18 Feb. 1988, p. 22; "What Makes an Environment 'Hostile'? Advice from Three Courts," *Fair Employment Practices*, 23 June 1988, p. 78.

13. "Sexual Harassment after Meritor Savings v. Vinson," *FEP Guidelines*, no. 264 (1987), p. 1. Used by permission.

14. J. N. Draznin, "Closings and Consolidations," *Personnel Journal* (Oct. 1981): 764–65; L. Chavez, "When ARCO Left Town," *New York Times*, 25 July 1982, pp. 15; G. L. Felsten, "Current Considerations in Plant Shutdowns and Relocations," *Personnel Journal* (May 1981): 369–72; N. R. Kleinfield, "Reinventing a Company Town," *New York Times*, 27 Mar. 1988, sec. F, p. 4; "Pro & Con: The 60-Day Notice Provision," *New York Times*, 8 May 1988, sec. E, p. 5; F. J. Solomon, "Citicorp's Big-City Tactics Leave Them Jobless and Angry in Indiana," *Wall Street Journal*, 19 Aug. 1982, p. 19.

15. G. W. Bohlander and H. C. White, "Building Bridges: Nonunion Employee Grievance Systems," *Personnel* (July 1988): 62–66; R. Folger and J. Greenberg, "Procedural Justice: An Interpretive Analysis of Personnel Systems," in *Research in Personnel and Human Resources Management*, vol. 3, ed. K. M. Rowland and G. Ferris (Greenwich, Conn.: JAI Press, 1985); "Improve Employee Relations with a Corporate Ombudsman," *Personnel Journal* (Sept. 1985): 12–13; T. Rendero, "Grievance Procedures for Nonunionized Employees," *Personnel* (Jan./Feb. 1980): 4–10.

16. "Employee Relations and Morale," *Bulletin to Management*, 23 July 1987, pp. 9–10.

17. L. D. Foxman and W. L. Polsky, "Ground Rules for Terminating Workers," *Personnel Journal* (July 1984): 32; G. B. Hansen, "Preventing Layoffs: Developing an Effective Job Security and Economic Adjustment Program," *Employee Relations Law Journal* (Autumn 1985): 239–68.

18. J. A. Gildea, "Safety and Privacy: Are They Compatible?" *Personnel Administrator* (Feb. 1982): 78–83; H. X. Levine, "Privacy of Employee Records," *Personnel* (May/June 1981): 4–11; "Respecting Employee Privacy," *Business Week*, 11 Jan. 1982, pp. 130–31.

19. "Privacy Policy Approaches and Pointers," *Bulletin to Management*, 20 Feb. 1986, p. 57. Reprinted by permission from *Bulletin to Management* copyright 1986 by The Bureau of National Affairs, Inc., Wahington, DC 20037.

20. "Soul-Searching at Ceiba-Geigy," *HR Reporter* (May 1987): 5–6.

21. G. E. Biles, "A Program Guide for Preventing Sexual Harassment"; R. H. Faley, "Sexual Harassment: A Critical Review of Legal Cases with General Principles and Practice Measures," *Personnel Psychology* 35 (1982): 583–600; O. A. Ornati, "How to Deal with EEOC's Guidelines to Sexual Harassment," in *EEO Compliance Manual* (Englewood Cliffs, N.J.: Prentice-Hall, 1980), 377–80.

22. "Smokers' Rights vs. Health Concerns: Smoking Emerges as New Controversy," *Resource* (Feb. 1987): 3. See also "ASPA–BNA Survey No. 50: Smoking in the Workplace," *Bulletin to Management*, 12 June 1986; M. L. Colosi, "Do Employees Have the Right to Smoke?" *Personnel Journal* (Apr. 1988): 72–82; A. I. LaForge, "Snuffing Out Smoking in the Office," *New York Times*, 22 Feb. 1987, F12–13; L. Reibstein, "Forced to Consider Smoking Issue, Firms Produce Disparate Policies," *Wall Street Journal*, 10 Feb. 1987, sec. 2, p. 41; E. Schmitt, "The Last Refuge of Smokers May Be No Place but Home," *New York Times*, 27 Sept. 1987, sec. E, p. 7; J. C. Stewart, "Corporate Smoking Policies: Today and Tomorrow," *Personnel* (Aug. 1988): 61–66.

23. "Worksite Smoking: Need for Dual Accommodation," *Bulletin to Management*, 25 June 1987, p. 201.

24. P. D. Johnston, "Personnel Planning for a Plant Shutdown," *Personnel Administrator* (Aug. 1981): 53–57.

25. Bearak, "Termination Made Easier"; M. Elleinis, "Tips for Employers Shopping Around for a New Plant Site," *AMA Forum* (July 1982): 34; B. H. Millen, "Providing Assistance to Displaced Workers," *Monthly Labor Review* (May 1979): 17–22; "Outplacement Assistance," *Personnel Journal* (Apr. 1981): 250; "Plant Closings: Problems and Panaceas," *Management Review* (July 1982): 55–57. The issue of plant closing notification and the employee's right to be informed is also important on an international scale for multinational corporations (R. G. Caborn, "Workers Have a Right to Know More . . .," *New York Times*, 3 Oct. 1982); T. Rendero, "Outplacement Practices," *Personnel* (July/August 1980): 4–11.

26. L. B. Baenen and R. C. Ernest, "An Argument for Early Retirement Incentive Planning," *Personnel Administrator* 27 (1982): 63–66; M. Harris, "A Lifetime at IBM Gets a Little Shorter for Some," *Business Week*, 29 Sept. 1986, p. 40; "ITT's Early Retirement Package Fails to Achieve Needed Staff Reductions," *Bureau of National Affairs White Collar Report*, no. 60, 19 Nov. 1986.

27. Labor Letter, *Wall Street Journal*, 1 Apr. 1986, p. 1.

CHAPTER

15

Unionization and Collective Bargaining

It's Time to Scrap a Few Outmoded Labor Laws

The Clayton Act of 1914 exempted trade union wage negotiations from antitrust laws. A conspiracy by competing companies to obtain monopoly prices is a violation of the Sherman Antitrust Act. Why should the efforts of unions in different companies to raise wages above competitive levels be treated differently?

People working for large, impersonal corporations often prefer to bargain over wages and work rules through unions rather than individually. In particular, workers who have spent many years with the same company may find a union helpful in protecting against management, especially new management, that tries to take advantage of the diffiulties senior workers face in finding comparable employment elsewhere.

However, these legitimate and important bargaining goals of workers are attainable through a union of workers in the same company. They do not require workers in different companies to act in unison. Japanese workers, for example, have greatly improved their wages and working conditions by bargaining through company unions.

Dubious Value

To allay the fear that company unions will bow to management, Congress and state legislatures can strengthen the right to a union shop and other protections for company union members. For example, if company unions were made fully subject to antitrust laws, right-to-work laws would not be desirable, even though they are a useful barrier between the workers and the power of unions that organize whole industries and occupations.

It is difficult to discuss unions dispassionately because they receive more credit and at the same time more blame than they deserve. Some unions have been a bulwark to workers against oppressive management, but advances in productivity, not unions, are mainly responsible for the improvement in earnings and working conditions of the average worker. Unions were unimportant in the American economy prior to 1930. Yet average earnings greatly increased from 1870 to 1930 despite the huge immigration of unskilled workers, who were more likely to be exploited than were native-born workers.

Unions that raise wages of their members above competitive levels lower economic efficiency by reducing employment in the unionized sector. And the higher earnings of union members usually come at the expense of poorer nonunion workers. Earnings gains to large numbers of union workers cannot mainly out of profits because corporate profits are less than 10% of national income. Still, despite these harmful effects, unions should not be blamed for inflation and sluggish economic growth. The 1950s and 1960s had little inflation and rapid economic growth, even though unions were at peak strength. Unions are not a major cause of the monetary expansion that produces rapid inflation nor of the slow advance in productivity that leads to sluggish growth.

Less Clout

The decline of trade union power during the past 30 years is as remarkable as it was unexpected. In 1955 one of every three members of the U.S. labor force belonged to a union, compared with 17% in 1987. This halving of union membership is partly due to structural changes in the economy and greater international competition. The growth of the service sector and the declines of manufacturing and mining in this period reduced the percentage of membership because service workers have not been easy to unionize. International trade expanded greatly during the past 30 years: Imports into the U.S. increased from 5% of gross national product in 1955 to 12% in recent years.

continued

Steel, auto, and other manufacturing industries lost out to imports from Asia and elsewhere partly because strong unions greatly raised costs of production.

But the most significant causes of decline in union membership since 1955 are laws that protect workers against unfair dismissal and the growth of unemployment compensation, Social Security payments, medicare, and other government transfer payments. Workers no longer need to rely on unions for protection against job loss and the expenses of ill health and old age.

Unions remain more powerful in Canada and Western Europe than in the U.S., but union strength also has begun to ebb rapidly in some of these countries. For example, during the past eight years unionized workers in Britain declined from about 50% to less than 40% of the work force, and Margaret Thatcher decisively defeated a long strike by the militant coal miners' union.

Union leaders were once powerful political brokers courted by members of both parties, but now they have less clout when challenged by business and other groups. A decade ago the National Football League could not have continued with replacement players, while almost all the regular football players were on strike, without fear of picketing violence and sympathy strikes. It is a good time politically to push for legislation that protects society against anticompetitive union practices and also strengthens a worker's right to join a union. Such a redirection of labor laws would help both the average worker and society at large.

SOURCE: G. S. Becker: "It's Time to Scrap a Few Outmoded Labor Laws," *Business Week*, 7 Mar. 1988, p. 18. Used with permission from *Business Week*, copyright 1988.

This "PHRM in the News" highlights several aspects of the union movement in the United States. One is that the union movement has played an important role in the economic development of the United States in this century. Another is that unions have traditionally helped their membership get better wages, benefits, and working conditions. A third aspect is that the current status of the union movement and labor laws in the United States is being called into question by some commentators such as Gary Becker. A final point is that in order to survive and possibly grow, unions are moving away from traditional blue-collar industries to health care and professional arenas.

Two major aspects of the union movement that are important to examine in depth are the actual processes of forming a union (unionization) and the characteristics of administering an agreement reached between the union and management (collective bargaining).

Unionization is the effort by employees and outside agencies (unions or associations) to act as a single unit when dealing with management over issues relating to their work. When recognized by the National Labor Relations Board, a union has the legal authority to negotiate with the employer on behalf of employees—to improve wages, hours, and conditions of employment—and to administer the ensuing agreement.[1]

The core of union-management relations is **collective bargaining.** It generally includes two types of interaction. The first is the negotiation of work conditions that, when written up as the collective agreement (the contract), become the basis for employee-employer relationships on the job. The second includes activities related to interpreting and enforcing the collective agreement (contract administration) and resolving any conflicts arising out of it.[2]

In this chapter, issues associated with both the establishment of unions (e.g., union attraction and organizing) and the administration of the agreement (i.e., collective bargaining) are discussed. Additionally, the legal umbrella under which union-management relations operate is discussed.

PURPOSES AND IMPORTANCE
OF UNIONIZATION

The existence or possibility of a union can significantly influence how an employer manages its vital human resources. Unions often result in management's having less flexibility in hiring, making job assignments, and introducing new work methods and technology. For large organizations, however, unions may be vital. Rather than negotiating with individual employees, management can cut the task down by negotiating with groups of employees through the unions.

For employees, unions can help resolve work problems and get what they want (higher wages, better working conditions, job security) from their employers. Unions may also assist employees, and consequently employers, in identifying work place hazards and ways to improve the quality of work life for employees.[3]

RELATIONSHIPS INFLUENCING THE UNIONIZATION
OF EMPLOYEES

As Exhibit 15.1 shows, the unionization of employees is related to many other PHRM functions and has an extensive set of legal relationships.

Relationships with Other PHRM Activities

Several PHRM activities have important relationships with the unionization of employees.

Relationships and Aspects of the Unionization of Employees in the Union-Management Relationship	EXHIBIT 15.1

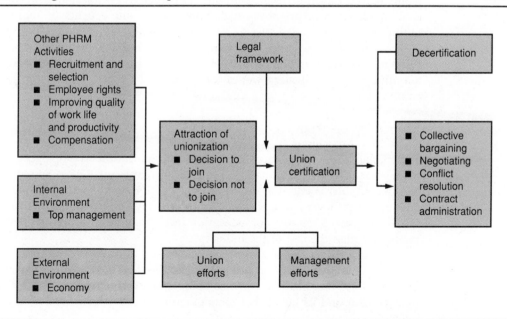

Recruitment and Selection.   Unionization may have a direct impact on who is hired and the conditions under which applicants are hired. In the construction industry, for example, union hiring halls are generally the source of employees for any employer hiring construction workers who are union members. In states with **union shop** provisions (approximately three-fifths of the states), employees must join the union (if the company has one for the particular group of employees) after a set number of days—often sixty or ninety. In the remaining states where **right-to-work** provision exist, employees do not have to join a union even if one exists.

Unions can also play an important role in deciding who is to be promoted, given a new job assignment, put into training programs, terminated, or laid off. This role is facilitated through the establishment of seniority provisions in union-management contracts.

Employee Rights.   When employers treat employees with fairness and respect, employees may be more inclined to exhibit loyalty toward their employers. Because treating employees fairly and with respect results from recognizing and observing employee rights, the more rights that employers recognize and observe, the better employees feel.[4] This suggests that an organization that wants to remain union free may choose to observe all the legal rights of employees and to recognize and observe many of the "humane" rights of employees desribed in Chapter 14. If employers fail to do this, employees may be more likely to unionize. Once unionized, the union will help ensure that many employee rights (legal and humane) are recognized and observed.

Improving Quality of Work Life.   Although not all unions support QWL programs, many programs are undertaken jointly by unions and managements. As indicated in Chapter 12, when this occurs, employers need to be sure that they have complied with the National Labor Relations Act.[5]

Compensation.   An important goal of employees is a decent wage and adequate indirect benefits. Because unions are perceived as causal in achieving this goal[6] employees who are not provided these wages and benefits are more likely to find unionization attractive. The threat of possible unionization, however, is often enough to cause employers to provide even more than a decent wage and benefits. Recently, unions have taken up the cause of comparable worth, attempting to get equivalent wages for males and females performing jobs of comparable worth.

Relationships with the Internal Environment

Top management is a major factor in the unionization of employees. If top management desires to remain union free, a great many PHRM activities will be directed to that end. For example, organizations may recruit and select individuals that they judge to be loyal to the company. Top management can direct this to happen. Similarly, compensation levels may be increased so that they are higher than the rest of the industry.

Top management can also set the stage for unionization by creating dissatisfied employees and thus promoting their desire for the protection that unionization offers. Unionization can also come about through the invitation of top management and its belief that managing unionized employees is better than managing nonunionized employees.

Relationships with the External Environment

As illustrated in the initial "PHRM in the News," the state of the economy has a significant influence on unionization. As national and international competition has increased, employers have looked to cutting wage levels as a way to stay competitive. Organizations have threatened to move if wage levels were not reduced. This environment, coupled with relatively high levels of unemployment, has given organizations a relatively strong hand in dealing with the unions. As a consequence, unions have granted wage concessions, and the size of the union movement has been stable at best. Helping to further stabilize and even reduce the size of the union movement has been the decline of manufacturing, a traditional source of union membership.

LEGAL CONSIDERATIONS IN THE UNIONIZATION OF EMPLOYEES

Prior to the 1920s, classic economic theory, in which the free operation of the law of supply and demand was considered essential, dominated management. It was assumed that control of wage rates by workers artificially inflated prices and ultimately harmed commerce, the community, and workers.[7]

Private Sector

These "fundamental values of society" were protected by declaring attempts by workers to form a union a conspiracy condemned by law (*Commonwealth v. Pullis*, 1806). By 1842, this condemnation was modified to include a "means test" (were the measures used by members to form a union harmful and pernicious?) In the 1900s, criminal law was replaced by civil injunctions. These injunctions, which affect unionization even today, were established to maintain the status quo. For example, workers can be forced back to work until the legality of a strike is decided. Injunctions were also important because they could be used to enforce **yellow dog contracts** (i.e., contracts signed by employees agreeing not to join a union) (*Hitchman Coal & Coke v. Mitchell, 1917*).[8]

Sherman Anti-Trust Act. To protect free trade, the Sherman Anti-Trust Act was passed by Congress in 1890. This act limited the ability of organizations including unions to engage in acts (mergers) that lessen competition. The Supreme Court applied this act to unions in 1908 (*Loewe v. Lawlor, 1908*). The meaning and application of the act for unions were reinforced by the Clayton Anti-Trust Act of 1914 (*Duplex Printing Co. v. Deering, 1921*).

Railway Labor Act. To prevent the serious economic consequences of labor unrest in the railway industry, the Railway Labor Act (RLA) was passed in 1926. This act was the first to protect the "fundamental right of workers to engage in labor organizing actively without fear of employer retaliation and discrimination. Other objectives of the act were to avoid service interruptions, to eliminate any restrictions on joining a union, and to provide for prompt settlement of disputes, and grievances.[9]

The act specified that employers and employees would maintain an agreement over pay, rules, working conditions, dispute settlement, representation, and grievance settlement. A board of mediation (later called the National Mediation

Board) was created to aid in the settlement of disputes through encouragement of negotiation, then arbitration, and finally the president's emergency intervention. A second board—the National Railway Adjustment Board—was created in 1934 to deal with grievances or the interpretation of agreements concerning pay, rules, or working conditions; it makes decisions and awards that are binding on both parties.

National Labor Relations Act.   The success of the Railway Labor Act led Congress to enact a comprehensive labor code in 1935. The purpose of the National Labor Relations Act (NLRA), also known as the Wagner Act, was to restore the equality of bargaining power arising out of employers' general denial to labor of the right to bargain collectively with them.[10]

The NLRA affirmed employees' rights to form, join, or assist labor organizations, to bargain collectively, and to choose their own bargaining representative through majority rule. It outlawed, however, the use of the **closed shop,** a procedure whereby an individual had to belong to a union *before* getting a job. Use of the union shop was affirmed except in states that have **"right-to-work" laws.** Under the **union shop,** employees generally have to join the union thirty days after they begin working. Under the "right-to-work," they are not required to join the union.

The second significant portion of the act identified five unfair labor practices on the part of the employers:

1. Interference with the efforts of employees to organize
2. Domination of the labor organization by the employer
3. Discrimination in the hiring or tenure of employees to discourage union affiliation
4. Discrimination for filing charges or giving testimony under the act
5. Refusal to bargain collectively with a representative of the employees

Court interpretations of these unfair labor practices have made it clear that bribing, spying, blacklisting union sympathizers, moving a business to avoid union activities, and other such employer actions are illegal.[11]

The National Labor Relations Board (NLRB) was established to administer the NLRA. Its major function is to decide all unfair labor practice suits and render decisions consistent with the NLRA. In 1974, the Supreme Court ruled in *NLRB v. J. Weingarten, Inc.,* that a union employee has the right to demand that a union representative be present at an investigatory interview that the employee reasonably believes may result in disciplinary action. In 1982 the NLRB ruled in *Materials Research Corporation* that unrepresented employees now have the right to demand that a co-worker of their choice be present at an investigatory interview, if the employee reasonably believes that the meeting may result in disciplinary action. As summarized by the NLRB in *Materials Research:* "[W]e concluded that the right enunciated in *Weingarten* applies equally to [union] represented and unrepresented employees."[12]

Construed as not favoring unions, this decision is consistent with the *Otis Elevator* decision, ruling that employers need not bargain with unions before choosing to transfer operations elsewhere if based on economics, not labor cost considerations (*Otis Elevator v. NLRB*, 1984). Recently the NLRB ruled that decisions involving plant closing and/or transfer of operations need not be bargainable, even if they are based on labor cost considerations (*Arrow Automotive Industries v. NLRB*, 1988). These are also consistent with the Supreme Court's decision stating that employees may resign from a union at any time, even during a strike or when one is imminent (*Pattern Makers' League v. NLRB*, 1985).

Labor-Management Relations Act.   Employer groups criticized the Wagner Act on several grounds. They argued that the act, in addition to being biased toward unions, limited the constitutional right of free speech of employers, did not consider unfair labor practices on the part of unions, and caused employers serious damage when there were jurisdictional disputes.

Congress responded to these criticisms in 1947 by enacting the Labor-Management Relations Act, often called the Taft-Hartley Act. This act established a balance between union and management power. The following were among the changes it introduced:

- Employees were allowed to refrain from union activity as well as to engage in it.
- The closed shop was outlawed, and written agreement from employees was required for deducting union dues from workers' paychecks.
- Unions composed of supervisors did not need to be recognized.
- Employers were ensured of their right to free speech, and they were given the right to file charges against unfair labor practices. The unfair practices that were identified were coercing workers to join the unions, causing employers to discriminate against those who do not join, refusing to bargain in good faith, requiring excessive or discriminatory fees, and engaging in featherbedding activities.
- Certification elections (voting for union representation) could not be held more frequently than once a year.
- Employees were given the right to initiate decertification elections.[13]

These provisions indicated the philosophy behind the act—as Senator Taft put it, "simply to reduce the special privileges granted labor leaders.'"

From time to time, amendments are added to the Taft-Hartley Act. For example, the 1980 amendments to the act provided for accommodation for employees with religious objections to union membership or support. For example, an employee may, based on religious grounds, contribute to a charity in lieu of paying union dues (*Tooley v. Martin-Marietta Corporation*, 1981).

Labor-Management Reporting and Disclosure Act.   Although the Taft-Hartley Act included some regulation of internal union activities, abuse of power and the corruption of some union officials led to the passage of a "bill of rights" for union members in 1959. The Labor-Management Reporting and Disclosure Act, or the Landrum-Griffin Act, provided for detailed regulation of internal union affairs. Some of the provisions include the following:

- Equality of rights for union members in nominating and voting in elections
- Controls on increases in dues
- Control on suspension and fining of union members
- Elections every three years for local office and every five for national or international offices
- Restriction of the use of trusteeship to take control of a member group's autonomy for political reasons
- Definition of the type of person who can hold union office
- Filing of yearly reports with the secretary of labor

The intention of this act was to protect employees from corrupt or discriminatory labor unions. The United Mine Workers, for example, held its first election of international officers in 1969. This event would not have been likely to occur even then without the provisions of the Landrum-Griffin Act.

Public Sector

Until recently, federal employee labor relations were controlled by executive orders issued by the president. Several rights of unions in the private sector are not included in public-sector regulations, although the content of these regulations is often lifted from private-sector acts.

Federal Employee Regulations.   The first set of regulations for federal employee labor relations was Executive Order 10988, introduced by President John Kennedy in 1962. This order prohibited federal agencies from interfering with employee organizing or unlawful union activity and provided for recognition of employee organizations. Employee organizations were denied the right to strike, however, and economic issues were not part of the bargaining process because these are fixed by the civil service classification system. Agency heads were made the ultimate authority on grievances, and managers were excluded from the bargaining units.

Executive Order 11491, issued in 1970 and amended in 1971 (EO 11616) and 1975 (EO 11838), addressed some of the difficulties presented by the first executive order. It created the Federal Labor Relations Council to hear appeals from the decisions of agency heads, prescribed regulations and policies, and created a Federal Services Impasses Panel to act on negotiation impasses. The council and the employee representatives could meet and discuss personnel practices and working conditions, but all agreements had to be approved by the council head. The council was restricted from interference, discrimination, and sponsorship of union discipline against an employee for filing a complaint and was required to recognize or deal with a qualified union. Labor organizations were also restrained from interfering, coercing management or employees, discriminating against employees, calling for or engaging in a strike, or denying membership to an employee.

These controls on employers and labor organizations are similar to those found in private-sector legislation. Yet federal employees do not have the same bargaining rights. They lack rights in four areas:

1. No provision is made for bargaining on economic issues.
2. Although the parties can meet and confer, there is no obligation to do so.
3. The ultimate authority is the agency head, rather than a neutral party.
4. There is no provision for union security through the agency shop, which requires all employees to pay dues but not to join the union.

In 1978 the Federal Service Labor-Management Relations Statute was passed as Title VII of the Civil Service Reform Act. It has been referred to as "the most significant change in federal personnel administration since the passage of the Civil Service Act in 1883."[14] Several significant changes were made by the statute, prime among them the following:

■ The president's ability to change the act through executive order was removed, and it was made more difficult to change the legislation.

- The Federal Labor Relations Authority (FLRA), modeled after the NLRB, was established as an "independent, neutral, full-time, bipartisan agency [created] to remedy unfair labor practices within the Government." Interpretation of the act is the province of the FLRA and the courts.
- An aggrieved person may now seek judicial review of a final order of the FLRA. The FLRA may also seek judicial enforcement of its order.
- Negotiated grievance procedures, which must be included in all agreements, must provide for arbitration as the final step.

State and Local Employee Regulations.   Employee relations regulations at the state and local level are varied. Not all states have legislation covering municipal employees as well. One widespread regulation can be noted: Collective bargaining is permitted in most states, and it covers wages, hours, and other terms and conditions of employment. The "other terms and conditions" have caused the most difficulty in interpretation. Managerial prerogatives are usually strong, especially for firefighters, police, and teachers. The requirement to bargain over certain issues is not as stringent in the private sector as it is at the state or local level. In addition, some twenty states have passed "right-to-work" laws, which prohibit union membership as a condition of employment.

Although the rights and privileges of public-sector labor organizations are not as extensive as those of labor organizations in the private sector, the greatest growth in unionization in recent years has come in the public sector. This will become an increasingly important area of labor relations during the 1990s.

Court Decisions

Several court decisions also are important. In *First National Maintenance Corp. v. NLRB* (1980), the Supreme Court held that an employer is not obligated to bargain with the union about a decision to close a portion of its business.[15] As discussed in Chapter 14, however, employers are now required to give their workers, unionized or nonunionized, sixty days' notice of a plant or office closing (Plant Closing Act, 1988).

In *Textile Workers Union v. Lincoln Mills* (1957), the Supreme Court held that the agreement to arbitrate grievances is the *quid pro quo* for an agreement not to strike through the year of the contract. This agreement, however, has been afflicted with the problem of unfair representation by the union of its members.[16] Over the past ten years, cases filed by employees with the NLRB against their unions for unfair representation (breach of duty) have more than *tripled* to several thousand annually. Although the union's obligation of fair representation is clear, the parameters of the specific duties of this obligation have been left unclear by numerous court decisions, including *Ford Motor Co. v. Huffman (1953); Vaca v. Sipes* (1967); *Hines v. Anchor Motor Freight Co.* (1976); and *Milstead v. Teamsters, Local 957* (1979) and by the NLRB ruling in *Miranda Fuel Co.* (1962).[17]

Finally, in the area of seniority systems, the Supreme Court has ruled that "bona fide" seniority systems are protected under Section 703(h) of Title VII of the 1964 Civil Rights Act. Recently, the sanctity of the seniority systems as related to layoff decisions was affirmed in *Firefighters Local Union 1784 v. Stotts* (1984).

The extensive legal considerations affecting unionization, however, do not ensure union membership. Unions must attract members, or employers must create unfavorable working conditions that produce dissatisfaction.[18] The results of these activities are reflected in the current state of unionization.

THE STATE OF UNIONIZATION

While the history of unionization in the United States is marred by conflict, today's environment is one of growing mutual cooperation. This is due to changes in membership, structure, and operation of unions and to their need to survive.

Decline in Membership

In 1988 the number of private and government employees belonging to unions or employee associations was about 17 million. As shown in Exhibit 15.2, all sectors of the work force include some components that are unionized. However, the proportion of the labor force represented by unions has declined steadily since the mid-1960s. In 1987, only 17.5 percent of all workers were represented by unions, down from 24.7 and 23 percent in 1970 and 1980, respectively.[19]

There are several reasons for the decline, including the increase in public-sector and white-collar jobs, both of which have historically had a low proportion of union members. This has been coupled with decreases in employment in industries that have been traditionally highly unionized (steel and manufacturing). It also seems that management initiatives have successfully met worker demands, lowering the need for unions. These are described in the initial "PHRM in the News."

In the future, economic conditions and legislation may make unionization more feasible in white-collar and public-sector jobs. Unions are now merging and expanding coverage in untraditional areas. This is one benefit that the AFL–CIO and the Teamsters anticipate from their recent merger.[20]

EXHIBIT 15.2

Union Membership

Union Members	Union Membership (in thousands)		
	Total Number of Workers	Members of Unions*	Percentage of Employed in Unions
All private nonagricultural wage and salary workers	77,044	11,227	14.6
Agricultural wage and salary workers	1,427	30	2.1
Private goods-producing workers	20,120	4,996	24.8
Private service-producing workers	20,167	1,331	6.6
Government workers	16,050	5,740	35.8

*Includes members of a labor union or employee association similar to union.

SOURCE: Bureau of Labor Statistics, 1988.

Distribution of Membership

Union membership has traditionally been concentrated in a small number of unions. In 1986, sixteen unions represented 60 percent of union membership, and eighty-five other unions represented just 2.4 percent. As shown in Exhibit 15.3, the Teamsters (IBT) continues to lead the pack with 1.9 million members. The National Education Association (NEA) is next largest and represents 62 percent of all public-sector unionized employees. The Food and Commercial Workers (UFCW) is now the third-largest union.[21]

The AFL–CIO

The major umbrella organization for national unions is the American Federation of Labor and Congress of Industrial Organizations (AFL–CIO). Representing 77 percent of total union membership, ninety-nine national unions currently belong to the AFL–CIO. Consequently, this organization has considerable clout and power.

The AFL was begun in 1886 and immediately assumed a leadershiip role in the union movement. As conceptualized by its president Samuel Gompers, the federation would work, only if:

- The national unions were to be autonomous within the AFL.
- Only one national union would be accepted for each trade or craft.
- The AFL would focus on the issues of wages, hours, and working conditions and avoid reformist goals.
- The AFL would avoid permanent political alliances.
- The strike would become a key weapon for achieving union objectives.

EXHIBIT 15.3

Unions Reporting 500,000 Members or More, Including Canadian Members

Organization	Members	
	1985	1982
Teamsters (IBT)	1,900,000	1,800,000
National Education Association (NEA)	1,700,000	1,641,354
Food and Commercial Workers (UFCW)	1,356,900	1,079,213
State, County (AFSCME)	1,100,000	950,000
Auto Workers (UAW)	1,029,900	1,140,370
Steelworkers (USW)	899,030	1,200,000
Service Employees (SEIU)	850,000	700,000
Electrical Workers (IBEW)	791,000	833,000
Machinists (IAM)	750,000	655,221
Carpenters (CJA)	628,000	679,000
Teachers (AFT)	610,000	573,644
Communications Workers (CWA)	515,000	650,000

SOURCE: Permission to reprint from *The Directory of U.S. Labor Organizations*, 1986–87 Edition, by Courtney Gifford, page 4, copyright © 1986 by The Bureau of National Affairs, Inc., Washington, D.C.

The AFL's endorsement of the free enterprise system allowed it to build a strong foundation among craft unions.

By comparison, the CIO was formed in 1935 and focused on industrywide unions. While the two union conglomerates were rivals for several years, this competition ended in 1955 when they merged. Unfortunately, the AFL–CIO marriage was not peaceful, and the anticipated growth in unionization did not occur. Eventually, the Teamsters and the United Auto Workers (UAW) left the organization, corruption among the remaining unions tarnished the image of the AFL–CIO, and high wage demands reduced public confidence.

Today, these problems are generally in the past. While membership continues to grow at a slow pace, hopes for large-scale unionization seem to be fading. In an attempt to increase union power in the 1990s, the UAW and Teamsters have rejoined the AFL–CIO.

At the heart of the labor movement are the seventy thousand or so local unions, varying in size from a handful of members up to forty thousand members. The locals represent the workers at the work place, where much of the day-to-day contact with management and the personnel department takes place. Most locals elect a president, a secretary-treasurer, and perhaps one or two other officers from the membership. In the larger locals, a **business representative** is hired as a full-time employee to handle grievances and contract negotiations. The other important members of the union local is the **steward,** an employee elected by his or her work unit to act as the union representative on the work site and to respond to company actions against employees that may violate the labor agreement.

THE ATTRACTION OF UNIONIZATION

To understand the union movement today, we must consider the reasons employees decide either to join or not to join unions.

The Decision to Join a Union

Three separate conditions have a strong tendency to influence an employee's decision to join a union. They are dissatisfaction, lack of power, and union instrumentality.

Dissatisfaction.   When an individual takes a job, conditions of employment (wages, hours, type of work) are explicitly specified in an **employment contract.** Unionization is considered a viable option when employees perceive that such employment conditions as pay and benefits, supervision, and job security are deteriorating, and individually they have little power to change them.[22]

Lack of Power.   It is important to remember that unionization is seldom the option of choice for employees. Usually dissatisfied employees approach management first with their concerns. Thoughts turn to unionization only when employees feel powerless—that is, when they feel their issues are being ignored by management. Therefore, communication of problems followed by responsiveness on the part of management helps defuse unionization attempts.[23]

Union Instrumentality.   Even when employees feel powerless, they may not turn to unionization. The likelihood that a coalition of dissatisfied employees will try to organize a union ultimately depends on whether they accept the concept of collective action and whether they believe unionization will yield positive rather than negative outcomes for them.[24]

Decision Not to Join a Union

Conversely, there are several reasons why employees may decide *not* to join a union. First, employees may have misgivings about how effective the union will be in improving conditions. If the union is not strong, its presence may generate more ill will than good feelings. Even if an employer does respond to union demands, the workers may be affected adversely. The employer may not be able to survive when the demands of the union are met, and thus the company may close down, costing employees their jobs. The organization may force the union to strike, inflicting economic hardship on employees who may not be able to afford being out of work, or it may attempt reprisals against pro-union employees, although this is illegal.[25]

Employees may also resist unionization because they identify strongly with the company and have a high level of commitment to it. They would therefore tend to view the union as an adversary and would be receptive to company arguments against unions. In addition, employees may perceive the goals of the union to be objectionable, intending to harm the company and the free enterprise system in general. They may object to the concept of seniority or even to the political activities of the unions. Moreover, certain employees—for example, engineers or college professors—view themselves as professionals and find collective action to be contrary to such professional ideals as independence and self-control.[26]

The decision not to unionize also can be influenced by management. Management practices that will dissuade employees from unionization include

- Practicing good management
- Involving employees in planning and decision making
- Having open, two-way communication channels
- Establishing procedures for handling employee problems and grievances
- Offering competitive wages
- Ensuring that work conditions are safe and hazard free.[27]

THE ORGANIZING CAMPAIGN

Under American labor law, the union that is certified to represent a group of employees has sole and exclusive right to bargain for that group. The process by which a single union is selected to represent all employees in a particular unit is crucial to the American system of collective bargaining. All employees are bound by the majority vote for union representation, and the employer is obligated to recognize and bargain with the chosen union.[28]

Because unions may thereby acquire significant power, employers may be anxious to keep them out. To add to this situation of potential union-management conflict, more than one union may be attempting to win certification as the representative of a group of employees, creating competition and conflict between unions. The stages in the certification process are detailed in Exhibit 15.4 and will be discussed next.

EXHIBIT 15.4	Certification Process

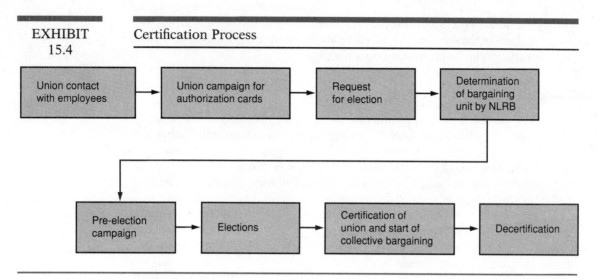

SOURCE: William D. Todor.

Establishing Contact Between the Union and Employees

Contact between the union and employees can be initiated by either party. National unions usually initiate contact with employees in industries or occupations that they have an interest in or are traditionally involved in. The United Auto Workers, for example, would be likely to contact nonunion employees in automobile plants and has, in fact, done so in the new plants that have been built in the South. In other cases the union is approached by employees interested in union representation, and the union is usually happy to oblige.[29]

At this point the company must be careful and avoid committing unfair labor practices. Accordingly, employers *should not*

- *Misrepresent the facts*—Any information management provides about a union or its officers must be factual and truthful.
- *Threaten employees*—It is unlawful to threaten employees with loss of their jobs or transfers to less desirable positions, income reductions, or loss or reduction of benefits and privileges. Use of intimidating language to dissuade employees from joining or supporting a union also is forbidden. In addition, supervisors may not blacklist, lay off, discipline, or discharge any employee because of union activity.
- *Promise benefits or rewards*—Supervisors may not promise a pay raise, additional overtime or time off, promotions, or other favorable considerations in exchange for an employee's agreement to refrain from joining a union or signing a union card, vote against union representation, or otherwise oppose union activity.
- *Make unscheduled changes in wages, hours, benefits, or working conditions*— Any such changes are unlawful unless the employee can prove they were initiated before union activity began.
- *Conduct surveillance activities*—Management is forbidden to spy on or request antiunion workers to spy on employees' union activities, or to make any statements that give workers the impression they are being watched. Supervisors also may not attend union meetings or question employees about a union's internal affairs.

- *Interrogate workers*—Managers may not require employees to tell them who has signed a union card, voted for union representation, attended a union meeting, or instigated an organization drive.
- *Prohibit solicitation*—Employees have the right to solicit members on company property during their nonworking hours, provided this activity does not interfere with work being performed, and to distribute union literature in nonwork areas during their free time.

However, employers *can*

- Discuss the history of unions and make factual statements about strikes, violence, or the loss of jobs at plants that have unionized.
- Discuss their own experiences with unions.
- Advise workers about the costs of joining and belonging to unions.
- Remind employees of the company benefits and wages they receive without having to pay union dues.
- Explain that union representation will not protect workers against discharge for cause.
- Point out that the company prefers to deal directly with employees, and not through a third party, in settling complaints about wages, hours, and other employment conditions.
- Tell workers that in negotiating with the union, the company is not obligated to sign a contract or accept all the union's demands, especially those that aren't in its economic interests.
- Advise employees that unions often resort to work stoppages to press their demands and that such tactics can cost them money.
- Inform employees of the company's legal right to hire replacements for workers who go out on strike for economic reasons.[30]

Authorization Cards and the Request for Elections

Once contact has been made, the union begins the campaign to get sufficient **authorization cards,** or signatures of employees interested in having union representation. This campaign must be carried out within the constraints set by law. If the union collects cards from 30 percent of an organization's employees, it can petition the National Labor Relations Board for an election. (Procedures in the public sector are similar.) If the NLRB determines that there is sufficient interest, it will schedule an election. If the union gets more than 50 percent of the employees to sign authorization cards, it may petition the employer as the bargaining representative. Usually employers refuse, whereupon the union petitions the NLRB for an election.

The employer usually resists the union's card-signing campaign. For instance, companies usually prohibit solicitation on the premises.[31] However, employers are legally constrained from interfering with an employee's freedom of choice. Union representatives have argued that employers ignore this law because the consequences for doing so are minimal—and they can effectively discourage unionism.[32] During the union campaign and election process, however, the personnel and human resource manager should caution the company against engaging in unfair labor practices. Severe violations by the employer can result in certification of the union as the bargaining representative, even if it has lost the election.

Determination of the Bargaining Unit

When the union has gathered sufficient signatures to petition for an election, the NLRB will make a determination of the **bargaining unit,** the group of employees that will be represented by the union. This is a crucial process because it can determine the quality of labor-management relations in the future:

> At the heart of labor-management relations is the bargaining unit. It is all important that the bargaining unit be truly appropriate and not contain a mix of antagonistic interests or submerge the legitimate interest of a small group of employees in the interest of a larger group.[33]

Professional and nonprofessional groups cannot be included in the same unit, and a craft unit cannot be placed in a larger unit unless both groups agree to it. Physical location, skill levels, degree of ownership, collective bargaining history, and extent of organization of employees are also guidelines to be considered.

From the union's perspective, the most desirable bargaining unit is one with pro-union members, so that they can win certification. Employers generally want a bargaining unit that is least beneficial to the union; this will help to maximize the likelihood of failure in the election and to minimize the power of the unit.[34]

The Pre-Election Campaign

After the bargaining unit has been determined, both union and employer embark on a pre-election campaign. Unions claim to provide a strong voice for employees, emphasizing improvements in wages and working conditions and the establishment of a grievance process to ensure fairness. Employers emphasize the costs of unionization—union dues, strikes, and loss of jobs.

The impact of pre-election campaigns is not clear. A study of thirty-one elections showed little change in attitude and voting propensity after the campaign.[35] People who will vote for or against a union before the election campaign generally vote the same way after.

Election, Certification, and Decertification

Generally, elections are associated with the process of determining if the union will win the right to represent workers. Elections can also determine if the union will *continue* to have the right to represent a group of employees.

Election and Certification.   The NLRB conducts the **certification election.** If a majority votes for union representation, the union will be certified. If the union does not get a majority, another election will not be held for at least a year. In 1980 the NLRB held 7,200 elections in which 478,000 employees were eligible to vote. By contrast, in 1986 there were only 3,300 elections representing 208,000 employees. Generally, about one-third to one-half of the elections certify a union, with less union success in larger organizations. Once a union has been certified, the employer is required to bargain with that union.

Decertification Elections.   The NLRB also can conduct **decertification elections** to remove a union from representation. This type of an election can be held if 30 percent or more of the employees in a bargaining unit request such an election. Such elections are most likely to occur during the first year of union representation when union strength has not been established.[36]

COLLECTIVE BARGAINING

Collective bargaining is a complex process in which union and management negotiators maneuver to win the most advantageous contract.[37] As in any complex process, a variety of issues come into play. How these issues are dealt with and resolved depends on the following:

- The quality of the union-management relationship
- The processes of bargaining used by labor and management
- Management's strategies in the collective bargaining process
- The union's strategies in the collective bargaining process
- Joint union-management strategies

These critical determinants of the collective bargaining process are described in detail prior to a description of the negotiation process.

Union-Management Relationships

An understanding of union-management relationships is facilitated by seeing them set in a **labor relations system.** The labor relations system is composed of three subunits—employees, management, and the union—with the government influencing the interaction among the three.

Each of the groups identified in the labor relations model has traditionally had different goals.[38] Workers are interested in improved working conditions, due process, wages, and opportunities; unions are interested in their own survival, growth, and acquisition of power, which depend on their ability to maintain the support of the employees by providing for their needs. Management has overall organizational goals (i.e., profit, certainty, market share, growth), and it also seeks to preserve managerial prerogatives (i.e., management rights to direct the work force and to attain the personal goals of the managers, such as promotion and achievement). Government is interested in a stable and healthy economy, protection of individual rights, due process, and safety and fairness in the work place.

These sets of goals, particularly those of union and management, are important because they can play an integral part in the nature of the relationship between union and management. Therefore, the possible relationships between union and management are now discussed in detail, starting with the adversarial relationship.

The Adversarial Relationship.   In the **adversarial** relationship, the goals of union and management are generally seen as incompatible. Labor and management each are attempting to get a bigger cut of the pie, while government looks on to protect its interests.

> In an adversarial system of union-management relations, the union's role is to gain concessions from management during collective bargaining and to preserve those concessions through the grievance procedure. The union is an outsider and critic.[39]

Historically, unions have adopted an adversarial role in their interactions with management. Their focus has been on wages and working conditions as they have attempted to get "more and better" job conditions from management. This approach works well in economic boom times but becomes difficult when the economy is not healthy.

The Cooperative Relationship.   High unemployment and the threat of continued job losses have recently induced unions, as well as management, to revise their relationship. In a **cooperative** system, the union's role is that of a partner, not a critic, and the union becomes jointly responsible with management for reaching a cooperative solution. Thus, a cooperative system requires that union and management engage in problem solving, information sharing, and integration of outcomes.[40] Cooperative systems have not been a major component of labor relations in the United States. Other countries—Sweden, Yugoslavia, and West Germany, for example—have built a cooperative mechanism into the labor system. On occasion, however, American management and labor have worked together to solve a problem.[41]

An example of what this cooperation can bring is the worker participation and involvement project at Ford Motor's plant in Edison, New Jersey:

> The innovation at Edison—other Ford plants are now installing the stop concept—is only the most visible symbol of a near-revolution in labor-management relations that started five years ago and has since become entrenched. Ford and the United Auto Workers have established what may be the most extensive and successful worker participation process in a major, unionized company. Thousands of teams of workers and supervisors at eighty-six of Ford's ninety-one plants and depots meet weekly to deal with production, quality, and work-environment problems.[42]

Regardless of whether union and management share an adversarial or a cooperative relationship, they still must engage in bargaining to arrive at a union-management relationship. For example, an adversarial relationship is more likely to accommodate distributive bargaining, while a cooperative relationship is more likely to favor integrative bargaining.

Processes of Bargaining

The most widely used description of the bargaining processes incorporates four types of bargaining in contract negotiations: distributive bargaining, integrative bargaining, concessionary bargaining, and continuous bargaining.

Distributive Bargaining.   **Distributive bargaining** takes place when the parties are in conflict over an issue and the outcome represents a gain for one party and a loss for the other. Distributive bargaining usually is associated with situations in which there is a fixed pot of resources and/or only one issue over which conflict exists. This classic approach to bargaining focuses on resolving one issue at a time, rather than on making trade-offs between issues.

Exhibit 15.5 details the distributive bargaining process. As shown, on any particular issue, union and management negotiators each have three identifiable positions. The union has an **initial demand point,** which is generally more than they expect to get; a **target point,** which is their realistic assessment of what they may be able to get; and a **resistance point,** which is the lowest

EXHIBIT
15.5

Distributive Bargaining Process

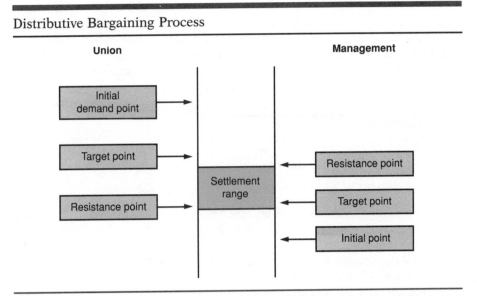

SOURCE: Adapted from R. Walton and R. B. McKersie, *A Behavioral Theory of Labor Negotiations* (New York: McGraw-Hill, 1965), 43.

acceptable level for that issue. Management has three similar points: an **initial offer point,** which is usually lower than the expected settlement; a **target point,** which is the point at which it would like to reach agreement; and a **resistance point,** which is its highest acceptable limit. If, as shown in Exhibit 15.5, management's resistance point is greater than the union's resistance point, there is a positive settlement range where negotiation can take place. The exact agreement within this range depends on the bargaining behavior of the negotiators. If, however, management's resistance point is below the union's, there is no common ground for negotiation. In such a situation, there is a negative settlement range, and the bargaining impasse exists.[43]

Using wages as an example, the union may have a resistance point of $8.40 per hour, a target point of $8.60, and an initial demand target point of $8.75. Management may offer $8.20 but have a target point of $8.45 and a resistance point of $8.55. The positive settlement range is between $8.40 and $8.55, and this is where the settlement will likely be. However, only the initial wage demand and offer are made public at the beginning of negotiations. The ritual of the distributive bargaining process is well established, and deviations are often met with suspicion.[44]

It is important to also remember that even when a zone of agreement exists and the bargaining ritual is followed, the parties may still not reach an agreement. Some factors that affect this process include time, calculation ability of the decision makers, memory, experience, lack of information, and expertise. Cognitive biases of negotiations will be discussed in a subsequent section.

Integrative Bargaining.   When there is more than one issue to be resolved, the potential exists to made trade-offs between the issues or to pursue integrative agreements. **Integrative bargaining** focuses on creative solutions to conflicts that reconcile (integrate) the parties' interests and yield high joint benefit. It can only occur when negotiators have an "expanding" pie perception—that is, when the two parties (union and management) value particular issues differently.[45]

Consider recent negotiations between the typographers union and management in which the union wanted a wage increase of $2.00 an hour and management wanted wage concessions of $2.00. An initial examination of this conflict might suggest that a negative bargaining zone exists and that a negotiated resolution would not be possible. In other words, the resistance points would not overlap, and an impasse would be reached.

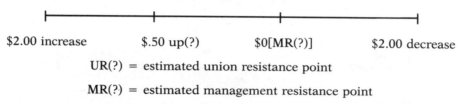

$2.00 increase $.50 up(?) $0[MR(?)] $2.00 decrease

UR(?) = estimated union resistance point

MR(?) = estimated management resistance point

As the negotiations proceeded, it became clear that the positions of the union and management *were* incompatible regarding wages. However, the *interests* of both were compatible. In future discussions what emerged were two issues of differential importance to the union and management: job security and holding the line on wages. The final agreement called for management to guarantee jobs for all employees with two or more years seniority and to retrain any of these employees who faced job obsolescence due to the introduction of computerized typesetting. In exchange for this, the hourly rate of pay would remain constant. However, a profit-sharing program would be established to reward labor cost savings. This solution met the needs of both the union and management.

Regarding the likelihood of integrative agreements, researchers have found that integrative agreements usually involve the development of novel alternatives, rather than reanalyzing known alternatives. In other words, creative problem solving is absolutely necessary for integrative agreements, which maximize the concerns of both parties, to emerge. If negotiators are unaware of the unequal value placed on an issue, then they are likely to fall back on the traditional distributive bargaining (i.e., fixed pot, win-lose) perspective. In reaching integrative agreements, there are five different strategies that can be pursued; these are listed in Exhibit 15.6.

As shown, one approach is to expand the number of options considered or the amount of resources available. Another is to trade or logroll issues; where one gives up something to gain something else. For example, the union discussed above agreed to no wage increase in exchange for job security. Nonspecific compensation is similar but involves trades between issues that are not central to the negotiations. For example, the union would get job security but would agree to a no-strike clause—an item not originally central to the pay–job security conflict. An example of cost cutting involves providing the union with job security but requiring that the union pay for training its members to meet the demands of the new technology. Finally, bridging involves the development of a new option that meets the underlying concerns of both parties. The solution above for the typographers union is an example of bridging.[46]

Concessionary Bargaining.   While distributive and integrative bargaining represent the primary approaches to bargaining, **concessionary bargaining** often occurs within these two frameworks. As the initial "PHRM in the News" suggests, concessionary bargaining is prompted by the severe economic conditions faced by employers. Seeking to survive and prosper, employers seek givebacks or concessions from the unions, giving promises of job security in

Strategies for Developing Integrative Agreements

EXHIBIT
15.6

Strategy	Definition
1. Expanding the pie	When additional resources are available, they can be obtained to meet the needs of both parties (e.g., hire more union members to reduce overtime expenditures). Does not work if the concerns are mutually exclusive.
2. Logrolling	Trading issues consists of having each party concede on low-priority issues in exchange for concessions on higher-priority issues. Each party gets the part of the agreement that is most important to it. Trading issues requires information about the interests of the parties, so that exchanges can occur.
3. Nonspecific compensation	One party gets what it wants, and the other party is paid on some unrelated issue. Nonspecific compensation is very similar to trading issues, except that additional issues outside of the original bargaining domain are brought into the conflict with the potential of making a trade.
4. Cost cutting	Calls for one party to get what it wants and for the other party to have its costs associated with the concession reduced or eliminated.
5. Bridging	Requires development of a new option that satisfies the most important interests underlying the demands of both parties. Neither party achieves its initially stated objective; rather, the parties search for new, creative solutions that are hidden by the original statement of the conflict. Involves a reformulation of the conflict by assessing a wider variety of potential solutions.

SOURCE: Adapted from D. G. Pruitt, "Integrative Agreements: Nature and Antecedents," in *Negotiating Inside Organizations*, ed. M. Bazerman and R. Lewicki (Beverly Hills, Calif.: Sage, 1983); M. Bazerman, *Judgment in Managerial Decision Making* (New York: Wiley, 1986).

return. During the past few years, this type of bargaining has been particularly prevalent, especially in the smokestack industries, such as automobiles, steel, and rubber, and to some extent in the transportation industry. In these industries, concessions sought by management from the unions include wage freezes, wage reductions, change in or elimination of work rules, fringe benefit reductions, delay or elimination of COLAs, and more hours of work for the same pay. Two-tier wage systems were tried in some industries, but problems of inequity and lower worker morale offset much of the savings from lower labor costs.[47]

Although some rank-and-file union members are not pleased with concessions and many are rejecting tentative contracts that have them, the alternatives are limited. Consider the plight of Eastern Airlines in 1989. Failing to get wage concessions from mechanics and machinists, a strike was held which was honored by Eastern pilots and backed up by "flying by the book" by other airlines. Ten days after the strike began, Eastern declared bankruptcy.

Another available alternative, and one that a few organizations such as Rath Packing of Waterloo, Iowa, and Great Atlantic & Pacific Tea Company have chosen, is having the employees buy the company or parts of the company. Such purchases can be facilitated through employee stock ownership plans.[48]

Continuous Bargaining.   As affirmative action, safety and health requirements, and other government regulations continue to complicate the situation for both unions and employers, and as the rate of change in the environment continues to increase, some labor and management negotiators are turning to **continuous bargaining.** A joint committee meets on a regular basis to explore issues and solve problems of common interest. These committees have appeared in the retail food, over-the-road trucking, nuclear power, and men's garment industries.[49]

Several characteristics of continuous bargaining have been identified:

- Frequent meetings during the life of the contract
- Focus on external events and problem areas rather than on internal problems
- Use of outside experts in decision making
- Use of a problem-solving (integrative) approach[50]

The intention is to develop a union-management structure that is capable of adapting positively and productively to sudden changes in the environment. This continuous bargaining approach is different from, but an extension of, the emergency negotiations that unions have insisted on when inflation or other factors have substantially changed the acceptability of the existing agreement. Continuous bargaining is a permanent arrangement intended to help avoid the crises that often occur under traditional collective bargaining systems.

Although the selection and utilization of a bargaining strategy is important in determining the outcomes of collective bargaining, so, too, is the actual process of negotiation, or negotiating the agreement.

Intraorganizational Bargaining.   During negotiations, the bargaining teams from both sides may have to engage in intraorganizational bargaining—that is, conferring with their constituents over changes in bargaining positions. Management negotiators may have to convince management to change its position on an issue—for instance, to agree to a higher wage settlement. Union negotiators must eventually convince their members to accept the negotiated contract, so they must be sensitive to the demands of the membership as well as realistic. When the membership votes on the proposed package, it will be strongly influenced by the opinions of the union negotiators.

A special form of intraorganizational bargaining, practiced particularly in the public sector, is multilateral bargaining. This form of bargaining involves more than two parties in bargaining but there is no clear union-management dichotomy. For example any public employee association may negotiate with division directors as well as the legislature. One result of this pressure is that the elected officials are forced to tell their negotiators to grant more concessions to the unions than they otherwise may have. Bargaining then becomes a process involving multiple levels.

NEGOTIATING THE AGREEMENT

Once a union is certified as the representative of a work unit or bargaining unit, it becomes the only party that can negotiate an agreement with the employer for all members of that work unit, whether or not they are union members. This is therefore an important and potent position. The union is responsible to its members to negotiate for what they want, and it has the "duty to represent all employees fairly."[51] The union is a critical link between employees and employer. The quality of its bargaining is an important measure of union effectiveness.

Negotiating Committees

The employer and the union select their own representatives for the negotiating committee. Neither party is required to consider the wishes of the other. Management negotiators, for example, cannot refuse to bargain with representatives of the union because they dislike them or do not think they are appropriate.

Union negotiating teams typically include representatives of the union local, often the president and other executive staff members. In addition, the national union may send a negotiating specialist, who is likely to be a labor lawyer, to work with the team. The negotiators selected by the union do not have to be members of the union or employees of the company. The general goal is to balance bargaining skill and experience with knowledge and information about the specific situation.

At the local level, when a single bargaining unit is negotiating a contract, the company is usually represented by the manager and members of the labor relations or personnel staff. Finance and production managers may also be involved. When the negotiations are critical, either because the size of the bargaining unit is large or because the effect on the company is great, specialists such as labor lawyers may be included on the team.

In national negotiations, top industrial relations or personnel executives frequently head a team made up of specialists from corporate headquarters and perhaps managers from critical divisions or plants within the company. Again, the goal is to have expertise along with specific knowledge about critical situations.

The Negotiating Structure

Most contracts are negotiated by a single union and a single employer. In some situations, however, different arrangements can be agreed on. When a single union negotiates with several similar companies—for instance, the construction industry or supermarkets—the employers may bargain as a group with the union. At the local level, this is called **multiemployer bargaining;** at the national level, it is referred to as **industrywide bargaining.** Industrywide bargaining occurs in the railroad, coal, wallpaper, and men's garment industries.[52] National negotiations result in contracts that settle major issues, such as compensation, whereas issues relating to working conditions are settled locally. This split bargaining style is common in Great Britain and has been used in the auto industry in the United States. When several unions bargain jointly with a single employer, they engage in coordinated bargaining. Although not as common as the others, coordinated bargaining appears to be increasing, especially in public-sector bargaining.

One frequent consequence of coordinated and industrywide bargaining is pattern settlements, where similar wage rates are imposed on the companies with employees represented by the same union within a given industry. Pattern settlements can be detrimental because they ignore differences in the employers' economic condition and ability to pay. The result can be settlements that are tolerable for some companies but cause severe economic trouble for others.[53]

A negotiating structure that exists in the contract construction industry is wide-area and multicraft bargaining. This bargaining structure has arisen in response to the need for unionized employers to be more price competitive and have fewer strikes and the desire by construction trade unions to gain more control at the national level. Consequently, the bargaining is done on a regional (geographic) basis rather than on a local basis, as previously done. In addition, it covers several construction crafts simultaneously instead of one. The common contract negotiations resulting from wide-area and multicraft bargaining help lessen the occasion for unions to **whipsaw** the employer (i.e., to use one contract settlement as a precedent for the next), which then forces the employer to get all contracts settled so that all the employees will go back to work. A frequent result of whipsawing is that an employer agrees to more favorable settlements on all contracts, regardless of the conditions and merits of each contract, just to get all employees back to work.[54]

Preparation for Bargaining

Prior to the bargaining session, management and union negotiators need to develop the strategies and proposals they will use.

Management Strategies.   In preparing for negotiations with the union, management needs to prepare in four different areas:

1. Preparation of specific proposals for changes in contract language
2. Determination of the general size of the economic package that the company anticipates offering during the negotiations
3. Preparation of statistical displays and supportive data that the company will use during negotiations
4. Preparation of a bargaining book for the use of company negotiators, a compilation of information on issues that will be discussed, giving an analysis of the effect of each clause, its use in other companies, and other facts[55]

An important part of this preparation is calculation of the cost of various bargaining issues or demands. The relative cost of pension contributions, pay increases, health benefits, and other provisions should be determined prior to negotiations. Other costs should also be considered. For instance, what is the cost to management, in its ability to do its job, of union demands for changes in grievance and discipline procedures or transfer and promotion provisions? The goal is to be as well prepared as possible by considering the implications and ramifications of the issues that will be discussed and by being able to present a strong argument for the position management takes.

Union Strategies.   Like management, unions need to prepare for negotiations by collecting information. Because collective bargaining is the major means by which a union can convince its members that it is effective and valuable, this is a critical activity.

Unions collect information in at least three areas:

1. The financial situation of the company and its ability to pay
2. The attitude of management toward various issues, as reflected in past negotiations or inferred from negotiations in similar companies
3. The attitudes and desires of the employees

The first two areas give the union an idea of what demands management is likely to accept. The third area is important but is sometimes overlooked. The union should be aware of the preferences of the membership. For instance, is a pension increase preferred over increased vacation or holiday benefits? The preferences will vary with the characteristics of the workers. Younger workers are more likely to prefer more holidays, shorter workweeks, and limited overtime, whereas older workers are more interested in pension plans, benefits, and overtime. The union can determine these preferences by using a questionnaire to survey its members (discussed in Chapter 16).

Issues for Negotiation

Although they vary by organization and union, the actual issues for negotiation are likely to be far more extensive than are those for the initial organizing campaign, described earlier in the chapter. As specified by the Labor Management Relations Act, wages, hours, and other terms and conditions of employment are **mandatory issues** for negotiation. Other mandatory items include subcontracting work, safety, changes of operations, and other actions management might take that will have an impact on employees' jobs, wages, and economic supplements.[56]

While historically there has been a debate over what specific topics fall into this category, the Supreme Court's decision on the *Borg Warner Corp. vs. NLRB* (1982) case suggests that the distinction between mandatory and permissive bargaining issues is based on whether the topic regulates the relations between the employer and its employees.[57] Any issue that changes the nature of the job itself or compensation for work must be discussed in collective bargaining. Mandatory issues therefore include subcontracting work, safety, changes of operations, and other actions management might take that will have an impact on employees' job, wages, and economic supplements. With the Supreme Court decision in *First National Maintenance*, management's obligation to bargain over plant closings has been substantially reduced.[58]

Permissive issues are not specifically related to the nature of the job but are still of concern to both parties. For example, issues of price, product design, and decisions about new jobs may be subject to bargaining if the parties agree to it. Permissive issues usually develop when both parties see that mutual discussion and agreement will be beneficial, as may be more likely when a cooperative relationship exists between union and management. Management and union negotiators cannot refuse to agree on a contract if they fail to settle permissive issue.[59]

Prohibited issues are those concerning illegal activities, such as the demand that an employer use only union-produced goods or, where it is illegal, that an employer employ only union members. Such issues may not be discussed in collective bargaining sessions.

The actual issues for negotiation can be expected to vary in different union-management bargainings. In contrast to organizing, where the critical issues are grievances, economics, job security, and supervision, there are a multitude of mandatory issues for negotiation, not to mention the permissive issues.[60] Most of the issues for negotiation are mandatory and are summarized below.

Direct Compensation. Wage conflicts are the leading cause of strikes. Difficulties arise here because a wage increase is a direct cost to the employer, as is a wage decrease to the employee. As discussed in Chapters 8 and 9, rates of pay are influenced by a variety of factors including the going rate in an industry, the employer's ability to pay, the cost of living, and productivity. All these are subjects often debated and discussed in negotiations.

Fringe Benefits.   Because the cost of fringe benefits now runs as high as 45 percent of the total cost of wages, they are a major concern in collective bargaining. Benefit provisions are very difficult to remove once they are in place, so management tends to be cautious about agreeing to them. Still, some of the most commonly negotiated fringe benefits are

- *Pensions.* Once management has decided to provide a pension plan, the conditions of the plan must be determined (when the benefits will be available, how much will be paid, and whether they become available according to age or years of service). Finally, the organization must decide how long employees must work for the company to receive minimum benefits (vesting) and whether the organization will pay the whole cost or whether the employees or the union will be asked to help.
- *Paid vacations.* Most agreements provide for paid vacations. Length of vacation is usually determined by length of service, up to some maximum. The conditions that qualify an individual for a vacation in a given year are also specified. Agreements occasionally specify how the timing of vacations will be determined.
- *Paid holidays.* Most agreements provide time off with pay on Independence Day, Labor Day, Thanksgiving, Christmas, New Year's Day, and Memorial Day. Several others may also be included.
- *Sick leave.* Unpaid sick leave allows the employee to take time off for sickness without compensation. Paid sick leave is usually accumulated while working. Typically one-half to one and one-half days of paid sick leave are credited for each month of work.
- *Health and life insurance.* The employer may be required to pay some or all of the costs of health and life insurance plans.
- *Dismissal or severance pay.* Occasionally employers agree to pay any employee who is dismissed or laid off because of technological changes or business difficulties.
- *Supplemental unemployment benefits.* In the mid-1950s, the United Auto Workers negotiated a plan to supplement state unemployment benefits and to make up the difference when these state benefits expired. Most contracts with this provision are found in the auto and steel industries, where layoffs are common, but workers in other industries are beginning to negotiate them as well.

Hours of Employment.   Finally, while organizations are required to pay overtime for work in excess of forty hours, unions continually try to reduce the number of hours worked each week. Negotiations focus on including lunch hours in the eight-hour-day requirement. Additionally, negotiations may focus on providing overtime after any eight-hour shift, rather than after forty hours.

Institutional Issues.   Some issues are not directly related to jobs but are nevertheless important to both employees and management. Institutional issues are those that affect the security and success of both parties.

- *Union Security.* About 63 percent of the major labor contracts stipulate that employees must join the union after being hired into its bargaining unit. However, twenty states that traditionally have had low levels of unionization have passed "right-to-work" laws, outlawing union membership as a condition of employment.
- *Checkoff.* Unions have attempted to arrange for payment of dues through deduction from employees' paychecks. By law, employees must agree to this in writing, but about 86 percent of union contracts contain this provision anyway.
- *Strikes.* The employer may insist that the union agree not to strike during the life of the agreement, typically when a cost-of-living clause has been included. The agreement may be unconditional, allowing no strikes at all, or it may limit strikes to specific circumstances.
- *Managerial prerogatives.* Over half the agreements today stipulate that certain activities are the right of management. In addition, management in most companies argues that it has "residual rights"—that all rights not specifically limited by the agreement belong to management.

Administrative Issues.   The last category of issues is concerned with the treatment of employees at work.

- *Breaks and cleanup time.* Some contracts specify the time and length of coffee break and meal breaks for employees. Also, jobs requiring cleanup may have a portion of the work period set aside for this procedure.
- *Employment security and job security.* This is perhaps the issue of most concern to employees and unions. Employers are concerned with restriction of their ability to lay off employees. Changes in technology and attempts to subcontract work are issues that impinge on job security. A typical union response to technological change was the reaction of the International Longshoremen's Association in the late 1960s to the introduction of containerized shipping. The union operated exclusive hiring halls, developed complex work rules, and negotiated a guaranteed annual income for its members.
- *Seniority.* Length of service is used as a criterion for many personnel decisions in most collective agreements. Layoffs, transfers, and promotions are most frequently determined by seniority. The method of calculating seniority is usually specified to clarify the relative seniority of employees.
- *Discharge and discipline.* This is a touchy issue, and even when an agreement addresses these problems, many grievances are filed concerning the way employees are disciplined or discharged.
- *Safety and health.* Although the Occupational Safety and Health Act specifically deals with worker safety and health, some contracts have provisions specifying that the company will provide safety equipment, first aid, physical examinations, accident investigations, and safety committees. Hazardous work may be covered by special provisions and pay rates.[61]
- *Production standards.* The level of productivity or performance of employees is a concern of both management and the union. Management is concerned with efficiency, but the union is concerned with the fairness and reasonableness of management's demands.
- *Grievance procedures.* This is a significant part of collective bargaining and is discussed in more detail later in this chapter.

- *Training.* The design and administration of training and development programs and the procedure for selecting employees for training may also be
  bargaining issues.
- *Duration of the agreement.* Agreements can last for one year or longer, with
  the most common period being three years.

Partly because there are so many issues over which to bargain, agreement
and contract settlement are not always attained without conflict. When this
occurs, forms of conflict resolution are utilized.

Factors Affecting Bargaining

The preceding discussion suggests that negotiations proceed in a rational manner and end in resolution when a positive contract zone—a set of outcomes that
is preferred over the imposition of a strike—exists. Unfortunately, negotiators
often fail to reach agreement, even when a positive contract zone exists. The
question is, Why?

To fully understand the negotiation process, it is important to examine the
decision processes of negotiators. By identifying the biases of negotiators, then
prescriptive approaches and training programs can be developed to improve
negotiations. Discussed below are the five most common cognitive limitations
to negotiator judgments.[62]

Mythical Fixed Pie.   All too frequently, negotiators believe that their interests
automatically conflict with the other party's interests. In other words, what one
side wins, the other side loses. However, most conflicts usually have more than
one issue at stake, with the parties placing different values on the different
issues. Consequently, the potential usually exists for integrative agreements. A
fundamental task in training negotiators lies in identifying and eliminating this
false "fixed pie" assumption and preparing them to look for trade-offs between
issues of different value to each side.

Framing.   Consider the following bargaining situation: The union claims that
its members need a raise to $12 an hour and that anything less will represent
a loss due to inflation. Management argues that the company can't pay more
than $10 an hour and that anything more would impose an unacceptable loss.
If each side had the choice between settling at $11 an hour or going to binding
arbitration, they are likely to be risk seeking and will move toward arbitration
rather than settlement.

Changing the frame of the situation to a positive one results in a very different
predicted outcome. If the union can view anything above $10 an hour as a gain,
and if management can view anything under $12 as a gain, then a negotiated
settlement is likely—at $11 dollars.

As the preceding example emphasizes, the frame (positive or negative) of
negotiators can make the difference between settlement and impasse. One solution then to impasses in bargaining is to alter the frame of reference such
that it is positive, rather than negative.[63]

Nonrational Escalation of Commitment.   Consider the following situation.
It is 1989, and Eastern Airlines mechanics and baggage handlers strike to obtain
wage concession from management. The union is willing to invest the temporary

loss of pay during the strike to obtain long-term wage gains. Unfortunately, without wage concessions no buy-out offers appear to be forthcoming from other airlines. To make matters worse, Eastern says that it will have to file for bankruptcy. The union is faced with the option of backing off and returning to work or increasing its commitment to the strike to try to force the concessions they desire.

In this example, the union has committed resources to a course of action and then is faced with escalating that commitment or backing out of the conflict. As we discussed previously (Chapter 7), escalation literature would predict that the union would probably persist in the course of action (strike), rather than taking the action a rational analysis would have dictated. And that's exactly what the union did. Even after Eastern declared bankruptcy, the machinists and baggage handlers remained on strike.

Negotiator Overconfidence.   Research demonstrates that negotiators, like other decision makers, tend to be overconfident and erroneously believe that their positions will prevail if they do not "give in." While only 50 percent of all final offers submitted actually can be accepted, negotiators consistently over-estimate by 15 percent the probability that under final-offer-arbitration, *their* offer will be accepted. As a result, negotiators are unwilling to settle, even when a positive bargaining zone exists. To counter this bias, the track records of management and union in arbitrations and grievances need to be recorded and utilized when evaluating the likelihood of a successful agreement.

Lack of Perspective Taking.   One important component of successful ne-gotiations is an individual's ability to take the perspective of his or her opponent. Not only can perspective taking increase one's ability to predict accurately the opposition's goal, but also it positively affects the concessionary tendencies of negotiators and the likelihood of a settlement. Unfortunately, many negotiators fail to see the world from their opposition's perspective. As a result, they fail to reach settlements when they are possible.[64]

CONFLICT RESOLUTION

Although the desired outcome of collective bargaining is agreement on the conditions of employment, on many occasions, negotiators are unable to reach such an agreement at the bargaining table. In these situations, several alter-natives are used to resolve the impasse. The most visible response is the strike or lockout, but third-party interventions such as mediation and arbitration are also used.

Strikes and Lockouts

When the union is unable to get management to agree to a demand it believes is critical, it may resort to a strike. A **strike** may be defined as the refusal by employees to work at the company. Management may refuse to allow employees to work, which is called a **lockout**.[65]

In order to strike, the union usually holds a strike vote to get its members' approval for a strike if the negotiations are not successful. Strong membership support for a strike strengthens the union negotiators' position. If the strike takes place, union members picket the employer, informing the public about the existence of a labor dispute and preferably, from the union's point of view, convincing them to avoid this company during the strike. A common practice is the refusal of union members to cross the picket line of another striking union. This gives added support to the striking union.

Employers usually attempt to continue operations while the strike is in effect. They either run the company with supervisory personnel and people not in the bargaining unit or hire replacements for the employees. Although the company can legally hire these replacements, the union reacts strongly to the use of "scabs," and they may be a cause of increasingly belligerent labor relations. The success of a strike depends on its ability to cause economic hardship to the employer. Severe hardship usually causes the employer to concede to the union's demands. Thus, from the union's point of view it is paramount that the company not be able to operate successfully during the strike and that the cost of this lack of production be high. In addition, the timing of the strike is often critical. The union attempts to hold negotiations just prior to the period when the employer has a peak demand for its product or services, when a strike will have maximum economic impact.

Although strikes are common, they are costly to both the employer, who loses revenue, and the employees, who face loss of income. For example, the 1989 strike at Eastern cost the airline an estimated $4 million a day. Costs were also substantial for other airlines because pilots "flew by the book," refusing landings without exact specification, and for employees. The result was delayed takeoffs and prolonged landings. Even when bankruptcy was filed, the economic hardship continued as Eastern resorted to $12 one-way shuttle fares to lure passengers back into the air. By the end of the strike, almost all of Eastern's routes were shut down.

Slowdown.   Short of an actual strike, unions may invoke a **slowdown.** The impact of slowdowns can be more effective than an actual strike. For example, the United Auto Workers recently orchestrated a work slowdown.

> In a contract dispute, union employees are refusing to install parts without blueprints, and they are working to the minimums of their job requirements. The union also is weighing a plan to stage mass grievances by having hundreds of workers blow whistles whenever a member has a complaint against a foreman.
>
> Although such tactics, viewed individually, might seem fairly mild, their cumulative effect has hurt the company and its earnings. Since the slowdown started, McDonnell Douglas has missed 10 delivery dates for MD-80 jets—though the company partly blames its production problems on parts shortages and the training of new workers. The union's actions have been "baffling and frustrating," says Sanford N. McDonnell, the company's chief executive, adding that he has fielded some phone calls from angry airline customers.[66]

Corporate Campaign.   Another indirect tactic in the form of a secondary boycott is called a **corporate campaign.** In the corporate campaign a union may ask the public and other unions to write letters to a company asking it to change the way in which it is bargaining with the union.[67]

Conflict resolution that avoids work stoppages or slowdowns, which may occur regardless of the existence of no-strike clauses, by interventions such as mediation, arbitration, and injunctions may therefore be desirable from several perspectives.

Mediation

Mediation is a procedure in which "a neutral third party assists the union and management negotiators in reaching voluntary agreement."[68] Having no power to impose a solution, the mediator attempts to facilitate the negotiations between union and management. The mediator may make suggestions and recommendations and perhaps add objectivity to the often emotional negotiations. To have any success, the mediator must have the trust and respect of both parties and have sufficient expertise and neutrality to convince the union and employer that he or she will be fair and equitable. The U.S. government operates the Federal Mediation and Conciliation Service (FMCS) to make experienced mediators available to unions and companies. For situations in which problems frequently reappear, a program is offered by the FMCS to eliminate the causes of recurrent impasses. The program, called Relationships by Objectives, utilizes aspects of attitudinal structuring to increase the likelihood of a cooperative relationship between union and management.[69]

Arbitration

Arbitration is a procedure in which a neutral third party studies the bargaining situation, listens to both parties and gathers information, and then makes recommendations that are binding on the parties. The arbitrator, in effect, determines the conditions of the agreement. Arbitration in disputes of the basic terms and conditions of employment is called **interest arbitration.** This type of arbitration is relatively infrequent in the private sector (occurring in only 1.3 percent of all cases) but is required in the public sector.[70] Arbitration of disputes involving the interpretation or application of laws, agreements, or customary practices is called **rights arbitration** and is quite common in both the private and the public sectors.

For arbitration to be considered a reasonable alternative, its potential costs must be considered as lower and its benefits as greater than those associated with a strike. Still, costs of arbitration are multiple. Because a third party is involved, there is increased uncertainty regarding the outcome. Second, fees and expenses of the arbitrator must be handled. These costs are in addition to the time and expense incurred by the union and management in meeting with the arbitrator. Finally, the quality of arbitrated outcomes is usually less because arbitrators most often recommend compromise decisions.

The major benefit of arbitration is that its use transfers the responsibility of the outcome to a third party. Arbitration is also a viable resolution to the **bargainer's dilemma.** That is, to save face, resolve the dilemma, and avoid the imposition of sanctions, negotiators may opt for arbitration.

Once the impasse is resolved, union and management have a contract by which to abide. Abiding by it is the essence of contract administration; however, at times during contract administration, arbitration is again necessary—namely, when a grievance is filed. This type of arbitration is referred to as **grievance arbitration.** Grievance arbitration in the private sector receives the most attention and concern. The role of the grievance arbitrator is considered in Step 4 of the grievance procedures in the discussion of contract administration.[71]

CONTRACT ADMINISTRATION

The collective agreement, once signed, becomes the basic legislation governing the lives of the workers.[72] Because it is impossible to write an unambiguous agreement that will anticipate all the situations occurring over its life, disputes will inevitably arise over interpretation and application of the agreement. The most common method of resolving these disputes is a **grievance procedure.** Virtually all agreements negotiated today provide for a grievance process to handle employee complaints.

Grievance Procedures

A **grievance** is a "charge that the union-management contract has been violated."[73] A grievance may be filed by the union for employees or by employers, although management rarely does so. The grievance process is designed to investigate the charges and to resolve the problem.

Five sources of grievances have been identified:

1. Outright violation of the agreement
2. Disagreement over facts
3. Dispute over the meaning of the agreement
4. Dispute over the method of applying the agreement
5. Argument over the fairness or reasonableness of actions.[74]

In resolving these sources of conflict, the grievance procedure should serve *employers* and *unions*, by interpreting and adjusting the agreement as conditions require; *employees*, by protecting their contractual rights and providing a channel of appeal; and *society* at large, by keeping industrial peace and reducing the number of industrial disputes in the courts.

As shown in Exhibit 15.7, grievance procedures typically involve several steps:

Step 1.   An employee who believes that the labor contract has been violated usually contacts the union steward, and together they discuss the problem with the supervisor involved.[75] If the problem is simple and straightforward, it is often resolved at this stage. Many contracts require the grievance to be in written form at this first stage. However, some cases may be resolved by informal discussion between the supervisor and the employee, and therefore do not officially enter the grievance process.

Step 2.   If agreement cannot be reached at the supervisor level, or if the employee is not satisfied, the complaint can enter the second step of the grievance procedure. Typically, an industrial relations representative of the company seeks to resolve the grievance. There is usually a time period in which a formal complaint can be filed.

Step 3.   If the grievance is sufficiently important or difficult to resolve, it may be taken to the third step. Although contracts vary, top-level management and union executives are usually involved at this step. These people have the authority to make the major decisions that may be required to resolve the grievance.

Step 4.   If a grievance cannot be resolved at the third step, most agreements require the use of an arbitrator to consider the case and reach a decision. The

Typical Grievance Procedure

EXHIBIT
15.7

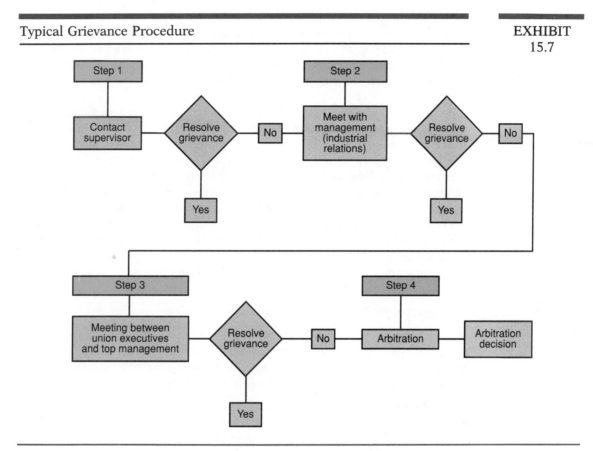

SOURCE: W. D. Todor.

arbitrator is a neutral, mutually acceptable individual who may be provided by the Federal Mediation and Conciliation Service or some private agency. The arbitrator holds a hearing, reviews the evidence, and then rules on the grievance. The decision of the arbitrator is usually binding. Because the cost of arbitration is shared by the union and employer, there is some incentive to settle the grievance before it goes to arbitration.[76] An added incentive in some cases is the requirement that the loser pay for the arbitration.[77]

Occasionally the union will call a strike over a grievance in order to resolve it. This may happen when the issue at hand is so important that the union believes it cannot wait for the slower arbitration process, which takes an average of 223 days.[78] This "employee rights" strike may be legal, but if the contract specifically forbids strikes during the tenure of the agreement, it is not legal and is called a **wildcat strike.**[79] Wildcat strikes are not common, however, because most grievances are settled through arbitration.[80]

Grievance Issues

The Taft-Hartley Act gives unions the right to file grievances on their own behalf or for their members if they believe rights have been violated. As noted previously, grievances can be filed over *any* issue that is subject to the collective agreement or over interpretation and implementation of the agreement itself.

The most common are grievances over **insubordination,** which focus on whether an employee failed or outright refused to do what a supervisor requested. If the supervisor's orders were clear and explicit, and if the employee was warned of the consequences, discipline for refusal to respond is usually acceptable. The exception is when the employee believes compliance will endanger his or her health.

Grievances of seniority relate to layoffs, job bumping, and rehires, and grievances regarding compensation for time away from work, vacations, holidays, or sick leave usually focus on how these benefits are calculated. Grievances may also be filed regarding overtime pay or even the requirement of mandatory overtime, scheduling, and pay for reporting to work when not scheduled.

Finally, a growing area of grievances is management rights—that is, its right to introduce technological change, use subcontractors, change jobs, or reassign workers. Occasionally other activities prompt grievances. For example, wildcat strikes or behavior that is considered to be a strike (mass absences from work, for example) may result in management grievances. The major focus of grievances, however, is on the administration of the conditions of the agreement.

Management Procedures

Management can significantly affect the grievance rate by adopting proper procedures when taking action against an employee.[81] The issue of just cause and fairness is central to most grievances. The following activities have been identified as being useful in reducing the likelihood of grievances:

- Explanation of rules to employees
- Consideration of the accusations and facts
- Regular warning procedures, including written records
- Involvement of the union in the case
- Examination of the employee's motives and reasons
- Consideration of the employee's past record
- Familiarization of all management personnel, especially supervisors, with disciplinary procedures and company rules[82]

Management also can avoid some grievance problems by educating supervisors and managers about labor relations and the conditions of the collective agreement.

Union Procedures

The union has an obligation to it members to provide them with fair and adequate representation and to speedily process and investigate grievances brought by its members (*Vaca v. Sipes,* 1967; *Hines v. Anchor Motor Freight,* 1976; *Smith v. Hussman Refrigerator Co. & Local 13889, United Steel Workers of America,* 1980). Thus, it should have a grievance-handling procedure that will aid in effectively processing grievances without being guilty of unfair representation.

Unfair representation, according to the National Labor Relations Board, is usually related to one of four types of union behavior:

1. *Improper motives or fraud.* The union cannot refuse to process a grievance because of the employee's race or sex or because of the employee's attitude toward the union.

2. *Arbitrary conduct.* The union must investigate the merits of the grievance. Unions cannot dismiss a grievance without investigating it.
3. *Gross negligence.* The union cannot display a reckless disregard of the employee's interests.
4. *Union conduct after filing the grievance.* The union must process the grievance to a reasonable conclusion.[83]

Because the employer can also be cited for unfair representation, management should attempt to maintain a fair grievance process.

Unions may have an additional interest in grievances as a tool in collective negotiation. Grievances may be a way to introduce or show concern for an issue in negotiations. In some cases, grievances may be withdrawn by unions in exchange for some management concessions, although this may be dangerous because it may be an unfair representation of the employee.

An important influence on the grievance process is the union steward. Because the union steward is generally the first person to hear about an employee's grievance, he or she can encourage an employee to file a grievance, can suggest that the problem is really not a grievance, or can informally resolve the problem outside the grievance procedure.[84] Since stewards are selected from the ranks of employees and may have little knowledge of labor relations, the union should provide training to improve their effectiveness.

PUBLIC-SECTOR COLLECTIVE BARGAINING

Collective bargaining in the public sector differs somewhat from that in the private sector. Federal employees do not have the right to strike. The recently passed Civil Service Reform Act, however, has changed the situation by creating an independent agency to remedy unfair labor practices. Yet federal employees still do not have the same collective bargaining rights as private workers. In the federal sector, management must bargain over a limited number of issues.

Arrangements for collective bargaining at the state and local level vary considerably. All but fourteen of the states have collective bargaining provisions. A wide range of coverage exists among states; some include municipal employees, some include state employees, and some include both. Special legislation for police officers, firefighters, and teachers is also often found.

One distinctive characteristic of public-sector collective bargaining is the tendency to have multilateral bargaining. Governments tend to have so many levels of authority that unions can sometimes go around the government negotiating team to higher authorities to seek a settlement. However, such actions tend to disrupt the bargaining process and can lead to distrust and difficulties in future negotiations.

The frequency of strikes in the public sector is nevertheless increasing,[85] partly because the penalty for striking has rarely been enforced in the public sector. The success of strikes or work stoppages in the public sector depends on both the political clout of the union and its ability to impose economic costs. Because many public-sector services are service-related, and because strikes can mean cost savings in terms of unpaid wages for the government involved, strikes of teachers or public employees have a lower success rate than do strikes in the private sector.[86]

TRENDS IN UNIONIZATION AND COLLECTIVE BARGAINING

Two trends to be described are assessing the process of collective bargaining and strategic involvement. Between these trends, strategic involvement is the more recent and is in the early stages of development.[87]

Assessment

The effectiveness of the entire collective bargaining process and the union-management relationship can be measured by the extent to which each party attains its goals. Difficulties are associated with this approach, however. Because goals are incompatible in many cases and can therefore lead to conflicting estimates of effectiveness, a more useful measure of effectiveness may be the quality of the system used to resolve conflict. Conflict is more apparent in the collective bargaining process, where failure to resolve the issues typically leads to strikes. Another measure of effectiveness is the success of the grievance process, or the ability to resolve issues developing out of the bargaining agreement.

Effectiveness of Negotiations.   Because the purpose of negotiations is to achieve an agreement, agreement becomes an overall measure of bargaining effectiveness. A healthy and effective bargaining process encourages the discussion of issues and problems and their subsequent resolution at the bargaining table. In addition, the effort required to reach agreement is a measure of how well the process is working. Some indications of this effort are the duration of negotiations, the outcome of member ratification votes, the frequency and duration of strikes, the use of mediation and arbitration, the need for government intervention, and the resulting quality of union-management relations (whether conflict or cooperation exists). Joint programs for productivity and QWL improvements could be regarded as successes resulting from the quality of union-management relations.[88]

Effectiveness of the Grievance Procedures.   The degree of success of a grievance procedure may be assessed from different perspectives. Management may view the number of grievances filed and the number settled in management's favor as measures of effectiveness. Unions may also consider the number of grievances, but from their point of view, a larger number rather than a small number may be considered more successful.

Although the views of management and the union may differ, an overall set of measures to gauge grievance procedure effectiveness may be related to the disagreements between managers and employees. Measures that might be included are the frequency of grievances; the level in the grievance procedure at which grievances are usually settled; the frequency of strikes or slowdowns during the term of the labor agreements; the rates of absenteeism, turnover, and sabotage; and the necessity for government intervention.

The success of arbitration is often judged by the acceptability of the decisions, the satisfaction of the parties, innovation, and the absence of biases in either direction. The effectiveness of any third-party intervention rests in part on its ability to reduce or avoid strikes because the motivation for third-party intervention is the realization that strikes are not a desirable form of conflict resolution.

Strategic Involvement

Critical to the success of many companies vis-à-vis competitors are their labor costs. In many industries today, companies face possible bankruptcy because of high labor costs. Helping to lower costs are wage reductions agreed on by unions and management. Recently American Airlines, Greyhound, McDonnell Douglas, Boeing, and Ingersoll-Rand have negotiated two-tiered wage systems to help reduce total costs by reducing labor costs. Without these jointly negotiated systems, these companies would not have survived. Thus, a company's relationship with its union can be critical to its survival, and the better its relationships are, the more likely it is to gain a competitive advantage.[89]

Crown Zellerbach Corporation and the International Woodworkers of America demonstrated, however, that a competitive advantage can be gained without reducing total wages. Based on a recent incentive pay plan agreed to by the union and management, workers earn about three dollars more per hour than before on straight wages. Because this incentive system makes the workers more productive, the company in exchange had to give the union greater worker involvement in work-related decisions. Thus, the workers gain in involvement and salary, and the company gains in cost reductions and greater competitiveness.

Ford Motor Company has engaged in a program of more worker involvement and more cooperative labor relations with the United Auto Workers. The results of this program are higher product quality than its competitors and a marketing campaign centered on quality as Job 1. As with the two-tiered wage systems, this program of more worker involvement gains competitive advantage through cost reductions and improved efficiencies. Similar results of high product quality and efficiency have been obtained at Westinghouse Electric Corporation, Warner Gear Division of Borg-Warner Corporation, and the Mass Transportation Authority of Flint, Michigan. In these companies, gains in quality and efficiency have resulted from employee commitment associated with quality circle programs. In addition to increased quality and efficiency, these companies have experienced fewer grievances, reduced absenteeism and turnover, lower design costs, higher engineering productivity, and fewer costly changes in design cycles.

INTERNATIONAL COMPARISONS

An examination of labor-management relations in Great Britain, other European countries, Canada, Japan, and Australia suggests that union and employee involvement in organization decision making is no isolated phenomenon. Many countries even appear to have *stronger* employee organizations than those found in the United States.

Great Britain

The industrial relations system in Great Britain differs markedly from those in both the United States and other European countries. Traditionally, the framework of labor law in Britain has been noninterventionist, fostering an essentially voluntary system of industrial relations. Under this system, employers have had no general legal duty to recognize and bargain with their employees, while employees have had no legally protected rights to organize themselves in unions.

Also, negotiated agreements signed between unions and employers are not enforceable as legal contracts. The collective agreements familiar to U.S. managers are more akin to gentleman's agreements in Britain and are based on social rather than on legal sanctions.

As with so many aspects of life in Britain, the explanation for this state of affairs is largely historical. The development of British labor law has progressed via the granting of immunities from existing restrictive statutes—such as immunity from prosecution for criminal conspiracy—rather than through the legislation of positive rights. Unlike their U.S. counterparts, British unions have not viewed the law as a positive and protective force guaranteeing their right to existence.

The tradition of legal nonintervention in industrial relations has, however, come under increasing challenge in recent years. Concern over the country's poor economic performance and a growing international reputation for labor strife sparked a vigorous debate among the major political parties in Britain during the 1960s and eventually led to the establishment of a royal commission of inquiry (the Donovan Commission). This commission, which reported in 1968, highlighted the growing importance of what it termed Britain's unofficial system of industrial relations. Under this system, terms and conditions of employment were increasingly being negotiated between local managers and informally elected shop stewards, rather than between management and paid full-time union officials.

Rejecting the Donovan Commission's recommendation that reform should be accomplished without destroying the tradition of keeping industrial relations out of the courts, a newly elected Conservative government made an ill-fated attempt in 1971 to reform Britain's voluntary system of industrial relations along U.S. lines. The Industrial Relations Act of 1971 included provisions to formalize the process of union certification through the establishment of bargaining units for which a designated union would be the sole bargaining agent. This reform was intended to replace the practice of voluntary recognition, which led to a complex pattern of multiunionism under which a single local management could find itself negotiating with as many as half a dozen unions at the same work place. Provisions were also included to make collective agreements legally enforceable, unless the parties included a clause to the contrary. (In practice, most negotiators did include such a clause.)

The 1971 legislation also defined and strengthened a number of individual rights, including protection against unfair dismissal. The rationale for this legislation was not merely to redress a perceived inequality in the balance of power between the individual employee and a management able to fire at will. Rather it was an attempt to limit the large number of unofficial wildcat strikes that were called, often with some success, to pressure management into reinstating a dismissed employee.

Active union hostility combined with management indifference to the 1971 legislation made it largely unworkable, and the act was repealed by a Labour government in 1974. Between 1974 and 1979, with the support of the unions, the Labour government introduced a number of pieces of legislation that took a significant step in the direction of creating more positive legal rights to protect and support trade union membership. Legislation also entrenched a variety of individual rights, including protection against unfair dismissal and discrimination on the basis of sex or race.

Many observers have seen this legislation as a form of *quid pro quo* for the cooperation of the Trade Union Council (TUC) (the central umbrella organization for Britain's unions) in the Labour government's incomes policy, which was in place between 1975 and 1978. Income policies in one form or another have acted as important constraints on management freedom in compensating employees in Britain during most of the 1960s and 1970s, but none has been based on the same degree of union cooperation.

By 1979, union power in Britain, measured by political influence and industrial strength as well as by membership, was undoubtedly at a postwar peak. Since the election of the Thatcher Conservative government in 1979, however, the industrial relations climate has changed dramatically. A process of step-by-step reform, including laws against secondary picketing, restrictions on the operation of the closed shop, and the establishment of secret union ballots before strikes, has effectively shifted the balance of power back toward management. High levels of unemployment have further undermined union bargaining power. Between 1979 and 1985, the percentage of the labor force in unions fell by about one-fifth from its postwar peak of about 55 percent. Despite some highly publicized disputes, which give an unduly inflated impression of Britain's overall strike proneness, strike activity has also fallen to historically low levels.

The full, long-run consequences of these changes are difficult to predict with any certainty. Managers in Britain still face a work force that is highly unionized compared with that in the United States, where less than 18 percent of the labor force are currently in unions. Managers in many parts of British industry must also negotiate with a multiplicity of unions the representational boundaries of which often owe more to craft tradition and the accidents of history than they do to the logic of efficient production. They must also operate on a day-to-day basis without the support of legally enforceable collective agreements. Important developments at the shop-floor level do, however, offer some clue to a changed future. On the union side, both the engineering and the electricians unions have been willing to sign single-union agreements that include no-strike clauses. They have also shown a preference for cooperative over confrontational relations with management. Perhaps significantly, the key movers on the management side of these innovative agreements have often been overseas companies setting up operations in Britain. Japanese companies such as Nissan, Hitachi, and Toshiba are notable examples, but innovative agreements have also been signed with some U.S. firms. This is a useful reminder that the behavior and attitudes of both sides determine the quality of labor-management relationships.

Other European Countries

The belief that worker interests are best served if employees have a direct say in the management of the company is called **codetermination.** Originally conceived in Germany, this philosophy of labor-management relations now exists in Sweden, the Netherlands, France, Norway, Denmark, Luxembourg, and Austria.

Codetermination means, for example, that unions are given seats on the boards of directors of corporations. In addition, managers are encouraged to consult with unions before making major organizational changes, whether they be mergers, investments, or personnel matters such as plant closings and relocations. If management disagrees with the union position, management prevails. However, unions may veto subcontracts by the company, and they have access to all company information.

Codetermination also has caused unions to propose asset formation. Such proposals seek to place under the control of the union funds provided by the employer. At this time, however, these proposals have been rejected by management.

Although the European ideas of codetermination and union-controlled funds will probably not be applied in the United States in the 1990s, increased cooperation may occur between labor and management on issues of productivity and quality of work life. An issue on which cooperation has been less evident, in both Europe and the United States, is that of the thirty-five-hour workweek. The extent of union-management disagreement on this issue is particularly evident in West Germany.[90] In Sweden, however, some progress has been made in hours reduction.

Canada

Approximately one-third of the Canadian labor force is unionized. About three-fourths of the union members are affiliated with the Canadian Labor Congress (CLC). As in the United States, the union local is the basic local unit. The CLC is the dominant labor group at the federal level. Its political influence may be compared with that of the AFL–CIO.

Although the labor laws in Canada are similar to those in the United States, noteworthy differences do exist. Since 1925, the majority of Canadian workers have been covered by provincial, not federal, labor laws, whereas in the United States over 90 percent of the workers are covered by the National Labor Relations Act. The Canadian Industrial Relations Disputes and Investigation Act of 1973, on the other hand, covers less than 10 percent of the labor force.

Canadian labor laws require frequent interventions by government bodies before a strike can take place. In the United States, such intervention is largely voluntary. Compulsory arbitration in Canada is governed by the Public Service Staff Relations Act of 1967. This law also allows nonmanagerial federal employees to join unions and bargain collectively.

The history of labor relations in Canada and the United States is similar because both nations follow British common law, except that provincial governments, rather than the federal government, have developed most of the Canadian labor laws. Since the decision in *Toronto Electric Commissioners v. Snider* (1925), Canadian workers have been governed primarily by provincial laws (except for employees working for the federal government and industries under federal coverage, as defined by amendments to the 1973 industrial relations act—for instance longshoring, seafaring, provincial railroads, Crown corporations, and airlines). Many of the features of the U.S. Taft-Hartley Act have been incorporated into the labor laws of the Canadian provinces.

For the union movement as a whole, the trend toward concessionary bargaining to avoid layoffs and plant closings appears to be less evident than it is in the United States.[91] At the same time, Canadian labor organizations affiliated with unions dominated by labor organizations in the United States are becoming increasingly autonomous. This trend was recently highlighted when the United Auto Workers in Canada became independent from the same union in this country.

Japan

The third sacred treasure of the Imperial House of Japan is what is known as the enterprise union. Unlike in the United States and Europe, where unions are organized horizontally and industrywide, almost all trade unions in Japan are formed on a company-by-company, or enterprise, basis. In 1978, as many as 70,868 labor unions could be found in Japan, with one existing in practically every company or plant to conduct labor negotiations at that level. Enterprise unions today account for nearly 90 percent of all Japanese union organizations. Also, four principal industrywide federations of workers serve as coordinators, formulators of unified and reliable standards, and sources of information.

Although the enterprise concept received a fair amount of attention in the United States during the 1920s and 1930s, such unions collapsed, primarily as a result of excessive management involvement and their narrow field of interest. The success of the enterprise union in Japan is attributed to two major differences. The first of these is the allocation of financial responsibility between the enterprise union and the trade or regional organizations, which reflects a difference in the organizational roles of Japanese labor unions. In Western countries, where centralized union control and authority is predominant, the national union receives union dues, decides how they are to be used, and returns a portion to the local unions for expenses. In Japan, the enterprise union controls the dues, passing on 10 percent or, at most, 20 percent to the federation.[92]

As a result of the enterprise union's role, problems in labor-management relationships can be dealt with more directly, without necessarily involving an outside body. The "mixed" union representation of all blue-collar and some white-collar workers also proves valuable in determining more representative concerns. As a result of greater union participation by employees of a given company, 15.7 percent of Japan's current top management have once been active labor union leaders. This should lead to better management understanding of the needs and interests of employees.

The second difference that accounts for the success of the enterprise union system in Japan is the greater company and national loyalty shown by each worker. Accordingly, workers do not look on the union solely as a negotiating body but use its structure to deal with such issues as industry and technical reforms, new plant and equipment investments, and matters of personnel and productivity development.

Australia

It is interesting to note that the institutional framework of both U.S. and Australian industrial relations evolved from similar historical circumstances: the need to compel strong employers to meet and deal with a weak labor union movement for collective bargaining purposes.[93] The legislative solutions to this situation that were enacted in each country were, however, quite different. American legislation in the 1930s carefully avoided imposing the decisions of a third party on labor and management by providing a detailed legal framework within which the parties were compelled to bargain in good faith with each other. In contrast, Australian legislation at the turn of the century provided government machinery for the making and enforcement of industrial awards.

Walker[94] has argued that the principal distinguishing features of the period which led to the establishment of the institutional framework of Australian industrial relations were as follows:

- The development of a strong and vigorous union movement which achieved industrial power and interunion solidarity earlier than in most countries. It is important to note that many of the nineteenth-century settlers who arrived in Australia had experienced the "dark Satanic mills" of industrial England, and some had been transported from Britain for participation in labor union activities.
- The complete defeat of the labor unions following nationwide strikes in the 1890s. This convinced the labor movement of the need for political representation and led to the formation of the Australian Labor Party (ALP), which rapidly became a major political party.
- The development of a labor movement which, despite its direct involvement in politics, was characterized by a pragmatic and nonrevoluntionary ideology.
- Acceptance by the labor movement of the concept of compulsory arbitration of industrial disputes.

The results of this process were twofold. First, the notions of conciliation and arbitration were written into the Australian Constitution which was enacted in 1900. Section 51 (XXXV) of the constitution limits the role of the federal Parliament to making laws "with respect to conciliation and arbitration for the prevention and settlement of industrial disputes extending beyond the limits of any one state." Second, the Conciliation and Arbitration Act of 1904 established the institutional framework of Australian industrial relations which is still in place today, making this system of conciliation and arbitration the oldest national labor relations mechanism in the Western industrial democracies. The centerpiece of this legislation was the establishment of a federal tribunal known as the Australian Conciliation and Arbitration Commission (ACAC).

The constitutional limitation of federal government intervention in industrial relations issues and the emphasis on the role of a federal tribunal in the Conciliation and Arbitration Act combined to give the ACAC a leading role in Australian industrial relations. This system was explicitly designed to encourage union organization, and labor union membership rapidly increased from less than 5 percent to over 50 percent.[95] Employers that operated outside of the system were excluded from tariff protection—a major economic penalty. Faced with a rapidly growing labor movement and a centralized industrial relations system, employers developed strong associations to represent their interests before the federal and state tribunals, and this remains a distinctive feature of Australian industrial relations.

The Australian industrial relations system is now over eighty years old, and while a strength of the present system is that the role of the ACAC allows for effective macrowage policy implementation, at the micro level serious labor market rigidities are apparent—for example, all companies in an industry face the same award, regardless of cost structure and market position, and individual companies cannot restructure a federal award through private negotiations with labor unions. The Business Council of Australia, one of the major employer representative bodies, has identified labor market failures as perhaps the single most important obstacle to improving the competitiveness of the Australian economy.[96]

In 1983, in recognition of these problems, the Labor federal government commissioned a committee of inquiry on industrial relations in Australia (generally referred to as the Hancock Committee in recognition of the chair, Professor Hancock). The Hancock Committee recommended a number of changes in the present system, such as the establishment of a new labor court and the extension of grievance procedures, but it did not recommend total deregulation of the current centralized system.[97] The federal government is clearly aware that change is necessary if Australia wishes to compete successfully for a share in the dynamic growth of the Pacific Basin. This awareness has been illustrated by such changes as the deregulation of the Australian financial markets in December 1983.

After much debate and delay, the federal government's response to the recommendations of the Hancock Report was presented in the Industrial Relations Bill of 1988. Although the bill supports the need for increased flexibility in the industrial relations system, it presents a much diluted version of the original reforms recommended. The main elements of this bill include an updated name for the ACAC (to be known as the Industrial Relations Commission), which now has the power to hear unfair dismissal cases, and provisions for greater opportunities for enterprise-level negotiations. Despite the different approaches of labor unions and employer associations to industrial relations, both groups have advocated reforms that allow for decentralization and greater flexibility within the present system.[98]

Given the collectivist and centralist traditions of Australian labor relations, dramatic changes are unlikely, and any assumption of convergence over time to a system based solely on plant or enterprise collective bargaining, as in the United States, would be unwarranted. Foreign companies doing business in Australia will still need to analyze the industrial relations implications of their business strategy in considerable detail.

SUMMARY

Employees are generally attracted to unionization because they are dissatisfied with work conditions and feel powerless to change these conditions. Some major sources of dissatisfaction are inequity in pay administration, poor communications, and poor supervisory practices. By correcting these, or by not allowing them to occur in the first place, organizations help prevent unions from becoming attractive. However, once a union-organizing campaign begins, a company can't legally stop it without committing an unfair labor practice.

Historically, unions and management have operated as adversaries because many of their goals are in conflict. But because conflict is detrimental to both management and unions, effective labor relations have been established to reduce this conflict. For instance, unions and management have begun to cooperate to achieve mutual goals. Although cooperation is not widespread, it may be the style of union-management relations in the future. Its effects are particularly apparent in collective bargaining, contract negotiation, and grievance processing.

In the United States collective bargaining relationships are currently at a critical crossroads. Global competition has brought about a greater emphasis on mutual survival. This has resulted in a shift from the traditional adversarial relationship between union and management toward cooperation. New bargaining strategies characterize this altered relationship. Productivity bargaining is an attempt to encourage increase effectiveness in the work place by passing some of the economic savings of modernization or increased efficiency on to the employees. Another innovation is continuous bargaining, where a joint union-management committee meets on a regular basis to deal with problems.

Although obstacles exist to union-management cooperation—a history of adversarial relations, hesitancy on the part of the union to give up the traditional roles of labor, and both parties' fear of losing power—present economic conditions and the threat of an influx of foreign products are prompting many organizations to act for their mutual benefit.

The quality of the union-management relationship can have a strong influence on contract negotiations. Labor and management each select a bargaining committee to negotiate the new agreement. The negotiations may be between a single union and a single company or multiple companies, or between multiple unions and a single company. Bargaining issues are mandatory, permissive, or prohibited. Mandatory issues must be discussed, permissive issues can be discussed if both parties agree, and prohibited issues cannot be discussed. The issues can be grouped into wage issues, economic supplements issues, institutional issues, and administrative issues.

Almost all labor contracts outline grievance procedures for handling employee complaints. The most common grievance is related to discipline and discharge, although wages, promotions, seniority, vacations, holidays, and management and union rights are also sources of complaints. Management can influence the results of grievances by developing a procedure that ensures their actions are just and fair. Written records of actions taken are useful for potential arbitration. Unions have a legal responsibility to represent the employee fairly in grievances; therefore, they also need a grievance-handling procedure.

The effectiveness of collective bargaining and contract administration is usually assessed by measures of how well the process is working. Bargaining can be evaluated using measures such as the duration of negotiations, the frequency of strikes, the use of third-party intervention, and the need for government intervention. The effectiveness of the grievance process can be assessed by the number of grievances; the level in the grievance process at which settlement occurs; the frequency of strikes or slowdowns; the rate of absenteeism, turnover, and sabotage; and the need for government intervention.

DISCUSSION QUESTIONS

1. Briefly state how the legal climate has changed with respect to organized labor since the inception of unions.
2. What steps are required for employee organizations to establish union certification?
3. What are decertification elections, and how do they affect organized labor and management?
4. Why have unions appealed to workers historically? Are the reasons today different from what they were fifty years ago? Explain.
5. What is the NLRB? How does the NLRB help promote the policy of "free collective bargaining" in the United States?

6. What kinds of topics would you expect to find in a typical collective bargaining agreement? Assume that you and the other students "organize." For what terms would you negotiate with your professors in your agreement?
7. Distinguish mediation from arbitration. How does grievance arbitration differ from interest arbitration?
8. From a public policy perspective, is it necessarily bad for union and management to regularly depend on interest arbitration to resolve conflicts?
9. What are the steps of a typical grievance procedure? Is this process formal or informal?
10. Why does the NLRB concern itself with the duty of fair representation? In what sense is the union steward caught in the middle on the issue of fair representation when representing a grievant?

CASE STUDY

The Union's Strategic Choice

Maria Dennis sat back and thoughtfully read through the list of strategies the union's committee had given her that morning. If her union were to rebuild the power it had lost over the past few years, it was time to take drastic action. If the union continued to decline as it had been the last few years, it wouldn't be able to represent the members who had voted for it to be their exclusive bargaining representative.

Maria had been elected two years before at her union's convention to be the international president of the Newspaper Workers International Union (NWIU). At the time she knew it would not be an easy job, and she had eagerly looked forward to taking on a new challenge. But she had no idea during the election just how difficult it would be to get the union back on its feet again.

The NWIU had been founded in the late 1890s, made up of newspaper typographers who were responsible for such tasks as setting type on linotype machines, creating the layout of the newspaper, proofing the articles, and printing the newspaper. Members of the union typically completed a six-year apprenticeship, learning all the different tasks involved in the printing process. Prior to 1960 the printing profession had been considered to be the elite of the industrial work force. The craft demanded that typographers be literate at a time when even the middle and upper classes were not. The combination of this literacy with proficiency in a highly skilled, highly paid craft made printers the "status elite" of manual workers.

Since the 1970s, however, the union had begun to decline. Literacy was no longer a unique characteristic, and automation had led to a deskilling of the craft. The introduction of video display terminals, optical character recognition scanners, and computerized typesetting eliminated substantial composing room work, and the demand for skilled union workers was reduced. The union experienced its peak membership of 120,000 in 1965. During the 1970s, however, membership began a substantial decline, and in 1988 the total membership was only 40,000.

The union's reduced membership resulted in other problems for the union. First, there were fewer members to pay dues to the union, which was their main revenue-generating function. Consequently, the union was having some serious financial problems and was being forced to cut some of its services to the members.

Second, the union was experiencing a significant loss in bargaining power with newspaper management. In the past the printers had been fairly secure in their jobs because there was a good demand in the labor market for individuals who could run the complicated printing equipment. But the recent switch to automation had eliminated many jobs and had also made it possible for employers to easily replace union employees. Anyone could be trained in a short time to use the new printing equipment. Therefore, if union members decided to strike for better wages, hours, and working conditions, management could easily, and legally, find replacements for them. In essence, the union was unable to fulfill its main mission, which is to collectively represent those employees who had voted for it. To solve the current crisis, Maria was considering five options.

- Implement an associate member plan through which any individual could join the union for a fee of $50 a year. While these members would not be fully represented on the job, they would get an attractive package of benefits, such as low-cost home, health, and auto insurance.
- Attempt some cooperative labor-management relations programs, such as trying to get member representation on newspaper boards of directors or employee participation programs in the work place.
- Put more effort into political action. For example, lobby for labor law reform or for new laws more favorable to unions. Try to initiate action that would result in harsher penalties against employers that practice illegal union-avoidance activities, such as threatening to move the business if a union is voted in or firing pro-union employees.
- Appeal to community leaders to speak out in favor of the union in order to improve public relations, to help recruit new members, and to encourage employers to bargain fairly when negotiating with the union.
- Search for another union with which they might merge, thus increasing their membership, strengthening their finances, increasing their bargaining power, and obtaining economies of scale.

Maria realized each of the above options could have both positive and and negative results and was unsure which strategy, if any, she should recommend for the union to pursue. In less than three hours, however, she would have to present the list to the council with her recommendations.

By Kay Stratton

Case Questions

1. What are the strengths and weaknesses of each strategy?
2. What strategies could be employed to get new bargaining units?
3. What other types of services could the union offer to its members?
4. What would your final recommendation be? Justify your response.

NOTES

1. For a more extensive discussion of unionization and the entire union-management relationship, see H. J. Anderson, *Primer of Labor Relations*, 21st ed. (Washington, D.C.: Bureau of National Affairs, 1980); R. B. Freeman and J. L. Medoff. *What Do Unions Do?* (New York: Basic Books, 1984); P. Cappeli, "Theory Construction in IR and Some Implications for Research," *Industrial Relations* (Winter 1985): 90–112; L. Troy and N. Sheflin, *Union Sourcebook: Membership, Structure, Finance, Directory*, 1984 ed. (West Orange, N.J.: Industrial Relations Data and Information Service, 1984).

2. For a good overview and in-depth discussion of collective bargaining, see L. Balliet, *Survey of Labor Relations* (Washington, D.C.: Bureau of National Affairs, 1981); J. Barbash, *The Elements of Industrial Relations* (Madison: University of Wisconsin Press, 1984); B. F. Beal, E. D. Wickersham, and P. Kienast *The Practice of Collective Bargaining* (Homewood, Ill.: Richard D. Irwin, 1976); N. W. Chamberlain and J. W. Kuhn, *Collective Bargaining*, 3d ed. (New York: McGraw-Hill, 1986); R. J. Donovan, "Bringing America into the 1980s," *American Psychologist* (Apr. 1984);

429–31; J. A. Fossum, "Union-Management Relations," in *Personnel Management*, ed. K. M. Rowland and G. Ferris (Boston: Allyn & Bacon, 1982), 420–60; J. A. Fossum, "Labor Relations," in *Human Resource Management in the 1980s*, ed. S. J. Carroll and R. S. Schuler (Washington, D.C.: Bureau of National Affairs, 1983); Freeman and Medoff, *What Do Unions Do?*; T. A. Kochan, *Collective Bargaining and Industrial Relations* (Homewood, Ill.: Richard D. Irwin, 1980); R. C. Richardson, *Collective Bargaining by Objectives* (Englewood Cliffs, N.J.: Prentice-Hall, 1977); A. Sloan and F. Whitney, *Labor Relations* (Englewood Cliffs, N.J.: Prentice-Hall, 1979 2d Edition); A R. Weber, ed., *The Structure of Collective Bargaining*, (New York: Free Press, 1961).

3. J. M. Brett, "Why Employees Want Unions," *Organizational Dynamics* (Spring 1980): 47–56; J. M. Brett, "Behavioral Research on Unions and Union Management Systems," in *Research in Organizational Behavior*, vol. 2, ed. B. M. Staw and L. L. Cummings (Greenwich, Conn.: JAI Press, 1980); W. T. Dickens and J. S. Leonard, "Accounting for the Decline in Union Membership 1950–1980." *Industrial and Labor Re-*

lations Review (Apr. 1985): 323–34; J. Fiorito and C. R. Greer, "Determinants of U.S. Unionism: Past Research and Future Needs," *Industrial Relations* 21 (1982): 1–32; C. V. Fukami and E. W. Larson, "Commitment to Company and Union: Parallel Models," *Journal of Applied Psychology* (Aug. 1984): 367–71.

4. P. Hersey and K. H. Blanchard, *Management of Organizational Behavior*, 3d ed. (Englewood Cliffs, N.J.: Prentice-Hall, 1977); E. P. Hollander, *Leadership Dynamics: A Practical Guide to Effective Relationships* (New York: Free Press, 1978); Ingrassia, "Union Rank and File Talk Bitterly of Their Bosses," *Wall Street Journal*, 12 Apr. 1982, p. 22; P. M. Podsakoff, "Determinants of a Supervisor's Use of Rewards and Punishments: A Literature Review and Suggestions for Further Research,'" *Organizational Behavior and Human Performance* 29 (1982): 58–83; P. M. Podsakoff, W. D. Todor, and R. Skov, "Effects of Leader Contingent and Non-Contingent Reward and Punishment Behaviors on Subordinate Performance and Satisfaction," *Academy of Management Journal* 25 (1982): 810–21.

5. The support, however, may be influenced by economic conditions and layoffs in the industry and the specific site where the joint QWL program is being conducted. See "How Power Will Be Balanced on Saturn's Shop Floor," *Business Week*, 5 Aug. 1985, pp. 65–66; and D. Sockell, "The Legality of Employee-Participation Programs in Unionized Firms," *Industrial and Labor Relations Review* (July 1984): 541–56.

6. R. W. Mondy and S. R. Preameaur, "The Labor-Management Power Relationship Revisited," *Personnel Administrator* (May 1985): 51–55.

7. A good discussion of earlier contributions to labor law can be found in R. D. Trussell, ed., *U.S. Labor and Employment Laws*, 1987 ed. (Washington, D.C.: BNA Books, 1987); and D. P. Twomey, *Labor Law and Legislation*, 6th ed. (Cincinnati: South-Western, 1980).

8. Balliet, *Survey of Labor Relations*, 44.

9. Twomey, *Labor Law and Legislation*.

10. Ibid, 77.

11. A. Sloan and F. Whitney, *Labor Relations*, 3d ed. (Englewood Cliffs, N.J.: Prentice-Hall, 1977).

12. D. Israel, "The Weingarten Case Sets Precedent for Co-Employee Representation," *Personnel Administrator* (Feb. 1983): 23.

13. J. A. Fossum, *Labor Relations: Development, Structure, Process*, 2d ed. (Dallas: Business Publications, 1982).

14. H. B. Frazier II, "Labor Management Relations in the Federal Government," *Labor Law Journal* (Mar. 1979): 133. See also T. J. Krajci, "Labor Relations in the Public Sector," *Personnel Administrator* (May 1985): 43–47.

15. "Companies Can Void Contracts if 'Burdensome' to Employers," *Resource* (Mar. 1984): 1, 10; P. J. Harkins, "The Fickle Nature of Employment Agreements," *Personnel Journal* (May 1985): 76–80; B. S. Murphy, W. E. Barlow, and D. D. Hatch, "A Successor Employer's Duty to Bargain," *Personnel Journal* (May 1985): 29–36.

16. G. W. Bohlander, "Fair Representation: Not Just a Union Problem," *Personnel Administrator* (Mar. 1980): 36–40, 82; J. P. Swann, Jr., "Misrepresentation in Labor Union Elections," *Personnel Journal* (Nov. 1980): 925–26.

17. "Unions are Getting Clobbered in the Courts," *Business Week*, 22 July 1985, p. 106A.

18. J. A. Fossum, "Union-Management Relations," in *Personnel Management*, 430–31; S. A. Youngblood, A. D. DeNisi, J. Molleston, and W. H. Mobley, "The Impact of Work Attachment, Instrumentality Belief, Perceived Labor Union Image, and Subjective Norms on Union Voting Intentions and Union Membership," *Academy of Management Journal* 27 (1984): 576–90.

19. "Beyond Unions," *Business Week*, 8 July 1985, pp. 72–77. C. D. Gifford, ed., *Directory of U.S. Labor Organizations*, 1988–89 ed. (Washington, D.C.: Bureau of National Affairs, 1988); D. Yoder and P. D. Staudohar, *Personnel Management and Industrial Relations*, 7th ed. (Englewood Cliffs, N.J.: Prentice-Hall, 1982); D. Yoder and P. D. Staudohar, "Assessing the Decline of Unions in the U.S.," *Personnel Administrator* (Oct. 1982): 12–15.

20. This forecast is not necessarily shared by all. For multiple views on the outlook for unions, see L. M. Apcar and C. Trost, "Realizing Their Power Has Eroded, Unions Try Hard to Change," *Wall Street Journal*, 21 Feb. 1985, pp. 1, 20; F. Carbry, "What Happened to the 'Threat' of White-Collar Unionization?" *Management Review* (Mar. 1985); 52–56; M. W. Miller, "Unions Curtail Organizing in High Tech," *Wall Street Journal*, 13 Nov. 1984, p. 35; W. J. Usery, Jr., and D. Henne, "The American Labor Movement in the 1980s," *Employee Relations Law Journal* 7 (1981): 251–59.

21. "Building Trades Lose Ground," *Business Week*, 9 Nov. 1981, p. 104–6; C. J. Janus, "Union Mergers in the 1970s: A Look at the Reasons and Results," *Monthly Labor Review* (Oct. 1978): 13–23; B. Keller, "Unions' Economic Troubles Are Spurring Merger Trend," *New York Times*, 13 May 1984, pp. 1, 26; "A Union Fight That May Explode," *Business Week*, 16 Mar. 1981, pp. 102–4.

22. For a discussion of the concept of met expectations and satisfaction, see A. C. Kalleberg, "Work Values and Job Rewards: A Theory of Job Satisfaction," *American Sociological Review* 42 (1977): 124–43; and E. A. Locke, "What is Job Satisfaction?" *Organizational Behavaior and Human Performance* 4 (1969): 309–35.

23. J. G. Getman, S. B. Goldberg, and J. B. Herman, *Union Representation Elections: Law and Reality* (New York: Russell Sage, 1976).

24. J. M. Brett, "Behavioral Research on Unions," in *Research in Organizational Behavior*, vol.2; Brett, "Why Employees Want Unions"; R. Dubin, *The World of Work* (Englewood Cliffs, N.J.: Prentice-Hall, 1958); W. C. Hamner and F. J. Smith, "Work Attitudes as Predictors of Unionization Activity," *Journal of Applied Psychology* (Aug. 1978): 415–21.

25. Getman, Goldberg, and Herman, *Union Representation Elections*.

26. F. Bairstow, "Professionalism and Unionism: Are They Compatible?" *Industrial Engineering* (Apr. 1974): 40–42; P. Felville and J. Blandin, "Faculty Job Satisfaction and Bargaining Sentiments," *Academy of Management Journal* (Dec. 1974): 678–92; B. Husaini and J. Geschwender, "Some Correlates of Attitudes toward and Membership in White Collar Unions," *Southwestern Social Science Quarterly* (Mar. 1967): 595–601); L. Imundo, "Attitudes of Non-Union White Collar Federal Government Employees toward Unions," *Public Personnel Management* (Jan./Feb. 1974): 87–92; A. Kleingartner, "Professionalism and Engineering Unionism," *Harvard Business Review* (Mar./Apr. 1971): 48–54.

27. J. H. Hopkins and R. D. Binderup, "Employee Relations and Union Organizing Campaigns," *Personnel Administrator* (Mar. 1980): 57–61.

28. For an extensive discussion of the organizing campaign, see Fossum, "Union-Management Relations," and W. E Fulmer, "Step by Step through a Union Campaign," *Harvard Business Review* (July/Aug. 1981): 94–102.

29. Getman, Goldberg, and Herman, *Union Representation Elections.*

30. "Dealing with Organizing: Do's and Don'ts," *Bulletin to Management,* 7 Mar. 1985, p. 8.

31. See E. L. Harrison, D. Johnson, and F. M. Rachel, "The Role of the Supervisor in Representation Elections," *Personnel Administrator* (Sept. 1981): 67–72; S. M. Klein and K. W. Rose, "Formal Policies and Procedures Can Forestall Unionization," *Personnel Journal* (Mar. 1982): 214–19; D. McInnis, "A New Chill on Organizing Efforts," *New York Times*, 30 May 1982, p. 4F; "Pros Who Try to Help Unions Win," *Business Week*, 23 Aug. 1982, pp. 96–100; M. Z. Sappir, "The Employer's Obligation Not to Bargain When the Issue of Decertification Is Present," *Personnel Administrator* (Feb. 1982): 41–45; and W. Serrin, "An Organizer Beset," *New York Times*, 19 Sept. 1982, p. 6F.

32. See "Testing a New Weapon against Litton," *Business Week*, 27 Dec. 1982, pp. 32–33.

33. Twomey, *Labor Law,* 134.

34. "An Acid Test at DuPont," *Business Week,* 14 Dec. 1981, pp. 123–27; W. Bitler, Jr., "Unionization of Security Guards: A Unique Problem," *Personnel Administrator* (June 1981): 79–83.

35. W. Imberman, "How Expensive Is an NLRB Election?" *MSU Business Topics* (Summer 1975): 13–18.

36. J. W. Hunt, *The Law of the Workplace* (Washington, D.C.: Bureau of National Affairs, 1984); S. R. Premeaux, R. W. Mondy, and A. Bethke, "Decertification: Fulfilling Unions' Destiny?" *Personnel Journal* (June 1987): 144–48; J. P. Swann, Jr., "The Decertification of a Union," *Personnel Administrator* (Jan. 1983): 47–51.

37. See Balliet, *Survey of Labor Relations,* especially pp. 106–48. What is best or most advantageous, however, is not necessarily what is best for only one party, although maximizing for one party may happen in an adversarial relationship. In a cooperative relationship, maximizing for both may be regarded as most advantageous.

38. See Brett, "Behavioral Research," in *Research in Organizational Behavior,* vol. 2; Brett, "Why Employees Want Unions"; Hamner and Smith, "Work Attitudes as Predictors of Unionization Activity"; W. Serrin, "Unions Are Shifting Gears but Not Goals," *New York Times*, 31 Mar. 1985, p. 2E; "Unions Are Turning to Polls to Read the Rank and File," *Business Week*, 22 Oct. 1984, pp. 66–67.

39. Brett, "Behavioral Research," in *Research in Organizational Behavior,* vol. 2, 200.

40. Ibid.

41. J. M. Draznin, "Labor Relations," *Personnel Journal* (Oct. 1980): 805; T. H. Ferguson and J. Goals, "Co-determination: A Fad or a Future in America?" *Employee Relations Law Journal* (Autumn 1984): 176–93; "Hot UAW Issue: Quality of Work Life," *Business Week*, 17 Sept. 1979, pp. 120–22; S. M. Jacoby, "Union-Management Cooperation in the United States: Lessons from the 1920s," *Industrial and Labor Relations Review* (Oct. 1983): 18–33; H. C. Katz, T. A. Kochan, and K. R. Gobeille, "Industrial Relations Performance, Economic Performance, and QWL Programs: An Interplant Analysis," *Industrial and Labor Relations Review* (Oct. 1983): 3–17; Mills, *The New Competitors,* 225–42; "The New Industrial Relations," *Business Week*, 11 May 1981, pp. 85–98; "A Partnership to Build the New Workplace," *Business Week*, 30 June 1980, pp. 96–101; "Quality of Work Life: Catching On," *Business Week*, 21 Sept. 1981, pp. 72–80; M. Schuster, "The Impact of Union-Management Cooperation on Productivity and Employment," *Industrial and Labor Relations Review* (Apr. 1983): 415–30; M. Schuster, "A Re-examination of Models of Cooperation and Change in Union Settings," *Industrial Relations* (Fall 1985): 56–68; P. V. Simpson, R. M. Patlison, and R. W. Novotny, "Collective Bargaining: Management's Opportunity to Improve Labor Economies," *Employee Relations Law Journal* (Summer 1985): 72–87; R. E. Steiner, "Labor Relations," *Personnel Journal* (May 1981): 344–46; "A Try at Steel-Mill Harmony," *Business Week*, 29 June 1981, pp. 132–36.

42. "What's Creating an 'Industrial Miracle' at Ford," *Business Week*, 30 July 1984, p. 80.

43. J. A. Fossum, *Labor Relations.*

44. M. Bazerman, *Judgment in Managerial Decision Making* (New York: Wiley, 1986).

45. M. Bazerman, *Judgment in Managerial Decision Making* (New York: Wiley, 1986); M. Bazerman and J. S. Carroll, "Negotiator Cognition," in *Research in Organizational Behavior,* vol. 9, ed. L. L. Cummings and B. M. Staw (Greenwich, Conn.: JAI Press, 1987); M. H. Bazerman, T. Magliozzi, and M. A. Neale, "The Acquisition of an Integrative Response in a Competitive Market" *Organizational Behavior and Human Decision Processes* 34 (1985): 294–313.

46. D. Pruitt, "Integrative Agreements: Nature and Antecedents," in *Negotiation inside Organizations* ed. M. H. Bazerman and R. Lewicki (Beverly Hills, Calif.: Sage, 1983); D. Pruitt, *Negotiation Behavior* (New York: Academic Press, 1981).

47. K. Jennings and E. Traynman, Two-Tier Pay Plans, *Personnel Journal* (March 1988), pp. 56–58.

48. "Can GM Change Its Work Rules?" *Business Week*, 26 Apr. 1982, pp. 116, 119; "Concessionary Bargaining," *Business Week*, 14 June 1982, pp. 66–81; J. F. Falhee, "Concession Bargaining: The Time Is Now!" *Personnel Administrator* (Jan. 1983): 27–28; R. F. Garrett, "Reducing the Adversary Relationship," *Personnel Administrator* (Feb. 1982): 31–32; "Give-Backs Highlight Three Major Bargaining Agreements," *Personnel Administrator* (Jan. 1983): 33–35, 75, 77; "A Year of Settling for Less and Breaking Old Molds," *Business Week*, 20 Dec. 1982, pp. 72–74.

49. Sloan and Whitney, *Labor Relations*, 3d ed.

50. Fossum, "Labor Relations," 395–96.

51. *1979 Guidebook to Labor Relations*, 18th ed. (Chicago: Commerce Clearing House, 1978), 282. See also H. Raiffa, *The Art and Science of Negotiation* (Cambridge: Harvard University Press, 1982); J. J. Hoover, "Negotiating the Initial Union Contract," *Personnel Journal* (Sept. 1982): 692–97.

52. Fossum, *Labor Relations*.

53. Fossum, "Labor Relations"; C. Hymowitz, "Coordinated Steel Talks May Collapse," *Wall Street Journal*, 4 Apr. 1985, p. 6.

54. P. T. Hartman and W. H. Franke, "The Changing Bargaining Structure in Construction: Wide-Area and Multicraft Bargaining," *Industrial and Labor Relations Review* (Jan. 1980): 170–84.

55. Sloan and Whitney, *Labor Relations*, 3d ed., 59.

56. E. Platt, "The Duty to Bargain as Applied to Management Decisions," *Labor Law Journal* (Mar. 1968): 145.

57. Fossum, "Labor Relations."

58. Ibid, 173.

59. Platt, "The Duty to Bargain," 144.

60. "The Demands Airlines Are Pressing on Labor," *Business Week*, 7 Dec. 1981, p. 37; "Tough Choices for the UAW," *Business Week*, 7 Dec. 1981, p. 105; "Detroit Gets a Break from UAW," *Business Week*, 30 Nov. 1981; M. H. Dodosh, "Companies Increasingly Ask Labor to Give Back Past Contract Gains," *Wall Street Journal*, 27 Nov. 1981, p. 21. "The IBT Pact Could Be a Model of Moderation," *Business Week*, 28 Sept. 1981, p. 38; "A New Moderation in Rail Talks," *Business Week*, 31 Aug. 1981, p. 50; "Why the URW Will Be More of a Team Player," *Business Week*, 28 Sept. 1981, pp. 97–99.

61. T. A. Kochan, "Collective Bargaining in Organizational Research," in *Research in Organizational Behavior*, vol. 2, ed. B. M. Staw and L. L. Cummings (Greenwich, Conn.: JAI Press, 1980):

62. M. Bazerman and M. A. Neale, "Heuristics in Negotiation: Limitations to Effective Dispute Resolution," in *Negotiating in Organizations*, ed. M. Bazerman and R. Lewick (Beverly Hills, Sage, 1983), 51–67; M. Gordon, et al., "Laboratory Research in Bargaining and Negotiations: An Evaluation, *Industrial Relations* (Spring 1984): 218–23; R. E. Walton and R. B. McKersie, *A Behavioral Theory of Labor Negotiations* (New York: McGraw-Hill, 1965).

63. M. Neale, V. Huber, and G. Northcraft, "The Framing of Negotiations: Contextual versus Task Frames," *Organizational Behavior and Human Decision Processes* 39 (1987): 228–41.

64. M. A. Neale and M. Bazerman, "The Effect of Perspective Taking Ability under Alternate Forms of Arbitration on the Negotiation Process," *Industrial and Labor Relations*, 36 (1985): 378–88.

65. J. Kennan, "Pareto Optimality and the Economics of Strike Duration," *Journal of Labor Research* 1 (1980): 77–94; T. A. Kochan and R. N. Block, "An Inter-Industry Analysis of Bargaining Outcomes: Preliminary Evidence from Two-Digit Industries," *Quarterly Journal of Economics* 91 (1977): 68–76; D. J. B. Mitchell, "A Note on Strike Propensities and Wage Developments," *Industrial Relations* 20 (1981): 123–27.

66. A. Kotlowitz. "Labor's Shift: Finding Strikes Harder to Win. More Unions Turn to Slowdowns." *Wall Street Journal*, 22 May 1987, p. 1.

67. J. Tasini. "For the Unions, a New Weapon," *New York Times Magazine*, 12 June 1988, pp. 24–25, 69–71.

68. T. A. Kochan and T. A. Jick, "A Theory of the Public Sector Mediation Process," *Journal of Conflict Resolution* 23 (1979): 209–40; H. A. Landsberger, "The Behavior and Personality of the Labor Mediator: The Parties' Perception of Mediator Behavior." *Personnel Psychology* 13 (1960): 329–47.

69. D. T. Hoyer, "A Program for Conflict Management: An Exploratory Approach," *Proceedings of the Industrial Relations Research Association* (Milwaukee: IRRA, 1980): R. C. Richardson, *Collective Bargaining*.

70. R. Johnson, "Interest Arbitration Examined," *Personnel Administrator* (Jan. 1983): 53–59, 73.

71. Ibid.

72. Fossum, *Labor Relations*.

73. S. H. Slichter, J. J. Healy, and E. R. Livernash, *The Impact of Collective Bargaining on Management* (Washington, D.C.: Brookings Institution, 1960), 694.

74. Ibid., 694–96.

75. D. R. Dalton and W. D. Todor, "Union Steward Locus of Control, Job, Union Involvement, and Grievance Behavior," *Journal of Business Research* 10 (1982): 85–101; D. R. Dalton and W. D. Todor, "Antecedents of Grievance Filing Behavior: Attitude, Behavioral Consistency and the Union Steward," *Academy of Management Journal* 25 (1982): 158–69.

76. B. R. Skeleton and P. C. Marett, "Loser Pays Arbitration," *Labor Law Journal* (May 1979): 302–9.

77. D. R. Dalton and W. D. Todor, "Win, Lose, Draw: The Grievance Process in Practice," *Personnel Administrator* (Mar. 1981): 25–32; J. W. Robinson, "Some Modest Proposals for Reducing the Costs and Delay in Grievance Arbitration," *Personnel Administrator* (Feb. 1982): 25–28.

78. F. C. Botta, "The Accretion Clause in the Supermarket Industry: Unit Determinations and Employee Rights," *Employee Relations Law Journal* (Summer 1985): 106–17; H. G. Heneman III and M. H. Sandver, "Predicting the Outcome of Union Certification Elections: A Review of the Literature," *Industrial and Labor Relations Review* (July 1983): 537–59; J. E. Martin, "Employee

Characteristics and Representation Election Outcomes," *Industrial and Labor Relations Review* (Apr. 1985): 365–76.

79. G. L. Tidwell, "The Meaning of the No-Strike Clause," *Personnel Administrator* (Nov. 1984): 51–61.

80. For the number and type of these arbitration awards, generally of a closed type, see *Bulletin to Management* 11 Nov. 1982, and contact the Federal Mediation and Conciliation Service, 2100 K Street NW, Washington, D.C. 20427.

81. S. R. Korshak, "Arbitration, the Termination of a Union Activist," *Personnel Journal* (Jan. 1982): 54–57.

82. Bureau of National Affairs, *Grievance Guide*, 4th ed. (Washington, D.C.: Bureau of National Affairs, 1972), 8–9; A. J. Conti, "Mediation of Work-Place Disputes: A Prescription for Organizational Health," *Employee Relations Law Journal* (Autumn 1985): 291–310; F. Elkouri and E. A. Elkouri, *How Arbitration Works*, 4th ed. (Washington, D.C.: Bureau of National Affairs, 1985); D. Lewin and R. B. Peterson, *The Modern Grievance Procedure in the American Economy: A Theoretical and Empirical Analysis* (Westport, Conn.: Quorum Books, 1986); D. A. Peach and E. R. Livernash, *Grievance Initiation and Resolution* (Cambridge: Harvard University Press, 1974).

83. Memorandum 79–55, National Labor Relations Board, 7 July 1979.

84. D. R. Dalton and W. D. Todor, "Manifest Needs of Stewards: Propensity to File a Grievance," *Journal of Applied Psychology* 64 (1979): 654–59.

85. H. Graham and V. Wallace, "Trends in Public Sector Arbitration," *Personnel Administrator* (Apr. 1982): 73–78; H. R. Northrup, "The Rise and Demise of PATCO," *Industrial and Labor Relations Review* (Jan. 1984): 167–84.

86. L. Ingrassia, "Municipal Officials Getting Tougher in Bargaining with Public Employees," *Wall Street Journal*, 18 Aug. 1981, p. 35.

87. R. S. Schuler, "Strategic Human Resource Management and Industrial Relations," *Human Relations* (1989), 157–184; T. A. Kochan and J. Chalykoff, "Human Resource Management and Business Life Cycles: Some Preliminary Propositions," paper presented at UCLA Conference on Human Resources and Industrial Relations in High Technology Firms, 21 June 1985; T. A. Kochan, R. B. McKersie, and P. Capelli, "Strategic Choice and Industrial Relations Theory," *Industrial Relations* (Winter 1984): 16–38; Mills, *The New Competitors*, 243–71.

88. M. F. Payson, "Wooing the Pink Collar Work Force," *Personnel Journal* (Jan. 1984): 48–53; J. Usaj and J. Howell, "Potential Issues Audit: New Channels of Communication in a Union Environment," *Personnel Administrator* (Sept. 1985): 40–41.

89. R. S. Schuler and I. C. MacMillan, "Gaining Competitive Advantage through Human Resource Management Practices," *Human Resource Management* (Fall 1984): 250–62. See also J. A. Fossum, "Strategic Issues in Labor Relations," in *Strategic Human Resource Management*, ed. C. Fombrun, N. M. Tichy, and M. A. Devanna (New York: Wiley, 1984), 343–60; and J. P. Goodman and W. R. Sandberg, "A Contingency Approach to Labor Relations Strategies," *Academy of Management Review* (Jan. 1981): 145–54.

90. J. M. Markham, "German Workers Watch the Clock," *New York Times*, 13 May 1984; P. Revzin, "Swedes Gain Leisure, Not Jobs, by Cutting Hours," *Wall Street Journal*, 7 Jan. 1985: 10.

91. D. J. Schneider, "Canadian and U.S. Brands of Unionism Have Distinctly Different Nationalities," *Management Review* (Oct. 1983): 31–32, p D4.

92. M. S. O'Connor, *Report on Japanese Employee Relations Practices and Their Relation to Worker Productivity*, a report prepared for the Study Mission to Japan, 8–23, Nov. 1980.

93. K. F. Walker, "The Development of Australian Industrial Relations in International Perspective," in *Perspectives on Australian Industrial Relations*, ed. W. A. Howard (Melbourne: Longman Cheshire, 1984).

94. For a comparison of laws governing union security in Australia and the United States, see B. Aaron, "Union Security in Australia and the United States," *Comparative Labor Law* 6 (1984): 415–41.

95. "Management Pressures for Change and the Industrial Relations System," Business Council of Australia submission to the Alternatives to the Present Arbitration System Conference, October 1984, Sydney.

96. *Report of the Committee of Review: Australia Industrial Relations Law and Systems* (Canberra: Australian Government Publishing Service, 1985).

97. For an analysis of these changes, see "Australia Vaults Ahead with Free Banking," *Wall Street Journal*, 4 Nov. 1985, p. 10 and 26.

98. This observation was drawn from S. Deery and D. Plowman, *Australian Industrial Relations*, 3d ed. (Sydney: McGraw-Hill, 1985).

Personnel Research

Measuring Matters at Mellon

"Our management reports used to be centered purely around profitability—now, we are also looking at how profitability is achieved," Candice Mendenhall, vice president, research, planning and information, Mellon Bank (Pittsburgh, PA) said.

"We began providing quarterly reports to senior management, consisting of corporate officers, legal entity presidents and department heads, on human resource management measures about one year ago. The reports are presented in aggregate form.

"We identify those departments doing exceptionally well in particular areas; for example, if a department's merit pay awards reflect performance appraisal ratings, we credit that department. We also identify general areas to probe into more deeply and provide assistance to those who want our help in addressing specific issues.

Impacts of Measurements

"We've found our reporting process has provided a high-visibility, powerful forum for emphasizing human resource management issues. We believe the responsibility for hr rests with line managers—but although you can encourage someone to manage according to the company's guidelines, it's sometimes tough to get things implemented. With measurements, the impact on the organization—and whether managers are carrying their share of the responsibility for hrm—becomes clear. Measuring is credible—managers are used to being measured, and they respond to measurement processes.

"Some of the impacts we've noticed include:

- Managers are incorporating our new management-by-objectives approach into their performance appraisals. This is not mandatory, but since we started measuring the number of such evaluations done on an annual basis, department heads are now acting.
- There's a healthy dialogue going on. We're asking more questions about the 'why's' behind the numbers we are generating. When we looked at the relationship of performance appraisal ratings to merit pay, we discovered we were not differentiating between levels of performance to the degree we'd like to be. Now, this issue is being addressed.

"We don't stress how this process is creating more of a demand for service from the hr department. In fact, our goal is to put ourselves out of business—to get to the point where line management is doing its own measuring, to where good hr management is part of the culture."

SOURCE: *HR Reporter* 4, no. 3 (April 1987): Used by permission.

THE trends noted in the preceding "PHRM in the News" toward measuring and incorporating PHRM practices into an organization's strategic planning represent challenges and opportunities. In many respects these challenges are attempts to address unresolved questions—questions that personnel and human resource managers can address through PHRM research and through playing the innovative and policy-formulating roles introduced in Chapter 1. As noted at Mellon Bank, without research there would be no knowledge to apply to the practical situation on the job.

This chapter reviews methods and procedures used in conducting PHRM research, discusses areas in which researchers are currently addressing unresolved questions, and describes recent PHRM research findings.[1] Although emphasis is placed on personnel assessments, it should be stressed that human resource program managers (e.g., managers in staffing, training, compensation, labor relations, and line positions), face all types of decisions. PHRM research is often very helpful in providing these individuals with information to assist in their decision making.

THE EMPIRICAL RESEARCH PROCESS

Individuals and organizations possess numerous beliefs about why people perform as they do. The question in such cases is, Which beliefs are true? One way to test our beliefs is to conduct research. Understanding the research process helps individuals to solve PHRM problems in organizations; to understand and apply the research results of others; to assess the accuracy of claims made by others concerning the benefits of new procedures, programs, equipment, and so on; and to evaluate the soundness of the theory relating to the performance of individuals in organizations.[2]

Exhibit 16.1 shows the five basic steps needed to conduct sound empirical research. Initially, the PHRM researcher will need to identify or be alerted to a problem and formulate a question or set of questions that will address the problem. At approximately the same time, the researcher will translate the research question into a testable **hypothesis**—a tentative statement about the relationship between two or more variables. Typically in PHRM research, one

The Empirical Research Process

**EXHIBIT
16.1**

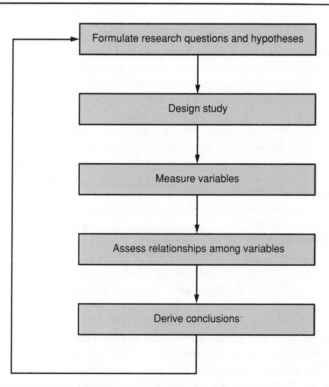

variable—the variable that the researcher has some control over or manipulates—is referred to as the **independent** or **predictor variable**. Examples of predictor variables are scores on selection tests or judgments of interviewers. The predictor variable is often hypothesized to have some effect on or relationship with a **dependent variable** or **criterion**. The criterion is frequently a measure of job performance, such as an accident rate, reject rate, supervisory performance rating, training score, or absenteeism or turnover rate.

The second major step—the design of the research study—focuses on the development of a strategy to examine the validity or truth of the hypothesis. Next, the PHRM researcher implements the study and obtains scores (numerical values) on the variables being examined. These scores are then collected and statistically analyzed to determine the observed relationship between or among the variables. Finally, conclusions are drawn as to whether or not the hypothesized relationships were supported, as well as to the implications of the results. The conclusions derived from the study often provide useful information for formulating new research questions.

PHRM problems can be examined in a variety of different ways. Some PHRM research is theoretical, designed to determine appropriate ways to measure constructs and variables important to understanding PHRM functions in organizations. To acquire basic knowledge about PHRM activities, research can be conducted in the laboratory. A field experiment is conducted in an organization, but as with laboratory research, one or more independent variables are manipulated to determine the effect on a dependent variable. PHRM researchers also conduct field studies that do not involve the manipulation of variables, but rather the systematic examination of relationships between different variables (e.g., satisfaction and performance; commitment and absenteeism).

Laboratory Research

In a laboratory study, the environment is carefully controlled to ensure that extraneous factors do not influence the results. Laboratory research also allows the researcher to control the assignment of subjects to experimental conditions. In this way, such factors as age, gender, job experience, and prior performance can be carefully controlled. Laboratory research also gives the researcher control over all variables that influence the dependent variable. Laboratory research has provided basic knowledge about PHRM selection decision making, performance appraisal processes, compensation decision making, human resource forecasting, and negotiations. Recently, it has been used extensively to acquire knowledge about how PHRM decisions are made.

Despite the wealth of basic knowledge acquired through laboratory research, many researchers and PHRM practitioners are critical of it, contending that it simplifies complex issues and fails to consider the effects of the organizational context on behavior. Others are concerned because student subjects are often used instead of managers. The argument is made that students can't possibly think like managers. Nor do they have the same political, social, and organizational pressures on them that managers do.

Proponents have shown that results found in laboratory settings are somewhat stronger, but point to the same conclusions as those found in applied settings. They also argue that laboratory research overcomes the limitation of study-specificity. That is, because each organizational setting is unique, it is difficult to determine whether differences found across studies reflect "real differences" or artifacts of the situation. By controlling the environment (via the laboratory), a body of knowledge can be built up that isn't muddled by contextual variables.[3]

Regarding student subjects, their usefulness depends on the type of decision being made. That is, they make decisions like any other naive decision maker. However, their use may not be appropriate if the objective of the study is to identify the simplifying rules used by experienced managers to make decisions. Still, PHRM researchers have shown that experts, like amateurs, fall prey to decision biases.[4]

Realistic Materials.   To overcome these concerns, laboratory researchers have done three things. First, many laboratory studies are carefully designed to mimic organizational events and contingencies. Consequently, experimental materials are carefully designed to parallel those used in actual settings (organizations).

Consider a recent laboratory study that examined the effects of decision context and anchoring bias (discussed in Chapter 5) on selection decisions. Student subjects evaluated the résumés and letters of applicants submitted in response to an advertisement by an actual computer company. Some subjects were told there were three openings for computer technicians; others were told there was only one opening. Some of the subjects were told they could compare one candidate to another (simultaneous evaluation); others were told to evaluate one candidate after another (sequential evaluation).

The number of openings was found to affect judgments about job suitability when the decision maker compared one candidate to another but not when candidates were evaluated sequentially. Additionally, the study showed that if rapid decisions are needed, then evaluating candidates sequentially (one at a time) rather than simultaneously is more expeditious. The down side of sequential evaluations was that the first candidates to be evaluated were evaluated more leniently than they objectively should have been. The study provided a number of insights about hiring quotas which would not have been acquired if the study had been conducted in an actual organization where information is less controlled.[5]

Managers as Decision Makers.   Another strategy is to use organizational decision makers, rather than students, as subjects. For example, a recent study examined the effects of rater and ratee characteristics on performance appraisal, pay, training, and promotion decisions. While prior research had examined the effects of single variables (tenure, gender, pay grade), PHRM studies had neglected examining the constellation of variables that affect these PHRM judgments. The subjects were 229 administrative, professional, and technical managers who worked for a northeastern city government. The study was conducted as part of a training session on performance appraisal. To add realism, the organization's actual performance manual and its rating and pay system, as well as performance information gleaned from PHRM files, were used as experimental materials. Performance profiles were constructed which varied in terms of four ratee characteristics (performance level, current pay, job tenure, and prior rating). Each manager evaluated five performance records selected from a pool of 480 profiles. In addition, information about the raters (sex, age, tenure, prior performance rating, and experience) was obtained.

The study showed that characteristics of the ratee directly affect evaluations, while characteristics of the subjects (raters) indirectly affect judgments. For example, ratees who received higher evaluations in the past got better evaluations in the present, regardless of the actual level of their performance. Female raters, more experienced raters, and raters who themselves had received higher ratings in the past all recommended larger pay increases for good performance than their colleagues did.[6]

Policy Capturing.   Finally, PHRM researchers have begun using **policy capturing**, a method that requires subjects to make holistic evaluations of multiattribute job alternatives, rather than direct estimates. This type of research is considered a major step forward because it parallels closely the complexity of PHRM decision making in actual organizations. Policy capturing studies have examined job choices of applicants, performance appraisal judgments, and compensation decisions. In a study of managerial salary-raise decision making, it was found that five factors (performance level, performance consistency, tenure, current salary, and external job offers) affected raise decisions, but that decision makers placed different degrees of importance on these factors.[7]

Field Experiments

A **field experiment** is conducted in an organization, rather than a laboratory. Like laboratory studies, the researcher still manipulates one or more independent variables and tries to maintain as much control as possible over the situation. While much more difficult to set up than laboratory studies, actual events in the organization serve as the foundation for such studies. Field experiments are particularly useful for understanding the effects of a specific organizational event on behavior. They can include such things as the introduction of new technology, a switch in management, or the implementation of a new performance appraisal or pay system. As mentioned in Chapter 11, field experiments are also helpful in assessing the usefulness of training programs.

For example, the safety project described in Chapter 13 was a field experiment in which one group received training on safety behaviors and another group did not. The study then compared the incidents of safe behavior in the two environments. Another field experiment examined the influence of training method and trainee age on the acquisition of computer software skills. For the latter study, an announcement offering the training was placed in a newsletter. Without the subjects' knowledge, two different types of training (tutorial and modeling) were conducted. Subjects were divided into age groups (younger and older), and their computer skill mastery was assessed. Older trainees exhibited lower performance than younger trainees did in both training environments. The study provided a number of insights regarding strategies that managers can use to help older workers overcome technological obsolescence.[8]

An interesting field experiment involved unionized workers employed by a state government that had problems with work attendance. Twenty workers were taught principles of self-management. Compared with twenty untrained workers with similar attendance problems, the employees given training in self-regulation were better able to manage personal and social obstacles to job attendance; the training raised their self-efficacy beliefs that they could control their behavior. The advantage of studies such as this one over laboratory research is that effects were found in the organization where a multitude of outside factors could impinge on or reduce the effectiveness of training. That training lead to better attendance despite the environmental conditions is noteworthy.[9]

Field Research

While the two strategies discussed above (laboratory and field experiments) are useful in determining the effects of specific variables on others or the consequences of organizational interventions, they may not lend themselves well to studying the broad research questions that frequently confront the PHRM researcher. Consequently, PHRM researchers conduct field studies, which do not involve the manipulation of variables. This type of study does, however, allow the researcher to systematically measure numerous variables and examine the relationships between these variables. In most cases, field studies gather data through questionnaires or interviews. An important consideration of the PHRM researcher using the field study is to intrude as little as possible on the organization, department, or individuals being studied. Organizational surveys and PHRM test validation studies (to be discussed later) are examples of different types of field studies.

Field studies have been used to examine a variety of issues. For example, researchers Thomas Lee and Richard Mowday were interested in identifying the factors that affect an employee's decision to voluntarily leave an organization. Relying on a theoretical model (see Exhibit 16.2), they generated hypotheses about the relationship between the variables. For example, one hypothesis predicted that there would be a relationship between a person's efforts to change a situation and job satisfaction, commitment and involvement. Another hypothesis predicted that a person's intentions to leave would be related to job satisfaction, commitment, involvement, and the importance of nonwork influences, attitudes, and turnover intentions.

A questionnaire containing items measuring constructs in the model was mailed to a random sample of the fourteen thousand employees who worked at a major financial institution in the western United States. There were questions about how well their expectations about work were met, the importance of job information, organizational characteristics (e.g., job content, co-workers), organizational experiences, job satisfaction, and the influence of nonwork factors on their job values. They also were asked about intentions to leave, job search activities, and perceptions of job opportunities. Job performance was measured by a single supervisory rating of overall job performance taken from company records.

The researchers collected the surveys and waited nine months. At this time the company generated a list of persons who had left and their reasons for leaving. Of the 445 employees who had completed the original questionnaire, 8 percent had quit. Using mathematical procedures to be described in the next section, they examined the relationships between the variables and tested the hypotheses. Results indicated that met expectations, job values, job attitudes, intention to leave the organization, and actual leaving were related. More important, the study found general support for the interrelationships proposed in the model. The study also showed that an employee's intention to stay or leave was the best predictor of actual turnover. For the manager concerned about employee turnover, the study clearly indicates that it is important to meet employee expectations and to ensure that employees are satisfied and that their commitment is high.[10]

Another study grew out of concern about the rapid growth in benefit costs and the low return on this investment. A team of three researchers first conducted interviews with PHRM specialists to find out about benefits practices—

**EXHIBIT
16.2**

The Steers and Mowday Model

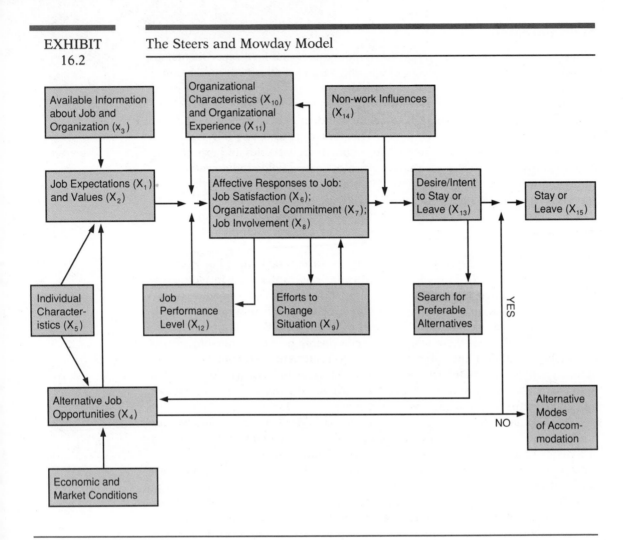

SOURCE: T. Lee and R. T. Mowday, "Voluntary Leaving an Organization: An Empirical Investigation of Steers and Mowday's Model of Turnover," *Academy of Management Journal*, 30 (1987): 721–743

life insurance, holidays, vacation, retirement and disability benefits, sick leave, insurance, and employee costs—in eight organizations. After determining the differences in benefits practices, the researchers surveyed employees in the agencies to determine their satisfaction with pay and benefits. Employees were also asked questions about their jobs and the level of benefits they received.

The study determined what average benefit levels were for law enforcement agencies surveyed. Additionally, it showed that satisfaction with benefits increased as benefits coverage increased but decreased as employee costs associated with benefits increased. The study concluded that investments must be made in benefits programs to inform employees about the value of their benefits relative to the costs employees must pay.[11]

THE VALIDATION PROCESS

Regardless of the method or site used to study PHRM issues, researchers need to be concerned about the reliability and validation of measurement devices.

Reliability refers to the consistency of measurement, whereas **validity** relates to the truth or accuracy of measurement. The concept of **correlation** is discussed prior to the issues concerning reliability and validity.

Correlation Coefficient

Both reliability and validity are measured by a **correlation coefficient** (denoted by the symbol r), which is the degree to which two or more sets of measurement vary. A positive correlation exists when high values on one variable (e.g., job knowledge test) are associated with high values on another variable (e.g., overall ratings of job performance). A negative correlation exists when high values on one variable are associated with low values on another variable. The correlation coefficient, which expresses the degree of linear relationship between two sets of scores, can range from positive to negative. The range is from $+1$ (a perfect positive correlation coefficient) to -1 (a perfect negative correlation coefficient). Several linear relationships represented by plotting actual data on personnel selection test–job performance relationships are shown in Exhibit 16.3.

The correlation between scores on a predictor (x) and a criterion (y) is typically expressed for a sample as r_{xy}. If we did not have a sample but were able to compute our correlation on the population of interest, we would express the correlation as ρ_{xy} (where ρ is the Greek letter rho). In almost all cases, researchers do not have access to the population. Therefore, they must estimate the population correlation coefficient based on data from a sample of the population. For instance, an organization may desire to know the correlation between a computer programming ability test (scores on the predictor, x) and job performance (scores on a performance appraisal rating form, y) for all its computer programmers, but decides it cannot afford to test all computer programmers (i.e., the population of interest). Instead the organization may select a sample of computer programmers and estimate the correlation coefficient in the population (ρ_{xy}) with the observed correlation in the sample (r_{xy}).

Scatterplots Indicating Possible Relationships between Personnel
Selection Test Scores and Job Performance Scores

**EXHIBIT
16.3**

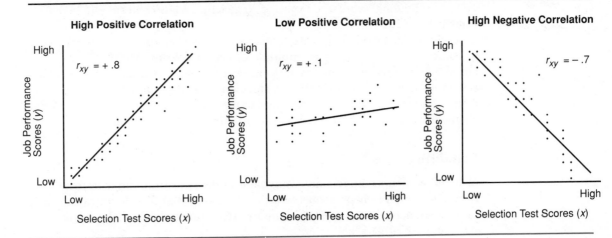

Each scatterplot in Exhibit 16.3 shows a solid line that best describes the linear relationship between the two variables. This line is described by the general equation for a straight line ($y = ax + b$, where a is the slope of the line and b is the point at which the line intercepts the y axis). The importance of this general equation, or **prediction equation**, is that it allows personnel researchers to estimate values of y (the criterion) from the knowledge of x (the predictor). For example, we may conduct a study to determine the correlation between sales performance (i.e., dollar sales volume) and a predictor (such as a number of years of sales experience) for a group of current job incumbents. Once we have developed a prediction equation, we can then estimate how well a sales applicant might perform on the job.[12] For example, the equation might read

$$\$\text{sales/month} = \$50,290 + \$2000 \text{ (years of sales experience)}$$

Therefore, a salesperson with ten years of experience could be expected to generate $70,290 a month in sales. A new salesperson with only one year of experience would be expected to generate only $52,290 a month in sales.

In many personnel research settings, researchers or decision makers often employ more than one predictor variable. This is noted in Chapter 5 when an organization uses a multiple predictor approach to make personnel selection and placement decisions. Similar to the single-predictor approach, the purpose of multiple prediction is the estimation of a criterion (y) from a linear combination of m predictor variables ($_y = a + b_1x_1 + b_2x_2 + \ldots + b_mx_m$).[13] Such an equation provides a **multiple-prediction** or **multiple-regression** equation. The b's are the regression weights applied to the predictor variables. In addition, the relationship between the predicted criterion score ($_y$) and the actual criterion score (y) is referred to as the **multiple-correlation coefficient.**

For example, if a manager believed that sales were a function of a salesperson's years of experience (exp), education level (ed), and gender (1 for females; 0 for males), information on each of these predictor variables could be collected along with outcome or criterion data. Using multiple regression, a regression equation such as the following could be generated:

$$\$\text{sales/month} = \$25,000 + \$1500 \text{ (exp)} + \$500(\text{ed}) - \$25(\text{gender})$$

A female salesperson with ten years of experience and a college degree (sixteen years of schooling) would be expected to generate $47,975 in sales [$25,000 + 1500(10) + $500(16) - 25(1)].

As will be discussed later, regression analysis has been used to determine how to combine information from multiple selection devices. Multiple regression has also been used to assess such things as the effects of rater and ratee characteristics (sex, experience, prior performance rating, rate of pay) on performance appraisal and pay decisions and to measure the effects of organizational characteristics (size, industry, sales) on PHRM planning and policies.

Reliability

As noted earlier, an important component in the use of measures in personnel research—particularly personnel selection tests—is **reliability.** If a measure such as a personnel selection test is to be useful, it must yield reliable results. As pointed out in Chapter 5, there are several ways of defining and interpreting test (i.e., predictor and criterion) reliability.

Each of these methods is based on the notion that observed scores (x) comprise true scores (T) plus some error (E), or $x = T + E$,[14] where T is the expected score if there were no error in measurement. To the extent that observed scores on a test are correlated with true scores, a test is said to be reliable. That is, if observed and true scores could be obtained for every individual who took a personnel selection test, the squared correlation between observed and true scores in the population (ρ^2_{xT}) would be called the reliability coefficient for that selection test.

One means of estimating reliablity ($\rho_{xx'}$) is **test-retest reliability.** This method is based on testing a sample of individuals twice with the same measure and then correlating the results to produce a reliability estimate. A potential major problem with the test-retest reliability estimate is the possibility of **carry-over effects** between the testing sessions: the second testing is influenced by the first testing. For instance, some people may improve between testing session. For example, students who retake the GMAT are likely to increase their scores by 40 to 80 points merely because they have been exposed to test materials previously.

Another means of estimating the reliability of a measure is to correlate scores on alternate forms of the measure. **Alternate test forms** are any two test forms that have been constructed in an effort to make them parallel, and they may have equal (or very similar) observed score means, variances (i.e., a measure of the spread of scores about the means), and correlations with other measures.[15] They are also intended to be similar in content and are designed to measure the same traits. The use of alternate or parallel forms, however, does not necessarily eliminate the possibility of carry-over effects related to response styles, moods, or attitudes.

A problem with test-retest reliability and alternate forms reliability is the necessity of testing twice. **Internal consistency reliability,** however, is estimated based on only one administration of a measure. The most common method, **coefficient** α (Greek letter alpha), yields a **split-half reliability** estimate. That is, the measure (e.g., test) is divided into two parts, which are considered alternate forms of each other, and the relationship between these two halves is an estimate of the test's (i.e., the measure's) reliability. The major advantage of internal consistency reliability estimates is that the reliability of a measure can be estimated based on one administration of the measure.

In summary, the PHRM researcher is interested in assessing the reliability of measures based on one or more of the previous methods because reliability is a necessary condition for determining validity. That is, reliability sets an upper limit on how high a measure can correlate with another measure because it is highly unlikely that a measure will correlate higher with a different measure than it does with itself.

Validity

As defined in the *Principles for the Validation and Use of Personnel Selection Procedures* (American Psychological Association), **validity** is the degree to which inferences from scores on tests or assessments are supported by evidence. This definition implies that validity refers to the inferences made from use of a measure, not to the measure itself. Three primary strategies have been identified to gather evidence to support or justify the inferences made from scores on measures: criterion-related, content-oriented, and construct validation strategies.

Criterion-Related Strategy.   A criterion-related strategy is an assessment of how well a measure (i.e., predictor) forecasts a criterion such as job performance. The two types of criterion-related validation strategies are concurrent and predictive—as shown in Exhibit 16.4.

Concurrent validation evaluates the relationship between a predictor and a job criterion score for all employees in the study at the same time. For example, this strategy could be used to determine the correlation between years of experience and job performance. PHRM would collect from each person in the study information about years of experience and performance scores. All persons in the study would have to be working in similar jobs, generally in the same job family or classification. Then a correlation would be computed between the predictor scores and criterion scores.

The steps in determining predictive validity are similar, except that the predictor is measured sometime before the criterion is measured, as shown in Exhibit 16.4. Thus, the **predictive validity** of a predictor could be determined by measuring an existing group of employees on a predictor and waiting to gather their criterion measures later, or by hiring a group of job applicants regardless of their scores on the predictor and measuring them on the criterion later. For either type of criterion-related validation strategy, it is important to demonstrate that the predictors and performance criteria are related to the duties of the job.

The classic example of a predictive validation study is AT&T's Management Progress Study.[16] In that study, personnel researchers at AT&T administered an assessment center, similar to the one described in Chapter 5, to 422 male employees, stored the results, and waited eight years before evaluating their predictions of how far these individuals would progress in AT&T's management hierarchy. For a group of college graduates, the predictions were highly accurate; a correlation of .71 was obtained between the assessment center predictions and level of management achieved. In addition, a twenty-year follow-up of the original predictions showed that the assessment center was still useful in predicting who would reach even higher levels in AT&T's management hierarchy.

EXHIBIT 16.4	Criterion-Related Validation Strategies

Criterion-Related Validation Strategies

Concurrent Study		
Time 1	*Time 1*	*Time 1*
Test (predictor) scores are gathered	Criterion scores are gathered	Correlation between scores on predictor (x) and criterion (y), r_{xy}, is calculated

Predictive Study		
Time 1	*Time 2*	*Time 2*
Test (predictor) scores are gathered	Criterion scores are gathered	Correlation between scores on predictor (x) and criterion (y), r_{xy}, is calculated

Another more recent and controversial predictive validation study involving preemployment drug testing is being conducted at the U.S. Postal Service. The Postal Service has tested over six thousand new hires for drug use and hired those who tested positive as part of their scientific study to see if past drug use correlates with poor job performance. Preliminary results indicate that there is no difference between the job performance of the identified drug users and that of hirees who did not test positive. It is likely that longitudinal predictive studies like this one at the U.S. Postal Service will yield more informative results than concurrent validation studies will. Unfortunately, the costs of longitudinal studies in terms of time, effort, and money often prohibit organizations from conducting such studies.[17]

Content-Oriented Strategy.   On many occasions, employers are not able to obtain sufficient empirical data for a criterion-related study. Consequently, other methods of validations are useful. One of the most viable is **content-oriented validation.** It differs from a criterion-related strategy in that it estimates or judges the relevance of a predictor as a sample of the relevant situations (e.g., behaviors or tasks) that make up a job. According to the *Uniform Guidelines*, A selection procedure can be supported by a content validity strategy to the extent it is a representative sample of the content of the job. The administration of a typing test (actually a job sample test is used for typists) as a selection device for hiring typists is a classic example of a predictor judged to be content valid. In this case, the predictor is a skill related to a task that is actually part of the job. Thus, to employ a content validation strategy, one must know the duties of the actual job.[18] As discussed in Chapter 3, information about job tasks and duties can be obtained using one or more job analysis procedures.

Construct Validation Strategy.   Instead of showing a direct relationship between a predictor (test, education, experience) and a job criterion (performance, performance rating, turnover, absenteeism), it is sometimes useful to determine if an individual possesses abilities and characteristics (psychological traits) that are deemed necessary for successful job performance. These underlying psychological traits are called **constructs** and include such characteristics as intelligence, leadership ability, verbal ability, interpersonal sensitivity, integrity, and analytical ability. Constructs deemed necessary for doing well on job criteria are inferred from job behaviors and activities (duties) indicated in the job analysis.[19]

A **construct validation** study attempts to demonstrate that a relationship exists between a test or a measure of the construct and the psychological trait (construct) it seeks to measure. For example, does a reading comprehension test reliably and accurately measure how well people can read and understand what they read? To demonstrate construct validity, one would need data showing that high scorers on the test actually read more difficult material and are better readers than low scorers on the test and that reading ability is related to the duties shown in the job description. Other evidence that the test is measuring the relevant construct could be obtained based on its relationship to other measures that assess both similar and unrelated constructs. In essence, construct validity is not established with a single study. Rather, it is assessed based on the cumulation of a body of empirical evidence. This evidence is likely to include information gathered from both criterion-related and content-oriented validation studies.

Estimating Population Validity Coefficients

As discussed in the section on correlation coefficients, if we were able to assess the relationship between a predictor and a criterion in a population of interest, with no measurement error, then we would have computed the true (population) correlation or validity coefficient, ρ_{xy}. Because we almost never have the population available and almost always have measurement error, our observed correlation coefficients (validity coefficients in personnel selection) underestimate the population validity coefficients between selection tests and job performance criteria.

Although predictor and criterion reliability have been noted as statistical artifacts that lower predictor-criterion relationships, other factors are also known to lower these estimated true relationships. Two other primary statistical artifacts, which obscure true relationships, are sampling error and range restriction. **Sampling error** refers to the inaccuracy in estimating the true population validity resulting from the use of a sample size that is less than the population when computing the validity coefficient. **Range restriction** relates to computing a correlation or validity coefficient between the predictor and criterion scores for a restricted group of individuals.[20] That is, the validity coefficient in personnel research is typically not computed on the entire range of scores for which the predictor will actually be used. This is evident when validity coefficients are based on a concurrent test validation study where only predictor scores obtained from the restricted group (i.e., current job incumbents as opposed to the entire range, which would include all applicant predictor scores) are used. We simply cannot hire all applicants and then relate their predictor scores to scores on a criterion measure such as a job performance rating. For this latter case, the resulting observed validity coefficient typically underestimates the population validity coefficient.

Formulas have been developed to remove the effects of predictor unreliability, criterion unreliability, and range restriction and for determining sampling error variance. That is, one would use the correction formulas to remove the influence of the previous statistical artifacts and, consequently, obtain a better idea of the predictor-criterion relationship in the relevant population. Recently, a number of studies have been conducted to examine the usefulness of these correction formulas in estimating population validity coefficients. These studies have examined the effects of variations in sample size, range restriction, and reliability on the size and variability of observed validity coefficient. These studies have improved our understanding of how observed validity coefficients are affected by measurement error and factors such as range restriction.[21]

Although this line of research has been helpful, most of the studies examined the impact of only one factor (e.g., range restriction). More recently, personnel researchers have been exploring the effects of correcting correlation coefficients for both range restriction and unreliability of measures. The hope is that continued research in this latter area will yield valuable information concerning the true relationships between our predictors and criteria.

Validity Generalization

Over the past fifty years, hundreds of validation studies have been conducted in organizations to determine the predictive effectiveness of personnel selection measures (e.g., ability tests) for selecting and placing individuals. Often the validity coefficients for the same or a similar predictor-criterion relationship differed substantially from one setting to another. Although personnel researchers were aware that these differences between the same or similar predictor-criterion relationships were affected by the statistical artifacts noted earlier (i.e., range restriction, predictor unreliability, criterion unreliability, and sampling error), only recently were corrections for these statistical artifacts integrated into systematic procedures for estimating to what degree true validity estimates for the same predictor-criterion relationship generalize across settings.

A series of studies has applied **validity generalization** procedures to validity coefficient data for clerical jobs, computer programming jobs, petroleum industry jobs, and so on.[22] In general, these investigations showed that the effects of criterion unreliability, predictor unreliability, range restriction, and sample size accounted for most of the observed variance in validity coefficients for the same or similar test-criterion relationship within an occupation (i.e., job grouping or job family). Thus, the estimated true validity coefficients (i.e., ρ_{xy} or corrected validity coefficients) were higher and less variable than when they were left as observed validity coefficients (i.e., r_{xy}s or observed validity coefficient not corrected for unreliability, range restriction, or sample size).

The implications of these findings are that inferences (predictions) from scores on personnel selection tests can be transported across situations for similar jobs. That is, if two similar jobs exist in two parts of an organization or in two different organizations, a given selection test should have approximately the same validity coefficients for both jobs. If validity generalization can be successfully argued, an organization can save a great deal of time and money developing valid, job-related predictors because the inferences from a predictor for a job have already been established.

More recently, the concept of validity generalization (or what is also commonly referred to as **meta-analysis),** has been applied to other areas of PHRM research than just selection.[23] This latter research has assisted the personnel and human resource field in gaining a better understanding of the true effectiveness of interventions such as training programs, goal-setting programs, and performance measurement (appraisal) programs. In addition to determining how well validity generalizes across settings, personnel researchers are interested in how stable their prediction equations are across samples.

Cross-Validation

As discussed in the section on correlation coefficients, personnel researchers often develop prediction equations (or regression equations) with multiple predictors. For the prediction equations to be of any practical use, they must produce consistent results. **Cross-validation** is a procedure for determining the amount of capitalization on chance that has affected the prediction equation (the **regression weights**). If the results were not stable, we might have to develop and use a different equation in each new sample or setting. This would be costly and time consuming for most organizations.

Traditional or empirical cross-validation typically involved holding out some of the data (sample). The equation developed in the initial sample could then be applied to the holdout sample to evaluate its stability. In general, this latter procedure has been shown to be less precise than formulas for estimating the stability of regression equations. The reason for the increased precision when using formula-based estimates is that all information (the total sample) is used at once in estimating the original weights.

As is the case in personnel selection, one is interested in how well the regression weights (the b's noted earlier) estimated in a sample will predict the criterion value of new subjects (e.g., job applicants) not used in the estimation sample. Assume we are interested in determining the criterion-related validity of three assessment center exercises (in basket, group exercise, and ability test) for predicting supervisory performance ratings. After collecting assessment center exercise scores and performance ratings, we may find a multiple correlation between the measures of .60. We are unsure, however, how useful the equation for predicting supervisory ratings will be in another sample. Using a formula to estimate this usefulness, we might find that our multiple correlation in another sample (based on the regression weights developed in the original sample) drops to around .40. Although lower than .60, this **population cross-validated multiple correlation** may still have substantial practical utility for the organization.[24]

DETERMINING THE USEFULNESS OF PHRM PROCEDURES

Armed with procedures to determine the reliability and validity of measurement devices, PHRM researchers have become concerned about demonstrating the usefulness of the methods and procedures they use. This is particularly important when PHRM activities and programs are vying for scarce financial resources. In order to justify finding, PHRM activities must be cost effective. This section addresses the process used to determine the usefulness of selection devices. Additionally, utility analysis, which assesses the costs and benefits of PHRM programs, is discussed.

Usefulness of Selection Devices

An important application of validity and reliability is in selection decision making. By examining the interaction between validity and reliability, as well as the selection ratio and cutoff scores, the usefulness of one selection device compared to another or to no selection device can be assessed.

Consider the diagram in Exhibit 16.5. The vertical line labeled x_c divides the applicant pool based on their performance relative to the predictor. Applicants who meet or exceed the cutoff score would be hired; those who score below the cutoff score would be rejected. For this example, 60 of 100 applicants would be hired. The horizontal line labeled x_y represents the division between successful and unsuccessful job performance. Using this cutoff score, if all 100 applicants were hired, only 45 would be successful. Thus, the base rate for this job is 45 percent.

Quadrants I and III contain correct predictions made by the predictor. In Quadrant I, a low test score is related to low job performance. This is referred to as a **true negative** prediction. [The test predicted low (negative) job performance, and it was true.] Quadrant III includes the scores of those applicants who scored above the cutoff score on the predictor and also were successful on the job. These judgments are referred to as **true positive** judgments. [The test predicted high (positive) job performance, and it was true.] The higher the

Scatter Diagram Showing Correct and Erroneous Selection Decisions
(Based on a Selection Ratio of .60 and a Base Rate of .45)

EXHIBIT
16.5

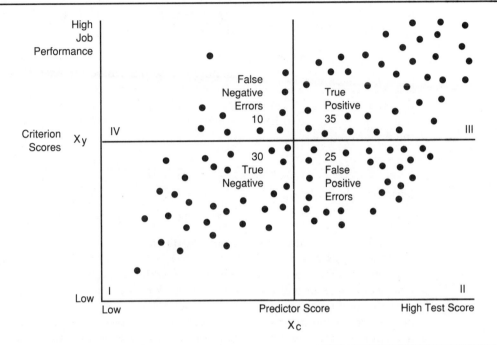

number of true positives and negatives relative to total applicants, the more accurate and useful the selection device is. In our example, the test made accurate predictions 65 percent of the time. This is a substantial improvement over selection by chance (45 percent).

However, because no selection device is perfect, errors in judgment occur. These fall into two categories. Quadrant II includes people who are hired based on their high scores but who are unsuccessful on the job. These are called **false positive** selection errors or erroneous acceptances. **False negative** selection errors (Quadrant IV) occur when individuals would not be hired because they scored low on the test. If hired, however, they would have performed well. For the selection device shown in Exhibit 16.5, there were 10 false negative selection decisions and 25 false positive errors.

An organization knows that using valid predictors will result in a greater success rate than not using them (i.e., a greater percentage of predicted successful employees will be hired—**predictor rate**—than if the organization had been selected applicants at random—**base rate.**) For example, if the base rate is .5 (half the applicants hired at random turn out to be good performers), and the predictor rate is .8 (80 percent of the applicants hired by using a particular predictor turn out to be successful), the percentage of correct predictions over and above the base rate is 30.

A series of tables was developed to portray the increase in the percentage of correct predictions over and above the base rate as the cutting score (i.e., the predictor score above which we predict success and below which we predict failure) is raised, given a **selection ratio**[25] (percentage hired) and correlation coefficient.[26] This increase in the percentage of correct predictions can be illustrated in using Exhibit 16.5. Exhibit 16.5 depicts the possible selection decision outcomes for a population of 100. The base rate of success is .45 or

$$\text{Base rate of success} = \frac{\text{III} + \text{IV}}{\text{I} + \text{II} + \text{III} + \text{IV}} = \frac{35 + 10}{30 + 25 + 35 + 10} = .45$$

That is, 45 percent of the applicants would be successful if we had no valid selection procedure and hired at random. To determine the usefulness of the selection device, the predictor rate needs to be compared to this base rate: If the predictor is useful, it should produce an improvement in selection. As shown below, the predictor in Exhibit 16.5 yields an improvement of .13 points over the base rate of .45:

$$\% \text{ increase in correct predictions} = \frac{\text{III}}{\text{III} + \text{II}} - \frac{\text{III} + \text{IV}}{\text{I} + \text{II} + \text{III} + \text{IV}} = .13$$

$$\frac{35}{35 + 25} - \frac{35 + 10}{30 + 25 + 35 + 10} = .13$$

where the first quantity is our predictor rate and the latter is the base rate.

Psychologists have also developed an elaborate set of tables, referred to as **expectancy tables** or **expectancy charts**, which convert the correlation coefficient to frequencies of correct predictions have been presented.[27]

At this point, we might ask the question, Does a 13-percent increase in predictive accuracy resulting from the use of any selection procedure always result in the same economic benefit to an organization? In answer to this questions, the usefulness of a selection device varies depending on where cutoff scores are set. By lowering a cutoff score, false and negative errors are minimized, but false positive errors increase. Conversely, raising a cutoff score minimizes false positive errors but increases false negative errors. Because of these trade-offs, an organization needs to carefully consider the cost of each type of error. Usually, false positive errors are the more costly because a poor performer is hired and trained and may have to be replaced. Still, as we will see next, the benefit of an increase in predictive accuracy is dependent on the costs to obtain it, as well as on the payoff associated with the correct predictions.[28] Thus, we now move from a concern with predictive accuracy to measuring the costs and benefits of predictions.

Utility Analysis

In addition, to assessing the usefulness of selection devices, correlation coefficients and validity information can also be used to conduct a utility analysis. Although it is not yet used by many organizations, **utility analysis** helps personnel and human resource managers determine what the cost/benefit of one selection device is over no selection device or over an alternate device. Utility analysis also can be used to determine the financial impact of PHRM-related events (performance appraisal program, absenteeism, turnover, training program, compensation plan).[29] In examining this research, bear in mind that it is primarily theoretical and mathematical in nature.

Utility analysis is premised on the assumption that individuals who are familiar with a job (supervisors) can estimate the dollar value of performance associated with someone performing at the 50th percentile, the 85th percentile,

and the 15th percentile. This is called the **standard deviation** (SD_y) of performance in dollars. Research indicates that the SD usually ranges from 16 to 70
percent of wages, with values most often being in the 40-to-60-percent range.
This means that an estimate of SD for a job paying $40,000 per year typically
ranges from $16,000 to $24,000. Studies have been conducted in which supervisors have provided estimates of SD for such jobs as sales manager, computer
programmer, insurance counselor, and entry-level park ranger.

In addition to estimating the SD, utility analysis also considers other factors
(e.g., number of employees, tax rates, and validity coefficient of the selection
device) that affect the value or utility of a selection process. The following
equation, which incorporates these economic concepts, can be employed when
comparing two alternative selection procedures or other PHRM options:

$$\Delta U = N_s \left[\sum_{t=1}^{T} (1/(1 + i)^t) \, SD_y \, (1 + V) \, (1 - TAX) \right. \tag{16.1}$$
$$\left. (\hat{\rho}_1 - \hat{\rho}_2)\bar{z}_s \right] - (C_1 - C_2)(1 - TAX)]$$

where

ΔU = total estimated dollar value of replacing one selection
procedure (1) with another procedure (2) after variable costs,
taxes, and discounting,

N_s = the number of employees selected,

T = the number of future time periods,

t = the time period in which a productivity increase occurs,

i = the discount rate,

SD_y = the standard deviation of job performance in dollars,

V = the proportion of SD_y represented by variable costs,

TAX = the organization's applicable tax rate,

$\hat{\rho}_1$ = the estimated population validity coefficient between scores on
one selection procedure and the criterion,

$\hat{\rho}_2$ = the estimated population validity coefficient between scores on
an alternative selection procedure and scores on the criterion,

$\bar{z}_s$ = the mean standard score on the selection procedure of those
selected (this is assumed to be equal in the equation 18.1 for
each selection procedure),

C_1 = the total cost of the first selection procedure, and

C_2 = the total cost of the alternative selection procedure.[30]

For illustration purposes, let us employ a portion of the utility analysis information collected at a large international manufacturing company, which we
will call Company A. Company A undertook a utility analysis to obtain an
estimate of the economic impact of its current procedure for selecting sales
managers as compared with their previously used interviewing selection programs. The current selection procedure was a managerial assessment center.
Although the assessment center had been in operation for seven years at the

time of the utility analysis, a value for T of four years was used because this was the average time (tenure) for the 29 (N in equation 16.1) sales managers who had been selected from a pool of 132 candidates. A primary objective of the utility analysis at Company A was to compare the estimated dollar value of selecting 29 managers with the assessment center with what the economic gain would have been if 29 sales managers were selected by an interviewing program.

Company A employed an interdisciplinary approach when estimating the various components of equation 16.1. For instance, values of V and TAX were provided by the accounting and tax departments, respectively. These values were $-.05$ for V and .49 for TAX. V was considered the proportion of dollar sales volume as compared with operating costs. Because there was a positive relationship between combined operating costs (e.g., salary, benefits, supplies, automobile operations) and sales volume, a value for V of $-.05$ was used in equation 16.1. In addition, the value for i, .18, was based on an examination of corporate financial documentation. The accounting department also provided the figure for C_1 (the total cost of the assessment center), \$263,636. Based on 29 selected individuals, the cost of selecting one district sales manager was computed to be about \$9,091. The estimated total cost to select 29 sales managers by the previously used one-day interviewing program was \$50,485 (i.e., the value for C_2 in equation 16.1). Let us now turn to the final four components of equation 16.1: $\hat{\rho}_1$, $\hat{\rho}_2$, $\bar{z}_s$, and SD_y.[31]

$\hat{\rho}_1$, the estimated population validity coefficient for the assessment center, was obtained by correlating five assessment dimension scores (i.e., scores for planning and organizing, decision making, stress tolerance, sensitivity, and persuasiveness) with an overall performance rating. The multiple correlation between the measures was .61. Next, the population cross-validated multiple correlation was calculated, using the formulas mentioned above in the section on cross-validation. This resulting value of .41 was finally corrected for range restriction and criterion reliability to yield an estimated value of .59 for $\hat{\rho}_1$.

Because Company A had not conducted a criterion-related validity study for the interviewing selection program, a value was obtained from the validity generalization literature.[32] The value of $\hat{\rho}_2$ for the interviewing program was .16. In addition, the standard score on the predictor ($\bar{z}_s$) was determined to be .872. This value was assumed to be the same for both the assessment center and the interviewing program.

The final, and traditionally the most difficult, component to estimate in equation 16.1 has been SD_y. As indicated earlier, SD_y is an index of the variability of job performance in dollars in the relevant population. The relevant population or group for evaluating a selection procedure is the applicant group, the group with which the selection procedure is used. When evaluating the economic utility of organizational interventions, however, the relevant group is current employees. Because the intervention would be applied to current employees, the appropriate value of SD_y is for this group. In this latter case, if the SD_y were estimated from the applicant group, it could be an overestimate. Consequently, the approximate value for a sales manager, \$30,000, will be used for SD_y in the present example.

Placing the previous values into the utility analysis equation would result in a value of approximately \$316,460. This value represents the estimated present value, over a four-year time period, to the organization from the use of the assessment center in place of an interviewing program to select 29 sales managers. Although the cost of the interviewing program is only about one-fifth of the assessment center cost, the estimated dollar gain from use of the assessment center instead of the interviewing program is substantial. This result is primarily due to the greater predictive effectiveness (i.e., higher validity coefficient) of the assessment center.

As demonstrated, utility analysis makes it possible for personnel and human resource managers to compute the dollar gains and losses that result from the use of employee selection practices. The same procedures can be, and have been, used to assess the usefulness of training, programs to reduce absenteeism, safety, and other PHRM programs. Despite the potential usefulness of utility analysis, very few firms have adopted these procedures. There are several possible reasons for this. First, practice tends to lag theory. Because utility analysis is rather new, it may not have filtered down to organizations yet. Second, opponents of utility analysis question the viability of measuring the standard deviation of performance by using managerial estimates. Finally, it was noted in Chapter 5 that validation studies were not conducted as often as they sould be. Without information regarding the validity of selection, training, safety, or absenteeism programs, utility analysis cannot be conducted.

OTHER INNOVATIONS IN PHRM RESEARCH

In addition to assessing the economic utility of organizational interventions, PHRM researchers and practitioners are making important progress in other research areas. Although many of these developments have been discussed in the chapters on job analysis, recruitment, selection, and compensation, three areas deserve discussion here: adaptive testing, procedural justice, and mergers and acquisitions.

Adaptive Testing

One area of computer technology that is currently receiving increased research attention among PHRM professionals is that of tailored or adaptive testing. **Tailored or adaptive testing** refers to the situation in which the computer program adjusts the test difficulty to the ability of the individual being tested:

> A computer-assisted or adaptive test uses a multi-stage process to estimate a person's ability several times during the course of testing, and the selection of successive test items based on those ability estimates. The person tested uses an interactive computer terminal to answer a test question. If the answer is correct, the next item will be more difficult; if not, an easier item follows. With each response, a revised and more reliable estimate is made of the person's ability. The test proceeds until the estimate reaches a specified level of reliability. Generally, the results both are more reliable and require fewer items than a paper and pencil test.[33]

A few researchers have examined issues concerning the validity of computer-administered adaptive tests.[34] One interesting study compared the Arithmetic Reasoning, and Word Knowledge subtests of the Armed Services Vocational Aptitude Battery (ASVAB) with computer-administered adaptive tests as predictors of performance in an air force mechanic training course.[35] The study found that computer-administered adaptive tests which are one-third to one-half the length of conventional (i.e., paper-and-pencil) ASVAB tests could approximate the criterion-related validity coefficients of these conventional tests. The importance of these findings is even more impressive when one considers that adaptive tests administer different items to different individuals.

Others have pointed out that increased measurement accuracy is not the only benefit of computer-administered adaptive testing.[36] Additional benefits include reductions in testing time, fatigue, and boredom, as well as cost savings in some cases over conventional paper-and-pencil testing.[37] A study conducted within the U.S. Office of Personnel Management placed the cost of adaptive testing at less than that of paper-and-pencil testing.[38] Moreover, a report prepared for the Canadian government estimated that even considering the capital investment in computer equipment, computer-administered adaptive tests could show a savings over conventional paper-and-pencil tests in one year.[39]

Although potential benefits are associated with computerized testing for making employment decisions, this form of assessment will probably be examined by the courts. Based on numerous and significant recent court decisions concerning employment testing,[40] continued legal scrutiny of employment practices is clearly a reality.

Procedural Justice

A PHRM research area that has been gaining in popularity concerns perceptions of justice and fair treatment at work. This line of research focuses on the process by which evaluation decisions (selection, performance appraisal, layoffs) or reward allocation decisions are made. In general, this research suggests that even when employees are satisfied with a PHRM outcome, they may or may not be satisfied with the process or procedures that were used to make the decision.

While research on procedural justice is only just beginning, initial findings suggest that procedures that are open, are specified in advance, treat similarly situated people similarly, and allow input from employees are more likely to be perceived as fair than are those violating these principles. Procedural justice is of greatest concern when outcomes are unfavorable.

While early research was conducted in the laboratory, field research may be helpful to PHRM practitioners in several ways. According to a recent survey on the importance of PHRM functions, policy adherence including assurances that proper administrative procedures have been followed in an equitable manner is one of the top four concerns of four PHRM constituencies (executives, supervisors, professional employees, and hourly employees).[41]

It can be further speculated that as organizations strive to exist in an increasingly competitive global economy, the fairness of procedures will become even more important. This is because allocation decisions will more often be unfavorable to employees. For this research to advance, practitioners need to team up with PHRM researchers to explore the factors that influence perceptions of fairness.

Mergers, Acquisitions, and Downsizing

As noted in the initial chapters, many U.S. organizations have been forced to cut costs and reduce size: to become "lean and mean" in order to survive. At the same time, the rate of mergers and acquisitions has greatly increased. Both these trends have important implications for PHRM practices and strategies. Because of the speed of these changes, PHRM research has lagged, rather than led, actions in the real world. Still, some knowledge has been acquired, and more can be expected about the changing structure of organizations.

Articles in practitioner journals on outplacement activities surfaced in the early 1980s and stimulated academic research on the consequences of job loss and job change. Some of this research has identified the conditions under which job loss is positive, leading to personal and career growth. Other research has focused on what organizations can do to reduce the stress associated with job loss or change through mergers and acquisitions.

On the flip side of layoffs, knowledge is beginning to be amassed regarding the reactions of retained employees to reductions in force. Several studies have shown that "survivor guilt" can lead to increased performance among survivors of layoffs. For example, employees with strong work ethics may increase their job involvement after even mild or temporary layoffs.[42]

Other research has identified the strategies used by organizations to reduce the size of the work force. For example, one study found that layoffs were by far the most common downsizing strategy used because personnel and human resource managers in the sample had less than two months, on average, in which to plan and carry out the reduction in employment levels. While research has not yet emerged, it would seem that personnel managers could become more expert and proactive in monitoring product life cycles, the business environment, and organizational strategy in order to anticipate needed staff changes. This is more likely to occur when PHRM is integrated in the planning process. There also is a need for more research on how downsizing is accomplished and on how employees respond before, during, and after the fact. Similar questions can be raised regarding mergers and acquisitions.[43]

COMMUNICATING WITH EMPLOYEES: ORGANIZATIONAL SURVEYS

According to a recent study by *Personnel Journal*, more than 90 percent of all personnel and human resource directors believe that employee research is helpful. The majority of these managers also believe that employee surveys are an effective way to collect information relating to many PHRM issues and concerns, including communications, motivation, organizational culture, effectiveness of supervisors, and satisfaction with work and compensation. Because employee satisfaction, involvement, and skill level can change, personnel managers must continually monitor these factors. Regular, periodic organizational surveys are one method of doing this.

What Surveys Measure

In many of the chapters thus far, the need for PHRM data has frequently been for either measures of job performance itself or predictors of job performance, such as tests and background characteristics. But the personnel manager often needs other types of data. For example, to develop ways to improve employee job performance, he or she needs to measure employee perceptions of organizational characteristics, including the consequences of job performance, organizational policies, frequency of feedback, job design qualities, task interference characteristics, aspects of goal setting, role conflict and awareness, and supervisor behaviors. Equally necessary is gathering data on the employee's reactions to the organizational conditions, the quality of work life, and reactions such as satisfaction and job involvement.

In addition to these subjective or reactive measures, concrete information is also useful in determining the actual or objective qualities (nonreactive measures) of the organizational characteristics.[44] For example, to make improvements in the design of jobs, one may need to know what the actual characteristics of jobs are that the employees perceive as highly repetitive. With this information and information about the employees' reactions, job design changes are more feasible. However, these changes can probably be made effectively only when other organizational characteristics are considered as well.

Other measures or variables that could be used to supplement organizational surveys are objective measures of employee reactions. Many of these reactions can be symptoms of employee stress, which include physiological measures such as blood pressure and heart rate. Because one of the criteria for the effectiveness of personnel and human resource management is employee health, these additional measures of employee reactions may become more common in organizational surveys. Besides these reactions, employee behaviors to be measured objectively include job performance, absenteeism, turnover, rates and types of accidents, and incidents of diseases.[45] In summary, organizational surveys are really efforts to systematically gather information on objective and subjective bases about organizational characteristics and employee reactions and behaviors for one or more of the purposes noted earlier. For instance, the Ford Motor Company is systematically gathering information on its managers to assist in their efforts to change Ford's corporate culture.[46]

> Ford is putting its managers (2,000 so far) through workshops where they take tests to determine their management style and how they cope with change. Each person's results are then displayed on his or her name tag. The workshops, which started last year, also include a session at which participants confide what it is they most admire about one another. "What we're trying to do is make this place the most loving, caring group of people in Ford," Joseph Kordick, the general manager of parts and service, says of the workshops held in his division.[47]

Steps in an Organizational Survey

The personnel and human resource manager—or an outside consultant—has several important steps and issues to consider when conducting an organizational survey. These become necessary, however, only after top management has given its support for the survey.[48]

As the first step, the personnel manager must consider the following:

- The specific employee perceptions and responses that should be measured
- The methods that will be used to collect the data, including observations, questionnaires, interviews, and personnel records
- The reliability and validity of the measures to be used
- The people from whom the data will be collected—all employees, managerial employees only, a sample of employees, or only certain departments within the organization

- The timing of the survey and the way to make the survey part of a longer-term effort
- The types of analyses that will be made with the data
- The specific purposes of the data—to determine reasons for the organization's turnover

This last consideration is important because by identifying the problem, the personnel manager can determine which models or theories will be relevant to the survey. Knowing which model or theory to use tells the personnel manager what data are needed and what statistical techniques will be necessary to analyze the data.

The next step is the actual collection of data. Three areas are important here: (1) Who will administer the questionnaire—the line manager, someone from the personnel department, or someone from outside the organization? (2) Where, when, and in what size groups will the data be collected? Both these considerations are influenced by the method used to gather the data. For example, if a questionnaire is used, larger groups are more feasible than if interviews are conducted. (3) Employee participation in the survey must be ensured. This can be done by gathering the data during company time and by providing feedback—for instance, by promising employees that the results of the survey will be made known to them.

The actual feedback process is the third step in the survey. As part of this process, the data are analyzed according to the purposes and problems for which they were collected. The results of the analysis can then be presented by the personnel department to the line managers, who in turn discuss the results with their employees. The feedback sessions can be used to develop solutions to any problems that are identified and to evaluate the effectiveness of programs that may already have been implemented on the basis of results of an earlier survey.

The extent to which employees actually participate in the development of solutions during the feedback process depends on the philosophy of top management. Organizations that are willing to survey their employees to ask how things are going are also usually willing to invite employee participation in deciding to make things better. This willingness allows organizational surveys to be used most effectively.

Sample Questionnaire

The most common method of obtaining survey data is the paper-and-pencil questionnaire.[49] Exhibit 16.6 is a questionnaire asking students to describe the degree to which they know what is expected of them (role awareness) and how much conflict they face in doing what is expected (role conflict). Measures of role awareness and role conflict have been used extensively in organizational surveys; typical items have been reworded here to apply to a classroom situation. To use this questionnaire, circle the appropriate numbers before reading any further.

Once you have completed the questionnaire, add the numbers you circled in items 1, 6, 7, 9, 10, and 12. This is your *role awareness* score. Now add the remaining numbers you circled to determine your *role conflict* score. Next, in the following display, circle the response that you think best describes your overall level of satisfaction with the class:

EXHIBIT
16.6

Role Awareness and Role Conflict Questionnaire

Read each classroom characteristic, and select the scale number that best reflects your opinion.

Definitely not characteristic of this class				Definitely characteristic of this class
1	**2**	**3**	**4**	**5**

1. I know what my responsibilities are. 1 2 3 4 5
2. I receive assignments without the time to complete them. 1 2 3 4 5
3. Part of my grade depends on a group project. 1 2 3 4 5
4. I have to go through all sorts of hassles to find out what's expected of me. 1 2 3 4 5
5. Good work or a good idea is not really recognized by the instructor. 1 2 3 4 5
6. I have been given clearly planned goals and objectives for this class. 1 2 3 4 5
7. I know how to study for this class to do well. 1 2 3 4 5
8. I do things that are apt to be accepted by the instructor at one time but not accepted at another time. 1 2 3 4 5
9. I feel certain about how much I am responsible for. 1 2 3 4 5
10. I know exactly what is expected of me. 1 2 3 4 5
11. I have to do things that can be done in different ways. 1 2 3 4 5
12. Explanations of what has to be done are clear. 1 2 3 4 5
13. I work on unnecessary things. 1 2 3 4 5
14. The amount of work I am expected to do is not fair. 1 2 3 4 5

SOURCE: Adapted from J. R. Rizzo, R. J. House, and S. I. Lirtzman, "Role Conflict and Ambiguity in Complex Organizations," *Administrative Science Quarterly* 15 (1970): 156.

	Strongly Disagree	Disagree	Neutral	Agree	Strongly Agree
All in all, I am very satisfied with this class	1	2	3	4	5

How does your score on satisfaction compare with your scores on role conflict and role awareness? Are you high on all three? Low on all three? Do you have a mixed pattern?

What is the importance of these scores? In most organizational surveys, employees are asked for their perceptions of and attitudes toward many aspects of the organization. These surveys generally reveal definite patterns. Satisfaction, for instance, tends to have a negative relationship with role conflict and a positive relationship with role awareness. Role conflict and role awareness are also frequently related to employee performance and stress.[50] Therefore, an employee's role conflict and role awareness scores reveal a great deal about the employee. Other variables—for example, descriptions of the employee's supervisor, the job, and the extent of the employee's perceived participation in decision making—also reveal important information about how the employee is reacting to the organization. Still other variables, such as employee perceptions of and attitudes toward group members, may indicate the quality of group relationships.

Organizational surveys, coupled with knowledge of the practical usefulness of organizational interventions, provide rich information for improving individual and organizational performance. Improvements in survey development will serve to make organizational surveys an increasingly important means for identifying problems, as well as feasible criterion measure for evaluating the effectiveness of organizational interventions.[51] In addition, future improvements in utility analysis, as well as continued cumulative research on the effectiveness of alternative organizational interventions, will assist the PHRM decision maker in increasing work force productivity and consequently increasing the efficiency of personnel decisions.

SUMMARY

PHRM research must be conducted in order to improve individual and organizational effectiveness, determine the success of PHRM programs, and compete for scarce organizational financial resources. Emphasis here is placed on describing the steps in the empirical research process and on explaining research strategies. Laboratory research helps managers acquire basic knowledge, provided the setting is carefully designed to mimic organizational reality. While difficult to set up, field experiments involve the manipulation of specific variables in actual organizations. By comparison, field studies examine interrelationships between variables without assessing the effects of interventions. Underscoring the effectiveness of PHRM research are issues associated with the reliability and validation of measurement and the evaluation of the usefulness and economic utility of PHRM selection and organizational interventions. Recent advances in PHRM research relate to adaptive testing, procedural justice, and mergers and acquisitions. Continued research efforts will further advance our knowledge of PHRM activities, as well as contribute to the steadily increasing importance of the PHRM function.

DISCUSSION QUESTIONS

1. Assume you wanted to determine the effect of quality circles on performance quantity and quality. How might you go about examining this issue?
2. Describe three methods for assessing the reliability of measures, and evaluate the practicality of each method.
3. Discuss the importance of decision-theoretical utility equations for estimating the economic utility of alternative organizational interventions.
4. How should an organization evaluate the predictive effectiveness of a particular personnel selection test battery (series of tests) in another situation?
5. How do organizational surveys serve as indicators of problems, as well as criteria for evaluating the effectiveness of organizational interventions?
6. Assume you want to test the hypothesis that situational interviews are more useful than traditional unstructured interviews are. How would you go about testing your hypothesis in the laboratory? In a field experiment? In a field, research study?
7. Identify a research question relating to mergers and acquisitions, and explain how you would examine the question.

NOTES

1. This chapter was originally prepared by Michael J. Burke, Stern School of Business Administration, New York University.

2. For a discussion of reasons for conducting organizational research, see J. E. Stone, *Research Methods in Organizational Behavior* (Santa Monica, Calif.: Goodyear, 1978).

3. J. E. Stone, *Research Method in Organizational Behavior* (Santa Monica, CA: Goodyear, 1978).

4. M. Neale and G. Northcraft, "Experience, Expertise, and Decision Bias in Negotiations: The Role of Strategic Conceptualization," in *Research in Bargaining and Negotiations*, 2d ed., ed. M. Bazerman and R. Lewicki (Greenwich, Conn.: JAI Press, 1989).

5. V. Huber, M. Neale, and G. Northcraft, "Decision Bias and Personnel Selection Strategies," *Organizational Behavior and Human Decision Processes* 40, (1987): 136–47; V. Huber, G. Northcraft, and M. Neale, "Effects of Decision Context and Anchoring on Selection Decisions," *Organizational Behavior and Human Decision Processes* 42 (1989).

6. V. Huber, M. Neale, and G. Northcraft, "Judgment by Heuristic: Effects of Ratee and Rater Characteristics and Performance Standards on Performance-Related Judgments," *Organizational Behavior and Human Decision Processes* 40, (1987): 149–69.

7. S. Rynes and S. Lawler, "A Policy Capturing Investigation of the Role of Expectancies in Decisions to Pursue Job Alternatives," *Journal of Applied Psychology* 31 (1983): 353–64; S. Rynes, D. Schwab, and H. Heneman, "The Role of Pay and Market Pay Variability in Job Application Decisions," *Organizational Behavior and Human Decision Processes* 31 (1983): 353–64; P. Sherer, D. Schwab, and H. Heneman, "Managerial Salary-Raise Decisions: A Policy-Capturing Approach," *Personnel Psychology* 40 (1987): 27–38.

8. M. Gist, B. Rosen, and C. Schwoerer, "The Influence of Training Method and Trainee Age on the Acquisition of Computer Skills," *Personnel Psychology* 41 (1988): 255–67.

9. C. Frayne and G. Latham, "Application of Social Learning Theory to Employee Self-Management of Attendance," *Journal of Applied Psychology* 72 (1987): 387–92.

10. T. Lee and R. T. Mowday, "Voluntary Leaving an Organization: An Empirical Investigation of Steers and Mowday's Model of Turnover," *Academy of Management Journal* 30 (1987): 721–43.

11. G. Dreher, R. A. Ash, and R. D. Bretz, "Benefits Coverage and Employee Cost: Critical Factors in Explaining Compensation Satisfaction," *Personnel Psychology* 41 (1988): 237–54.

12. For a summary of the conditions under which each type of correlation coefficient is used, refer to M. J. Allen and W. M. Yen, *Introduction to Measurement Theory* (Monterey, Calif.: Brooks/Cole, 1979), 36–41.

13. G. V. Glass and J. C. Stanley, *Statistical Methods in Education and Psychology* (Englewood Cliffs, N.J.: Prentice-Hall, 1970).

14. F. M. Lord and M. R. Novick, *Statistical Theories of Mental Test Scores* (Reading, Mass.: Addison-Wesley, 1968).

15. E. E. Ghiselli, J. P. Campbell, and S. Zedeck, *Measurement Theory for the Behavioral Sciences* (San Francisco: Freeman, 1981).

16. For a discussion of the AT&T Management Progress Study, as well as an overview of assessment centers, see A. Howard, "An Assessment of Assessment Centers," *Academy of Management Journal* 17 (1974): 115–34. A twenty-year follow-up study of AT&T's original Management Progress Study predictions was reported in A. Howard, "Cool at the Top: Personality Characteristics of Successful Executives," paper presented at the Annual Convention of the American Psychological Association, August 1984, Toronto.

17. See S. J. Osterlind, "Using CRTs in Program Curriculum Evaluation," *Educational Measurement: Issues and Practice* 7 (Fall 1988): 23–30. A critical commentary on competency-based tests is provided by M. C. Ellwein, G. V. Glass, and M. L. Smith, "Standards of Competence: Propositions on the Nature of Testing Reforms," *Educational Research* 17 (1988): 4–9. An early review of criterion-referenced testing was provided in the special Fall 1980 issue of *Applied Psychological Measurement* entitled "Contributions to Criterion-Referenced Testing Technology."

18. R. S. Barrett, "Is the Test Content-Valid: Or, Does It Really Measure Construct?" *Employee Relations Law Journal* 6, no. 3 (1981): 459–75; R. S. Barrett, "Is the Test Content-Valid: Or, Who Killed Cock Robin?" *Employee Relations Law Journal* 6, no. 4 (1981): 584–600.

19. A method for assessing construct validity based on correlation coefficients between the relevant construct measure (i.e., the measure being validated) and measures of similar and unrelated constructs is the multitrait-multimethod matrix. This method requires that at least two constructs be measured by minimally two methods. An assessment of construct validity is based on the degrees of convergence (i.e., the correlation coefficients between measures of the same construct) and divergence (i.e., judged by higher correlation coefficients between two methods of measuring the same construct than between correlation coefficients of two constructs measured by the same method). For a discussion of the multitrait-multimethod matrix, refer to D. T. Campbell and D. W. Fiske, "Convergent and Discriminant Validation by the Multitrait-Multimethod Matrix," *Psychological Bulletin* 56 (1959): 81–105. A more concise discussion of the multitrait-multimethod matrix is presented in A. Anastasi, *Psychological Testing* (New York: Macmillan, 1976), 156–58.

20. R. A. Alexander, G. M. Alliger, and P. J. Hanges, "Correcting for Range Restriction When the Population Variance Is Unknown," *Applied Psychological Measurement* 8 (1984): 431–37; R. A. Forsyth and L. S. Feldt, "Investigation of Empirical Sampling Distri-

butions and Correlations Corrected for Attenuation," *Educational and Psychological Measurement* 29 (1969): 61–71; R. L. Linn, D. L. Harnisch, and S. B. Dunbar, "Validity Generalization and Situational Specificity: An Analysis of the Prediction of First-Year Grades in Law School," *Applied Psychological Measurement* 5 (1981): 281–89.

21. P. Bobko, "An Analysis of Correlations Corrected for Attenuation and Range Restriction," *Journal of Applied Psychology* 68 (1983): 584–89; R. Lee, R. Miller, and W. Graham, "Corrections for Restriction of Range and Attenuation in Criterion-Related Validation Studies," *Journal of Applied Psychology* 67 (1982): 637–39.

22. For a review of validity generalization research, see M. J. Burke, "A Review of Validity Generalization Models and Procedures," in *Readings in Personnel and Human Resource Management*, 3d ed., ed. R. S. Schuler, S. A. Youngblood, and V. L. Huber (St. Paul: West, 1988). See also F. L. Schmidt and J. E. Hunter, "Development of a General Solution to the Problem of Validity Generalization," *Journal of Applied Psychology* 62 (1977): 529–40. Alternative validity generalization procedures have been presented in J. C. Callender and H. G. Osburn, "Development and Test of a New Model for Validity Generalization," *Journal of Applied Psychology* 65 (1980): 543–58; and N. S. Raju and M. J. Burke, "Two New Procedures for Studying Validity Generalization," *Journal of Applied Psychology* 68 (1983): 382–95.

23. G. V. Glass coined the term *meta-analysis* to refer to the statistical analysis of the findings of many individual studies in an article titled "Primary, Secondary, and Meta-Analysis of Research," *Educational Researcher* 5 (1976): 3–8. Although numerous articles and books are beginning to be written on the subject of meta-analysis (of which validity generalization can be considered a subset), two original and frequently cited texts in this area are G. V. Glass, B. McGaw, and M. L. Smith, *Meta-Analysis in Social Research* (Beverly Hills, Calif.: Sage, 1981); and J. E. Hunter, F. L. Schmidt, and G. Jackson, *Meta-Analysis: Cumulating Research Findings Across Settings* (Beverly Hills, Calif.: Sage, 1982).

24. P. Cattin, "Estimations of the Predictive Power of a Regression Model," *Journal of Applied Psychology* 65 (1980): 407–14; J. G. Claudy, "Multiple Regression and Validity Estimation in One Sample," *Applied Psychological Measurement* 2 (1978): 595–607; K. R. Murphy, "Cost-Benefit Considerations in Choosing among Cross-Validation Methods," *Personnel Psychology* 37 (1984): 15–22.

25. The selection ratio refers to a population parameter representing the proportion of successful applicants or, more specifically, the proportion of individuals in the population scoring above a cutting score. Typically, the selection ratio is equated with the hiring rate (a sample description), which can lead to errors. For a discussion of the distinction between the terms *selection ratio* and *hiring rate*, see R. A. Alexander, G. V. Barrett, and D. Doverspike, "An Explication of the Selection Ratio and Its Relationship to Hiring Rate," *Journal of Applied Psychology* 68 (1983): 342–44.

26. H. C. Taylor and J. T. Russell, "The Relationship of Validity Coefficients to the Practical Validity of Tests in Selection: Discussion and Tables," *Journal of Applied Psychology* 23 (1939): 565–78.

27. J. Tiffin and E. J. McCormick, *Industrial Psychology*, 5th ed. (Englewood Cliffs, N.J.: Prentice-Hall, 1965).

28. H. E. Brogden, "On the Interpretation of the Correlation Coefficient as a Measure of Predictive Efficiency," *Journal of Educational Psychology* 37 (1946): 65–76; H. E. Brogden, "When Testing Pays Off," *Personnel Psychology* 2 (1949): 171–83. At a later point, the cost of testing was incorporated into the equations developed by Brogden in L. J. Cronbach and G. Gleser, *Psychological Tests and Personnel Decisions* (Urbana: University of Illinois Press, 1965).

29. See B. D. Steffy and S. Maurer, "Conceptualizing and Measuring the Economic Effectiveness of Human Resource Activities," *Academy of Management Review* 13 (1988): 271–86, for a presentation of alternative approaches to evaluating the economic impact of PHRM programs. See also J. W. Boudreau, "Decision Theory Contributions to HRM Research and Practice," *Industrial Relations* 23 (1984): 198–217; and J. W. Boudreau and C. J. Berger, "Decision-Theoretic Utility Analysis Applied to Employee Separations and Acquisitions," *Journal of Applied Psychology* 70 (1985): 581–612. Also, discussions of why decision-theoretic utility equations were not widely applied relating to (1) the belief that data did not fit the assumptions of the equations, (2) difficulty in estimating equation components, and (3) the inability to generalize validity coefficients are presented in J. E. Hunter and F. L. Schmidt, "Fitting People to Jobs: The Impact of Personnel Selection on National Productivity," in *Human Performance and Productivity*, vol. 1, *Human Capacity Assessment*, ed. M. D. Dunnette and E. O. Fleishman (Hillsdale, N.J.: Erlbaum, 1982); and F. L. Schmidt, J. E. Hunter, R. C. McKenzie, and T. W. Muldrow, "The Impact of Valid Selection Procedures on Work-Force Productivity," *Journal of Applied Psychology* 64 (1979): 609–26.

30. For more information on the economic components of this equation, see J. W. Boudreau. A study that has employed this full equation and provides useful information for estimating the economic components as well as the true validity coefficients is presented in M. J. Burke and J. T. Frederick, "A Comparison of Economic Utility Estimates for Alternative SD_y Estimation Procedures," *Journal of Applied Psychology* 71 (1986): 334–39.

31. J. E. Hunter and R. F. Hunter, "Validity and Utility of Alternative Predictors of Job Performance," *Psychological Bulletin* 96 (1984): 72–98.

32. R. J. Niehaus, *Computer-Assisted Human Resources Planning* (New York: Wiley, 1979), 222.

33. For summaries of research related to adaptive testing via the computer, see D. J. Weiss, "Improving Measurement Quality and Efficiency with Adaptive Testing," *Applied Psychological Measurement* 6 (1982): 473–92.

34. J. B. Sympson, D. J. Weiss, and M. J. Ree, *Predictive Validity of Conventional and Adaptive Tests in an Air Force Training Environment* (AFHRL 81–40), Brooks Air Force Base, Tex., Manpower and Personnel Division, Air Force Human Relations Laboratory.

35. C. L. Hulin, F. Drasgow, and C. K. Parsons, *Item Response Theory: Application to Psychological Measurement* (Homewood, Ill.: Dorsey, 1983).

36. For a critique of the espoused benefits and problems associated with not only adaptive testing but also computerized psychological testing in general, see M. J. Burke and J. Normand, "Computerized Psychological Testing: An Overview and Critique," *Professional Psychology*, 3(1987): 42–51.

37. V. W. Urry, "Tailored Testing: A Successful Application of Latent Trait Theory," *Journal of Educational Measurement* 14 (1977): 181–96.

38. D. R. Budgell, "Preliminary Analysis of the Feasibility of Computerized Adaptive Testing and Item Banking in the Public Service," unpublished report, Public Service Commission, Ottawa, Canada, 1982.

39. L. S. Kleiman and R. H. Faley, "The Implications of Professional and Legal Guidelines for Court Decisions Involving Criterion-Related Validity: A Review and Analysis," *Personnel Psychology* 38 (1985): 803–33. See also the January 1987 issue of *Personnel Administrator* for a series of articles on how recent court decisions have affected management policy.

40. R. J. Bies, and D. L. Shapiro, "Voice and Justification: Their Influence on Procedural Fairness Judgments," *Academy of Management Journal* 31 (1988): 676–85; J. Greenberg, "A Taxonomy of Organizational Justice Theories," *Academy of Management Review* 12 (1987): 9–22; J. Greenberg, "Reactions to Procedural Injustice in Payment Distributions: Do the Means Justify the Ends?" *Journal of Applied Psychology* 72 (1987) 55–61.

41. L. Greenhalgh, A. T. Lawrence, and R. I. Sutton, "Determinants of Work Force Reduction Strategies in Declining Organizations," *Academy of Mangement Review* 13 (1988): 241–54; A. Nahavandi and A. R. Malekzadeh, "Acculturation in Mergers and Acquisitions," *Academy of Management Review* 13(1988): 79–90.

42. J. Brockner, "The Effects of Work Layoffs on Survivors: Research, Theory, and Practice," in vol. 10, ed. B. M. Staw and L. L.Cummings (Greenwich, Conn.: JAI Press, 1988), *Research in Organizational Behavior) 213–55;* J. Brockner, S. L. Grover, and M. D. Blonder, "Predictors of Survivors' Job Involvement Following Layoffs: A Field Study," *Journal of Applied Psychology* 73 (1988): 436–42; J. Brockner, S. Grover, T. Reed, R. DeWitt, and M. Malley, "Survivors' Reactions to Layoffs: We Get By With a Little Help for Our Friends," *Administrative Science Quarterly* 32 (1987): 526–4.

43. For a discussion of these types of measures, see E. J. Webb, D. T. Campbell, R. D. Schwarts, and L. Sechrest, *Unobstrusive Measures: Nonreactive Research in the Social Sciences* (Chicago: Rand McNally, 1972). See also G. R. Oldham and J. R. Hackman, "Work Design in the Organizational Context," in *Research in Organizational Behavior*, vol. 2, ed. B. M. Staw and L. L. Cummings (Greenwich, Conn.: JAI Press, 1980), 247–78; and comments by G. R. Oldham at the National Academy of Management symposium entitled "Personnel Programs for Productivity and QWL Improvements," 1982, New York."

44. M. T. Matteson and J. M. Ivancevich, "Organizational Stressors and Heart Disease: A Research Model," *Academy of Management Journal* 4 (1979): 347–57; R. S. Schuler, "Definition and Conceptualization of Stress in Organizations," *Organizational Behavior and Human Performance* (Apr. 1980): 184–215.

45. Although categorized here as objective data, performance data can often suffer from many subjective rating errors, as described in Chapters 6 and 7.

46. For a series of articles on corporate cultures, see the special January 1986 issue of *Personnel Administrator*.

47. "Labor Letter" *Wall Street Journal*, 4 Dec. 1985, p. 25.

48. E. J. Bernetisn, "Employee Attitude Surveys: Perception vs. Reality," *Personnel Journal* (Apr. 1981): 300–305; R. B. Dunham and F. J. Smith, *Organizational Survey* (Glenview, Ill.: Scott, Foresman, 1979); W. Martin, "What Management Can Expect from an Employee Attitude Survey," *Personnel Administrator* (July 1981): 75–79, 87.

49. Dunham and Smith, *Organizational Surveys*, 13.

50. For an extensive discussion of these relationships, see R. S. Schuler, " A Role and Expectancy Perception Model of Participation in Decision Making," *Academy of Management Journal* 23 (1980): 331–50; and M. Van Sell, A. P. Brief, and R. S. Schuler, "Role Conflict and Role Ambiguity: Integration of the Literature and Directions for Future Research," *Human Relations* 34 (1980): 43–72.

51. For a helpful discussion of what a proper, professionally designed survey should look like, as well as a presentation of the functions (e.g., employee development, assessment of change, a management audit) a well-designed survey serves in contributing to the overall planning process, see D. R. York, "Attitude Surveying," *Personnel Journal* (May 1985): 70–73. Some words of caution about misinterpreting attitude survey data are offered in R.C. Ernest and L. B. Baenen, "Analysis of Attitude Survey Results: Getting the Most from the Data," *Personnel Administrator* (May 1985): 71–80.

Summary Cases

NORTHEAST DATA RESOURCES, INC.

PEOPLES TRUST COMPANY

**THE TALL PINES HOTEL AND
CONFERENCE CENTER**

Northeast Data Resources, Inc.*

George Wellington closed the door behind him and slumped into his desk chair with an air of resignation. He had just returned from a meeting of the Executive Committee of Northeast Data Resources where personnel layoffs had been decided upon. As director of personnel at NDR, he realized that he would be responsible for both developing the process by which the layoffs would take place and assisting the managers responsible for the actual implementation. It wasn't a pleasant task, particularly in light of the human resources program that he had begun to implement over the past four years.

Wellington pulled out a pad of paper from the top desk drawer and began to scribble notes. He had found that in times of pressure it was best to get some perspective on the situation before taking action. The drastic character of this situation required a review of the growth of Northeast Data Resources from its inception in 1969 to the present. It was the first crisis the young company had been forced to face.

BACKGROUND OF THE COMPANY

In 1969, four young engineers formed a partnership to form the basis of NDR. Three of them had worked for a large, national data-processing company. They had recognized the high potential in the computer industry particularly for a product which filled a vital need in this growing field. Another engineer working

---

*This case was prepared by D. Jeffrey Lenn, The George Washington University. It is not meant to be an example of effective or ineffective PHRM but an example for teaching and discussion purposes.

in a research program with a large university was asked to join them because of his expertise in the computer field.

Jack Logan was the prime mover of the new company. He had been working for nearly five years on a project within the large company to develop ways to protect its computer systems from being copied by competitors. The primary objective in this project was to ensure that a customer would have to purchase the entire system rather than being able to make use of a number of different systems. Jack saw the opportunity to sell a service to customers that would do just the opposite—provide a mechanism that would link various competing systems into an integrated unit.

He and a colleague, Charlie Bonner, developed a "black box" which had the capacity to connect at least two types of computer systems already on the market. They had worked in Jack's basement over a two-year period to perfect this instrument. Another six months of testing found that it was very effective. The two other engineers had begun to work with them in order to expand the box to tie together three other systems with which they had experience.

The four men decided to strike out on their own and found that their innovation and daring paid off. The first two years were both exhilarating and demanding. NDR subcontracted the production of the black box to a small manufacturing company while the partners divided responsibilities between marketing and continuing research. Jack and Charlie carried the marketing and organizational functions while George Miller and Al Grant worked to streamline the instrument itself.

Early success in securing contracts with some key customers and fears about loss of the exclusive information about the unpatented invention led to a decision to go into full production. An old plant was leased and renovated and workers were hired to begin the process of building the black box for distribution. Within two years the company had grown from four partners to nearly 100 people. By 1979 NDR had expanded to about 700 people and had become the focus of attention for a number of investors. The invention, now dubbed Omega I, had become a product competitors emulated but with little success.

Logan assumed the responsibilities of chairman and president with Bonner as executive vice-president in charge of operations. Miller and Grant stayed in the lab with more interest in research and development, being willing to act more in advisory capacity on managerial decisions.

Logan saw the need to consolidate and expand the overall operations of the company. Production and distribution now overflowed into three buildings separated by nearly ten miles. He negotiated a contract with the economic development committee of Newbury, a New England town about 40 miles away, to help construct a new building to house headquarters and plant. The town agreed to help NDR through reduced taxes, water, and sewage hookups at a minimal charge, arrangements with local banks to secure a loan for construction of the plant, and development of a federal grant to train new workers at the plant. In exchange NDR agreed to move its entire operation to Newbury within the next two years. It helped Newbury in its search for new industry while assuring NDR of a secure base of operations for the future.

The Newbury headquarters was only 40 miles from the old facilities so NDR lost few of its present staff because of the change. But the growth in business demanded an increase in personnel. Engineers with sophisticated skills in computer science were hired to expand the system capability. Often, international engineers were the only ones available and the importation of English and

Australians with a spattering of Europeans gave an international flair to the small company. New factory workers from Newbury and surrounding towns were hired so that the production shifts could be expanded from one to two. The training grants secured by the town helped to equip new workers and the integration with more experienced workers moved smoothly. Empty managerial slots required hiring from the outside mostly. A new vice-president of manufacturing came from a large industrial company in the Midwest. The new vice-president of finance had a solid resume which included most recently financial experience with a large conglomerate but before that two stints with growing companies much like NDR. The staffing of the growing company proceeded professionally.

FUTURE OF THE COMPANY

The phenomenal growth of NDR in old industrial New England rivaled the computer companies developing in California's Silicon Valley. The workforce had evolved from 4 in 1969 to 100 in 1971, 700 in 1976 and 1,350 by 1982. Sales increased from two small initial contracts in 1969 of $75,000 to nearly $20 million by 1982. The opening price of 7 moved to between 8 and 9 and hovered there in 1981. But a feature article in a national stock advisory report about NDR led to an upward move in the summer in 1982 to 15. Even without paying a dividend in its 13 years of existence, it had become an attractive investment.

Logan had taken time during the summer of 1982 to begin the process of strategic planning. Convinced that he and his executive committee could and should do this alone, he decided not to engage outside consultants to develop a costly set of plans. His projection was that the computer industry would grow nearly ten times in size over the next decade. Conservatively the company could expect to hold its share of the market which meant a doubling of sales in five years to $40 million and up to $70 million by 1992. Expansion was the key to maintaining market share and holding its own against the handful of competitors which had begun to appear by 1982.

In shaping the strategy, Logan began to map out a new marketing plan which would guarantee NDR's position in the national market instead of the eastern market alone. He saw new customer possibilities in the fields of insurance, financial institutions and state and local governments. He negotiated an option to buy the factory of a watch company moving South. Its building was about 35 miles away in the heart of another old industrial New England town with a pool of skilled workers available to be retrained. He began to develop some ideas about how many new staff would be needed and the kind of capital necessary to finance this expansion.

GEORGE WELLINGTON'S CAREER AT NDR

George stopped his writing and reviewed the rapid growth of NDR up to this point. He remembered vividly his first few months at the company in 1977. He had moved to a nearby town to retire in the serenity of New England. His career had begun immediately after completing his MBA from a leading eastern university where he had concentrated on management and personnel. He had begun work in the personnel area with a major corporation located in New York. Six years in the field had led him next into marketing and then strategic planning with another company. The last seven years had been with a prestigious consulting firm in New York where he had focused on a variety of problems for a host of clients. His decision to retire had been prompted by a dislike for traveling and a desire to settle down in the area where his children had located.

While retirement continued to bring part-time consulting work, George still found the travel excessive. But his ideas of relaxation in retirement quickly exposed his own need to be fully active in business to be happy. His search for a part-time job was successful as Jack Logan met him at a Chamber of Commerce luncheon in Newbury and hired him as a consultant to help with the transition from the old to the new facilities. He remembered the challenges associated with coordinating not only the efforts of NDR personnel but outside contractors and town officials as well.

The flawless nature of the transition into the new plant made the president recognize that he needed George full-time. Wellington agreed to stay only another six months as a special assistant to Logan. He carried out a variety of projects for Logan and quickly became an integral part of the management team at NDR.

The president called in George one day and showed him an organization chart which he was reworking. "George, I know that your six months are nearly up but I need you around here on a permanent basis. I just don't know where to put you on this chart. How about becoming director of Personnel for NDR? That is the only important position which we haven't filled here in the past few months and it would allow me to have you close at hand for help on those big decisions."

George asked for some time to think through his decision and within a week agreed to a full-time position. While Logan still saw Personnel as a somewhat unnecessary staff function, there would be a chance for George to help him understand the importance of human resources to this company.

Wellington began immediately to develop a plan for human resources at NDR. Logan encouraged him but wasn't excited about the use of the term "human resources." "I don't understand why you have to complicate this whole business of Personnel with a new name. Why not still use the old 'Personnel' for the department?" Logan asked. George saw a futile battle in this naming process so he clearly defined his function as that of director of Personnel.

His plan for that function at NDR had three major elements:

1. **The Program**

   ■ *Gathering employee information*
   He had his staff develop a file on each employee with a record of hiring date, previous experience and employers, salary, job title, etc. This was stored in a computer so that he could have rapid recall for evaluation.

   ■ *Performance appraisal system*
   He developed a new appraisal system which incorporated a three-page form to be completed twice a year by immediate supervisors. The annual review was tied to salary and bonus decisions. He experimented with it in two engineering sections over a two-year period and then was able to get Logan to mandate it for all of NDR beginning in 1981. The results from the 1981–82 year were compiled and filed for future use.

   ■ *Personnel policy manual*
   In 1981, a new personnel policy manual was developed that detailed the policies and procedures as well as benefits for all personnel at NDR. There

was some initial negative reaction by those who had enjoyed a variety of benefits from the early days of the company. But the imprint of Logan on the manual quelled the complaints and ensured uniformity in the policies.

■ *EEO and Affirmative Action (AA) program*

The highly technical character of the NDR business and its presence in a small New England town made both EEO and AA difficult to pursue. A visit to Wellington by an EEO field investigator regarding the case of a former worker led him to move quickly to formulate this program. The data was gathered on minority hiring and promotion and then a plan designed for increasing the percentage of minorities in all categories and the number of women in management in particular. Logan resisted the immediate implementation of the program with the argument that the Reagan administration would soft-pedal civil rights in employment so that business people did not need to worry. George accepted this decision with reluctance but got an agreement to update the plan periodically as well as pursue informally a goal of more integration of the workforce.

■ *Management development program*

The rapid growth of NDR created many new managerial positions. Hiring from the outside became one method by which to increase the number of managers, but George believed that the key to the company's future lay in developing them from within. He negotiated a contract with a professor of management at a local university to design and teach a course in management for selected employees. George and the professor team-taught a six-week course for 20 middle level managers in 1980. Its success led to an offering three times a year to both managers and potential managers.

2. **The Staff**

George became director of personnel in the spring of 1979. He selected four professionals and two secretaries to work with him. Two professionals came from outside of NDR and two from within. All four had human resources management experience but needed more training. One was encouraged to enter an MBA program on a part-time basis with a concentration on human resource management. The other three were sent to local and national seminars to upgrade skills and understanding in the various areas of HRM. But at the heart of their training was George Wellington, drawing on his vast experience and encouraging his younger colleagues to learn through experimentation and discussion.

3. **The Office Location**

The final design of the NDR headquarters had not been decided when George became a consultant to the project so he had taken primary responsibility for the design of the corporate office area. Later, as director of personnel, he negotiated some changes in the office assignments so that personnel was located at one of the major entrances and exits of the building. It was a primary thoroughfare for engineers and managerial personnel arriving in the morning and leaving at night. It was also a stop along the way to the new cafeteria that had just opened.

George had chosen this location for a reason. He felt that human resources departments must have high visibility and availability. Being in the middle of a key thoroughfare allowed people to recognize the central function of personnel in the operation of NDR. It encouraged questions about policies and procedures. It also gave the HRM staff the chance to get to know all of the managers and professionals within a short period of time. This provided instant recognition and a capacity to deal with problems on a much more personal basis. George himself was always at his desk working before most of the staff arrived and usually left after 6:00 P.M. This gave him considerable visibility with managerial personnel who often worked late.

The images of the first few years were succeeded by thoughts about the past two months with his staff. He had begun to engage them in the planning process by asking them to think about NDR for the next five years. He had sketched out the growth projections of Logan and then provided some parameters within which to think about staffing. Each of his professional staff was to develop a short presentation on four consequences for HRM:

1. Impact on the size of our workforce
2. Impact on the mix of skills needed in the workforce
3. Impact on the recruitment efforts from outside NDR and development efforts from within
4. Impact on the working conditions within the company itself, both physically and organizationally

The first meeting four weeks ago had produced some very good reports. With one exception, the four had done a lot of homework and some imaginative thinking about the future with regard to how HRM plan would fit into the NDR overall strategic plan. George had collated and refined the projections and re-distributed them to the professional staff asking for further thought and more specific targets for the next five years. He asked for input for his own report to the president, which he had hoped would be ready by December 1982.

THE PRESENT DILEMMA

That work had now come to an abrupt halt although he had not alerted the staff to the discussion taking place within the executive committee until the day before. Logan's projections about the future had been overly optimistic.

Two weeks ago, Logan had asked George to meet him at 8:00 P.M. He laid out a report on the results from the first quarter of this fiscal year and then a chart which traced the sales of the last nine quarters. The last two quarters showed a significant decline. Logan indicated to George that, "The decline is now a trend and not simply a blip on the screen as I had thought." The loss of five key contracts totaling nearly $3 million dollars over the past six months plus the entry of a new competitor in the southeastern market had been responsible for the dramatic sales drop. At the same time, profits had suffered as well because of the increased expenses from a decision to increase the size of the engineering and financial service departments. The president admitted that his projections had been too optimistic and that something had to be done immediately. The cash flow problem had emerged as the most important pressure in this situation. The budget had to be pared while efforts to increase revenue were intensified.

George studied the figures carefully and agreed reluctantly to both the con-clusions and recommendations reached by Logan. The two men took some time to sort through the various options available but it always came back to drastic cuts in personnel. He urged Logan to call a meeting of the executive committee in the morning and provide the data to them with encouragement to diagnose the problem and solutions to it. He argued that any solution must be a product of consensus of the committee.

The meeting caught everybody by surprise as they had accepted the president's projections of growth despite a temporary decline in sales. Two weeks of intensive debate among the executives led to the meeting this morning which defined the exact personnel cuts to be made. It was agreed that 25 engineers, 50 production personnel (workers and supervisors), and 25 others from various departments would be laid off within the next two weeks. In addition, 15 new marketing and sales personnel would be added as soon as possible to carry out a new marketing thrust aimed at a different market segment.

There had been heated discussion about the exact number to be laid off and hired with considerable friction between the vice-presidents of production, engineering, and marketing. The blame for the crisis was shouldered by Logan who asked that the executives recognize that they had to work together to resolve this problem if the future of NDR was to be assured. Wellington as the director of personnel was given the task of coordinating the identification of the people to be laid off although the actual decision would rest in the hands of the three vice-presidents. There were no criteria for the decisions although all agreed that loyal and trusted employees who had been with NDR for a number of years should be released only as a last resort.

THE DIRECTOR'S RESPONSIBILITY

The acrimonious debate of the morning still echoed in George's ears that afternoon. He tore the pages on which he had been writing off the pad and began a new one as he started to determine how the layoffs should be handled. It was a far cry from the exuberance with which he had begun the process of developing a five-year human resource plan just two months ago. Cutbacks in personnel demanded the same precision and careful thought in planning and action as hiring and promotion. There was less excitement about retrenching than growing because it affected the livelihood of so many people.

George jotted down the important questions in three different areas as he mapped out his thinking on this problem.

1. **The Layoffs**

   ■ Criteria to be used?
   ■ Data available on employees?
   ■ Impact of EEO and AA on decisions?
   ■ Severance pay and benefits?
   ■ Procedure for layoffs?

2. **The New Hires**

   ■ Skills needed in marketing and sales?
   ■ Available resources for positions?
   ■ Salary and benefit package?
   ■ Procedure for hiring?

3. **The HRM Plan**

   ■ Immediate impact on HRM five-year plan?
   ■ What if only temporary reversal of growth trend? (commitments to rehire or not?)
   ■ Impact on employee morale now and in future?

George recognized that he had a lot of work to do. He struggled to regain his sense of professionalism as he began to detail the options available to each of the questions. His days as a consultant and manager had given him little experience in the arena of layoffs. But Logan had given him the responsibility and he knew that the future of NDR would depend heavily on how it handled this crisis.

Peoples Trust Company*

The Peoples Trust Company first opened its doors to the public on June 1, 1875, with a total salaried staff of eight members: a treasurer; a secretary; and six assistants (three of whom held the positions of day watchman, night watchman, and messenger). Located in a large, midwestern city, the original company had occupied the basement floor of a new five-story office building with an electric-bell system, steam heat, and steam-driven elevator.

During its early years, the Trust Company had concentrated its activities on providing vault services to its customers for the safekeeping of tangible items and securities. Management had been able to develop the reputation of being a highly conservative trust company that concentrated on a relatively small and select market of wealthy individuals from the local area. In the years following, the vault service had been retained as an accommodation to its customers, but the company's emphasis had slowly shifted from vault service to a wider range of banking and trust services.

Until the early 1900s, banking services had overshadowed trust services in terms of asset volume. Following the turn of the century, trust assets had begun to grow at an increasing rate. Over the years, the company had been able to achieve an impressive record of sound and steady growth. According to a story often told in banking circles: "Peoples Trust was so conservative that they prospered even during the Depression!"

In 1963, with the appointment of a new president, a new era began for Peoples Trust Company. Between 1963 and 1978, trust assets under supervision rose by $145 million, while deposits increased by more than $20 million in savings deposits.

---

*This case was prepared by Hrach Bedrosian and is used here with his permission.

Accompanying this recent growth has been the company's desire to fashion a new image for itself. In 1979, Mr. Robert Toller assumed the presidency of Peoples Trust. In 1982, he remarked: ". . . it should be said that the old concept of a trust involving merely the regular payment of income and preservation of capital is largely obsolete." Accordingly, the Investment Division of the company had been expanded and strengthened. Similar changes had been effected in the Trust and Estate Administrative Group and other customer services. Among these were the improvement of accounting methods and procedures, the installation of electronic data processing systems, and complete renovation of the company's eight-floor building and facilities. Most recently, the company has extended its services into the field of management consulting. This had been acknowledged as a "pioneer" step for a banking institution. The president recently characterized the company as "an organization in the fiduciary business."

At the time these data were gathered, the company had a total of 602 employees. Of this number, 109 were in what is considered the "officer-group"* positions of the company. The company's relations with its employees over the years have been satisfactory, the People Trust is generally recognized by city residents and those in suburban areas as a good place to work. The company hires most of its employees from the local area.

In the period before 1980 Peoples Trust had provided satisfactory advancement opportunities for its employees, and it had been possible for a young, high-school graduate who showed promise on the job to work his way up gradually to officer status. Graduates of banking institutions were also sought for employment with the company. Ordinarily individuals were considered eligible for promotion to the jobs above them after they had thoroughly mastered the details of their present positions.

Prior to 1980 the total staff of the company was small enough so that there was no need to prepare official organization charts or job descriptions. Virtually all of the employees knew each other on a first-name basis, and they were generally familiar with each other's area of job responsibility. New employees were rapidly able to learn "whom you had to go to for what."

In 1980 the company management called in an outside consultant to appraise its organizational structure and operations and to confer on the rapid expansion and diversification of banking services that the company had planned. The presence of the consultants and the subsequent preparation of organization charts and job descriptions reportedly "shook up a lot of people"—many feared loss of their jobs or, at least, substantial changes in the nature of work and assignments. However, there was little overt reaction among the officer-level employees in terms of turnover and/or other indices of unrest.

Over the years it had been the policy of the company to pay wages that were at least average or a little above the average paid by comparable banking organizations in the area. This, combined with favorable employee relations and the stable and prestigious nature of the work, resulted in a low turnover of personnel. The bulk of employee turnover occurred among the younger employees who filled clerical positions throughout the company's various departments.

Since 1980, the personnel picture at Peoples Trust has been shifting. Several changes have taken place in the top management of the company. By adding

---

*Membership in the officer group is determined by an employee's being legally empowered to represent the company in a transaction.

several new customer services, the company has altered the very nature of its business. This has resulted in a trend toward "professionalization" of many of the officer-level positions in that these positions now require individuals with higher levels of education and broader abilities. The impact of these changes on current employees has been a matter of concern to several executives in the company, particularly to Mr. John Moore, Manager of the Organization Planning and Personnel Department. Mr. Moore described his picture of the situation to the researcher as follows:

Interview with John Moore, V.P., Organization Planning and Personnel

Our problem here is one of a changing image and along with it the changing of people. As a trust company, we had no other ties with an individual's financial needs . . . we could only talk in terms of death. We wanted to be able to talk in terms of life, so we got active in the investment-advisory business.

The old wealth around here is pretty well locked up, so we wanted to provide services to new and growing organizations and to individuals who are accumulating wealth. Our problem is one of reorientation. We used to provide one service for one customer. We now want to enter new ventures, offer new services, attract new customers. The problem has become one of how to make the change . . . do we have the talent and the people to make the change?

We have a "band" of people (see Exhibit C.1, C.2, and note opposite) in our organization . . . in the 35-50 age group who came in under the old hiring practices and ground rules. Given the new directions in which our company is moving and the changing job requirements, it's clear that, considering their current qualifications and capabilities, these individuals have nowhere to go. Some have been able to accept this; and this acceptance includes watching others move past them. Others have difficulty accepting it . . . a few have left . . . and we haven't discouraged anyone from leaving. For those who can't accept it, there is the problem of integrating their career strategy with ours. We've articulated our objectives clearly; now individuals need clarification of their own strategies.

As I see it, change caught up with these individuals. They had on-the-job training in their own areas, but that doesn't help them much to cope with the new demands. New functional areas are being melded on top of old ones. For example, marketing is new; so is electronic data processing. They both require qualities that our existing employee staff didn't have.

To date, we have not approached any of these people in an individual way to discuss their problems with them. Our objectives are to further develop these people, but we'll first have to get the support of the department managers who supervise them.

We want to find ways to further develop personnel of the kind represented by this group through a variety of approaches. I am thinking here not only of formal job training in management development, but also of management techniques that would help individuals identify new kinds of qualifications or possible new standards of performance they must take into consideration in planning their own personal growth.

Note: Mr. Moore drew from his files a list of ten individuals who he felt were representative of the group whose lack of appropriate experience or qualifications created a road block to their future development and advancement with the company. These individuals are described in Exhibit C.1.

EXHIBIT
C.1

Name	Age	Education	Date of Hire	Positions Held
Linda Horn	37	2-year technical institute of business administration	1975	Messenger Clearance clerk Accounting clerk Unit head (working supervisor) Section head (supervisor)
Richard Gaul*	30	2-year junior college program in business administration	1977	Business machines operator Section head (supervisor) Operations officer
Fred James	35	B.A. Degree local university American Institute of Banking	1976	Loan clerk Teller Accounting unit head (working supervisor) Section head (supervisor)
Fran Wilson*	35	1 year at local university	1981	Methods analyst Operations unit head (working supervisor) Systems Programmer Property accounting dept. head
Martin Pfieffer*	32	Prep School	1977	Messenger Accounting clerk Section head (supervisor) Department head
James Klinger	38	B.A. Degree from local university	1972	Messenger Accounting clerk Records clerk Unit head (working supervisor) Administrative specialist
Karen Kissler*	35	B.A. Degree from local university co-op program	1974	Messenger Real property specialist Assistant estate officer
Charles Ferris	42	2-year jr. college program in business administration American Institute Banking	1962	Messenger Deposit accounting section head (supervisor) Unit head (working supervisor)
William Jagger	54	High School	1949	Messenger Trust liaison clerk Accounting clerk Bookkeeping section head
Thomas Geoghigan*	42	2-year jr. college program in business administration	1969	Messenger Securities accountant Property custodian Office manager Assistant operations officer

* = Officer

EXHIBIT C.2   Peoples Trust Company Organization Chart (June 1983)

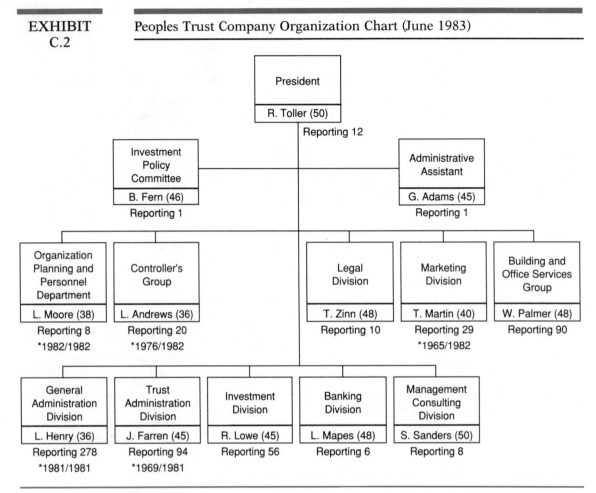

Note: Numbers in parentheses indicate manager's age. These are included for planning purposes only. Numbers below each position indicate number of subordinates.

*Indicates year in which manager joined the Company and year in which he assumed current position. For example, Mr. Larry Andrews joined Peoples Trust Company in 1976, and became Controller in 1982.

We also have to find ways to provide more opportunities for minorities and women in the organization, particularly at the officer level. Although Peoples Trust is not a federal contractor, we would like to be seen as and be an affirmative action employer and an organization where everyone has an equal chance for employment and promotion.

We have to change the conditioning of old times throughout the company. A recently hired MBA is now an officer. Years ago that couldn't have happened so rapidly. And not everyone here is in agreement that the appointment I just mentioned *should* have happened the way it did. We have to develop support in our company for the new recruiting image.

There are two things which really concern me most about this whole problem:

1. We have a problem in under-utilization of resources.
2. There is a problem which is presented to the growth and development of the company in having some of the individuals I have been discussing settled into key spots.

The company really bears the responsibility for the current situation as I described it. In addition, what this all means to me is that our personnel function may change considerably over the coming year.

After this interview with Mr. Moore, the researcher talked with other company executives to learn their views of the problems outlined by Mr. Moore. The findings from these interviews are presented below.

Interview with Fred Bellows—Human Resource Planning

Historically we have been conservatively managed . . . you might say "ultra-conservatively." But now we want to change that image. Several years ago there was a revolution in top management. In 1979, Mr. Toller took over and brought in young people, many not from the banking field but from other types of business and consulting organizations. Our employment philosophy may be stated as follows: "We want above-average people . . . for above-average pay . . . and we want to give them a chance to learn and grow and move with the organization." This applies mainly to those in whom we see management-level potential.

They are told in their employment interview that if they don't see opportunity with us, then they should leave. This is in contrast to the old philosophy that this is a secure place to work, that you can stay here by keeping your nose clean, and that you can sit and wait for pot luck to become a trust officer.

Many people are caught in this changing philosophy. A case in the Trust Administration Division is a good example. There we have an employee in a Grade 10 job who has been with the bank eight years. We just hired a new person out of college who we put in that same Grade 10. Now they're both at the same level, but they're entirely different people in terms of education, social background, etc.

Now the Head of our Trust Division bucks this sort of thing. She argues that we don't need all "stars" in the company. Yet, the president wants young, dynamic individuals who can develop and be developed. So I'm trying to get the Trust Division to define: what does the job really require?

We have a number of people with two years of accounting training who have been with the company anywhere from six to nine years. Under our old system they'd be okay, but under the new system they're not. They're not realistic about their future. Our problem is that we're being honest, but few are getting the message.

We bring in a new individual . . . ask others to train that person . . . and then promote that person over their heads. We have people whose jobs we could get done for a lot less money. When, if ever, do we tell them to go elsewhere?

Interview with Larry Andrews—Controller

There is no question but that there has been a complete revolution around here. In the past, we were in business to serve the community; to handle small accounts; to help the small investor who needed investment service. Our motto was "help anyone who needs help." Our employees were geared to this kind of work orientation and felt at home with it. They could easily identify themselves with this sort of approach to doing business. Most people were quite comfortable; their personal goals coincided with the company goal.

But we found that we couldn't make any money conducting this kind of business. So, we've had to extend our services to attract people who have money and can afford our service. Now the company goal has changed. For example, the Trust Department is now concerned with the management of property in general. The "dead man's bank" has become the "live people's service organization." So we've had to create a kind of snob appeal that too many of our people can't identify with or don't believe in.

Many problems have emerged from these changes. Before, individuals' knowledge of the details of their jobs was their greatest asset. They worked to develop that knowledge and protected it. Now—and I'm speaking of supervisory jobs—the important factor is to have some familiarity with the work but to be able to work with people; to get others to do the detail. Too many of our people still don't understand this. . . .

The route to the top is no longer clear. Over a five-year period this organization has changed. There have been reorganizations, new functions created, and some realignment of existing functions. Many who felt they had a clear line to something higher in the organization now find that that "something" isn't there anymore.

We've had lots of hiring-in at higher levels. Many old-timers have been bypassed. In some cases, the new, outside hirees came into jobs that never existed before, or were hired into a job that had previously existed, but which is now a "cut" above what it was before. What used to be a top job is now a second or third spot.

What we need now are people who are "professional managers"—by that I mean a supervisor versus a technical specialist. Years ago supervision could be concentrated in a few key individuals . . . but in the past five years we've grown 20% to 30% and have a management hierarchy. A person used to be able to grow up as a technical specialist and develop managerial skills secondarily.

To a small extent it's a matter of personality too. We have a new president, and what is acceptable to him differs from what was acceptable to his predecessor. There's a new mix of personal favoritism that goes along with the new vogue. Technical specialists are "low need" as far as the company is concerned. I estimate we now have about 30 people in this category in officer-level jobs.

Interview with Tom Martin—Marketing Division Head

There have been many changes over the past six years. Mr. Toller took a look at the entire organization . . . and then hired a consultant to do an organizational study. It was sort of an outside stamp of approval.

His hope was to move some of the dead wood . . . the senior people who were past their peak and didn't represent what the company wanted anymore in its managerial and officer staff. Few of these individuals have the capacity to change, and for others it may already be too late to change. Many had leveled off in their development long before these changes came about, and the changes just made it more apparent. Early retirement has been given to some of those over 60. Others remained as titular head of their departments, but in essence report to a younger person who is really running the department.

Banking used to be a soft industry . . . you were hired and never fired. If you were a poor performer, you were given a lousy job that you could stay at. No one was ever called in and told to shape up. The pay was so poor it attracted people who wanted to work in a sheltered area, and they were satisfied to try and build a career in that area. So it was a job with low pay, high prestige, and some opportunity.

Our biggest problem is to convince people that they are not technicians anymore, that they are to *supervise* their subordinates and work to develop them. Apparently, for many older individuals, and younger ones too, this is an impossible assignment. They can do the jobs themselves, but having anyone else do it in any other way runs against their grain.

If our rate of personnel growth over the next ten years is as fast as the previous ten years, I'm afraid we can only absorb about 50% of our most promising people.

Interview with Jane Farren, Trust Administration Divisions Head

We have several people for whom there is very little opportunity anymore. We just don't see any potential in these people. There are about fifteen of them who are in their 40s and are really not capable of making any independent decisions. We're trying to get them to see other opportunities . . . both inside and outside the company. For example, our Real Estate group was big in the 1960s and 1970s. We're trying to make it important again, and there may be some opportunities in that area.

To give you an idea of the problem we're faced with: One individual is really a personality problem. He's an attorney but he can't get along with others. He wants people to come to him; he focuses on detail too much; and he has great difficulty in telling others what to do and how to do it. He has to do the job all by himself.

Another individual: We gave him a section to supervise but he really hasn't measured up. But, he was the president's pet. I suppose we'll let him continue on . . . he's 57 . . . and then retire him early.

Interview with Mr. L. Henry, General Administration Division

The company has been undergoing basic change. In the past, if people demonstrated technical competence they were promoted, and that was fine while the company was a small, stable group, and everyone knew what the other was thinking. But then, many in the senior group began to retire. With this "changing of the guard" and the growth of the company, many of us have lost communication with our counterparts. Many of us are new in this field, new to this company, and, of course, new to each other. But we recognize this, so half the communication problem is solved. In a sense, we're not constrained by "how it was done before."

My people have reacted to all this change by sitting back and waiting, seeing which way things are going to go, then I guess deciding whether they are going to join you or not. Most of my people are relatively recent employees—as a matter of fact, of the 278 people in my division, only 11 have been with the company more than 10 years. Conversion to EDP will really create a lot of changes in my area.

The Tall Pines Hotel and Conference Center*

Gordon McGregor sorted through his morning mail to find the report from Natalie Sharp about the open house sponsored by the hotel for job applicants. With the sounds of hammering and the smell of fresh paint all around, he was eager to get a picture of his new staff as he neared the opening of the hotel in about two months. He pushed aside samples of carpeting left by a subcontractor this morning to read the five-page report from Natalie.

As hotel manager, Gordon was faced with the last of the major hurdles in getting Tall Pines open—the filling of about 315 positions ranging from bellhops and butchers to clerks and chambermaids. The grand opening scheduled for May first made it imperative to bring his full staff on board and get them trained and operational quickly. He had brought in most of his managerial and supervisory staff over the past six months. Many had come from other hotels in the nationwide chain. Some he had worked with in other parts of the chain in his fifteen years in the system, so there was a sense of excitement about being together as a team to create something brand new. Today marked the beginning of the final phase of his plan to manage his own hotel successfully.

THE TALL PINES HOTEL

Gordon had been involved in the planning of the hotel for about two years. Corporate management had selected the site four years ago on the basis of a

---

*By D. Jeffrey Lenn, School of Government and Business Administration, George Washington University, 1986. This case is based on an actual situation, but the names, location, and other significant data have been altered to provide anonymity. Its purpose is not to focus on effective or ineffective management but to provide a basis for teaching and discussion.

careful study by its market research staff of the southeastern part of the United States. They were interested in launching a new concept in hotels and had chosen the city of Riverton (pop. 95,000), located in the suburbs of Roosevelt City, a major city in the Southeast. The entire metropolitan area had grown dramatically since the early 1960s to a total population of about 1.9 million, with further growth forecast for the next fifteen years before a leveling off would occur.

Riverton comprised about half the area and two-thirds the population of one of the counties that surrounded Roosevelt City. Growth in population, wealth, and industry had been concentrated in the suburban counties, although there was new interest in the revitalization of the old downtown area. Riverton had been especially aggressive in its plan to attract new industry with the creation of an economic development committee, which had been successful in enticing a number of high-technology firms to open offices or build small facilities within the city limits. Many offices had moved from Roosevelt into the suburbs to take advantage of lower taxes, new buildings, and a pool of skilled workers. Shopping centers, restaurants, and housing developments mushroomed to meet the demands of the population shift.

Corporate management saw the opportunity to fill a niche in the suburbs because of lack of hotel and conference space. They purchased an eighteen-acre tract on a major highway that entered Roosevelt City from the south on the west side of Riverton. It was to be developed as a campuslike setting with the preservation of two major pine groves and the expansion of a natural lake. The hotel had been constructed in line with these plans to include 350 rooms, two swimming pools, three restaurants, small shops, and a small exercise and weight room. An outdoor jogging trail was being completed as well. The conference center was built to cater to corporate meetings with secretarial services, teleconferencing facilities, and even access to personal computers. The entire facility was oriented toward comfortable stays of extended periods as well as overnight lodging.

An architect of national reputation had designed the building to become a focal point for the surrounding area. Twin towers jutted through the pines to provide the foundation for a five-story atrium. The glass enclosure provided light and freshness to the restaurants and public space below. The building was striking as viewed from the interstate in both directions, standing boldly against the horizon and rising from the pine groves. Tall Pines was a particularly appropriate name for the entire center, which could act as a comfortable retreat from both city activity and corporate life.

The building had also been controversial. The Riverton Board of Architectural Review was besieged by complaints about the design. But support from the city council and the mayor dissolved the opposition quickly. Projections of a $3.8 million payroll and annual tax bills of $350,000 for the city and $420,000 for the state made the entire project highly appealing. The board voted unanimously to accept the architectural plans.

NATALIE SHARP, DIRECTOR OF PERSONNEL

Last November, Gordon had hired Natalie Sharp to become his director of personnel. She had worked for two other hotel chains after college and then been hired three years ago to help with the opening of a new one-hundred-room hotel in the Southwest. She had done an outstanding job of staffing this hotel set in the center of an older city undergoing major renovation. Corporate management was enthusiastic about her potential and had urged Gordon to consider her for the job. Two days of interviews at Tall Pines confirmed this potential as well as the experience he needed in opening a new hotel.

Natalie was given the responsibility for the entire staffing process, although Gordon had made it clear that his department managers had the final authority for those working in their departments. Supervisory personnel were hired with Natalie confirming managerial decisions and working out job descriptions, salaries, and other specifics for each position.

Her major task was the recruitment and hiring program for the bulk of the staff to ready the hotel for opening on May first. She and Gordon had met in the middle of January to review her plan. She had worked closely with the state Department of Employment Services as well as Riverton's Employment Options Office to arrange for a Job Fair on February fifteenth. Held at a local school on a Saturday, the fair was designed to attract candidates and provide a screening session and even some first-round interviews. Tall Pines would provide a good package of benefits on top of a competitive wage:

- Blue Cross/Blue Shield
- Paid vacation (after one year)
- Pension plan (vested after seven years)
- On-site job training
- Educational benefits

Natalie had convinced Gordon that although minimum wage would be the controlling factor for many entry-level positions, the promise of raises in six months was needed as an inducement for retention of good employees.

Natalie believed that the primary pool of candidates would be found in Roosevelt City and Riverton. The figures provided by a local governmental agency supported her belief that a number of people would apply for the various positions to be filled.

Local Unemployment Rates*	
Metropolitan area	3.7%
Roosevelt City	8.1
Riverton	5.0
All suburbs	3.7
*December figures.	

An advertising campaign directed toward the larger metropolitan area, coupled with state and city support, should yield at least double the number of candidates needed for each position. Natalie had shown Gordon a series of articles in the *Metro Star*, the major daily, about a large hotel opening last year in the center of Roosevelt City. Over 11,000 applications were made for 350 positions; the articles included pictures of long lines of people trying to get through the door for interviews. Tall Pines would find an eager group ready to work at its hotel.

THE DISAPPOINTING REPORT

The note of optimism of last month was missing from the short report on yesterday's Job Fair. Just over 200 people had applied for the 315 positions. Of these, only 75 had been screened and interviewed. Most had little experience in the hotel business but seemed capable of on-the-job training. The applicants were mostly from the surrounding towns in the county and Riverton, with a few from Roosevelt City.

Natalie had done an informal survey of her small cadre of interviewers late in the afternoon. Applicants had concerns about wage scales and transportation. Unskilled workers with some experience found it difficult to believe that they would start at minimum wage, saying that they could get more at many fast-food chains. Three employees from Big Tex, a regional hamburger chain, had come to the fair together and reported that the chain had just upped starting salaries for counter help to seventy-five cents above minimum wage. Natalie's follow-up call to Big Tex, as well as her conversation with a representative of the county chamber of commerce, had confirmed that many employers were offering hourly wages in excess of minimum wage simply to fill empty positions.

The concerns about transportation were more difficult to bring into focus. Natalie pieced together a picture of Tall Pines being out of the way for most people using public transportation. A few asked about whether the hotel planned to provide bus transportation into Roosevelt City. It had taken them nearly an hour from home with a transfer from a subway stop onto a bus, which dropped them off about three blocks away. Riverton residents indicated that it took thirty minutes to get over from the east side of the city, which meant crossing the interstate because the bus route ended there. Location clearly was a factor in keeping applicants away.

THE STREAM OF TELEPHONE CALLS

Gordon's optimism about his gala opening was suddenly deflated by this report. Natalie's conclusion was concisely stated in one sentence:

> I have arranged another Job Fair in ten days with the hope that our results will be better this time.

He wondered whether there would be enough candidates for the remaining positions and whether there would be enough time to train them after all of the necessary personnel paperwork had been completed.

His thoughts were interrupted by a call from his secretary indicating that a reporter was on the line from the *Riverton Telegram*, asking questions about the Job Fair. He directed the call to Natalie's office. A call from the *Metro Star* was also redirected. But he did take a call from the Riverton mayor's office to assure them that the hotel had the hiring situation under control with the opening still set for May first. Later in the afternoon, the director of one of the associations scheduled to hold a conference at the hotel during the first week called to ask about the opening. Bad news travels fast! thought Gordon as he hung up with another set of assurances to the anxious director.

Natalie sailed into the office to report on the two phone calls from the press. Both had received information about the disappointing turnout at the Job Fair and were interested in both the reasons and the impact on the opening. She thought that it would be difficult to assess the impact of the publicity until the morning editions were out. Gordon suggested a breakfast meeting with the hotel's top staff to discuss the problem and work toward a solution.

THE BREAKFAST STAFF MEETING

Both papers covered the story with short articles hidden away in the second sections. The *Telegram* headline read:

NEW HOTEL NEEDS 240 WORKERS

It briefly described the low turnout at the Job Fair with a listing of the positions still available. A quote from Natalie indicated that another fair would be held in the near future. The story was done in a generally favorable light with emphasis on new business within Riverton, which the hotel should attract.

The *Star* headline was more critical:

NEW SUBURBAN HOTEL SURPRISED TO
FIND FEW APPLY FOR 315 JOBS

The new twin towers were pictured along with a sheet from the fair that listed the jobs available at the hotel. Natalie was quoted about the continuing search to be carried out as well as the types of benefits offered by Tall Pines. A representative of the Roosevelt City Office of Job Services was quoted: "It's not so much that people here won't look in the suburbs; it's that once you cross over that city line, there is a mental barrier about being away from home. Employers have to offer good jobs, good transportation, and a lot of encouragement to get people to apply." A union office spokesman wondered whether people were discouraged because Tall Pines is a nonunion hotel. A man who had been offered a second interview at the fair indicated that he would rather work close to his home in Roosevelt City, but had been out of work for four months and needed the job.

Gordon and Natalie agreed that neither article gave a negative perspective on hotel management, but questions could be raised about postponement of the opening. Clearly, it was important to follow up with the Riverton mayor's office as well as meeting planners who had scheduled the hotel opening for May and June to assure them that the situation would be under control. Contact with the Roosevelt City Office of Job Services was mandatory now.

At the meeting, Gordon asked Natalie to review her report as well as the press clippings for the assembled department heads. They both answered a number of questions about the Job Fair and the type of applicants at the fair. Gordon suggested that they delay the discussion about the future until later in the meeting so that all of the facts surrounding the problem could be sorted through carefully. It became clear that many departments could operate for the first two weeks in May on a reduced staffing pattern using supervisory personnel to fill in. But a full staff was essential to accommodate the anticipated increase in business.

The meeting then turned to a brainstorming session to help Natalie develop a strategy for attracting people who would be good candidates to fill the remaining positions. The group agreed that four areas merited further consideration:

- *Advertising campaign*
  Directed particularly toward Roosevelt City and Riverton with focus on benefits of working at Tall Pines.
- *Upgrade of wage scale*
  Additions to minimum wage for entry-level jobs in order to be competitive. Necessity for incentive pay to retain good employees.

■ *Transportation system*
  Necessity for assistance to workers coming from both Riverton and Roosevelt City in particular because of their reliance on public transportation.
■ *Cooperation with public agencies*
  Cultivation of relationships with a number of agencies to identify other applicant pools.

Gordon asked Natalie to make use of these ideas in the development of a plan to fill the 240 remaining positions. He assured the managers that he would call them the next day with a finalized plan to meet the objective of full staffing by May first. In the meantime, he would handle the public relations aspect of the issue through his office. The meeting adjourned with an agreement that any hotel was only as good as its personnel.

REFLECTIONS OVER LUNCH

As manager of Tall Pines, Gordon enjoyed a number of perquisites unavailable in other jobs. Today, he was delighted to initiate one of those—access to the best meals from the hotel kitchens. Jack Sanders, the sales and convention manager, wheeled in a cart of delectable dishes prepared by one of the French chefs interviewing for the position as head chef. Expecting to join Gordon for lunch, he set a small table for two and uncorked a bottle of wine. As he settled into one of the chairs and pulled out his napkin, Gordon interrupted: "Sorry, Jack. This is a working lunch for me with all of this hiring mess on my mind. You're welcome to take a plate back to your office, but I need to be alone to get a handle on this situation." Jack excused himself, a full plate and wineglass in hand, while Gordon settled into his chair.

The meal was excellent, with the wine chosen for its appropriate balance with the food. Gordon thought about his fortunate managerial situation—no fast-food lunches, no traveling throughout the week, and no narrow job responsibilities. All of these were left behind for any hotel manager. There was a sense of excitement about what lay in store for him both here at Tall Pines and within the larger national organization as it expanded.

But the past day had drowned out much of that excitement. What seemed so close to completion was now filled with a number of questions. Could Tall Pines attract a good staff? Could they be trained and on the job by May first? How costly was it going to be to pay a competitive wage? Could he instill within the staff a sense of pride about Tall Pines? Could the hotel open on May first?

The smell of paint, the carpet samples, and even the faint sound of hammers now came into fuller focus as he asked the last question. Where had he gone wrong in the development of his plan to open the hotel? Why didn't he foresee a potential problem about staffing earlier? Getting the right people seemed like the easiest of his plans to implement. Now it looked like an impossible task. With a cup of coffee in hand, he moved back to his desk to begin the process of solving the problem he faced.

Legislation, Court, and NLRB Decisions Affecting Personnel and Human Resource Management

LEGISLATION/BASIC PROVISIONS

Employment Legislation

Act	Jurisdiction	Basic Provisions
Fair Labor Standards Act (1938) and subsequent amendments—FLSA	Most interstate employers, certain types of employees are exempt from overtime provisions—executive, administrative, and professional employees and outside salespeople	Establishes a minimum wage; controls hours through premium pay for overtime; controls working hours for children
Minimum Wage Law (1977)	Small businesses	Sets graduated increases in minimum wage rates
Equal Pay Act (1963 amendment to the FLSA)	Same as FLSA except no employees are exempt	Prohibits unequal pay for males and females with equal skills, effort, and responsibility working under similar working conditions
Civil Rights Act (1964) (amended by EEOA 1972)	Employers with fifteen or more employees, employment agencies, and labor unions	Prevents discrimination on the basis of race, color, religion, sex, or national origin; establishes EEOC
Equal Employment Opportunity Act (1972)—EEOA	Adds employees of state and local government and educational institutions; reduced number of employees required to fifteen	Amends Title VII; increases enforcement powers of EEOC

Act	Jurisdiction	Basic Provisions
Executive Order 11246 (1965) as amended by Executive Order 11375 (1966)	Federal contractors and subcontractors with contracts over $50,000 and fifty or more employees	Prevents discrimination on the basis of race, color, religion, sex or national origin; establishes Office of Federal Contract Compliance (OFCC)
Revised Order Number 4 (1971)	Federal contractors	Defines acceptable affirmative action program
Executive Order 11478 (1969)	Federal agencies	Prevents discrimination on the basis of race, color, religion, sex, or national origin
Age Discrimination in Employment Act (1967)—Revised 1978; 1986	Employers with more than twenty-five employees	Prevents discrimination against persons from age forty and states compulsory retirement for some workers
Rehabilitation Act (1973) as amended 1980	Government contractors and federal agencies	Prevents discrimination against person with physical and/or mental handicaps and provides for affirmative action
Prevailing wage laws—1. Davis-Bacon Act (1931) and 2. Walsh-Healey Act (1935)	Employers with government construction projects of $2,000 (Davis-Bacon) and government contracts of $10,000 or more	Guarantees prevailing wages to employees of government contractors
Legally required fringe benefits— 1. OASDHI (1935 and amendments)	Virtually all employers	Provides income and health care to retired employees and income to the survivors of employees who have died
2. Unemployment compensation (1935)	Virtually all employers	Provides income to employees who are laid off or fired
3. Workers' compensation (dates differ from state to state)	Virtually all employers	Provides benefits to employees who are injured on the job and to the survivors of employees who are killed on the job

Act	Jurisdiction	Basic Provisions
Occupational Safety and Health Act (1970)—OSHA	Most interstate employers	Assures as far as possible every working man and woman in the nation safe and healthful working conditions and to preserve our human resources
Employee Retirement Income Security Act (1974)—ERISA	Most interstate employers with pension plans (no employer is required to have such a plan)	Protects employees covered by a pension plan from losses in benefits due to: ■ mismanagement ■ plant closings and bankruptcies ■ job changes
Freedom of Information Act	Federal agencies only	Allows individuals to review employers' records on them and bring civil damages
The Pregnancy Discrimination Act of 1978 (1987 Civil Rights Act Amendment to Title VII)	Same as Civil Rights Act (1964)	Pregnancy is a disability and, furthermore, must receive the same benefits as any other disability
Privacy Act of 1974 (Public Law 93-579)	Federal agencies only	Allows individuals to review employer's records on them and bring civil damages
Uniform Guidelines on Employee Selection Procedures (1978)	Same as EEOA (1972)	Updates EEOC 1970 guidelines to more clearly define adverse impact and test validation
Guidelines on Sexual Harassment (1980)	Same as EEOA (1972)	Defines standards for what constitutes harassment
Vietnam Era Veterans Readjustment Act (1974)	Government contractors with contracts in excess of $10,000	Provides for affirmative action in the employment of Vietnam era veterans
Civil Rights Act of 1866 Section 1981	All citizens	It gives all persons, regardless of race, alienage, and national origin, the same contractual rights as "white citizens." Does not apply to sex-based discrimination
Civil Rights Act of 1871 Section 1983	All citizens	As the Civil Rights Act of 1866 but does apply to sex-based discrimination

Act	*Jurisdiction*	*Basic Provisions*
The First Amendment, U.S. Constitution	All citizens	Guarantees freedom of speech and religion
The Fifth Amendment	All citizens	No person shall be deprived of life, liberty, or property without the due process of law
The Fourteenth Amendment	All citizens	Prohibits abridgment of federally conferred privileges by actions of the state
Employee Polygraph Protection Act (1988)	Private Employers	Prohibits most employers from polygraph testing without reasonable suspicion.
Plant Closing Act (1988)	Employers with more than 100 employees	Requires 60 days notice of plant or office closing

Labor Relations Legislation: Private Sector

Act	*Jurisdiction*	*Basic Provisions*
Railway Labor Act (1926)—RLA	Railroad workers and airline employees	Provides right to organize; provides majority choice of representatives; prohibits "yellow dog" contracts; outlines dispute settlement procedures
Norris-LaGuardia Act (1932)	All employers and labor organizations	No yellow dog contracts; no injunction for nonviolent activity of unions (strikes, picketing, and boycotts); limited union liability
National Labor Relations Act (1935)—Wagner Act	Nonmanagerial employees in private industry not covered by Railway Labor Act (RLA)	Provides right to organize; provides for collective bargaining; requires employers to bargain; unions must represent all members equally
Labor-Management Relations Act (1947)—Taft-Hartley	Nonmanagerial employees in private industry not covered by RLA	Prohibits unfair labor practices of unions; outlaws closed shop; prohibits strikes in national emergencies; requires both parties to bargain in good faith

Act	*Jurisdiction*	*Basic Provisions*
Labor Management Reporting and Disclosure Act (1959)— Landrum-Griffin	Labor organizations	Outlines procedures for redressing internal union problems
Amendments to Taft-Hartley Act (1974)	Labor organizations	Specifies illegal activities within union

Labor Relations Legislation: Public Sector

Executive Order 10988 (1962)	Federal employees	Recognizes employees' right to join unions and bargain collectively; prohibits strikes. Requires agency to meet and confer with union on policy practices and working conditions
Executive Orders 11616 (1971) 11838 (1975)	Federal employees	Expand EO 11491 to cover labor-management relations: cover disputes of bargaining rights; order elections; consolidate units; limit scope of grievance and arbitration procedures
Civil Service Reform Act Title VII (1978)	Federal employees	Defines grievance procedure and requirements for goal-type performance appraisals; establishes Senior Executive Service (SES)

COURT AND NLRB DECISIONS/BASIC PROVISIONS

Title/Date

Stringfellow v. Monsanto Corporation (1970)
Established the precedent for giving credit to the employer for making performance appraisal-based decisions on the basis of evidence that the appraisal uses definite identifiable criteria based on the quality and quantity of an employee's work.

---

*This set of court cases is meant to provide a sampling of those mentioned in the text. For descriptions of these and of the other cases, see J. Ledvinka, *Federal Regulation of Personnel and Human Resource Management* (Boston: Kent, 1983); J. Bernardin and W. Cascio, *Annotated Bibliography of Court Cases Relevant to Employment Decisions 1980–1984* (Boca Raton: Florida Atlantic University, 1984); M.D. Levin-Epstein, *Primer of Equal Employment Opportunity,* 3d ed. (Washington, D.C.: NA, 1984); M. McCarthy, ed., *Complete Guide to Employing Persons with Disabilities* (Albertson, N.Y.: National Center on Employment of the Handicapped at Human Resources Center, 1985).

Phillips v. Martin Marietta Corp (1971)
Whether a BFOQ exists is whether it can be shown that the qualification is demonstrably more relevant to job performance for a woman than a man.

Diaz v. Pan American World Airways, Inc. (1971)
The primary function of an airline is to transport passengers safely from one point to another. Therefore, not hiring males for flight attendants is discriminatory. *Business necessity* is established.

Griggs v. Duke Power (1971)
Test for hiring cannot be used unless job related. Organization must show evidence of job relatedness. Not necessary to establish intent to discriminate.

Board of Regents of State Colleges v. Roth (1972)
Protects workers from discharge when due process hasn't been given.

Richardson v. Hotel Corporation of America (1972)
Dismissal on grounds on conviction record resulted in adverse impact. But since conviction record argued (not shown) to be related to business necessity (not job performance) dismissal is okay.

Spurlock v. United Airlines (1972)
Use of college degree as a selection criterion valid because job related, even though no performance data provided.

Rowe v. General Motors Corporation (1972)
All white supervisory recommendations were based on subjective and vague standards which lead to a lack of promotions for black employees. Indentified 5 discriminatory factors.

Hodgson v. Robert Hall Clothes, Inc. (1973)
Pay differentials between salesmen and saleswomen justified on the basis of profitability of area in which employees work.

McDonnell Douglas Corporation v. Green (1973)
Employer's test device constitutes *prima facie* case of racial discrimination under four different criteria.

Brito v. Zia Company (1973)
Zia violated Title VII because they laid off a disproportionate number of a protected group on the basis of low performance scores on measures that were not validated.

Sugarman v. Dougal (1973)
The due process and equal protection clauses of the Fifth Amendment also apply to aliens in public employment.

Hodgson v. Greyhound Lines, Inc. (1974)
Could discriminate without empirical evidence on basis of age. Good faith used to show older people would make less safe drivers.

Corning Glass Works v. Brennan (1974)
The Equal Pay Act is violated by paying male inspectors on the night shift a higher base wage than female inspectors on the day shift.

Baxter v. Savannah Sugar Refining Co. (1974)
Subjective appraisal form is viewed as discriminatory

Green v. Missouri Pacific R.R. Co. (1975)
Applying the lessons from *Griggs v. Duke Power,* the court and the EEOC have found it unlawful to refuse to hire job applicants because of their arrest record except for certain circumstances *(Richardson v. Hotel Corporation of America).*

Kirkland v. New York Department of Correctional Services (1975)
The use of quotas was rejected as a method of determining promotions except as an interim measure to be used until nondiscriminatory procedures to determine promotion are established.

Stamps (EEOC) v. Detroit Edison (1975)
Title VII does not provide for an award of punitive damages. Back pay and attorney fees are the explicit provisions of Title VII.

Rogers v. International Paper Company (1975)
Subjective criteria are not to be condemned as unlawful per se because some decisions about hiring and promotions in supervisory and managerial jobs cannot be made using objective standards alone. This opinion, however, is somewhat contrary to those in *Albemarle Paper Company v. Moody* (1973); *Baxter v. Savannah Sugar Refining Corporation* (1974); and *Rowe v. General Motors* (1972).

Green v. Missouri Pacific R.R. (1975)
Applying lessons from *Griggs v. Duke Power,* the court and the EEOC have found it unlawful to refuse to hire job applicants because of their arrest record except for certain circumstances.

Albemarle v. Moody (1975)
Need to establish evidence that test related to content of job. Could use job analysis to do so, but not evidence from global performance ratings made by supervisors.

McDonald v. Santa Fe Trail Transportation Co. (1976)
Requires consistency in dismissal policies due to absenteeism

Mastie v. Great Lakes Steel Corporation (1976)
As with *Stringfellow,* the court said that the objectivity of evaluation can be established by demonstrating that the company performed and relied on a thorough evaluation process intended to be used fairly and accurately.

Smith v. Mutual Benefit Life Insurance Company (1976)
Employer is not discriminating if refusing to hire male appearing to be effeminate.

Chrysler Outboard v. Dept. of Industry (1976)
Employer refuses to hire a worker who had leukemia because he was prone to infection. Court said he had to be hired because he was qualified.

Watkins v. Scott Paper Company (1976)
Performance data to validate tests that are derived from graphic scales are too vague and easily subject to discrimination.

Robinson v. Union Carbide Corporation (1976)
These two require written standards for promotion to help prevent discrimination.

Patterson v. American Tobacco Company (1976, 1978)

Wade v. Mississippi Cooperative Extension Service (1976)
Performance scores used to decide promotions and salary issues not valid because no job analysis.

Washington v. Davis (1976)
When a test procedure is challenged under constitutional law, intent to discriminate must be established. No need to establish intent if file under Title VII, just show effects. Could use communication test to select applicants for police force.

Castaneda v. Partida (1977)
Prima facie evidence of discrimination established when evidence of both statistical disparity and discriminatory selection procedures vis-à-vis the gross population figures.

General Foods Corp. (1977)
Corporatewide team program of employee-employer cooperation does not violate the National Labor Relations Act because program established to promote efficiency, not forestall unionization.

James v. Stockham Values and Fitting Company (1977)
An apprenticeship program was viewed as discriminatory since selections were made by supervisors who were given guidelines.

Barnes v. Costle (1977)
All of these state that sexual harassment is a form of sex discrimination under Title VII, Section 703, and employer is responsible if takes no action on learning of events.

Mistretta v. Sandia Corporation (1977)
Employment decisions suspect when based on evaluations that reflect only best judgments and opinions of evaluators rather than identifiable criteria based on quality or quantity of work or specific performances that are supported by some kind of record.

Hazelwood School District v. U.S. (1977)
Labor market comparisons must be based on relevant labor-market and not general labor market.

International Brotherhood of Teamsters v. United States (1977)
Bona fide seniority systems maintained without discriminatory intent are exempt from Title VII liability if established before 1964.

United Air Lines, Inc. v. McMann (1977)
Employer can force retirement before age of sixty-five if has bona fide retirement plan; since AEDA (1978) can't force retirement before age of seventy.

Yukas v. Libbey-Owens-Ford (1977)
All of these against nepotism, especially close relatives and spouses, are non-discriminatory, especially in same department and/or as in supervisor-subordinate relationship.

Flowers v. Crouch-Walter Corporation (1977)
Plaintiff established *prima facie* evidence that a discharge was discriminatory and not based on performance.

Donaldson v. Pillsbury Company (1977)
All of these three require clear establishment and communication of job requirements and performance standards.

James v. Stockman Values and Fittings Company (1977)
Applicants to apprenticeship program selected by white supervisors without formal guidelines is discriminatory. Need more discrete performance appraisal.

Dothard v. Rawlinson (1977)
Height requirements not valid, therefore constitutes discriminatory practice.

Bakke v. Regents of the University of California (1978)
Reverse discrimination not allowed. Race, however, can be used in selection decisions. Affirmative action programs permissible when prior discrimination established.

Los Angeles Department of Water v. Manhart (1978)
Employer is required to provide equal benefits to employees under both Title VII and EPA.

United States v. City of Chicago (1978)
These three require in promotion cases specific promotion criteria that are related to the job to which being promoted.

United States v. City of Chicago (1978)
Specific promotion criteria must be used which are related to the job to which being promoted.

Detroit Police Officers Assn. v. Coleman Young (1979)
Court holds in favor of goals and quotas to reverse previous discrimination.

Oshiver v. Court of Common Pleas (1979)
Without objective or extrinsic documented evidence of poor performance or evidence not hastily developed, an employment decision is suspect if based on the notion of "poor performance."

Milstead v. Teamsters Local 957 (1979)
Leaves open question of a union's obligation.

Charles L. Maehren v. City of Seattle (1979)
Upheld practice of setting goals and quotas to reverse previous practices of discrimination.

Marshall v. Barlow's, Inc. (1979)
Employers are not required to let OSHA inspectors enter their premises unless they have search warrants.

Schultz v. Wheaton Glass (1979)
The employer's lower wage rate for women is in violation of the Equal Pay Act when the wage differentials are based on artificially created job classifications that differentiate otherwise equal jobs.

Steelworkers v. Weber (1979)
Quota system to admit employees into a training program may supersede seniority provisions as long as the program is a temporary one to correct past employment practices and does not trample the interests of the more senior employees.

State Division of Human Rights v. Rochester Housing Authority (1980)
Although religious preferences cannot be used for discrimination, an employer may defend not hiring an applicant because of religion by showing that a reasonable attempt was made to accommodate the applicant.

Fullilove v. Klutznick (1980)
Congress can impose racial quotas in handing out federal money (10 percent) to federal contractors who are minority owned (51 percent).

Ensley Branch NAACP v. Seibels (1980)
Training scores can only be used to screen out, not select job candidates.

City of St. Louis v. U.S. (1980)
Upheld use of quotas and goals.

EEOC. v. United Virginia Bank (1980)
Prima Facie evidence of discrimination established on the bases of statistical disparity vis-a-vis the relevant labor market (i.e., comparably qualified individuals).

Weahkee v. Perry (1978) and *Weahkee v. Norton* (1980)
Use of quotas in performance evaluation not objectively used or enforced so not justified in using if discrimination results. Weahkee was reinstated, but no finding of discrimination.

EEOC v. Sandia Corporation (1980)
Discrimination against employees protected by ADEA in regard to a decision on work force reduction required by budget restraints. Used a subjective (ranking) evaluation form for their scientists, engineers, and technical employees. Statistical impact and informal comments indicated bias.

EEOC v. United Virginia Bank (1980)
Prima facie evidence of discrimination established on the basis of statistical disparity vis-à-vis the relevant labor market (i.e., comparably qualified individuals).

Marshall v. Whirlpool (1980)
Employees have right to refuse job assignment if constitutes clear and present danger to life or limb. Employer, however, not required to pay if, as a result, employee sent home because of no work.

Backus v. Baptist Medical Center (1981)
A defense of bona fide occupational qualifications was extended to permit the hiring and staffing of only female nurses in an obstetrics and gynecology department in a hospital.

NLRB v. Wright Line, Inc. (1981)
In cases where an employee is fired for what may appear to be union-related activities, the employer must show (to be vindicated in the dismissal) that the discipline imposed is the same as in other cases where union activity was not an issue.

American Textile Manufacturers Institute v. Donovan (1981)
OSHA need not do cost benefit analyses before issuing working health standards.

Tooley v. Martin-Marietta Corporation (1981)
Must be religious accommodation for employees who object to union membership or support (as long as no undue hardship on union).

Los Angeles Dept. of Water v. Manhard (1981)
Rule against department rule of having female employees contribute more to a retirement plan than men.

Clayton v. United Auto Workers (1981)
When a union member feels unfairly represented and only the employer can grant the relief requested, the employee need not exhaust internal union remedies before suing the employer.

Lehman v. Yellow Freight System (1981)
Informal affirmative action not permissible although formal voluntary one such as *Weber* is okay.

Northwest Airlines, Inc. v. Transport Workers (1981)
An employer found guilty of job discrimination cannot force an employee's union to contribute to the damages, even though the union may have negotiated the unequal terms.

United States v. Trucking Management, Inc. (1981)
Same as in prior above *Teamsters* case, but adds exemption from EO 11246 also.

County of Washington, Oregon v. Gunther (1981)
It can be illegal (under Title VII and EPA 1963) to pay women unfairly low wages even if not doing same work as men (not a comparable worth case).

First National Maintenance v. NLRB (1981)
Management does not have to negotiate with unions in advance over closing plants or dropping lines.

Texas Department of Community Affairs v. Joyce Ann Burdine (1981)
A defendant in a job discrimination case need only provide a legitimate, non-discriminatory explanation for not hiring or promoting a woman or minority, and need not prove that the white man hired was better qualified. The burden of proving intentional discrimination rests with the plaintiff.

Fernandez v. Wynn Oil Company (1981)
Title VII does not permit employers to use stereotypic impressions of male and female roles as a BFOQ defense to sex discrimination. Employer can't use customer preferences for working with male employees as a defense of discrimination.

Connecticut v. Teal (1982)
Employers must defend each part of a selection process against adverse impact and not just the end result of the entire process (the bottom line).

Spirit v. TIA/CREF (1982)
Retirement annuities must be equal, regardless of sex.

Borg Warner Corp. v. NLRBC (1982)
Distinction between mandatory and permissable. Terms depend on whether topic regulates the employer-employee relation.

American Tobacco v. Patterson (1982)
Bona fide seniority systems without discriminating intent are exempt from Title VII liability.

Newport News Shipbuilding and Dry Dock Co. v. EEOC (1983)
If an employer supplies any level of health benefits to female workers' husbands, the employer must also supply the same level of benefits to male workers' wives, and that includes pregnancy benefits. This, in effect, reverses the Supreme Court's ruling in *General Electric v. Gilbert,* where the court said that pregnancy benefits need not be given the same treatment by employers as other health and disability programs.

Arizona Governing Committee v. Norris (1983)
Pension pay-outs by employers should be equal for women and men, and past unequal treatment of women must be cured by retroactive funding of pensions. This decision is in essence the other half of the issue. The first half was rendered in the Supreme Court decision of *Los Angeles Department of Water and Power v. Manhart,* where the decision was made that requiring larger contributions by females than males into pension programs is discriminatory.

NLRB v. Transportation Management (1983)
Employees are protected by the NLRA when helping organize employees. If an employee claims to be fired for trying to organize a union but the employer claims it was poor performance, the employer has the burden of proof. In cases where such "mixed" motives for employer action may exist, the employer must prove the case.

Firefighters Local Union No. 1784 v. Stotts (1984)
In this decision, the Supreme Court upheld the bona fide seniority system over an affirmative action consent decree in a situation of layoffs. Thus, the employees most recently hired could be subject to layoff even though this action could compromise the affirmative action efforts.

Otis Elevator v. NLRB (1984)
Employees need not bargain over a transfer of operation if move is based on economics not labor cost, consideration

AFSCME v. State of Washington (1985)
State had systematically paid jobs dominated by women less than their value according to job evaluation. Court of appeals over turned this decision saying state could not be forced "to eliminate an economic inequality that it did not create."

Pattern Makers' Leage v. NLRB (1985)
Employees may resign from a union at any time, even during a strike or when one is imminent.

Garcia v. San Antonio Transit Authority (1985)
Extends coverage of FLSA to state and local governments.

Scott v. Sears Roebuck (1985)
Woman unsuccessful in sex harassment suit based on acts by co-workers. Woman did not complain to supervisors. Court ruled only responsible for acts of co-workers if they knew or should have known of acts and took no action.

Horn v. Duke Homes (1985)
Court endorsed principle that employers have strict liability for sexual harassment by supervisors (company claimed that it was not liable because it was not aware of the behavior). Court supported full back pay (plaintiff had been terminated).

Glasgow v. Georgia Pacific Corp. (1985)
Court accepts sexual harassment argument on basis of creating hostile work environment (no *quid pro quo*). Company was found by Court to have made sexually harassing environment a condition of employment because harassment went on for long period of time with organization doing nothing. Court outlined four-point test for sexually harassing work environment.

1. Harassment was unwelcome
2. Harassment was because of sex
3. Harassment affected terms and conditions of employment
4. Knowledge of harassment is "imputed" to employer

Wygant v. Jackson Board of Education (1986)
The Court ruled that white teachers were illegally dismissed in order to hire minority teachers in the School Board's efforts to fulfill a voluntary affirmative action program.

Philbrook v. Ansonia Board of Education (1986)
Defined reasonable accommodation for religious preference.

Barns v. Washington Natural Gas (1986)
Employer fires an employee because he was believed to have epilepsy. Awarded two years back pay and reinstatement.

Local 28 of the Sheet Metal Workers v. Equal Employment Opportunity Commission (1986)
The Court approved a lower court order requiring a New York City sheet metal workers' local to meet a 29 percent minority membership goal by 1987. The Court also held that judges may order racial preferences in union membership and other contexts if necessary to rectify especially "egregious" discrimination.

Local 93 of the International Association of Firefighters v. City of Cleveland (1986)
The Court held that lower Federal courts have broad discretion to approve decrees in which employers, over the objections of white employees, settle discrimination suits by agreeing to preferential hiring or promotion of minority-group members. It upheld a decree in which Cleveland agreed to settle a job discrimination suit by black and Hispanic firefighters by temporarily promoting black and Hispanic workers ahead of whites who had more seniority and higher test scores.

Meritor Savings Bank v. Vinson (1986)
The Court held that sexual harassment is a form of sex discrimination prohibited by Title VII of the Civil Rights Act and that employers may be liable for condoning a hostile work environment. However, the Court made it clear that employers will not be automatically liable for sexual harassment by supervisors or employees.

Philbrook v. Ansonia Board of Education (1986)
An employer may choose its own method of religious accommodation over a plan suggested by the worker as long as the employer's plan is reasonable.

Johnson v. Transportation Agency, Santa Clara County (1987)
The U.S. Supreme Court ruled that the county was justified in giving a job to a woman who scored two points less on an exam than a man. The county had an affirmative action plan that was flexible, temporary, and designed to correct the imbalance of white males in the work force.

School Board of Nassau County, Fla. v. Arline (1987)
The U.S. Supreme Court ruled that contagious diseases are not automatically excluded from coverage of the handicap provisions of Section 504 of the 1973 Rehabilitation Act.

Luck v. Southern Pacific Transportation Company (1987)
The court ruled that the company wrongfully discharged Barbara Luck for refusing a drug test on the grounds that it violated her rights to privacy. Subsequently, the company stopped its random drug testing program.

U.S. v. Paradise (1987)
The U.S. Supreme Court affirmed the affirmative action plan for the state troopers of Alabama in which promotion and hiring quotas were established in order to correct racial imbalances even though it may result in discrimination against an individual because of race or color.

Chalk v. U.S. District Court for Central District of California (1987)
Although handicapped because of AIDS, the teacher was otherwise able to perform his job within the meaning of the Rehabilitation Act of 1973 and, therefore, should be allowed to teach.

O'Connor v. Ortega (1987)
Supreme Court recognized workplace privacy for the first time.

EEOC v. Commonwealth of Massachusetts (1987)
A Massachusetts law requiring entry-level motor vehicle examiners to be aged 35 or younger does not violate Age Discrimination in Employment Act because it is a bona fide occupational qualification (BFOQ).

Watson v. Fort Worth Bank and Trust (1988)
The U.S. Supreme Court held that all selection procedures—objective or subjective, scored or unscored—should be subject to adverse impact analysis, compelling a demonstration by the employer that the procedure is job related if adverse impact is shown.

Kraszewski v. State Farm (1988)
Out of court settlement. Firm agrees to set aside half of its new sales jobs to women for 10 years and to pay damages and back pay.

Arrow Automotive Industries v. NLRB (1988)
Do not have to bargain on plant closings even if based on labor cost considerations.

Wards' Cove Packing v. Atonia (1989)
Concentration statistics were used to prove adverse impact. Court rule that burden of proof should not shift to employer unless it can be proved that a specific policy created the disparity.

Index